The Bradshaws in about 1946 (clockwise from back left):
Franklin, Marilyn, Robert, Elaine, Frances, Berenice.

**Here is the full and shocking story of how—
and why—Frances Schreuder, New
York socialite and board member of the
New York City Ballet, masterminded
the murder of one of the richest men in
Utah—her father. Her chief accomplice cold-
bloodedly pumped two bullets from
a .357 Magnum into the old man, killing
him instantly. The murderer was 17-year-old
Marc Schreuder— Frances's son and
Franklin Bradshaw's grandson.**

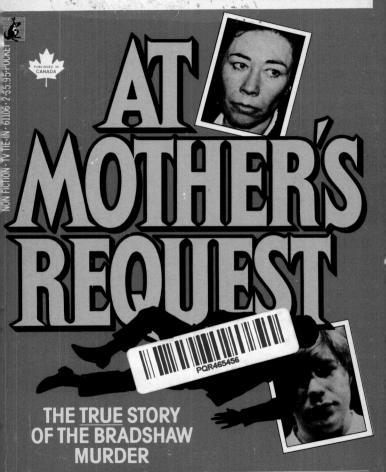

PUBLISHED IN CANADA

NON FICTION • TV TIE-IN • 61106-2 $5.95•POCKET

AT MOTHER'S REQUEST

THE TRUE STORY OF THE BRADSHAW MURDER

BY JONATHAN COLEMAN

"A gruesome, fascinating tale…BRILLIANT"— Ken Follett

Of the Two Major Books Chronicling the Shocking Bradshaw Murder Case, *Newsweek* Prefers *AT MOTHER'S REQUEST* . . . "HARROWING AND CONVINCING . . . BY FAR THE MORE SOLID BOOK."

And Our Most Important Critics Agree . . .

"The obvious model for both books was Tommy Thompson's 1976 epic Texas melodrama with the title that said it all: *Blood and Money*. . . . Paradoxically, Coleman's book is closer to what Thompson probably would have written. Essentially a cop book . . . gathering momentum based on solid reporting and colorful writing . . . I'd pick Coleman's *AT MOTHER'S REQUEST*."

—*Chicago Tribune*

"In some . . . areas—notably in tracking the detectives and lawyers—Mr. Coleman proves the more indefatigable reporter. . . . He has dredged up some interesting material that Miss Alexander largely or completely ignores. . . . Mr. Coleman . . . lends the case an extra dimension . . . with some interesting speculation about the family's pathology. . . . PROVOCATIVE."

—*New York Times Book Review*

"Jonathan Coleman provides a straight-ahead journalistic account. . . . Comparisons to *The Executioner's Song* are inevitable. . . . THERE IS AMPLE IRONY AND MORDANT HUMOR IN THESE PAGES, ENOUGH TO KEEP A READER UP HALF THE NIGHT."

—*San Francisco Chronicle*

A Book-of-the-Month Club Alternate Selection

(More . . .)

THE CRITICS CHOOSE
AT MOTHER'S REQUEST . . .

AT MOTHER'S REQUEST

JONATHAN COLEMAN

PUBLISHED BY POCKET BOOKS NEW YORK

Distributed in Canada by PaperJacks Ltd., a Licensee
of the trademarks of Simon & Schuster, Inc.

Excerpts from *Adolescence: The Farewell to Childhood* by Louise
J. Kaplan, Ph.D., copyright ©1984 by Louise J. Kaplan, Ph.D.
Reprinted by permission of Simon & Schuster, Inc. Lines from
"Musee des Beaux Arts" by W. H. Auden, copyright 1940,
renewed 1968 by W. H. Auden. Reprinted from *W. H. Auden:
Collected Poems,* edited by Edward Mendelson by permission of
Random House, Inc. Lines from "Epilogue" by Robert Lowell,
copyright © 1977 by Robert Lowell. Reprinted from *Day by Day*
by permission of Farrar, Straus & Giroux, Inc.

POCKET BOOKS, a division of Simon & Schuster, Inc.
1230 Avenue of the Americas, New York, N.Y. 10020
In Canada distributed by PaperJacks Ltd.,
330 Steelcase Road, Markham, Ontario

Copyright © 1985 by Jonathan Coleman
Cover artwork copyright © 1986 Bill Purdom

Published by arrangement with Atheneum Publishers
Library of Congress Catalog Card Number: 84-45616

ISBN: 0-671-61106-2

First Pocket Books printing January, 1986

10 9 8 7 6 5 4 3 2

POCKET and colophon are registered trademarks
of Simon & Schuster, Inc.

Printed in Canada

For KATHRYN,
who has always believed,

and for
IAN HAMILTON and ANGUS CAMERON,
friends and mentors,
who have meant far more to me
than they will ever know

Author's Note

Quotation from written material appears, with few exceptions, without the editorial [*sic*]. When it seemed that a word was inadvertently missing, it has been added for the sake of clarity. Mistakes in punctuation, grammar and spelling have been corrected in certain instances, but in others it was felt that retaining an error would help convey the flavor of a document and the style of the person who had written it.

Prologue

On a late summer's day in 1975, a gaunt figure, dressed in thrift-shop clothes and carrying some money in his shoe, sat under a bare lightbulb in the back of a weather-beaten, brick warehouse in Salt Lake City, Utah. Nearly as old as the century and one of the richest men in the state, Franklin Bradshaw was sifting through the morning mail when he came across something that disturbed him—a letter from his wife:

Aug. 30th, 1975

FRANKLIN:

Here are some correspondence for you to look over with this explanation. As I have told you I have one ambition left in these last days of mine and that is to see that my grandchildren are raised properly and well educated.

We are rich people and there is no reason why we should not share our wealth with our own flesh and blood. The time to share with our family is now, when they need it, not twenty years from now. The Drukman family seem to be doing a fine job on their own. They have never asked for help, they prefer to do their own thing in their own way. For 25 years money has been spent on educating Marilyn, I think she has had her share. We have three (3) fatherless grandchildren who need us and our help, personally and financially. Marc and Larry are now young men, a critical time in their lives. Now is the time for making the kind of high quality men of these young boys we

1

want them to be. They have no one to [look] after them, to support and encourage them but us. They are looking to us for this guidance and development. I'm dedicating myself to giving them my all, my best. The very least I can do is finance their education. You let them down last year (1974–1975) by not paying their schools. It was a desperate struggle for their mother, with no husband and no income, to keep these boys in these fine schools.

I finally got wise, it took a long time. You have told me many times, I cannot spend all my income. With this worth-while interest in my grandchildren, I want to share this "vast wealth" with them. Why should they suffer while we linger in our old age with more wealth than we know what to do with? Doug said to me: "You folks can't spend the interest on your money." What is to happen to all this wealth? Why can't we and our family enjoy some of the fruit of our whole-life's labors? We are in our 70's, how old do you have to be to "be old"? If I had my way we would sell everything we own and divide it up with our families and we start living and they enjoy life a little more. Now I know this will never be, you will not change and how sad. I think you are making a big mistake not to liquidate the Auto Parts business. There is no one to carry on that business. As Doug says: "After the Mr. goes there will be a blood-bath." How well we both know. How sad to let this happen when it can be avoided by taking care of our business affairs *now*. I think everyone in the organization is wondering what is going to happen to the business and to them personally when you die. There is no feeling of security with three (3) violent, unfriendly daughters waiting to gorge the life-blood of our 50 years of work. Think about this, are you doing the right thing?

I promised my grandsons I would take care of their schooling. As you will see by the enclosed copies I have taken care of this year's, 1975–1976. You offered me $5000 for my American Savings and Loan stock. If you can give me $5000 for my stock you can give me $5000 without my stock. You are choking to death in stock, still you have your hand out to take away from me any sign of property I might own. You don't want me to "own anything" or have "anything" of value. I'm just supposed to work up to my last day for my board and room. I intend to change that. My stock is not for sale.

I made a trip down to Lehi and went to the bank. I found my signature is as good as yours in that bank. Also I found my bank balance to be over $38,000. I had four cashier checks made; one for $3800 for Eastern Military Academy, one for $3200 for Allen-

Stevenson school, two for $300 each for the boys (some school clothes) and $200 cash for myself. This leaves a balance of about $30,791.15.

I have a wonderful feeling knowing I have done the right thing. I intend to share my wealth and income with those I love,

BERENICE J. BRADSHAW

Part One//

Children begin by loving their parents.
After a time they judge them.
Rarely, if ever, do they forgive them.

—OSCAR WILDE

1 // All mornings should be as bright, cloudless and peaceful as July 23, 1978, was in Salt Lake City. It was a Sunday and it was going to be a hot one.

Many found it a perfect day to drive to one of the canyons, like Millcreek or Little Cottonwood, for a picnic, or to noisier places like Lagoon, for its amusement park, or to the Great Salt Lake to "float like a cork" in America's version of the Dead Sea. If they were Mormon—and two of every three people in Utah are—many would have been at their local ward attending Sunday School in the morning, and, later, they might have put the finishing touches on floats for the annual parade down Main Street the following day. While July 24 was just another Monday in the rest of America, it was Pioneer Day in Utah, commemorating the day in 1847 when Brigham Young, lifting himself up from his covered wagon, took in the Salt Lake Valley for the first time and uttered those now-famous words to his faithful followers: "This is the place whereon we will plant our feet and where the Lord's people will dwell."

Utah was part of Mexico then and didn't become a United States territory until three years later. The Indians, of course, had been there first, and so had Spanish explorers, fur traders, Captain John Charles Frémont, and the ill-fated Donner-Reed Party, among others. But with the exception of the Indians, eventually forced off their lands as they were elsewhere, none of these people had chosen to try to colonize what they saw as a land of desert and sagebrush—isolated, arid, uninviting. But then again, they were not Saints, come to establish the Kingdom of God on Earth.

It was still cool outside that Sunday morning when Franklin Bradshaw rose before six and began his daily regimen of one hundred push-ups and jumping rope. For a man of seventy-six, standing six feet tall and weighing 163½ pounds, he not only was in remarkable shape, but planned to live forever. A man of rigid habit, he took his daily dose of choline and inositol (to ward off senility), then sat down to a bowl of oatmeal with Karo syrup and warm milk (in order, he once told an employee, "to open my veins"). It was a routine Norman Rockwell might have approved of.

In his reddish-orange sport shirt, polyester pants and olive-green shoes, Bradshaw had not gotten up this early to enjoy a leisurely Sunday. He was doing what he did every day of the year—something that gave him more pleasure than any picnic in a canyon could. He was going to work. But Sunday mornings were special, "his little baby," his time to have at least two hours alone at the warehouse before his first employee arrived at nine.

Though his wife, from her bedroom, noticed it was quarter to seven when he left the modest house they had lived in since 1937, she did not stir. While they would be married fifty-four years that October, they had led separate lives for quite some time. Berenice Bradshaw knew her husband was wealthy, but neither she, nor anyone else for that matter, knew the full extent of that wealth. Besides the thirty-one auto-parts stores he owned in Utah and other ventures, he was one of the largest holders of federal oil and gas leases in America, having accumulated the mineral rights to roughly a million acres of land in thirteen states. It was hardly surprising that his wife called him "Utah's Howard Hughes."

Driving to the west side of town in his green Ford Courier pickup truck, his lunch of meat loaf and bran muffins on the seat next to him, Bradshaw arrived at the warehouse that bore his name a little past seven. Built around 1900, the building was beginning to deteriorate badly, as was the area

7

surrounding it—the transient-filled part of Salt Lake where, someone would later say, people "sleep in the fields and they die in the fields."

Someone else had risen early that morning, after a restless night. Instead of wearing the T-shirt and Levi's he said he would, he decided to look as "dapper as a CIA agent," putting on a yellow shirt, dark pants and a blue blazer. The polished oak handle of a .357 Magnum protruded slightly from the jacket's inside left pocket. As Bradshaw pulled up to the concrete loading dock and got out of his truck, a cool set of blue eyes watched him, waiting for the old man to pick up the *Salt Lake Tribune* in front of the door and go inside.

Bradshaw was surprised to see his visitor. They talked for fifteen minutes or so about things that mutually concerned them. Feeling he might be unable to shoot him face to face, the visitor hoped Bradshaw would turn around for a second— all that he would need. When Bradshaw finally did, the gunman fired one bullet, at close range, into his back, and then, as the old man was slumped on the green linoleum floor, another into the back of his head. But he wasn't through. There was a plan—and he was obliged to follow it.

Rolling Bradshaw over onto his back, he turned one of his pockets inside out and scattered the contents of his leather, Western-style wallet around the floor: some gas credit cards, a Blue Cross/Blue Shield card, a claim check for a prescription, a list of things he wanted to accomplish, some loose change. Nothing unusual, just the ordinary elements of a person's life. It was meant to look like a robbery, so he did his best to paint the crime scene that way.

One shot, as it turned out, would have been enough. But Franklin Bradshaw's grandson didn't know that. All he knew was this: he didn't want to have to come back and do it again. In fact, he confided to a friend, "the first thing that came to my mind was how easy it was, that it happened so quickly. I thought there would be the agonizing death scene, but he just died, almost as if he were asleep."

It had been a perfect Sunday all right, perfect for a lot of things—including murder. When Bradshaw's sister Bertha asked Berenice a few days later who she thought might have done this, Berenice had an answer: the oil Mafia. But Bertha, other members of the family, and loyal employees were still haunted by the memories and the stories of the nightmare summer of a year before. And though some of these people conveyed their suspicions to the police, the investigation into the killing of Franklin Bradshaw was considered inactive within a couple of months. And inactive it would remain— until something occurred to change all that.

But what happened on the morning of July 23, 1978—and, in a larger sense, what happened to the entire Bradshaw family—had its beginnings a long time before.

2// In Utah, Mormons love to tell the story of the farmer's son from western New York who had a vision—the First Vision. His name was Joseph Smith, Jr.

His parents were Bible-reading New Englanders who moved the family in 1816 from Vermont, where young Joseph had been born eleven years earlier, to New York State—first to Palmyra, then to Manchester. While religiously inclined, the Smiths, like many of their neighbors in that frontier territory, belonged to no specific denomination. This was of great concern to the various religious leaders during that period, who launched a fervent and, at first, united crusade to convert the unconverted, not only in New York, but from New England to as far south as Kentucky.

While some members of his family joined the Presbyterian Church, Joseph was confused by what he called "a strife of words and a contest about opinions." So he turned to his Bible and read the Epistle of James, first chapter and fifth verse: "If any of you lack wisdom, let him ask of God, that giveth to all men liberally, and upbraideth not; and it shall be given him." So Joseph decided to do just that.

Walking in a wooded area near his home, "on the morning of a beautiful, clear day, early in the spring of 1820" (he later wrote), Joseph knelt in prayer. "I had scarcely done so, when immediately I was seized upon by some power which entirely overcame me, and had such an astonishing influence over me

9

as to bind my tongue so that I could not speak. Thick darkness gathered around me, and it seemed . . . as if I were doomed to sudden destruction." Then he went on, "I saw a pillar of light exactly over my head, above the brightness of the sun, which descended gradually until it fell upon me. . . . I saw two Personages, whose brightness and glory defy all description, standing above me in the air. One of them spake unto me, calling me by name and said, pointing to the other—*This is my Beloved Son. Hear Him!*"

When Joseph asked these Personages—God the Father and His Son, Jesus Christ—what sect he should join, he was told to join none of them. A few days later, when Joseph innocently spoke of this to one of the preachers involved in the crusade, he was treated with contempt and soon became the object of ridicule and persecution. But the farmboy doggedly clung to his story, joined none of the faiths, and "found the testimony of James to be true."

Three years later, during the night of September 21, 1823, Joseph was lying in bed when he was visited by an angel named Moroni (son of Mormon), whose loose robe was of a "whiteness beyond anything earthly I had ever seen" and who told him, in Joseph's words, "that God had a work for me to do. . . ." The angel mentioned a book, written on gold plates, which told of "the former inhabitants of this continent, and the source from whence they sprang." The book was deposited with two transparent stones, set in silver bows and attached like eyeglasses to a breastplate. Known as the Urim and Thummin, the stones were used as "seers" in ancient times, the angel told Joseph, and would enable him to translate the writings that he would find on a hill nearby—the hill where Moroni had buried them.

Four years later, Joseph received from the Angel Moroni all that he said would be there, "with this charge: that I should be responsible for them; that if I should let them go carelessly or through any neglect of mine, I should be cut off. . . ." Leaving the Hill Cumorah, Joseph proceeded to translate this precious record, dictating it to scribes from behind a curtain. It was published, in late March of 1830, as the Book of Mormon; and a few days later, on April 6, the Church of Jesus Christ of Latter-day Saints was organized.

Within seven years, in a tradition that continues to this day, the young prophet dispatched missionaries throughout the globe to "call the world to repentance," to spread the gospel that God had once again spoken from the heavens in a last dispensation of truth before the Second Advent of the Savior, and to enlist members for the new sect.

Not long after this, a young Englishman named Samuel Briggs, drifting from job to job, heard two missionaries preaching near the town of Bolesover, in the county of Derbyshire. He began talking with them, soon agreed to convert, and was baptized into the Church in 1849.

"It was just borne upon my soul that the things those men were saying was correct," Brigg's son recalled his father saying. "I have never had occasion to doubt it from that day to this." The son also recalled a song his father used to sing.

> When I was a little boy to Sunday School I went,
> With my Bible and my Testament I used to be content.
> They taught me to believe all things, whatever the Books
>   would say,
> But many of the things I did read, they said were done
>   away.
> So to Zion we will go, to Zion we will go.
> We'll leave these old sectarians, and to ZION WE WILL GO!

Shortly after his baptism, Samuel Briggs, Franklin Bradshaw's maternal grandfather, began the long journey with his wife to the land of Zion—to the green valleys and red-clay deserts of Utah. His fellow Saints had already suffered a great deal. In 1831, hoping to escape intolerance of their religious beliefs (especially their practice of polygamy), Joseph Smith and his followers moved from New York to Kirtland, Ohio, where the first Mormon Temple was completed five years later, while others moved to Jackson County, Missouri, near Kansas City. But mobs kept after them, taking their belongings and, in many cases, their lives. Seeking refuge in Illinois in 1838, they established the city of Nauvoo on the banks of the Mississippi, and Smith soon became its mayor. Not exactly unambitious—after all, here was a man who said he had conversed with God and His Son—Smith announced his intention in 1844 to run for President of the United States on an independent ticket.

His campaign was short-lived. Smith and his brother Hyrum were falsely accused of treason, were imprisoned in Carthage, the county seat, and, while awaiting trial, were killed by a mob of angry citizens who stormed the jail. So Brigham Young, a Vermont glazier and cabinetmaker, was chosen to be the new Prophet, and led the group west to Utah.

Samuel Briggs arrived in Great Salt Lake City (its name until 1868) in October 1852 and moved south to the town of Lehi—named after a prophet in the Book of Mormon—the same month. A farmer, Briggs forged a close friendship with Porter Rockwell, who was a bodyguard for both Joseph Smith and Brigham Young and to whom Smith had given the following advice: if he, like Samson, wore his hair long, no enemy would have power over him. "Many times Father braided Porter's hair," Briggs's son Azer recalled in a biographical sketch of his father. "Father related that he saw a man come to his place and tell Porter he was going to kill him. Porter stood in the doorway of Father's place; the man fired at him three times, and each bullet missed Porter. . . . The man, after his third attempt failed, turned and fled. The words of the Prophet had been verified in this instance, as in many other instances."

Though young Franklin never met his grandfather—who, at the time of his death in 1898, had become a high priest in the Church—both Grandmother Briggs and his mother would tell him this and other Mormon stories as he was growing up.

The Salt Lake Valley ends and the rolling farmland of the Utah Valley begins at a place called Point of the Mountain, the geological link between the Wasatch and Oquirrh ranges, about twenty miles south of Salt Lake City. In gazing out at the Utah Valley, which measures about forty miles from north to south and fifteen miles from east to west, it is easy to understand why it was enthusiastically described to the King of Spain in 1777 as "the most pleasing, beautiful, and fertile site in all New Spain."

On a clear day, the sky above Mount Timpanogos, to the east, and Mount Nebo, to the south, is vast and slightly unreal in feeling, as if its cerulean color had been freshly painted that morning. If one lies on the grass and gazes skyward, as

Franklin and his younger sister Bertha used to do, what clouds there are seem as white as Angel Moroni's exquisite robe and low enough to touch.

Lehi is one of a number of towns in the valley—towns with names like Pleasant Grove, Springville, Payson and, the largest, Provo—and the place where Franklin became the seventh of ten children of John and Emma Briggs Bradshaw on April 3, 1902. His father built the red-brick Victorian house he was born in, and while the brick has since been painted over, the horse chestnut, weeping birch and cherry trees still provide marvelous shade.

Farming was the main occupation at the time and the raising of sugar beets had led to the building of the Lehi Sugar Factory in 1890. The factory became so successful that Lehi was widely known as the first sugar city in the West, and President Benjamin Harrison made a whistle-stop tour of it a year later.

By the time of Franklin's birth, Utah officially had been a state—America's forty-fifth—for only six years, and Lehi a town for a mere fifty-two. The population was barely over two thousand. The Utah Southern Railroad with its "iron monster" cut through Lehi in 1872, followed by the Denver & Rio Grande nine years later. They ran parallel to the two streets that claimed to be the town's main thoroughfare, and therein lay a problem. State Street was in "upper" Lehi and Main Street in "lower," and it was perfectly possible to drive through town on one and not know the other existed. In fact, this became such a topic of conversation—and is still mentioned to this day—that Brigham Young apparently offered his opinion that if the main street wasn't along State, the city would always be divided. In this one instance, perhaps because Main Street already possessed the name, the people of Lehi went against the advice of their Prophet.

"You were not raised. You just grew under sagebrush," Franklin's mother had told his father once, and she was right. Possessing rugged good looks, easy charm, and the raw energy and heart of a true pioneer, John Bradshaw was orphaned at the age of three and started work when he was twelve, herding horses and sheep. His "stubborn, independent disposition" (which passed on to his son) led him to become a cowboy, a buckaroo, and one of the first settlers of Rexburg, Idaho.

Realizing that he "had the cage, but not the bird," his thoughts drifted back to Lehi and a "special girl" he had danced with and who had once become his valentine. From Idaho he sent her letters, saying he was thinking of coming home for a visit, and she replied that he would be welcome. He bought himself a suit of clothes, never having had one before, and arrived home in the fall of 1888. It wasn't long before he and this "special girl"—Emma Briggs—decided to get married.

The couple moved back to Idaho briefly, had a child that lived but three days, and then lost their log cabin and few belongings in a fire. Without a home, they returned to Lehi with a sewing machine and Emma's wedding band—the only things they had salvaged—and lived in a tent on John's grandfather's farm. John got a job hauling rock for the Lehi Sugar Factory, began planting sugar beets, onions ("I believe that I planted the first acre of onions ever raised in Lehi!"), cabbage, tomatoes and potatoes, and slowly acquiring sheep and cattle. In no time at all he prospered, becoming the second person in Lehi to purchase an automobile.

Around the time Franklin was born, the Canadian province of Alberta was being settled. His father's pioneering spirit and sense that it would be "a cattleman's paradise" carried the family to the town of Magrath in March of 1904. Emma told people "she had selected a diamond in the rough," her husband would recall, "and when the busybodies tried to persuade her not to go she said, 'I don't think my diamond is fully polished yet.'"

Success came quickly to this enterprising rough diamond. Shortly after arriving in Canada, he purchased ranch land as far as the eye could see, raising hundreds of cattle and thousands of sheep. A train station on the Canadian Pacific Railroad was given the name Bradshaw, and he became president of a trading company and eventually bought the town of Caldwell. The young orphan boy had come a long way.

Franklin learned a lot from the "sales talks" his father gave him from time to time: the importance of hard work and having good credit, and the stern advice that he should always make his word "as good as gold." But of all the things he gleaned from the father he adored and would try to emulate, one experience played as big a part as any in shaping the man he would become.

One night, on the Bradshaws' farm, their bulldog tangled with a "half wolf dog" from the Canadian Mounted Police. "It was a terrible fight," Franklin wrote later to two of his sisters. "The next morning, both dogs had scars and were bleeding. The half wolf dog won. It probably would not have won but our bulldog was getting old. From then on our bulldog just laid around all day long and was not interested in hunting coyotes or going with us. A short time later, he died. I talked to Father about this and he told me that human beings were the same way. If a person worked for years to build a business and then it failed, sometimes the man would lose all interest in life just like the bulldog. That was the reason a person in business should never fail, and should work all the harder if necessary, but he should never fail."

Shortly after that, on a train trip with his father, the porter told Franklin that an older couple, boarding at the next town, would need a berth, and he wanted to know if Franklin would be willing to part with his. Franklin agreed to, but cagily "added a couple of dollars" to the price. "Of course, I gave Father the price of the berth," he said in that same letter, "and kept the couple of dollars."

He was learning fast.

When John Bradshaw first proposed going to Canada he had promised his wife that if she would pioneer with him for a while, he would bring her back to America and build her a home more beautiful than the one they were leaving in Lehi, anywhere she wanted to be.

Since she wanted the children to be raised in the Mormon Church, they came back to Lehi, and John Bradshaw (who would become the director of a bank, and the president of drug, cereal and cosmetic companies) was good to his word, building a house in 1914 that was considered the finest in town at the time. Located right on State Street, it had a porch in front and back, white-tiled floors in the kitchen and bathroom, steam heat, a full basement (where Franklin lived and kept his motorcycle), and a most unusual and controversial feature: painted murals of Canada, Utah Lake, and two seductive Grecian women in filmy clothing, each with a breast exposed, all done in oil by a French artist named Pierre Rochard, adorning the walls of the dining room, living room, and hall. To complete the ambience, the ceiling was painted sky blue with a smattering of clouds and birds. (When John Bradshaw was away in Canada once, his wife had the Grecian women "covered up.")

Often employing four in help, the family used to have many parties at the house, and Franklin would often bring a comely dark-haired Mormon girl with a rich alto voice. Her name was Gail Webb, and they both attended Lehi High School. She was a cheerleader and he played guard on the football team, graduating in 1922 with the highest honors among all the boys in his class. He would pick Gail up in his father's eight-speed black Cadillac and take her to basketball games in nearby American Fork, to silent movies starring Rudolph Valentino, and, on special occasions, to Salt Lake City to go dancing.

"We danced cheek to cheek," Gail Webb Ross remembered. "He was delightful, cheerful and very well liked. He was his father's son. He was very ambitious and wanted to make money. He always said he would be successful. And he really was. He made the grade.

"I couldn't swear to it, but I think I was his first sweetheart," she said with affection. "In some measure he proposed to me, but I wasn't ready to settle down."

Years later, Bertha would maintain that if only her brother and Gail Webb had gotten married, he would have had a different life. But it never came to pass. So in the fall of 1922, having boldly informed his mother that he did not want to go off on a mission for the Church, Franklin, slightly heartbroken but charged with drive and ambition, entered the University of Utah. Eighteen months later, he met a stunning girl from the Midwest on a Salt Lake City streetcar. She had lovely blue eyes and her brown hair had a marcel wave. Her name was Berenice Jewett—the girl he was to marry.

3// In the fall of 1638, the *John of London* set sail from Hull, England, bound for America. On board were about twenty hardy Puritan families, "nonconformists" fleeing the religious persecution of the Church of England—much in the way Joseph Smith and his group of Latter-day Saints would flee New York State two centuries later.

Two of the people headed for the New World were sons of a well-to-do Yorkshire cloth manufacturer. Arriving in Boston at the beginning of December, they and their families were among the first to settle and name the little town of Rowley, Massachusetts, the following year and the first to "set upon making cloth in this western world." Their names were Maximilian and Joseph Jewett, descendants of the House of Juatt of England and from Henri de Juatt of France.

The tradition of affluence these early Jewetts had begun in England and carried to America had not sustained itself by the time Florence Roberts Jewett gave birth to her first child, Berenice Harriet, in Sioux City, Iowa, on May 12, 1903.

Berenice's father drifted from job to job, moving the family around like a band of gypsies. From Sioux City to Alta, Iowa; twice to Denver, and twice to Salt Lake City, and in Idaho to Payette, Eagle and Boise. Though Berenice was, by her own admission, shy, she and her younger brother, Bill, were "social climbers." Eagle, Idaho, had two churches, Baptist and Methodist, and they would attend Sunday school at whichever one was having a party. "Religion never did sink in very deeply for either of us," Berenice wrote in her unpublished autobiography. "Everytime we moved, which was oftener than I care to relate, we attended Sunday school nearest our home. My religious training included a variety of Christian churches. Not knowing which to believe left me an agnostic and [I] still am."

When they lived in Boise, her parents scraped together enough money to send her to an Episcopal school for girls, many of whom came from well-to-do families. "They drove to school in their live pony carts," Berenice wrote, "invited us to

17

their beautiful homes for little teas after school and birthday parties. Their homes were staffed with maids and butlers and I tried to put my best foot forward and let on like I was used to this luxury. 'You can't make a polished diamond from a lump of coal but you can improve its appearance.'"

Berenice was such a pretty girl that it wasn't long before boys began taking full notice of her. In Denver, in the seventh grade, she "found little love notes in my coat pocket like, 'I love you,' 'You are pretty. I like you.' . . . Of course this sent a trickle down my spine but I was so shy I would walk a long ways out of my way home for fear [a] boy might show up and try to talk with me." Though many boys would pursue her, one in particular would later break her heart.

In Salt Lake, Berenice's mother began a successful career selling women's ready-to-wear. "She liked pretty clothes and her extra income kept the two of us well dressed," Berenice wrote with envy, then resentment. "Mother was not a home-body. . . . As I look back on those days I feel I was robbed of my girlhood. I really didn't care much about those pretty clothes; it was nice to be the best-dressed girl in school but I would much rather have had my mother home when I got home from school than always coming into a dark, dingy apartment that had been closed up all day, breakfast dishes still in the sink. Other kids went out to play after school but I always had [to] dash home to wash dishes, straighten up the house and start our evening meal. On Saturday I cleaned the whole apartment thru. My mother never had to ask me to do these things I just felt it my duty. I always washed the dinner dishes, my mother never had to ask me to do this either, not once. From those days on my life was never carefree and easy like so many young people. . . . My brother was not the help he should have been. He teased and tormented me to death at times but mother always protected him and wouldn't let my father administer the discipline he needed. This was to his determant because it turned other members of the family against him."

The making of a martyr had begun. And, in time, some of her children would say similar things about her.

* * *

18

When Berenice was fifteen and about to enter the ninth grade, her Aunt Lillian and Uncle Lloyd came from Oregon to Salt Lake for a visit. World War I was on, her uncle was going off to fight, so her aunt asked the Jewetts if they would let Berenice come and spend the school year with her in the small town of Redmond in the central part of the state.

The nine months she spent in Redmond were the "most important" of her life. Her aunt gave her advice about boys, and it wasn't long before she was "the envy and jealousy of all the girls in town. The boys were flocking around for dates, little did they know how terrified I was inside. Life started to blossom for me and I loved it.

"I made the terrific mistake of dating two different fellows for the same nite and the same dance but Aunt Lillian came to the rescue and helped me 'lie' out of the one I did not want to go with. I went to the dance with a tall, dark, handsome fellow named Arthur Tuck. Who was the first person I should look in the face but the fellow I had rejected. Confusion dominated my first few weeks so I finally decided to settle for the one I liked best and reject all others. Arthur was a gentleman and I felt I could trust him. He showed me a wonderful time everywhere we went so my choice turned out to be him. Arthur was a senior and the top athlete of this small high school. He was looked up to by all the students and considered the prize catch by all the girls. We never missed a week end going to something. We went out every Fri., Sat., and Sun. nite, but on school nites I studied. He was my date for all school and social functions. I was the only freshman girl at the football banquet that year. He had an old model 'T' Ford and we just lived in his Ford. He kept my desk supplied with rich chocolates I nibbled on during study hour when the teacher wasn't looking."

Since Arthur was "such a big-shot in school" Berenice felt determined to "make him proud of me." She tried out for the school operetta and captured one of the minor leads. Tryouts were announced for the school declamatory contest, and she surprised everyone, including herself, by winning first place on the night of her sixteenth birthday.

But Arthur was hard to keep pace with—literally. He entered the state track meet in Eugene and took *thirty-two* first places—the *entire* meet. (A few years later, this feat made its way into *Ripley's Believe It or Not.*) When he returned to Redmond, the whole town turned out at the train station to welcome him home. "They showered him with flowers," Berenice wrote, "the station was filled with excitement and joy. As he alighted from the train, he had a large bouquet of red roses and several loving cups and 32 gold medals dangling. I felt insignificant with all this fuss going on and I did not want any attention that was his to be drawn my way so I rather slinked in the corner of the station. The girls were crowded around him pulling at his coat and carrying on. He stood for this just so long then he started to look for me. When I saw him looking I knew it was for me and I came out from hiding and he handed me the red roses. At this point the damsels of the town knew they were licked and they didn't have a chance. The town officials put both of us in a car and we were driven up and down Main Street just like real celebrities. Arthur was modest and didn't care for all this fuss, his one thought was for us to be alone. Finally he got his Ford and we slipped away by ourselves to our favorite romantic solitude. When we were alone he said to me, 'Do you remember your promise to me before I left?' I said, 'No, what was it?' 'You promised me a kiss for each *first* I won.' I had forgotten about the promise and when I made it I thought the most he would win would be 3 or 4. When he said, '32,' I nearly fainted. It was a pleasure to keep my promise for both of us."

Just before Berenice was due to leave Redmond and her whirlwind year with Arthur behind, he proposed to her "in a most dramatic, romantic way, just like they do in the movies." Thrilled and practically speechless she accepted, eagerly anticipating "the day when we would always be together."

But that fall, while Arthur was starring in football and being pursued by sorority girls at the University of Oregon, Berenice was back in Salt Lake and miserable, both at East High and among the Mormons. ("In the state of Utah," she wrote, "the Mormons dominate: the grade schools, the high schools, the Universities and even the government. They have their clicks they form at their church and it is next to impossible for a non-Mormon to break thru. It is sad but true.") No longer quite as shy now, perhaps because she was engaged to the famous Mr. Tuck, Berenice threatened to run away from home. Not anxious for their only daughter to do that, Berenice's parents told her she could go to any school of her choice, and she picked Westminster, a Presbyterian school, for her junior and senior years. Though she and Arthur were still writing to each other, "and I was as much in love with him as ever," his letters became less frequent.

In the summer of 1920, Arthur stopped in Salt Lake on his way to, and back from, the Olympic Games in Belgium. "Naturally I was all aflutter but our romance was dying gradually," Berenice rationalized. "We were too far apart and his college life was more sophisticated than my immature high school days. . . . If we could have been together our romance might have survived two or three years but separated as we were, miles apart, living in entirely different environments, it just wasn't in the cards."

But something disturbing happened on Arthur's way back to Redmond, something involving Berenice's mother and "one of her 'sneaky tricks.'" While Arthur and Berenice went to her grandmother's canyon cabin so that they could hike and be alone, Berenice's mother went through Arthur's pockets ("she was used to going thru Dad's pockets so this was just another pocket for her to pick") and discovered a letter he had written to a girl back in Redmond but never mailed. She not only read the letter, but copied it and hid it in one of Berenice's drawers. "A few days after Arthur left," Berenice wrote, "I was in a vocal recital at Westminster. Mother, Dad, and I took the street car out to school for this program. On the way out my mother said to me: 'Who is Mildred Smith?' Well, the only Mildred Smith I had known was a girl in Redmond, she was in Arthur's class at school, and I think she would have given her eyeteeth to have gone with him when I did. . . . I asked my mother why she wanted to know but she just passed it off by saying: 'She just wondered.'" The following day Berenice was straightening her drawers and found the copied letter. "There were no names attached but the minute I read it I put the whole story together. He had told her in this letter he could hardly wait to get back to her and his Ford. . . .

"I threw myself on my bed and cried all one day just as hard as I could cry. When I could cry no more I resolved that

21

that was the end and that I must adjust myself to a new life, one that did not include Arthur. I wrote him a very sarcastic letter and . . . never heard from him again. A broken love affair is very devastating and it took me several years to get over this. Every nite when I went to bed I shed a few tears [and] dreamed of him, but in the day time I worked very hard to conceal my feelings. I spent many hours playing the piano and singing, I doubled my efforts in school, all this to try to forget my heart-felt broken romance."

The "new life" Berenice was determined to have would begin two years later, in the fall of 1922, when she decided to attend the University of Utah.

4// The home is the center of civilization. The goal of the college girl should be to attain the highest position of woman, that of homemaker, wife and mother. A practical knowledge of the preparation and relative values of foods, the making and proper use of clothing, the furnishing and building of a house, the care and feeding of children, are necessary qualifications. The curriculum of the modern university permits the girl to equip herself with this necessary training. The welfare of the race depends upon her wisdom in choosing the correct preparation. The college girl should become all that the word implies—queen of the home.

If one didn't know these stern words had been written by Miss Lucy M. Van Cott, the formidable dean of women at the University of Utah, one might think they were lifted verbatim from a pamphlet explaining the Mormon Church's view of a woman's role in society.

If homemaking and motherhood were destined to be her future curriculum, Berenice was determined that "fun, the boys and social life" be her current one until, as her father had said once, the old grind began.

In the same yearbook that Dean Van Cott stated her views for eternity, a quote from Ralph Waldo Emerson would hold special meaning for a six-foot-two-inch freshman. With thick, wavy brown hair, he had a rock-hard physique, was strong enough to pick up a motor block, and proudly possessed the last name of Bradshaw.

> Life is too short to waste,
> 'Twill soon be dark;
> Up! mind thine own aim, and
> God speed the mark!

Franklin not only possessed his father's work ethic and frontier mentality, but had a vision, born of instinct and cleverness, that could be uncanny. And, over the years, especially with his oil dealings, he had what everybody needs a little of: luck.

"Where most people can't see to the end of the street, Frank could see to the end of the street and around the corner for miles and miles," Doug Steele, an affable bulldog of a man who worked for him for thirty-two years, recalled in admiration after his death. "Frank was a pioneer, a plugger, a builder from day one. He was the kind of businessman who made this country great."

It was during his freshman year that his vision first bore fruit. He was taking a chemistry class and found that he couldn't get some of the chemicals he needed locally and had to send elsewhere for them. Deciding that Utah needed a chemical distributor, he persuaded his father to invest some money to form one, and, along with the Thatchers (one of whom was his professor), they started the Wasatch Chemical Company. (Even before Franklin got to the university, he had developed such an interest in mining and geology that he managed to complete, in one year, a correspondence course in geological studies that normally took three.)

He played on the freshman football team, joined both the Pi Kappa Alpha (social) and Alpha Kappa Psi (business) fraternities, and met his bride-to-be in the spring of his sophomore year. Franklin and Berenice were introduced by a mutual friend and he soon asked her to his fraternity formal. When he came to call for her in a tuxedo, white silk muffler, and gloves, driving the same black Cadillac he used to take Gail Webb around Lehi in, Berenice recalls how "handsome" he looked and that her mother told her, "Now *there,* that is the first real fellow you have ever had."

"I liked him because we could talk," Berenice said, remem-

23

bering that first date nearly sixty years later. "He was the first fellow I'd met that I could just sit and talk with. That's what attracted me to him. Most of those kids in those days were 'punters' and punting—silliness—was the campus rage. Franklin was not a punter and that pleased me."

But their first date was not a total success. He was disappointed that she didn't know what kind of car he was driving; she was dismayed that with only one seat in front for the driver, you couldn't drive *and* neck at the same time. They went together the rest of that spring and summer, but by the fall of their junior year, Berenice became edgy and felt Franklin was taking her for granted.

"Every Friday afternoon the school had open matinee dances," she wrote. "I loved to dance and suggested to Franklin we go. Why he would not go to these dances I don't know but we would sit on the lawn and quarrel (I don't know about what, he managed to find something) until the dance was over, then he would be nice to me and we would make up and he would take me home. This used to make me furious. On weekends he'd go chasing down to Lehi to see his father. I never dated on school nites, which meant weekends were for dating. It was a campus knowledge we were going together 'steady' so no other fellows would 'cut in.' I was left without a date many weekends and I didn't like it. They say true love never runs smooth, so I guess this was true love manifesting itself. I always said: 'We got married so we could stop quarreling.' That worked for a while."

One October evening, walking home together from the library, Franklin told Berenice his parents (Franklin's mother had died during his freshman year and his father was now remarried) were going to California for the winter and suggested it would be nice if they could go with them.

Berenice took a long look at him before saying, "Why, *what* would people think?"

"Oh, I mean for us to get married," Franklin reassured her.

"Now that was *his* proposal," Berenice said decades later, the bemused disappointment barely hidden by time. "This other fellow had given me a *real* romantic proposal and I was

24

just thrilled. But him, it was, 'Let's go to California,' and we were not panting for breath at this point either."

This was her version.

The other story—Franklin's, as related by his sister Bertha and one of his daughters—went like this. Another of Fred Jewett's business ventures was failing; Berenice's mother was urging a family move to California, and told Berenice that if Franklin loved her he would surely follow. But Berenice had been through one broken romance and didn't want another. So she proposed to *him*. He said that he wanted to finish school first, but she insisted they could still be married. He then said he wanted to establish himself in business, but she was not to be deterred. Knowing that her parents could not afford a grand wedding and would disapprove of her marrying at that point, Berenice and Franklin decided to elope.

They agreed to rendezvous on the last day of October at the drinking fountain in front of the Park Building on campus. Franklin drove Berenice home (her mother was at work), and she put on her best outfit—a black velvet dress with a matching hat. He went to her father's sinking dry-cleaning operation, where he had left a suit to be cleaned, and "brazenly" asked Mr. Jewett if he could change his clothes there. He went back to pick up his bride, then they stopped at the jewelry store to get their rings and headed north toward Ogden.

When they arrived, they went immediately to the county clerk's office to obtain a license, and said that they did not want their marriage listed in the official records. Asked where they wanted to be married, they said the courthouse in the building would be fine. While they assumed that no one could marry them there but a judge, they did not confirm that. After what seemed like hours in a waiting room, a man and two witnesses finally appeared and the legal ceremony proceeded.

What Berenice didn't learn until she looked at the marriage certificate months afterward was that they had been married by a Mormon bishop. "They had *slipped* in a Mormon, another sneaky Mormon trick," she shouted years later to a visitor. "*They* could have at least asked us what religion we preferred, and *we* didn't have sense enough to say we wanted a judge. When my mother found out that it was a Mormon bishop, she hit the ceiling. And of course I've always been ashamed of that on there, because those were *not* our intentions."

Try as one might, it seems there was no escaping the Mormons—at least in Utah. Nevertheless, Franklin and Berenice became Mr. and Mrs. Franklin J. Bradshaw on Halloween Day, 1924—a day that would hold significance of a different kind fifty-nine years later.

They not only had eloped, but decided to keep their marriage a secret for a while. When Berenice's father left for California about a week later, he warned his only daughter that if she got married while he was gone, he would never forgive her. "I was so heartbroken because I was already married," she wrote. "To my knowledge this is the only time I ever defied my parents. It wasn't right and I have regretted it all of my life. Parents deserve better treatment than this."

When they finally told their parents, Berenice's mother cried all night, and Franklin's father, being a practical man, merely inquired how his son was going to support her. They finished the quarter at Utah, and Franklin began working at Wasatch Chemical Company full-time. But relations with the Thatchers were somewhat strained, so in the spring of 1925, in an Overland ("the frog") that, Berenice claimed, had no brakes and front wheels that shimmied so badly she was amazed her husband could keep it on the road, the Bradshaws started toward Challis, Idaho—the beginning of their "hobo trip"—where Franklin had heard that the Bayhorse Mine was hiring and paying good money.

Just before they left, Berenice's sorority, Gamma Phi, gave a dance in their honor. Berenice scraped together enough money to buy a new dress and asked Franklin to buy her a corsage. But he refused, an indication not only of their financial situation at the time but, to some degree, of the tight leash he would try to keep her on in the years to come.

"Once the preacher ties the 'knot,'" Berenice wrote, "the courtship frills are frayed strings."

Traveling through southern Idaho and choking on dust, they arrived at the Bayhorse Mine only to be told that women were not welcome. They stayed the night in Challis and pushed on to Leadore, a "godforsaken" place, Berenice recalled, with no trees, no grass, just a single two-story building and a blacksmith's shop. Franklin pawned a gold nugget (which actually was a fake) for a room and $3. And the next day, before driving to the mining town of Butte, Montana, he pawned his father's watch. Since the watch, like the nugget, was of little value, they left Leadore like Bonnie and Clyde, with Berenice looking intently out the rear window "in case the watch stopped and we would be apprehended before we got out of town."

The quarreling that Berenice had hoped would end with their marriage started up again as they both felt the frustration of their predicament. Franklin could have easily gone back to Lehi and built a future on the solid foundation of the Bradshaw name, but he was his father's son, proud and determined to make it on his own.

Franklin landed a job in Butte running an electric motor in the mines, pawned their car (which they recovered a month later at an interest rate of 800 percent!), and rented a room in a downtown hotel. Convinced that the only work a married woman could get was "homework," Berenice removed her wedding ring and tried to get a job. She spent one day as a stenographer before answering an ad and going door to door, asking the good women of Butte if they wanted to order silk-knitted dresses by mail. When the five dresses she had managed to take orders for began arriving at her customers' houses, Berenice's phone started ringing off the hook with calls of complaint about their fit. She was not prepared to take the little money she had and mail the dresses back, so she told Franklin, who was not happy at the mine, that they had to leave town.

But before leaving Butte, a place where prostitution, gambling and bootlegging ruled the day, Franklin wanted to show his wife how "the wild of Butte lived." In an uncharacteristic display of playfulness, he dressed Berenice up in *his* clothes and took her to the red-light district of town. Walking along the street, Berenice recalled how these "naughty girls would reach out and try to drag the males into their dens. One grabbed me, I became frightened and started to run, then they realized I was a decoy. Franklin was disgusted with me because I ran, but at this point my fright overcame me. What was supposed to be a 'jolly' evening ended abruptly."

They pushed on, traveling north through Deer Lodge, Montana, and soon arrived in the small northern Idaho town of Kellogg. The mine wasn't hiring, so they pitched a pup tent on the outskirts of town, and simply drank in the scenery for a while. In Spokane, Washington, with only a nickel in their pockets and $20 in a Butte bank, they came across a sign that said "ALL THE BUTTERMILK YOU CAN DRINK 5¢"; so Berenice, who would rather have starved than drink the stuff, told Franklin to use the nickel and "tank up," while she arranged through a local bank to get her money.

Still moving west, over the Cascades, they felt carefree, Berenice recalled, despite not knowing where their next meal or job was coming from. But when they reached Seattle, they both realized it was time to bring out one of John Bradshaw's blank checks that Franklin had been carrying. He had brought his fraternity directory with him, and spotted the name of a man who was president of the largest building-and-loan company in town. He went to see him, gave him the Pi Kappa Alpha secret handshake, and cashed a check for $25. "This is the first time we had sought help," Berenice wrote with pride. "That $25 looked like a million and in those days it went farther than a hundred does today."

Tacoma was the next stop. Franklin found a job working over a hot blast furnace, and they met a couple from California with three children. Their names were Vern and June Hunt. The Hunts and the Bradshaws decided to form a "caravan" and go to the Yakima Valley to pick fruit. But they never got there. They had gone in the wrong direction. Disillusioned at this point, they drove toward Olympia, Washington, instead, stopping at every service station along the way to ask for work. Once they reached Olympia, they were told that people were being hired to cut down trees in a forest about five miles from town. So once again, Franklin and Berenice pitched the pup tent and called it home. While the men cut down the pine trees and sawed them into foot-length pieces, the women peeled the bark with

28

heavy crowbars. They received $6 a week per couple and lived on pancakes, potato soup, rice and beans.

It wasn't long before Berenice tired of this hand-to-mouth existence and told Franklin that she had had enough. So they parted company with the Hunts and decided to go south to Portland, where Berenice's aunt and uncle lived, the same people she had lived with during her romantic year in Redmond. Looking like "a pair of tramps," they arrived in time for a Sunday dinner of pot roast, potatoes, gravy and *real* butter. Long afterward, Berenice could describe that meal as if she had just eaten it.

For a while they felt they were in paradise. They house-sat for two weeks while Berenice's relatives went on vacation; Franklin began working for a contractor, and Berenice got a job at the Meier & Frank department store. They rented an apartment, and after two more construction jobs, Franklin began working for the Ford Motor Company, where he started on the assembly line and soon became a supervisor.

But Berenice developed emphysema and was told that she needed to leave the damp climate of Portland for a drier one. So they picked up once more and headed for California, where Franklin's father and stepmother were spending the winter, and where the Jewetts had moved earlier that year.

Berenice was overjoyed to be back among her family. "They were 'fun' people to be around," she wrote, and then leveled one of the many jabs she would take at the Bradshaws over the years. "Franklin's people were religious, their customs and outlook on life were very different from my people. My people were free from ritual living, no inhibitions."

If she did not feel comfortable among the Bradshaws, he did not feel at home among the Jewetts. But Franklin was not outspoken about it. "Dad *didn't* gossip," his daughter Elaine said. "He didn't like people telling stories on each other. He would never tell stories that reflected badly on Mother. But she told *lots* of stories. Her story was that he said to her, 'Your family drinks and they party and that's *not* my lifestyle,' and she would get irate. This was one of his rare occasions of trying to confront something directly and being very honest about it. But his problem was that after that he fell apart and Mother cried. She felt he was demolishing her. He didn't *stick* by his guns. It was always a problem with him—not wanting to hurt people's feelings."

For six months, they lived and worked in Los Angeles, Franklin with a trucking company and Berenice in the jewelry department at Robinson's. But Franklin felt that he wasn't getting anywhere, and so he made a decision: he was going back to Utah, and he told Berenice that she could either go with him or she could stay. Berenice didn't want to leave her family, but she felt that her place was with her husband.

Like the marriage proposal, this story has another version, and this is the way Franklin's sister Bertha would like it to be remembered: "Franklin told her that he was *not* taking her back to Utah, and was leaving her in California with her mother. He said that it was a mistake that they married. She went into a tirade and said, 'Oh, no, you're not. You're *not* leaving me. We're married and I'm going with you.' He told me, 'I couldn't do it, I just couldn't get away from her. She wouldn't allow it.'"

Whichever version is correct, the hobo trip of more than a year was over. In July of 1926, Franklin and Berenice headed back to Utah—back to the state where he would ultimately amass his fortune and where, one year later, they would have their first child and only son.

5// Three days after leaving Los Angeles, they arrived in Lehi, Franklin's hometown. Franklin started working for the Lehi Cereal Company, of which his father was president, they rented a house from a woman that John Bradshaw used to stay with as an orphan, and they had no pressing financial worries. But Berenice found life in Lehi confining and "foreign," and longed for the city living of Portland, Los Angeles, or even Salt Lake.

Because of her background ("free, liberal, unreligious")

she did not, and could not bring herself to, enter into Lehi's community affairs and religious activities. It was against her nature, and she didn't accept this way of life. Though she insists she did not antagonize or provoke anyone, there are many in the Bradshaw family who remember her impassioned airing of her views at Sunday dinners at the family house on State Street. "She would do anything except in the Mormon way, if she could. She would do her washing on Sunday, her biggest work jobs, things to be contrary," Bertha recalled.

Though Franklin and his father were not devout Mormons ("jack-Mormons" is the most common term), the family as a whole were. Sensing his wife's feeling of isolation, Franklin urged Bertha to try to involve Berenice with the Church. "He would say to me," Bertha remembered, " 'Take Berenice to church, to Sunday School, to Relief Society.' He wanted in the worst way for her to go. But she would say, *'Me* go to church? *What* would I do?' She was lonesome. If she would have gone, she would have known women and she would have got involved in the wonderful art projects they had. Not even once would she set foot in the door. And that's when Franklin said, 'She's a Mormon hater.' "

Since Mormons are notoriously passionate about their religion and their desire to convert people to it, it is not hard to understand the uneasiness Berenice felt. But it is one thing not to be a Mormon in Utah (especially in a place like Lehi in those days) and quite another to be so outspoken against them. Berenice had come a long way from the shy girl she had been as a child. She had a wonderful, boisterous personality and could easily entertain a roomful of people all evening if she had to. She was strong and she was forthright, but she was sailing against the wind.

By Christmas of 1926 Berenice was pregnant, and the following August, just before midnight on the 10th, Robert Jewett Bradshaw was born. Though the baby was strong and healthy, Berenice was furious with Franklin. He had her admitted to the hospital about six hours earlier, but disappeared for a while during her labor pains, an indifference she claimed would mark the births of their other three children as well.

By the following summer, his passion for geology as strong as ever (in time his reputation as an amateur geologist would be known far and wide), Franklin decided to do some prospecting in American Fork Canyon, leaving his young bride and baby with his parents in Lehi. "To my recollection," Berenice wrote, "he did not ask his father if we were wanted, he just dumped us there. . . . I was the 'goat.' They worked the tail off of me. I felt like a servant being used to the utmost. Every Saturday, Father and Sylvia [Bushman, Franklin's stepmother] would leave early for a day in Salt Lake and before they went out the door they would turn and say to me: 'We are leaving the Saturday cleaning to you.' Every Sunday Sylvia would invite some of her relatives to dinner and I was expected to wash a kitchen full of dirty dishes while they retired to the front room. After I finished the dish job they would insist that I entertain their guests by playing the piano and singing. One Sunday I fooled them. The dishes washed, the baby down for a nap, I ducked out the back door and disappeared. When I returned my father-in-law said: 'Well, you didn't have to sneak off.' I was so unhappy, so homesick, if I had had the money I would have taken my baby on a bus and gone home to my parents in California."

When Franklin finally descended from the hills and got himself into a bath, Berenice had something to tell him. "Your father says it is time you got a job and supported your family."

No sooner had Franklin gotten dry than he announced he was going to Salt Lake to find work. He saw an ad in the paper—"EMPLOYEE WANTED TO WORK IN PARTS STORE. CHANCE FOR ADVANCEMENT."—and went to apply at the Mendenhall Auto Parts Company. But when he walked in, there was a large stack of applications already sitting on the desk. Mr. Mendenhall told him that he wasn't simply looking for an employee, but someone that could help build up the business. Franklin stated that he was the man for the job and recalled, in a 1975 letter to his employees, that "he hired me and didn't even bother to look over or study the other applications."

His auto-parts career had begun.

The Bradshaws moved to Salt Lake and into a tiny house Franklin's father had loaned them on Downington Avenue.

There was another baby "in the basket," and they had little money. "We were so poor and destitute that winter," Berenice wrote, "I didn't dare take 10¢ and ride the bus to town. For 25¢ I would go to the store and buy a head of lettuce, loaf of bread, a bunch of carrots and that was our supper. If I had an extra 10¢ I'd buy us a soup bone."

Robert was a difficult baby, she recalled, and it was a struggle to get him to sleep. He would cry in the night for no apparent reason and "wore me to a frazzle." Franklin was working long hours and was the employee Mr. Mendenhall hoped he would be, but he was not satisfied working for someone else. He decided that he wanted to be in business for himself, and a two-day trip to Provo for Mendenhall's enabled him to see that city's need for an auto-parts store.

So with a loan of $12,000 from his father and the grittiness needed to make it work, Franklin Bradshaw opened his first Bradshaw Auto Parts store on 333 West Center Street in Provo in the summer of 1929. He was finally about to run something; it would be *his*, and in time it would become, in different ways and for different reasons, considerably more than that.

On July 6, late that summer evening, the Bradshaw family expanded to four. A "plump, healthy" baby arrived and they named her Marilyn, after the dancer and actress Marilyn Miller. Franklin was not home when Berenice went into labor—he had been called back to the store for an emergency—and her mother, who had come to visit, stayed with Robert while Berenice's uncle took her to the hospital.

The problems they were having with their son continued. He still wasn't sleeping, was hard to toilet-train, and would wander away if not watched carefully. "We would tie him up in the yard with a strong rope," Berenice wrote, "and when we would check on him there would be the rope but no boy. A large irrigation canal ran thru town only a block away. The canal was the first place we would look, always expecting to see him floating lifeless. . . . Three blocks from our house were the railroad tracks. That was the second place we would look, expecting to see a crushed body. . . . One day he was found a mile from home. The business district was only two blocks away so he would wander up there and come home with new toys. One day he rode home on a new tricycle. I would call Franklin in frantic but he would inform me he could not leave his business. Many a time I had to leave a tiny baby alone while I searched for Bob. One day I had him tied up and a small Boy Scout came along and with indignation he chastised me for tying a little boy up. I said: 'I tied him up because I loved him.'"

On March 14, 1931, Berenice called Franklin at the store and insisted he come home.

"What for?" he asked.

"Guess what for?" she snapped, but he did not come home until it was time to close the store.

They named their third child Elaine, and she barely grazed the scales at five pounds. At the hospital, Berenice was put into a large room with four or five other mothers. During visiting hours, she recalled, the babies would be brought in so the visitors could see mother and child together. "The visitors would look at these darling new babies, with heads of dark hair and dimples. They raved and commented on the beautiful babies, then they would look at this thin, weasel-looking baby of mine and say: 'Aren't they sweet?' From then on I covered her up, she wasn't on exhibition. The nurse would bring Elaine in to nurse; the poor little thing would suck and chop but get nothing from me. They would take her away, hungry. It always worried me for fear they would forget to give her a bottle. I was glad to get her home, she started filling out and became a darling looking baby. Elaine was the sweetest baby, she never cried. She would sleep so long I would wonder if she was still alive."

Berenice had had three babies in a little more than three and a half years. When asked how it had happened, she would reply jauntily, "I was too tired to resist."

There were five Bradshaws now and very little money. Elaine was born just before the 1931 "bank holiday," and banks had been failing nationally at an alarming rate. The two banks in which Franklin had his deposits—in Provo and Lehi—closed in the same week. He had empty boxes on the shelves—a ploy on his part to make customers think he was loaded with stock—and little money to get new merchandise.

He was working long days, "from early morning until late at nite, seven days a week," Berenice wrote. It was a routine he would adhere to, with little exception, for the rest of his life. "The children were my complete responsibility and care," she continued. "Bob was still running off and, on occasion, taking Marilyn with him. One day, just before Elaine was born, they had disappeared in the morning and had not returned by three in the afternoon.

"I was frantic but felt too miserable to start hunting. I kept thinking they would get hungry and come home, so I stayed home waiting. Finally I could stand it no longer and . . . found them blocks from home. Bob had taken his tricycle but it was not with them. With a stick I whammed Bob every step of the way home. Then I demanded he show me where he left his tricycle." He led her to a grocery store, where the clerk told Berenice they'd been there for hours, had wanted candy, but she hadn't given them any. Berenice was disgusted and implied the woman should have sent them home. "I never went after Bob again. When he ran away I just waited for him to come home. I had Marilyn and Elaine to look after, I could not be constantly leaving these babies and go on the prowl looking for Bob. When I quit looking he quit running away. Bob was always a sweet boy, never did naughty things like other boys. He would never strike another child even in self defense. But he was hard to raise. He was five years old before we could get him toilet trained. One day Franklin put him in the bath tub and took the broom to his behind. Another time we went up the canyon on a family picnic, Bob messed his pants, Franklin took his clothes off and ducked him in the cold mountain stream. When I think of all the cruel things we did to that boy trying to toilet train him, I just shudder.

"Those were trying days, three small children to care for. It was work, work, work. I loved my children dearly," she wrote, then added, almost defensively: "I did everything I was told to do by the doctors for their health and well being. I did not neglect them, ever."

When Franklin had to leave Provo to collect merchandise or deliver parts, the family on occasion went with him. In summer, they sometimes drove to Saratoga, a natural-springs resort a short distance away on the shores of Utah Lake, to swim. But most of the time, she said, she was alone. "Sundays I would watch the neighbors go off in their cars with their families and picnic lunches," she wrote. ". . . Many a Sunday afternoon for years I would throw myself on the bed and cry. Cry for someone to show an interest, to relieve me of my constant burden. In the last fifty years I have cried enough tears to float a battleship. The well has dried up now but the emotions are still there."

It would be just such a Sunday when they came to tell her the news about Franklin.

Berenice's life brightened for a while when the family moved into an apartment above the store. Though Franklin constantly ran down the stairs to service a customer who might ring the bell after hours, this living arrangement brought the family closer together than they would be in the years that followed their move to Salt Lake City.

"Dad would come upstairs at night, sit in his chair with his newspaper, and I'd wiggle into his lap," Elaine remembered with pleasure. "Mother played the piano and sang for a long time. I had to learn all the Shirley Temple songs and have my hair done in ringlets. I was supposed to *be* Shirley Temple, you see, but after I got sick it was all over."

At the age of four Elaine contracted rheumatic fever. Berenice said they took her to a heart specialist but that neither he nor the pediatrician who diagnosed it told them to keep her in bed. So Berenice took the three children to San Diego for the California Exposition, feeling that Elaine especially would benefit from exercise and fresh air. "The result of our ignorance [and a distrust of doctors to begin with] and the doctors' failure to advise us," Berenice wrote, "left Elaine with a damaged heart."

Since Berenice loved dancing, it was natural that she would want to interest her children in it. Filled with the hope that Marilyn could be a dancer like the woman she was named after—Marilyn Miller—she enrolled her, as well as Robert, in a dance class. But Marilyn did not live up to her mother's expectations. "All my early years of effort proved useless," Berenice wrote with disappointment. "After four years of lessons my Marilyn could not 'hippity-hop.'" Though it wouldn't happen until many years later, Berenice's dream of having a dancer in the family would be fulfilled: her only granddaughter would one day dance at Lincoln Center in New York City with the New York City Ballet.

In the spring of 1937 the entrepreneur in Franklin was visualizing expansion, and Salt Lake seemed the obvious place to go. He began looking for a suitable building and a house in which to live. Being a product of the Depression, Franklin would have been content to go back to the tiny house on Downington Avenue they had lived in when he worked for Mendenhall's, Berenice said, but she and his father talked him out of it.

The dark-purple brick house they finally settled on was located at 1327 Gilmer Drive on the East Bench. One of a row of houses with tidy lawns in a staunchly Mormon neighborhood, it had a front porch, a yard, and more room than they had ever had. If a person walked a few yards up the street in an easterly direction and turned around, he would be able to see the rays of the Utah sun glinting off the Great Salt Lake in the far distance and spectacular sunsets just before nightfall.

"I thought it was terrific to have a house with fruit trees in the back, poplars along the side, and spruce trees along the street," Elaine recalled. "I liked to sit up in the trees and smell the blossoms. I had a little apricot tree that was all *mine* and planted a cherry tree with a pit. We also had a marvelous apple tree right in the middle of the backyard with a branch you could hang from. But Mother eventually took away the fruit trees because they were messy."

The family moved into their new home in late May of 1937. After the many places and conditions Franklin and Berenice had lived in and under during their hobo trip and in the years following it, they were finally establishing a home from which they would never move. They had had problems in their marriage and had come close to parting in California. But they had a family of three now, a deep sense of responsibility toward them, and divorce, in any case, was not something people, regardless of their religion, rushed into as quickly as they might today.

But what could they have envisioned were the dramas

that awaited them—dramas that would unfold after the birth of their fourth and last child, Frances Bernice, on April 6, 1938.

It had been seven years since Elaine was born, and Berenice was both surprised and dismayed to learn in the summer of 1937 that she was pregnant. "This was unexpected because I was looking forward to having all my kids in school that coming year," she wrote. "What freedom I would enjoy. That first Christmas in Salt Lake was the bleakest I have ever known in my entire life. I took the only 50¢ we had to buy some candy for the children's stockings. Santa brought Bob a cheap little red wagon, the girls each a doll, and that was all. Franklin gave me the devil for buying those few toys, saying I could buy them cheaper after Christmas. What a horrible thing to do to children, deny them one toy each for Christmas. Franklin was so on edge that winter, he was horrible to live with. Expecting a baby under these conditions was almost more than I could bear. I wanted to die many times. But as life goes on in spite of our choosing, we survived the storm. Franklin said there were days on end he ate no lunch or dinner to make financial ends meet.

"When it came time for the baby and me to come home Franklin had to go out of town. He told me to take a taxi home, with a new baby and all the equipment you go to the hospital with, say nothing about my physical weakness. As usual I was left alone to take care of my own burden. I was terribly upset to think he could not come and get this new baby and me. My sister-in-law happened to call me that day and asked if there was anything they could do to help me? I said: 'Yes, I have no way to get home.' She sent her husband, Floyd, to the hospital to pick me and [the] baby up. Was he indifferent. He was as onry as Franklin. He didn't even help me out of the car. I tumbled out, baby and all. My children were not allowed to visit the maternity ward so naturally they were all eyes and very excited to see our new baby. Marilyn loved bathing and dressing her, she was Frances's other mother."

Not long after Frances was born, Marilyn had a question for her mother.

"Was Frances's birth a mistake?"

"Marilyn, I'd hate to think that any child was a mistake."

But Berenice would come to say that if abortions had been legal, she wouldn't have had any of her children. And she would have her reasons.

6// In the autumn of 1939, Elaine again came down with rheumatic fever. Her parents did not identify the symptoms at first, and when she began falling down a lot and having a difficult time feeding herself, her mother scolded her for being clumsy and messy. Elaine was told that the pains in her knee joints were simply of the growing variety, but in fact she had chorea—also known as St. Vitus' dance—and that, along with the rheumatic fever, kept her bedridden on and off for more than two years.

"The boy next door used to come over and say, 'I have a secret to tell you, but you must promise you won't tell anybody.' He would lean over and whisper, 'You're going to die.' He was serious. As it turned out I was grateful," Elaine said, "because it challenged me. For a while, I cried every night, but I couldn't let on that I knew, because that might implicate him. But as soon as the door was shut and the lights went out, I would cry." Eventually, with the same kind of resolve and determination both of her parents possessed in their own ways, she decided she was going to live.

Yet even before her illness set in and physically isolated her from her peers, Elaine felt another kind of ostracism. When she was in the first grade, her teacher asked each of the students to stand and state their religion. While each cherubic, soap-polished face rose up and said "LDS," Elaine stood and innocently said "Unitarian," to an immediate warcry of "What's that?"

For a child of six the effect was devastating, and she would come to feel that she would have been better off had she been raised a Mormon.

* * *

·Not long after Elaine was confined to her room, Robert began having epileptic seizures. In medieval times, epilepsy was thought to be caused by demons. Whatever was causing Robert's seizures in 1941, the sad fact remains that at first neither Franklin nor Berenice wanted to accept and deal with their son's problem. That was left to Marilyn, who was moved from the room she had shared with Elaine to one in the basement so that she could be near her brother.

"He would often have the seizures in the morning when he had something to do," Marilyn said, the memory still fresh in her mind. "In the basement there were washtubs and we used them as sinks. Bob and I had our toothbrushes and towels down there. When he would have a seizure, I would run out and grab a towel—he used to get so red in the face—and wet it with cold water and wipe his face with it, and talk to him. 'It's going to be all right. Don't worry about it. Everything's okay.' I have no idea whether he heard me, and I did not always tell the folks he'd had one. Seeing somebody have a seizure is a frightening thing. Even as much as I saw it and took care of it, it still was discomforting. For years after I moved to New York, if I woke up in the middle of the night, I'd stop and listen to the sounds to see what woke me up. Because that's what would happen: I'd wake up and hear Bob thrashing around."

By the end of 1941, following the bombing of Pearl Harbor, the United States had entered World War II. Since Franklin was needed to help keep vehicles on the road, he was gone from home much of the time. His absence, along with the problems Elaine and Bob were having, took their toll on Berenice. She suffered what she termed "nervous exhaustion."

"Going into a building I had a feeling of the walls falling in on me," she wrote, "or that I would smother if I didn't get out doors. At night I couldn't go to sleep because of sinking feelings, as tho each breath were my last breath. I kept Franklin awake talking to me; if I could hear his voice I knew I was still alive. I trotted from doctor to doctor with no relief. Their advice was to rest. How can a woman with four children and a nine-room house rest? So it was decided to send Bob and Marilyn away to boarding school. This would relieve the workload at home."

Berenice contends that it was impossible to get a house-keeper during this time, because everyone was involved in the war effort. But Marilyn and Elaine remember clearly that their father wanted to get a Mormon woman to come in, but their mother wouldn't hear of it. So once again the burden—and the role of mother, especially Frances's—fell on Marilyn's strong and willing shoulders.

"I did a lot of baby-sitting and taking care of Frances. I was the oldest girl and it was always my responsibility to see to it that dinner got started, if Mother wasn't going to be home. It was up to *me* to watch over the kids, it was up to *me* to take care of Frances. Elaine got unhappy because she wanted to take care of the baby. I accepted this as *my* responsibility. I respected my father and I matured in that way. So I was asked to do this and I was asked to do that. I did it, I didn't question it. I accepted what my father told me and I did what my mother told me."

For the Bradshaw children, Elaine recalled, home was a pretty desolate place during this period. When their mother was there, she stayed in her room most of the time. When she wasn't, she was often, on the advice of a physician, taking singing lessons, and she found that it really helped her—"like bringing sunshine into the soul," Berenice wrote. And even when their father was in town he would not come home for dinner, though Elaine contends she got used to that.

"It seemed the way things were supposed to be. I *wanted* him around more, but he wasn't. What we all wanted to do was go down to work with him, which meant always being around him, on *his* turf, where he could always be more comfortable than he could at home. I think we all understood he wasn't comfortable at home and that it wasn't *our* fault. I perceived it early on. It was not quite like that in Provo, it got worse in Salt Lake, and really bad after Frances arrived.

"Because of Mother's breakdown, primarily from having Frances, and her inability to deal with things, Frances learned very quickly that anything she wanted she could get by throwing a tantrum. And Mother would give her anything to get her out of the tantrum. Or Frances would say, 'You don't love me, Mother,' from the time she could talk. Mother would get all flustered, showing her guilt, and say, nervously, 'Of course I love you, I'll give you anything.'

"Kids pick up and sense things. She knew the prime person to take care of her was Marilyn, and she was exploiting the fact that Mother never wanted her. She always knew how to orchestrate guilt from day one."

Much later, long after she had moved to New York, Frances told a friend that she was a "change of life" baby. She would write her mother a letter and sign it this way:

The child no one wanted—ever

7 // In the fall of 1942, Bob and Marilyn (fifteen and thirteen) went off to Wasatch Academy, a Presbyterian boarding school about two hours southeast of Salt Lake in the town of Mt. Pleasant.

Marilyn and Elaine had been doing their best to persuade their parents to get help for Bob, who was having academic problems as well as the occasional seizure at school. But Franklin and Berenice's dislike of doctors was exceeded only by their feeling about psychiatrists.

"I was desperate to get him help. He was probably my closest sibling," Elaine recalled, finding it painful to talk about her only brother. "We used to take nocturnal walks— we were both insomniacs—and I taught him to dance. He was bright and very sensitive—*too* sensitive—and he was disturbed, beyond having epilepsy. No one had ever taken him to a doctor, except to a chiropractor. . . . I don't think my parents turned their backs on him really, they just didn't know how to deal with it. Each, in their own way, tried. But then again, they weren't together on anything."

Even before Bob and Marilyn left for Wasatch, what Elaine refers to as her mother's "divide and conquer" tactics had begun. When Berenice and Franklin disagreed over something, Berenice, like a military strategist, would invariably try to enlist her children as allies. If Bob was having a problem at school and Berenice couldn't sort it out, Elaine recalled, "she would come home and scream and yell at Dad, 'Why don't you *do* something?' His response, being descended upon like that, was to run. Mother was *always* trying to get support for *her* position, which was always different from Dad's position. I'd refuse to take either side, and this really made her crazy. Dad would simply state his position. He didn't ask me to choose sides."

The religious alienation that Elaine had felt in the first grade Frances would encounter in the second and third. "Our neighborhood being solid Mormon," Berenice wrote, warming to her subject, "she had no protestant friends to play with. The public schools and teachers in Salt Lake maintain there is no religious discrimination but our children were always ostrasized and even persecuted by the Mormon children in our neighborhood. [They] taunted Frances for two years on her way to and from the Uintah School. One noon she came home with her coat ripped. It seemed the Mormons way-laid her in the alley and ripped the belt off her coat and threw it in the bushes. I was washing and looked like the 'wrath of God' but I pulled the electric cord and marched straight up to that school. The principal was very busy preparing for a PTA meeting but she halted everything to listen to our complaint. I was furious and I told the principal what Frances had gone thru for two years and said: 'My child does not have to go to school, I'll keep her home.' Miss Ryberg was very sympathetic and she called every child living in our neighborhood into the office right then and there and we had it out with these 'belligerent Mormon brats.' Frances was never bothered again, but she was never one of the crowd as far as the neighborhood gang was concerned."

Her problems with the Uintah School aside, Frances was the most troublesome of her four children to raise, Berenice said. "Her temperament made her the most difficult. Marilyn was even-tempered and easy to live with. And always the best one to me. Frances would be at odds with me a lot. When she gets down about something, all hell can break loose. She can be both lovely and vindictive. I think she was born with a vindictive streak.

"When Frances was eight or nine, I planned a surprise birthday party for her. Frances has a *very* uncanny sense of knowing when something is going on. And she got the sense I was drumming something up, and she has a way of confronting you and you have to tell her. When I said I was, she asked who I had invited. When I told her, she went to the phone, called everyone of them up and told them to stay home. I never tried to give her a party again. That was the end of that. She was different," Berenice said with a sigh, "she was different."

Family vacations were a rare occurrence for the Bradshaws. The first—and only—one all six of them ever took together was to Yellowstone National Park in August of 1946. Instead of staying a week or more, they were back in a few days. The other trip, some years later, was to Denver, where Franklin had some geological research he wanted to do.

Berenice recalls that her husband was edgy and irritable on the first trip and anxious to get back to his business. Elaine recalls that what made both trips so unhappy was Frances.

"She never allowed anything to be an obstacle. She always wanted center stage. We could be having a good time and she would sit and sulk and pout, because somehow something was happening and she wasn't *it*. She wanted all the focus to always be on her. If it wasn't, she would march off. It is *always* in my memory this way. The more she got her way, the more she wanted to get her way, and the worse it became."

Robert, meanwhile, was trying hard to be his father's son. Just as Franklin prided himself on self-education and devoured all he could about geology, Robert taught himself Russian and Chinese. He loved to play with lead soldiers as a boy and became knowledgeable about Russian and military history as well as radio electronics; he learned how to play the piano and drew cartoons. He was considered brilliant by all who knew him, but in a self-possessed and singular way. Quiet and withdrawn, he stood six feet tall, had a large mouth (a Bradshaw trademark) and wide smile, and had his father's dark wavy hair and blue eyes.

But his problems continued. He spent only one year at Wasatch Academy—he had a number of seizures there and was asked not to return—and, after graduation from East High in 1945, enlisted in the Navy. But he had not informed the Navy of his epilepsy and was discharged two months later, "one of the great disappointments of his life." He took some classes at the University of Utah, was active as a scoutmaster for the Boy Scouts, taught a class in radio electronics for the Utah National Guard, and began working part-time for his father. But he couldn't draw clear of his mother's web.

"Berenice used to work Robert up," Bertha said. "She used all the children as sounding boards. She didn't have special friends to go to, so she complained to them that their dad wasn't doing this and this and this. She kept him worked up the way she kept Franklin worked up."

On one occasion, Robert got so agitated that he and Franklin got into a fight. "Bob had a look in his eye you would worry about," Franklin's nephew Howard Bradshaw, who worked for him at the time, remembered. "He used to beat the hell out of Frank at the store. Frank would say that he fell on the railroad tracks but would finally admit that it was Bob. I think that's why he was given the lobotomy."

Before Robert was given a frontal lobotomy, Franklin and Berenice, finally and reluctantly, had sought psychiatric help for him. The people he was drawing cartoons of no longer had faces. The piano pieces he was playing were dark and funereal. They told the doctor their son had epilepsy. The doctor told them that he was a schizophrenic.

Franklin's prescription was to jog with his son in the park, hoping that would help "to straighten out his thinking" and make him calmer. He moved Robert into a hotel downtown so they could be together, away from Berenice, but she contends that her husband never stayed there with him.

"My husband *never* accepted his illness," Berenice began testily one day. "The psychiatrist told me my husband *couldn't* accept reality. He thought he could walk him around the block and he'd be all right. The hotel he moved him into was a fleabag. Franklin wanted no burdens of any kind. He never went near him. He never stayed there with him. Poor Bob was in that fleabag hotel, having seizures, and nobody to look after him.

"*I* was always the one to look after him," she shouted. "*I* was the one. I was the one who got him in the hospital. I was the one who always went to see him. Franklin would only go to see him twice a year—on his birthday and on Christmas. I'd make him go."

(On one occasion, Bertha recalled, Franklin was summoned to Provo by the doctors. They told him that he had to keep Robert away from Berenice. When she came to visit him, they said, she would get after the doctors, make certain demands, and she would get upset. Robert would then get upset and tell his father to "take me out of here. Take me home."

Yet the doctors chastised Franklin for not having spent more time with his son as he was growing up, Marilyn said. "Dad had pictures of himself standing with fish he'd caught. He did those things as a kid, but he never took Bob to do them." Asked why, she replied defensively: "Because he was working.")

"The worst fight we *ever* had in our *whole* life was when I made him go to [the state hospital in] Provo to visit his son on his birthday," Berenice continued, still shouting. "The worst fight we ever had. I was so upset that I felt like opening the car door and falling out. He was so abusive. He just resented going to see him. He just couldn't *face* reality. He never could."

If Gilmer Drive was essentially a place for Franklin to sleep, Bradshaw Auto Parts and the oil and gas lease business he soon immersed himself in were his life.

Some of his employees became very close to him over the years, closer in many ways than the members of his own family. One of them was Doug Steele. A native of Salt Lake, Steele was twenty-three when he went to work for Franklin in 1946, and he never left. Steele learned a number of things very quickly about his boss, and two of the most important were these: Franklin had a unique and eccentric way of doing business, and Doug's job would require him to be more than just a loyal and dependable employee.

"In the old days, when I first started out," Steele recalled with amusement, "the boys who opened up were the janitors, along with everything else we did. When we got there first thing in the morning, we'd sweep the floors. One morning there was a ten-dollar bill on the floor and I took it over to Frank and said, 'From now on I get to sweep the floors. Here's a ten-dollar bill I found. If the janitor is going to get that every morning, I want the job full-time.'" Franklin thanked him for the money; it wasn't until later that some of the older employees told Doug that was a trick of his to see if a person was honest.

When the man he called "the Godfather" tried it again thirty-one years later, Doug would not be so amused.

One night in the early 1950s Doug was woken by an urgent phone call.

"Doug, I need your help." It was Franklin, and he sounded desperate.

"What's the problem?" Doug said sleepily.

"Bob's acting very violently. I'd like to take him to the hospital and wonder if you could come and help me."

Doug knew why Franklin had called him. Robert had gotten to know Doug at work and trusted him. When Robert would have his seizures and be "stretched out on the floor," Doug would help him. When Doug arrived at Gilmer Drive he found Robert "all bleary-eyed and way out" and suggested that the three of them go for a ride. They drove down to the County Hospital and had Robert admitted. Though Robert had calmed down at this point, he still managed to convince the attending physician that Doug and Franklin were the ones who were behaving strangely, not he.

It wasn't long before Doug was called on again. Franklin asked him if he would take Robert up to Ogden for a medical appointment at the Dee Hospital.

"This upset me greatly," Doug remembered. "They had a new surgery at that time to cut into the brain to relieve tension. It was for a preliminary look-see, and instead of taking his own son, he had me take him. I don't know why he wouldn't go. I spoke to the psychiatrist and the doctor, who asked me what my position was. When I said that I was an employee they were shocked and said, 'This is hard to rationalize.' Even to this day, I remember how amazed the doctors were that Frank wasn't there himself. He used me on a lot of his little errands."

* * *

Lobotomies were considered "the new promise" at the time, and Berenice was hoping, Elaine recalled, that Robert would become calmer and less abusive as the result of having one. "He and Mother got into it an awful lot," she said. "So he, like Dad, tried to stay out of her way, but they'd get into it, and it was very hard for her. But after his lobotomy, I thought he was dead. I kind of mourned for him then. Even when somebody's very angry and disturbed, at least there's a person there, there's *feeling* there, there's something going on. But he just wasn't there anymore."

Over the years Robert was shifted between the state hospital in Provo and the Veterans Administration hospital at Fort Douglas in Salt Lake. In an effort to help him, Franklin had him come down from the V.A. to the warehouse on occasion in the evenings, after the other employees had gone home. What Franklin wanted more than anything was for Robert to be able to work on a regular basis and eventually take over the business. And that's what Robert wanted as well—to carry on the legacy, to do what he thought was expected of him.

Yet nothing reveals so much about Robert Bradshaw—his anxieties and his hopes—than one of his own impassioned, earnest letters to his family from the hospital.

GREETINGS;

. . . The Dr.s pointed out that my one. bad habit was always tending to make fun of myself while trying to build up others in their own eyes. . . . This could well be the explanation of so many of my troubles? As you remember, the only explanation I can give in description of my 'Fore-Warnings' is that I am immediately aware of a situation closing in around me that screems of Dad, & the stores. It is so eeirry that I can-not describe it! All I know is, sometimes if I can detect it soon enough, sometimes I can take measures that mite stop it all together. Too often, though, these *things* give no advance warning. (tilt)

I still remember when Dad & I founded the Roosevelt store. We had set up the Vernal store, or ground-work, & then went over to Roosevelt and looked through some old buildings on some last legs. Dad found what he wanted & I was immediately put to work (I hope this agrees with Dad's version.?). I still remember the thrill I had when I got my first shot of Hotel life. This was also to be my first view of the Uinta country.

It will be tough for a while, but I still can not get over my desire to be the 100% parts-man that Dad could count-on. . . . Enough of this scandalsheet & talk about rotten eggs who live off of the Familie'S labors. . . . I would like to see some of the family as soon as possible. It sure gets lonesome down here.

My love to all
ROBERT

Frank Bradshaw was not a typical businessman, and did not stand out in a crowd as the multimillionaire he would become. No sooner had Doug Steele passed Frank's honesty test than he, like other Bradshaw employees before him, began to witness the other habits, quirks and examples of financial acumen that, in time, became the stuff of legend. Doug would understand why Berenice called her husband "Utah's Howard Hughes."

The briefcase he took to work was a Coors beer carton he had rooted out of the garbage like a scavenger. The letters he wrote were often on pieces of paper he had cut off the bottoms of letters he had received. His employees knew better than to throw envelopes away, because he used them as file cards for his oil and gas lease business. In order to dodge taxes, which he did with relish all his life, he would stuff royalty checks from those holdings into secret places and forget where he put them—sometimes for fifteen years. He catalogued practically everything he ever came into contact with, from auto parts to shoes. The shoes, like many of his clothes, were often secondhand or worse, and usually purchased from Desert Industries, the Mormon Church's thrift-shop outlet. It is hardly surprising that many customers who came into the store would ask, "Who's that old guy you got working back there?", think he was the janitor, and be amazed to find out otherwise.

In winter, with the heat turned down low in the warehouse to save money, he often worked in an old gray corduroy jacket with a red ski cap pulled down over his ears. The zipper on the jacket didn't work, so he tied a rope around himself to hold it closed.

"He dressed *worse* than the janitor," Berenice recalled with a mixture of horror and amusement, wanting to set the record straight. "He looked poverty-stricken most of the time. He had some peculiar ideas. He'd go to bed, when he had his own bedroom, with two to three layers of stuff on and that cap on his head. Oh my God, you'd think he was going to Klondike! I tried to shame him one time and said, 'You know, you certainly have no sex appeal,' but he said nothing and kept on wearing it."

He couldn't stand to think that there was any part he didn't have in any of his stores. A customer came in once looking for a set of points for an old Durant and said that he had been all over the Western states with no luck in finding it. "Frank would say, 'Well, what are you worrying about? We have that at the warehouse,' " Wally Glover, who went to work in 1937 as the manager of one of his Provo stores, remembered. "That would tickle him to death more than making ten thousand dollars—to sell that guy a set of points for an old Durant." Another customer would tell a woeful tale of being laughed out of every junkyard from Brigham City to Provo looking for a distributor cap for a 1925 silent-engine Packard. Frank calmly told the man that he knew he had one but had to think where it was. Could he come back around lunchtime? The customer did and Frank had unearthed the part.

In the towns where he had two stores, he named the second one All Car Parts Company. That way, if someone was considering opening up an auto-parts business, he would think there were two different companies already there, and probably leave town disappointed.

When he started out in Provo, Frank sent his employees to all the produce people in town to ask for their discarded orange and lemon crates, which he used as shelves or containers to hold parts. (These crates had colorful labels that were illustrated by some of the country's artists during the Depression years. "Honeymoon Brand" of Los Angeles showed an orange sun, trees and a castle; "Barbara Worth" of Riverside, California, revealed a fetching woman with a hat on, set against a desert backdrop dotted with cactuses; "Silver Lake" of Tulare County, California, had a deep-blue lake with mountains; "Gold" had a scale with gold piled on one side and lemons on the other. Frank was prescient about many things, but not even he foresaw the value these crates ultimately had as collector's items.)

When he traveled to his stores he often hitched rides with salesmen or took the bus and, upon arriving at night, slept either in the station—which was usually in the lobby of a hotel—or in the store, where he always kept a sleeping bag or a rug to cover himself with. He ate only two meals a day (before he began eating a steady diet of meat loaf and bran muffins for lunch, he used to get the Blue Plate Special at the Denver & Rio Grande station that was near the warehouse), the second one no later than four in the afternoon, so that his food would be digested by bedtime. He loved jello, craved peanut butter and candy bars, and often ate cold SpaghettiOs right from the can. He devoured the *Wall Street Journal* and would one day be mentioned in it, but he was not willing to buy it. So he asked his brother Fred, a prominent Salt Lake banker, to hold a week's worth of copies, and every Friday he went and collected them. He was so concerned that Berenice not know his credit rating—the highest one could have—that he tore the page with his name on it out of his copy of *Dun & Bradstreet.*

Frank and Berenice battled over a number of things and one of them was cars. She was always hounding him for a new car and he would generally be able to hold her to one every ten years. If she couldn't get anywhere with Frank, she would go around him and appeal to his managers. One day in the 1960s, Wally Glover, as easygoing a man as his name suggests, got a long-distance call from Berenice.

"Wally, I'm a disgrace to my neighbors. Frank won't buy me a new car. Will you buy me one?"

"Berenice, I'll be glad to, *if* Frank will okay it."

"Well, I'm going to work on him tonight."

As soon as Wally hung up he realized that he shouldn't have told Berenice that. "For three days there was such hell in my life," Wally recalled. "That phone was ringing every fifteen minutes. First it would be Berenice: 'Now you go get me that car, Wally.' Then it would be Frank: 'Don't you buy her that car.' Here I was in the middle of this thing. Finally I told Frank: 'Why don't you sleep on it and decide what you want to do? I'm right in the middle.' And of course he was *blaming* me for even mentioning I would buy her a car.

"Next morning, he called me and said, 'Well, maybe I've been selfish. This old wreck of ours is kind of bad. Do you think *you* can afford it?' I think I 'only' had one hundred and ten thousand dollars in the bank at that time. It was *his* money. So I said, 'Yes, Frank, we have no problem.' 'Well, maybe you better go buy it.' So I called Berenice and said, 'I am going to buy you a car.' And she said, 'Well, get everything on it.' So I went up and got her a new Plymouth."

Frank and Berenice both loved dancing, and though she could never get him to those Friday dances at the university while they were students, they took up square dancing around 1948, and soon became one of the leading couples in the entire Salt Lake area.

"He loved to square dance," Berenice said, sitting on a couch in the living room of her house. "We did it for several years, gave it up and tried to go back again, but we couldn't do it. We'd fight all the way there and all the way home. He didn't like dancing with me. He liked dancing with the other ladies, because they would flatter him and tell him what a good dancer he was. So he yanked me around over the floor. I didn't enjoy dancing with him either. But he loved it. He even took records down to the warehouse and was teaching the employees how to dance. He would get people up here, even on this carpeting, which I objected to, and he was trying to run square dancing around here. He was just *nuts* about square dancing. *Nothing* would stop him from square dancing. He didn't care where you were or who it was. But as I said, he didn't like dancing with me."

Years later, Wayne Hacking, one of Franklin's cousins and managers, would say, "When they gave up square dancing, it was the worst thing that happened to him and them."

Following World War II, Franklin once again went prospecting. In an old pickup truck—a sleeping bag, pots and pans, a Geiger counter and, on occasion, Robert on the seat next to him—he traveled all over the state, prospecting by day and sleeping under the stars at night.

The uranium rush that began after the war culminated in 1952 when Charles A. Steen made his world-famous Mi Vida find in San Juan County. Prospectors couldn't get themselves, let alone their mules, quickly enough to the land of Zion and the penny-stock boom that awaited them there. People could buy stock for a penny a share one day and sell it for four cents the next, and the whole area was caught up in the get-rich-quick fever.

Frank formed a company called BAPCO—after Bradshaw Auto Parts—put some uranium claims in it, sold stock for two cents a share and raised about $300,000. Though his uranium interests would eventually cease, the company's stock rose, at one point, to as high as thirty-five cents a share.

But Frank sensed that the future was in oil, not uranium, and he was right. With the cash he had accumulated during the war, he saw that both oil and gas leases would be a very good way to shelter him from taxes.

There are two kinds of leases—federal and state—and three ways to obtain one, entitling the leaseholder (in the case of federal leases, which were the majority of Frank's) to the mineral rights (the right to drill for oil and gas) to a parcel of land for a maximum period of ten years:

—*over the counter,* in which the first person to pay $10 and a year's rental (it was fifty cents an acre until 1975, then raised to $1) obtains the lease on what is usually considered to be unpromising land;

—*filing for it in a lottery system* (which was set up in 1960), a form of gambling in which the person pays a tax-deductible filing fee (it was $10 for a number of years, now it is $75) for the right to have his entry drawn from the kind of huge rotating drum that is used on television quiz shows (it is now operated by computer);

—*open, competitive bidding,* generally engaged in by the major oil companies and large independents, on "known geologic structures"—tracts of land considered most likely to yield oil and gas.

After paying a year's rental, a leaseholder can either drill on his land or sell that right, to an oil company or to anyone who wants to buy it, in exchange for a royalty (a production override) that generally does not exceed 5 percent. If oil or gas is found during the ten-year period, the seller will continue to receive that royalty as long as the wells are productive.

Frank, who was extremely active in both buying over the

counter and filing in the lottery, devised a system based on careful research and discussion with other people. But what other people, not to mention geological surveys, often considered to be a dry hole (a duster) would turn out to be a bonanza for Frank. When the lottery system became more and more competitive, Frank used the names of his wife, daughters, relatives and employees in order to increase his chances of being the winner. This was illegal—and one of the reasons some members of Congress have been pushing to abolish the lottery—but Frank knew that other people did it, so he did too.

"He was lucky, but he was a very smart man," Nancy Jones, his oil secretary at the time of his death, said in 1983. "He knew what was going on. He was a geologist. The whole thing was a game to him, and he worked hard at it. He would often drop a lease, refile on it, then pick it up again. He knew what was good, bad, and what things were worth. He made money but he also spent money. Not on food and clothes and having a good time with the family, but on giving it back to the government, trying to win. It was like gambling. And he just kept playing the game. Win and sell. The big oil companies—Texaco, Conoco, Davis Oil, all the majors— would call and want to talk to him. They would talk to me first and I'd put the lease out. They *knew* that if they wanted to deal with Frank Bradshaw, they had to come up with top dollar, or he'd hang on to it."

He stood for the little guy—the independent who was making it—and loved the fact that "the heavies" pursued him, gleefully announcing that "they're really coming to my door now." (But whenever a representative of one of the oil companies did want to meet with him, he didn't want them coming to the warehouse. He was embarrassed by where he worked, but he never did anything about it. So he tried to arrange meetings with these people in restaurants or hotels, appearing in the pressed blue suit he always kept hanging on a hook for occasions like these. But if they insisted on coming to the warehouse, he always met them out front on the loading dock and never invited them inside.)

He confided to Bertha that he was not just after his first million, but she feels that what excited him even more than making money was the recognition he received for his accomplishments and the fact that people sought him out for his opinions at oil seminars and meetings of the Utah Association of Petroleum and Mining Landmen.

When Bertha tried to persuade him to slow up and enjoy life more, she was wasting her breath. "I've got a lion by the tail and I can't let loose," he told her. Whatever was missing from his marriage to Berenice was more than filled by his love of work and achievement.

Yet, Marilyn says, "We didn't think of Dad as being successful. He was a hardworking man. And he always *told* us how hard he worked. He would say, 'I guess I'll just have to work a little harder,' when he wanted something. But we knew. He didn't come home. And it wasn't because he was out playing. You could always find him at work."

Frank paid his employees low wages, but promised each person he hired that he would receive a priceless financial education. He got many of them involved in filing for leases and buying the right stocks. Neil Swan, who, like most of Frank's employees, remembers him as generous with his time, if not his money, and a superb listener, won a lease once: 640 acres of land for which he paid $320 a year. He got a phone call one day from Exxon, which offered him $40 an acre for it. He told them that he needed to check with his "landman" and get back to them. Frank told him that he should get at least $50 an acre and not to sell. Neil told Exxon that, and a few days later was offered $45 an acre. Once again, Frank told an increasingly anxious Swan to hold out. So he turned it down. Another few days passed and Exxon phoned again, offering $47.50 an acre. Neil immediately jumped at it, but Frank insisted that he call back and tell Exxon he'd changed his mind. For three months, Neil's phone never rang, and he felt he had really lost a chance to score, as his mentor did so often.

But one day there was a call for him. It was Michigan-Wisconsin Gas, offering $50 an acre for his land. Over those past few months, Neil had cursed himself for listening to Frank, but Frank had been right. He usually was.

When he wasn't poring over geological surveys and maps on the aluminum picnic table he used as a desk, he was buried in the pages of *The Value Line Investment Survey* and other business publications, plotting his next move in the stock market. He loved watching the Big Board at J.A. Hogle, invested heavily in energy stocks, and built his employees' retirement plan on them; when the Arab oil embargo took effect in 1973–74, the dividend checks—which he would often stash into old copies of *Life* magazine—came rolling in. But he remained a product of the Depression his whole life, always crying the blues, claiming that he was borrowed and invested to the hilt and telling everyone who would listen that "someday you have to pay the fiddler."

"Frank had no conception of how to spend money on material things," Doug Steele said. "Most guys have big homes, big cars, a winter place or a summer place, extended vacations. That wasn't important to him. He didn't give a damn what anybody thought. In the thirty-two years I worked for him I don't think he ever went to see one movie. This guy didn't waste his time."

"I went to him for a raise once," Nancy Jones recalled. "I was making a dollar sixty an hour, and when he gave me a ten-cent raise he said I was living outside my budget if I couldn't live on four hundred dollars a month. When I told him my house payment was four hundred dollars a month, he almost died. When I asked for the raise, he said that I didn't save him enough money for a meal ticket. And it made *me* feel bad, and I could never figure out why *I* should feel bad."

As Berenice said, Frank had some peculiar ideas.

8// By the fall of 1950, Marilyn had graduated from the University of Utah, where she had majored in speech, and Elaine from East High the year before, with a passion for art. Elaine had plans to go to New York with a friend and attend the New York School of Interior Decorating. But the friend backed out, so Marilyn, who had been thinking about going to graduate school at Syracuse, decided to accompany her sister to New York instead, secretly harboring a dream of one day living in a penthouse.

Most young people who leave Utah eventually return there

to live, marry, and raise a family. But Marilyn never did and Elaine did only briefly, before moving to California. Whatever they may have been able to tell themselves about the kind of family life they had had so far, they were able to accept reality in a way their parents could not. The social ostracism they both felt, their mother's constant working on their emotions, a father who cared about them in his way but was never there, parents who were united on almost nothing—these things combined to make it possible for them to envision a future far from the emptiness of 1327 Gilmer Drive and from the clear air and alluring surroundings of the Salt Lake Valley.

As sisters they had not been particularly close, and being only twenty months apart in age created a lot of sibling competitiveness between them. But it was not long before the divide-and-conquer game that they were barely able to avoid growing up forced them together as allies in a way they could not have imagined as they left the land of Zion.

If Marilyn and Elaine could understand, if not totally accept, why their father wasn't home much, Frances apparently could not. She would tell her mother that she wished her daddy would come home for dinner like other daddies. Berenice would tell her that he was working and making money, but then ask the same rhetorical question that she had of her other children: "If your father has all this money, why can't we spend it?"

Never one to keep her feelings to herself, she would air her unhappiness with Frank to anyone within earshot. The ally she had tried so hard to make of Marilyn and Elaine she finally made of her youngest daughter—"her golden idol," Doug Steele said. The child she perhaps felt most guilty about began to have her full attention.

Frances had brown hair and the same lovely blue eyes her parents, brother and sisters did. She took piano and dance lessons and played the cello in the school orchestra in junior high, but her mother claims that all her artistic endeavors ended with "the same lack of perseverance." At East High her friends knew her as "Frankie"—a name she would eventually rid herself of—and one of them remembered her as being "the life of a party. She smoked and drank and was kind of wild." While physically plain, the friend said, she was "attractive because of her gregariousness."

Like most of her classmates, she attended dances and sporting events, and, on the surface, was leading a fairly ordinary high school life. "She was a fun, outgoing, happy child, well liked and popular," one of her teachers said. But she also was remembered by others as a private person. A neighbor remarked that the Bradshaws were not the sort of people you could press your friendship on, and a friend of Frances's recalled being invited to her house on one occasion. "I heard a banging on the other side of the door and Frankie said, 'Oh, that's my brother. We have to contain him.' That was the only time I was invited over."

She got off to a slow start academically in high school, but pulled her grades up and made her parents proud. She received A's in French, Latin, zoology and bookkeeping and a B in English (from a D in tenth grade), was a member of the French Club and Dance Club, and had an IQ of 120.

Like her sisters, she was determined to flee Utah and she set her sights high. She applied to Radcliffe, Wellesley and Bryn Mawr, with the University of Colorado her backup choice. When she was invited, a few months later, to become a member of the class of 1960 at Bryn Mawr College, she accepted. For eighteen years she had experienced one kind of life, and now she was eager and ready to experience another.

9// If Frances was going to go to an elite school like Bryn Mawr, Berenice was going to see to it that her youngest daughter went east with the best things the stores in Salt Lake had to offer. Berenice no doubt had to battle with her husband over this, but she prevailed, and Marilyn remembers how things had begun to change—at least as far as Frances was concerned.

"When I went away to Wasatch Academy, I had five blouses and five skirts, and every Monday morning I would wash and iron my blouses and press my skirts so I would be all set for school for that week. When Frances went to Bryn

Mawr, she had a whole trunkful of new clothes from the skin out."

Before leaving for college, Frances worked for her father at the warehouse that summer of 1956. Nothing pleased him more than for members of his family to work, especially if they came and worked for him.

"Frances was a good worker," Doug Steele, no slouch himself, said one day in the warehouse as he reached for a muffler. "Frank imposed rigid guidelines and she worked fast and efficiently." But Doug also recalled something else about having Frances at the warehouse. "She had to be domineering in any situation, fully in charge. She was very brilliant. You only had to pass it by her one time and she would pick it up. They say, though, that when you're up that high you're close to the edge the other way."

Frances was not the only Bradshaw about to do something exciting that fall. Elaine, who was attending college at San Francisco State, was planning to marry Mason Drukman, a curly-haired Jew from the Boston suburb of Canton with political leanings distinctly to the left.

They had met at a Unitarian social and political gathering on campus, begun living together, and soon decided to marry. But beyond the fact they were in love, Mason knew very little about the family of which he was soon to be a member—the Bradshaws' first in-law.

"Elaine didn't talk much about her childhood when we were courting," Mason recalled. "She remembered very much being bedridden—that is the crucible period of her childhood—and older-sister competitiveness with Marilyn. I think there was a period in Elaine's late adolescence when she kind of went her own way. She thinks of herself as being overlooked during that period.

"Coming from the East Coast, where your mother was Mom or Ma, I had never heard anybody call their mother Mother before. I got a sense that there was little love in the household by the way Elaine interacted with her mother. From this, I sensed an austere relationship with her. But I didn't know how much import to give it, or how it had scarred the whole family, or to what degree it scarred Elaine. I later found out it scarred her badly."

Marilyn flew from New York for the wedding and met Frances and her mother in San Francisco. Frances and Marilyn were going to be bridesmaids. Frances had had a green silk dress made by a Japanese seamstress for the occasion; Marilyn made her own. The night before the wedding everyone went out to dinner, and Mason remembers it as a "jovial, cheerful occasion. I had no notion—either psychologically or financially—of what the family was about."

Mason's parents didn't attend the wedding because they couldn't afford to. Franklin didn't come because he either couldn't or wouldn't afford the time. Elaine was not surprised; she knew her father hated social occasions, but she also assumed that he didn't approve of the match. Nevertheless, she held out hope to the last minute that he would appear, deciding that if he didn't she would have a private ceremony.

So late in the afternoon of September 13, with no one there to offer her hand in marriage, Elaine Bradshaw, wearing a white, lace-trimmed silk dress, became Mrs. Mason Drukman.

After the wedding, Frances went to New York to stay with Marilyn for a few days. But it wasn't until after Marilyn had taken her youngest sister down to Bryn Mawr that she discovered what Frances had been doing. During the day, while Marilyn was at her job at NBC, Frances had been opening up charge accounts and buying clothes. This piece of information came to Marilyn in a letter from Berenice. The letter also asked a favor: would *Marilyn* please get in touch with Frances and convey their parents' displeasure about this.

The role of mother that Marilyn had long hoped to escape seemed to be trailing her in the same way her brother's seizures still did in the middle of the night. As for Frances, Marilyn said: "I didn't resent her having clothes. She was going to a posh college. What was annoying was what she had was not enough. And you will find that pattern from then on."

Part Two//

Most fathers wouldn't talk or act the way Dad does even if their daughter was a murderess—it's only over money—oh, excuse me, I shouldn't say "only money" because it's very important to you.

—FRANCES (in a letter to Berenice)

10 // The Main Line of Philadelphia lies west of the city in one of the most affluent pockets of America, and the Gothic wonder of Bryn Mawr College is nestled right in the heart of it. Founded in 1885 by a number of Quakers, the college is one of the group of schools known as the Seven Sisters. In addition to its high academic standards (when Katharine Hepburn was there in the 1920s, she was told that if she didn't pull her grades up she wouldn't be permitted to perform in any theatrical productions), Bryn Mawr adheres to a rigid honor code; while that code allows each student a great deal of freedom, the student in turn is expected to uphold the college's trust in her.

In Frances's freshman year, because of an overflow of students, she was living with twelve other women in a small residence called East House, and one of those women remembers her clearly. "Frankie had incredible mood swings. One time she would be terribly joyous, twirling and whirling and dancing about. Another time I walked past her room and she was sobbing her heart out on her bed. I asked, 'What is it? What is it?' and she said, 'It's just everything, everything, everything.'

"I liked her very much. She was someone desperately in need of affection, someone you wanted to hug. She seemed alienated and spoke of how difficult it had been to be a non-Mormon growing up in Utah. She would talk about it all the time. To me this seemed silly, because, though she didn't know it, my parents and I were survivors of the Holocaust. I knew what it was like to be a Jew in a world that didn't want you. Rejection to me was when people wanted to kill you.

"Frankie had an infectious smile and beautiful eyes," her classmate continued. "She had wonderful dreams of being a ballet dancer and would wear her leotards and pink tights a lot. She didn't work very hard, had extraordinarily expensive clothes—tweeds and cashmere sweaters—but she was unkempt in an endearing way. There would be always a spot on her clothes or her stockings would be falling down or she would be unraveling in some way.

"She said she loved her mother very much, and her mother was mad for her, doted on her, writing and calling all the time. She said she feared her father, who was terribly penurious. But there always seemed to be money for what she needed, and I wondered why she was so unhappy."

"I felt she was like Don Quixote," another classmate began, "always fighting windmills. She was very solitary and unto herself, a rebel bucking the system. If there was a rule, she broke it. [For safety reasons, smoking was not permitted in the rooms at Bryn Mawr, yet Frances did, putting her butts in a mug high up on a shelf.] Doors were always open at Bryn Mawr. I didn't even have a key to my room, yet she would lock herself in. She was a puzzling creature, a poor lost soul."

While Bryn Mawr attracted students from all over, the majority came from the Northeast. As a Westerner, Frances was "free from tiny hierarchical concerns," a self-proclaimed Puritan and friend recalled with envy. "She was the equivalent of a cowboy and her program was not the one we were handed out with the grind aspect attached to it." But, the friend added, "she was given to these inexplicable bouts of alcohol. It went outside what I could relate to. It was amusing to fool the warden"—a gradute student who was in charge of the women in each residence—"but I didn't understand her need to go beyond this."

After her sophomore year, Frances decided she wanted to work in New York City for the summer of 1958 before returning to Bryn Mawr in the fall. So she took a room at the Barbizon Hotel for Women on East 63rd Street, a place with its own set of rules, and called a friend from Bryn Mawr on the phone.

"Camilla, this is Frankie Bradshaw. I'm in New York and staying at the Barbizon. Could we get together?"

Camilla was two years older than Frances, had just graduated, and was going to Europe for the summer. She knew Frances as someone who enjoyed life and wanted to live it fully, who was extravagant with money, liked to have a lot of jewelry all over her and wear expensive things. At Bryn Mawr, she felt Frances was trying hard, too hard perhaps, to make it with the "Northeastern rich types, the debutantes" and had an inordinate interest in who was riding horses with whom. But Camilla liked Frances and drove down to the Barbizon to meet her.

When Camilla arrived, Frances suggested they go and get a drink, complaining about the Barbizon's confining rules on the way. They walked south on Lexington a couple of blocks and into a restaurant between 60th and 61st called Gino. Then, as now, Gino was a place that New Yorkers flocked to—not for four-star cuisine, but to watch others and be watched. For a couple intent on carving out a social identity for themselves in the world of New York, Gino was a good starting point. For a bachelor with money to burn, it was perfect.

Frances and Camilla were sitting having a drink and remarking about the restaurant's distinctive zebra wallpaper when a short man, five and a half feet tall with a foreign accent and glasses, began sweet-talking them. He was a regular and knew they were not.

"I have a brand-new Mercedes parked outside. Would you girls like to take a ride?" he offered.

It was a postcard-perfect June afternoon, but Camilla, a streetwise New Yorker, was dubious. Knowing that "Frankie was a hick in the big town and was flattered," and seeing that she was determined to go, Camilla went along to "protect" her.

The Mercedes was a sleek, jet-black convertible with red upholstery, and the top was down. As they tooled around the streets, Frances was excited by the man's attention.

"Let's go to my apartment," he suddenly said to his two

companions, indicating that it was on East 54th Street, between Park and Madison.

Camilla warned Frances that that would not be a good idea, but once again Frances prevailed.

Frances and he began drinking a great deal, and the man started offering her and Camilla all kinds of jewelry. He was in the imported jewelry business with his uncle, a flamboyant character named Luigi Borrelli who had sold pearls to Aristotle Onassis and was known throughout the trade as "King of the Pearls." He insisted that they both have a gift, and Camilla, who announced she was leaving, reluctantly accepted—not a piece of jewelry, but a hat made of straw. She made one last attempt to dissuade Frances from staying, but it was no use.

The man drove Camilla to her car, and that was the last she ever saw of Frances and the older man she seemed so infatuated with.

Though small in stature Vittorio Gentile was large in his spending habits, and Gino was not the only place in town where the thirty-one-year-old bachelor was a regular and known by name. But Gino was his favorite restaurant, and they ate dinner there that evening. Knowing what to order and what to avoid, Vittorio took responsibility for their food and drink. When he told Frances that the best bottle of wine the house had to offer was on their table, she smiled. After all, that was why she had come to New York: to be in a place like Gino, and in the company of a man who would introduce her to the kind of things of which her father disapproved.

From Gino, they went on to a party. By the time they arrived, the place was filled with drunken Scots wearing kilts. Vittorio and Frances had been drinking all day, but the Scots appeared, at first glance, to be a few steps ahead of them.

"We drank ourselves senseless," Gentile said. "For an Italian to meet a girl from Salt Lake City was adventurous." By the time they left the party it was one in the morning and past the Barbizon's curfew time. Gentile offered to take her back to his apartment and she agreed. "I put her to sleep in the living room and I went to sleep in the bedroom," he said. "In the morning I brought her a cup of Italian coffee and said,

'Now, if you want, we can make love.' 'Yes,' she said, 'because you were such a gentleman last night.'"

Before Camilla left for Europe, she heard from Frances a couple of times. Frances told her that she was in love with Vittorio and had been with him ever since. She said that Vittorio was so debonair and knew all the headwaiters at places like Delmonico's, the Colony and El Morocco, and that her summer with him had been the most wonderful thing that had ever happened to her.

When Frances returned to Bryn Mawr for her junior year, her relationship with the dashing pearl merchant continued. If she wasn't coming up to New York for a weekend, Vittorio would zip down to Philadelphia in his Mercedes at breakneck speed. He would stay at one of the city's best hotels, the Barclay, and always bring food from Gino with him, so that he and Frances could have a picnic on the lawn at Bryn Mawr.

If her schoolwork got little attention before, it received even less now. She had tasted a kind of life in New York that was intoxicating to her, and she was in love with a man who could continue to provide it.

Though Bryn Mawr had its rules, it was actually a very liberal place. If a student wanted to leave campus and stay away overnight, there was a book to sign out in. The college did not necessarily disapprove if a student wanted to stay with a man from Haverford or Swarthmore for the weekend, provided she left word where she could be reached. Nevertheless, when Frances came to New York, she signed out to her sister's apartment, but stayed with Vittorio.

One Friday afternoon in October, Marilyn received a phone call. The college wanted to know where Frances was, but would not say why. Marilyn told them that she wasn't certain, but suggested Vittorio's.

Two days later, Marilyn received another call. The college asked her to come to Bryn Mawr as soon as possible. Frances was being suspended.

Marilyn knew that her sister had been seeing a psychiatrist the college recommended, but not exactly why, and knew of her repeated violations of parietal rules. But she was unprepared, as were her parents, for something as dramatic as this, and worried too by something Frances had said to her once:

66

"If I can't go to Bryn Mawr, I'll kill myself." Perhaps that was said in jest, but it stuck in Marilyn's mind.

Marilyn drove out to La Guardia that night with her boyfriend and bought one plane ticket to Philadelphia and two from there to Salt Lake. When Marilyn arrived at Bryn Mawr the next day, she went to the main administration building. Though Marilyn didn't know it at the time, suspensions were rare at Bryn Mawr. The college would not tell Marilyn why Frances was being suspended, but they did tell her that the suspension was to last for the rest of the school year, and that Frances could not be considered for readmission unless she had intensive psychiatric help.

Marilyn was given the name of a psychiatrist in Salt Lake and told that her sister was in the infirmary. Upon arriving there, she found her sister crying.

"I guess I've really done it this time," Frances said.

"Yes, you have," Marilyn said. She packed a bag for Frances—the rest of her belongings would be shipped—and they left for Salt Lake.

As their cab drove away from Bryn Mawr College and the changing colors of a Pennsylvania autumn, Frances was leaving behind not only a place of learning but one that had allowed her great freedom. But she had abused its privileges, violating the trust that the institution had placed in her. And, as it turned out, she had done a lot more than that. Now she was going home, back to Utah, and she was none too happy about it.

No sooner had Marilyn gotten Frances back to Salt Lake than her parents sent out a rare cry for help to Elaine, who came home from San Francisco. The Salt Lake psychiatrist Bryn Mawr had recommended suggested a hospital in Colorado Springs as a suitable place for treatment. Berenice felt that Frances had had a nervous breakdown, and she later blamed it on Vittorio. But when Berenice had had her collapse not long after Frances was born (and another one during a trip to a number of Mediterranean countries during the summer of 1957), *she* had never entered a hospital, and she wasn't about to send her youngest daughter off to one. She and Franklin already had one child in a mental institution, and one was enough. So they sought another opinion, and were told that Frances could be treated twice a week right there in Salt Lake.

Elaine went to see the psychiatrist who was treating Frances and was told that her sister had been sent home "for criminal misconduct, with instructions that she be hospitalized or allowed to be prosecuted." Though she knew that her father "bailed her out of her criminal offenses," Elaine didn't ask what Frances had done, nor would her parents have told her. (In addition to Frances's repeated violations of the rules, she was, as Elaine suspected, forging classmates' checks, and she was also stealing.) The doctor told Elaine that "someone *has* to say to her, 'Stop. You can't continue to behave the way you are.' He said if that meant turning your back on her, then it must be done. He described her to me as being either a psychopath or a sociopath." (According to *Webster's New World Dictionary*, a psychopath is a person whose behavior is largely amoral and asocial and who is characterized by irresponsibility, lack of remorse or shame, perverse or impulsive—often criminal—behavior, and other various personality defects, generally without psychotic attacks or symptoms; a sociopath is someone with a psychopathic personality whose behavior is aggressively antisocial. While many professionals refrain from using these terms altogether, when they are used they are often used interchangeably.)

Elaine's conversation with the psychiatrist also covered the relationship Frances was having with Vittorio. Frances told the psychiatrist that Vittorio had beaten her at times when she lived with him during the previous summer and when she saw him that fall. The psychiatrist told Elaine that it was a relationship of *choice*. "He said that Frances wanted to be beaten, that she hated men—her father in particular—and wanted to be punished for it. I felt that it was because of Mother, and the way she tried to use Frances against Dad."

When Elaine left the psychiatrist's office, she knew that she couldn't put her sister in jail or in a hospital. All she could do was follow his advice and try to persuade her parents to do the same.

But her parents showed the same reluctance to deal with Frances as they had with Bob, and Elaine was furious. "I startled them, because I just blew up. I really gave it to my father for the first time in a long time. I decided *I* had to follow the doctor's advice—*not* dealing with Frances and *not* relating to Frances—and Mother has held it against me ever since.

"Dad *wasn't* strong—he couldn't dig in and meet things head-on. Mother would get irrational and start ranting and raving, and Dad's reaction to that was to run. He didn't know how to deal with it, he didn't learn how to deal with it, he didn't really want to deal with it, I guess."

Elaine left Salt Lake and went home. She had answered the call for help, but when her parents did not want to accept what she told them, she felt defeated. "They were stuck with each other," Elaine said years later, "and not too happy about it. They always had trouble, they always had Frances. She was always there keeping them stirred up, keeping them at each other's throat, so they had no peace at all."

While Elaine and the rest of the family were concerned about Frances, Frances began missing appointments with the psychiatrist and had even gone back to New York for a long weekend with Vittorio. What she had said to the psychiatrist about Vittorio was one thing. What she did was another. She was in love with Vittorio, was determined to be with him in New York and to continue the romance that she had told her friend was the most wonderful thing that had ever happened to her.

In November, not long after Frances came back from that weekend, Berenice found a couple of items in her daughter's purse. One was a plane ticket to New York—one-way—and the other was an application she had filed to recover some "stolen" Wasatch Chemical stock. Franklin bought stock for all his children, not only in Wasatch Chemical, but in American Savings and Loan (his brother's bank) and other interests. The certificates were in the children's names; they received the dividends but he kept the certificates, because he didn't want them to sell them. The stock Frances had claimed was stolen wasn't. When Franklin found out about it, he exploded. It was one thing for her to be suspended from Bryn Mawr. But now she was doing something that would affect his business interests. And as anyone who ever worked for

Franklin Bradshaw knew, you didn't do *anything* that would cause him to lose a dollar.

Ironically, both he and Berenice now seemed prepared to follow the psychiatrist's advice that Elaine had conveyed to them earlier and they had stubbornly rejected. But Frances didn't leave town without providing them with one more surprise. Just before she boarded the plane that would take her to New York and Vittorio, she opened up a locker at the airport. Crammed into it were plastic bags full of brand-new clothes she had charged to her parents and secretly stashed away. She had planned her getaway well.

Years later, her mother, recalling that period, said, "Frances wants to do what she wants to do when she wants to do it. And nobody under heaven is going to stop her."

Nobody did. When she was confronted at the gate and told she couldn't go aboard with all those things, she informed the attendant that she *had* to and pushed through.

After all, she knew what her parents did not: she was going to be married to Vittorio Masimo Gentile (whose brother was the Italian Ambassador to Egypt at the time) and had to get back to New York to be at the engagement party at L'Aiglon that his uncle was giving for them.

11 // On December 27, 1958, an announcement of Frances's engagement ran in the *Salt Lake Tribune,* along with a serene-looking photograph. Two days later, Frances wrote her father a letter, apologizing for her actions before she left Salt Lake and asking his forgiveness. She expressed the hope that he would come to her wedding, and thanked him for some money he had sent to help with the cost of it.

The wedding was set for Friday, January 9, at four o'clock at St. Patrick's Cathedral in New York. The day was brilliant and cold, and it was almost dark outside as Marilyn, a bridesmaid, proceeded down the aisle to a side altar in the huge and elegant cathedral. Frances came next, radiant in an Empire-style white satin dress and wearing a set of pearls

Vittorio had given her. The dark-suited man who accompanied her was not her father, but a granduncle.

"She married me because she was a social climber," Gentile began one day at Gino, where he often conducts his business from the pay phone. "My brother was an Italian diplomat. I taught her about clothes, shoes and places to go. We had dinner every Thursday here, with drinks at the bar first, and would meet on Fridays for lunch at the Red Devil, a Neapolitan greasy spoon on West 48th Street. We always held hands."

Right from the start, though, "it was stormy," he said. "She had suicidal tendencies. She would throw tantrums, screaming and yelling, and try to get out of the Mercedes while it was moving, even before we got married. She was always jealous, but I never had any other girlfriends."

One day during the summer of 1959, Vittorio had to drive a customer to Idlewild Airport and got caught in the afternoon rush-hour traffic. He tried to call Frances five or six times from locations just off the Van Wyck Expressway, but each time he did she hung up. When he finally arrived home, Frances, who was pregnant with their first child, wasn't there. He immediately went to Marilyn's apartment on East 63rd Street, but Marilyn said she hadn't seen her. "Marilyn was always defiant and never sympathized with me," Gentile explained. "She always stuck up for Frances. I called Dr. Robbins at nine o'clock. He called back and said Frances was in New York Hospital and was having a miscarriage. He told me I should go and see her. I brought her roses—*always*—stuffed toys, a favorite nightgown: everything to make her feel warm and wanted and loved."

A doctor had apparently told Frances she was going to lose the baby and not to worry about it, Gentile said. But Dr. Robbins, who ultimately delivered the child, told Vittorio that the other doctor had been wrong; she was going to be fine.

Marilyn recalled the same incident in a different way on a piece of yellow legal paper.

Saturday, July 18, 1959

At appx 230AM V. called & asked if I knew where F. was—I said no. She left him because she thought he had been unfaithful. I called

71

V. Sat. morning around 9AM & he still didn't know where she was. She was finally located under the name of Todd at the Allerton House. She wasn't taking calls—I went over and she agreed to see me. We talked for a little while. She said she still loved him but couldn't live with him. There was a bruise over her left eye—what was left of a beating V. gave her the previous weekend and one reason they didn't come back to the city until Elaine & Mace had left town.

When I got home around 1PM I called Dr. Robbins and he said F. was going to the hospital as she was bleeding. It had started right after I left (according to her). V. called & I told him where she was but the Dr. didn't want him to go to the hospital and upset her so I had him call the Dr.

V. called about 10PM & said that everything was okay again.

That same summer, Frances found herself at New York Hospital again. According to Vittorio, she had locked herself in the bathroom, swallowed half a bottle of aspirin, and had to be rushed to the emergency room to have her stomach pumped.

Not long after Frances and Vittorio arrived home from a belated honeymoon in Italy, Marilyn had a serious accident. She was on a skiing trip over New Year's weekend with a group of friends and was staying at the Adelphi Hotel in Saratoga Springs, New York. One evening, after skiing all day, she went to a cocktail party, had dinner and was starting up the stairs toward her room. She apparently slipped on a step, fell over the low banister, and dropped to the lobby on her head. Rushed to a hospital in Schenectady about twenty miles away, she lay in a coma for five days.

A month later, on February 6, 1960, a son was born to Vittorio and Frances Gentile at Doctors Hospital on East End Avenue. They gave him the name Lorenzo Jewett and took him home in their arms to their new apartment at 110 East End Avenue. Whatever troubles the Gentiles may have been having in their marriage, they were not sexual ones. Within six short weeks, Frances was again pregnant.

After Marilyn had her accident, she hired a lawyer to file suit against both the hotel and the insurance company representing it. Though she eventually lost her suit, she fell in love with the lawyer. So on June 16, 1960, she and Robert Reagan were married in a judge's office in Brooklyn.

Seven years older than Marilyn, Reagan was the son of a Quaker minister and private-school headmaster from Poughkeepsie, New York. Divorced from his first wife and the father of two daughters, he was a soft-spoken, rather timid, well-meaning individual whom Marilyn affectionately describes as a Caspar Milquetoast, the character in H. T. Webster's comic strip.

Like Frances and Elaine, Marilyn was choosing a husband who was different from her father in many ways. And like Mason Drukman and Vittorio Gentile before him, Robert Reagan would come under Berenice Bradshaw's close scrutiny and soon be the object of her caustic tongue. But unlike the others, he would be called on to perform an additional function—one that he would later regret.

Four days before Christmas of 1960, another son was born to Frances and Vittorio, and they named him Marco Francis. When her mother wrote that Frances "had her hands full," she was not exaggerating. Frances not only had two babies to take care of, but her battles with Vittorio were continuing.

On the evening of February 26, 1961, Frances showed up at Marilyn's apartment. In a signed affidavit that was later introduced in her sister's separation proceedings from Vittorio, Marilyn Reagan gave her account of that evening.

My sister appeared at my home severely beaten and her face disfigured. She had severe bruises and marks about her face, arms and legs. She informed me that her husband had been drinking heavily since 10 o'clock that morning and that he had passed out at about 6:00 p.m. That when he had awoke at about 8:00 p.m. he became irritated because my sister had already eaten her dinner, and thereupon he became vicious and commenced pummeling her with his fists across the face, twisted her arms and had thrown her to the floor.

I immediately took pictures of my sister with a camera that I had in the house showing the condition of my sister with the existing injuries. [The pictures were attached to the affidavit.]

I know of my own knowledge that my sister's husband on many occasions was drunk and disorderly. I have been present in their home on innumerable occasions when he was under the influence of liquor and was belligerent to my sister. On an occasion during the summer of 1960, I saw my sister's husband pass out at the dinner table because of excessive drinking.

A lawyer who has done negligence work knows that a picture truly can be worth a thousand words and help win a case for his client, but that if the picture is not good enough, it should not be entered into evidence. While Bob Reagan, who fit that category, later lamented the quality of those Polaroid color photographs, Marilyn backed off from her extreme description (saying "she was certainly bruised, with red marks on her face and arms, but if you saw her on the street, you wouldn't do a double take"), and Vittorio admitted that he would slap Frances when she went into "hysterical convulsions," but denied that he ever beat her, Frances's marriage to him—her relationship of choice, as the Salt Lake psychiatrist had told Elaine—continued for more than two years after that evening.

The year 1963 began with both Berenice and Franklin still reeling from a traumatic Christmas Day. Berenice had insisted she was going to have their son home from Provo and Franklin had told her it would be a mistake. In a letter to the family on January 4, he wrote: "We clashed pretty heavy three or four times on it. I thought I had talked her out of it." But Berenice changed her mind and told him that Bob was coming home and she was preparing a big Christmas dinner for six o'clock on Christmas Eve. His letter continued

I just knew Bob was going to give trouble but he was calm until your Mother went into a raving streak which she just loves to do but had nothing to do with me or against me. This got Bob started and he tore into me, blaming me for several things. . . . But I knew this was coming and I didn't want Bob home.

Your Mother informed me not to get angry as everything Bob was telling me was the truth. This would have gone on for hours if I hadn't stopped it. I told Bob that I didn't want him home Christmas, not because I don't like him and wouldn't do everything I could to help him but for his health and my health I thought it best. . . . The next afternoon I received a telephone call from Mrs. Anderson next door. She said that your mother was in a state of nervous shock. She had to give her a sedative and I had better come home. Bob was out of control and wasn't going to go back to his Provo rest home. I went home and took Bob to Provo. . . .

We were met at the door by a very nice lady with lots of personality. She greeted Bob and asked him what kind of Christmas he had. He said terrible. So my Christmas was ruined, his was ruined, and your Mother's was ruined, but I just couldn't talk her out of it.

He wrote that the Provo hospital in the past had requested they write letters monthly but make only three or four visits a year, not to exceed a half hour each time. "Your mother has agreed with neither request but goes down weekly for a couple of hours at a time. Bob would use pressure to come home. She would promise to bring him home next week even though Bob's health wasn't near as good after he would come home. They think your Mother's an intelligent person. They also think that a lot of parents are over emotional when it comes to children. Instead of taking a long-range view [they] let their emotions control their thinking."

Time and again, Franklin Bradshaw would tell his children that if there was something bothering them, the best thing to do was to just get it out of their heads. When his sister Bertha and her husband were in an auto accident in May of 1962, he offered them money, a place to stay, employment if they wanted it, and the following advice: "The number one problem for people that have had such a shock as you and Art have had, is to keep busy and forget the incident as fast as possible."

This was the way he looked at the world. There had been many crises in his own life that he would try to forget by absorbing himself in his work and in simply being Franklin Bradshaw—oilman, respected geologist, canny stock investor, auto-parts magnate, the little guy who took on the big boys and became a millionaire under a lightbulb. But all his self-discipline would ultimately not be enough to alter his fate.

12// Like the character of Neddy Merrill in John Cheever's "The Swimmer," Vittorio Gentile arrived home one humid summer evening in late June of 1963 to find nobody there.

His wife and two children were gone. All the furniture in the apartment had been removed, except for a bed, a table and some linen. On the walls, scrawled in lipstick, were swastikas and the words "Heil, Hitler!" and "Heil, Mussolini!" Stunned and confused, he immediately phoned Marilyn, who coldly told him that Frances didn't love him anymore and didn't want to see him. What she didn't tell him was that some moving men had transported Frances's furnishings to a tiny apartment on East 89th Street. Frances had plotted the move for weeks, but waited until her new apartment could be occupied.

Getting no cooperation from Marilyn or Berenice, Vittorio tried to think of some way to find Frances and his sons. He walked through Carl Schurz Park, across the street from his apartment, hoping they might come there during the day, as so many mothers do with their children, and along the promenade by the East River. But they were nowhere to be seen. After about a week, he made a phone call to a diaper service. He stated his name and address and asked where they were now delivering diapers to Mrs. Vittorio Gentile. Upon receiving the information, he went over and pounded on the door.

"She wouldn't let me in," Vittorio recalled. "The kids were screaming and she was yelling, 'Get out of here or I'll call the police!' I loved her too much. I told her that I wanted her back but she said, 'No, my mind is made up.'"

Perhaps they both loved each other too much—too much to continue living together. By the third week in July, Vittorio was served with a subpoena informing him that Frances was filing a lawsuit for an official separation (the required first step at that time toward getting a divorce). The person who delivered it was none other than his *bête noir*, Marilyn.

By the following May, the marital life of Vittorio and Frances Gentile was being unfolded to all of New York in the pages of the *Daily News*.

Frances was being represented by Howard Cerny, a short, muscular figure who could easily pass for a Marine drill sergeant or a Robert Duvall lookalike. Cerny, whose future clients would include the controversial financier and exile Robert Vesco and the fried-chicken king Colonel Sanders, was battling against Irving Erdheim, who was building a reputation as one of the formidable divorce lawyers in New York (and would later be cited in *Harper's Bazaar* as one of the four best in the country).

Prior to the court proceedings, Frances had received a temporary support settlement from Vittorio, partly based on the contents of the affidavit Marilyn had signed. On Friday, May 1, dressed in a pink woolen suit, "the blue-eyed brunette, daughter of a western oil operator," as the *Daily News* referred to her, told the court of a weekend in 1959, their first year of marriage, that she and Vittorio spent at a private country club at Montauk Point. He was taking a nap and when she woke him up, she testified, he screamed at her for disturbing him, pounded her with his fists, slapped her about the face and neck, threw her on the bed, and sat on top of her.

On the next court day, her litany against Vittorio continued. Her legal papers called him a "habitual drunkard," and she contended that his liquor bill was $300 a month, including wine and brandy that cost $12 a bottle.

"This is your testimony, that your husband never drew a sober breath when you lived together?" Justice Wilfred A. Waltemade pressed her.

"The only time he was sober was when he woke up in the morning," Frances replied, saying that he had orange juice then.

"Was there ever a day when he did not drink?" Justice Waltemade continued.

"Only once, when he was sick," Frances said.

She told of other beatings she had received, and Cerny tried to introduce the color photographs the Reagans had taken of Frances that February evening in 1961 when she appeared at their door. But he was unsuccessful; the judge sustained Erdheim's strenuous objections that they were not proper evidence, because color shots can be misleading if they are overexposed.

The following day, Frances continued to testify about Vittorio's drinking, saying he would drink until he was senseless and would pass out, and then launched into another area—their sex life. She said that after the spring of 1962 she had sex with her husband only once, in the spring of 1963. When Cerny pushed her to go into detail, she said, "I talked to him about the lack of sex and I asked him why he did not like to have sex with me. I asked if he was having sex with someone else and he said he had an allergy, that he was allergic to sex. He accused me of being unfaithful."

Frances said that Vittorio suspected her of having sex with her dentist, her doctor, her neighbor, and that "he was even jealous of the P.T.A." at the nursery school that Marco and Lorenzo attended, because he thought she might rendezvous with someone there.

She admitted, however, that before his "allergy," Vittorio had worked his office hours around the time that she preferred to make love, which was after her breakfast. Vittorio would leave for work at seven-thirty, then return home no later than eleven in order to accommodate her.

She also admitted to making a "mock" suicide attempt six weeks after their marriage in 1959, but said she did it only to get her husband's attention. She claimed he was throwing plates against the walls and screaming that he didn't love her. Justice Waltemade broke in to say that it seemed she was getting a good deal of attention, but Frances was not deterred. She said the suicide attempt "was like putting cold water on his face to sober him up."

When the swastikas and allusions to Hitler and Mussolini were brought up, Frances said she had made them because of the disagreements they had over international politics. Vittorio would emphatically say years later that he was *not* a Fascist, and claim that she hated both Jews and Italians.

When Vittorio finally had his day in court, he said that he loved his wife very much and wanted her back. Asked if it was true that they had made love only once during the last year and a half of their marriage, as Frances had indicated, he said they made love once a week.

"I was the aggressor on all occasions," Vittorio said, his deep accent filled with the indignation of a man whose role as a husband had been challenged. "She refused me several times during this interval because she was very nervous and afraid."

Justice Waltemade called a recess and spoke with Frances and her lawyer in an anteroom. He asked if she wanted to reconcile with Vittorio, and she indicated she did not. When the judge again took the bench, he rendered his decision: he was dismissing the suit for lack of proof. He said both parents displayed a certain immaturity that made them "unable to cast aside their own selfish interests in order to make a peaceful home." He went on to say that Frances's allegations of daily intoxication on Vittorio's part were not entirely credible.

"I am sure there was drinking by both of them and that this has been greatly exaggerated." Instead of the $300 liquor bill that Frances testified about, he said the highest monthly bill seemed to be about $77.

Frances would continue to have custody of Lorenzo and Marco; Vittorio was granted visitation rights between ten a.m. and five p.m. on weekends; and the question of permanent custody and support would be determined at a future point.

Vittorio might have gained a victory, but it would prove to be a Pyrrhic one.

From the time that Frances left Vittorio, her parents were sending her about $1,000 a month to cover rent and utilities, the children's school fees, clothing and medical bills, and Frances's various needs. Franklin was not happy about this, and once she lost her separation suit (which meant that she could not get alimony, only child support), her father suggested she either go to work or move back to Utah with her sons. That was the last thing she would ever do, and besides, she felt the court would want the boys to stay in New York so that Vittorio could visit them.

While Frances and Vittorio were continuing to battle,

Marilyn and Robert tried to be Franklin's go-between in New York—Robert on legal matters, Marilyn on domestic ones. Much of Marilyn's correspondence with her father was intended to be kept from Berenice, because she felt her mother could no longer be objective about Frances. The sides she had refused to choose while growing up she could no longer avoid choosing now.

DEAR DAD,

[Frances] is so resourceful that she can appologise to her Mother, whom she has just taken over the coals royally, and get Mother to come and be on her side again. I feel very sorry for Mother, because she is so happy that her Frances is speaking to her. I don't like to sound pessimistic, but I feel sure that as soon as Frankie has what she wants, she will turn against Mother again. . . .

Needless to say, this letter is confidential, because Mother doesn't like to read or hear disparaging comments on her favorite child and in my opinion, one and only love. . . .

Love,
MARILYN

Berenice often departed on trips when the family's crises either got too much for her or she was rebuffed in her attempts to help. Frances's loss of her lawsuit was one of those times, and on this occasion she forced Franklin to go with her. Berenice had been down at the warehouse one day and saw a letter indicating Bradshaw Auto Parts had won an all-expenses-paid trip to Las Vegas for three days and two nights. In the past, Franklin had never told her about these free packages and would give them to one of his employees to use. When she found out about this one, she insisted that they were going.

She had seen these kinds of things given away to lucky recipients on television game shows, but never dreamed she would experience one. No sooner had they gotten to town and checked into a deluxe room—$17 a night in 1964—than Franklin wandered away to a stockbroker's to watch the Big Board, while Berenice helped herself to all the cocktails she could drink; in the evening, they took in the free nightclub shows and stuffed themselves with food.

But at the end of their three-day package, Franklin was ready to go home and she was not. Johnny Carson was going to perform that evening, and Berenice wanted to see him. Franklin told her that they couldn't afford the hotel room, so he left town while she checked into a less expensive room in a motel across the street.

"The bed had a meter you put 25¢ in and it would jiggle you to sleep so I didn't miss a bed companion," she wrote. "I got the last reservation they could possibly squeeze in for Johnny that nite. His wife sat close to me, Johnny was delightful and I had the thrill of my life. The next day I took the plane home."

A letter was waiting for her when she got there. It was from a psychiatrist in New York whom Frances had been referred to by a social worker at Family Court:

DEAR MRS. BRADSHAW:

A few months ago your daughter, Mrs. Frances Gentile, applied to me for psychiatric treatment. . . .

She has had nine office visits, and I believe that her need for treatment is urgent—her problems are serious.

She said to me during her seventh visit that you had refused to provide her with the necessary financial aid required for her treatment. On a subsequent occasion she mentioned that you had changed your mind.

I am writing to you with Mrs. Gentile's permission in order to ask you what your plans are in this regard, and what in your opinion would be the best thing for her and her future.

From the thrill of Las Vegas back to reality.

Marilyn wasn't the only one who had been sending her father confidential letters. Her brother, who had not given up his dream of becoming a successful businessman of whom his dad could be proud, was writing them as well. In a letter from Provo, he told his father: "I am still pushing my programme of cutting-myself-off-from-my-mother's-skirt's as you suggested last Time I saw you. (seems like an eternity). The programme is still being pushed even-Though my love for the family has not deminished any." In another letter he said how disappointed he was that he did not receive a reply to his letters and wondered if his mail got through at all.

AnoTher look aT The situation also Tells me That I have never been independent since I can remember!? How's ThaT for Training a boy To become a man? Especially an independenT business-man? (send me To any corner of The sTaTe—please) (As I said before, ninety percenT of The paTienTs here are ex-con's!) LiTTle wonder Then ThaT I would like to geT myself on The 'family-payroll' and sTarT living in some 'Boarding-House' or apartment near here (and a loT come aT $50:00 a month, furnished!) (I am sure my work-ideas are worth more Than That!?)

I sTill would like To organize a small fronT corp. which would be part of B.A.P. co. Inc., but operate as a semi-night-shift in UTah county (aT firsT) and let me show "my stuff." . . .

I have done alloT of Talking and 'hand-shaking in be-half of B.A.P. co. Inc. lately. . . . This salesman is noT asleep and will not leT anyone else sleep eiTher! A liTTle helP from you and This aTomic-source could be on The 'family pay-roll.'? Don'T under-raTe me because, There will be a day in The fuTure when This family will need all The skill you can give me now! . . . (In the lasT 12 years I have had no independence I could call my own.?!) . . .

Love,
Robert

Though Franklin had known for a long time that his only son could not take over the business he had started in 1929, the reality of that was still difficult for him—and for Robert—to accept.

her father one. She warned him that the issue of genealogy aroused the frenzy from Vittorio was going to be trouble some. The court had asked Frances to produce her business records—containing oil leases and stock—her father had paid for—and remain in a position to prevent that, if she didn't

13 // By the end of 1964, Frances had moved from her small apartment on East 89th Street to one with two bedrooms and a study at 85 East End Avenue, just down the street from the building she and Vittorio had lived in. Frances loved the Upper East Side of poodles and poohbahs, and in years to come would live in three other buildings all within the same area. Sharing her mother's interest in genealogy, she, like Berenice, became a member of a number of societies, including the Huguenot Society of America (which she would later make sure Marilyn could not join) and the Daughters of Founders and Patriots in America, and she became a fundraiser for the Republican Party in New York, rubbing elbows with the Rockefellers. If going to Bryn Mawr had been the first step, living in New York had been the logical second.

In every sense, it was a world and a way of life far removed from the one she had known in Mormon Utah. And it was a world and a way of life that her father had a hard time understanding. New York represented one thing to Franklin Bradshaw: it was damn expensive. If Frances couldn't get a job to support her family and supplement the money he was sending, then he wanted her to pack up and come home to, in his mind, a more sensible way of life.

Her problems had so consumed Berenice that Franklin complained of it in a letter to the family after Thanksgiving in 1964. (Though his daughters often sent him confidential letters, he usually wrote an open letter to the whole family or wrote to one member and sent copies to others.) In it, he said that Berenice had "Francis' problems on her mind 18 to 20 hours a day for the last 16 months and that is all she would think and talk about and do quite a bit of raving besides. Now she refuses to even talk about it and I think she has found out that she has got to try her hardest to completely get it out of her mind if possible." He closed the letter by saying, "Her health and probably life is at stake."

No sooner had this letter been received than Marilyn sent

her father one. She warned him that the issue of permanent support for Frances from Vittorio was going to be troublesome. The court had asked Frances to produce her business records—containing oil leases and stocks her father had paid for—and Franklin was determined to prevent this. If he didn't even let his own wife know what he had, he certainly wasn't going to let any New York court put his holdings under a legal microscope and into the center of a matrimonial battle that he didn't approve of in the first place. Marilyn wrote:

If this thing ever gets settled, then she will be sued for beating up one of Vittorio's baby sitters. He was ordered by the court to take the boys himself and not hire a baby sitter. He had a teenage girl bring the boys home a couple of times and on one occasion Frankie took a picture of the girl returning the children in her apartment building. . . . The story she told Mother was that she took the girl's purse to get her name and address but didn't touch the girl. . . . The law suit says that Frankie gave the girl a black eye, pushed her to the floor, beat her and pulled her hair. Now we don't believe that she did all of that but she must have done some of it, because they will either have pictures of the black eye or a doctor that examined the girl and be able to prove some of it. . . .

She does not want to go back to Utah and will fight it in any way she can. I think that if you give her the alternative of coming back to Utah or going to work—*full time*—then she might go to work. . . . One of her arguments against going to work is that Vittorio gets the boys on Saturday and Sunday so when would she see her boys. . . . If she goes to work I'm sure that the Judge will change Vittorio's visiting previliges. . . . The children are the only mutual link they have and they have been using them to get back at each other.

Vittorio was very hurt by this episode but he has now moved to a new apartment in a new building and drives a very expensive car—the lawyers think that he spends about $6000 a year for the apartment and upkeep of the car. He is getting very busy with his own life now. Unfortunately I think Frankie is jealous of his way of life. He used to take her to expensive places dressed in her expensive clothes. She still has all of the clothes but no place to go. She sneaks around and spies on Vittorio—I can't see what she hopes to accomplish or prove.

It is a horrible, mixed-up mess. I think Frankie is torn between loving her children and wanting to go to parties, have fun and play.

Mother knows only the love of children side and cannot believe that Frankie would put anything above that. I hope I am wrong, but I think Frankie would put the children second if there was something that she wanted to do. . . .

Battles were being waged on all fronts, but perhaps the most crucial one was between Lorenzo and Marco.

"They were constantly fighting," Berenice recalled. "Lorenzo wanted air at night and Marco didn't, but Marco had to put up with whatever Lorenzo wanted, because he seemed to be superior physically to Marco. He was always trying to destroy Marco. They were bad characters and shouldn't have been raised together. I did see Lorenzo push Marco's head through a plate-glass window, but fortunately it didn't cut him. One time they were at the ocean, and Frances said he tried to drown Marco."

"I was a rowdy, hyperactive kid," Lorenzo would say with no emotion years later. "It wasn't because of the attention I was getting, it was because I wanted to dominate. As long as I can remember I was never Mom's favorite. Marco was always her star, her pet. I think she hated my guts. She never liked having me around the house and felt I was too hard to handle. She complained that I ate too much, drank all the liquids, and said she couldn't support me. My mother said my father was violent, drank too much and beat us up. But she used to push us around when we were little, and beat me up a lot. She was just kind of violent at times."

He remembered one of those occasions as if it were yesterday. It was not long after they had fled to East 89th Street, and Marco and he, roughly three and four, were playing in Frances's bedroom. "We spilled all her perfume on her bed. She picked me up high in the air and threw me hard on to the ground. She did the same thing to Marco. There was blood on his face. It is my first memory of life."

After Frances had left Vittorio, Marilyn suggested she come to All Souls Unitarian Church, on the corner of 80th Street and Lexington Avenue, as a way to meet people. The church had a group called the Guild that met after services on Sundays, and it was at one of those kaffeeklatsches in 1963 that Frances met Richard Behrens, who was thirty-seven, unmarried, a graduate of Lafayette College, a former student of violin at Juilliard, and the son of a doctor from Jersey City, New Jersey. Short, stocky, rambling in his speech, and looking very much like an absent-minded professor, Behrens worked for a microscope company and lived in a rent-controlled railroad apartment nearby.

When Frances wanted to spy on Vittorio, Behrens often went with her on what Lorenzo called "secret missions." Vittorio had met a woman whose parents lived about fifty miles upstate from New York City, and one time Frances and Behrens drove there in search of the family house. On the surface, they seemed an unlikely pair of sleuths; but Frances represented adventure to a man whose life had little in it, and he in turn showed her how to slip away from the detectives whom Vittorio had following her—by getting on at one subway stop and suddenly jumping off at the next—and how to know when people were following her in the first place.

From the start he was a figure of mystery in her life—"the invisible man, the guy in compartment C," he would later say of himself. When she introduced him to her sons, they were told to call him Uncle George, so that Vittorio would not know who he was. When their father saw them on weekends, Marco and Lorenzo spoke of Uncle George—and Vittorio would be both baffled and infuriated.

Richard Behrens and Frances Gentile would drop in and out of each other's lives. He would introduce her to other men, would become a confidant, a keeper of secrets, and would always try to be there if she needed him. She would confide in him, among other things, that her father had destroyed her brother, Robert, and that her mother tried to smother him with love. She in turn would help him to stop drinking. He would be both sympathetic to her problems yet clear-eyed about her, learning from experience that she could be sweet and lovely one minute and turn on a person the next. As time went on, they became two figures who fed on—and reinforced—each other's paranoiac outlook on the world. If she was unpredictable, so was he. To understand Richard Behrens is *not* to understand Richard Behrens, someone would later say.

* * *

While Franklin was continuing to use Marilyn as a secret informant, he also began to deal directly with his youngest daughter, whose name he constantly spelled like a man's—Francis. On January 9, 1965, he wrote her that "everybody has good points and bad points and there is no such thing as a perfect person." Her good points, he said, were that she was "quite a good looking gal and an attractive person. You wear your clothes nice and you have personality plus when you want to use it." Her bad points, he listed in a businesslike 1-2-3 style, were that she didn't keep promises (she promised "time and time again" to go to work, but hadn't); she didn't appreciate things other people did for her—especially the amount of money it took to send her to a "swanky" college; she was "a poor business lady" (by continuing to draw money out of the oil account he had set up for her, she was hurting her and her sons' future); and she was "nervous and high strung, and those kinds of people often make poor decisions and don't meet reality, especially if they are the baby girl and spoiled." One of those poor decisions, he said, was leaving Vitro (as he called him):

There is an old saying that the first marriage has only a fifty-fifty chance of proving out, the second marriage the chances are 75 percent against you, the third the chances are 90 percent against you. Personally I think Vitro had some very good qualities. (1) He had a college education, could speak about three languages, that means he was a very intelligent person. (2) He had business ability which he proved by taking a business over and making it profitable. (3) He did provide a nice apartment and a very good school for the boys and all the medical help that was necessary. He was very good taking you out a couple of times a week to expensive cafes. The above qualities only fit about 5 percent of the people in the country. . . . I was told by a couple of other persons that no matter who Francis married she would get tired of them and want new thrills. I didn't believe it at the time, I sure do now.

Francis, in plain words I am real hurt. . . . I don't think you have been considerate of me in the past and I don't think you are considerate of me now and I don't think you will ever know the value of money until you go to work and earn it yourself which you have no other choice than to do.

Four days later he sent her another letter, telling her that the boys needed a father and that if she left Vittorio on "account of your mother building up feelings against your husband," then she showed poor judgment. "She wouldn't let her mother run her life and you shouldn't yourself." As for Vittorio's drinking, Franklin told her that "a smart woman just doesn't divorce a man for drinking unless he gets completely out of hand." He closed the letter by warning her not to draw any more checks on her oil account and sending a stamped air-mail envelope for her reply.

That reply did not come for a while, and Franklin was becoming increasingly concerned about the effort of Vittorio's lawyers to get a full accounting of Frances's holdings—technically part of his. So he urged Marilyn to take Vittorio, whom he had never met, out to dinner, let him do 90 percent of the talking, and show him some of the letters he had been sending to Frances. "In this way we may or may not get any leads to work on," he wrote. He said that if she didn't want to, maybe Bob could, and he would gladly pay for the meal.

Marilyn replied that taking Vittorio out to dinner would accomplish nothing because "he would just plead with me to try to get Frankie to come back to him. This she will never do and I don't think she should." She again raised the issue of the assault on the baby-sitter, and the possibility of Frances's being sued. "Under these circumstances, I think it best to quit putting any thing of any value in her name. . . . She said to me once when she was going to college—'If Dad has all that money, why can't we spend it!' My answer was, 'If you don't know by now—there is nothing I can say.'"

By the beginning of April, Franklin still had no reply from Frances. He wrote her that she had copies of all her holdings and that for the lawyers to come to Utah would be "just like taking some green backs and touching a match to them." A few days later, on Frances's twenty-seventh birthday, he wrote again:

DEAR FRANCIS:

. . . Please advise me when you are going to work. What plans are you making? If I don't get an answer I will be back to New York to spend a couple of weeks and it looks like I am going to be Vitro's witness not yours. You are not going on the way you are. I have enough proof that you are completely responsible and you should go back to Vitro and unless you go to work at once you are going back to Vitro so I expect an answer by return mail. I have tried for 5 days to get you on the telephone, . . . are you afraid I am calling you up on the phone, or what is the reason you are not answering the telephone? . . .

DAD

Franklin was not the only one upset with Frances. Berenice was too, and for once they were united on something. Two days after Franklin's letter, Berenice fired off one of her own:

April 8, Thurs.

DEAR FRANCES:

. . . You are living like Mrs. Astor on our money. This has to stop and the only way it can be stopped is to close [your oil] bank account because you refuse to heed warnings.

Frances, you are not facing life realistically. You have two boys to support. So far you have made no effort on your own to support them. You have been told by legal authorities and you know thru experience you can not rely on Victor [Vittorio] for support. The only way to make him assume his financial obligation is to throw him in jail a few times but no one in N.Y. has the guts to get tough with him. . . . In the meantime you will have to find a way to make some money. Other women do, why can't you?

I have risked everything to help you; home, husband, financial standing, and all I've gotten from you is abuse. I have never been more horribly treated by anyone than by you on my last stay in N.Y. . . . I'm so ashamed of the way you treated me this last time I haven't told a soul. . . . Can you imagine what your family would think if they knew all that happened? You laid me out verbally several times, the first time in front of Bertha. I was so heart broken from that tongue lashing I told Bertha I was going home. It was Bertha who talked me into staying. Bertha said: "Mrs. Bradshaw, your daughter needs you, she is very lonely."

The summer you left Victor you called me one day, you were crying, and you said; "Isn't some one going to help me?" From that day to this I have done everything in my power to help you and I'm the only one who has helped you. Then you had the audacity to tell me to my face that: "I thought I could buy my way into your lives." This slap in the face after I had spent thousands helping you and the boys. . . . They say people destroy the thing they love. I could even stand to be destroyed if I thought there was some love behind it. The only explanation I can see for this is that you are sick of mind, for which I feel deeply sorry. I want to help you overcome this illness or personality emotion, call it what you will, but you won't let me. I think before you ask me for help again you should ask for my forgiveness, which I will gladly give, but it must come from *you* to ask. You are raising two children, they may treat you that way some day, they say chickens come home to roost. . . .

Dad has had a report from N.Y. that you are doing considerable chasing with men and that you stay away all nite with a man. We are horrified. Women who do this are called "hores." You may think your sons are too little to know what you are doing but I'm telling you that what you do now is leaving a picture on their minds and when they grow up they will have no respect for you. . . . Dad and I have tried calling you many many evenings and no one answers. Can it be you are leaving your boys alone while you tom-cat around? . . . I warned you once before about getting in men's apartments but you didn't listen, so you ended up marrying a dego and ruining the lives of many people, including your own and children.

Dad and I appreciated the darling Easter cards from the boys and Grandpa's cute birthday card. You can do such nice thoughtful things when I'm not around. . . .

All my love to you and the boys. Hope you all have a nice Easter also. I'm sending out my usual money cards to the children.

MOTHER & GRANDNANA

When Frances got backed into a corner, Richard Behrens said, she was a true desperado who would come out fighting. This was such a time, and she was ready to reply.

April 10, 1965

DEAR MRS. BRADSHAW,

I received your lovely birthday letter. It didn't surprise me since I've received letters like that for two years from you. I agree that your visits are quite terrible. . . . No normal, sane, healthy balanced woman can stand to be dominated like a small child by her mother when she is adult and has her own house and own family. You would be scared to death to go to Marilyn's apartment and pull the shit you do with me. . . . Alone and struggling to raise two children, [I] have been dependent morally and financially, and in exchange I'm supposed to show my gratitude by letting you rob me of every ounce of self esteem and be a helpless baby daughter once again. You will have to realize that neither I nor any of your children will, as adults, permit you to dominate and suffocate them as if they were infants.

Your visits are sickening. I wish I had another mother who would be kind and to whom I could say "Oh please come stay with us." . . . You don't give a damn about anyone's feelings at all. . . . Do you consider how my son felt when you said he was born bad and wicked to his little face? No wonder you have a son in a mental hospital.

Yes, you do buy affection with money. In your letter you said I had no right to defend my house and home, to tell you when you do something wrong because you "spent thousands of dollars on me." Well, keep your money and take it to your grave with you. I prefer my serenity, and peace of mind. You say I don't treat you with love, and feeling, and respect? Well you "created" me and as you say "chickens come home to roost," for you've never ever treated your children with love or respect. Children learn from infancy to give as much love and respect to their parents as they themselves have in turn been given. My most vivid memories of childhood are of being completely alone, listening to you talk to yourself like a maniac all day. My psychiatric test says: "My mother was too engrossed in her own neurotic problems to give her children the *proper* emotional and psychological attention that children require." The test results have paragraph after paragraph describing what a "bad" mother you were and are. You sent me so many disgusting, vulgar, insane, sick, cruel letters that you've just about destroyed any feelings I have for you. Your a great one to moralize. You never had to get a job or face this problem so how do you know anything? You didn't have to leave your children when we were young—although it would have been better if you had. You say I married "a dego and ruined everyone's life." Who did you marry? How many lives did you ruin? Well, you married a man who cares about objects and things. . . . Did you see that we got a father? No, Dad will do anything to save his money (all he cares about in exchange for ignoring his children). He was too busy to come to my wedding, to give me a kiss or do any of the things that normal fathers do—the rest of the world is shocked at his insanity. . . .

You say I ruined lives? Where's your son? You say I'm a bad mother? Thank god my sons aren't helpless, emotionally crippled szchophrenics, locked up for life in a mental hospital. Oh yes, it's true that bad genes and physiological factors such as chemicals in the blood play a part, but all the evidence that medical science has found says that it *also* takes "emotionally sick" parents to produce a son like you molded yourself. If you and Dad want to go on kidding yourselves go ahead, but no one else believes otherwise and in your heart, you know it's true.

Don't you ever say I've ruined lives for you've left a whole trail of destruction throughout your life. Your paranoid delusions of all the suffering that you say that others inflict on you has every ounce of it been self-inflicted on yourself in your own twisted and warped mind and soul. . . . I would have to go a long way to be as sick as you and I think you need intensive psychiatric care immediately and desperately. . . . Yes, I have a few emotional problems but I'm working mine out with my analyst, thank you. Thank god I'm reasonably normal, sane and healthy of mind and body. My children and I basically lead a quiet serene and peaceful life and there is nothing you can possibly do or say to destroy or take our serenity away from us. My one hope in life is never, never to be in my old age as sick, neurotic, and cruel as you are. . . . You were asking for this letter and if you want to sit down and cry and feel sorry for yourself in your usual fashion go right ahead. . . .

Also, what's this business about staying away all night and "tom cating" around? You repeat that again, either to my face or to my back, and god damn your asking for trouble and I mean TROUBLE. You'd either better shut your vile mouth or go into a court of law and prove that what you're saying is true and defend yourself against charges of slander. . . . If I don't want to answer my phone it's my right. . . . If there's an emergency anyone can send a telegram. . . .

I have problems—financial, legal etc. etc.—but I can face it all because I learn more and more every day to have peace or serenity in my soul and mind and respect for myself as a worthy human being on this earth. Dad can testify against me, but he can never take away my soul and my tranquility. Money is all you think of—your prized possession—and you would sell your daughter to the devil for touching your money. Keep it and take it to your grave—you'll need it, for you will be very lonely. Most fathers wouldn't talk or act the way Dad does even if their daughter was a murderess—it's only over money—oh, excuse me, I shouldn't say "only money" because it's very important to you. . . .

Sincerely,
MRS. V. GENTILE

The same day that Frances wrote the nine-page letter to her mother, she wrote a four-page one to her father.

April 10, 1965

DEAR DAD,

I received your letter of April 6th. I tried very hard in the past to get a job and I agonized over the various solutions to the problem, especially whether or not to work all night and, above all, who and how to get someone in the home to take care of my children. . . . I don't want to leave my children all day so I started to look for part-time work while the children are in school in the morning. Meanwhile I got engrossed in court matters. I'm glad that I did because I might have taken a job and left my children without their mother. I will never leave my children to take a job until my children are old enough to stay in school all day (two years from now). God bless my children, my two little boys who are my very heart and soul to the core. If I'm such an intolerable burden to you I will be most happy to go to the public relief authorities and they will investigate my needs. My children and I are quite lucky, for all the laws of this country, whether you like it or not, support the matter of *mothers staying with their children.* . . .

You are perfectly welcome to come and testify for Vittorio. . . . Judge Waltemade would feel great sympathy for me should you testify against me because he already doesn't care for you. You see, he cross-examined me and asked me various questions, among which are that you never even bothered to attend the wedding of any of your children, that you've never met Vittorio and that you never bothered to give any of your children any love as other "human beings" know of it. Judge Waltemade knows that you never bother to see your children, but we all know that you'll pay for a plane trip East if you think it will save you some money somewhere. If pounding the "shit" [out of] your daughter obtains a few extra bucks for you go ahead, I'm waiting for you. So is the N.Y. City police waiting for you. It's against the law to beat your daughter. . . .

Sincerely,
FRANCES B. GENTILE

The fallout was immediately felt. Berenice fell apart, and Franklin came rushing to her defense as well as his own. He wrote Frances that as soon as Berenice received her letter she called him up "in a complete nervous condition. . . . I rushed home as soon as possible after work and found her sobbing . . . and she was still sobbing late at night when I went to bed. I was very hurt that you would write a letter like that to your mother."

Stern and forever practical, he went on to tell her that when companies hire people they often inquire into the prospective employee's background, including one's relationship with his parents. "If the employee has feelings against either one of his parents they know 90 to 95 percent of the time it is the child, not the parent, to blame for that, and that person just isn't hired. I want Francis to always remember that.

"Your mother is a very nervous, high-strung person; of course, one third to two thirds of all mothers are. It is up to the children to understand those nervous traits and to accept them; after all, she is the one that brought the children into the world and raised them. Your mother has a lot of good features. She is a good-looking lady, she dresses nice, has a very outstanding personality, she likes the social part of life . . . she has quite a few lady friends that enjoy her and she enjoys them, she enjoys her three times a week trip to the spa, she enjoys very much her yard and flowers, she likes to go to operas and shows, and she enjoys the Jack Paar show in the evening. I think she laughs harder than anybody at some of his jokes." He said that Frances needed her mother's help "awful bad," but that he wouldn't let her come to New York unless she was completely welcome.

Frank Bradshaw may have been an obsessed workaholic and a father who was rarely home while his children were growing up, but he could not be accused in 1965 of not caring about Frances and her situation. Nearly every day that April he wrote her a long businesslike letter (often more than one), letters that revealed his values and the way he looked at the world. In his letter of April 14, he informed Frances that he *was* planning to come to New York (where he had never been) on Sunday, the 25th, with six orders of business on his agenda.

The first was to try to get the lease canceled on the East 89th Street apartment she was no longer living in. The second was to try to find a lodger for the one she was living in and paying $305 a month for. The third was to investigate the report that she had been doing considerable drinking. ("There is an old saying," he wrote, "that a person can't go two directions at one time. . . . Most people that drink are admitting that they love themselves more than [their] children. So if you are drinking again it is like a man going north and south at the same time.") The fourth was to do something about her living "completely above your means" (implying that it meant she didn't love her children, and that Berenice's practice of sending her money in the past without his knowing about it was going to stop). The fifth was to try to stop her from making so many long-distance phone calls. And the sixth was a request that she specifically not call her mother anymore, repeating what he had told Marilyn: "her health and life is at stake."

Two days later, he wrote Frances about a girl named Dee whose father had divorced her mother and deserted the family, and who had worked for Frank during high school. When Dee graduated from West High with honors and won a scholarship to the University of Utah, she told him how much she had appreciated the opportunity to work and that Bradshaw Auto Parts was like a second home.

The reason he was telling Frances about Dee, he wrote, was that Dee often reminded him of her: Frances was "just as good looking," had an "outstanding personality," and was "sharp and bright." But the difference between them, he said, was that Dee couldn't have gone to college without that scholarship and working part-time for him. "I think people who struggle as she did to make it and make their way in life build up character and become some of the finest people there is." He reminded her how she had pulled her grades up in her last two years of high school and said, "I was so thrilled that you dug in and ended up as an honor student at East High but I have wondered since if it wasn't a mistake for you to go to a fancy eastern school. The cost . . . was terrific and I think Francis ran the cost up way higher than it should have been. . . .

"I have been pounding you heavy to go to work because . . . you would do real good at it if you put your mind to it. Somebody tending the children for 4 to 6 hours a day would give you a break, and if you did get to work, you would make almost twice as much as you would paying for the person tending the children. . . . I still think if Francis had to make her own living, which a lot of other women do when they get a divorce, it would just make a swell person out of you and build up that extra character. Francis, I write these letters in a hurry and it is hard to put my points over, but many times I write a letter when I am trying to help, not criticize. I have some other good employees, the reason I am talking about Dee is that you have every bit as much ability as she has, but you don't have the advantage of having to make your way in life."

Marilyn had planned to stay out of things, but found that she couldn't. On April 17, she sent her father a special-delivery letter, trying to persuade him to do what Elaine had tried and failed to get both her parents to do more than six years before: turn his back on Frances.

April 17, 1965

DEAR DAD,

. . . I am going to quote from a book written by an outstanding doctor here in New York: "ANTISOCIAL SOCIOPATH—This term refers to the chronically antisocial person who is always in trouble, profiting neither from experience nor punishment and maintaining no genuine loyalties to any person, group, or code. He is frequently callous and hedonistic, showing marked emotional immaturity, and lacking a sense of responsibility. His judgment is poor, and he often attempts to rationalize his behavior so that it appears warranted, reasonable, and justified." We had read a definition of a psychopath, which we can't find right now, which was quite similar to this one. These people will do anything necessary to accomplish what they want now, with no regard to other people or others' feelings. However, let anyone else treat them the same way and it is an entirely different story. I am not trying to diognosis Frankie's problem, because these are just general terms anyway, but in my opinion and in the court's opinion she is sick. Vittorio is sick also.

At this point it is pretty obvious to me that she does not want to have anything to do with any of us. I felt sure that this would happen at what ever time the money ran out. . . . I had thought at first that it would be good for you to come to New York and get a little bit of this inhospitable treatment that she can give out, and maybe you would go home realizing how impossible this situation is. Any little talks that you might have with her would mean nothing to her. . . . I believe if either you or Mother come she will close the door on you and not let you in her apartment. She won't have anything but cruel insults to say to you and I think it would be a waste of your time and money. . . .

As hard as it will be to do, I think you both would be wise to write Frankie off as a lost cause for the time being. If anything changes, for better or for worse, I'm sure you will hear about it. . . .

Love,
MARILYN

By planning to go to New York, Frank Bradshaw was, perhaps for the first time in his married life, putting his family above his work. For years he had endured his wife's accusations that he was a weak and uncaring father and husband, and he was finally about to assert himself—not by letter, not as a businessman with a checkbook, but in person as a father who was concerned about his youngest daughter. But that daughter was warning him that nothing more inviting than "New York's Finest" awaited his arrival, and another was bluntly telling him that nothing could possibly be gained by his trip. Berenice, however, was all in favor of his going and felt he should have gone a long time before to pull Frances out of her marriage to Vittorio. Yet her approval of his decision to go was not free of strong criticism at the same time—and she had a secret plan of her own.

"Dad would never go back with me on any of my trips and he doesn't want me to go with him this time," Berenice wrote in frustration to Marilyn on April 18, unaware of Marilyn's letter to her father. "He is always talking about team work, but what he really means is dictatorship. Everyone has got to agree with him, go along with his ideas, or he won't function.

Now this is not 'team work' as I see it. 'Team work' is more than one person's ideas, opinions, objectives, motives, procedures, etc. He sends me back to N.Y. to handle things; then when I come home and tell him how I find things, he won't believe me." She said that "he will only believe the things that coincide with his peculiar way of thinking," and "refuses to believe that Victor was mean to Frances and . . . the boys."

She told Marilyn of her concern that Frances had pawned all of her sterling silver (which Berenice had given to her when she married) and very expensive pearls, and of her desire to redeem them. ("It makes me sick to think of all that silver being donated to a loan shark. For chicken feed.") She said that Franklin was willing to "meet and talk with anyone who wants to talk to him. If you think of any one he should talk to, lawyer, doctor, etc., maybe you should make some appointments for Dad to see them. You know Dad, he won't stay one minute longer than he has to, so if you do make appointments they should be close to his arrival. I wish there was one certain person we could talk to, but I don't know who it would be. . . .

Dad says things in fits of anger and [I] wonder how much of it he means. Just recently he said if he went back to N.Y. he would make Frances go back to Victor. Now you and I know this would be wrong for many reasons. In the first place she should live her own life and no one should demand she live with a man under the conditions she was living under. They are too much alike from an emotional stand point. We know it would be absolutely disasterous for her to attempt to go back to him. He would simply torture her to death. And for the children's sake she can't live with him. When your father gets mad he has a violent temper and if she goes against him and starts argueing or defies him he might not control himself. He says he would beat her too. This beating business I think is horrible. It shows weakness of character and dominance of will.

Now, Marilyn, please don't mention this, but I'm thinking strongly of taking a plane the next day after Dad leaves for N.Y. I will stay in the back ground and let him take over Frances, but I do feel I should be there; I know my way around N.Y. so well and I know all the people he might be contacting. Now please don't give me away. I have tried so hard for so long to get him back there handling this thing, and if he thought I would go back he wouldn't. If I come I will get myself to your place. Just act surprised to see me. I'm in hopes Dad can have some good talks with Frances and help her to see what she is doing to the family by her horrible treatment of all of us. If he can't do it, no one can. . . . .

I'm so very worried about Frankie's condition. You know and I know Dad does not recognize mental illness, and if she were raving mad he would say: "If she would get a job she would be alright." He used to walk Bob around the block and try to talk him out of his schitsfranic (can't spell it). We know this is ridiculous. He will be the last one to recognize she needs help. This is the main reason I feel I should be there. If you and I feel she needs help we will have to gang up against him. This has gone on too long, something should have been done a long time ago.

I must close for now. Don't give my secret away.

Berenice never had an opportunity to carry out her plan. Five days before Franklin was due to leave, he received a letter from Frances; it was much calmer than her letter of April 10, but just as firm. She told him, in the same 1-2-3 style that he often wrote her, that she had just about sublet the vacant apartment, and that his coming would be "highly detrimental," because the judge might ask him about things he had apparently said to Vittorio. She guaranteed him that Vittorio would never give his permission for her to leave New York with the children, and said that if she were Vittorio she wouldn't either. She added that she would not come home "under any circumstances. . . . I don't think it's a healthy environment and I will never permit my children to be raised there." As far as his accusations of her drinking she said, "I don't know what you mean about drinking unless you are refering to my typewriter which is broken." She said that if he came to New York, he could use it and see for himself. She closed by saying that she realized her expenses had been too high, but she hadn't kept track of the checks she was writing and had no idea it was so much. She signed the note, "Love, Frances."

Whether it was Frances's saying she had sublet her vacant apartment—a beacon to Frank that she was taking action and meeting reality—or her threats or Marilyn's advice that kept

Frank from flying to New York on April 25, he regretted his decision immediately. He received another of Frances's bank statements and a frosty call from an exasperated Chemical Bank telling him that the bank could no longer allow her to have overdrafts. Proud of his own excellent credit rating, Frank took this as a personal slap in the face.

Yet with all the heartache and anger Frank felt about Frances's depleted assets, he never lost sight of a chance to make money.

May 8, 1965

DEAR MARILYN:

If Francis is borrowing on her American Savings, maybe I should lend to her indirectly, even though I am in bank loans myself. Why don't you call up Francis and ask her if there's anything you can help her with and if she mentions money, tell her you will be glad to loan on some of her savings if it would help her out. If she's got it in hock, find out the details and we may have to loan her enough to get it out of hock. I can advance you the money and loan it to her in any way you suggest. Marilyn, if you loan her some money on her stock, have her endorse it. Give her a receipt for it and I would charge her at least six per cent interest. That is what I am now paying the bank.

Love,
DAD

Perhaps you should charge her 7%. That will give you a 1% commission.

Berenice couldn't stay angry with Frances for long, and Frances knew that. Whether or not it was her own guilt over not wanting Frances in the first place—a guilt that Frances knew how to exploit—that kept Berenice rushing to her daughter's side, the fact is that, with rare exception, she did each time. The divide-and-conquer game that Elaine said Berenice had engaged in while her children were growing up had now become Frances's turn to play.

If it seemed in April that Franklin and Berenice were both resolved to shut a financial door on Frances, one month later

Berenice had slipped out the back and was funneling money to her again. When Franklin found out about it, he was furious and wrote to her in New York, where Frances had summoned her from a White Shrine of Jerusalem convention in Miami.

DEAR BERNICE,

Before you left here I had you promise about six times that you absolutely would not send Francis any more money. . . . This has been going on for two years and I know you don't want to hurt Francis, but it is hurting her all the time instead of helping her. . . . She knows her mother is an easy mark and knows just how to handle her. . . . [If you] give Francis any more money without my permission . . . I am going to close out your bank account.

Everybody grows up and is still growing up when they are 70 or 80 years old. I am afraid Francis has not grown up in some ways and I am afraid that her mother is stopping that growth. When she was a little girl she put on temper fits. You always gave in to her and you still are. . . .

Bernice, I know you don't do this on purpose, it is part of your nervous system. . . . I don't think [Frances] will ever grow up until she has to work and make her own living. . . . Please don't keep stopping her from growing up. Please write me all details.

Love,
DAD

As he was writing this letter, Berenice was writing him one from New York about problems with the landlord over the sublet that Frances had arranged. Such problems were new to Berenice, and she told Franklin what residents had known for years: "This is the damdest town. The landlords are tougher than hell. You see people's furnishings setting out in the street all the time here. They were ready to put Francis's things in the street when she called me in Miami.

"I told Francis I'm going to get her on her feet; then, if she can't pay bills, they can put her in jail. There is one thing I'd like to do and that is send a check to this building every month for her rent; then I would feel sure they have a roof over there head and won't be threatened with eviction every month. What happens to her from there on is up to them. If she goes out on a limb with her spending she can suffer the consequences."

What she would tell her was one thing; what she would do for her was another. Berenice wanted to be all things to all people. She wanted Franklin to believe she was with him on the matter of Frances, but she wanted to help Frances as well. She was a wife and a mother, and in this situation it was hard, if not impossible, to keep from being torn apart.

The troubles with Frances affected every member of the Bradshaw family, not just Marilyn, Berenice and Franklin. Robert was so upset, according to Marilyn, that he escaped once from the Veterans Administration hospital, hopped a freight train, and tried to get to New York to help straighten things out. It was winter, and he got no farther than Wyoming, where he almost froze to death.

Berenice often went to California to see the Drukmans and two of her grandchildren (Sam, born in 1958, and Max, born in 1963) for "open-ended visits," spending much of the time crying and complaining about Frances. "It was more wanting sympathy than really wanting answers," Elaine said. "Most of her friends told her to go to a psychiatrist. She would say, 'The doctor wanted to talk about me and I wanted to talk about Frances.'"

Elaine's husband, Mason, recalled those visits as well. "Elaine would get enormously upset. Berenice would complain how ill-used she was by Frances—the sheer travail of it all. I don't know when I figured out this was all a game. On the one hand, Berenice tortured herself and was tortured; on the other, she came back and asked for more. She was rejected, but felt she had to embrace Frances at the same time.

"There was an interregnum—a period of less tension between her and Elaine, between her and me, where she did seem to relax a bit—when I could see the possibility of enjoying her. If you can have 'the good time' with Berenice, which she likes, and blot everything else out for a concerted period of time, then it's all right."

But for all of them, those periods, sadly, were few and far between.

14 // The phone rang one summer evening in 1965 as Vittorio was having dinner.

It was Frances.

She told him that she was sorry, he said, and wanted to get back together. He thought it was a trap and immediately phoned his lawyer. Erdheim told him he should see her if he wanted to.

"I'm a Neapolitan, a jerk," Vittorio said. "I told her to come to the apartment"—he was living at the Pavilion, on the corner of 77th Street and York Avenue—"clad *only* in the seal coat I'd bought her. She did. We made love, trying to relive the early part of our relationship."

The next day happened to be a court appearance. According to Vittorio, he told Erdheim about the evening, Erdheim told Howard Cerny, and Frances was livid. Neither Erdheim nor Cerny recalls this specific incident, both saying it was so many years and court cases ago, but Cerny does recall that they continued to have sex. "It was one bright spot in her life. She loved the guy."

She might have loved him, but she had no intention of going back to him. And despite his efforts to be conciliatory (he had appeared as a character witness for her in the suit that the father of the baby-sitter brought, because he did not want her to have a criminal record*) his chances of winning legal custody of his children were slim. He fell further and further behind in the payments he was ordered to give Frances for child support, and began missing court appearances. By May of 1967—nearly four years after Frances had moved out— Vittorio Gentile had closed his business and fled the country, virtually broke and in contempt of court.

* * * *

---

*He was not successful. On December 16, 1964, four months after the incident occurred, Frances was convicted in Criminal Court of third-degree assault. On February 4, 1965, she received a sixty-day suspended sentence—a decision later upheld on appeal.

No matter how often Franklin pleaded with Berenice for teamwork in his attempt to cut Frances off from money so that she would either work or come home, Berenice continued to bypass him and use her own devices to get money for her. While Berenice was away in California visiting the Drukmans, Franklin found a letter one evening in August 1965 when he came home from work. It was from the Tracy-Collins Bank and Trust Company and addressed to Berenice. When he opened it, he discovered that she had arranged a loan but had neglected to sign something. Franklin was livid and typed a short note to Marilyn and Bob the next morning.

August 6, 1965

Dear Marilyn and Bob:

I am enclosing a statement received from Tracy-Collins Bank and Trust Company which was quite a surprise to me. I have even threatened to beat up your mother but I just can't handle her. I wouldn't have got this mail if your mother had been home; she has done this in secret.

Love,
Dad

Four months earlier, he had admitted to Marilyn that Berenice had been "so hysterical at times that I have had to slap her face several times to calm her down which I have never done before. I wouldn't have done then, only that I just didn't know any other way to handle the situation."

Franklin hated confrontation of any kind. But he saw himself being slowly conquered in the deadly game that Frances had learned so well, and he was, literally, fighting back.

One person who was no longer fighting back in his sad and lonely battle to be the "100% parts-man" of whom his dad could be proud was Robert. On Father's Day of 1966, Franklin and Berenice went up to see him at the V.A. hospital, not far from the university where they had met and fallen in love. Robert had gotten very heavy, and Berenice blamed it on the hospital's starchy food. He was hardly seen anymore without the American Legion cap he proudly wore on his head, and he was always delighted when his parents came to visit him together. They sat on the lawn, had ice cream and refreshments, and enjoyed the brilliant June day—the last one they would ever spend together.

On the evening of June 25, the phone rang at 1327 Gilmer Drive, and Berenice went to answer it. It was the hospital calling. Seven weeks short of his thirty-ninth birthday, Robert had died of heart failure.

Franklin did not want to tell anyone what had happened. Berenice reminded him that their son was "not a dog." If it was necessary for people outside the family to know, he argued, there was no need to have a funeral service, especially since they were going to give Robert's body to the university's anatomy department. But despite his peculiar wishes, a memorial service was held at the Unitarian Church on Thirteenth East, the one that all of their children had attended and where Robert had been scoutmaster of Troop 138 for a number of years.

"It was a very cold and impersonal ceremony," Doug Steele recalled. "Bang, bang, alakazam. We Mormons reveal our whole history at our funerals." And Wayne Hacking's wife said it was "the saddest thing. Not even a prayer. Of course we believe in prayer and Berenice doesn't and maybe that's the difference. But there wasn't even beautiful things said."

They might not have been said, but in her little book Berenice wrote, "'O death where is thy sting and grave thy victory'? The sting is in the hearts of those who loved—and stand in silent bewilderment and anguish for a life that has vanished and the victory belongs to Mother Nature, that selfish individual who demands a return of all that she gives. . . .

"His poor health was a source of heart ache to us, and the saddest cross we had to bear. He was a dear, sweet son, loved by his family and friends. His hopes and suffering had come to an end. . . .

"To his great disappointment, he spent one-half of his life in the confine of a hospital, always dreaming of the day when he would be able to show the world his eagerness to achieve production and a status equal to his heritage and his family position in the community."

The service was held in the morning, and when it was over Franklin went back to work. His blood heir was gone.

Robert Jewett Bradshaw's death certificate stated "Coronary Occlusion" as the cause of death. Elaine had her own conclusion: he simply gave up.

15 // On blistering summer days in New York City, many Upper East Side mothers take their children to swim at the John Jay pool on the corner of 77th Street and East End Avenue. One day Marco accidentally fell into the water and a woman, fully clothed, jumped in to save him. When Frances saw the woman and her son a few days later in Carl Schurz Park, she invited them to dinner that evening but said she needed to borrow $10 to buy the food for it. The woman was very surprised, because Frances was living in an apartment that cost more than five times the $59 a month that she was paying for one on East 84th Street.

As they got to know each other, Ilona Baranyai found she loved to be in Frances's company, but also felt sorry for her. Frances didn't feel that she was very pretty, Ilona later recalled, and always "wanted to spend more than she had and was miserable that she couldn't. Maybe she was not loved as a child, maybe not enough attention was given to her. Maybe she was not as beautiful as a sister or a brother?

"Her apartment was a mess," Ilona continued. "She hated to wash dishes and there were cigarette butts all over the place. One room she did not want me to see was the boys' bedroom. There were crayon marks on the walls and toys all over. She cared for those children. She loved them. But they were loved in the wrong way. She transferred her insecurities and her misery to her boys, who were gorgeous and shockingly blond. Marco was like a little worm, always moving around. Lorenzo would sit in the corner, self-absorbed. They were warm in the winter and in the summer they were cool, but I felt she would be capable of controlling them in the wrong way.

"Her eyes never smiled. My son Tommy said, 'Mommy, she's a very nice lady, but very sad.'" Ilona also remembered that Frances was very secretive, that she loved to talk about food, fashion and the kids, but *never* about herself or her ex-husband. One time Frances asked Ilona to get something for her in a drawer, and Ilona came across the *Daily News* pieces about her separation battles. When Ilona asked Frances about it, Frances started to cry, said that it was a very sad story, and promised to tell her about it one day. "She started to shake," Ilona said, "and smoke one cigarette after another. She was always shaking."

Though Ilona became a friend of Frances's, it was really her son who got to know all three of them well. Frances had bought Tommy an ice-cream cone when she first met him, and he soon spent so much time at Frances's apartment playing with the boys that he called her Mommy. He ate there about three times a week and was allowed to take food from the refrigerator.

"I was lower-middle-class and liked her jet-set apartment with its big beds, nice carpeting—brown shag with a white rug on top—and fancy furniture," Tommy said. "I was envious. She dressed well and had jewelry."

Yet Tommy remembered another side of Frances. One time all five of them went to see the movie *Berserk,* starring Joan Crawford. Frances said she didn't have enough money, so his mother, who had never gotten her $10 back but had seen Frances get into a limousine once, paid for it. What confused Tommy was that when he was at her apartment, she often left him alone with Marco and Lorenzo, went shopping, and brought back lots of clothes.

But one thing sticks out in Tommy's mind more than any other. "We were watching 'Batman and Robin' on television and I tried a judo move on Lorenzo. He wound up flipping onto the part of the floor where there was no carpet, and he was unconscious. Frances started screaming, 'Oh my God, what have you done, you killed my son.' I ran all the way home, but the next day she called to say he was okay."

Lorenzo wasn't okay, but it was not because of anything that Tommy had done.

* * *

Frances had told her parents that she wouldn't get a job until both her sons were in school full-time, and she meant it.

By the time Marco was in first grade in the fall of 1967, Frances's divorce, ultimately obtained in Idaho, was final. She was taking classes in stenography and shorthand, and Franklin was more than happy to give her the money for them. In a letter to him just before Christmas, she said she was planning to find work after the holidays.

"Even after I start working," she wrote, "I intend to continue my classes as it is a valuable skill that is 'marketable.' . . . If you can take dictation you can always get a job as you have a definite, tangible skill to offer. I'm very pleased with my decision, and I feel good that I'm devoting my energies toward such a positive goal that will pay off dividends for me in the job world."

Now *this* was music he could dance to. After all the letters and bad feelings, maybe this was the Frances he remembered from the times when she had worked for him.

But no sooner had Frances gotten a job and began working than Berenice and Marilyn collaborated on something that Frances would never forgive them for. Berenice was in New York at the time, and was concerned that Frances could not cope with having a job and taking care of the children too. As her mother had once been, Frances was reluctant to entrust her children to a housekeeper. So with Marilyn's help—Berenice insists it was Marilyn's idea, Marilyn says it wasn't—they "kidnapped" Lorenzo and Marco, and Berenice took them on an airplane to Salt Lake. Just as Vittorio had returned home that night in 1963 to find no one there, so did Frances. Within hours, Frances flew out to Salt Lake, and there was an awful scene. Furious, she slapped her mother and pushed her up against the hutch in the living room with such force that a framed picture that Berenice had saved up Green Stamps to buy fell down and lay broken on the floor. Frances took the kids back to New York and sent her father the bill.

For Frances, it was Catch-22. Her father had railed against her for not working and not coming back to Utah. So once she got a job and partly appeased him, her mother attempted to take her children away. Nearly three years had passed since her angry letters of April 1965, and now she was ready to send another one.

"Dear Bernice," Frances began her February 26 letter on the stationery of Burnett, Appleby and Woodruff, the Madison Avenue company where she had a clerical job.

Well, now it seems to be my turn to write little "notes" but since it is the last one I ever intend to write to you, I will make it as brief, concise, and as much to the point as possible.

1. You completely fail to realize the gravity or serious consequences of your act in every single respect, and your judgment seems to be severely affected lately.

2. You can't and never seem to have been able to accept the fact that all your children are . . . adults and you will have to treat us as such if you wish harmony with any of your children (which you haven't had too much of). . . .

3. Besides the severe legal implications of kidnapping children that aren't yours, morally, ethically, legally, and spiritually, you took it upon yourself to make a decision that you have no right to make. . . . Apparently my children were, in a neurotic fashion, supposed to fill some sort of void in your life when you got home.

4. Besides not being able to cope with my children, they would have been severely homesick in one week or perhaps two weeks maximum. You fail to take into account the fact that my children love me very much, as much as I love them, and it would have been very damaging to pluck them away from their mother. . . . No material comfort can replace their knowing that they are not abandoned by their parents.

5. You have never had such a horrible life as I and you have no conception of my own personal anguish, fears, and problems. For the past five years I have fought and fought all alone the most horrible battle in behalf of my children and I wouldn't have had to fight it if I didn't have children. I could have given up the fight and given my children to Vittorio if I had wanted to escape responsibility, or if I didn't think my children's best interests were served by being with me. Your sense of judgment must have been very bad if you could have deluded yourself into thinking for one moment that I was going

(after five years of agony) to permit you to kidnap them without causing the most horrible bitterness to arise.

6. . . . We could starve to death and live in a slum and be much healthier and happier than you, because . . . even though we don't have all your material advantages and possessions . . . we have possession of love, feelings, and sincere emotions. . . .

7. . . . To arrive home and find that my own mother had chosen to deceive, lie, cheat, and sneak around and commit what I consider to be the most horrible of all crimes is more than I can ever absorb psychologically as a shock. . . . It goes without saying that you have destroyed all my confidence in you and that I can never feel the same about you or have any faith or confidence in you again. You burned all your bridges behind you as I would have been willing to send the children home for vacations, etc., but as you know that is all finished now.

8. In many ways I will be much happier now, because I don't have to account to you for anything and everything I do I do with my own sweat and blood. This is good for me psychologically as I have a feeling of independence, and even if we don't have much I'm an adult 100%.

9. If I were you I would go to a psychiatrist on a steady weekly or biweekly basis, because every action of yours points to very severe imparement of judgment.

10. . . . Don't ever bother to write to me or contact me in any way, shape, or fashion as I have no intention of acknowledging it. It will not be too long before you will never be able to contact us, because you will not know where we are. . . . I shall tear up every letter [of yours] and put it in the incinerator before opening it or reading it. . . .

In late June of 1968, Franklin arrived home in time to see the local news at ten. As he sat down with a bowl of jello, he began to read a letter from the director of the Children's Day Treatment Center and School in New York, where Lorenzo was just completing second grade.

The director said that he wasn't certain whether Franklin knew of some of the difficulties the agency was having with Frances in arranging for Lorenzo's care. "I did not know . . . whether you were fully aware of our opinion as to the seriousness of Lorenzo's condition and I, therefore, secured your daughter's permission to discuss the matter with you. . . . Lorenzo is a very seriously disturbed child whose sense of reality and of personal identity is so precarious as to warrant the diagnosis of psychosis."

For nearly thirty years, from the time Robert had his first seizure, there had been problems in this family, Franklin perhaps thought as he sat there in disbelief, problems that no amount of business success could ever overcome. He had lived through Berenice's nervous breakdowns and Elaine's illness; he had been told by doctors and psychiatrists, whom he would no sooner trust than a man with proven bad credit, that his son was schizophrenic, and he had agreed to the lobotomy; he had been informed that Frances was a sociopath, had witnessed her stealing from him—stealing that in part was fueled and aided by his own wife—and had clashed with her over money and the work ethic he had lived by for so long. Now he was being told that one of his grandsons was mentally ill.

"We are convinced that he is properly placed in this setting," the letter went on, "but only if the conditions in his home are such as to afford him the stability and support required at the end of our school day. Since his mother works, this condition means that there should be at all times an efficient and warm person like a housekeeper in the home to provide him with the nurturance and support that he needs. As you probably know, such services as I have outlined above are quite expensive and I have not been impressed with Mrs. Gentile's success in finding suitable persons to be with the boys."

The letter told him that Frances had trouble understanding that the center's fees needed to be paid promptly, and that even its lowering of Lorenzo's fee had no effect. While he was sympathetic to Frances's contention that Vittorio should be responsible for the fee, the fee could not go unpaid indefinitely. The director's conclusion was that it was bad for both Lorenzo *and* Frances for the situation regarding a housekeeper to remain uncertain, and that a definite long-term plan was essential.

The center's fee eventually got paid, but its advice was not taken. As much as Frances did not want to be dependent on her parents, and despite her telling her mother in February that she would never see her or her grandsons again,

Frances's threats were idle ones. She needed them, and Berenice knew it.

Frances sent the boys out to Salt Lake for the summer, first Marco, then Lorenzo. Franklin and Berenice hadn't had children in the house for quite some time, and Franklin broke from his daily routine to spend time with them. Gramps and Granny, as the boys referred to them, took them to Lagoon for swimming and to the Utah State Fair for the amusement rides. Berenice, intrepid as ever at sixty-five, took them on long hikes in the mountains. Franklin told them stories in the evening about Colorado (and the U.S. Mint in Denver), Idaho, Nevada, California and his boyhood years in Canada; about the Platte, Colorado, and Mississippi rivers and fishing for salmon. They loved to build things, so he brought boards and nails home from work. In a letter to Frances, Berenice wrote:

Marco and Lorenzo will be difficult boys to handle for a few more years but they are much better than they used to be. Grandpa and I feel we have accomplished something as far as discipline goes. The Andersons [their neighbors] say they can see a big difference in the boys since they have been here. . . .

The boys spend a big part of their day in the sunshine and fresh air. Their bodies are as brown as Indians. They have gained in weight and I feel sure they have grown an inch. Our lovely back yard with its lawn, shade and large tree is simply heaven to them. . . . Royalty couldn't have been entertained any more than these boys have been. . . .

Grandpa fills a great void in their lives. They have his telephone number and they are permitted to call him after six. Lorenzo loves having his grandpa teaching him things. We can hardly get him to go to bed. Lorenzo asks Grandpa to stay beside him until he is asleep. Marco sleeps in my room since Lorenzo came. Before that, Marco had two months of sleeping beside Grandpa; now Lorenzo is demanding his turn at everything, including the front seat of the car. Once in a while Marco has a nitemare but they are getting less frequent and don't last as long. These boys can be simply darling and they can be devils too. But we are trying our best in every way to help them because we love them. We have given them love, security, health and happiness this summer. We have given them everything

112

but their own mother's love, which nothing can replace, and I'm sure they miss their Momie very much. They wish she was here in God's country instead of them being in that dreary, pent-up apartment in N.Y. [The doctor at the center who wrote to Franklin] couldn't be more wrong when he says (if he did) these children are better off pent up in a gloomy old N.Y. apartment than with "old folks in Salt Lake City."

Then, just in case Frances missed her point, she closed by saying, "These 'old folks' in Salt Lake have done more for these children and their happiness than anyone else in their short lives. They both have expressed a desire to stay here and they are welcome."

Franklin was even less subtle than Berenice had been. He wrote Frances, "You do not have the time to spend with the boys. You don't have the income to support them. [He had previously told her that he was "thrilled" she was working, but worried that she didn't have enough schooling to get a better-paying job.] A apartment house is not a good place for children nor is a air Polluted city, so why don't you do the following. Let us help you with the boys until Christmas time. . . . It could mean much to Lorenzo's health and future happiness."

In another letter he urged her "to come home at least for the next few months. If you don't want to stay in Salt Lake you could move to Nevada and Arizona," then listed the monthly expenses of living in New York, Utah, and Nevada or Arizona, which he had worked out and done some research on:

	#1 New York	#2 Utah	#3 Nevada-Arizona
Rent	$400.00	None	$100.00
Housekeeper	$400.00	None	$100.00
Living Expense	$500.00	None	$300.00
Lorenzo School	$200.00	None	None (Public Schools)
Marco School	$200.00	None	None
School Transportation	$ 50.00	None	None
Total	$1,750.00	None	$500.00

* * *

At the same time Berenice and Franklin were trying to persuade Frances to leave the boys with them, Berenice was secretly telling Marilyn of their plans for Marco and Lorenzo and of their continuing concern over Frances. She wrote that they were going to enroll both of them in school—Marco at Uintah, where his mother had gone, and Lorenzo in a special school—and *then* tell Frances about it. "If you tell her in advance she wrecks everything. Next week the sheriff will be after her [for a bill she hadn't paid F.A.O. Schwarz for toys she had bought the boys for Christmas in 1966] and the apartment people will do something. We will suffer more than she will, but we have no other course. We simply can not finance her living. It just has to stop. I can't imagine what will happen in the next few weeks.

"How one person can cause so much trouble, so much heart ache, so much anxiety, so much worry is just inconceivable. We have suffered over this mess for so long I'm absolutely numb. I can't think. I can't talk any more. I'm just a cabbage."

But Frances wasn't the only reason she felt like that. The idyllic portrait of that summer that Berenice had painted for Frances in her letters does not resemble her memory of it. If Marco and Lorenzo didn't come home when they were told to, Berenice, in an effort to discipline them, would lock them out. But they'd break a window and get in anyway. She had a whole load of sand dumped in the backyard for them to play in, and she helped them make a tree house. Franklin and she did everything to make them happy, she claimed, but they were impossible. In addition to the window, they broke some lights, wrecked a lampshade, and turned her home into a shambles.

Frances proposed a compromise to her parents' suggestion that her sons stay in Utah: she would leave Lorenzo with them, but wanted Marco, who had been hit by a car and suffered a concussion, to return home. The boys were too difficult to raise together. Control was important to Frances; by picking the one she could more easily exert it over, she was reaffirming a choice whose effect, on all three of them, would be felt in the years to come.

* * *

Lorenzo loved being in Salt Lake with Gramps and Granny. He made friends with a boy in the neighborhood, and together they organized a Vote for Nixon rally. Lorenzo might not have been Mormon, but that neighborhood, including his grandparents, was overwhelmingly Republican, so he was in favor. Being cared for and having attention paid to him were important to Lorenzo, and he got plenty of both in Salt Lake. When he first arrived, Franklin and Berenice took him to be examined by various doctors. One doctor told them he could not give a complete prognosis because they could not provide enough information about Lorenzo's background. But he did say Lorenzo was someone who would push to do what *he* wanted and nothing else. He suggested a special school for him and said, according to Berenice, that the right kind of home atmosphere with a man at the head for stability could help him a great deal.

Lorenzo started off in the special school in second grade but switched, after a few weeks, to public school in third—the level he was supposed to be at—with special teachers to help him if necessary. He joined the Cub Scouts, went swimming at the YMCA on Saturdays, washed Granny's Oldsmobile for her, made Gramps a jack-o'-lantern for Halloween, and learned how to play bingo. In the winter he went ice skating and learned how to ski, though he broke his leg.

"We grew so attached to him that he seemed like our own son," Berenice wrote. But by spring of 1969, Lorenzo was becoming homesick. He was nine years old and had been away from his mother since the previous August. So when the school year was over he flew back to New York and found someone new in the house—a stepfather.

16 // It was a gray winter afternoon, the second of February 1969, when Frances Gentile married Frederik Willem Schreuder at New York's Marble Collegiate Church on the northwest corner of 29th Street and Fifth Avenue. It was a small Dutch Reformed wedding, and no one was there to give Frances away. She looked striking with a flower in her hair, and was beginning to resemble the actress Lily Tomlin more and more.

Tall and slender, Frederick (though Dutch, he preferred the American spelling) was nine years older than Frances, divorced, spoke a number of languages, and had been engaged in diplomatic work for the Dutch government. At the time of their marriage, he was working for Chromalloy, but was unemployed when Lorenzo returned home that summer. By autumn, though, he had been hired by the management consultant firm of Booz Allen & Hamilton, and was asked to move to Holland.

Before Frances went over for a few weeks in November to help him get settled, she asked her mother to come to New York and look after the boys, who were attending St. Hilda's & St. Hugh's, an Episcopal school near Columbia University.

As she had the year before in Salt Lake, Berenice found the two boys difficult to manage together, so Lorenzo was sent to stay with Aunt Marilyn and Uncle Bob.

One day, Berenice got a phone call from the school. Marco and Lorenzo were upsetting their respective classes, and their teachers felt unsure of how to handle the situation. Berenice went up to the school immediately and met for an hour and a half with school counselors, who questioned her about her grandsons' home life.

"Both boys are very attached to Frederick & now that he is gone they are unhappy & have really 'fallen apart,'" Berenice wrote Franklin. "With their mother gone too—they more or less felt abanded & were reacting by being difficult at school." She said that the school was on the verge of throwing the boys out, so she wrote to Frances and told her to come home at once.

While Marco's trouble turned out to be a temporary antic, Lorenzo's was far more serious. The school told Frances, once she got there, that Lorenzo had tried to gouge a girl's eyes out with a pair of scissors.

"This is on the school record," Berenice wrote; "the girl's parents know about it & [the teacher] told Frances she is lucky the girl's parents didn't sue her. Another thing they have caught Lorenzo doing—taking the girls' pants down and asking to see their female parts. The school is watching

Lorenzo very carefully. Someone is doing things to school property—such as destroying children's lunch boxes; they also suspect Lorenzo."

The following day, on her way to the school for another appointment, Frances had a car accident but refused to stay at the scene to provide the necessary information. As soon as she got to St. Hilda's & St. Hugh's by taxi, she phoned her mother, who leaped into a cab to meet her. Frances was hysterical, Berenice wrote Franklin, and "in such a rage she acted out like she was out of her mind." When one of the policemen handling the car accident met with Frances later, he asked Berenice for permission to take her daughter to the hospital for observation, and Berenice gave her consent.

Lorenzo told a counselor at school that his uncle was hitting him and he did not know why. Marilyn, who said that Bob was *not* hitting him, only "biffing" him, spoke with Bob about it and blamed her mother for getting "worked up about it and getting Frances worked up about it."

But Bob, who had had some unpleasant experiences with both boys, later confessed, "I really did hit Lorenzo, but I never hurt him. I felt it was better for him to be made to understand. He hadn't had much discipline when he was little, so it was hard for him."

While Berenice was trying to be strong and hold everything —and everyone—together, she was also beginning to feel sorry for herself and slip back into her role of martyr. In that same letter to her husband, she wrote, "I feel I have been gone a long time & I'm sure the empty house is lonely—how do you think I feel sitting in that empty house 365 days a year? We never go any place or do anything. We have no personal friends—no one who cares a damn—not even your shirt-tail relatives. I feel if I can be of some help to our family that is where I should be. I should come home now to get ready for Xmas but if I can help Frances in this ordeal of getting them off to Holland I should. At last she is getting out of N.Y.

"She can't decide what to do with Lorenzo. They can't have these boys together; even the school says they should be kept apart. Lorenzo is very homesick for his mother and

Frederick. Frederick suggested Lorenzo come over later until he heard of Bob hitting and slapping. Now he wants Fran to send him by plane at once."

Frances did just that. With a passport and little else, Lorenzo, not quite ten years old, was taken directly from school one day in December and put on a plane to Amsterdam.

Marilyn did not always know if Lorenzo would be home for dinner. Sometimes he got off the bus with Marco and had dinner at 85 East End Avenue, returning to Marilyn's only to sleep. When her phone rang that evening, it was Berenice who gave her the news.

Marilyn had grown very attached to Lorenzo. He was the child she never had. Bob and she had talked about having children, but Marilyn indicated she never wanted any; she had done more than enough mothering of her brother and two sisters when she was younger.

When the school bus stopped for Lorenzo the next morning, the driver buzzed and asked, "Where's the boy?"

"The boy doesn't live here anymore," Marilyn said, crestfallen, angry and nearly in tears.

The boy had arrived at the Amsterdam airport, but there had been no one there to greet him. Whether Frances was unable to contact her husband about Lorenzo's time of arrival or Frederick was detained for some business reason is unclear.

This is not: alone, Lorenzo waited at the airport for eight hours.

While Frances was busy preparing to move with Marco to Holland, her lawyer was filing papers to have her sons' first and last names changed. There were a number of reasons cited, the main one being the actions of her ex-husband: the petition said that Vittorio Gentile had failed to support his children (claiming he was in arrears about $15,000); had been held in contempt of court approximately seven times and that commitment orders had been issued seven times; had disappeared in the spring of 1967 and left no forwarding address, only a message with the building's managing agent that he was leaving the country and going to Italy "where his wife would not be able to obtain money from him"; and had not made any contact with his children since that time.

It also said that the children were caused much anguish by other children due to the fact that they had a different last name than their mother's husband and acting father; and that it was desired to have their first names changed so they would not imply a different nationality than that of Frederick Schreuder.

The petition was successful. As of February 8, 1970, Lorenzo Jewett Gentile and Marco Francis Gentile officially became Lawrence Jewett Schreuder and Marc Francis Schreuder.

Frances's desire to keep the boys apart resulted in Larry (as he would come to be known) being enrolled at the International School Vilsteren in Holland and Marc at the British School of Brussels, where the Schreuders moved in the summer of 1970. At first, Marc and Larry got along fairly well with their new father; though it wasn't long before their feelings changed, Larry could still recall that Frederick taught him all about inflation and spurred his interest in stamps. But what Larry remembered most were the terrible fights, both verbal and physical, over money—her excessive spending of it—that Frederick and Frances would have.

So Frederick turned to his new father-in-law for a loan, and Franklin was willing to provide one. Frederick was a businessman who spoke Franklin's language, and Franklin liked that. He and Berenice were pleased that their two grandsons now had a man in the house, and they wanted Frances's second marriage to work. For all of Berenice's harping about Franklin's being a tightwad, the truth is that he often came through with money—but it would never be enough.

On November 15, 1970, Frederick sat down to write a letter to Franklin, whom he had never met but referred to as Father. The former diplomat's letter, full of both good and bad news, was formal and very smooth.

He apologized for not having written sooner, but he knew that Frances's "30 and 40 page works about life in Brussels" were keeping him and "Mother" fully informed. He said that he traveled a lot and often worked seven days a week, and that when he got home both Frances and Marc, "warm-hearted boy that he is," were desirous of his attention.

He told Franklin about his new job and how interesting he found it, but said that "Frances feels a little out of the water here because Brussels is not very stimulating and friendly, and people hardly speak any English, so that she feels a little isolated and cut off socially. Also, we are living on an extremely tight budget, our apartment is tiny (one room basically) and we have no money for winter clothing or much clothing in general for that matter, and no woman feels happy in those circumstances. Still, she tries valiantly, grits her teeth, and is a good, warm-hearted wife to me and a good inspiring mother for our boys.

Marc is doing very well at school, I am proud to say, and for months was number one in his class. . . . We have not been able to give him the attention he deserves so that he gets quite nervous from time to time, but he is a good boy and we both are quite proud of him. . . .

Larry is a more difficult boy, he is still torn by his childhood experiences and the things done to him, and although I can reach him most of the time, I cannot all the time. He needs a home badly, and although he is very happy with our family stability, he sometimes tries to subvert it. We show him what a family unit is, yet although he responds with warmth and affection, he cannot stand the presence of Marc. I love the boy, he knows it and thrives on it because he too needs a daddy, yet he will sometimes try to hurt me just out of sheer rebelliousness. Frances and I try and try, but we are sometimes a bit discouraged. On the other hand, he does well at school and . . . we hope that between ourselves and the school he will find more and more happiness. We don't give up so easily and have a firm purpose in mind. . . .

Now the bad things and I will give you the facts straight, Father. My transfer to Brussels on top of my not working in New York for many months last year have been a severe drain on our resources. We are living on a tight budget so that I have been able to make a lot of repayments already, but I cannot make it and our creditors are drawing closer to my office and have started sending open letters and cables there, which one day soon is going to explode in my face and cost me my job.

He asked Franklin for another loan, telling him that the European laws were "merciless," that if a person didn't pay his debts he was whisked off to jail or thrown out of the country. "Believe me, I am ashamed that I have to ask you this and I do so only because you are my father; I will repay but at a slower rate. . . . May I ask the question urgently because we are down to $100.

"It would help me enormously because I work under great pressure with a lot of responsibility, and this gnawing fear in the back of my head undermines my self-confidence and ability to work effectively in my job. Frances has nightmares and lately wakes up tearful, with knots in her stomach. . . ."

He said he was sorry to have to end with "the bad things," urged Franklin to reread the first part of the letter and "be assured . . . we are a close family and full of fighting spirit," and closed with "thanks, Father, for anything you can do."

The letter worked. Franklin took the bait and replied immediately, saying how much he appreciated the attention Frederick was giving the boys. He realized it was expensive to raise boys, he said, and told Frederick that he would pay for the boys' schooling and various other things and that there was no need to pay him back. He also sent along some of Frances's stocks in Mountain Fuel, suggesting that it would be foolish to sell them because their value would only go up, but that they would be solid collateral if he needed a loan.

There were things, however, that Frederick had carefully avoided telling Franklin in his letter—disturbing things he would not bring out until later, when Frances was suing him for a separation and divorce on the grounds of physical maltreatment, mental cruelty and financial nonsupport. He would claim that in June of 1970, "the police of the Hague [where they lived prior to moving to Brussels] recommended that she be placed under psychiatric observation when she had the telephone lines in our home checked on the grounds that they were tapped by the FBI because of her imagined meetings with a Polish secret agent"; that two months later, in Belgium, "she was found wandering the streets one Sunday clad only in a negligee, and was again picked up by the police"; and that in the fall of that year "she was obsessed by fear of a TV camera mounted for advertising purposes on the

121

facade of a restaurant above which we then lived, thinking that it was a spy camera of the CIA. As a result she did not leave the apartment."

During roughly the same period that Frederick said these things were occurring, a man in Italy said he received a phone call.

Vittorio Gentile had been living in Italy since May of 1967, first in Torre del Greco, where he was born, and then in Rome. In 1968, he married the woman he had met four years earlier and whose parents' house Frances and Richard Behrens had gone in search of.

In 1970, Frances wrote to Vittorio's brother, asking for Vittorio's address and phone number. Knowing that Vittorio's divorce was final, his brother saw no harm in giving her the information. According to Vittorio, Frances phoned and invited him to Belgium. She said that she wanted to have another child and wasn't having any luck with Frederick, and asked if he wanted to accommodate her.

Vittorio, who still loved her, said he'd have to ask his wife. But when Frederick found out about Frances's request, plans for the tryst were canceled.

Franklin turned sixty-eight in April of 1970, and Berenice was concerned that he had never made a will. In 1961, Robert Reagan, at Berenice's urging, had sent Franklin a skeleton will to look over, a will that listed Berenice and Marilyn as co-executors. If Franklin wanted to execute it, Bob wrote him at the time, he simply needed to have it gone over by a Utah lawyer and witnessed by two people. Franklin never acted on it.

Nine years later, tired of his wife's pestering, he finally decided to make one. The will was divided into two trusts—marital and family—and stipulated that if Berenice survived him, she would be the sole beneficiary. But instead of making her and Marilyn co-executors, he named the Walker Bank and Trust Company.

By spring of 1971, Berenice wanted to see how her family was doing in Europe and, of course, have a vacation. She first went to London to meet Frances and Marc, who was on spring break, and the three of them spent two glorious weeks there. They rode the double-decker buses; ate dinner at the top of the Post Office Tower; toured Westminster Abbey, 10 Downing Street and the Houses of Parliament; went to the theater; and stayed on Eaton Place.

But vacation was not the main reason they were there. Frances, suffering from serious kidney trouble, had appointments to see some doctors. Berenice wrote Franklin that if an infection developed the doctors might not be able to save her. "Her life is at stake," Berenice wrote, using the same phrase he had used so often in regard to her, "and she is a *very* sick woman. . . . She is going to need money to get out of the hospital. Mine is going fast. I do not expect to see Europe—don't care if I do. If we ever get this family on their feet—first it's money, then it's health. . . . We must try to save her so she can raise these boys. If she goes, who will raise them?"

Her letters began to have a do-or-die quality, and Franklin could never be certain what was real and what was not. But he replenished her account, and Berenice continued trying to put out the fires that Frances, in large part, felt her mother had started in the first place.

Marc wasn't the only one who had a spring vacation. Larry did as well. But instead of joining them in London, he was left behind, alone during the day while Frederick was at work.

When Berenice, Frances and Marc arrived back in Brussels, Berenice was determined that Larry have some real vacation too. So she took him on some local tours around Brussels; to Waterloo, the site of Napoleon and Wellington's famous battle; to Ghent, where they visited churches and looked at paintings; and then to the ancient shipping port of Bruges, where they had lunch outside.

But it quickly became apparent to Berenice that what Frederick had written to Franklin the previous November was true: Larry was finding it difficult to be part of the family. "He disrupts the family," she wrote Franklin. "They can not tolerate him at home. He has a psychotic problem & they do not expect him to be any better. . . . It is very sad & my heart bleeds for him."

While Marc would later tell a friend that living in Europe

was "like being in a romance novel," Larry looks back on this period with mixed feelings. Though he felt lonely and deserted—in addition to waiting alone at the airport that time in Amsterdam, he slept at a train station in Brussels one night because nobody came to pick him up—the stoic in him proudly says it forced him to learn to do things by himself (buying tickets, getting on the right train, making connections) and to be more independent that he might have been.

He was building a shell for himself, a shell of self-protection. But inside, the shell was empty and, in time, the outside would begin to crack.

Frances went back to London for an operation, and Berenice went with her. When they returned, Frederick accompanied them on a trip to Switzerland that turned out to be emotionally stormy. But the clash that nearly had them thrown out of their hotel there was minor in comparison to what Frederick would later claim (in his court papers, when Frances was suing him for divorce) occurred that spring and summer of 1971:

One Saturday in the spring of 1971, after we had a verbal argument, she followed me to the office, went berserk and severely damaged the walls, doors and light fittings by smashing at them with the heel of her shoe. The incident was hushed up by my company.

Around that time her French physician, Dr. Antoine Germain, and his Swiss psychiatric consultant, Dr. Willy Adler, strongly recommended to her that she place herself voluntarily under observation, but she refused.

In June of 1971, when she attacked me during my sleep, I called for an ambulance whereupon the police, after consultation with her doctors, forcibly committed her [on the 13th] to the Brugmann Clinic, a mental hospital. . . . Struck with pity for her, I managed to override the authorities and obtained her release in my care.

Frances spent the summer of 1972 at Point O'Woods on Fire Island. Marc and Larry were with her, and Frederick was there for part of the time. But at the end of the summer not all of the Schreuders went back to Europe. Once again Frances was making a choice: Marc would stay in

New York with her and attend the Allen-Stevenson School, while Larry would continue going to school in Europe. But Larry wasn't the only one returning to Europe. So was Frederick.

Shortly afterward, Frances learned that she was expecting his child the following April.

17// The Allen-Stevenson School was founded in 1883. Occupying a five-story red-brick building on East 78th Street, it is a boys' school of strong tradition and classical curriculum, where blue blazers, neckties and leather shoes are expected to be worn at all times, and the students are reminded by a scroll in the front entrance that "An Allen-Stevenson boy is a scholar and a gentleman."

The majority of students in Marc's class had been attending the school since the first grade, so when he entered in the sixth there were hurdles he needed to overcome.

"People generally didn't welcome him," Henry Boehm, a classmate who became his friend, recalled. "Any new student had to make an adjustment, and Marc was not a conforming-type person."

But if Marc was a nonconformist (which, along with his intelligence, was one of the things Boehm liked about him), he did a number of things to draw attention to himself. Prep schools are traditionally big on nicknames, and Marc collected two of them while he was there: Butterball, because he was overweight, almost pearlike, and Hulk, because he imagined himself as the Incredible Hulk, a character of superhuman power.

Recalling how Marc often admired violent characters, Boehm said that some classmates would keep Marc captive in a closet, but he would manage to free himself, emerging from bondage as the character he loved, fists flying, throwing desks around and hurling his captors aside.

"One time he brought a hundred-dollar bill to school," Boehm said, "and I felt it was an attention-getting device. He had a desperate need to attract attention. Someone dared him once to throw the chrome handle of a desk out the window on to East 78th Street and he did."

Though Marc had nice clothes—Frances always dressed the boys as well as she dressed herself—he was remarkably unkempt. His shirttail was invariably out, there were food stains on his tie, his dark-blond hair was often unwashed, and he once wore his pajamas under his school uniform. His eating habits were equally sloppy, and his appetite huge. A friend later recalled that when Marc ate he looked like "a little King Henry VIII without a beard," consuming each meal as if it were his last.

He became interested in coins (Canadian maple leafs would become his favorite), stamps, chess and photography, collected comic books, and followed the stock market as avidly as his grandfather. At school he was a member of the Chess Club and Art Club, and learned a number of other things as well—not all of them academic. One of his friends taught him how to use a plastic credit card to break into the science lab. (When the photo darkroom, which was in the lab, was later broken into and a student's camera equipment was stolen, many students, including his "teacher," and, later, his mother, suspected Marc. He denied it then and long afterward.) The same friend once gave him mousetraps and instructed him in the precise art of placing them in people's mailboxes.

When Marc applied himself, he was a very good student. He was often the butt of many class jokes, but he had a good sense of humor and the ability to poke fun at himself. He wrote compositions that tended to be macabre and, on certain occasions, acted them out as he read aloud in class.

"Marc's English compositions would become theatrical performances," Henry Boehm said. "Gothic horror tales, reminiscent of Poe. 'Malevolence' was one of his favorite words." Boehm remembered one of these as clearly as if he had written it himself. "It's dark. A man walking down the street hears footsteps behind him and quickens his pace. The footsteps become louder; he doesn't know who's behind him. He ends up at the steps of a monastery, pounding on the door. In perhaps an ending out of *Don Giovanni,* he finds himself taken down into Hell by some demonic force." On another occasion, one of Marc's characters had been shot and he acted out the character's death throes, eventually turning over a number of the desks in the room before he collapsed on the floor.

"He radiated enthusiasm and had a lot of energy," Bob Brown, another classmate and friend, said. "He was quite a character, something of an oddball. He had a keen, active mind, colorful speech patterns, and had a great deal of interest in words—words like 'lugubrious' and 'cacophonous' that other people never used. He was fascinated by them and used them in any way he could."

Marc played football at Allen-Stevenson, and though he was not particularly good, one of his coaches recalled, he loved the contact. "Football was a good outlet for him," Bill Landis, who also taught him English, said. "It allowed him to take out a lot of his pent-up frustration."

Asked why Marc might have been frustrated, Landis did not hesitate in his reply. "He used to come to school kind of beat-up with scratches and marks, and was tardy quite often. It was almost common knowledge that his mother slapped him around. This occurred more than once. He would flinch if you walked up close to him, as if he was about to be struck. We sensed that his relationship to his mother was strange and not normal."

The relationship that had been developing between Marc and his mother was very strange indeed. If Larry was on the outside—cut off and isolated because he was unable and unwilling to be controlled—Marc, her "prize," was on the inside, expected to cater to her every whim and forced to absorb, verbally and physically, the immense frustration and anger she had built up over the years. If football was Marc's outlet, he was his mother's.

When Frances's psychiatrist moved to Canada, she became hysterical, Marc later said. In addition to being her son he became, at thirteen, something else. "*I* became her psychiatrist," he told a psychiatrist. "She needed a friendly ear and I felt I had to solve all her problems. If I didn't do everything she asked, she'd get angry, lay a guilt trip on me, make me feel shitty. She was hard to please and would beat me if my grades were not good enough. I always tried my best for her.''

He said that he was expected to get straight A's, get her up in the morning (she lived on black coffee and cigarettes, staying up much of the night and spending much of the day in bed), do the grocery shopping, clean the apartment, and do the laundry.

When Marc was older and could drive, there was an altercation that Bob Brown remembered. "Marc had driven somewhere and went inside to get something. He left the car lights on and the battery went dead. She just started screaming and got red in the face."

Brown also recalled something else: he never even knew Marc had a brother.

"Marc had a subtle way of letting you know *not* to ask questions about his life. When I called his house once, someone answered and said it was Marc's brother. Marc got on and said it was a friend who was just fooling around." (For the Schreuders to answer their phone—or even their apartment buzzer—was rare; often the calls or visits were from bill collectors.) On another occasion, Brown was trying to reach Marc, and when no one answered the phone, he went to Marc's building to leave a note. "The doorman told me that he and his brother had just gone out. When I asked Marc about it he denied it, and I didn't press further."

Questioned about this in the summer of 1983, Larry said matter-of-factly, "Mom didn't want Marc to admit he had a brother, because she thinks I'm disturbed and a bad person." She had told him in 1974, he said, "You're not as good as Marc. I don't want anything to hurt his chances of getting ahead."

Larry returned home from Europe for Christmas vacation in 1972, but he stayed at Marilyn's and was allowed to see his mother only when she invited him over. A couple of months later, somebody else returned from Europe—Vittorio Gentile, with his wife and two children. His wife's parents lived in Shrub Oak, about an hour's drive north of New York City, and Vittorio, a city person, did not want to be confined to life in the country during the week.

He had heard that Frances was back from Europe, and he tried to phone her. The phone had been cut off, so he called in person at her apartment on 75 East End Avenue, one building south of where she lived before moving to Europe.

He gave the doorman a couple of dollars and went upstairs to knock on the door. There was no answer, but the door was open. "The apartment was a mess," he recalled. "She was sleeping and woke up when I entered. She jumped up and said, "What are you doing here?""

He told her that he was back for a visit, and she opened up a bottle of Dom Pérignon. It was moments like these that had brought them together in the first place, before the four years of battling in the courts had torn them apart.

Vittorio did not just spend a leisurely afternoon with Frances, seven months pregnant at the time. "I moved in!" he exclaimed. "I couldn't stay in Shrub Oak." How would the pearl merchant explain this to his wife and in-laws? He told them he had to be with Marco (whom he hadn't seen for six years and who was understandably cool toward him); but would come to Shrub Oak on weekends. When he asked Frances why his sons' names had been changed—a blow to his Italian pride—he said she told him that she wanted their names "to end in a consonant, not a vowel."

To say that Vittorio's wife was a saint throughout all of this would be a vast understatement. No amount of reason could untangle this triangle of love. When the Gentiles were ready to go back to Italy at the end of their six-week stay, Frances, in an effort to express what Vittorio called her "high admiration" for his wife, gave her a hair dryer.

On April 10, 1973, four days after her thirty-fifth birthday, Frances brought a blue-eyed baby girl into the world and gave her a name that would befit royalty—Lavinia Tacy Alexandra Schreuder.

Berenice said that she and Franklin had hoped for a granddaughter, and Frances didn't disappoint them. Invited or not, nothing would stop Berenice from rushing to New York to see the family's newest member. "It was so thrilling holding this tiny baby," Berenice wrote, "just like holding a doll."

Berenice may have been thrilled by Lavinia's birth, but neither she nor Franklin had been happy when they first found out Frances was pregnant—one of many things that Frances reminded her of in a long and angry letter written shortly after Berenice returned to Utah from her trip.

DEAR MOTHER,

. . . You have done nothing but harass my family for two solid months in vain. I most strongly request you to stop before it will reach a level you shall regret. . . .

You discuss [in a letter] my daughter, whom you fought to have killed with an abortion. You discuss my son, whose reputation for his character and personality is something I am truely proud of. Everywhere I go people ask me if I'm Marc's mother and when I say "yes" they tell me what a well-mannered, fine boy he is. . . .

You can't even meet your own family in the same room anymore. You criticize Marilyn to Bob, Bob to Marilyn, Marilyn and Bob to me etc. etc. You criticize your children to my Dad and you viciously condem Dad behind his back to friends, employees and family. It was the same thing Bob Bradshaw did, isn't it? Who taught it to him? His mother, of course.

I can fully understand why I was so lonely as a child and never saw my Dad. His sanity alone would make it necessary to not always be at home as much as he would like. I survived too. I even went down to my father's office after school every night and I have good memories of that. Later I spent a lot of time at the home of very fine people in the community, Alfred and Inez Todt. I studied there and ate meals there. . . . Mr. Todt would drive me home every evening and they didn't like to hurt me by discussing it too much but they really loved me and they knew how cruel it was for me to be there. Inez asked me to call her mother and she became my mother. They still send me Xmas cards signed "Mom and Dad." . . .

You always write me letters that my health is poor, I'm going to die etc. (you can't deny it because I still have them going back for *10 years*—the more significant ones in a safe in a bank). Well, my health is excellent. For years Elaine was supposed to die also, but her health is now excellent too.

Since I have not responded to your offers of money you now write to my husband (the man you say you "don't trust," is "sneaky" and "vile") and ask for understanding, attempt to flatter him (you will never like any man, you always say how "wicked" all men are) and place offers of money with a copy to me. You are so dishonestly playing one person off against another as you do with everyone. . . .

You tried so hard when I was a child to convince me that my father was wicked and evil, and it made me very sad. It was only when I grew up and got older [that I had] the freedom to decide for myself that my father was and is a very nice person indeed. You should be grateful and happy with all the things you have, but you appreciate nothing. Instead, you escape from reality by taking frenzied vacations, even if the psychiatrist warns you not to go because you're having a "nervous breakdown." Afterwards, sometimes you admit that you are unable to recall anything that happened on your frenzied vacation. . . .

Although I needed my rest [when Berenice came to visit] you could only think about yourself. No one could have attempted to be more diplomatic and soft spoken than myself. Although I tactfully explained that I didn't have the time to have candlelight dinners etc. as you wanted, I still took time to speak to you so beautifully. All in vain, as you wallow in self-pity and selfishness. . . . One night you were not sleepy, you were agitated and tense for *no* reason whatsoever, and instead of getting my rest, I . . . had to keep on going without sleep as you ranted and raved around this household. . . .

Even the grandchildren are around for your own self-gratification and needs and you are incapable of considering their needs. . . . I know what your psychiatrist means when he says "you want a baby." You want a helpless baby of any age to gratify your needs, even if that baby has to be a Bob Bradshaw, who now rests in peace. "You don't like 'babies' who talk," who are independent, have a mind of their own, and can think for themselves. You put Bob in that role, no matter what his age, and that is why he is dead today. . . .

Love, respect, honor, and trust cannot be "forced," nor can it be purchased as you would like. Nobody is perfect and everyone makes mistakes from time to time but we have to work and earn by our behavior, trust, love, and respect.

FRANCES

The same divide-and-conquer tactics that Frances maligned her mother for using are ones she herself used in a letter to her father, written about the same time.

She gave him a progress report on Lavinia and Marc and

131

praised him for trying to keep Berenice "under control here in New York." She told him Berenice "disobeyed" and proceeded to list many of the same things she had said in her letter to her mother.

"It just became so bad," Frances wrote, "that I finally left instructions downstairs [with the doorman] about my mother not entering so I could have a few days of peace and tranquility to help my children get back to a normal, healthy schedule around here."

She said that her mother's vacations had increased to an "almost abnormal amount" and that she had gone "from the North Pole to the South Pole in six months." (This was an exaggeration, but only a slight one.) These trips, she told her father, were "simply an escape from facing herself and from facing reality—just as alcohol can be. . . . Her almost compulsive escape from home is not normal."

When her mother visited them in Europe, Frances said, she "almost sent Frederick to a nervous breakdown. People are simply bewildered by her and can't cope with her and something has to give somewhere. . . .

She is really incapable of giving any love and I think it is marvelous that you have been able to withstand all of these years and do as well as you are, Dad. . . . She plays one person off against another and has everyone so worked up that everyone blames everyone else. . . .

Mother never gave you the warmth and affection you needed and she is getting worse. Just some words of practical advice, *look after yourself first, Dad*, and don't let her . . . jeopardize your health. . . .

I don't like to write such a sad letter, but you have been very, very wise in the past and perhaps you can attempt once more to use your wisdom to help mother and indirectly yourself as well to a happier life. Intelligence in life is so very important but it is using intelligence with wisdom that counts the most.

As soon as I have a picture of Lavinia I will send one to you. I don't know when Father's Day is, but in any case, Happy Father's Day.

But her love letter did not close without a request of her own. She said that she wanted to purchase a new car, had no money, and asked for "some suggestions." Reminding him of how much she and the kids loved to drive into the country-side, she wondered if he could arrange a deal to get one wholesale, and help her finance it. She signed the letter with love from her, Marc and Lavinia, added Larry's name almost as an afterthought, and then wrote the following P.S.:

. . . We don't want anything to happen to my Dad because you are fine and I think I understand you better than you perhaps are aware that I do. God bless you, Dad, I love you, and you take care of yourself, because we only have one dad and nobody can ever take your place for me.

> All my deepest love,
> Your daughter, FRANCES

Elaine always felt her younger sister had missed her calling in life—that she was a truly magnificent actress who would have found real happiness on the stage. On the other hand, Franklin was not a particularly sentimental person, and he had seen this performance before. He was all too aware of his daughter's ability to be sweet and charming one minute and turn on a person the next.

By the summer of 1973, Larry and Frederick were back from Europe, but it was decided, once again, to send Larry away to school. While the school wasn't too far from New York City, it was not an ordinary boarding school. It was the Eastern Military Academy, located in the Long Island town of Huntington, and Larry would spend the next five years there, from eighth grade through twelfth.

Frances and Frederick had been together on and off since the previous summer, and during that time, Marc told a psychiatrist, his mother aired her dislike of Frederick to him and complained about being alone. Once she threw Frederick out for good in February of 1974, Marc essentially took Frederick's place in her life. She came to rely upon him almost totally, and he even spent the next year in her bed.

Though she discouraged him from making friends, Marc told the doctor, "I always had Mom for company. We went everywhere together."

* * *

In April of 1974, Frederick was living in Room 510 at the Roger Williams Hotel on East 31st Street, a two-minute walk from the church where he and Frances had been married five years before. As Vittorio had before him, Frederick wanted to patch things up with Frances and told her so in a Western Union Mailgram—one that also expressed concern for her health:

IF THERE IS POSSIBILITY OF YOUR SERIOUS ILLNESS I WANT TO BE RIGHT WITH YOU FOR PROTECTION AND REASSURANCE. STOP ALL NONSENSE AND REFERENCES TO PAST AND PARENTS. CALL ME EVENING AT 689-0600 FOR EARLIEST DAY AND TIME TO GET TOGETHER AGAIN, PREFERABLY FOR GOOD. YOU ARE MY WIFE AND MY LOVE, AND I DON'T WANT ANYTHING TO HAPPEN TO YOU.

FREDERICK

As they had during her long battle with Vittorio, Berenice and Franklin were pulled into the skirmish. It was a replay of bad memories—legal and otherwise. Money inevitably became the central issue, and once again Franklin took the husband's side. In a letter to Frances on May 10, he reminded her that he simply didn't believe in divorces, especially when children were involved, said that he personally felt Frederick was "a very sensible fellow," and warned her that she could no longer keep "bleeding me of my working Capital."

A warning like that was hardly about to stop Frances.

Frederick continued to fight back. In two separate pleas in September of 1974 to New York's Family Court—pleas that included his allegations of what happened while they were living in Europe—he tried to counter Frances's charges against him of physical maltreatment, mental cruelty and financial nonsupport. His second plea, on September 26, was a letter written directly to Judge Edith Miller. Having referred to Frances, in his papers of September 10, as an "emotionally disturbed person who often is completely out of mental control, at other times reverts to childhood" and one who "has been under psychiatric care and has been committed already once to a mental institution," he told the judge that "I am writing you in some desperation, as a last resort, to ask for your intervention to protect my three young children against the grave carelessness and irresponsibility of their mother, who is mentally disturbed."

Even the most discreet matrimonial lawyers will admit that gross exaggeration and lack of truth inevitably mark most divorce cases. The cases generally become bitter and nasty battles—particularly when children are involved—and each party's tale of woe is always held in question. Were it not for the fact that certain things Frederick Schreuder accused Frances of in this letter have been borne out by both of her sons and by other people—people with no specific ax to grind—it would be gratuitous and wrong to mention them here. But since many of them are true and help in understanding what would later be called a "pathological family constellation," they bear mention.

He told the judge (referring to a letter he had written to his lawyer in June and had attached) that Marc and "Sugar"—his name for Lavinia—were being maltreated. He said that Frances did not get up to prepare Marc's breakfast and rarely prepared dinner, so he had to do his own cooking; that she was "repeatedly absent" when he came home from school, the door would be locked, and he would either sit in the stairwell or roam the streets; that it was his job to do the home cleaning while she lay in bed; that she usually kept Marc up until one in the morning for company, so that "he is often white as a sheet from fatigue"; that she did not take care of his personal habits so he was most often "dressed like a bum"; that she "periodically attacks him when she is angry, and on several occasions pounded the boy senseless"; and that she "periodically takes off and leaves the baby unattended."

The letter to his lawyer also told of the building management's concern about the situation. He wrote that Marc is "unwashed and stinks so badly that tenants have reported it"; that he "wanders the streets at night in search of an open delicatessen store to buy some food"; "has been found sleeping in the hallways on several floors as late as 12:00 P.M. because she was out or had locked him out"; that Frances "continuously screams at him so that tenants have reported it"; that "the baby has been found crying for many hours so that tenants have called the police who found that she deserted the child"; that Frances "periodically, through negligence, leaves the apartment front door open," but when the superintendent closed it one night she called the police and accused him of theft. The incident was on file, he wrote, with the building's management corporation.

He told Judge Miller that Mr. Ralph Manzi, an investigator for the Society for the Prevention of Cruelty to Children (SPCC), had made a detailed investigation (following his letter to his lawyer) and that "his report clearly establishes that the situation is sufficiently serious that temporary removal of the children from their mother's care is indicated as well as the need for her psychiatric observation. My wife's attorney however managed to stop this report from reaching you.

"I have since been advised by the building management on September 5 that there was continued screaming and bottle throwing in the apartment all through the night, and again on September 24 that my boy Marc, aged 13, was locked out (for five hours) . . . and in his emotional agony defecated in the building's hallway (enclosed is copy of the Church Building Management's telegram of the SPCC)."

The mailgram was sent on September 24, and received by the SPCC the next day. Copies were sent to a number of people, including Franklin. The message read:

BASED ON INFORMATION AND BELIEF, EMERGENCY SITUATION CONTINUES TO EXIST CONCERNING THE ABOVE CAPTIONED REFERENCE [RE: CHILDREN OF FREDERICK AND FRANCES SCHREUDER NYSPCC CASE NUMBER 635352] CHILD LOCKED OUT OF APARTMENT FOR MORE THAN ONE HOUR. SITUATION WORSENING. IMMEDIATE STEPS MUST BE TAKEN BY YOUR AGENCY.

In contacting Judge Miller directly, Frederick was not adhering to standard court procedure. But he was frustrated and told the judge, in closing, that "nobody apparently cares enough to break through legal niceties to act for the protection and welfare of these children.

"As a father I therefore appeal to you directly, however irregular that may be in terms of legal procedures, to bring these children's plight to your urgent attention. I do so as a last resort because I know of no other way, and hope that this may result in a personal discussion [of] how we all can act to safeguard these three children."

By the time Judge Miller received the letter, Frances and her children were preparing to move. She wanted to have a lavish life-style, Marc told a psychiatrist, and whether she had the money or not was secondary. She felt she had to live better and better, he said, and if anybody threatened the life-style she felt she was entitled to, she became very depressed and suicidal. On one occasion, Marc recalled, she ran to the bathroom, locked the door, and threatened to take sleeping pills. After a half an hour of pleading with her to come out, she did.

They were leaving a $600-a-month apartment and moving into one on the eighteenth floor of the Andover, a brand-new building at 1675 York Avenue, between 88th and 89th Streets, that cost $1,000 a month and had three bedrooms. While Berenice once again managed to come through with the money for it, she also warned Frances that the money—and Franklin's patience—were running out. "It was just plain stupid," Marc told the doctor. "We always had to move up and up."

Though Marc was in charge of the move, Frances didn't take everything with her to the Andover. From her four-year legal struggle with Vittorio, she had become savvy in the ways of the courts. Anticipating an ongoing battle with Frederick, she was hiding various papers with a friend, a man whom Marc saw as a rival for his mother's attention—and would later want to kill.

If Frances had found a safe haven of sorts, Marc had found one at Coleman's Delicatessen, a family-run operation on East End Avenue. He would buy comic books there, and loved seeing and hearing coins go into the cash register. His passion for collecting them prompted him to ask the owners' daughter to check the coins and give him a call immediately if certain ones dropped into the till.

When he was not sitting quietly on a box, reading a book, he was carrying out some of the practical jokes he had learned

137

at Allen-Stevenson. When the owners' daughter was up on a ladder, he would place a banana peel in a strategic spot on the floor. Or he would make a pyramid of certain items and then be temporarily banished by Mr. Coleman when they fell down. But his daughter, Susie, found his mischievous ways "charming" and liked his "winning smile and superior intelligence." Ten years older than Marc, she became a combination of friend and concerned, doting sister. It was a relationship that he not only needed, but one that would grow in importance as time went on.

Just as his grandfather would run back to his warehouse when he felt Berenice's pressure at home to be too great, Marc would seek refuge at Coleman's. But not always by choice. When he was locked out, there was nowhere else to go.

In her new apartment building, Frances was seen as a rather mysterious and erratic figure. One time she tipped one of the building workers nearly $200 for washing her Oldsmobile; the next time she gave him nothing. She developed a reputation along York Avenue for bouncing checks, and when the one for rent was not made of rubber, it was usually late. When the Schreuders first moved in, Frances left food burning in the apartment. Andrew Fuleki, the building's superintendent, received a complaint from a neighbor, and he and his son, Bobby, went up with fire extinguishers. They found drawing on the walls, and the only clean room in the apartment belonged to Lavinia, who was "treated like a saint," Andrew Fuleki said. "She had everything there was in the book."

There is a large lawn in front of the building's entrance, and Lavinia used to throw her toys off the terrace. Marc tossed a *watermelon* down once; fortunately, it landed on the roof of a car. Instead of admitting it, he told Bobby Fuleki that his sister had done it. When Larry came home from military school, which wasn't often (there was "an unspoken understanding," Larry said, that he was to come home only once a month), the rivalry between Marc and him for Frances's attention would reignite. On one occasion, Frances asked Larry to beat Marc up. He complied, though he later said he felt guilty about it. He might have been unwilling to be controlled by his mother, but he wanted her love nonetheless.

He hated military school, and, aside from his mother's cruel treatment of him, the main thing he held against her was that she had sent him there. "I wish I'd had a normal high-school environment, with girls my own age. Mom knew I was better and smarter than Marc, but he was always the favorite."

Like Marc, Larry was also interested in coins. He collected wheatback pennies (pennies before 1959) and had accumulated more than five hundred of them. Since money from home was coming less often now, Frances took them from Larry and exchanged them for their face value, not the two cents for each one they were worth to some coin dealers. He then began collecting them again, and within a period of time he had six thousand. But his mother seized the collection once more and exchanged them at the bank for $60. "I'll never forgive her for that," Larry said. "I begged her not to. You just don't do that to a person. It was terrible, because I had worked very hard on that."

Throughout 1974, one person who continued to work very hard was Franklin Bradshaw. Financially, he was riding high. The Arab oil embargo of 1973-74 drove up the amount he could command from "the heavies" for his oil leases, and the energy stocks he owned skyrocketed in price.

He had never posted a sign that indicated when his warehouse opened or closed, because his steady customers knew that they could usually find him there. But there had been some brutal murders in April of that year in Ogden—murders that occurred during the robbery of a stereo store and became known as the "Hi-Fi Murders"—and Franklin, for a time, closed up before dark. His warehouse was in the part of town where transients aimlessly roamed the streets and often slept in Pioneer Park, a few blocks away. The Denver & Rio Grande railroad station was close by, and hobos would occasionally jump off a freight train, rob a store, and go on to their next destination. Berenice had never liked the area and was trying to get Franklin to sell his auto-parts business anyway. But he wouldn't hear of it.

If he had had only the possibility of robbery to worry about, that would have been enough for any businessman. But the financial pressure that Frances had always exerted on him now took the form of a suit she was threatening to file. She had stocks in her name, but he held and owned the certificates. She wanted the certificates, as well as certificates in her children's names. Hoping to appease her, he sent one hundred shares of Mountain Fuel. At the same time, he began pressuring her once more to come back to Utah. He decided not to pay for the boys' schooling for the 1974–75 school year, and both of their accounts were seriously in arrears. Money was his only weapon against Frances—words meant nothing: if he could push her up against a financial wall, she would have no choice but to come home, culminating more than ten years of effort to get her to do so.

That was his hope.

But Frances was as stubborn as her father—and she still had Berenice. On May 21, 1975, she sent her mother a desperate mailgram:

DEAR MOTHER

BOYS CANNOT TAKE FINAL EXAMS OR GRADUATE UNTIL BILLS ARE PAID. DAD HAS WITHHELD DIVIDENDS CHECKS ETC., SO YOUR GROCERY MONEY JUST ABOUT SAVED OUR LIVES LAST WEEKEND. . . . SITUATION CRITICAL. COULD YOU POSSIBLY FIND A WAY TO SEND $950.57 TO ALLEN-STEVENSON SCHOOL . . . AND $1529.31 TO EASTERN MILITARY ACADEMY. . . . I HOPE YOU CAN HELP US DURING THIS DIFFICULT TIME. LOVE

FRANCES

Berenice had warned Frances that the money supply wouldn't last forever, and she reinforced that idea in a letter the next day.

DEAR FRANCES:

Dad tells me that he sent you within the last six months 100 shares of Mt Fuel and you received a stock dividend for 400 shares; that makes a total of 500 shares at $35 a share, a monetary total of $17,500.

I am enclosing another 100 shares of stock that Dad willingly

140

handed to me to send to you. This makes a total of $21,600 you have received in the last six months. Dad has another 100 shares broken into 10's (shares) but he didn't want to give you too much at once. My stock is practically all gone & I want a *little* bit for future emergency. So I can not send money at this time. If you will give a complete accounting on the $21,000 maybe I can use my influence on Dad, but he requires an accounting of where the money is going.

> Hope this meets your needs,
> All my love
> MOTHER

On June 5 Frances wrote back: "I can put together an accounting of these boys' medical, clothing, etc. expenses that would put F.J.B. to shame in any court. Romney [George J. Romney, a Salt Lake attorney] feels it is sheer spitefulness on F.J.B.'s part and Romney knows pretty much what I spend taking care of my children, so to force me to spend months trying to go back five years for an accounting of every penny is vindictive and petty. . . .

"I feel as though F.J.B. purchased a marriage. There wasn't anything he wouldn't do for Frederik and I resented it. All Frederik had to do was snap his fingers and F.J.B. would loan him money. Frederik cannot account for it and he cannot account to me either for the money I loaned him, nor did he ever repay me. F.J.B. is so pro-male and anti-female that he expects me to pay for an obligation that Frederik personally has with him. That is really criminal. I am beginning to feel as though I hate all men.

"I have loaned Frederik enough money and he left me to pay for everything Lavinia has. He didn't even buy his daughter a 50 cent baby toy when he came back to America. Dad thinks that's okay and I am supposed to go on paying for Frederik's debts by hitting me for a loan Frederik made with F.J.B. These two men can go rot in hell before I will pay a penny for a debt of Frederik's. I'll fight Dad in court until he regrets it. Just what do these men think? I am paying for three fatherless children and if F.J.B. wants me to pay some more of Frederik's debts, he must have sawdust in his head instead of brains."

But it was not just the present situation that concerned

Frances. She had begun to think about the future. She knew that Marilyn had been learning about the complicated world of estates and trusts (Marilyn had already attained an M.B.A., and was now working toward a paralegal certificate at New York University with a particular focus on this area), so Frances had been arming herself with some knowledge of her own. Part of Berenice's will, drawn up at the same time as Franklin's, established a trust fund that would give her *grandchildren*—five in all—the interest from the principal in the fund, while her great-grandchildren (in the event there would be some) would receive the principal in full. Though this generation-skipping trust was an ideal way to save a vast amount of money in taxes, Frances thought it was a dreadful idea and told her mother why in a letter:

"What you have done is bypass your daughters, leave funds (interest) to go directly to the grandchildren without any parental supervision over their lives or what they do with the money, and finally upon the death of the grandchildren, the principle in full going to yet unborn great-grandchildren. . . .

"Four of the five grandchildren are males who in this world of ours must and should do their best to get a college education and learn how to get a job, so that they can learn how to appreciate the effort that goes into making a living without turning into playboys and wayward children who can just run off and do whatever they wish because they will have the financial resources from the interest of the trust fund. . . .

"Any grandchild that turns into a playboy, etc. is very vulnerable to being 'persuaded' into marriage by a woman who does not love them but wants their hands on their money."

Frances had a suggestion. For the "love and goodwill [and] welfare of your daughters," she said, "I strongly suggest the following trust which I feel is the most fair and morally correct and just." Frances's proposal would give her, Marilyn and Elaine equal shares of the interest from the trust and Berenice's grandchildren would receive the principal in full upon the daughters' death. (In Marilyn's case, she said, the principal should be divided among the grandchildren, and *not* be given to her husband.)

This way, she stressed repeatedly, she and Elaine could

control their children's activities and continue to raise children of whom Berenice could be proud.

"Nobody can be a mind reader," Frances continued, "and predict what is going to happen to either your daughter, grandchildren or great-grandchildren, but I believe this is the best way to handle all these generations and see that there are still people around to be able to exercise a little guidance over their best interests and future. . . .

"Needless to say, I will never cease to remind my children during my lifetime of exactly where their money really comes from—their grandmother—and just which side of the 'family' it comes from."

Frances was right about one thing. Nobody in 1975 could have predicted what would happen to any of them.

18 // In September of 1975, Elaine and her family decided to move to New Zealand, where Mason had been hired to edit a magazine. They had lived for a number of years in Portland, Oregon, where Mason had been teaching political science at Reed College, and they later had edited the *Oregon Times,* a political monthly of a decidedly liberal persuasion. With the exception of Berenice's "open-ended visits," as Mason called them, their occasional trips to Utah, and the "family letters" that Franklin sent them, they had managed to keep a safer distance from the ongoing troubles with Frances than Marilyn and Bob Reagan had.

But just before she and her family left, Elaine had a set-to with her father over the phone. Franklin had sent her one of Frances's bills, so she could see proof of what he was up against. The stock of Mountain Fuel—which Franklin had in abundance and had parceled out to his children and grandchildren—had just split, so Elaine had received some as a result.

"My father called me," Elaine said, "and asked me to send

him the stock. I asked why and he said he'd keep it for me. I got mad and said, 'Dad, I'm *not* Frances. I won't sell it.' I really felt like Frances had poisoned everything. He was so afraid of what Frances would do; he assumed I might do it too."

The Drukmans, as it turned out, weren't the only ones leaving the country. Frederick Schreuder, as Vittorio had in 1967, did too, and Frances attempted to have the Internal Revenue Service locate him. Frederick, it seemed, had vanished, and by the spring of 1976 Frances was granted a divorce.

Berenice spent the 1975 Christmas holidays in New York, shuttling back and forth between Frances's and Marilyn's apartments. The relationship between the two sisters had been strained for some time, and their mother seemed to be their only link. But that didn't prevent Berenice (who loved to say that Salt Lake was "dead from the ground up") from having a good time in New York—going to the theater and the opera, the ballet and the Ice Capades, eating out, taking long walks along the Hudson, and shopping for clothes. At seventy-two, she had boundless energy, and people much younger became exhausted trying to keep up with her.

Berenice spent a lot of time during the holidays with Marc, Larry and Lavinia—but especially with Lavinia. "She could not say Granny so it comes out 'Danny,'" Berenice wrote. "She liked to have me dress her in the morning. She loved to slop around in my shorts. She mimics everyone no matter what you are doing. She always followed me into the bathroom, she liked for me to comb her hair, dab some face creme in her cheeks and a little powder. She would brush her teeth with me. Once she got in the bath tub with me, she was so funny. Every place I washed she had to wash . . . .

"[Larry] looks so impressive in his military uniform. . . . Marc is the 'father' of the family, he is a great help to his mother and sister, she could not get along without him. Both boys are doing well in school, study diligently. Larry has a beautiful trophy for championship mile run. He now is wrestling.

"Frances did so much to make my stay with them enjoyable

and pleasant," Berenice continued in her autobiography, painting a far brighter picture of their relationship than the grim one many of the letters between them did. "She is a gourmet cook. My visit with Frances would not be complete if we did not talk genealogy. She has done a marvelous job collecting data on our ancestors . . . We are now eligible for many exclusive hereditary organizations due to her laborious work of several years and hundreds of dollars on research help. We are both very thrilled and we hope to write a book some day with this material. We both have been accepted into 'The 1903 Order of Americans of Armorial Ancestry.' A most difficult order to get into and difficult to prove eligibility."

Marilyn flew to Salt Lake for a week during April of 1976. She was not there just to pay her parents a social call, but for a purpose: to discuss their estate and help them do some planning. But Marilyn also wanted something else: she wanted her father to change his will and appoint *her*, not the bank, to be executor of his estate. With her education in this area, she felt that she could do a solid job, and she told her father that. She admired him and all that he had accomplished. She wanted to be her father's daughter, and this would enable her to get close to him, learn from him, and win his approval. Since she knew he disliked paying lawyers, she felt that a family executor, as opposed to an impersonal bank, made more sense.

But when she raised the subject, he told her, "Marilyn, your mother and your sister [Frances] would not like it." He had lived through enough to be right about that.

When Marilyn got back to New York, though, that was not the sentiment she expressed to her sisters in a letter about her trip. She reminded them about the experience she had, and said that she felt capable of looking at the arrangements their parents had made and offering her advice on ways to improve them. She told them that in the week she was there, she was able to determine from their parents that their wills and trusts did *not* achieve the purpose that they in fact desired. She said that she and Berenice had had two conferences with Alma Boyce, their father's attorney (he was married to a Bradshaw, but had not drawn up the wills); that she hoped to begin compiling an inventory of their parents' assets; and that she hoped to work with her father and an experienced estate planner.

"As progress is made, I will advise you and if your opinion is required, it will be solicited," Marilyn wrote in a terse, businesslike manner. "This is quite a challenge for me and one that I am very interested in spending the necessary time to accomplish. While Mother & Dad seem to be in excellent health, they will not live forever."

By the time Marilyn's little letter made its way crosstown to 1675 York Avenue and into Frances's mailbox, it was like a ticking time bomb, just waiting to explode.

19 // Van Cott, Bagley, Cornwall & McCarthy is the largest of Salt Lake City's law firms. Occupying three floors of 50 South Main Street, a minute's walk from Brigham Young's statue and the Mormon Temple, the firm's offices bespeak its considerable success. Carpets of deep rich green with orange, blue and beige patterns are set into polished parquet floors, giving the reception area an antique look. Through the windows one can see the magnificent gold-domed state capitol to the north, the doughnut-shaped Salt Palace to the west, and the city's many banks to the south and east.

People often joke that the reason the statue of Brigham Young at Temple Square (the official center of the city) does not face the Temple but faces Zions First National Bank is a subtle acknowledgment of the Mormon Church's considerable wealth and the Mormons' interest in making money (one-tenth of which all strict Mormons tithe to the Church). And down at the Chamber of Commerce, a visitor is told that one reason Salt Lake is still America's best-kept secret, and has not become overgrown like Denver, is that outside companies, seeking new locations, openly express their fear of the "Zion Curtain."

Of the many clients that Van Cott, Bagley represented, a good number were banks, and one of them was the Walker Bank and Trust Company—the executor of Franklin and Berenice Bradshaw's estates.

In the fall of 1975, Berenice had asked David Salisbury, the Van Cott lawyer who had prepared and witnessed the Bradshaws' wills five years earlier, to explain certain things about them to her, and to tell her something she had wanted to know for quite some time—how much her husband's estate was worth. He fulfilled her first request in a letter on December 11, but could not satisfy her second. "We do not have any idea as to the nature and extent of your husband's estate," he wrote.

Lawyers who specialize in estate work often find it difficult, if not impossible, to stay removed from the sometimes nasty fights that can erupt within families over the issue of a will—especially when a great deal of money is at stake. When David Salisbury returned to his office from the July Fourth weekend in 1976, celebrating America's 200th birthday, there was a fifteen-page, single-spaced letter waiting for him from Frances Schreuder. A phone call between them had enabled Salisbury to get his feet wet, but now, like it or not, he was about to be tossed into the deep end.

Frances stated that her mother did not understand legal jargon or terminology and had been frustrated and confused in trying to put her legal affairs into order. She explained that the will Berenice currently had "does not reflect her desires or wishes," and attached a copy of her May 2, 1975, letter to Berenice that proposed how she could change her trust—a letter, Frances said, that was "a culmination of our discussions.

". . . My mother's frustration and unhappiness has been further compounded by the fact that my sister, Marilyn Reagan, has 'appointed' herself, without any legal power of attorney or written consent of any contractual basis, as an 'estate planner' for my parents. . . .

"She has taken full discretionary and decision-making powers for herself and has not been completely honest or candid with my parents and myself as to the details, goals, scope and ultimate aims of her so-called 'estate planning.'"

Her mother, Frances said, was "rightly resentful that my sister is demanding all records, delving into private financial affairs and has stopped at nothing, including copies of all income tax returns. . . .

"Unfortunately I will be very frank and state that with my many years of knowledge of my sister's character and stated intentions as well as past deeds, I can only come to the conclusion of deliberate fraudulent misrepresentation and undue influence with the intent of benefiting for herself unduly . . . at the expense of others. . . ."

She then moved on to the subject of her father, who, she said her mother had told her, was not "totally adverse" to Marilyn's efforts.

My father has a rather distinctive and unique personality and might be fairly characterized as highly eccentric. Furthermore, his whole life is absorbed with his work to the point where he is so compulsive/obsessive about his work that he does not like to take the time or trouble with anything else in the world. This includes also such matters as wills, and he refuses to take the time to put his businesses in order so that a smooth and orderly transition in his business affairs can take place upon his death. He refuses to face such a possibility and devotes 365 days a year to his work, refusing to consider anything else in life. I doubt very much that my father will ever truly put his affairs in order as he is fearful of death, imagines he will live forever and cannot conceive or make provisions for anyone else taking charge of things upon his death (he has always refused to properly delegate authority in business and insists on keeping total control of everything . . .) . . . .

At the same time, he is demonstrating more and more poor and quite frequently unsound, even childlike judgement about practical everyday matters of almost any nature. . . .

Although he has not granted my sister power of attorney or placed any instrument in writing to her, being totally consummed with his own narrow world, he is willing to sit back while my sister does all of his thinking for him. . . .

My father is extremely loathe to spend money for anything except business and business reinvestments in a compulsive manner. With this in mind, perhaps you can understand that he likes to obtain, as much as possible, everything for free. A will and proper estate planning and arrangements are, as I am certain that you well know, proper, wise and sound business investments in terms of money spent and time delegated. My father with his narrow outlook, however, does not consider that in its proper prospective. He cannot stand anything of any nature that takes time away from his current obsessive interests and in fact considers anything that takes his time away from his business as a threat and is highly resentful. . . .

Sadly enough, she said, her father did not "possess the practical sophistication to realize that while he sits back and lets her do his thinking for him, she can, is and probably will continue on a course that will leave a path of irrovacable havoc" from which her father might not be able to recover.

"Although it might appear unwise, childish, foolish and perhaps a serious lapse of sound judgement on my father's part," she continued, "my mother should not be bound in anyway by my father's folly, lack of judgement and potentially tragic mistake."

Frances then launched another attack on Marilyn, claiming that her sister became "viciously angry" when someone didn't agree totally with her plans or ideas. "Since my mother desires family harmony and neither desires to be caught in the middle of a family disagreement nor incur the wrath of my sister, she does not exactly find it pleasant to tell her to mind her own business."

But her concern about Marilyn didn't stop there. It extended to Marilyn's husband, Bob, and the provision for him that Frances felt Marilyn had been trying to ensure. She claimed that the main reason her mother skipped her daughters as beneficiaries of her trust was fear that "son-in-laws— more specifically Robert Reagan—[might] inherit her property." Frances claimed that Marilyn made "veiled and not so veiled threats" about the matter and told Berenice that "wills are meant to be broken."

She raised the issue of Marilyn wanting to be executor of her father's estate, with full power of attorney. She felt that Marilyn and Bob would try to take over his oil business "which she has wanted to control since her marriage to her husband." She expressed her concern that Bob would become the estate's legal adviser and take legal fees for himself, not to mention the cost of business offices, plane fares, rented cars, and corporate salaries they would both accrue.

"Although my father has not changed his will yet and I hope he doesn't, I do not believe that my mother should leave part of her estate to my father for two reasons. *Firstly, he has no economic necessity to benefit from it. Secondly, any part of my mother's estate that would go to my father could possibly be controlled by Marilyn and Robert Reagan, if my father continues to succumb to my sister's pressures to [re]write his will, be executor and generally take control of his estate."* If he did change his will as her sister wished, Frances cautioned Salisbury, and if her mother were to leave part of her estate to her father and died before him, *"my mother would rise out of her grave as Robert and Marilyn Reagan spend my mother's share that has been left to my father."*

In closing, she told him, "I have tried to give a general picture of a situation that is far more complicated and difficult than I have been able to convey in this letter."

By September, Marc was preparing to leave home. He was not happy about it and told a friend that he wanted to "live with Mom forever."

Having graduated with honors from Allen-Stevenson, he was going to attend the Kent School, located about a hundred miles north of New York City in the small northwestern Connecticut town of Kent. The Reverend Frederick Herbert Sill, a former cockswain from West Park, New York, founded the Episcopal school in a farmhouse on the banks of the Housatonic River in 1906, and it is often referred to as the most English of American prep schools: a fairly strict, tightly structured community in which each student is required to do a job, attend chapel, and participate in athletics; a student in charge of a residence is a "prefect"; a tenth-grader is in the "fourth form"; and upperclassmen can "sting hours" on lowerclassmen—a form of punishment that can range from cleaning out horse stables to chipping ice on the coldest day in winter.

While school officials and students concede that the school is not quite on the same academic level as Andover, Exeter or Choate, many stress that Kent "pays more attention to the whole person" and that it "toughens" the individual. "Direct-ness of purpose, simplicity of life, and self-reliance" is the school's motto, and its graduates have included former Secretary of State Cyrus Vance, the lawyer Whitney North Seymour, Jr., the writer James Gould Cozzens (who wrote about it in *Children and Others)* and the actor Treat Williams.

Like her father, Frances believed strongly in the value of education. Since she had driven Marc to get good grades at Allen-Stevenson and wanted him, in three years' time, to attend an Ivy League college, sending him to a place like Kent was a sensible next step.

At Kent, like many prep schools, the students who play varsity athletics are the gods, and often receive their nectar in the form of special treatment. Since Marc would never be held in that kind of esteem, he would have to distinguish himself in other ways.

Marc wasn't at Kent long before his disheveled figure was easily recognizable on the lush 1,533-acre campus near the foot of Mount Algo. With his tie askew, he was the same paradox of nonconformist and attention seeker that he had been at Allen-Stevenson. He seemed to have more laundry than any boy at Kent. Doing laundry was a major social activity, and while most boys carried theirs in a knapsack, Marc was a drayhorse on roller skates, pulling a huge suitcase on wheels with a ropelike harness toward the local laundro-mat. Just as he had acted out his Poe-like English composi-tions a few years before, he gave an interpretation of William Wordsworth's "Ode: Intimations of Immortality from Recol-lections of Early Childhood" that one of his English teachers would long remember.

Judson Scruton called on Marc one day while a visiting headmaster from England was observing the teacher's class. "Marc took off on this jag about the influence of the child fathering the man," Scruton recalled—the epigraph to the poem begins with the line "The child is father of the man"—"and the presence of childhood in adulthood. He clearly had a very powerful, emotional response to childhood memories, because he was drawing inferences about them and their relation to immortality. His interpretation was

151

blatantly subjective yet brilliant. He was so convincing and interesting that I let him go." On another occasion, a guest artist was demonstrating how to do tai chi. Most of the kids, Scruton remembered, were very self-conscious, and that prevented them from "letting themselves go." But not Marc, who flung himself into it in a performance that is still talked about by the people who witnessed it.

"Marc was either a genius or a con artist or both," Scruton said at Kent one July day. "He was not a clear rebel, but enjoyed being an oddball. He had a crazy grin halfway between a leprechaun's and a Halloween jack-o'-lantern. I found him absolutely engaging, charming and zany." But other teachers, Scruton admitted, had different opinions of him, and Marc soon developed a reputation for being quite strange. Of all the faculty members who got to know Marc in his three years at Kent, perhaps Father Michael Bullock, Marc's adviser and one of the school's assistant chaplains, knew him best.

"Marc was a scared, gnomish kid when he came to Kent," Father Bullock recalled. "He was away, in a sea of people. He wasn't an athlete. He wasn't handsome. He had memorized his Shakespeare in order to gain acceptance. But people didn't laugh with him and he didn't realize that. I would tell him in effect: stop being an ass in trying to get attention. You don't have to be a fool to be accepted. It was a conversation we had often. By senior year he had become the character he created—the class fool, a drunken Charles Laughton. He played a role so often he exceeded the boundary line."

While Bullock said Marc was very immature, he also saw him as more like a sixty-year-old man than a teenager. "His ace in the hole—his way of dealing with the world—was his cleverness. He was not someone you could get close to. He was his own worst enemy. He was very lonely and not loved. He had a complete disregard for himself, and for his uniqueness.

"Kent was *not* a positive influence on him. He was aware of, but couldn't accept—and ignored—his limitations. When he would study, he would just amass facts—a human word processor—and not gain insight. He was what the kids call a 'shiteater.' He was always nervous and hyperactive. He would come in to pick up his grades like he would eat his food—drooling, ready to devour."

Frances and Lavinia came up to see Marc on a Parents Weekend, and Bullock remembered the visit well. He had had a number of phone calls from Frances, usually at eleven at night. While Bullock encouraged his advisees' parents to call him, the phone calls from Frances were so long and rambling that "I'd listen and then put the phone down on a wing chair, because it was always meaningless. The conversations would sometimes be about Marc's erratic behavior and his getting 'stung.' She wasn't a parent I looked forward to hearing from."

When Bullock met Frances, he could see that Marc had gotten his tightness and nervousness from her and that he himself became nervous around her. As they were all sitting and talking that weekend, a classroom bell suddenly went off. There was nothing unusual about that, except what followed: Lavinia, who reminded Bullock of a marionette that might have been cut out of a children's magazine and inflated to life-size, practically went through the ceiling and began screaming hysterically.

To Bullock, Marc and Frances were people who "refused to be honest about themselves. There was such a gaping hole with Marc needing parenting and his parent needing parenting. What we give our children," Bullock said, quoting an anonymous passage, "are roots and wings. These kids [not just Marc] come into Kent before they are sophisticated enough to cover up the crassness of their parents' values. Our job was to pass along what is important about life. Kent reached out in every way to kids; they were given every opportunity to flower." But Kent, Bullock reiterated, was not a positive experience for Marc. "He was a weak person. There was a cowardliness to him, and that's why I found it hard to feel compassion for him. Marc grasped onto a concept of success—a very American thing—worshiped it, and it became a warped sort of evil."

Bullock felt that Marc should have been able "to separate himself from a parasitic mother." But the physical distance between Marc and his mother meant little. The emotional link between them was unshakable. She expected phone calls almost daily—calls that lasted from one to three hours with Frances talking nonstop. She talked to him about her woes and crises, as she had done when he was living at home, and would demand that he get good grades. It was Catch-22, Marc told a psychiatrist: she wanted him to get the grades, yet the considerable amount of time he was obliged to spend on the phone interfered with his study time.

Their phone calls sometimes became so angry that people, who happened to overhear them and were upset by the way Marc spoke to his mother from a public pay phone, wrote notes to Father Bullock. When Bullock questioned him about it, Marc always tried to downplay it.

"It was just a misunderstanding," Bullock said Marc assured him. "I must write her and apologize."

Two thousand miles from Kent, angry arguments were also taking place. Berenice and Franklin were beginning to clash right on the loading dock in front of the warehouse—and the employees could hear what was being said. One time, the warehouse intercom was left on accidentally, and everyone could hear Franklin, normally a very private person, screaming at Berenice on the phone. The subject was always the same: money for Frances. He was once again paying for the boys' schooling, and he was sending Frances her monthly rent of $1,000; Berenice, meanwhile, was sending her up to $2,000 a month for expenses. In Franklin's mind that was plenty, and the leash around Berenice was starting to tighten.

In the past when Berenice wanted to take her mind off Frances's problems but wasn't able to travel, she had thrown herself totally into all sorts of chores. She would paint the house by herself, or do all the yard work, and she had recently remodeled the kitchen. At first Franklin was oblivious to the fact that she was doing the remodeling; but when he finally discovered a bill she had left for him, he wrote her a disapproving note: "YOU WANTED IT. YOU PAY FOR IT."

He had successfully stymied her efforts to spruce up the warehouse, but she won a small victory in the summer of 1976 when Franklin decided to expand his space on Pierpont Avenue. On Sunday afternoons she went down and scrubbed the floors and toilets; during the week, she bought some new office furniture and curtains, as well as a used refrigerator. The employees had never had one.

Most of the employees had great affection for Berenice, but Nancy Jones, Franklin's oil secretary, seemed to be the closest one to her. Berenice would bring Nancy gifts back from her vacations and would often pour her heart out to her as well.

"I got real close to Mrs. Bradshaw," Nancy said. "She was like a grandmother. She was always worried about what Frances was doing to herself. But she couldn't see what Frances was doing to her. She never thought about that. Frances needed Mrs. Bradshaw, and I think Mrs. Bradshaw needed Frances, because as a person you need someone to need you.

"Frances would tell her that she was going to kill herself, and then Frances wouldn't answer the phone. So Mrs. Bradshaw would be afraid she did commit suicide.

"Frances would want money. As long as Mrs. Bradshaw sent her money, she was fine. Mrs. Bradshaw would send gifts with money in them, and Frances would take the money and send the gifts back. Frances always upset her in this way."

At the end of 1976 Berenice wrote, "We are off in 1977 with thousands of new government officials. Utah has a new governor (another Democrat), the Nation has a new president (a peanut farmer and Baptist holy-roller), may the lord help the rest of us. Let us hope all will not be gloom and doom in 1977."

This marked the last thing written in Berenice's autobiography. The years to come for the Bradshaw family would be recorded in other, more public ways.

20// It had been nine years since Marc and Larry had
spent the summer together in Salt Lake, and now
they were returning in 1977 to work for their grandfather and
live at Gilmer Drive. Both boys had been doing well in
school, and Franklin proudly showed their report cards to his
employees any chance he got. Though he had never succeeded in getting Frances to move with his grandchildren
back to Utah, having Marc and Larry for the summer would
give him a chance to spend time with them and give them a
chance to learn about his world.

Wally Glover, his manager in Provo, felt certain Franklin
was sorry he hadn't spent more time with his own children,
and that this would give him an opportunity to be a real father
to these boys. They were his flesh and blood, and no matter
how great the tension was between him and their mother, he
didn't fault them.

A few months before they were due to arrive, Berenice
wrote Larry a letter:

. . . We are looking forward to sharing our home with you, and
Grandpa says he needs you boys. He puts in very long hours, his age
is telling on him and he is getting worn out. I wonder sometimes how
much longer he can keep up this pace. Your Grandfather has huge
business operations and he needs you boys to share these interests.
With four Grandsons, there should be one or two of you interested in
carrying on his business operations.

This of course had been Franklin's dream for Robert, and
Berenice was rekindling its extinguished flame.

But Marc and Larry almost didn't get to Utah. In May,
Frances and Berenice had a flare-up on the phone about the
usual topic—Frances's financial problems—and Frances hung
up, but not before announcing that the boys would not be
coming to Salt Lake after all. Now that Marc and Larry were
old enough, they represented a new outlet for Berenice to air
her feelings of anger and frustration. The old divide-and-

conquer game was alive and well, and in writing to Marc and Larry about their mother she was writing to two boys who were already being indoctrinated into it:

. . . If it wasn't for me your whole family would be sitting out in the street, starving to death. I am her only source of income. Why should I be treated like this? This kind of treatment is cruel and unnecessary and I suffer. . . .

In her out-burst of anger . . . she said you boys are not coming to S.L. this summer. Is this your decision or hers and why? Grandpa and I were planning on you coming we will be very disappointed. Where does she plan to get the money to feed all of you this summer? At least if you come to S.L. you won't be hungry. I hope I haven't stirred up a hornet's nest, I'm only trying to help and I worry about the living of your family very much. With no income what would you do without me?

All my love,
GRANNY

Berenice's hope for 1977 had been that all would not be "gloom and doom," and it wasn't. On June 12, a Sunday, Frances and Lavinia were baptized into the Episcopal faith, and Berenice wanted both of them to know how she felt about it:

DEAR FRANCES AND LAVINIA:

I'm deeply impressed you both are taking unto yourselves a religion, especially the Episcopal Church. I'm pleased my dear, darling granddaughter has drawn you to commit your lives to something inspiring, something higher than man. . . .

My "non-belief" is a mark of my birth . . . and no amount of education, reading or association has brought me around to accepting anything "beyond my control." Many times I feel like I'm just dangling, nothing to cling to. Those who have a religion to "fall back on" have a source of enlightenment that can't be counted on by man. . . .

Frances, your life has been most "unfortunate, most difficult and at times most horrible." Now that Lavinia has shown you the way, I hope you will be happy in your new life. I hope your life will be enriched. Lavinia is a lucky girl to find her "niche" early in life. I'm sure it will bring her happiness, contentment and strength to live by.

You are the first of our family to be baptised in a Christian religion. You are true "Huguenots," of which we are descendants. . . .

All my love,
MOTHER & GRANNY

Whether Berenice's letter was the reason Frances changed her mind about sending Marc and Larry to Salt Lake is doubtful. When Berenice went out to the airport later that month to pick them up, they-arrived with nothing but the clothes on their backs. And so the nightmare began.

Part Three//

Come to the place of gathering, even
in flocks, as doves fly to their windows
before a storm.

—BRIGHAM YOUNG

21// Frances assumed that her mother would buy Marc and Larry everything they needed—and she was right. But Berenice was not happy about it. After she picked them up that day, she was "on fire" as she zoomed down to the warehouse to tell everyone how her grandsons had just arrived looking like the hobos she and Frank had been fifty years before.

Frank's plan for the boys was this: Marc was going to work under Doug Steele and Larry under Clive Davis. He was entrusting his grandsons to two men who between them had been with him for more than sixty years. Loyal and hardworking, they were closer to him than the members of his own family. They knew all his foibles and eccentricities and just how far they could push him. Doug, who had a short fuse, was practically the only person who would really stand up to him if they had a serious difference of opinion, and Clive had threatened to quit on more than one occasion. But they both stuck by him. They respected him as a businessman, and they profited, if not from their wages, from the financial education he had given them. The two men knew of the many crises that he and Berenice had been through over the years, and Doug, of course, had been in the dangerous middle of many of them—so many in fact that he called himself the "family peeing post." Though they both liked Berenice, they felt that her marriage to Frank was not right for either of them, and that if Frank were more happily married, perhaps he would spend less time working and enjoy the considerable amount of money he was making.

As hard as they both worked, Doug and Clive, both Mormons, spent a great deal of time with their families, and they always felt that Frank should have spent more time with his.

They had heard Frank talking about his grandsons coming and how proud he was of their performance in school. They had heard him say that he was going to take them around Utah, show them the various stores, and tell them about the Bradshaw heritage—how proud he was of it and all that the Bradshaws had accomplished. These boys were from the city, and Frank was going to show them the kind of people who really built this country. They had heard all of it, and it *sounded* great.

But they were still dubious.

On his first day on the job, Marc was sitting with Doug in Doug's office, doing a classification of certain parts. Just before lunch, an employee sauntered in, carrying a bag that she put into Doug's bottom drawer. The canvas bag contained about $2,700 that Doug's daughter was to deposit in the bank when she came in that afternoon. Like Frank, Doug rarely took much time for lunch and usually spelled people at the counter for an hour or so. He returned to his office about two, and his daughter arrived shortly afterward to pick up the bag.

No sooner had she left, it seemed, than Doug received a phone call.

"Dad, we're short fourteen hundred." It was Karen, calling from the bank.

"Oh, come on, you can't be," said Doug, stunned. He paused for a minute and then said, "Put everything back in the bag and come back immediately."

As soon as Karen returned, Doug went to see "the first employee," as he sometimes referred to Frank. He told Frank what had happened and said he could see only three possibilities.

"Either my daughter took it," Doug said, "or someone

161

came in off the street, took the fourteen hundred, and tied the bag back up, leaving the other thirteen hundred there." Doug stopped, reluctant to go further.

"What's the third possibility?" Frank demanded to know.

"Your grandson. He saw the bag brought in, knew where it was, and had all the time in the world to do it."

"No way, no way." Frank was adamant.

"Well, what are we going to do?" Doug said. "Are we just going to let this stand?"

"I want you to tighten up your security and get your desk fixed so you can lock the drawer," Frank shot back, telling Doug that Marc would no longer be his responsibility.

When Frank closed up that night, he followed his usual routine—hiding the cash that had been taken in from lunchtime on in different places. Then he and the two boys drove home.

The following morning, a cash count turned up more shortages. Frank decided that he wanted *all* the employees to take lie-detector tests. Employees had stolen from him in the past, and he was determined to catch the thief.

After Frank told Doug of his idea, Doug said, "That's fine, Frank, but let me tell you something. You understand that if *we* do this, *you'll* have to take one, and your boys will too." Frank agreed and then marched off.

About fifteen minutes later, Frank reappeared in Doug's office, singing a different tune.

"Oh, well, let's just forget about it," Frank said, then started to walk away.

As diplomatically as he could, Doug told Frank that he should hide the money when his grandsons weren't around—possibly in the basement.

A few days later, Doug came to work and found a $20 bill and a $10 bill under his desk. He immediately recognized his find for what it was: Frank's old trick of planting money on the floor to test his employees' honesty. He had pulled it on Doug in 1946, but it wasn't going to work now. Doug was furious and confronted Frank about it.

"I must have dropped it by accident while I was putting away the cash," Frank said unconvincingly.

"Don't lie to me, Frank. You've done it purposely. After

thirty-one years, I'm worth more to you than thirty bucks, aren't I? You're hurting my feelings."

Frank had put blinders on. He was too proud to accept the reality of what was happening. While his employees grew increasingly resentful and were on the verge of mutiny (one employee found Marc rifling through her purse, but, knowing how Frank felt about his grandsons, did not report him; another quit when told he could no longer use the till), he was paying Marc and Larry better than most of them. He took Marc and Larry to the railroad station for lunch and let them take naps in the afternoon. He took them down to Provo and introduced them as the two boys who would take over the business someday. He was trying to be a father to them, yet all the while they were abusive, to both him and Berenice, in their language and their actions.

Berenice did everything she could to make them happy. She took them to Park City one day, and the trip was a disaster. They taunted her all the way there, she said, and she almost took them back before they arrived. Yet even after they arrived, they kept it up.

"So I ditched them," Berenice said, still cringing at the memory of that day, "and lay down under a tree for about an hour and a half. When I got back to the car they had smashed one of the windows. Why oh why didn't somebody see them, stop them, or report them to the police?"

There had been problems with Marc and Larry during the summer of 1968, but those were pleasant memories compared to what Frank and Berenice were enduring now.

One night something strange happened.

Frank and Berenice were asleep in their separate bedrooms when Berenice heard her husband cry out. She came into his room and found Marc standing over him. It was a particularly still summer night and Marc had wandered upstairs from the basement, where he and Larry stayed, because he apparently couldn't sleep. When Frank happened to wake up, he was startled to see his grandson and hollered for Berenice. Marc said that he wanted to sleep on the cool floor, but was told to go back downstairs.

Frank couldn't get back to sleep that night and had trouble

sleeping the rest of the summer. From that moment on, he told Doug Steele and Nancy Jones, he was afraid of Marc— and years later Berenice said she was convinced he had been trying to poison the air.

The situation at the warehouse grew worse. Doug told Marc and Larry that if they continued using foul language to their grandparents he would slap them. "I can't describe what two spoiled brats they were," Doug said later. "They had no manners and they had no scruples. I think Frank wanted to help the boys that summer form some kind of character and get to know them better. But," Doug paused, "they were long gone by the time they got to Frank."

Frank was a stubborn man, though, and he continued to stand by them. But something occurred on the first day of August to change that. The previous night, Marc had been showing his grandparents some home movies he had taken with his Canon Super 8. Both he and Larry were interested in photography, and they had been taking hundreds of photographs that summer—everything from the city dump to the breathtaking scenery. On Sundays in particular, Marc would take photographs of the warehouse, inside and out, and on one occasion, Larry took a picture of Marc, who was taking a picture of his grandfather opening up early in the morning.

Marc was running the movie projector that July evening when something appeared that suddenly caught Frank's eye. He asked Marc to stop the projector. On the frozen frame were stock certificates, spread out on the floor of the warehouse. Marc had obviously put on the wrong reel. He told his grandfather that he had found the certificates inside some old copies of *Life* magazine, and had simply taken some pictures of them. Nothing more was said that evening.

The next morning, Nancy Jones was going through the July statement from the bank in Lehi where Franklin kept a checking account and where his father had been one of the first directors. Like most of the employees, she had been having a miserable summer and was looking forward to Marc and Larry's going back to New York.

She came across a check made out to cash for $10,000. Then she came across *another* one. Then she found one made out to Lavinia Schreuder (who was four years old) for $500. There was something wrong, and she knew it.

Frank *never* made out checks to cash. She went next door and got Doug. "The summer had been hell anyway," Nancy recalled, "and I figured here was one more blowup. Doug went and got Mr. Bradshaw and he came up to the front to my office. When he saw them he just started yelling, 'Oh my God, oh my God,' and began to cry. He said, 'You call that bank and tell them to stop payment on any more checks coming from New York.'"

The checks had been forged and had been deposited in a New York bank. There were eight checks in all. In addition to the three that Nancy came across, there were five others: four more made out to Lavinia and one to Dr. M. R. Brand, Frances's psychiatrist. The eight checks totaled $22,320.00. Franklin kept blank, unnumbered checks in an unlocked box under the desk in his oil office, and somebody had found his hiding place.

Frank told Doug to call Berenice and tell her and Larry, who was home that morning, to come to the warehouse at once. He couldn't avoid reality any longer. When he got Marc and Larry together he asked Doug to take them upstairs and talk to them. Doug had been put in this position many times before, but that didn't make it any easier. It was Frank's responsibility to take them to the woodshed, but he shied away from it. But while Larry was upstairs with Doug, something else was happening downstairs.

Frank discovered that his file cabinet had been broken into and that a lot of cash was missing. When Doug returned with Larry, Franklin confronted his grandsons. He didn't show his anger very often, but this was one of those times.

"Look, it wasn't the Salt Lake City boys," Franklin began, finally defending his employees. "We don't break into people's private files and take their cash, their stocks and their papers out. *You* did. We saw those films last night by mistake. You said you found those stocks in some *Life* magazines. So show me where they are. You *find* them."

Marc began taking merchandise off the shelves and piling it up. This was the first time Doug had heard about the home movies and what had come up on the screen. He realized that Franklin had them "cold-turkey." Finally, Marc had everything off the shelves, the place was a mess, and no stock certificates to show for it. Both Franklin and Doug told him to stop.

Doug then took Marc upstairs to talk with him. "He was cool as a cucumber," Doug remembered. "Neither one of them was breathing heavy. I laid it all out in front of him from day one. I talked about their coming in at nights, stealing keys and getting them made, and how their grandfather had even told me he'd 'lost' his keys. I told him, as I had told Larry: 'Protect your position. Just admit it. You'll be wealthy someday.' But they denied everything. They were as cold as Toby's backside. I couldn't believe it."

Franklin didn't blame the boys so much as he blamed Frances. He was certain she was behind it. The bank in Lehi said the money could be credited within forty-eight hours, but in order to do that the FBI would have to be involved. When Doug told him that, he backed off. Frank had been in this situation before with his youngest daughter, and considered it a private matter. He'd handled it before and he would handle it again.

By late August, Larry had decided to go home ahead of Marc. He had bought a bluish-green 1961 Chevrolet Impala for $380 from one of Frank's employees. Larry loved cars, especially Chevys, and had been slowly accumulating parts from the warehouse and putting them into his trunk. Doug had seen a number of "high-ticket items" collected together one day, and he mentioned his suspicion to Frank. Frank didn't do anything until the night before Larry was ready to leave, when Marc told his grandparents that Larry had indeed been stealing parts. While Larry was asleep, Marc and Frank unloaded the trunk and put everything into Berenice's car. She drove the parts back to the warehouse the next day and told everyone, "These goddam kids don't own the place yet."

When Larry was asked about this six years later, he laughed. "I started out on Interstate 80, heading east, and I felt the car was kind of light. I opened up the trunk and the parts were gone." Actually, he said, they had really done him a favor. "I got rid of all those dumb parts. If I hadn't, I would've broken down in the mountains."

Marc and Larry had been sent to Salt Lake City that summer on a mission—a mission for Frances. About a week before they had gone out there, their mother had given them their marching orders and told them about all their grandfather's secret hiding places.

"My mother really had us so hyped up," Larry recalled, the excitement of the summer clearly still with him. "We thought we could do anything we wanted. You name it, we did it. She said, 'Send me money, send me stock certificates, do this, do that. Break into the warehouse, get the keys—come on, Larry, come on, Marc.'"

She also suggested how they treat their grandmother. "She told us to treat Granny roughly and show her who's boss," Larry said. "To put our foot down with her or else she would try to *control* us and boss us around. We treated Granny very badly that summer. The second day we were there we were in Pioneer Park and she was crying and was upset. We drove her crazy, we tormented her, we made fun of her. She told us to go to the library and we brought home about ten books on sex. She returned them the next day."

At the warehouse, Larry said, "Marc and I were loafers. My grandfather was a miser and a hoarder. We were ripping that place blind. If it moved, we took it. If it was loose, we took it. If it was in place, we'd rip it off." There was a time clock that Larry and Marc had to punch, and Larry figured out a way to get paid twice as much. In the evenings, they would say they were going to a movie, but usually went back down to the warehouse on their "midnight raids." Collecting keys and picking locks were activities that Marc had begun to excel in at Kent, and he applied those talents to get into the warehouse.

Marc's recollection of that summer was similar to his brother's. While Larry called it a "great" summer, Marc said it was a "dirty" one. " 'Don't listen to Granny—she is a bad influence on your personality,' " Marc told a psychiatrist his mother told them. "Mom worked on us and I believed her." She was not getting any money, he said, so they had to steal for her—blank checks, thousands of dollars' worth of stock certificates, and cash. He said she told them there were sacks of money in the warehouse, and where to find it. When they sent the blank checks back to New York, she forged them. They also sent her all of the stock certificates and most of the cash, keeping some for themselves.

Frances's scheme had worked. With part of the money, she rented a summer house called Dragon Hall in Southampton, New York—an exclusive town on Long Island—for three months at a total cost of $20,000. She was living lavishly and eating caviar, Marc said, and calling them daily with instructions to get more and more money and tips on new places to search. When she didn't call them, they called her. On July 10 alone, they made seven calls to New York. The total amount of the calls was $77.90, and the longest one cost $39.05.

"I felt like a piece of shit," Marc said. "The employees knew what we were doing and looked at us like scum. Gramps hated us, the employees hated us, but Mom said it was right and she became like the only person in my life. When I asked permission to come home, she said, 'What are you trying to do, starve me and Lavinia?'"

The boys were gone. What Franklin and Berenice had hoped would be a lovely summer was a total disaster. He had wanted them to experience his world, but they had simply knifed him in the back. He had been down this road before with Frances, but this was supposed to be different: these were his grandsons. Two months before he had boasted to people how they were going to take over the business. But he had missed the point: they might have been his grandsons, and he might have loved them, but they were their mother's sons first, and their allegiance was to her.

"I seen him," Nancy Jones said of the period that followed their departure. "I looked at him. He was depressed. He wasn't happy. He used to smile and kid you a little bit. I think they left a bad mark with him and he never recovered from it. He was wore out, he slept more, he was losing weight, and he started to age."

Wally Glover remembered the trip Frank made to Provo after the boys left. "Frank was too proud to tell us too much, but he was really upset that Frances and the boys had taken him so badly, when he had trusted them so much. He just didn't want to believe it. When he came down to talk to me, he was embarrassed. He'd been down in the mouth before and done all this bragging. He brought the kids in and said, 'These are the boys who are going to eventually take over the business.' Us guys were wondering what was going to happen to us. Us guys had been there forty-some-odd years. You can imagine what that one statement meant to us at the time."

When Franklin got back to Salt Lake the employees at the warehouse had a message for him: if his grandsons came back to work the following summer, they would quit. They were angry that he initially had blamed them for the thefts, and they had endured a summer none of them would forget. Berenice was as bitter as her husband. Not only had the boys taunted and tormented her, but they had secretly tape-recorded conversations she had with them about Frances. And that's who the summer of 1977 finally came back to, Doug said. "Frances programmed this. She created these monsters." A long time before, Berenice had told Frances that if she ever wanted money from her father she would have to take it. Frances had certainly followed that advice. Her "monsters" had taken about $200,000.

Franklin decided to strike back. He made it clear that he would not pay for the boys' schooling that year. In fact, he said he was going to turn his back on Frances and her family completely. As always, but especially now, he hoped that Berenice would be in agreement with him on this. After all, she had suffered as much as he had during the summer.

After the forged checks had come in, Franklin had begun reviewing the bank statements himself and had closed out Berenice's checking account at the Walker Bank as a precautionary measure. As he was looking over the checks that were written in the month of September, he came across two, both dated September 17, that he had not signed. One was made out to Eastern Military Academy for $2,300, the other to Kent School for $5,520. He was dumbstruck. Nancy was out sick that day, so he asked another woman who worked for him if she had made them out and she said no. He told her to ask Nancy the next day if she had. When Nancy came in and was told what had happened, she told Franklin that she hadn't either. The nightmare wasn't over. This time it seemed his wife had forged his signature, and he told Nancy to get Berenice on the phone and tell her to come to the warehouse. Nancy called Berenice at home, but did not tell her why her husband wanted to see her. When she arrived, Nancy showed her the checks and said, "Mrs. Bradshaw, Mr. Bradshaw knows that you made these checks out and sent them to the boys' schools."

Berenice immediately began to cry, telling Nancy, "He said he'd pay for their education and then he said he wouldn't."

As Doug had been so often, Nancy was caught in the middle. "I didn't want to be," Nancy said. "*He* should have talked to her. I felt sorry for her. He just didn't like to confront her."

When asked in 1983 about the forgeries, Berenice said, "I just went down to the Bank of Lehi and made out checks for their schooling. I said nothing to him about it. He was angry, but I figured it was just as much my money as his. This thing of men thinking they've got control over *all* finances is hogwash. And that's why nine-tenths of the women work. They say, 'Oh, I can't stay home,' and I say, 'Uh, huh.' Nine-tenths of the women work because they're living with a stingy man. They're stingy. That's my personal opinion."

One morning, not long after he discovered the forged school checks, Frank asked Nancy Jones to type something on one of those half-sheets of paper that he loved to cut off the bottoms of other letters and use as if they were new. The message was this:

A) On my death it is my wishes that my 100% of my parts business is to be incorporated into two or more companies and there is to be a mother holding company. I do will $2,000.00 of that stock to each of my 30 year old employees. All employees working in my unincorporated stores will have another option to buy $2,000.00 shares of stock and the 30 year employees $4,000.00 shares of stock.

B) On my death I do appoint Douglas Steele as co-administrator to my estate, in the case of his death or inability to serve I do appoint Clive Davis to take his place, on his death or inability to serve I do appoint Neil Swan to take his place, on his death or inability to serve I appoint Walker Bank & Company to take his place.

On my death I do appoint my daughter Marilyn Reagan to act as co-administrator of my estate, on her death I appoint my daughter Elaine Drukman and on her death or inability to serve I appoint Walker Bank & Trust co. to take her place.

Nancy gave this back to Franklin and he made a few copies. He then went to the back of the warehouse and sat down at his typewriter, the one he had used so often over the years to send his "family letters." Underneath what Nancy had typed, he typed the following:

Gifts in stock 20 year Service Employees $1000.00 30 year $2000.00
Stock Options "   "   "   " $1000.00 "   "   "
Gifts Trust Fund $n Stock $20,000.00
                        F.J.B.
    ⅓ of my estate to Berenice J. Bra ds haw ⅓ to
Marilyn Reagan an ⅓ to Elaine Drukman.

Frank went back to the Xerox machine and made a number of copies of this. He called Doug over and let him see the memo. Doug couldn't believe it. It stated not only that Frank was apparently intending to make Doug co-executor of his will, but that he was going to change it in such a way that Frances could not benefit from it. His will was currently set up so that if Berenice survived him, she would get everything. But if Berenice was funneling most, if not all, of her oil-lease royalties to Frances at the present, Frank knew that amount of support would probably increase after his death.

"You really mean it, don't you? Are you really going to cut her out of your will? Do you really mean it?" asked Doug in amazement.

"You bet. You betcha I am," Frank said, and told Doug that he wanted him to drive him downtown.

"When do you want me to take you downtown?" Doug asked.

"I'll come over and get you when I'm ready," Frank said.

"Where are you going?" Doug asked, curiously.

"I am going to see a lawyer," Frank said.

While Doug was waiting to take Frank to the lawyer's, he showed Neil Swan a copy of the memo Frank had given him. Neil had just begun reading it when Frank came in with his briefcase and said he was ready to go. So Doug drove him to

Second South and Main, dropped him off at the corner, and returned to the warehouse. While Frank was gone, the warehouse was abuzz. He had made enough copies "to sink a battleship," Doug said, and they were just lying around.

If Franklin was serious about this, Frances would not be the only one affected. Berenice would be too. Her inheritance would be reduced to one-third. On top of that, he would be giving Marilyn part of what she desperately wanted— executorship of the estate, a decision bound to rankle his wife and youngest daughter.

But was he *serious?* Or was he just trying to send a message to Frances to back off, a message she would doubtless receive from Berenice, who was beginning to spend more and more time at the warehouse, would probably hear about the memo from one of the employees, or would see it herself?

The question was further complicated when, later that day, he took *another* copy of the memo that Nancy had typed and simply signed his name to it. Underneath his signature were some further notations by hand relating to retirement money for employees, but no mention of the proposed one-third split. What was Frank Bradshaw up to? It was uncharacteristic of him to be so public about his family affairs, and it was unlikely that he would go outside the family—to Doug—in organizing his estate. But it had been an awful summer, and maybe he felt he needed to show his employees that he was capable of striking back in order to regain their confidence, respect and loyalty. But then why the "afternoon memo," as it would come to be called? Had he changed his mind during the course of the day? Or had something caused him to?

When Larry got back to New York, ahead of Marc, his mother had some news for him. He could *not*, under any circumstances, stay at the apartment until school started, nor could he stay at the house in Southampton. She gave him no reason, he later said, and he saw it as just another example of his mother's unpredictability and cruel treatment of him. He had done her dirty work during the summer, and this is what he received in return. Since he had been left on his own before, he knew how to fend for himself.

As a measure of his intelligence, Larry says he has been reading the *New York Times* since he was twelve years old.

That may be, but he had never had to use it for warmth before. For the next few weeks, he slept outside in Carl Schurz Park (where his mother used to take him as a child) and in Central Park, the newspaper of record his only blanket on those late-summer nights. When it rained and both he and his newspaper got soaked, he either headed for his car or for the stairwell at 1675 York Avenue, curling up on the eighteenth floor (where his mother's apartment was) or the thirty-fourth (the top floor), where he was less likely to be discovered. He even spent a few nights at the apartment of Richard Behrens (his "Uncle George" from childhood), who provided him with spaghetti dinners as well as company.

Initially, Frances had rented Dragon Hall for three months, but she decided to extend the rental to the early part of 1978. When Marc returned from Salt Lake, he joined his mother and Lavinia there for three weeks, before going back to Kent for his junior year. He found out that she had already "burned" a lot of the money he and Larry had sent her, spending $50,000 at Tiffany's alone for one set of earrings.

He also found out that Larry had been banished. Marc told a psychiatrist his mother might have done that because Larry had blamed him for doing most of the stealing. But he felt the real reason was so that Larry, whom Frances was fearful of, could not be in a position to influence him any longer. He was so afraid of being locked out, he told the doctor, that when he was younger he preferred being beaten.

When Larry went back for his senior year at Eastern Military Academy, he found out that his mother had sent strict instructions to the commandant that he not be allowed off the school grounds. This made Larry furious, not only because she would do that but because he hated the school. Since he had a car, though, he left on weekends anyway, often resuming his "comfy" perch in the stairwell.

By Christmas, Larry was still cut off from the family and his car had been stolen. While Frances, Marc and Lavinia spent the holidays at Dragon Hall, Larry was permitted to stay at the apartment because his school was closed over the vacation period. He not only was alone, but had little money.

A few weeks before, his grandmother had written him a letter. She told him how sad and concerned she was about his family's financial situation and that she was sending "all the money I can get my hands on to your mother," including her monthly Social Security check. She expressed the hope that he and Marc would find jobs, reminding him that Frances "had no way of feeding you boys last summer. We have paid for your schools thru your entire education, your dental and doctor bills, rent, etc. It costs at the very least $35,000 to $40,000 a year to support your family in N.Y. and with all your private schools. How can you possibly justify this fabulous sum and no one works? No one in this whole world would attempt such a thing. I only wish I had my hands on lots of money, your family would get every cent."

Shortly after the new year began—cold and bright and full of the usual resolutions—Berenice still could not forget the summer. In another letter to Larry, on January 8, she wrote:

Last summer you and Marc would taunt me, agravate me, jag me into a frenzy, causing me to become very unnerved and at times hysterical; then when I lost self-control, you proceeded to tape my distraut verbal feelings on your tape recorder. You took these tapes home and ran them off for your mother to hear. How very, very unkind, inconsiderate, a horrible thing to do to me, your grandmother. Because of this horrible act on your part she has severed all ties with me. . . . She says to me: "What will Lavinia think when she hears those tapes?" Imagine she plans to perpetuate this horrible act thru all generations to come. To turn my granddaughter against me for a horrible act you boys committed against me. . . .

I'm asking you to destroy ALL those tapes you made in Salt Lake last summer. . . . As long as those tapes are preserved and audited there will be a continued conflict and hatred in our family. Do you want this? It is only a few steps to the incinerator and I suggest you walk those few steps and throw them all down the shute. . . .

Though Larry was the only member of Frances's family who was corresponding with Berenice, she was not giving up on the rest of them. She was *never* going to give up on them. In order to help them, though, she knew there was only one alternative left. She told Frances her plans in a letter on Sunday, January 29, and sent copies to Marc and Larry:

Sunday, Jan 29th, 1978

DEAR FRANCES:

I think I have some good news for you. Dad is in the process of [in]

174

corporating the Auto Parts Stores. I've decided I'm going to get in on this—put my finger in the pie. He says it will take a month to accomplish this project. Mr. Wood [an accountant at Peat, Marwick that Franklin had been dealing with] is working on this. I'm going to make an appointment with Mr. Wood and tell him I'm desirous of being on the board of directors or what ever it is that governs this legal proceedure.

I've raked my brain trying to figure out how I can help support your family. My finances are depleted—even the oil checks don't come in, so I have a new approach. I've decided to go to work for Bapco. Yes, at 74 I'm going to work, for your family. I asked to be put on the pay roll and Dad said as soon as the corporation is completed, which should be in about a month, I can be put on the pay roll. In the mean time I'm going to work for him, and I told him I want pay for it. He keeps saying he is so far behind, maybe my efforts will be appreciated. It is strange, the minute I mentioned "work" he lit up. . . . I'm going to put in as much time as possible down there and see if I can't learn and earn something. . . .

I finally wrote to one of my big oil companies to see why my income had stopped. I'm lying awake nites trying to figure out how to get some income coming in so I can help your family. I am not doing this for myself, every dime of it will go to your family. All I need now is my board and room, which I'm assured of. . . .

I'm devoting my remaining years to helping you and your family in anyway possibly I can. All I ask in return is some respect. If you want to spend the rest of my life hating me you are only hurting yourself. There is no hate in my heart for any of you and I could think of some if I tried.

. . . I think all of us need to bury the past, nothing is gained by dwelling on the past. The future is all that should concern us now. Forgive and forget what has gone on in the past, that is water under the bridge. . . .

All my love,
GRANNY

She said she wanted to see "if I can't learn and earn something." As far as earning, she punched a time clock and got her pay just like every other employee. She received her education in a different way.

Franklin had a new file cabinet in the back—a replacement for the one that his grandsons had broken into the previous summer. The cabinet was just outside the ladies' bathroom, and one day Nancy Jones was in the bathroom and heard somebody trying to open it. Since Franklin was going out of town that day to visit one of his stores, she thought it must be him.

When she came out of the bathroom, she found Berenice.

"Mrs. Bradshaw, Mr. Bradshaw hasn't left town yet," Nancy told her. Berenice shut the drawer, locked it up and took off. "I must have scared her," Nancy recalled, "because she didn't know I was in the restroom. She must have got the key out of his pants and had one made. She knew there was money and checks in there.

"She'd ask how much money we had in our ledgers and we'd show her. We felt, as a wife, she had every right to know. He wouldn't tell her. But after a while, he came in and told us *not* to let her know." Nancy smiled. "I don't think *he* even knew how much he had."

Craig Bradshaw was Franklin's grandnephew and had become very close to him in the past few years. But it hadn't always been that way. Craig's father had been the manager of the Richfield Corporation (which included four of Franklin's stores in southern Utah), and there was very little that Jack Bradshaw and Franklin agreed upon. Jack had a 43 percent share in that corporation and badly wanted to have a controlling one, but Franklin had thwarted his efforts to do so. When Jack committed suicide in 1968, Craig was in his early twenties and wanted to make sure that his mother would be protected financially. Intent on trying to get what his father wanted, Craig had clashes with Franklin over this, and it was not until Craig realized his granduncle was not a man to be crowded that they began to get along fine. In fact, they developed such a fondness for each other that Franklin practically thought of Craig as his own son.

In the early 1970s, Craig and Franklin would drive down to corporation meetings in Craig's old Volkswagen (Franklin was still hitching rides) and Franklin would sit back and hold forth about the old days and his theories on how to make money and succeed in business. He would tell Craig about his oil ventures, how oil was going to be found someday under the pastures they were driving by, and that if somebody was smart he would persuade the farmers to sell their mineral rights. He said how much he had respected his father (John Bradshaw), especially his ability as a businessman. He told of how he would go on the train with him to cattle auctions and of the pride he felt when he was introduced to his father's colleagues as John Bradshaw's son. And he told Craig about how, even as a young boy, he wanted to make money and would dream up ways to do it and tell his father about it.

"Most of the things he talked about," Craig reflected one day, "were the things he accomplished on his own—the self-study he did, and the progress he had made in geology. He felt he had achieved a status in geology greater than most professors at the university [of Utah]. I think he was able to take such pride in the fact that he could pick up on a subject, devour all he could about it, talk circles around experts, and still not have graduated."

At the end of 1976, Franklin decided, partly based on Marilyn's advice, to form limited-partnership trusts for his children and grandchildren as yet another way to shelter his holdings from taxes. He called them F & B (for Franklin and Berenice) and showed his faith in Craig by naming him the trustee.

Craig would often stop at the warehouse at about eight in the evening on his way home just to chat with Franklin and see how he was. "There was *never* a time when he wasn't there," Craig said, "sitting in the back, one little lightbulb burning above him, working on his oil leases. During one of our conversations he asked *me* why *I* was going home so late. I said I had been doing paperwork. 'Let me tell you,' he said, 'what I've learned in this life. The most important thing in life is the family. Make sure that you spend time with them and you do things with them and you enjoy and appreciate them.' This shocked me, because here he was, sitting in his warehouse, which *was* his life. I had always felt he placed work first. His love of achieving financial success and building an empire was what made him happy. I had just assumed that family was not that important to him."

Perhaps the summer of 1977 had made Franklin Bradshaw realize that the Mormons were right after all about the importance of family; had made him realize just how distant he had become from his own, and how empty, finally, the empire he had so brilliantly built was. But if any or all of these things had occurred to him, it was too late—far too late—to change any of that.

22// Berenice seemed to be getting nowhere in her efforts to communicate with Frances. Apparently the previous summer's tapes had destroyed whatever remained of their turbulent relationship. Marc was aligned with his mother so closely that Berenice could not appeal to him either. So she continued to write to Larry. In a Valentine's Day letter, she told him that she had sent his mother some money from the F & B trust, and that she was upset to learn about a car accident Frances and Lavinia had been in just before Christmas and to receive a present back, unopened, that she had sent.

If she had taken a club and beat me over the head she could not have hurt me more than to send that present back "unopened." Why???? must she hurt me like this? . . . I can't sleep, eat, I cry half of the day. I believe if you boys had let me know about her horrible accident I could have come back to N.Y. and "possibly" made her see I am her friend, her very best friend. . . . You can't imagine what I have been thru over the years to help your family—and now I'm hated. Marc has all the same hated feelings towards me his mother has, because she has thoroughly indoctranated him with her feelings.

My grief, my heart ache is more than I can bear. When and how will this all end? If she would receive me I would take the next plane back to N.Y. tomorrow and put my arms around my daughter and granddaughter and love them with all my being. . . .

Please help me, Larry, to bring our family back together. . . . You must try to make her see I'm doing my best to help her and your family. You will have to be very *suttle* about it; she must not think we are trying to gang up on her in any way or it will back-fire and she will be all the worse. . . .

All for tonite, Larry, destroy this letter so no one will ever see it.

Six days later, Berenice was back at the typewriter again. She was sending her letters to Larry at school, and was pleased that he was responding so quickly. But in a way she was wasting her time. Larry was as much on the outside as she was. Even if he had been sympathetic to her feelings and wanted to help, there was not much he could do. But Berenice had no other outlet, so she kept trying.

Monday Feb. 20th, 1978

DEAR LARRY:

You have been very faithful about writing to us and we appreciate it very much. If you didn't write we would never know what is happening to your family. I hope you will continue to keep us informed. You are *our* family and we are concerned about all of you. "Blood is thicker than water" and you don't errase blood ties. . . .

Your mother is causing all of you to suffer because she wants to punish us. For what? Grandpa and I said things, told you boys things we should not have but she has said things about me, done things to me that were pretty horrible too. . . . . I'm never allowed in her house (the door will be bolted shut she says), she intends to turn Lavinia against me by letting her hear the tapes (what is on those tapes, I don't know), she says she is going to tell Lavinia everything (what that means, I don't know). She is hitting on all the meanest things she can think of to destroy me (and she is succeeding, I'm crushed beyond words). . . .

I want to see Lavinia so badly. I sent Frances a check for over $800 so that should help her a lot. I have sent her $100 to $200 every week, what ever I could rake up, plus I nearly always add a few "green backs" in small amounts so she will have bus fare or quickly-needed groceries. If your mother is ever in the hospital again, and she will be, please let me know; maybe at such a time I can pound some sense in her head and make her understand she needs me. Please do this whether she wants you to or not, it's the only way I can think of to bring our family back together. . . .

I went to the grocery store today and the prices of the fruits and vegetables were so terribly high I came away without buying anything. I came home and warmed up some home-made vegetable soup I had on hand and cut up some fruit I had on hand (orange, grapefruit and canned pineapple)—that was my supper. I have quit cooking for myself. About every two weeks I get a beef soup bone (very little meat on it, all I can afford) and cook up a pot of vegetable soup which lasts me about two weeks. . . . I don't buy fresh meat any more. . . . I refuse to pay the price for coffee, I drink tea at home, and when invited out I drink 2 or 3 cups to make up for what I don't have at home. When I go down to the warehouse, which is nearly every day, I drink their coffee. . . .

Your grandfather is still working his long hours but he is ageing and is not well. He hardly eats anything, is getting thinner and thinner. I am worried about his health. He is in the process of getting his auto parts stores cooperated, it is taking longer than he thot it would take. I hope this is accomplished and soon. . . .

all for now, all my love,
GRANNY

A few days after sending this letter to Larry, she wrote Frances that for some reason an oil royalty check that should have come to Gilmer Drive had gone to the warehouse instead. The check was for $15,000 and represented eight months of payments that had been mysteriously "suspended." (Franklin, of course, had diverted all of her oil money to him so that she couldn't send it on to New York. She knew that, but pretended she didn't.)

"What we couldn't do with this amount of money," she wrote. She then said that Franklin had paid a school bill of Larry's and an insurance company premium of Frances's, and that F & B had sent both her and Marc a check. She complimented Larry for staying in touch with her, but closed by telling Frances, "No matter how much we help you, you show no concern for our feelings. All we ask for our generosity to you is appreciation. Is that asking too much?"

Apparently so. The emotional passage she was so desperately seeking back into her daughter's heart remained closed to her. And no amount of money, it seemed, was likely to rectify that.

During Larry's spring vacation in April, he got a job with the Ace Inventory Corporation. The job paid $2.65 an hour, required Larry to take inventory of various supermarkets in New York City, and enabled him eventually to get a room on weekends at the YMCA's Vanderbilt branch on East 47th Street. Not only had Frances (except for one brief period) not changed her feelings about allowing him to stay at home, but she had told him that he would be on his own after he graduated in June.

Though he had little, if any, communication with his mother, he continued to receive Granny's cries for help. On April 9, one day before Lavinia's fifth birthday and three days after Frances's fortieth, Berenice wrote to Larry again.

Dear Larry:

. . . I called your home several times during the Easter vacation and each time Marc answered. Your mother never answers the phone, I wonder how she keeps in touch with her friends. Marc refused to let me talk to her, saying: "She is out or she is asleep." I dread getting Marc on the phone, he is like "talking to a vegetable." . . . Your mother has Marc so brainwashed he doesn't dare say "his soul is his own." I wanted to talk to you, but he always said you were not there or he didn't know where you were. He did let me talk to Lavinia once for a few minutes, but she started calling me "offensive names" so I hung up. I was totally shocked and heart broken my own granddaughter would call me offensive names. I called back a few minutes later and asked Marc who taught Lavinia to call me names and he said: "I don't know." He said you boys were going to get Easter dinner. I said: "What are you preparing for dinner?" He said: "I don't know"—the usual answer. . . . See what I mean about talking to a vegetable. . . .

Thursday was your mother's birthday. I started calling early in the morning and tried all day and evening but she never answered once. Did you get the $100 check I sent to you for Easter? Before Easter I sent your mother $1,000 and each of you kids I sent $100 for Easter and vacation money. Sent a check for $1,100 for Dr. Nelson, her dentist. Last week I sent her another $1,000 plus a $100 check from Grandpa for her birthday and $100 for Lavinia's birthday, which is tomorrow. That makes a total of $3,600 I have sent to her within the month. Never does she write or call and tell me she got all this money and *never* a THANK YOU.

I am working nearly every day. I put in 3 to 5 hours at the warehouse, I get paid $4 an hour, that brings me in around $200 twice a month. Every cent, plus my $200 Social Security, I send to your mother. I got a check from F & B for $2,400 and every cent was sent to your family. . . . So you see I *am working for your family*. Even if she doesn't want to give me credit for helping you. . . .

181

Grandpa is so pleased to have me working down at the warehouse, he "purrs like a kitten.". . . . He is looking very old and is so tired, he still goes to work at 6 A.M. and [comes] home between 8 and 9 P.M. every day. Those are very long hours for a man 76. He still does his morning exercises. I wonder how much longer he can keep this up? Monday April 3rd he was 76. Not one in your family sent him a birthday card. You boys should remember your grandfather on his birthday, April 3rd, and "Father's Day" with a card or a note. . . .

I think you should contact your grandfather regarding your college financing. You have spoken of this scholarship you are "hopeful" of getting. Your grandfather says he does not plan to finance your and Marc's college education. He says you boys are to earn your way thru college. Before you sign up for any college you had better determine how you are going to pay for it. All these years your mother has stuck her kids in expensive private schools and sent us the bills. Never once has she consulted us as to school payments before hand. She is still doing it. She plans to put Lavinia in expensive private schools but she *never asks us if we will pay for it.* Just sends us the bills. . . . No one else in this whole world lives like this. . . .

I think your mother has had a very sad life, she has such poor health also. Your family is on my mind constantly. I love Frances very, very much. . . . There is nothing I would not do for Frances and her family, you mean everything to me. . . .

Between you and me I think she is suffering from a mental break down. I would give my life just to help her. She hates her parents and every relative she has. . . .

All for now. Once more I suggest you destroy my letters; if they get in her hands she will only hate me more.

All my love,
GRANNY

Not long after Larry received this letter, he got one of a different kind: one that said he had won a Reserve Officers Training Corps scholarship to Lehigh University, one of the top engineering schools in the country. The scholarship would pay his tuition and his grandparents were thrilled. Berenice wrote to congratulate him, and to tell him that she too had had a triumph of sorts—Frances had finally deigned to speak with her. She said that if his mother continued to prohibit him from coming home he was welcome in Salt Lake at any time; but she also reinforced Franklin's idea that Larry should get a job for the summer with one of the oil companies. "Forget about that $2.30 [$2.65] an hour in New York," she wrote. "That is crumbs for the chickens."

The Drukmans had returned from New Zealand after more than two and a half years there, and were planning to visit Franklin and Berenice in June. When they arrived with their two sons, Sam and Max, an amazing thing happened. Franklin agreed to take some time off from work, provided it included a little business.

So they all piled into Doug Steele's pale-blue 1968 Belair station wagon and headed south on Interstate 15. They stopped in Lehi, where Franklin was born, then went on to Orem, where he had a store, and finally to Provo and his stores there. Franklin thought they were driving back to Salt Lake after that, but Berenice had other plans for him.

"We really hi-jacked him," she wrote to a cousin of hers, explaining that she had hidden a picnic basket in the car. So they drove on to Provo Canyon and American Fork Canyon, where they had their lunch under the trees. "Grandpa was riding in the back seat, he had to go where the car went," Berenice wrote. "It did Dad good to get away for a day, and the only day he spent with his family."

Three generations of Bradshaws, out for a summer day. Elaine and Mason had heard about the troubles of the previous summer—from Doug, Nancy and Berenice, and in letters from Marilyn—but that did not become a topic of conversation. Not that day. Even Franklin seemed to relax, Mason recalled, and agreed to pose for a picture. The pictures they took of him that day—one of which found its way onto Berenice's mantelpiece next to one of Ronald Reagan—were the last images the Drukmans had of him, and that trip to Utah was the last time they saw him alive.

Concern was growing about Franklin's health. His whole face would get beet-red at the warehouse, and he was becoming quite thin. Berenice was telling everyone, including the Drukmans that he was "wore out" and wasn't eating properly, but that she couldn't get him to a doctor.

Elaine and Mason, however, thought he looked fine. From their bedroom in the basement they could hear him upstairs, well before sunrise, doing his push-ups and jumping rope. But Berenice was certain there was something wrong with him. So she called Franklin's nephew Don Bradshaw, who owned the insurance business where Craig Bradshaw worked and whom she knew Franklin trusted, and pleaded her case.

"Franklin is sick and he won't admit it," Berenice said.

"How do you know he's sick?" Don asked.

"Well, he has these spells and the employees think he's having seizures. He gets very red in the face, he's actually going purple, and I can't get him to go to the doctor."

"Well, what do you want me to do?" Don asked, knowing from experience the danger of getting involved with this branch of the family.

"Maybe you can influence him and get him to go," Berenice said.

Don agreed to try. He called a geriatrics man to ask if he could see his uncle on short notice. The doctor said he could, and then Don called Franklin. He told him that he wanted to pick him up and show him "something," but was not specific. Franklin said fine, and when he got in the car later that day and learned where Don wanted to take him and why, he didn't fight it.

The doctor examined Franklin, and after about twenty minutes, the two of them emerged.

"Your uncle's fine," the doctor told Don. "The only problem is that he's taking a pill an osteopathic doctor told him to take, twenty-five years ago, for the rest of his life. The pill is loaded with nicotinic acid and it's poisoning him to death. That's why he's getting red and having the spells. So I've told him to stop taking it."

When Franklin got back to the warehouse, he boasted to everyone, including Berenice, that he had received a clean bill of health.

The Drukmans weren't the only visitors to Gilmer Drive that summer. No sooner had they left for Manzanita, Oregon, a small town on the coast where they had a house, than Larry boarded a Trailways bus in New York, bound for Salt Lake.

He had just graduated from Eastern Military Academy as the class valedictorian and had given a five-minute speech.

Though he had spent five unhappy years there, this was a proud moment for Larry—one his mother chose not to share with him. "She never cared about my life at EMA," Larry claimed. "She never said anything. I was the black sheep of the family."

When his grandmother told him in her letter that her home was his home, she had done so without consulting Franklin. When he learned that Larry might be coming back to Utah, he agreed to the arrangement on one condition—that Larry get a job, a job far from the Bradshaw warehouse. But once Larry arrived in Salt Lake, he slept late and did not try very hard to find one. He did get one offer—pouring tar for a construction crew—but Berenice refused to let him accept it. "He was not going to bring that kind of dirt in here, no sir," Berenice, a fanatic about cleanliness, said in her living room five years later, still shuddering at the idea.

Instead of making Larry find a "cleaner" job, she decided to let him take flying lessons—a decision that ultimately cost her $3,500. Initially, she was able to pay for the lessons with an oil royalty check she had managed to get her hands on; after Franklin's death, that was no longer a problem.

On Thursday, July 13, the phone rang at the warehouse and Nancy Jones answered it. Marc was calling collect from New York and wanted to speak with his grandmother. Nancy wasn't sure if Berenice was at the warehouse, so she asked the operator to hold. She went in the back and Franklin told her that Berenice was at the spa. So Nancy got back on the phone and gave the number there.

Within minutes, it seemed, Berenice appeared at the warehouse and stormed to the back to find Franklin. Nancy had seen and heard these confrontations before, but this one was beyond earshot. After a while, Franklin came up to the front, where Nancy's office was, and told her to make out a check for $3,000 in the name of Lavinia Schreuder and send it to Frances.

"Nancy, this is the *last* check we'll ever have to send them," he assured her. "Marc said if we send this check they'll *never* have to ask for any more money."

Nancy didn't believe it. She had typed up more checks for

Frances than she could remember in the seven and a half years she had worked for Franklin Bradshaw, and she was certain that by next month she'd be typing another one.

About a week later the phone rang again. Neil Swan, who was working the counter, picked it up. Like the previous week's call, it was for Berenice, collect from New York. Neil asked the operator to hold on and went out to the loading dock, where Berenice and Franklin were standing.

"Mrs. Bradshaw, you have a long-distance call from New York. Do you want to take it?"

Berenice took two steps in the direction of the phone and then stopped.

"No," Berenice said, perhaps thinking it was yet another request for money, "I don't want to talk with her. She's been chasing me all over town." Finally, it seemed, she was taking a stand behind Franklin.

When Swan got back to the phone, there was no one on the line. But just as he began to wait on a customer, the phone rang again.

"Mrs. Bradshaw is not here," Swan told the operator. "She was, but she must have left."

"It is imperative that I talk to Mrs. Bradshaw," the caller said. "I *have* to talk to her. This is her daughter."

"Well, I know she has three daughters," Neil said in his slow drawl. "Which one is it?"

"This is Frances. I've *got* to talk to her."

Frances was extremely upset, but Neil stuck to his story and finally, after some effort, was able to get her off the phone.

On Saturdays, Bradshaw Auto Parts usually closed around four in the afternoon. But as long as he'd been in business, Franklin had never believed in shutting the door on anybody —including his grandson.

All the time that Larry had been in Salt Lake that summer, Franklin, complying with his employees' wishes, had not let him come down to the warehouse to work. But on that Saturday, according to Larry, he called Berenice and asked her to bring Larry down late in the afternoon, when most of the employees would be gone, to help restock certain items.

So Berenice and Larry went to the warehouse and he

worked for a few hours, filling in brake parts and oil filters. At about quarter to eight, they asked Franklin if he wanted to have dinner with them at the Old Spaghetti Factory, but he said no. He had already eaten his meat loaf and bran muffins earlier in the day and said he would see them later.

When Franklin got home from work, he usually watched the local news before going to bed. As he went to sleep that hot July night, he had no way of knowing that it was the last one he would ever spend in the house he had lived in for forty-one years.

23// Dan Schindler was up early that Sunday morning and made a phone call a little after eight o'clock. He needed to get an auto part for a friend of his, and he wanted to see if his old boss Frank Bradshaw was open yet. Schindler, a husky man of twenty-eight, knew that the store didn't open until nine on Sundays, but he also knew Bradshaw was often there long before that. He let the phone ring for a bit, but there was no answer. Maybe he was late this morning, Schindler thought, or down in the basement and couldn't hear it. He decided to wait for a little while, then just drive over.

He got there a few minutes before nine and found a man waiting just inside the front door. His name was Kirk Taylor.

Taylor told Schindler that he had been there for a few minutes, and that no one seemed to be around. He had called out a hello a few times and had begun looking for some fiberglass on the shelves in front of the counter when he thought he heard a rustling noise, then a cough, coming from the rear of the building.

"Oh, that's probably Mr. Bradshaw, working in the back," Schindler said, unconcerned. "I used to work here, and he always lets me look up my own parts behind the counter."

The counter was high and looked even higher because of all the parts catalogs stacked on top of it. When Schindler stepped behind it, he saw something that neither he nor Kirk Taylor would ever forget.

Franklin Bradshaw, seventy-six years old, was lying stretched out on his back on the green linoleum floor in a pool of blood. His eyes and mouth were wide open. His wallet, some change, keys and credit cards were on the floor next to him.

Schindler instantly reached for the telephone by the cash register and dialed the operator. But he hung up quickly and dialed the emergency number, 911, instead. Within a minute, it seemed, Larry Stott, a Salt Lake City police officer, and some paramedics arrived.

No sooner had Schindler and Taylor been escorted outside than Neil Swan, who worked the Sunday shift, drove up.

"What's happened?" Swan asked. He had heard police sirens as he exited from the freeway on Sixth South.

"Mr. Bradshaw's been shot," Schindler said.

"Well, is he dead?" Swan wanted to know. Told that he was, Swan asked to see the body, but at first the police wouldn't let him. When they finally did, he stared a long time at Franklin's face. What he saw would become permanently etched in his memory; Franklin looked like a man who had been terrorized.

Doug Steele didn't work on Sundays and had gone next door to the neighbors that morning for a visit. He had just sat down to have a cup of coffee when his wife came over to tell him he had a phone call. Someone named Dan Schindler was calling, and said it was important.

Doug of course knew Dan as a former employee and now as a customer, but he had never called Doug at home before.

"Doug, I'm sorry to disturb you on a Sunday, but I thought I should let you know. Mr. Bradshaw's been shot. He's dead and the police think it was a robbery."

Doug was stunned. After taking a few seconds to collect himself, he said he would be there just as soon as he could. He drove to the ward to get Clive Davis, who was a member of the bishopric and who Doug knew would be there at that time on Sunday.

Together, they drove to the warehouse, lost in thought. When they arrived, Schindler, Taylor and Swan had already been taken to the police department to give official statements. Doug and Clive were met by Joel Campbell, a handsome, rather cocky, thirty-one-year-old homicide detective who had been assigned to the case. Campbell asked them who they were, and they identified themselves as men who had worked for Frank for more than thirty years. They asked Campbell if they could go inside the warehouse, but he said no. He wanted to know if they knew Berenice well, and when they said they did, asked them to go with the police chaplain and break the news to her.

From the moment Officer Stott first arrived on the scene, he and the other policemen who answered the call had been busy. Don Aldous, from the department's crime lab, had been taking photographs of the inside and the outside of the warehouse and checking for "latents"—latent fingerprints. A partial palm print was lifted from the inside of one of the double doors to the warehouse and from the front left side of the desk next to which Franklin was lying.

Officers Keller and Phelan drew diagrams of the crime scene. Blood samples were taken, a metal fragment was removed, and Sergeant Brent Davis and Lieutenant Roger Kinnersley (who had graduated from high school with Frances) did a search of the roof and building, and checked to see if the other doors were locked. Other officers checked the Sparks Hotel nearby, Pioneer Park, which was a haven for transients, and even a black man walking on the street and innocently carrying three bags of candy and a can of Vienna sausages. (He was quickly released.)

Detective Carl Voyles had arrived at the warehouse at about nine-twenty that morning, roughly twenty minutes after Larry Stott. It had been extremely hot in Salt Lake for the last few days, and as he walked into the warehouse, which did not have air conditioning, he noticed the temperature on a thermometer inside the front door: eighty sweltering degrees, and rising. When he went over to examine Franklin's body, he could tell that Franklin had been shot in the back of the skull. But it wasn't until a little later, when he examined him again, that he noticed a small hole in the back of his shirt, rolled it up, and saw that he had been shot in the back. Two shots at extremely close range—no more than two feet at most.

Everything pointed to a robbery, the police felt: the warehouse was in a high-crime area; the cash register was open; and one of the victim's pockets had been rifled through, its contents strewn about the floor. Yet Roger Kinnersley couldn't erase from his mind what a cold, violent feeling the crime scene had to it. And like Neil Swan, he remembered the look on Franklin Bradshaw's face. "Every crime scene has a feeling to it," Kinnersley said five years after the murder, "and this one felt like an execution."

When Doug and Clive went up with the chaplain to see Berenice and tell her what had happened, she was practically in a state of shock. Doug, knowing that she was "a high-strung gal," gave her some tranquilizers that he knew she had. He was particularly keen to know where Larry was, and she said he had left not long before to go flying out in West Jordan. Doug tried to call Don Bradshaw, but there was no answer, so he called Craig, who was at his local ward, and Craig promised to contact Don and other family members.

The chaplain was trying to help Berenice reach her three daughters, but none of them seemed to be home. He also made arrangements for the bishop of the Yale Ward, just up the street from Berenice and the place where Franklin's sister had often tried to take the girls to Sunday School, to come and pay her a visit.

The chaplain stayed with Berenice while Doug and Clive drove back to the warehouse. By now, Franklin's body had been taken to the Larkin Mortuary, so the police let them search the place.

The first thing Doug did was to go in the direction of his office, which was to the west of the front door. A separate door led to the outside from the area in front of Doug's office, and he noticed that the padlock in the hasp was undone.

"Who unlocked this door?" Doug wanted to know.

"Not us. What's wrong?" one of the officers said. He said that they had checked earlier to see that the building was secured. The lock was in the hasp (as it often is on barn doors) and, from a distance, it *looked* locked. But it wasn't.

"That padlock *had* to have been unlocked," Doug said, quite sure of himself.

"Are the keys missing?" the officer asked. "Where are they usually kept?"

"In Clive's top drawer, right side," Doug said. "Let's go look." They went over to Clive's desk and the keys were there.

"How do you know it wasn't unlocked the night before?" Doug was asked.

"Because I was on the afternoon shift yesterday," Doug explained. "We kept our money in my locked desk drawer. When they ran out of quarters and dollar bills I had to run back to the office to get the change for the till. Every time I'd walk through there, I'd see the padlock locked."

"Are there any other doors you want to check?"

"The back, where the radiator hoses are."

So they walked back to the rear of the warehouse and found that lock in the same position—in the hasp, but unlocked.

"Okay, they covered their asses front and rear," Doug blurted out, "but they made this mistake. It had to be someone who knew where the goddam keys were to those locks."

"Who knew where the keys were?" he was asked.

"Besides Frank, Clive and myself, only the two grand-sons," Doug said. "And Larry is here in Salt Lake."

When Detective Campbell asked Doug to elaborate, he told him a little bit about the previous summer.

Clive Davis and Neil Swan were much more circumspect. When Campbell asked them if they knew of anyone who might want Frank Bradshaw dead, they said no. But asked if it might have been someone in the family, they were less adamant and just shuffled their feet and coughed nervously.

Back at Gilmer Drive, the first family members to reach the house were Don Bradshaw and his wife, Jean. Don is a tall, engaging man with a wide smile and an appealing twinkle in his eye. His way with people and his genuine curiosity about them had made him one of the most successful insurance men in Salt Lake.

Don began quizzing Berenice about the events of the morning. She told him and Jean that Franklin had gotten up and fixed his oatmeal and that his bowl was still in the sink. She said that she got up and fixed Larry's breakfast right after that, because he was flying that day. Berenice asked them if they knew that Larry had been flying that summer and they said they hadn't.

Larry had returned from flying and Berenice introduced him to Don and Jean, who had never met him before. Larry told them that he had been flying over the house, had seen a number of cars parked outside it, and wondered what was going on.

Not long after that, Doug reappeared at the house. He told Don that he had found $331.40 from Saturday afternoon's business in a cardboard box, and asked if Don would come back to the warehouse with him. Clive had gone home, and Doug didn't want to go back there alone. Don agreed to go, while Jean, who was extremely fond of Berenice and had gone to the spa with her on a few occasions, said she would stay behind and help do the dishes.

As soon as Don got into Doug's car, Doug said, "Do you know who the culprit is?"

"No, who?"

"Larry."

"You floored me," Don said. "Tell me about it."

So as they drove down to the warehouse—Doug's third trip there that day—Doug filled Don in about the summer of 1977.

Doug pulled his keys out to unlock the front door to the warehouse. But he didn't need them.

"My God, what's going on?" Doug said. "I locked this door when I left. Am I losing my mind? Did I put this key in and turn it?"

"No," Don said. "You started to, but it pushed open."

They had taken about twenty steps in the direction of Doug's office when Doug suddenly wheeled around and said, "Let's get out of here. *Fast*. There's somebody in here."

They rushed back outside and Don said, "Doug, what's wrong?"

Doug explained that he *always* locked the first door—the heavy door that separated the main part of the warehouse from Doug's office area—when he left, and that he had locked it when he left with Clive an hour before.

"Someone's been in and opened that fire door," Doug insisted. "That's why the front door is open."

At that moment a police car drove by, and Don flagged it down. Doug called Clive, and he returned to the warehouse. Detective Campbell was contacted and, when he arrived, verified that Franklin had had his keys with him when he was murdered. But that didn't satisfy Doug. The suspicion he had about Larry was beginning to deepen.

Doug, Clive and Don decided that all the locks should be changed, and someone from Glens Key, Lock & Safe Company agreed to come over immediately. After that was done, Doug drove Don back up to Gilmer Drive. But before Don got out of the car, clutching a new set of keys that he was going to give Berenice, Doug cautioned him: "Don't let Larry know that those keys have been changed."

When Don walked into the house, the first thing he asked his wife was what Larry had been doing.

"He's a strange kid," Jean said. "He's like a cat and a mouse—he's here, and the next thing I know he's disappeared. I don't know if he's outside or downstairs. I think he's probably left this place a couple of times. Each time Berenice asked him where he'd been he said, 'Oh, just downstairs.'"

Don then told his wife of Doug's suspicions.

"I wouldn't doubt it," Jean said, "the way he's been acting around here."

Don made sure that Larry wasn't around and walked into the kitchen to give the new set of keys to Berenice.

But they didn't stay in her hands long. Don looked around and there was Larry, who not only had heard the conversation but quickly took the keys from her.

Oh brother, I sure blew that, Don thought to himself. He had to have been a cat walking up behind me.

It had been a long and confusing day, and Don suggested to Jean that they should think about going home. But Jean felt they should stay a little longer.

For the first time all day, Berenice started to break down and really cry, having wept briefly earlier when she washed Franklin's oatmeal bowl and the pan he prepared it in. She had had no luck in reaching any of her daughters; in helping her try to contact Elaine, Don had even called and left an

193

urgent message with the sheriff of Tillamook County in Oregon to have Elaine call the second she got home. Don and Jean were just sitting there with Berenice when she tearfully blurted out, "Oh, there is going to be terrible trouble."

"Why is there going to be terrible trouble?" Don wanted to know. "Marilyn is well trained in these estate matters and she's very capable."

"Marilyn will try to take over," Berenice said, "and the others won't let her. There'll be trouble over that."

"Well, you have a whole bunch of nephews—several of whom are attorneys, all of whom will help you," Don assured her.

But Berenice didn't hear him. She just kept telling Don and Jean how they had *no* idea of how much trouble there was going to be.

"My kids don't get along," she told them. "They hate each other. I wish to God abortions had been legal in my day because I would have had four of them. I *never* wanted children. They've been nothing but problems and grief to me." And she went on, Don remembered, ranting and raving about how they had never brought her happiness—just unhappiness and unpleasantness. She even went so far as to suggest that Marilyn's husband wanted Franklin dead so that he could inherit money.

As Don sat there and listened to her, certain memories came back to him. He was about the same age as Robert Bradshaw and they had occasionally played with lead soldiers together. But his mother had told him that Berenice didn't want him to come around too often, because she didn't want Robert to be too influenced by Mormons. In recent years Franklin's secretary would call him and ask him to go by the house to get Berenice's signature on bond applications. More often than not she would say, "I sure wish to hell I knew what I was signing," then ask him, as she practically did the entire town, if he knew what her husband was worth. What he did know, as did many members of the Bradshaw family, was that Frank and Berenice had not had a happy marriage, and that his uncle was "chintzy" with money. After all, it was Don's father who had saved the *Wall Street Journal* for Frank all those years. He had heard that Berenice was still making her own drapes from sackcloth and knew of how often she would try to secure loans from his brother and cousin, who were bankers, without Frank's knowledge. But he had never known, until that day, the extent of the family's problems and unhappiness as she described it.

At that moment the phone rang, bringing Don back to the reality of the day. It was Elaine.

She and Mason had been away for the weekend in Washougal, Washington, just over the state line, and their neighbor had told them the sheriff had been by.

"Elaine, there's been some trouble," Don said calmly. "Your father's been shot."

"Is he dead?"

"Yes."

"Oh my God," she said. "Was it a robbery?"

"I think they think that," Don said. "I don't know, but that's what it indicates." He didn't say any more, but as it turned out, he didn't have to.

"I'll get there as soon as I can. How's Mother?"

"We've been here most of the day, as have many other members of the family. People have brought food for her."

Elaine asked Don for suggestions about the funeral—whom to use and who would be a good person to give a talk. He told her that someone had mentioned Craig Bradshaw, and suggested a family member should formally approach him. Then they said goodbye.

When Elaine got off the phone and told her husband, his first thought was the same as Doug's—Larry had done it. He didn't know whether to say anything to Elaine about his suspicions, but when he did, "she jumped on it, because we knew Larry was there." They not only knew that, but they had heard, just a month before, about the disastrous summer of 1977.

Elaine cried all night. But when the morning came she was composed, ready to go to Salt Lake—and there was plenty she wanted to say.

Marilyn and Bob had left their weekend house early on Sunday afternoon and spent the day with some friends in Brooklyn. No sooner had they gotten home to their apartment on West End Avenue that evening than their phone rang.

"Aunt Marilyn," Larry said, "Granny wants to talk with you."

Berenice got on the phone and told her the news.

As soon as Marilyn hung up she began to sob. "They killed my father," she told Bob. "They killed my father."

Bob tried to comfort her and ask her what happened. All she knew was that her father had been killed early that morning, she said. But by the time they went to bed that night they too had their own suspicions, and Marilyn had made a decision—one that both surprised her husband and hurt his feelings.

She was going to Salt Lake without him the next morning.

Berenice finally reached Frances, who had been away on Long Island all day. Berenice said that the funeral was going to be on Wednesday; Frances said she would be in Salt Lake no later than Tuesday, and that Marc would stay behind and take care of Lavinia.

A few hours earlier, in the late afternoon, Berenice and Larry had been taken by the police chaplain to the eighth floor of the Metropolitan Hall of Justice to be interviewed by Joel Campbell and Carl Voyles.

As Larry waited outside, Campbell took Berenice into an office, told her to try to forget about the tape recorder, then started firing away.

"Is there anyone who would want to hurt your husband?"

"That's what we can't understand," Berenice said. "He didn't have an enemy in the world to our knowledge." Franklin had been dead less than twelve hours, and here she was, trying to explain her husband to two strangers. "He thought a great deal of his employees," she went on. "He always said he didn't care whether he made a cent, his employees came first to him, so there couldn't possibly be any problem there that I know of. . . . And as for friends, everybody liked him, that is, I can't imagine anyone having anything against him."

They wanted to know about his daily routine and she told them that he was always at the warehouse by six o'clock, but that he would get there a little later on Sundays.

Could she pin down what time he had left that morning?

"I would say I heard the car start up and I looked at my clock . . . it was about a quarter to seven. It seemed to me that's what it was."

They asked her when he would open the doors on Sundays. "Well, as soon as he got there," she said. "It appears that this was maybe somebody that was waiting for him. . . . He'd wait on anybody, any time of day or night. . . . He never refused to wait on anybody, and as much as that phone would ring, he'd always answer it and say, 'We're closed, but what can I do for you?'"

When they asked her if he had mentioned any special projects or appointments with anyone for that Sunday, she figured she better set these boys straight. "You know, that man would go to work before six and come home at eight at night and he was so tired, he was so worn out that we did very little talking. Lots of times he'd come home, look at TV and go to bed. We wouldn't exchange two words. . . . There was lots of things I'd like to talk about but I never did because he was just too tired, he just simply was worn out." She told them he worked every day of the year and never took a vacation.

They wanted to know if it would be difficult for someone to obtain his work schedule or if it was pretty well known. She said that not only was it pretty well known, but when he used to stay at the warehouse, sometimes until midnight, she worried about him and wondered why he was never held up.

"Had he had any robberies or burglaries?"

She said that there had been robberies, but not when anyone was there. "Someone has suggested the fact that he was shot in the back," she said. "Maybe they ordered him to get the money and that's why he got shot in the back." She said that was possible, because he never carried much money with him. "Shoot him three times for ten or twenty dollars?" she asked in seeming disbelief. Somehow Berenice had gotten the impression that he was shot three times instead of twice, but Campbell said nothing to correct that. He was moving to the subject he was most interested in discussing—Larry. Having confirmed that Berenice had three daughters and that Larry was Frances's son, Campbell asked: "Okay, what brings Larry down from New York?"

"He came down here to stay with us for the summer."

"Somebody mentioned that he was working at the—" Campbell began.

"No, he isn't working," Berenice broke in.

"—at the store?" Campbell finished.

"No. He's taking air flight lessons right now," she said.

"Air flight?" Campbell asked.

"He wants to get his pilot's license," she said.

"Did he *ever* work down at the store?" Campbell would not be deterred.

"He did last summer," she said.

"Did things go pretty well for him, or were there any problems?" Campbell prompted her.

"Oh no, they had some problems," Berenice admitted. "His brother was here too. . . . The two of them just messed things up down there. . . . That's one reason he isn't down there working now. The employees figured that they took advantage of their grandfather and the other employees didn't, so then his grandfather said, 'Well, look, you can't work there this summer 'cause they don't want you.'" But then she added, "He did go down and help his grandfather a little while yesterday, and his grandfather was pleased to think that he was working and he was pleased to think he was back in the store."

Campbell told her that in the course of investigating the murder it would be his job to look into "every aspect or angle that possibly comes up as to why or why not this crime took place," and wanted her to understand they might have to ask some questions of a sensitive nature. She was seventy-five years old, and he was paying her the proper deference.

"Getting away from store activities," Campbell began, "is there any problems with the family that you know of . . . anyone that wants to get at the money your husband has . . . or someone wants to take over the business and he may be uncomfortable with that, or anything like that at all that might be within the family?"

"Not on that angle," she began, then said: "Frances in New York and her father were not on good terms. They had a falling-out a few years ago, but it wouldn't have anything to do with business."

Campbell took her word on that and simply probed no further. Instead, he switched again to the employees and asked her about Doug Steele and Clive Davis. She assured him that they were "fine, wonderful men. They were behind us one hundred percent on everything."

"Who was going to be executor of the estate?" Campbell asked all of a sudden.

"I don't know that," she said.

"Do you have an attorney for the family or for the business?"

She told him that Alma Boyce, a nephew by marriage, had handled their legal affairs from time to time, but did not mention Dave Salisbury of Van Cott, Bagley.

"Do you know if your husband and you have composed a will, if one is available?"

"He has got a will someplace," she said. "I've seen it, and he had me draw up a will a couple of years ago but they didn't like it and they wouldn't accept it. . . . My family didn't like it and he didn't like it and so it is still there but nobody likes it."

"You don't know where it's at?"

"No, I don't know," she insisted, "but we haven't started to look, really. He has got file upon file down there. I've got a file in my basement, which I haven't even had time to look into, and we've got about three file cabinets downstairs and I just haven't had time. I have had nothing but callers and phones and no time to go down there and look. . . . My daughter [Marilyn], when she was home last Christmas, went through the files pretty much and sorted things."

"Your husband, did he include his employees in his will?"

"Not that I know of," she said.

"Just family?"

"I would say," she said, but then backed off slightly. "I don't know, but I don't think he would."

". . . Somebody mentioned that Larry left basically about the same time as your husband did this morning. Do you know if they left together?"

"Oh no, Larry didn't get up. My husband left home at a quarter to seven and Larry didn't get up until nine." This story conflicted with what Don recalled her saying earlier—that Larry had gotten up "right after Franklin."

"What time does he go to his flight lessons?"

"He was to be there at ten-thirty. He left home about ten," she said.

"About ten?"

"Yes, and he had no sooner left than the doorbell rang and it was these men to tell me about the tragedy," she said. She then asked the police if *they* could imagine who would do such a thing and if there were any eyewitnesses.

They said there weren't, and told her that these cases could be very difficult and take a lot of time to solve.

"You know," she told both of them, "our courts are not rough enough. After they get them, they don't do anything to them. Our jail is full of people just being fed by taxpayers' money that ought to be shot. I believe in capital punishment, so help me." (Utah is one of thirty-eight states that have the death penalty. At that time, executions in Utah were either by firing squad or by hanging. In 1980, hanging was abolished and replaced, three years later, by lethal injection.)

They tried to assure her that if they found out who did it, there would be some justice. But Berenice was skeptical and, in her own forceful way, told them so.

They thanked her for coming down and said they'd be in touch with her in a few days.

Campbell and Voyles had warmed up with Berenice and were ready to confront Larry. Or so they thought. Sitting in front of them was a cool, strong-looking young man of eighteen whom Campbell would later describe as the most unemotional person he'd ever met.

They asked him about his flying, and he said he'd left the house at ten, later had flown over it and seen a number of cars, but had thought nothing of it.

Asked if he had any idea of who might want to hurt his grandfather, he said, "I don't see who would have anything against him. He was a very nice man. He worked hard and he just did his thing."

Campbell asked him about the previous summer and if there had been any problems.

"Well, yeah, a few problems with scheduling and that kind of stuff," Larry said, unshakable.

"How about with the rest of the employees? Any conflicts, friction, anything like that?"

"No, not really," Larry said. "Not me anyway. I never really got to know anybody very well."

Campbell had a slight opening, but he didn't walk through it. He switched to Frances.

"Does your mother work?"

"She gets support from my grandmother."

"Have your mother and your grandfather ever had any problems?"

"No, not really," Larry said, adding paradoxically, "They never really speak to each other. They have never really spoken as long as I can remember."

"They must not like each other, huh?"

"Well, I don't know," he said. "You know, my grandfather doesn't really call, you know. I mean nobody really calls him and he doesn't call his children, if that's what you mean."

Was his mother connected to the business? Campbell asked.

"Well, no. She used to in 1960," Larry said. "She used to be in the oil business, she used to get dividend checks, she had Mountain Fuel stock . . . between him and her but that ended in the late sixties. There were problems or something, you know, I'm not really sure of exactly what."

"Problems between her and your grandfather?"

"Yeah," Larry said. "It pertained to money and all that."

"Was she bitter toward your grandfather?"

"No, but she never speaks about him. It is strictly a business problem, you know, nothing more. I'm not really sure, though."

Larry told Campbell and Voyles that he had been in ROTC and was going to college on an Army ROTC scholarship.

"Did you have any firearms training when you were in the ROTC?"

"Ah, yeah." Larry was slow to answer. "We used to practice. We went to Fort Devens and Fort Dix and we shot the M16 and then we had marksmanship with a .22-caliber rifle and we used to do that every spring."

"Anything larger than that?"

"No, it was just a marksmanship rifle we used," Larry said. He had won a medal in marksmanship two years in a row, but didn't tell the detectives that.

"Do you own any handguns?"

"No."

"Does your grandmother have any up at the house?"

"No, we don't," Larry said. "There are no handguns at our house." He added that his grandmother had wanted his grandfather to buy one and keep it at the store, but he never did.

"Did he ever seem like he was worried about anything lately or depressed?" Campbell asked, his last question of the interview.

"Well, he seemed sort of tired, that's about it. He didn't really seem, you know, like he expected anything, he was just tired. . . . He was worried about his finances, you know, his taxes . . . and he was just worried about the business, you know, how it was going along. He was always worried about it."

Larry then switched roles with the detectives and fired a question at them.

"Do *you* know anything about what could have happened?"

If they had answered in any detail, their answer would have been that Doug Steele had mentioned "the bath of '77" and hinted that they look carefully at the family itself. But they of course didn't tell Larry that. He was their leading suspect.

24// Monday was Pioneer Day in Utah, the biggest holiday of the year. But Clive Davis and Neil Swan didn't feel much like celebrating. They both had had sleepless nights as they reviewed in their minds the events of Sunday. They got together in the morning, talked for a while, and decided to call Joel Campbell. They told him they wanted to come by and that it was important. Clive had mentioned to Campbell on Sunday that he had caught a burglar in the warehouse about two weeks before, but had released him. The next morning, however, some items were missing, and Clive assumed that the burglar had had a confederate hiding in the basement.

When Clive read in Monday's paper that the police thought the individual he had described to them—"male, white, 18 years old, thin build, medium blond hair, 5 feet 10 inches tall"—might be connected to the shooting, he decided to contact Campbell. He didn't want the detective to trail too far from the track Clive felt he should be on.

So late that afternoon, more than twenty-four hours after they had first met Campbell at the warehouse and were rather vague in response to his questions, Clive Davis and Neil Swan found themselves in front of a tape recorder.

Nervous and apprehensive, they told Campbell of their concern that they might be considered suspects. At that point in the investigation *everybody* was a suspect, so the detective couldn't allay their fears.

They had discussed it, they said, and just didn't feel anyone would have shot Franklin for money, "unless it was some guy that just happened to bounce in there and they were drunk and just happened to do it accidentally." No, they said, they just couldn't think of anyone who would have anything against Frank Bradshaw.

So why were they there? What was so important that they needed to see Campbell *that* day? Campbell had a homicide that he was trying to solve. If they could help, fine; if they couldn't, he'd be in touch with them.

Then it came out—what had only been hinted at the day before.

Clive said they didn't really want to get involved with the family, "but he has had this trouble with his daughter back in New York for a long time. Frances. And the two grandsons were out here last summer and they stole quite a bit of money and other things from Mr. Bradshaw, which amounted to an awful lot." They told Campbell about the forged checks, and he asked if it had ever been determined who had actually stolen them.

"I think the whole family was in on it together," Neil said. Then Clive added that if Frances put her sons up to stealing the checks, "she might have put them up to other things."

If Campbell was already considering that possibility, he certainly didn't let on to the two employees. When he asked them more about the checks and if anyone had been prosecuted, they told him that Frank, "for some reason," hadn't wanted to. They said that Nancy Jones would know more about it and would be at the warehouse on Tuesday.

"How would this daughter Frances gain in having him killed?" Campbell asked.

"That's the part we just can't figure out," Clive said. Neil added that "she has us really concerned," but didn't mention the "morning memo" that Doug had shown him more than six months before—the one that would have changed his will and not made any provision for Frances.

They asked if he could have been killed by a "professional," and Campbell said that was a very good possibility, that it could have been somebody who knew Bradshaw would be there alone.

Hearing that, they told him that Marc had charged hundreds of dollars of camera equipment to Franklin the previous summer, and that every Sunday Larry and he had been down there taking pictures of the warehouse. Hence their concern "that someone had hired someone to come down there and kill Mr. Bradshaw."

Once again, Campbell said that it was possible, and agreed with Davis and Swan that it was probably not a real robbery but that it had been made to look like one. Only one pocket had been emptied out, and the papers from Bradshaw's wallet "looked like they had been deliberately laid," he said. "If somebody was frantically getting into a wallet, they wouldn't have been in that order."

The two men again said there wasn't anybody in Salt Lake who would have wanted to kill him, and this brought Neil back once more to the family and the fact that both Mr. and Mrs. Bradshaw argued a good deal of the time with Frances. At Clive's urging, Neil told Campbell about the phone call he had answered a couple of days before the murder—the one from Frances that Berenice did not want to take. He also said that Berenice often sent Frances "quite a bit of money" and that Frank, if he found out about it, would get upset. "Maybe that's one angle," Neil said, trying to be helpful. "That she thought without Frank she could probably get a heck of a lot more money."

Campbell said that he wanted them—and Doug Steele—to take polygraph tests and asked if they had any objection to that. (By law, a person cannot be required to undergo one.) Actually, they said, they would feel much better if they did. Before leaving, the two men couldn't resist coming back to the murder itself, and they were successful, in their own unobtrusive way, in eliciting Campbell's opinions. The detective said that if he were going to *rob* the place, he would do it at the end of the day because it would be dark and there would be a better chance of getting more money. But Campbell said if he were going to *kill* a man, he would do it in the morning, when the streets were quiet. Clive and Neil agreed with him, adding that if someone studied their "system," they would find that nobody except Frank was there on Sunday until nine, that Sunday in fact was "probably the ideal time to kill."

As to whether it was a spur-of-the-moment thing or a planned murder, Campbell said, it was almost impossible to tell. "If a Mafia guy came from New York to kill him, he's gonna kill him just about the same as a robbery really."

But, Campbell concluded, "somebody wanted to make sure he was dead. That is the thing that keeps sticking in my mind. They weren't just shooting to defend themselves or anything else, they just wanted to make sure he was dead."

Detective Joel Campbell would make a certain number of mistakes in his investigation into the killing of Franklin Bradshaw, but this line of thinking would not be one of them.

Elaine and Mason had left Manzanita early that morning for the two-hour drive to Portland's airport. But when they arrived they didn't have enough time to make their flight and park the car as well. So Mason dropped Elaine off and took the next flight after hers to Salt Lake. But as it turned out he got to the family home on Gilmer Drive ahead of her.

Larry and Berenice had met Elaine at the airport, and they all decided to wait until Marilyn's flight arrived from New York. Larry kept pulling Berenice over to the side to talk with her, away from Elaine. Finally, Elaine became perturbed and said, "Mother, *what's* going on?" At first, Elaine remembered, her mother said nothing at all. Then she said, "Larry wants to drive by the warehouse on the way home and check the keys to the door."

Elaine was floored. She couldn't believe what she had just heard. Since the phone call with Don Bradshaw the night before, she had had her suspicions, and they only had increased during the flight from Portland. And though Larry eventually drove them all directly to Gilmer Drive, this little episode certainly did nothing to change them.

Wally Glover had come up from Provo that day and was sitting on the front porch with Mason when Larry came back with his grandmother and two aunts. Like Doug Steele, Clive Davis and Neil Swan, Wally felt certain Frank had not been robbed. He had known Frank long enough to know that he never carried much money with him, and he also knew the details of the previous summer.

Don and Jean Bradshaw had not been the only ones troubled by Larry's strange behavior. Craig Bradshaw had been at the house on Sunday when Larry returned from flying and recalled that Larry received the news of his grandfather's death as if he were getting a weather report. Noticing that Larry was "high as a kite," Howard Bradshaw had called Joel Campbell, pressing him to check whether Larry had actually gone flying. (Campbell did, and Skyhawk Aviation confirmed that Larry had booked and paid for two hours of time—from ten-thirty to twelve-thirty—and checked out a plane, but could not say for sure that he had actually flown.)

Just as he had on Sunday, Larry would be there one minute and gone the next. Mason and Elaine were going to sleep in the basement that night, and at one point during that Monday, Mason was down there and aware that someone else was too: Larry, who had been on the phone for a very long time.

"He had this funny smile on his face," Mason remembered. "I thought about eavesdropping. Elaine and I had our suspicions, but when you face it straight on, you can't do it. The thought seemed so horrible to me. Maybe I didn't want to listen for fear of hearing what I thought I might hear."

What everyone did hear was that Frances was unaccountably detained and wouldn't be arriving until the next day—a clear signal to Elaine and Marilyn that they had better get moving. So, along with Berenice and Mason, they went down to the warehouse to begin rummaging through Franklin's belongings. Before they began their search, Doug gave them two things—$1,000 from the till because they were broke, and something else. He took Elaine and Marilyn aside and showed them the two memos that Franklin had drawn up regarding his will and that Doug had kept in his private file. When Elaine saw these, certain things began clicking into place in her mind.

As Doug watched them work their way through the warehouse like a tornado, he was a dejected man.

"I was frustrated as hell," Doug said, "and felt our world had been destroyed. All of a sudden the Godfather was gone—what happens now? It was a helpless feeling, a feeling of loss, of some security that had been taken away from you after thirty-two years. The fact that you put up with him for that long," he said with a half-smile, "shows you have a lot of compassion, a lot of feeling for the guy."

The body was not even cold, yet the family was packing Franklin's belongings into boxes and examining his files. They were searching for cash and stock certificates, and, though Berenice didn't know it, they were searching primarily for a new will—one that he might have drawn up after he had done that "morning memo" of intent. They knew that under the original 1970 will Berenice would get everything, but under the "new will"—if there was one—Marilyn and Elaine would receive a third apiece. They looked everywhere, from the top of the warehouse to the dark basement, and they couldn't find it. All they could find was the 1970 will, but even with that there was a problem: they could find only *copies* of it, not the original.

Families react to death in strange and different ways. Marilyn and Elaine were reacting by instinct. They knew that once Frances got to town, things could change and change quickly. They knew that no matter how awful Frances might have been to their mother in the past, she possessed the capacity, at any time, to have Berenice eating out of her hand for as long as she desired.

With the long history of the family and its problems clearly etched in their minds, Marilyn and Elaine were doing what they felt they had to do, what they were entitled to do, and, perhaps, what their father would have wanted them to do. But that did not make their activities in the warehouse any easier for the employees to accept.

As much as Nancy Jones liked both Marilyn and Elaine, she resented all the upheaval. "They just moved right in on top of us and upset everybody," she recalled. "They got boxes and started throwing things away. They were just going through *everything*—every piece of paper and envelope they could find. They hadn't even had the funeral yet."

Berenice found some coins, and Doug recalled how sad it was, standing there and watching her carefully count them. Marilyn put her hand into an envelope with a 1950s postmark and found four $100 bills. Elaine, feeling that the old orange and lemon crates with the artists' illustrations on the side that her father used to hold parts were "a piece of history," began to gather a number of those together.

"It was an amazing experience," Mason recalled, "the utter chaos of that warehouse. *This* is where his life was: spare socks, peanut-butter jars, changes of clothing, a suit, money scotched away in various places. When one area got too cluttered, he'd carve out space somewhere else. It was like a catacomb—only a totally unintelligible one to me. There was a room in the basement, totally enclosed, with stuff from the early forties—auto parts and various records— as well as money and silver dollars." After a long pause he said, "It must have been a ball for those kids—to find money in all sorts of places."

Marilyn and Elaine were not the only two people to arrive from out of town on Monday. Franklin's only living siblings, Bertha Beck and Emma Marie Monson, came from California. When Berenice phoned Bertha that Sunday to tell her the news, Bertha told her that when she got to town she was coming to see her directly.

"I wanted to see her before the girls got there. I tried to talk with her in the way Franklin might have. I told her to work with the attorneys and *not* to go all the way with any of the daughters or there would be perfect hell in the family."

But the family had something to tell Bertha—something that deeply upset her. They were not going to bury Franklin.

They were going to cremate him and simply have a memorial service on Wednesday. Mormons believe strongly in burial, in viewing the body, in long funerals in which they recite their history, and, of course, in the hereafter—and Bertha was certain that Franklin would want a proper burial. He might not have been as religious as his sister would have liked, but he was still a Mormon, Bertha felt, and cremation was repugnant to her—a final slap in the face.

Bertha appealed strenuously to Berenice, but she said it was up to Marilyn. Marilyn and Elaine felt they understood their father's religious beliefs far better than their aunt, and told Bertha they were sure he would have wanted it this way. He hated funerals anyway, they felt, and wouldn't want a big fuss—nor a big expense—made for his own. Bertha offered to pay for everything, but was turned down. Five years later Don Bradshaw said, "I don't think Frank would have given it any thought either way. I think the incident was just the marshaling of people against people at that point—the survivors feeling nervous about the Church people."

So the body of Franklin James Bradshaw was transported north to the Aultorest in Ogden—the town where he and Berenice had married and where he had one of his auto-parts stores. When his ashes came back to Salt Lake, they were in a brown wooden box.

On Tuesday afternoon, at ten minutes past two, Marilyn began her interview with Joel Campbell. She was sitting in the same room at the police department where Clive Davis and Neil Swan had been the day before, and where her mother and Larry had been taken the day before that. Elaine and Mason were waiting outside; as soon as Marilyn was finished, it would be Elaine's turn.

Marilyn wanted to talk about the confusing situation regarding her father's will and Campbell was more than happy to let her, having learned enough in forty-eight hours to know that the issue of money was of great concern to everyone involved. She explained about the 1970 will and the memo that Doug had given her—"the outline of what he wanted to do," she said.

"Okay," Campbell said, "so this doesn't include, what's

that one sister's name?" He'd been on the case two days and was still having difficulty keeping everybody's name straight.

"Frances," Marilyn said.

Campbell wanted to know if she felt there was anybody who would want to kill her father.

"Nobody."

"Not a soul?"

"The only one that I know that would act irrationally, and I'm not sure—"

"This is strictly confidential," Campbell assured her.

"The only . . ." Marilyn hesitated. "My sister and her family have been supported off and on by my parents. She has played Mother against Dad for years." There it was, out in the open.

"This is Frances?"

"Frances. She is not living in a modest manner. She is living in a very expensive way. She has no income at all. This has been a problem for my parents to support her and her family for years. She forged some checks last summer on Dad's bank account. And that made him very angry and that's why he rewrote the will." The mysterious will that nobody could find.

Marilyn assured Campbell that even though her father hadn't prosecuted Frances for the forgeries, she was going to make sure that the lawyer for the estate understood it was not a gift.

"What was the relationship between Frances and Mrs. Bradshaw?" Campbell probed.

"Off and on," Marilyn said.

"Mr. Swan told me that Thursday, before this happened, he received a long-distance call, a person to person to Mrs. Bradshaw from Frances, but . . . that Mrs. Bradshaw didn't want anything to do with her at that time."

"She is tired of discussing family matters over the telephone in front of employees and other people," Marilyn said. "That is why she refused the call at that time, which, of course, would do nothing but make Frances madder."

Campbell asked about the funeral arrangements and the viewing of the body, and Marilyn told him that her father was going to be cremated, much to his family's distress, and that a memorial service would be held on Wednesday at noon. "It would fit with Dad," she said. "He would not pay for a coffin, he would not pay for embalming, and he would not want his body viewed."

Campbell said that he wanted to have a plain-clothes officer at the service, asked if there would be a guest book, and was told there would be.

Did Marilyn think Frances would be against talking to him when she got to town? Campbell asked.

"No," Marilyn said, but cautioned him: "Handle her carefully."

Campbell came back to the "new will" and asked Marilyn if she felt *positive* that Doug Steele, Clive Davis and Neil Swan knew about it.

"I don't know about Swan, I think so. Yeah, Clive knew about it. Doug definitely knew about it. He drove Dad down to Walker Bank. And Dad said, 'I'm going to do it today,' and when he came back Doug said, 'Did you do it?' and Dad said, 'Yes,' and he said, 'Did you remember the fifteen dollars?' and he said, 'Yes,' meaning leaving her fifteen dollars." (Marilyn was referring to a *separate* trip from the one Frank and Doug made to Second South and Main to see a lawyer on the morning Frank had shown Doug the memo; this trip to the bank was apparently to have his "new" will witnessed—if, of course, there was a "new" will.)

"As a joke?" Campbell asked.

"As a gesture," Marilyn said. "In other words, intentionally writing her out."

Campbell was troubled. He sensed that some of these employees knew a great deal more than they were letting on to him. So he asked Marilyn what she thought about Doug and Clive, and she said she had no suspicions of them whatsoever, that they had worked with her father for years and that he had helped them to make money, which was true. Still, Campbell couldn't dismiss anyone or anything at this point in the investigation.

Marilyn told Campbell that she and Elaine had been through many of her father's files, both at home and at the warehouse, and were going to continue sorting through things that evening at the Deseret Inn. They had spent Monday night at the house, but when their mother told them that

Frances said she wanted to spend time with her alone when she arrived, Marilyn suggested they move out and avoid any friction.

"There is no one in his immediate sphere," Marilyn, anxious to drive the point home, said of her father before the interview ended, "who would have any reason . . . to want to do him in, [except for] the one suggestion that we have made and I hate to think about it."

In Elaine Drukman, Joel Campbell found a woman much less reluctant to express her feelings than her sister initially had been. When Campbell asked her if there was anyone, assuming it was *not* a robbery, who might want to kill her father, she said, "Well, when I first found out how my father died, something did flash into my head, because there is one person who would want to hurt him."

"And who is that?"

"My sister Frances," Elaine said, "and what flashed into my head was, 'Oh my God, Larry's there.' "

"You thought maybe Larry had some connection to it?" Campbell asked, playing the innocent.

"That was just what flashed into my head because I know what he did last summer. He hurt my father terribly last summer."

She told him what she knew of the previous summer, much of which Campbell had heard before, and added that Frances had been forging her father's signature for many years.

Campbell wanted her opinion of Doug Steele and Clive Davis, and she, like Marilyn, said she trusted them and that her father did as well. Campbell assured her that he wasn't trying to draw any conclusions, but had to look at all angles. He then switched back to Larry.

"On the morning this happened, Mrs. Bradshaw told us that Larry had gone out to the airport for flying lessons and didn't leave the house until ten in the morning. Is there any reason why she would ever want to protect him in any way?"

"Yes." Elaine did not hesitate.

"Would she?"

"She told me two different stories."

"About Larry?"

"Yes."

"What did she tell you?"

"She told me what you just told me—second. First she told me that on Sunday morning she heard Dad leave and that shortly after that Larry left, and *then* she told me about the flying lessons. . . . I thought maybe when she said Larry left shortly afterwards she could have telescoped her time, I didn't know. I think she would protect him, and I feel terrible because I worry that, you know, I'm too suspicious. It's a terrible thing to be suspicious of somebody like that, and so I just reckoned that she'd telescoped her time and mixed it up."

"Now she told us that he didn't wake up until nine o'clock," Campbell said. "Has she said anything to you about that?"

Elaine said she hadn't, but added that she hadn't really been able to sit and talk with her in a relaxed way.

"If you get a chance to bring that up again," Campbell suggested, "you know, casually. I don't know if you will or not, it is kind of touchy, but if you do, try and get a feeling for that."

"A couple of glasses of wine will do it," Elaine said, "but I haven't had the chance."

"That's terrible," Campbell said, appalled. Like all strict Mormons, Campbell followed Joseph Smith's Word of Wisdom, and abstained from alcohol, coffee, tea and tobacco.

"It's a terrible business," Elaine reminded him. She told him how chaotic things were at the warehouse, then dropped another bomb on him.

"There was one thing that had bothered me when I was picked up at the airport. Larry was trying to make excuses to get back to the warehouse and to try the keys, he said. I don't know why or what was happening."

"That was when, this morning?"

"No, yesterday."

"Yesterday? Larry was with Mrs. Bradshaw?" Campbell knew that the locks had been changed, but he didn't know that Larry did.

"Yesterday morning," Elaine said. "Trying to persuade Mother they should go to the warehouse."

"To try what keys—do you have any idea?" Campbell was alarmed.

"I don't know," Elaine said, "I don't know. See, Doug immediately changed keys."

"Yeah," Campbell said, "he told me he had a locksmith come in."

"Yeah," Elaine said, "Larry wanted to try the keys."

"That's strange," Campbell said.

"Anyway, that worried me a bit," she said, and stood up to leave.

"I'm sorry if you're upset," Campbell said, trying to be compassionate.

"How could I help . . ." she began to say, then dropped her voice. "My father had another ten years. He was a healthy man. He didn't deserve it. Nobody does."

A little over two days had elapsed since Joel Campbell had arrived at the Bradshaw Auto Parts warehouse at nine forty-five on that Sunday morning to begin his investigation. As he conducted his interviews, the message he got had begun as a hint and soon became a clear instruction: look in the direction of Frances and her family. Elaine was even suggesting that her own mother might somehow be involved.

Frances was arriving later that day. As Campbell drove home that afternoon, he recalled what Marilyn had told him: *Handle her carefully.*

Few things in Frances's life seemed to go smoothly. She couldn't get a direct flight to Salt Lake that Tuesday, so she flew to Chicago. But when she got there, the flight she was planning to take turned out to be overbooked. So she flew to Los Angeles and then back to Salt Lake. By the time she arrived at 1327 Gilmer Drive she was exhausted. Her mother suggested that she sleep in her father's room, but she chose to stay in the basement, where Larry was.

The following morning—the day of the memorial service—Frances was in the basement, wearing her bathrobe and preparing to go upstairs. She hadn't seen Elaine since her suspension from Bryn Mawr and was nervous about it, as well as seeing the rest of the family.

"I can't go up and face them," Frances said to her mother. "They hate me."

"They should be ashamed of themselves," Berenice replied, and persuaded her to go up.

When the two sisters saw each other, Frances said coolly, "You are Elaine, I presume."

"Yes, I am," Elaine said, equally cool, the emotional distance between them far greater than the twenty years since they had last seen each other. Beyond this superficial greeting, they had little to say. In another hour they would be sitting on either side of their mother at the memorial service.

The service was held at Eastman's Evans & Early Chapel, a Masonic establishment of the family's choosing and another snub to Bertha and the rest of the Bradshaw family. It was another steamy July day, just like the one Franklin had been murdered on, and the chapel was filled to overflowing. The warehouse was closed that morning and many of his employees were there, as well as business associates and friends throughout the community. It had been decided that Wayne Hacking, Franklin's cousin and the manager of one of his Provo stores, and Craig Bradshaw would each speak during the services.

"I have heard it said that each of us, as we walk through the sands of time," Craig began after Hacking's brief comments and a vocal solo of "In the Garden," "leaves some kind of mark. I believe we are thinking and speaking today of a man who left some very distinct footprints in those sands."

Craig compared his granduncle's life to a great novel and told of how "industrious" and "ambitious" Franklin was. He talked about his "desire to excel" and his "generosity," citing contributions to departing LDS missionaries and money to family members in need. He talked about Franklin's "wealth" and that he was "a frugal man in his management of that wealth," which brought a smile to a number of people's faces. He told the gathering what a good listener Franklin was and how he would often stop by the warehouse on his way home from work for a chat and that Franklin was always willing to give of his time.

He mentioned how proud Franklin was that his business provided a living for two hundred families across the state, how much Franklin had contributed to the good name of Bradshaw throughout Utah, and how much Craig appreciated that.

"There is grief in losing a loved one," Craig said, "but the grief belongs to those who are left behind, not the one who departs." Wanting to comfort her mother, Elaine reached to take Berenice's hand, but her mother pulled back and took Frances's instead. Frances was sobbing loudly, her mascara running down her face. "We grieve," Craig continued, "because we have lost something that will be missed: a father, a husband, a counselor, an adviser, an employer, a friend and a patriarch."

Craig then spoke of the hereafter, and how God "gives us a hope that when we leave this life we are welcomed elsewhere by others who have gone before." As she sat there, Bertha remembered how she had told her brother many times that when he got to heaven there wouldn't be any auto-parts stores and oil wells waiting for him, and how he had always smiled.

Saying that he believed this to be the message of the Twenty-third Psalm, Craig read it, at the request of the family. After a vocal solo of "Goin' Home" and a closing prayer, the service was over.

Back at Gilmer Drive there was tremendous tension. Frances spent a great deal of time in the basement during the open house, and a number of people were aware of it. One of them was Nancy Jones, who had never met Frances before but felt as if she had known her for years.

"She was on the phone most of the time I was there," Nancy remembered. "Everything was in a whisper." Nancy, who said later that she "just knew" that Larry had come back to Salt Lake to kill his grandfather, felt Frances was responsible for the murder as well and asked Berenice whom Frances was talking with. Berenice said she was speaking with Marc, who was back in New York with Lavinia.

When Frances wasn't on the phone, she was ignoring Larry. That wasn't lost on Doug Steele, who had been observing them closely. "I don't have much to do with him," Frances told him. "I've just dismissed him from my mind."

Later that afternoon, she and Berenice began shouting at each other about Larry and the possible change of his name from Schreuder to Bradshaw. (In 1974, after she separated from Frederick, Frances suggested to Larry that he think about changing his name, but that he should wait until he was eighteen. Larry liked the idea and began etching the initials L.J.B. into the walls and desks of Eastern Military Academy, "just to get used to it." By 1976, he began to refer to himself as Larry Bradshaw in *The Occupier,* a family newspaper that he had begun writing and publishing once, sometimes twice, a month two years earlier. Since Larry was now eighteen and entering college the following month, Berenice was about to begin the legal paperwork for his name change in Salt Lake.) But why were she and Frances shouting at each other about it? And why of all times now? If it could be proved that Larry had murdered Franklin—and nearly everybody at the house that day thought so—changing his name yet again was certainly not going to prevent his arrest and prosecution.

Frances had agreed to meet Joel Campbell later that afternoon, and the detective began his interview with her at ten minutes to five. He started out slowly, asking her what she thought and how much she'd heard about her father's death.

"I've heard very little," Frances said, "until I got home last night and I saw a newspaper clipping and my mother called me on the phone and she didn't know too much and then she called later on and we spoke and, you know, I've learned more and more information this afternoon."

Joel asked *what* exactly she had heard.

"He never knew what hit him," she said bluntly.

"Pardon?" Perhaps he hadn't heard her properly.

"He never knew what hit him," she repeated.

"Probably not," Campbell said. "Do you know how he died? Have you been told that?"

She said she had.

"Do you have any idea who might have wanted to kill him?"

She said she hadn't.

"Any idea at all?" he pressed.

217

"No," Frances said, but then added, "I only have one thought that goes through my mind and that is that my father was a stubborn man. He could be difficult if he wanted to, but everyone loved him. . . . For years and years everyone begged him to stop working so late at night because of the bad neighborhood, and he wouldn't. . . . It was his way of life. He was what you call a compulsive worker." She then told him how, as a little girl, she used to go down after school and work for him and that even then it was pretty "sleazy" in that area with drunks walking the street.

Campbell could tell she was nervous and told her to "just relax, if you can." He asked if she had heard the family discussing what they thought might have happened or who might want to kill him. She said she hadn't heard them discussing anything nor did she have any ideas of her own. Campbell was on a fishing expedition, but Frances wasn't even nibbling at his bait.

Undeterred, he moved to the thorny topic of the previous summer.

"I understand that last summer there was some bit of a problem with the boys working at the company. Do you have any idea of what that was about?"

"I was furious at them," she said without hesitation.

"You were what?" Campbell was having trouble hearing her.

"Furious with them," she repeated, "but they are basically very fine boys." She said that while her mother's intentions were good, she had a habit of screaming at them and didn't know how to handle teenagers. She said that she was reluctant to let her sons come out to Salt Lake to work, but after saying no to her mother in 1976, she relented in 1977.

"What kind of trouble did they have down there?"

She said that each one blamed the other, but after a second said, "You know, Larry—" then stopped herself. "I don't want to, you know—"

"Now this is strictly confidential," Campbell assured her, quietly confident that he was about to advance his investigation.

"I don't care," Frances said, "they're my sons." So she proceeded to tell Campbell how Larry would punch in the time clock and go off to the park and read the *New York Times*. But Campbell was after answers to the major things he'd heard about.

"Was there some property stolen during that time? Did the boys steal some things from the company?"

"I heard that there was something stolen," Frances said, battening down the hatches.

"Do you have any idea what that was all about?"

"No," she replied.

"Don't you?"

"No," she repeated.

Campbell decided to stop being coy. "Well, were there some checks stolen from your father?"

"Yes," she admitted.

"Or some forgeries?"

"Yes," she said.

"Okay," Campbell said, finally getting somewhere, "now tell me what that was all about."

"No," she said, then gave her reason: "Because my mother has done it for years."

"Your mother?" Campbell was surprised.

"I'm sorry," Frances apologized. "I don't want to say anything more about that."

"Okay," Campbell said, backing off. "Did that get all worked out? Did that problem get solved?"

"Yes," she assured him.

Not the most aggressive homicide detective in the department, Campbell didn't push it further. Instead, he asked if her father might have made some enemies in the course of doing business.

She said that he was a very competitive person and that people got annoyed at him because he always held out, in his oil dealings, for the best price. But, she said, she could not think of anyone who didn't respect him.

"Were you pretty close to him yourself?"

She said that depended on what he meant by close.

"Well, did you have a good relationship with him? So that you knew—"

"I had a very good relationship with my father," Frances cut him off, "and through the years we disagreed very much about some personal things. Other than that we were very close, very, very close. I knew my father better than anyone, even my own mother."

Campbell decided to test another troublesome item on his agenda. "Do you know if he left a will?"

"My sisters are trying to find his will. They found one will yesterday, but there is an updated one I think they haven't found yet." She said that to the best of her knowledge he had signed a new will *that year,* and that she probably knew about it from her mother, "because she usually writes me at the time something happens."

Instead of asking her about the memo he had been shown, and whether her mother had told her about *that,* Campbell simply asked if she knew how her father's will was divided. She was not entirely certain, she said, but she in no way indicated she might not be in it. She did say, however, that the new will was "completely changed over" from the 1970 will, which she claimed not to understand. "It's Greek to me, you know," Frances said, trying to persuade Campbell of her legal ignorance.

Campbell wanted to know how she derived her income and supported her family. Instead of answering him directly, she said she'd had a rather complicated life—two husbands, two divorces, occasional jobs. She said she wanted to get a legal degree through New York University's School of Continuing Education, but that her parents were against the idea. They told her she had a very young daughter, and should wait at least a year. So they paid her rent, she said, because they wanted her to stay home with her daughter. She said that her mother had been sending her money and that she had been getting her own stock in Mountain Fuel in order to keep her and her family afloat. She had planned to go into hospital administration, she said, but then she had a car accident in December that still caused her pain and might require surgery.

Campbell was about to wind up the interview and asked Frances if there was anything else she wanted to say before she left. She said she was upset and couldn't think of anything, but did suggest he might ask specific questions. Instead of seizing the opportunity to ask again about the summer of 1977 or even the memo that Marilyn had given him a copy of, he asked about her father's oil dealings and if there was any chance that someone, whose name he had used on a lease which he eventually made a lot of money from, would be angry enough to want to hurt him. She said it was possible, but that she didn't know all the names he had used over the years.

He asked if she would have any objection to taking a polygraph test. No, she said, but wanted to know if it could be done in New York. He said that he'd be in touch with her if it was necessary.

Before she left, she asked about the lead the newspaper said the police had—the one referring to the burglar who had been caught in the warehouse a few weeks before the murder.

"We have lots of leads to follow," Campbell said, "but nothing concrete yet."

She reminded him that burglaries in that area and employee thefts of merchandise were common occurrences, implying, as no one else had, that robbery was the probable motive in the killing of her father.

The rambling interview was over. The next time Campbell spoke with her, they were not sitting across a table with a tape recorder between them. They were on opposite ends of a long-distance telephone call. He asked to speak with Marc, and Frances hung up on him.

25// In the days following Franklin's memorial service, the family was faced with a number of problems. They had a photostat copy of his 1970 will but not the original one. Unless the "new will" that everyone was talking about could be found, the family could either declare Franklin intestate or agree to enter the will they did have into probate.

At Marilyn's urging, one of her cousins, who was also a lawyer, went to the Pioneer branch of Walker Bank to see if anyone there remembered witnessing a will that her father might have brought in. Nobody did. Nor did any lawyers in town come forward to say they had a copy of it in their files. Franklin had bought a book about how to make a will, Doug Steele told everyone, and the feeling was that he might have done it himself. Either the new will had vanished or, Marilyn and Elaine felt, somebody had stolen it. Much as they disliked the notion, they were suspicious of Larry and their mother, especially when they found out that she had been caught snooping in Franklin's locked file cabinet earlier in the year. That Berenice and Larry were at the warehouse the night before the murder certainly did nothing to allay those suspicions.

The family also faced tax problems. There were two reasons why Franklin Bradshaw could boast that he had *any* auto part, new or old, people were looking for: because it was true, and because the more he had in inventory, the less he had to declare as profit and pay in taxes at the time. Craig Bradshaw had warned him that this was going to be a problem when he died, but Franklin told him not to worry. He must really have believed he was going to live forever. When he died, his only life insurance was a policy worth $7,000. "It is ironic," Craig Bradshaw said, "that for a guy who hated to pay taxes as much as he did, a huge percentage of his estate went to taxes in the end because he hadn't completely faced his problems."

Even before Franklin died, Berenice and Frances were concerned that Marilyn was trying to take over. She wanted to be executor of his estate and learn more and more about his financial dealings. He had paid for her to get an M.B.A. and a paralegal certificate and she wanted to follow in his footsteps. Within hours after her husband's murder, Berenice was expressing her concern about this to everyone—and her determination not to let that happen.

But Marilyn was an equally determined, headstrong woman. If the new will naming her as co-executor could not be found, she was going to have to move quickly to establish a foothold in the Bradshaw empire. She wanted to oversee the management of F & B; she mentioned to some shareholders in the Bradshaw Investment Company (consisting of real-estate holdings and some of Franklin's huge array of oil and gas leases) that she was interested in eventually buying their stock from them; and, according to her husband, she wanted to become involved with the auto-parts business as well (feeling she could work well with Doug and Clive). While she was not planning to move to Salt Lake, she did take out a lease on an office in the Crane Building, across the way from the warehouse, in order to have a central location when she came to town.

As Craig Bradshaw said later, "I feel Marilyn wanted to take over where her dad left off—at the top of the empire—and run it, but I think she found it was more involved than she first thought." She certainly did. No sooner had she taken the lease on the office, which Berenice ironically agreed to pay for at first, than she learned that her mother had canceled it.

But ambition was not the only reason Marilyn decided to stay on in Salt Lake after her sisters went home. She was becoming obsessed with the idea that Larry had murdered her father, and didn't want to leave him alone with her mother in the house. When Larry wasn't around, she searched the house for anything she could find—keys, the gun, the new will, any sort of clue. She watched Larry's every movement and was eager to know when he was planning to go home. He said that he was going to stay until he got his pilot's license, and so Marilyn decided that she would stay too. When he first began flying, Larry had said that he wanted his grandparents to be the first passengers he took for a ride when he got his license. Since that was no longer possible, he took Berenice and Marilyn for one. Though they were both extremely nervous, an idea came to Marilyn while they were in the air: maybe Larry had flown over the Great Salt Lake that Sunday morning and dropped the gun into it.

Bertha Beck did not leave Salt Lake right after the memorial service either. Still unhappy about being defeated in her efforts to stop her brother's cremation, she was determined to have a say in where his ashes would be buried. Bertha wanted them to be put into the ground in the tree-shaded cemetery in Lehi. She did some checking and discovered that one grave remained in the family plot.

Franklin's father and mother were buried there, and so was one of his brothers. Knowing how much he loved Lehi, Bertha told Berenice, she was sure that he would want to be laid to rest there. Berenice agreed with her, and so on August 1 the brown wooden box that contained his ashes was taken to Lehi and given a proper burial.

Bertha was still upset, though, and wanted to tell Berenice: "Well, are you pleased with yourself, bringing him home to Lehi in a little box?" But she didn't. The important thing was that she finally had her brother back—back on Mormon soil and, to her mind, back home where he belonged.

Each morning that Lieutenant Roger Kinnersley walked into the homicide division of the Salt Lake City Police Department, he asked the same question: Who killed Franklin Bradshaw? Joel Campbell did not have the answer. He had opinions, his own and other people's, but no evidence. And he knew that if he couldn't advance his case in any substantial way—and fast—he would not be able to continue work on it fulltime. Since it was summer, a number of detectives were on vacation, and Campbell would soon have to help on other unsolved crimes as well. Carl Voyles, the other detective who had begun working the Bradshaw case with him, was pulled off it for just that reason. So Campbell was essentially handling it alone.

The morning after his interview with Frances, he spoke with Nancy Jones. She told him about things he had already heard but provided some new information: when Franklin had presented her with the draft of a new will she typed up a "formal letter," eliminating Frances from it. (Later, she said that by "formal letter" she really meant the memo.) She said that she was keenly aware of the tension between Franklin and Frances; he not only confided in her more than he did in Berenice, but she had seen a substantial amount of correspondence between them. She told him about the phone call Marc made on July 13 to Berenice and the $3,000 check they sent so that Frances would not be evicted from her apartment. And she also told him that an employee had been fired recently from one of the branch stores for "unknown reasons."

After Nancy left, Campbell interviewed Berenice and Larry again. She was growing impatient with the detective's questions and said there was no doubt in her mind that Larry did not get up until nine that morning and did not leave home until ten. She was certain of that, she said, because she woke him up so he wouldn't be late. When Campbell spoke with Larry it was an exercise in frustration, so he asked Larry if he would take a polygraph test the following week. Larry said he would, but then failed to keep the appointment.

Campbell had previously spoken with the boy who delivered the *Salt Lake Tribune* to the warehouse. First he said he delivered it about seven-thirty that Sunday, then changed his story to say that it was actually an hour and a half earlier. But he insisted that he hadn't seen anything.

The question of the two unlocked doors had troubled Campbell ever since Doug Steele pointed them out that morning. He sought out the last employee to leave that Saturday night and the young man told him he left at twenty minutes past six, that Mr. Bradshaw was still there and had requested that he secure all the doors and make sure that they were padlocked. He said he was positive he had done that. When Campbell asked Larry about it, he flatly denied that he had opened any doors.

When Larry did finally submit to a polygraph test, the results were interesting: they indicated that he was truthful about not shooting his grandfather, but untruthful when he denied possessing "undisclosed knowledge" concerning his death. Opinion has always been sharply divided about the accuracy of these "truth tests" (their results, in most states, are not automatically allowed into evidence at a trial, if at all), but Campbell at least had one more tantalizing, yet troubling, scrap of information to add to his file.

The two bullets taken out of Bradshaw's body were determined to be .38 caliber with a copper jacket, and one of them, the forensic scientist said, could be "preserved sufficiently to identify a weapon having fired that shell if ever located." *If ever located.* That and the fact that Campbell had no witnesses (none of the Bradshaws' neighbors could even recall seeing Franklin leave the house that morning, let alone Larry) were the main problems. If Larry had thrown the gun into the Great Salt Lake, as Marilyn speculated, Campbell would probably never find it and the case might never be broken.

In the course of his investigation, Campbell had also contacted the Washington office of Interpol—the international criminal police organization based in Paris—and asked for information about the Schreuders' life in Brussels. Campbell learned that they had arrived in Brussels on July 3, 1970; that on June 13, 1971, Frances had been admitted to a psychiatric institution; but that Interpol could not determine if Larry had been admitted for any type of treatment as well.

Campbell felt he should make a trip to New York in order to interview Marc and do some extensive checking on Frances's life there. Marilyn, who had already offered a $10,000 reward on behalf of the family, was even willing to pay his way. When he suggested this to his superiors they were dubious, but said they would discuss it. A police department operates like any business—it has a budget and a certain limit to its resources. Cops like to talk about "getting some bang for our buck," and in the opinion of Joel Campbell's superiors, they were not going to accomplish that by sending Campbell on a fishing expedition to New York City—and they certainly weren't going to allow a possible suspect to finance the trip for them. They simply didn't feel that Campbell had enough to go on. If a break was going to come in the case, they reckoned, it would probably come from deep within the family.

Within two months of the murder of Franklin James Bradshaw, case #78–56129 was officially considered inactive by the Salt Lake City Police Department—a decision that angered and frustrated a number of family members, but didn't prevent Marilyn from trying, almost single-handedly, to keep the case alive.

26// The search for Franklin's new will had been fruitless, so the family agreed to enter the 1970 will into probate and accept the photostat copy as being valid. Doug Steele had gone to visit Alma Boyce, the lawyer whom Franklin went to see on occasion, and showed him the controversial "morning memo." Boyce simply told Doug, who by now had read the 1970 will, that the family had accepted it. Doug had been urged by Marilyn to file a suit on behalf of the employees, and that is why he had gone to see Boyce. But as he drove back to the warehouse, he realized that "we didn't have a Chinaman's chance. We were through."

The lawyer at Van Cott, Bagley whom the family would now be dealing with had never met Franklin, nor did he have a last name that was likely to inspire trust in a client. But Stephen D. Swindle, an affable thirty-eight-year-old native of Salt Lake, would get to know the Bradshaw family to a far greater degree than his predecessor, David Salisbury, had. He had his work cut out for him: the will he began grappling with concerned an estate said to be the largest ever to come under probate in Utah

Frances struck quickly. Less than a month after her father's murder she petitioned the estate for a family allowance of $3,000 a month. To support the petition she testified, in an affidavit, that "prior to and at the time of his death, Franklin J. Bradshaw, my father, provided the sole and complete means of support for myself and for my children through direct payment to me and through payments to me forwarded from my father by my mother, Berenice J. Bradshaw." She said she received neither alimony nor child-support payments from her ex-husbands, and that she was physically unable to support herself or the children, listing her various ailments as well as an extensive description of the family's expenses— "the amounts which would be needed to enable me to maintain the standard of living which I enjoyed under my father's support."

Marilyn and Elaine, anticipating problems with Frances and the dispensation of money to her from the estate, obtained a copy of Frances's petition and were both dismayed and amused by the kinds of things Frances requested money for: $66 a month for fifteen loads of wash per week (they did not exactly remember her as the perfect housekeeper); $4,300 a year for family vacations; $1,500 a year for "community and social obligations and commitments." They felt their sister's budget was padded beyond all proportion, but they also felt that if Frances received the money she requested she might not be quite as huge a financial drain on their mother. They raised no objection to her petition and it was granted.

Elaine and Mason had moved to Berkeley, California, and mail that had been sent to them in New Zealand was just beginning to arrive at their new address. As Elaine was going through it one day in September, she discovered something that only reinforced her suspicions about her father's murder. The dividend checks that her sons received quarterly for the eight hundred shares they both had in Mountain Fuel stock were roughly half of what they should have been. (At one time, they had had only four hundred shares each, and Franklin, as was his habit, held the certificates; but when the stock split the number of shares apiece doubled, and Elaine was sent the new certificates on their behalf—the ones Franklin had wanted her to send him before she left for New Zealand, but she refused.) Thinking that maybe there had been an error, she did nothing until the next envelope, containing September's dividends (the previous one had been June's), arrived a few days later. Once again, it showed the same reduced amounts. She immediately contacted a lawyer in San Francisco, who said he would write to the Mellon Bank (the stock transfer agent for Mountain Fuel), and that she should speak with the FBI.

On November 6, she was interviewed by two of the bureau's agents. She related the story to them, and, because she now felt certain that the stock certificates were among the ones that her two nephews had stolen for Frances during the summer of 1977, she recounted the events of that summer for them, told them that her father had been murdered in July, and said that she suspected Larry, Frances and her mother of having something to do with it.

Family squabbles are not normally the domain of the FBI, but the interstate transport of stolen securities is, and the agents said they would investigate the matter further.

Back in Salt Lake, sitting at the same typewriter on which she had pounded out so many emotional letters in the past, Berenice had written to her family and relatives on September 19. There was a natural concern about how she was managing now that her husband of nearly fifty-four years was gone, but after reading her letter, the family was left in little doubt that Berenice was getting on with her life.

DEAR FAMILY AND RELATIVES:

Everyone is wondering how I'm getting along so I'm going to try to give you a picture of things pertaining to my adjustment. Many things are different, some things not so different. They have no leads to Franklin's assailant.

Six days a week Franklin was up, out of the house and down at the warehouse before 6 A.M.; he let the janitor in every morning at 6 o'clock. He would get up around 4:30-5:00 o'clock, do a hundred push-ups and other exercises, then get his own breakfast. I seldom saw him before he left home in the morning. For years he worked down at the warehouse until 10, 11, 12 o'clock at nite. . . . On Sunday he was down there at 7 A.M. and home generally around 9 P.M. This was 365 days out of the year. So I saw very little of him. I ran the house and raised the kids almost alone. Everywhere I went I was alone. My friends thought I was a widow and an orphan. . . . So my daily life now seems like a continuation of the way I've lived most of our married life. But he did come home to sleep and this is the hours I miss him. . . . He was getting so tired he was almost exhausted when he came home these last 2 or 3 years. Sometimes he would throw himself on the floor, too exhausted to undress for bed. . . . [At the warehouse] Franklin would be so tired he would sprawl on top of a desk in the back to take a nap or lay his head on his desk and catch a wink or two. . . . Everyone urged and urged him to take some time off, go some place, enjoy life a little. He would say:

"But I am enjoying myself." Work was his obsession and pleasure.
. . . Nothing else mattered.

What is my life like now? In some ways not much different. Now
that our cool weather has set in I get up to a cold house instead of the
warm house as Franklin left for me. I no longer go down to the
warehouse except to drop in and say "hello" to everyone. Since
Franklin's death, a special crew has been hired just to go thru and
sort out all his 30 years of accumulation, automotive catalogues, a
whole division of shelved papers, envelopes; Franklin never threw
out an empty envelope, a magazine or newspaper or box. . . . He
stached money and checks away in magazines, so every leaf of every
magazine has to be examined. They have a stack of old, uncashed
checks that go as far back as 1949. . . .

Franklin owned 3600 oil leases. A crew of oil people from Denver
was hired to come over here and they worked from 9 in the morning
until 10:00 at nite for 4 or 5 days just inventorying his oil leases. They
took this inventory back to Denver and are now trying to value his oil
holdings. These oil holdings could go from $25,000,000 to
$100,000,000. Then there are 25 [31] automotives stores! No one can
understand how one man could accomplish so much in a life time. He
was a genius and a work horse. I had a husband but not a
companion. . . .

I have made reservations for a ship tour around the world next
winter. I'm very excited about this fabulous trip. It is on the S S
Rotterdam, one of the biggest ships, if not the biggest, and [it] has the
reputation of being the best. I have a large outside cabin all to my
self. Everyone says: "Are you going alone?" I say, "Indeed I am and
love it." . . . It will be near the first of June before I return to
S.L. . . .

Love to everyone,
BERENICE

At the time Elaine had given her consent to allow her
father's 1970 will to be admitted to probate, she was ill (her
rheumatic heart was unable to withstand the shock of Franklin's murder, and she was hospitalized briefly) and did not feel
entirely equipped to think about such a delicate matter
clearly. What the problem over her sons' stock certificates
(though she didn't have proof at that point that Frances was
involved), the 1970 will and the long history of Frances's

financial demands on her parents made her realize was this: even though her mother *technically* inherited all of her father's estate, Frances probably would be able to obtain as much money as she wanted. Her mother had funded Frances in the past, and now that her father was no longer an obstacle, the money would rain on Frances like manna from heaven. Elaine realized that she had been naive to think that Frances's $3,000 monthly family allowance would satisfy her. A Salt Lake lawyer advised Elaine there was only one thing to be done in order to protect her and Marilyn's respective interests and to stop things from progressing further: petition the court to vacate the order admitting the will to probate.

On October 10, 1978, in an eleventh-hour move, Elaine's lawyer found a judge at home and made such a motion. If successful, the motion could only derail things for a short time—enough time, Elaine hoped, for the new will to turn up in some old magazine at the warehouse. If the employees were still finding cash and royalty checks down there, why not a will?

Despite Elaine's telling her mother she might do this, Berenice was furious when she discovered that Elaine actually had. She called Elaine and told her that it was a terrible thing to do, and that she was sure Marilyn had put her up to it. Elaine reminded her mother that she had been ill and just wanted some more time to think about things. Elaine suspected that her mother was so exercised about it because Frances was. Perhaps Frances was afraid, Elaine thought, that Marilyn and she had found the new will. And if they had, it would be damaging to both Frances and Berenice.

Berenice was not the only one upset about Elaine's petition. So were Steve Swindle and the Walker Bank. As executor of the estate, the bank did not believe good cause existed for pulling the will out of probate, especially since there was nothing to take its place. While Swindle was preparing the bank's countermove, Berenice petitioned the court, through Walker, to receive no less than the whopping sum of $10,000 a month. Elaine was staggered by this, and felt sure that Frances was behind the request. (Just a month before, Elaine and her mother were discussing how much Berenice should ask for, and Berenice, who had been informed that any trips she took would be paid for separately, said she thought $1,000 a month would be plenty.) She was also concerned about a number of meetings that Frances and her mother were having with lawyers in Salt Lake. In an attempt to achieve harmony among her daughters, Berenice had tried to get all three of them back to town that fall for a little while. Elaine felt too unwell to come, but Marilyn and Frances did. Unfortunately, Berenice's plan backfired. There was nothing but frostiness between her daughters, and the rift that Berenice had tried to mend only grew wider. But to Marilyn and Elaine, their mother was just reaffirming her "choice" of Frances, the one who needed her most—the one who they felt wouldn't allow her to be mother to all three of them.

Thus Elaine and Marilyn came face to face with the reality of their father's estate. Without a new will, the only way they felt they could prevent Frances from getting everything was to persuade their mother to renounce her interest in the family trust—one of the two trusts under the will, the other being the marital trust—so that the three sisters would share in that equally. Elaine and Marilyn had no idea of how their mother was going to react to this. But they knew that if she fought it, the whole thing could become ugly and vicious, and they were banking on their instinct that she wouldn't want that.

Indeed, the last thing she wanted to do with her remaining years was to continue spending long periods with bankers and lawyers—and to be in the middle of three daughters who she felt were "so rabid, so violent and so unfriendly." On November 10, Berenice agreed to disclaim her rights, powers and beneficial interests in the Franklin J. Bradshaw Family Trust—with the exception of the power to remove and change the trustee. Since this trust was the one from which all taxes and other costs would be deducted, its true percentage of the estate was not 50 but a little over 28, making Berenice's marital trust worth a little less than 72 percent. She would have plenty to live on.

She was busy remodeling her house and preparing to go around the world. In the seventy-sixth year of her life, she was still the spunky, attractive girl from Sioux City, Iowa, she had always been. While she said she missed her husband coming home to sleep at night (even in a separate room) and turning on the heat in the house before he left for work on cold mornings, the inescapable truth was that whoever murdered Franklin had, intentionally or not, set Berenice free—or so it seemed.

27// From their location on South Mountain, the ivy-covered buildings of Lehigh University overlook the aging steel town of Bethlehem, Pennsylvania, home of the famous steel company of the same name. In late August of 1978, Larry entered Lehigh's freshman class to pursue a degree in engineering—the university's best-known school, whose graduates include Lee Iacocca, the chief executive of Chrysler.

Larry came to Lehigh with an impressive, well-rounded secondary-school record and was excited, though anxious, about being in a fully coeducational environment for the first time as a young adult. He had been in school with girls in Europe, but that was before his five unhappy years at Eastern Military Academy, about which he still had nightmares.

Soon after he arrived at Lehigh, Larry became the object of administrative confusion. He insisted that his last name was Bradshaw and urged everyone to call him that. He was even listed in *The Freshman Register* as Bradshaw. But the official school records listed him as Schreuder. If he wanted to become Lawrence Bradshaw, he was told, that was fine with Lehigh. But he would have to change his name legally and produce the appropriate papers before the university could alter its records.

That was exactly what Larry had been trying to do. Berenice had begun the paperwork in Salt Lake three weeks before Larry left to drive east, and then offered Robert Reagan $100 to continue the process in New York. The papers Larry signed and had notarized stated that neither his father nor stepfather "had shown any interest or taken any action to provide for my support, care or maintenance. . . . I therefore wish to take the surname of that part of my family which has provided me with maintenance, support, care and love and with which I am most closely associated." When Berenice contacted him, Bob thought the whole idea was extremely odd. Like his wife, he suspected Larry of the murder, and thought to himself that to murder somebody for his money and then change your name to his was simply insane behavior—and probably inculpatory to boot. But Bob Reagan had witnessed a lot of strange behavior in the eighteen years he'd been a member of the family, and, not wanting to get on the wrong side of Berenice, he agreed to do it.

As the application papers awaited a New York judge's signature, Bob received an urgent mailgram from Frances on September 18. It told him to "cease any work on the change of name order." She said that if he were to proceed it would cost her "considerable time as well as money" to straighten things out. She was in possession of other documents that had to be processed first, she said, and claimed that Larry agreed with her in making this request. So Bob followed her instructions and sent the papers to Larry at Lehigh. It was six more months, though, before Larry, acting alone, finally had his name changed in New York City to Lawrence Jewett Bradshaw—"a good American name," he says proudly.

During his freshman year, the one tangible thing Larry had to offer his dormmates was a car, and he later admitted that having Doug Steele's old blue Belair station wagon—which he bought for $1 and nicknamed "the Moonatron" for the juvenile art of long standing—probably made him more popular than he would have been without it.

He loved Lehigh, and though his grades for the first semester only ranked him 456th in an engineering class of 514, he was eager to return from the Christmas holidays and begin the spring semester.

For the second year in a row he spent the holidays alone. Just as he had spent the Christmas of 1977 at York Avenue, while the rest of the family was in Southampton, Frances gave him money to spend his three-week vacation this year at a branch of the YMCA on West 34th Street. He was very lonely, he remembered, and quietly collected wheatback pennies he loved, just waiting to return to school. Shortly after he got back, he wrote to someone whom he had been friendly with at military school. At the close of the letter Larry asked his friend, who was two years older, to keep in touch: "You never know," Larry wrote, "someday I might need a lawyer." He signed the letter "Sincerely, Larry, THE PRESIDENT OF THE UNITED STATES OF AMERICA 2000."

Marc returned to Kent School in the autumn of 1978 and began filling out applications to colleges. He was particularly excellent in history, and during the year just missed winning the school's history prize. Determined that he attend an Ivy League school, Frances remembered that Marc's uncle (Vittorio's brother, the Italian Ambassador) had done research at Yale for one year on a Fulbright scholarship, and she decided to write Vittorio a letter. She had kept in touch with him and his wife since their permanent return to the United States in 1975, but allowed Marc to see him only occasionally and Larry hardly at all.

He was still miffed that she had changed their names, but did not disregard the bold favor she asked of him in the letter. She told him how important she felt it was that their son get into Yale and asked if he would approach his brother about putting in a good word for Marc with the proper people. When his brother's reply came back from Europe, it was bristling with Italian indignation. He said he would be more than happy to do as Vittorio had asked—provided, of course, the applicant's name was Marco Gentile.

In late January of 1979 Berenice was ready at last to take the trip around the world she had eagerly looked forward to for months. Before leaving Salt Lake she decided to throw a bon-voyage party for herself at Gilmer Drive and sent out invitations. On the back of the invitations she wrote: "Mormon relatives are coming in the afternoon, the bankers, lawyers & my drinking friends are invited for the evening."

In the six months since her husband's death, Berenice had not seen much of Franklin's family. They had offered their help and assistance right away, but Berenice, independent and stubborn as ever, did not accept it. She was reaching out to them now, though, thinking this party might be a good way to get many of them together at once.

She was wrong. Despite what the invitation said, it still was perceived to be a party with liquor, and "one thing you *don't* have," a family member said later, "is a wine-tasting party for a Mormon family." Hardly anyone from the family came and Berenice was quite bitter about it. But that wasn't going to spoil her fun, and the people who did attend enjoyed the expensive champagne she had to offer.

When Berenice set off on trips during her marriage she not only tried to escape her life in Salt Lake for the enjoyment of being in new places, but, more important, tried to escape the family problems—usually concerning Frances—that never seemed to leave her alone. She wasn't gone three weeks on her trip around the world before Marilyn wrote to her of the latest crisis.

Elaine had finally discovered, without the FBI's help, what had happened to her sons' Mountain Fuel stock dividends. Frances had gotten a copy of Elaine's birth certificate, obtained a New York driver's license (which did not require a picture until 1984, the last state in the country to do so) in her sister's name, and opened up, again in Elaine's name, accounts at two New York banks as well as one at the securities firm of Bache, Halsey, Stuart and Shields. In April of 1978, using Larry's Social Security number for Sam and a fictitious one for Max, she forged Elaine's signature and sold all but one hundred of the eight hundred shares through Bache. She then took the check she got from Bache and went to her own bank, Bankers Trust, and received $23,694.99 in cash. This made both Bache and Bankers Trust liable, and unless Elaine was willing to indemnify them, they would have no choice but to press legal action against Frances. Elaine's position was very simple: if Frances replaced the stocks, she would sign a waiver that essentially said it was "a family misunderstanding." In addition, she wanted to be reimbursed for her legal fees and, along with Marilyn, wanted Frances to reimburse the estate for the more than $22,000 worth of checks she had forged in 1977.

In response, Frances unhappily agreed to have her Salt

Lake attorney petition the court for $55,000—to be funded from the estate and deducted from her share of the family trust—citing "substantial liabilities" and a "dire need for funds."

Marilyn did not go into this kind of detail in her letter, because she did not want to alarm her mother unnecessarily. Berenice was aware of the problem before she left, and had asked Marilyn to monitor the situation. All Marilyn told her mother was that Bankers Trust had put Frances's account on hold, but that she was getting enough money separately from F & B to get by.

Berenice was having a wonderful time on her cruise, and she was not about to let family problems ruin her fun. She loved the ship, she wrote everybody on Valentine's Day; it was the ultimate in luxurious living, she cooed; the most heavenly experience on this earth. "We are waited on hand to foot—18 hours a day. They do everything but think for us & sometimes we have to rely on them to do that." She was making friends and learning to do the cha-cha, was excited that Lynn Redgrave was on board, and thought the food was "out of this world." And each night when she went back to her cabin, she found her bed turned down and a paper doily on her pillow which read "Sweet Dreams" and had a piece of chocolate on top of it.

But when the *Rotterdam* docked in New York on April 23, she was not on board. She left the cruise on March 27 and boarded a plane in Athens, bound for New York. Frances had cabled her on the ship that she must return immediately. Even though Frances had said she would comply with her sisters' wishes, the FBI was still trying to interview her.

When Berenice returned, she was convinced that Marilyn and Elaine were out to blackmail Frances and ruin her. On April 14, after calming down slightly, she wrote Marilyn that "what went on while I was gone has hurt me deeply. I would not do to a dog what Elaine and you did to your sister. I can never forget nor forgive what you two did. A lot of feeling and money could be spared with a little understandable talk and I think it is time we did more talk and less law-applying. Even though I feel a great wrong has been done I feel nothing can be gained by carrying a hatred in our hearts." She told her that they must always be friends and that nothing could break blood ties. Anger, hurt, suspicion and hatred may crop up, she said, but they can be overcome with human feeling, consideration and sympathy. She assured Marilyn that she was welcome to come to Salt Lake anytime—that Gilmer Drive was the family's home—and reminded her that she had always been her "mainstay," and that it would be "asinine" for them to part ways.

Whatever her three embattled daughters may have felt toward her (Marilyn, in particular, felt convicted without being properly confronted), Berenice was trying her damnedest, in her own way, to pull the three of them together. She had experienced—and contributed to—her share of tragedy and unhappiness in her life, and she was determined to put all of that behind her in the hope that tomorrow would be a better day.

By the second half of his senior year at Kent, Marc began to do a number of strange things. If Father Michael Bullock, his adviser, was the faculty member who knew him best, Jack Hartman, a classmate, insists that he knew Marc better than anyone at the school. Hartman, like most people, was attracted to Marc because of his intelligence, his ability to memorize things, and his facility with words. Jack was an excellent chess player and helped Marc to perfect his game. Like Marc, Jack was not a varsity athlete, not popular, and resented the preferential treatment he felt athletes received from certain faculty members. By senior year they both felt angry at the school.

While he did not entirely discount the negative effect that Kent may have had on Marc and the pressure Marc may have felt to get into the right college, Jack Hartman emphasized that Marc's behavior during their last few months together at Kent was more than just the result of academic and social factors.

"The first thing I realized was that Marc had a split personality. He was basically a good person, but there was an evil side to him as well. He'd be talking in a normal conversation, nice and friendly, and he'd start to tell a joke, or someone else would, and he'd start to laugh. Somewhere in the laughter he would lose control of himself and he would

238

start to look and act more like a troll, becoming sort of mean and malicious. He was the type of person people were afraid of because he was noticeably and demonstrably insane."

When told that that was a strong word, Hartman did not hesitate. "It's a very strong word and I mean it as a very strong word. I do not mean it as, 'Oh, he's wild and crazy, he likes to go partying.' If you saw him on the subway or street corner, you'd move away."

People might have been afraid of Marc, but he had difficulty in standing up to superiors. One teacher in particular, Hartman said, used to pick on Marc in the dining hall for his atrocious table manners and Marc was terrified of him. Needing a release for his frustration, Marc would take it out on a friend. Hartman had been selected by his history teacher to go to Washington for an event called Presidential Classroom for Young Americans. Marc had gotten a higher mark than Hartman on an advanced-placement history exam and felt that he should have been selected instead. But the teacher felt that his "puppydog" (the teacher's name for Marc) was physically unpresentable, Hartman said, and chose Jack. Because of Jack's pale complexion, the teacher had given him a nickname as well—Deathman. Jack had been struggling in advanced-placement physics that semester and worried that his being away would only cause him to fall further behind. But this was an honor, and Jack was not about to refuse it. When Jack returned, he found his physics notebook right in the center of his desk and could see that someone had been making all sorts of drawings in it—drawings of Jack hanging from a noose and of graves with his name on them.

Hartman was furious. The nickname had almost petered out, and now someone—Marc, as it turned out—had revived it and was reminding him that he was dying in physics. But this was minor compared with something else, something that convinced Jack that Marc was obsessed with the idea of death—Jack's own.

It was the night of their senior prom and Marc, Jack and one of their friends did not have dates. They were depressed about that and decided to go over to the school chemistry lab. Marc had gotten the key to the lab and they let themselves in. Keys are particularly important items in boarding schools.

They represent illicit freedom, unlocking doors to places where students aren't supposed to be. Marc had developed quite a collection (some he found, others he stole) and was admired by his friends for his prowess in this as well as for his ability to pick locks. Of course keys were an important symbol in his own life—mainly because he hardly ever had one to the New York apartments his mother lived in, and he knew the terrifying experience of being locked out. Doors can be locked and doors can be opened, his mother told him once, and he never forgot that.

Marc was having some difficulty in his advanced-placement chemistry class and said that he wanted to work on some experiments, prior to the final exam. The experiments he began doing were less experiments, Jack recalled, than mini-fireworks displays, and Jack indicated that he felt too depressed to participate.

Marc, perhaps inspired by the People's Temple massacre in Guyana the previous autumn, suddenly pulled down a vial of cyanide and told Jack he ought to drink it and commit suicide. Jack declined Marc's suggestion and told him to put the bottle back on the shelf. "I was depressed," Jack said, "but when I saw that, depression fades very fast."

Suddenly, a teacher walked in. He had seen a light on and wanted to know what was going on. He thought they had been smoking marijuana, but when he saw the chemicals he seemed pleased. "A group of little scientists here," the teacher remarked, nevertheless telling them to leave.

Jack and the other boy went back to Hartman's room. Marc came in later with some sodium, a chemical that explodes when it comes into contact with water, and said he wanted to flush pieces of it down the toilets throughout the school.

Jack couldn't believe it. First Marc had encouraged him to kill himself, and now he was thinking of demolishing the school's plumbing system. As Jack sat there, other things flashed in his mind—things that had happened earlier in the year. He knew that Marc had a low opinion of himself, because Marc had told Jack that he felt he was ugly and was never going to have a girlfriend. Still, Jack was startled one day to see Marc trying to get rid of his acne by washing his face with ammonia. On another occasion, Marc walked into Jack's room and said he thought he was losing his mind and was in great trouble. Jack didn't say anything to him at the time, but he was certainly going to say something to him now.

He and the other boy tried to reason with Marc. They said that even though they were depressed and angry with Kent too, there were only two weeks to go until graduation and he should just grit his teeth, because when he got out it would be a whole new world. But if you do this, they warned him, you'll be kicked out of school and your whole life will be ruined.

Marc finally backed down and the three of them walked to the bridge over the Housatonic River that separates the boys' campus from the town. Peering down at the dark water below, they tossed the sodium over the side, heard it fizz, and watched Marc's planned act of defiance and potential destruction burn itself out.

After that night, Jack did his best to stay away from Marc. The more he thought about the incident in the chemistry lab, the angrier he became. "The cyanide I interpreted as an outright attempt to murder me," Jack said. "But not in the normal sense that you'd think of murder. I think it was psychological and that it was related to his insanity. I think it was an attempt at suicide that he couldn't bring off on himself—and that he was projecting onto his best friend."

During the last weeks before graduation, Marc kept his distance from Jack Hartman too, and began spending more time with John Kantor, a senior with whom he often studied and who was the prefect of Marc's dorm.

Kantor enjoyed hearing Marc tell of his mischievous acts— like getting into the school's business office and picking the safe—and delighted in the danishes, tea and cookies Marc would steal from the school's kitchen when they were studying late at night. Kantor had his own grievance with Kent, and it had to do with a political petition he and another student were sponsoring in an attempt to ease social restrictions between the boys' and girls' campuses and to achieve certain reforms in the student government.

Marc had one last act of revenge planned against the school, and he encouraged John Kantor to be a part of it. On the night before graduation, they broke into the school store and stole sneakers, pens and money. The school reported the theft to the state police, but when Trooper James Caputo drove over from the local barracks to investigate he was unable to apprehend the culprits. The next day, the store manager discovered that the store had been entered again; this time, some faculty members traced it back to Marc. In his room were some of the missing items, some of the cash, and a number of keys that Marc had collected during his three years at Kent. This time—unlike the summer of 1977—Marc was being arrested for what he had done. When Caputo drove him to the barracks for booking, he noticed how pleased and fascinated Marc seemed that he had almost pulled it off. Kantor was arrested later that day. Marc claimed it was all Kantor's idea. Kantor said that he was merely a "lookout." Both boys were charged with two counts of third-degree burglary and one count each of second- and third-degree larceny, and were released on bail.

Kent ultimately decided against pressing legal action (since Kantor, unlike Marc, was under eighteen, he was considered a juvenile in Connecticut and his name was eventually expunged from the record), but dealt with the matter in its own way. Since the two boys had both graduated, Kent couldn't prevent them from doing that. What they could do was make it appear as if Marc Schreuder and John Kantor had never been in the class of 1979. They did not allow their photographs to appear in the yearbook as members of the graduating class (though their pictures do appear in group shots), or their names ever to be listed in the school's alumni directory.

For Marc, there was one further form of punishment. He had not been accepted by an Ivy League college, but the school he had chosen to attend—Trinity College in Hartford, Connecticut—now said that he could not enter that fall and would have to stay out a year and reapply. Before Marc left Kent for the last time, Father Bullock and others wanted to know why he had done it. Marc told them that he was angry at the school and had done it simply to prove that he could.

So Marc left Kent with part of what he had come for—the attention he always sought to bring to himself—and with his unique appearance and personality forever engraved in the minds of his teachers and the few friends he had. And though he had been deleted from the history of the school, certain events in the future would not be forgotten.

As soon as Larry's exams were finished in May, he headed south to the Lone Star State and began a love affair with the Sun Belt that would never fade. Larry had researched unemployment rates and decided that Dallas was a place where he could get a good-paying summer job. Berenice and Frances were renting a house in Southampton from July through September, and since Larry was not to be included in the family's plans he set off on his own—a role of forced independence to which he had become accustomed. Like his grandmother, Larry loved to go on trips and take hundreds of photographs. He took pictures of *everything*—even highway exit signs—almost as if he felt compelled to prove he was there.

When he arrived in Dallas he lived in his car for about three weeks in a vacant parking lot near Southern Methodist University, before landing two jobs (one at a lead-recycling plant, the other as a survey taker) and getting a place of his own.

"I was successful," Larry said, having made $6,000 altogether. "I still had my car and it still worked. But I didn't like being alone. That was the thing I didn't like."

On August 10, Larry left Dallas and drove to Juárez, Mexico. Fascinated by the country and by how the people were able to get by on very little, Larry vowed to return someday. He arrived back at Lehigh on August 20 and decided to "surprise" the family in Southampton. Granny had told him they were living on Ox Pasture Road, but not exactly where. When his Moonatron pulled into town, he cruised the main street, hoping to see either his family walking along or his mother's Oldsmobile. He then repeated this routine along Ox Pasture, without success. He was just about to turn around and drive back to Lehigh when he happened to see Marc, shuffling along the road with a copy of the *New York Times*.

Larry came up behind his brother and surprised him. Marc couldn't believe it. "How did you find us?" he asked.

"Granny told me it was on Ox Pasture Road," Larry said.

But when Larry walked into the house, neither his grand-mother nor his mother was happy to see him. His mother's cold reaction he could understand, if not accept, but not Granny's. He felt she had been turned against him by his mother.

Larry stayed for one tense hour, Berenice gave him $50, and he spent the night on the beach. The next day, rejected again, he drove back to Lehigh for his sophomore year—one that he would not complete.

Berenice didn't leave for Southampton that summer until all the remodeling and construction she was having done on her home was completed. It was freshly painted (she did that herself) and air-conditioned (for the first time). A new garage replaced the old wooden carport, and a new driveway re-quired more cement than her contractor had ever poured before at someone's residence. She was thrilled with her "new house," her new car ("I feel like Mrs. Astor driving down the street"), and her "new life," she wrote her family, and was taking people out to dinner and bringing them back not only to show them the house but the pictures from her cruise as well.

"I intend to keep going," she wrote Marilyn and Bob "If [older people] give up then it is too late." And keep going she would, planning a trip to Acapulco in late October with her wine-tasting club.

But before she boarded the *Sun Princess* that month she made a business decision that once again shook the precari-ous balance she was trying to maintain with her three daughters. She wrote to the president of Walker Bank that she intended to make Morgan Guaranty Trust in New York the new trustee of the marital and family trusts of her husband's estate and of the F & B limited-partnership trusts as well. All legal questions were to be referred to her two lawyers in New York, John B. Loughran and Peter J. Wallison of the distinguished firm of Rogers & Wells.

"I think it will ultimately prove to be in the best interests of my family as it is in my own best interests," she wrote. "I do not intend to discuss this decision with anyone."

This was a bombshell, and the impact was felt from New

York to California, when Marilyn and Elaine opened their respective copies of the letter. They were certain that, once again, Frances was behind this—that the decision had been discussed with her and was in *her* interest—and they were prepared to fight it all the way. If their mother (who was beginning to spend more time in New York) was allowed to do this, they felt, it would mean that Frances would have greater control of things by having a bank on her turf.

Steve Swindle helped Marilyn and Elaine in their struggle, and they were partly successful. Berenice agreed to compromise: she would move all her oil and gas holdings and the F & B account (though Craig Bradshaw would remain as trustee) to Morgan, while grudgingly allowing the marital and family trusts to remain in Salt Lake with the Walker Bank.

One more ordeal had been weathered—barely. If Berenice wanted to handle her own affairs, Marilyn and Elaine felt, that was fine. But if those affairs affected them, they didn't want them being stage-directed by Frances.

Berenice had always longed to have a dancer in the family, and though none of her daughters showed real talent, Frances was the one who had maintained a passionate interest in it. She started Lavinia in ballet class at an early age, and it wasn't long before she displayed true promise and was accepted to the prominent School of American Ballet.

But Frances wanted to be more than just a ballet mother. From the time she came to New York more than twenty years before, she had wanted to belong—to be a part of the city's glamour and society. She especially wanted a significant role for herself in the dance world, one that carried a certain amount of status, one that could perhaps bring her into contact with such major figures as George Balanchine and Lincoln Kirstein, the cofounders of the New York City Ballet. The Huguenot Society of America was one thing, the prestigious world of that dance company quite another. Just as her mother was now traveling first-class on airplanes, happy to be separated from "the common herd," Frances coveted a spot on the company's board of directors—a group that included such people as Mrs. Ahmet Ertegün (wife of the head of Atlantic Records), Mrs. Thornton F. Bradshaw (wife of the head of RCA) and W. McNeil Lowry, a former director of the Ford Foundation.

Essentially there are two ways one gets appointed to the board—through individual accomplishment (and the expectation that one will be able to raise money) or through the ability to donate that money oneself. With that goal in mind, Frances had already begun contributing thousands of dollars of Berenice's money to the company, and was actively involved in trying to raise more.

Perhaps anticipating the upset Marilyn might feel when she discovered this, Frances invited Marilyn and Bob to a special benefit to open the 1979 fall season. Marilyn was both stunned and suspicious. The general committee was listed on the back of the invitation, and Marilyn found her sister's name among a number of people she had either heard of or read about: Mrs. Patricia Kennedy Lawford, Mrs. Mollie Parnis Livingston, Mr. and Mrs. Georges de Menil, Mme. Vera Stravinsky.

Though Marilyn had come to New York nearly thirty years before "to seek her fortune," she knew, as she looked at the names, that this was not the world she lived in, but that it had always been the one her youngest sister had aspired to ever since she came east to Bryn Mawr.

Marilyn was upset. Not because she didn't feel the ballet needed the money. She was upset because she couldn't help wondering what her father would think if he were alive—after all, she felt, this was *his* money—and because it was yet another example of the incredible control that Frances had over Berenice, of her mother's seeming desire to grant her sister's every wish.

If eventually belonging to the board of the New York City Ballet was the public image and life Frances was attempting to fashion for herself, her private life, away from the bright lights of Lincoln Center, was darker and extremely troubled. One night, during the Thanksgiving holidays, she was very upset and screaming hysterically. Telling Marc that she had no reason to live, she suddenly emptied a number of pills from a bottle she was holding and swallowed them. Marc had witnessed his mother's suicide threats and attempts before.

246

Often they would result from her asking him to do something and his refusing. She would then say that she didn't love him anymore. If that didn't work, she would threaten to kill herself. On one occasion, in front of Marc, she had threatened to jump out the window with Lavinia in her arms—just as she once had threatened to do with Marc in front of Vittorio many years before.

Marc reached for the phone to call for an ambulance. Paramedics arrived within minutes, and Frances was saved.

28// The fall semester at Lehigh had been an odd combination of frustration and excitement for Larry. He was living in McClintic-Marshall House with a Lebanese-American transfer student named Farid Salloum. Fred (as Larry and others called him) and he had been assigned to live together in room B-225, but each had his own set of friends, and they had little in common. While Fred was extremely studious, Larry was much more interested in meeting girls and, ideally, having a steady relationship. Not only was Lehigh coeducational, but so was M & M, as the dorm was called. During his freshman year, Larry had been interested in a girl from Guatemala, but the relationship never extended beyond a friendship. But this year, he hoped, would be different.

Two freshmen in particular were the object of Larry's attention. Kathy Van Tyne and Judy Sare were roommates and lived on the same floor as Larry, but on the other side of the building. Of the two, Larry was especially interested in Kathy, an engineering student from New Jersey with black hair and brown eyes. She had a hometown sweetheart, and Larry knew that. Still, Larry was determined, hoping that Kathy would eventually forget about this rival for her attention. Though Larry was rather handsome, he felt awkward around girls, had no self-confidence and, by his own admission, was pushy in order to disguise that fact. If Kathy and Judy were trying to be friendly toward him, Larry would invariably read far more into their actions than they had intended. In no time, it seemed, he began to feel that they both were extremely interested in him, and were even beginning to fight over him. Kathy often went home on weekends to be with her boyfriend, and Larry, who seized any opportunity to get in his car and travel, as well as to be with her, drove her there on two occasions. Despite Kathy's weekend absences, Larry felt sure he was making headway and that she would be his steady after the Christmas holidays.

Kathy Van Tyne and Judy Sare were not the only things on Larry Bradshaw's mind that semester. In October he received a long-distance phone call that jarred him back into reality. Detective Joel Campbell wanted Larry to take another lie-detector test. After the one he had taken in Salt Lake, which suggested that he had knowledge of the murder, Campbell had tried to bring Larry in for another one before he left for New York. Larry had refused at the time and now Campbell, suddenly turning up again like a bad penny, was pressing him once more. Though Larry again said no, he couldn't help wondering what, if anything, had prompted the detective to call.

Larry tried to forget about Campbell's phone call, but when he returned from class in late November he found a note on his door. The Bethlehem Police Department's Charlie Team—a group of investigators who cover the area in Bethlehem that includes Lehigh—wanted Larry to contact them.

Larry ignored their request. He had nothing to do with his grandfather's murder, and better things to do with his time than be cross-questioned by some detectives. What really concerned him was a growing fear on his part that Russia was going to start a nuclear war with the United States. Larry, a Republican, felt that America's military strength under President Carter was not nearly what it should be and blamed his administration for the current hostage crisis in Iran. From his constant reading of the *New York Times* and his interest in foreign affairs, he told two friends, he was certain that the Russians knew *now* was the best time for them to achieve "global domination."

* * *

Exam time was approaching and Larry found it more and more difficult to concentrate. By mid-December he was starting to have nightmares. But this time they weren't about military school. He woke up about three in the morning, turned on the light, and began packing.

"What are you doing?" Fred said.

"Don't worry about it," Larry said. "I'm packing a suitcase because there is going to be a nuclear war and I'm going to Mexico."

Fred, who had begun to feel afraid of Larry before this, persuaded him to go back to sleep. But in the morning Larry wanted to talk. "He really wanted to make me believe that we were going into war with Russia," Fred would say later. "His vocabulary was, 'You gotta look into my eyes when I say this and you gotta believe me because it's true.'" Larry was not certain of when war was going to break out, but he told Fred it could happen before the end of the year. By going to Mexico, he felt, he would escape the radiation that would be traveling from east to west across the middle of the country.

But when Larry woke up in the middle of the following night, the subject he was shouting at Fred about was not nuclear war.

"Fred, wake up, wake up," Larry said. "You gotta stop it. You got to give it back. It's your fault I can't get it up anymore. Those poor girls are suffering because of it, so you gotta stop."

Fred was not only afraid but bewildered. He didn't know what Larry was talking about. He was angry that Larry was robbing him of his sleep, and once again he persuaded Larry to go back to bed without pressing him to explain exactly what he was accusing him of.

If Fred had become afraid of Larry, the feeling was mutual. Larry felt that Fred had been staring at him over the past few weeks, draining him of his energy and trying to gain control of his mind. Larry also felt that Fred was robbing him of his masculinity and was trying to change him from a man into a woman—to make him his wife. If that happened, then Larry wouldn't be able to become Kathy's or Judy's boyfriend or be able to have sex with them.

A few hours later, at about seven in the morning, Larry woke up again and repeated what he had said earlier. This time Fred was not able to quiet him, and so he quickly got up, grabbed his blanket and pillow, and knocked on the door of B-201, directly across the hall.

Larry followed right behind Fred, but Fred's friends let him in and shut the door before Larry could get into the room. Fred was shaking and began to cry. His friends, Michael Weaver and Kenneth Heinick, tried to calm him down and ask what had happened as Larry continued to knock on the door, saying that he needed to talk to Fred *alone*. But they wouldn't let him in. Fred told them that Larry had "gone nuts on me again," was now blaming him for some trouble with two girls, and that he didn't know how to deal with it.

Shortly after that, one of the boys opened the door to talk with a friend and the friend didn't shut it when he left. Larry, seeing the open door, entered the room.

"Larry, did you knock?" Fred asked.

"No," Larry said belligerently.

"Well, maybe you better leave."

"You're definitely a little strange," Larry said, then walked over toward the window and began staring outside.

"Larry, why don't you go and let these guys sleep?" Ken Heinick said gently.

"No." Larry was adamant. "I'm not going to bother anybody." He turned from the window and began staring at Fred.

"Larry, why don't you get out of here?" Mike Weaver said.

"No, it's okay," Larry tried to assure him.

When Weaver again told him to leave, Larry walked over to Mike's bed and stared down at him. "Please, Mike, let me stay for a few minutes. Fred's my roommate."

Weaver was angry now and told Larry to leave or else he and Fred would throw him out. Larry agreed to go and went to see Judy Sare. It was still early in the morning, a Saturday, the 15th of December.

"Larry came in and said that he had changed and was different from the night before and thought that Fred was going to kill him," she recalled. "He said something like Fred had taken everything from him and that he couldn't get it up anymore. He asked me if I saw that he was different. He made some comment about what was going to happen in Iran. I told him that I thought he should see the counselor. He said he was confused about things on different occasions. He also said that Fred was a woman and was feminine."

Judy was disturbed about the encounter and tried to avoid him for the rest of the weekend. Fred, meanwhile, had asked the advice of a senior, who told him to try to stay clear of Larry and consult the school's psychologist about it the following week. Fred knew that it was good advice, but he was so preoccupied with studying for his exams that he didn't follow it.

Larry's two closest friends at Lehigh were Dave Dubosky and Rob Rouland, his roommate from freshman year. Dave and Rob roomed together, and throughout the current semester, Larry went to visit them practically every day. He talked a great deal about Kathy and Judy and assured Dave and Rob that Kathy felt the same way about him as he did about her. He claimed that Judy liked him a lot, but that he did not feel as strongly about her. To prove his claim, he said that Judy had become so jealous of his relationship with Kathy that she remained in bed for a time because she was so upset.

Dave was extremely skeptical of what Larry was telling him and decided to ask Judy about it. Judy said that Larry was failing to tell him that she was ill during that period and, more important, that neither she nor Kathy had ever had any interest in their friend.

Larry finally admitted to Dave and Rob that Kathy had rejected him and asked Dave if he would "analyze many of her statements." From everything Larry told him, Dave could only conclude one thing: Kathy wanted nothing to do with Larry. Dave tried to tell him that, advising Larry "to look for another girl." But Larry refused to accept his friend's advice and told him that his relationship with Kathy was too "complicated" and "involved" for Dave to understand. So despite Dave's warnings that he would become, if he hadn't already, known as "a jerk on A-2" (Kathy's hall), Larry continued to visit her.

Just as he had tried to warn Fred, Larry told his two friends of the nuclear war that was coming. But whenever Dave and Rob attempted to challenge Larry about this, he would not be interested in hearing their point of view and would leave the room. Whereas before they had simply thought of Larry as "goofy," Dave now began to feel Larry's actions were "insane."

After Larry saw Judy Sare that Saturday morning he went to visit Dave and Rob. This wasn't the first time that Larry had dropped in on them unexpectedly and woke them up, but on this occasion Larry appeared very depressed. He told them that he had gone to bed the night before feeling "very content" because of a "most pleasurable conversation" he had had with Judy. But he began to feel "quite scared" of his roommate, he said, and told them what he had just told Judy: that he thought Fred was going to try to kill him. He added that when he woke up earlier that morning he felt "totally drained of all his emotions," as if Fred "had taken them into himself," and repeated his concern that he "couldn't even get it up anymore."

Dave's advice to Larry was the same as Judy's—seek professional help—and Larry seemed to accept it as he left their room.

But over the next few days, whenever Dave or Rob phoned Larry, their conversations were disjointed; Larry made statements that were incomprehensible; and the calls ended abruptly when he simply hung up.

By Tuesday, December 18, Larry had practically emptied his room of his belongings. He drove to New York and had dinner with his mother at a restaurant near the apartment. It wasn't often that he could spend time with her alone and they actually had a pleasant evening. She gave Larry a check for $150 as an early Christmas present, then surprised him by suggesting he come home for the holidays—just as soon as Berenice went back to Salt Lake. Larry did not accept or decline her invitation, nor did he tell her about his plan to go to Mexico. But he did tell her, in some detail, about the war that was about to break out and some of the reasons why.

As Frances went back to her apartment that night and Larry impulsively decided to return to Lehigh, she was genuinely concerned about her older son.

It snowed quite heavily on Wednesday—the day he was planning to leave for Mexico and thinking of asking Kathy to join him—and Larry knew that without snow tires it would be dangerous to attempt a long trip. He made a purchase at the hardware store, drove to the Union Bank to withdraw some money, and decided to leave his blue 1972 Impala (his Moonatron had died a few weeks before and Larry had gotten another Chevrolet) parked there, because the road conditions made it impossible for the car to climb back up South Mountain to the parking lot behind his dorm.

Early that evening he suddenly walked in on Fred. Fred was startled to see him because he thought Larry, who had decided to skip a couple of exams, had left for the holidays. Fred, who had already made arrangements for a single room the following semester, asked Larry why he was back and Larry said he wasn't sure. Larry again wanted to discuss the war and insisted that Fred look into his eyes. What Fred saw were eyes that were as "blank and glassed over" as any he could imagine.

"Larry said that he was planning to spend the night at Brodhead House with Dave and Rob," Fred told Mike Weaver, but then admitted his fear. "Mike, I'm afraid he will come back on me tonight."

Mike shared Fred's concern and, since his roommate had already left for the holidays, said that Fred could sleep in his room if he wanted to.

"Okay, I will," Fred said, grateful for the offer, "but I will be up late studying for the math exam."

Larry phoned Judy Sare in Scranton, Pennsylvania, that Wednesday evening at eight forty-five. She had left on Tuesday to go home for a few days before returning to school for one more exam. Judy's father answered and told her who was calling.

"I took the phone and I was really short with him," Judy said, "I was not pleasant. He said he wanted to talk with me—it was very important and I had to listen to him." Judy asked him what he wanted, and he said he wanted to drive to Scranton the next day and meet her in front of her house at twelve noon. He said he did not want to come in, but just wanted to see her.

"I got a little upset and told him no. I asked him if he had a talk with his friends from Brodhead and he said yes. I told him to believe what they said and I said goodbye and hung up. That was the last I heard from him."

Larry went to see Dave and Rob late that evening, and they, like Fred, had assumed he'd returned home for the holidays and were surprised to see him. He told them he had gone home, but was now on his way to Mexico at last.

So instead of sleeping in their room, he made his way back to his snow-covered car, filled to overflowing with everything he had moved out of his room—far more than most students normally packed for a three-week vacation. Larry tried to fall asleep but was having a difficult time. The snow had stopped falling, but the temperature had dropped sharply. Larry grew more and more restless, and sleep simply would not come. He couldn't stop thinking about Fred and the increasing control he felt Fred was exerting over him. Gradually, Larry began to feel "drawn" back to his room—drawn by Fred's "alpha waves" that he felt were trying to destroy him.

It was about three in the morning when Larry began his trancelike walk back up the snowy hill to M & M and to room B-225. When he let himself in, he did not turn on the light but locked the door and lay down on his bare mattress, a poster of Cheryl Tiegs on the wall above him. Fred had not gone to Mike Weaver's room after all and appeared to be asleep. If it had not snowed, Larry lay there thinking, I would be on my way to Mexico—and to safety.

"I've got to go study with Laura Penrod," Fred said, interrupting Larry's reverie as he suddenly jumped up and began to collect his books.

Larry sprang up like a cat behind him, and before Fred had a chance to turn around, Larry pulled something out from underneath his coat and began to hit Fred over the head with it—again and again.

Tom Morog was in the second-floor bathroom, brushing his teeth, when he heard a yell. It sounded like Fred's voice, Tom thought, but he wasn't sure. He continued brushing his teeth, then heard it again. He stepped into the hall, listening intently. This time it was unmistakable—a thumping noise, followed by the agonizing sound of human moaning, coming from B-225. Tom stood in front of the door and heard it again. He quickly ran to the women's side of the floor, where the two Gryphons (students in charge of the dorm) lived, Lynne Andreach and Kathy Ignar. Tom frantically banged on the door, and Lynne, who was studying in Kathy's room, came to answer it. He told Lynne that someone was getting beat up in Fred and Larry's room and that she should call the police. While Lynne made that call, Kathy instinctively phoned for an ambulance. But she was reminded that in such situations only the campus police could determine if an ambulance was needed.

Tom had already gone back to the other side of the hall and woke his friend Joe Griffin, who lived next door to Fred and Larry. They stood in front of the door, and Tom began pounding on it, demanding that someone open up.

Inside a voice said, "Wait a minute. I'm trying to help this guy." Tom recognized Larry's voice. Each time Tom told him to open up, Larry repeated this over and over—and the more Fred moaned, the more Larry kept hitting him. Lynne and Kathy were outside the door now, along with Keith Conley, the male Gryphon from upstairs whom Lynne had gone to get. The hall, both girls would later say, was shaking from the force of the blows. Other students began milling about. The window in Larry's room faced a parking lot, and they heard it begin to open. Tom Morog rushed down the steps and, just as he got outside, saw Larry preparing to jump—a drop of only about seven feet to the ground. Larry fell onto a car and then tumbled to the ground.

"Larry, come here," Tom yelled.

"No," Larry snapped, surprised that somebody had seen him.

Tom walked over to Larry, who was not trying to run, and put his arms around his chest. "Larry, let's go inside," Tom said as gently as he could.

"No, I can't go inside," Larry insisted.

"Larry," Tom repeated more firmly, "let's go inside."

Larry managed to break free, but Tom, who had no shoes or shirt on, tripped him and held him on the ground, yelling for Joe Griffin, who was watching from the window of his room, to come out and help him.

Tom and Joe brought Larry into the lounge area and

255

pinned him up against the wall. They demanded that Larry give them the room keys, which he was clutching in his right hand, and he finally but reluctantly did.

The keys were given to Keith Conley, who had now assumed charge of the situation, and he opened the door. The room was dark and the window wide open, cold air pouring in from the outside. On the floor, face down, was the crumpled, bloody figure of Fred Salloum. On the bed just above him was a brick-red, four-pound stonemason's hammer with a light oak handle—Larry's hardware-store purchase of the day before—covered in blood and hair.

There was a blanket on the floor, and Conley slowly turned Fred over and gently placed his head on it. He reached for a towel and began to wrap it around Fred's head. He stared at the hammer for a second, then placed it on the floor next to Fred's body. Fred was miraculously still alive, semi-conscious and moaning.

Two university policemen, Sergeant Neil Schlottman and Officer Pedro Torres, arrived and summoned both an ambulance and backup help from the Bethlehem Police Department. Out in the lounge, Larry, still pinned against the wall, shouted, "The guy tried to kill me. I'll tell the truth." But his dormmates told him to keep quiet. When Schlottman went over to handcuff Larry and read him his rights, Larry initially said nothing, then repeated what he had told his peers—that Fred had tried to kill him.

Back in the room, a student with first-aid training was applying bandages to Fred's head. Officer Torres wrapped the hammer in a towel and put it on the dresser. William Kinch of the Bethlehem Police Department arrived about five minutes after the university officers, but the ambulance was not as speedy. It took nearly twenty-five minutes to get there (a fact that later, despite the icy roads, became the subject of an article in the school newspaper). Fred was taken to the emergency room of St. Luke's Hospital; Kinch followed the Lehigh officers, who had Larry in handcuffs (and the hammer in a cardboard box), down to their Webster Street headquarters. Schlottman again advised Larry of his rights and asked him if he had anything to say. Since Larry said he wasn't sure, Schlottman, a former Philadelphia police officer, advised him to say nothing. Tom Morog and Keith Conley both gave statements, and Larry was turned over to Officer Kinch.

Officer Kinch was part of the Charlie Team, the same unit that was supposedly trying to contact Larry less than a month before. In addition to feeling that Fred had taken everything from him, Larry now had become convinced that Fred had been planted by the Bethlehem police to spy on him. It all fit: Fred would report Larry's activities to them and they in turn would be in contact with Joel Campbell out in Utah. Though Larry didn't express this suspicion openly until a few months later, he believed it was one of the main reasons that the university had contacted the local police in the first place.

When Kinch brought Larry into headquarters, he was met by James Ammend, acting head of the unit that week. At five forty-four, Kinch read Larry his rights (the third time Larry had heard them in two hours), and once again he declined to say anything. Staring straight ahead, he began rocking back and forth in his chair. Wherever he was, Kinch would say later, nobody was there with him. Larry then started to hyperventilate and his eyes glassed over. Asked if he was under medication for any illness or under the influence of narcotics, Larry said no. While Kinch and another officer took Larry to the Muhlenberg Medical Center to be examined, Ammend decided to call in another member of Charlie Team, the one person who Ammend felt could possibly "reach" Larry when he returned.

Harold J. Smith joined the Bethlehem Police Department in 1966 and had been an investigator for two years when he got the call that morning shortly before six. "Smitty" had the sort of relaxed, friendly manner that would charm even the most hardened criminal. Prior to taking on the Bradshaw case, Smitty's biggest investigation dealt with the arrest of a Pentecostal minister from the Miracle Valley Chapel who was raping women and having the assaults filmed on a video camera with the help of two-way mirrors. Though that case was much harder for Smitty to crack, within hours he would decide that the Bradshaw case was even more bizarre.

When Smitty got to headquarters, he was informed of what

had happened and told that Fred Salloum was in critical condition. He had been hit a total of eleven times, and his skull was fractured in seven places. Larry wasn't back yet, so Smitty and another detective went up to Lehigh and began interviewing all of the people who had been at the crime scene. Since Pennsylvania law required that Larry be given a preliminary arraignment within six hours of the time he was first apprehended, Smitty wanted to collect as much information as he could while people's memories were still fresh—and before he had to face the little man nearly everyone in Bethlehem affectionately called "the Judge."

If one didn't know John Gombosi was the busiest magistrate in Bethlehem, he could easily be mistaken for a butler in a Hitchcock drama. Prior to the preliminary arraignment before the fifty-nine-year-old, cigar-smoking magistrate, Smitty told Larry, "I think I can understand how this could have happened." Larry, who had stopped hyperventilating but had been rocking back and forth in his chair ever since he got back from the medical center, turned to look at him. Smitty's words seemed to have a soothing effect and broke his trance.

"You can?" Larry said, clearly surprised. "Well, if you can, then I'm going to tell you the whole thing." Smitty could see that a confession was coming, and told him to wait until the magistrate had finished the arraignment (setting bail at $25,000) and left the room.

So at nine-fifty, after waiving his rights to have an attorney present, Larry began to tell Smitty and William Kinch his account of what had happened. He told them all the things that he felt Fred was doing to him and how Fred's alpha brain waves had drawn him up from the car, with the hammer, earlier that morning. He insisted that Fred was destroying him by turning him into a woman, and said he was merely defending himself. Then he turned to Smitty and, eyes aglow, told him something Smitty would remember for years to come: *"I hit him and I hit him and I hit him and I hit him."*

Smitty quickly notified the offices of the District Attorney and the Public Defender that he had a confession. He processed Larry so that he could be transferred to Northampton County Prison and went to get a search warrant so that he could look through Larry's room, which had been locked and was under guard. Kinch and Ammend accompanied Smitty up to Lehigh, and though the only thing they found in the room was Larry's keys, it is what Kinch found somewhere else that gave them pause.

Officer Torres had told them that Larry had some personal belongings in a property room downstairs, and so they went to take a look. In a black wooden trunk, Kinch found a scrapbook. But it was not filled with pictures. In it were all the articles that had ever appeared about Franklin Bradshaw's murder. At this point, none of them knew that Larry was a suspect in the murder. If somebody from Charlie Team had left a note on Larry's door in late November, they didn't know about it.

"It gave us an inkling that something was amiss," Kinch said. He felt it was unusual for someone to keep so many articles about a relative's murder as opposed to keeping the articles about the arrest and trial of the person's assailant. Kinch might have had a point—except no one had been arrested.

The other thing they found was a diary recounting Larry's life at military school—entries in Larry's childlike writing about how much he disliked it there, especially the control the school tried to exert over him, and how much he wanted to be living in New York with his family. Between the diary, the scrapbook, the bizarre story Larry had given them and the act he had committed, Kinch said, it made them look at the case somewhat differently than they might the average assault.

When the officers returned to headquarters, they learned that their captain had already told someone to call Joel Campbell and tell him that Larry had been arrested. Campbell, who had previously contacted the Bethlehem police about Larry, was elated but cautious. He had felt all along that Larry was his man, and now reasoned that anyone who could hit someone over the head repeatedly with a hammer was clearly capable of killing his grandfather. But he still had to prove his case. He told the officer that he would try to get permission to fly east to interview Larry, and the officer assured him that the department would be in touch if anything significant turned up in the course of their investigation.

Later that day, Stanley Vasiliadis, the Public Defender assigned to Larry's case, went to visit him in prison. Advised that Larry had made an oral confession to Harold Smith, he asked Larry to tell him what happened, and Larry repeated the story he had told the investigator. While Larry was recounting the chain of events, his lawyer made the following note: *Defendant became increasingly agitated, rocking back and forth during the course of the interview. He appears to be genuinely insane.*

He asked Larry for his mother's phone number, having decided that he would try to have Larry involuntarily committed to the Allentown State Hospital. In order to do that he would need to have Frances's permission for Larry to be examined by someone who could then recommend that a mental health review hearing be held. But when Vasiliadis tried to reach Frances he discovered the number Larry had given him was incorrect.

Larry phoned Frances himself and told her what had happened. She said she would try to come as soon as she could, but did not manage to get there until a week later. The day before she was due to arrive she phoned Vasiliadis and told him three things: she wanted to hire him on a private basis, she didn't plan to bail Larry out, and she agreed with his suggestion that Larry be committed if possible.

Vasiliadis picked Frances up at the Holiday Inn the following day and she went to see Larry. They had a short, tearful meeting, and Frances was then interviewed by Dr. David Marvi, a psychiatrist in Northampton County's Mental Health and Mental Retardation Division. She told the doctor, according to his report, that Larry did not show any concern about his situation, or any understanding about what he had done. "Either it had to be his life or mine," Frances said Larry told her. She had met with Larry on December 18 and noticed that he was unkempt, appeared not to have bathed, was distracted, agitated, trembling, and complained of not sleeping for weeks. He appeared to be very frightened and told her that "the Russians were coming" and "we are in great danger." Larry was not responding appropriately to her conversation, she said, and was in and out of touch with reality. She told Marvi that Larry had been emotionally disturbed from the beginning of his life, attended special classes for two years, had a very bad temper, and used to hit his brother with the slightest provocation.

Marvi then interviewed Larry. He noticed that his facial expression and smile were "inappropriate," and that he could not maintain eye contact. Larry told Marvi essentially the same story he had told Smitty, Vasiliadis and his mother, but he went further. He claimed he was *still* afraid of Fred, and showed no concern about Fred's being in the hospital in critical condition. He informed Marvi that his parents separated in 1963 because his father had "a drinking problem" and said that his mother had been "mentally ill" and had tried to commit suicide.

In the concluding paragraph to his December 28, 1979, report, Marvi wrote:

I feel that this patient is delusional and I do consider him suffering from schizophrenia, paranoid type. He told me that he had smoked marijuana three times but he never used any alcohol heavily and does not believe in taking drugs. I do not feel that his delusional idea or his psychosis are drug or alcohol related. I do feel that he is in need of treatment.

When Larry spent the previous Christmas and New Year's at a New York City YMCA, alone and collecting wheatback pennies, even he, given the rich fantasy world he inhabited, would have been hard pressed to imagine spending the holidays this year in a Pennsylvania prison.

29// On January 2, 1980, Frances, Marc and Lavinia drove to Easton, Pennsylvania, for Larry's mental health review hearing at the Northampton County Prison. Only Frances was allowed into the hearing, so Larry never saw his brother and sister that day. Frances's testimony was similar to what she had told Dr. Marvi the previous week, but she particularly stressed the cruel physical treatment Larry had received from his father as a young child. Despite Frances's and Dr. Marvi's testimony, the master (the man who presided over the hearing) did not seem convinced that Larry should be committed to the state hospital. In fact, he seemed perturbed, because Larry, who had not been asked to testify, appeared quite normal and composed. But as Larry was leaving the room, he said there was something he wanted to say. Since the master had not made his decision yet, Stanley Vasiliadis, convinced that commitment was the proper course of action, asked Larry about what had happened early that December morning. Once Larry began talking about the alpha waves emanating from Fred's brain and controlling him, Vasiliadis felt sure that the master would commit Larry. He did, for a period not to exceed ninety days.

After the hearing, Vasiliadis learned that Frances did not want to hire a private attorney for Larry after all. Larry was entitled to have a public defender by law because he was a college student with no assets of his own. But Larry already had told Vasiliadis that his family had money and that his grandmother controlled it. Vasiliadis's feeling was that if the family could afford private counsel, Larry should have it. He tried to explain all this to Frances, but, as he later wrote in his notes recapping the day, "it appears that client's mother is crazier than client and impossible to deal with."

The following day he wrote Berenice a letter. Berenice had called him after the incident at Lehigh, and now he was writing in an attempt to urge *her* to get Larry not only a private attorney, but a private psychiatrist who could act as an expert witness in the preparation of Larry's defense.

"It appears that you exercise financial responsibility for Larry and his mother," he wrote. "Mrs. Schreuder, in my opinion, is incapable of exercising this kind of responsibility. I have become frustrated in efforts to work with her in a meaningful way."

Larry spent nearly seven weeks at the Allentown State Hospital. During that time he pleaded with his family to get him out on bail, but they took the position that if he was still considered dangerous they weren't prepared to do that. According to a doctor's report, he showed no remorse about what he had done, continued to contend he had acted in self-defense, and stated that he did not feel he was mentally ill.

"On the ward he has been maintained without any medication," a thirty-day diagnostic summary said. "He is found to persist with a rather inappropriate grin all the time. This appears to be his defensive style. He appears to be trying to live in a world of his own so that he can deny the act or the consequences of his act. He does not form relationships with the other patients. He is very much isolated. He is on the telephone quite a bit. He walks with a swing in his hips and tends to stride up and down the hallway with his swinging hips and his big grin. He has persistently made requests, like wanting to be interviewed for a census-taker job, and has expressed irritation that he was not to have his [preliminary] hearing, because he felt that he should be able to get back to Lehigh University to start the second semester. His plans at this time are to return [there]. He seems to have no doubt that that will be a possibility.

"There is evidence that his mother is somewhat scattered and perhaps flighty, but she has not been interviewed in depth at this time."

On February 2, the day before that summary was written, Larry wrote a letter to Kathy Van Tyne. He told her there was "a good chance" he would be back at Lehigh in September and hoped he could "since much of my future is at stake." He said that some of his friends from Brodhead had come to see him (they also came to be interviewed by the staff) and that he was having a rough time because of "all those mental patients who keep on staring at me. . . .

"I didn't meant to upset you about those comments on the Attollyah and Russia. I'm not sure how much you saw in me last semester but I've certainly learned a tremendous lot about myself in the past couple of weeks. I never quite realized how much my feelings had so much affect on everyone. . . .

"I feel kind of bad celebrating my 20th birthday alone this Feb 6, but I'll manage."

Larry did spend his birthday alone, but his mother came to visit him the day after it, bringing a box of chocolates and a book on, of all things, the Russian Revolution.

At a staff conference meeting on February 14, Larry was the topic of discussion. In the written report that summarized it, a caseworker stated that he had interviewed Frances (three times over the phone), Larry, Lehigh students, the dean of students, the police and Stanley Vasiliadis. He emphasized that Frances was given to exaggeration, and that information obtained from her was to be accepted with considerable reservation.

While Frances placed a lot of blame on Vittorio ("an alcoholic who was described as being reckless with patient and his younger brother but especially abusive towards Larry"), on Frederick ("a wife beater") and on Larry himself, she never gave the caseworker the slightest impression that she might have contributed to her son's condition or, with the exception of the time Larry went to the Children's Day Treatment Center in New York, that she had sought any other kind of professional help for him.

Larry's friends, the report said, described him as "socially isolated, immature and awkward" and as someone "rejected by most circles." They befriended him, in a "protective, sympathetic way," but also because he was "entertaining and goofy." While he was rarely invited anywhere, he was "used" for his car when they needed transportation. His freshman roommate did not want to room with him again, because it was like "being a father all the time."

In the section of the report dealing with Larry's psychiatric examination at the hospital, Larry characterized himself as "a normal, average, intelligent guy. I don't belong here, I'm not like all the other patients you have." When questioned about details of the hammer assault, Larry was vague and full of I-don't-know responses, but offered something he had not said before in his story of self-defense: Fred had "lunged" at him. At no time while he was at the hospital did Larry inquire about Fred's condition. He seemed to lack insight and judgment, the report said, as he totally ignored the consequences of his actions.

During two sessions with a psychologist, Larry denied that he was a loner, but the psychologist concluded that "it is unlikely that he is able to maintain any meaningful, lasting relationship. . . . He is somewhat distrustful of others. He does not admit to even ordinary feelings as he tends to repress and deny any hostile and aggressive feelings. The data further suggests the strong probability of unrewarding family relationships throughout childhood, which has caused a lack of emotion and distrustful attitude toward others. This in turn may have caused Schizoid tendencies (sometimes termed the burnt-out child reaction). . . . In situations of extreme stress and frustration his internal controls become weak, his defenses break down, and he may explode."

Larry wasn't thinking about exploding, he was thinking about escaping. Security at Allentown State Hospital was loose, and Larry, who still had a nice nest egg in the bank, had already been given an "open side" one day, which meant he could leave the grounds for a certain period of time. But the day he was planning to escape was the same day the hospital decided to send him back to prison. They felt he was capable of understanding the charges against him, of helping Stanley Vasiliadis prepare his defense, and that he was nonpsychotic during his seven-week stay and did not require medication. But they concurred with Dr. Marvi's original diagnosis that he was a paranoid schizophrenic. Larry's discharge summary contained the warning that he was considered to be "quite dangerous, in that under conditions of crowding he could potentially have another acute episode in which a similar incident could occur."

So on February 19, Larry was returned to Northampton County Prison.

Over the next few weeks Larry's condition deteriorated. He refused to eat or wash for short periods of time and was increasingly upset that his family, whom he was having trouble reaching on the phone, would not post bail for him. On March 7, Stanley Vasiliadis received a phone call from Ron Madsen, a Salt Lake City lawyer who represented Frances in dealing with her father's estate. He was calling on behalf of Berenice, he said, and was planning to fly to Bethlehem the following week. Larry had had a preliminary hearing four days earlier and it was now official: he would be formally arraigned on three charges—criminal attempt to commit criminal homicide; aggravated assault; and recklessly endangering another person. The bright news for all concerned was that it was not a murder charge. Farid Salloum was out of danger. He was paralyzed on one side of his body, but was expected to make a full recovery. The surgeon who operated on him remarked to a Bethlehem policeman that if Salloum hadn't had such an unusually thick skull he probably wouldn't have lived.

When Madsen met with Vasiliadis and his boss, Chester Reybitz, he explained that Larry *had* been considered a suspect in his grandfather's murder. (Reybitz was under the impression—a correct one—that he still was.) Madsen tried to assure them that the Utah authorities had questioned Larry at the time and that he was cleared by his grandmother's alibi. The family was prepared to obtain the services of a psychiatrist to aid Vasiliadis in the insanity defense he was hoping to raise, but it was unlikely a private attorney would be hired because of their concern that a civil suit might be filed against the family by Farid Salloum's parents.

Chester Reybitz didn't like what he was hearing. A high-priced lawyer with high-powered resources flies in from Utah (he thought at the time), full of concern for Larry Bradshaw, yet they don't want to hire a private attorney for him. Public defenders are for people who need them, and Reybitz felt that the family had Larry right where they wanted him.

"They always said, 'We want to do the best for him,'"

Reybitz recalled, " 'we want to do the best for him.' If they wanted to do the best for him they could have hired a private lawyer, they could have gotten him out on bail, and they could have put him in some private institution. I said I didn't see how they could sue the grandmother, even if she paid for his defense in the criminal case.

"Keep him off the street and protect our pocketbook. That's what it looked like. And, frankly, I wished at the time that I wasn't the Chief Public Defender," he said with sarcastic honesty, "so that I could have gotten on the gravy train."

On April 3, a prison report noted that Larry was "more agitated, unrealistic, and angry." He began to write letters during the next two months in the hope that he could somehow avert the trial that was soon to take place. He wrote to the president of Lehigh and told him, as if the president needed reminding, that he was the student who had attacked Fred Salloum—an act he said he regretted but did not feel guilty about. After all, he said, Fred was a transfer student and Lebanese—"unAmerican." He gave the president all the by now familiar reasons he had done it, and requested his personal involvement in the investigation because the dean of students had mishandled it.

At the same time, he wrote a series of letters to the dean of students, maintaining his innocence. He told the dean that he didn't belong in prison ("this ugly disgusting criminal environment"), and that his case—"a very personal one"—should be dealt with by the university, not the state. He said that he continued to be worried about a war with Russia; and after Russia's invasion of Afghanistan (a few days after Larry was arrested), even more so. He complained that Stanley Vasiliadis had no idea what he was doing or how to handle his case and wouldn't take his phone calls. He told the dean that his family "doesn't really care as you know," and that he was "already scared that this has damaged me psychologically and mentally."

He said that Fred had been spying on him for the Bethlehem police—a relationship they were trying to cover up. The police were "probably investigating" his grandfather's death, he said, and mentioned both the call he received from Joel

Campbell in October and the note that "C Team" wanted to see him in November as evidence of that. He said he refused to take another lie-detector test because he had had nothing to do with the death.

Not only did he claim Fred was jealous of Kathy Van Tyne but he said he had recently learned that Fred had "seduced and, in my opinion, raped" her about midnight on November 17.

That is why, I see now, everything went wrong during the last month of the semester. No one ever told me. She was apparently too ashamed to say at the time. My previous letters show how my roommate then started acting towards me. He felt, I see now, very guilty and wrong at what he had done. He ruined Kathy Van Tyne's life and my life, Lawrence J. Bradshaw. I wished I had killed him instead of just injuring that *faggot*. . . .

The main reason I am writing you all this is to clear me completely of any wrongdoing and to get the record straight.

I also would wish you could make a quiet call to the D.A. Office or the Bethlehem Police and tell them to get me out of jail on the basis of new and obviously very important factors.

I really don't know what to say. But please get me out of jail so I can pick up my shattered life again, which I very desperately want to do. Never once did I think that I belonged in jail.

Farid Salloum should be put in jail for the rest of his life for what he did to me.

The dean of students and the university's president were not the only people to receive Larry's letters. He continued to write and phone Kathy (who sent his letters to the dean and told Larry she did not want to hear from him again). He was in touch with Chester Reybitz, telling him how incompetent he felt Vasiliadis was and asking for a new lawyer to represent him. Reybitz wrote back immediately, saying that he felt his colleague was putting forth every effort on his behalf, that it was against his office's policy to switch counsel, and that if he wanted another attorney he should write his grandmother and request one. In another letter to Reybitz after that, Larry told him that Kathy Van Tyne was seven months pregnant with his child and that she had been "waiting for months for me to get out of jail." He said that he had tried to tell Vasiliadis about this new information, but that he had hung up on him.

Angered by what he saw as his lawyer's lack of interest, he decided to appeal directly to the District Attorney's Office. He went over the same ground in his letters to them and said that he had gotten "badly stuck" in the bureaucratic system. If they would just come and discuss the situation with him, he urged, they would see that the "wisest course of action" would be to refer his case back to Lehigh. If they did that, he implied, he would move to some other part of the United States. "This part of the country is too cumunistic for me," he wrote.

He accused the Bethlehem police of having "a very biased opinion" of him because of Utah's continuing investigation into his grandfather's murder. He said that it was illegal for them to have used Fred to spy on him without his knowledge. In connecting his argument that he had hit Fred only in self-defense with his fear of nuclear war, he said that he had to make "a preemptive strike."

He pleaded with them to get him out of prison, because "all these criminals around me" were constantly threatening him. All he wanted to do, he said, was go back to New York to get some sunshine.

Getting Larry out of prison was the last thing the District Attorney's Office planned to do. They felt they had an airtight case against him. Since the defense was planning to plead insanity, the state would have the burden of proving, beyond a reasonable doubt, that Larry Bradshaw was *not* insane at the time he committed the crime—that he in fact knew what he was doing, that he knew the difference between right and wrong. (In Pennsylvania, the test for legal insanity is the M'Naghten Rule. It relieves the defendant of criminal responsibility if, at the time of committing a criminal act, he was laboring under such defective reason, from a disease of his mind, as not to know the nature and quality of the act he was doing, or, if he did know it, as not to know what he was doing was wrong.)

On May 9, Dr. Robert Sadoff—the psychiatrist whom Ron Madsen had hired and who was reputed to be one of the top forensic psychiatrists in the country—examined Larry in prison and told Stanley Vasiliadis the following things in a letter.

1. Mr. Bradshaw is seriously mentally ill. He has a diagnosis of paranoid schizophrenia and that is a psychotic mental illness.

2. Mr. Bradshaw does pose a danger to himself and/or to others in the sense that he is not dealing with reality and that he is responding to hallucinations and delusions of a paranoid nature.

3. It is my opinion that because of Mr. Bradshaw's psychotic mental illness he requires medication to help with his thought disorders. If he does not receive medication his mental condition will likely deteriorate. This will be so whether he remains in Northampton County Prison or whether he is in a hospital without medication.

4. Mr. Bradshaw can benefit from further psychiatric treatment and hospitalization if he receives a combination of medication and psychotherapy.

He said that Larry did understand the "nature and object of the proceedings against him and can work with counsel in preparing a rational defense"—the legal words used to establish a defendant's competency to stand trial. But he also said that with respect to Larry's state of mind at the time of the incident, "it is my opinion that Mr. Bradshaw, as a result of his mental illness, was incapable of knowing the quality of his act, although he knew the nature of it—that is using a hammer. He did not know the quality of his act because he was responding to a delusional belief that his roommate was out to harm him and was spying on him and was homosexually involved with him."

The doctor added that Larry, as a result of his serious mental illness, was also incapable of "knowingly and intelligently" waiving his right to remain silent when he told his story to Smitty that morning.

With this letter, Stanley Vasiliadis had what he needed to proceed to trial. But there was a legal hitch. In Pennsylvania, a defendant must be tried within 180 days of the time a criminal complaint is filed—or he goes free. That period was due to expire on June 16. Vasiliadis had to be away for two weeks on National Guard duty and was not scheduled to return until June 23. Either the trial could proceed with another Public Defender in his place or Larry could probably get a continuance. It was up to him.

Ever since Larry had been arrested he had been unhappy with Vasiliadis, and, of late, he had decided that his constitutional rights were violated when he was arrested. If he couldn't persuade the authorities to have his case dealt with in the more private setting of Lehigh University, then perhaps the best thing to do, Larry thought, was to have his trial over and done with as quickly as possible.

At a hearing on Tuesday, June 10, Chester Reybitz pushed for a continuance. He told the court that not only was Vasiliadis away, but Dr. Sadoff would not be available to testify if the trial was held that week. But Larry, who was confused and acting strangely (at one point, he sat on the floor and had to be put back in his seat), told the court two things: he wanted to have the trial, but *didn't* know if it was the best decision to do so. Ironically, Larry got his wishes granted. He would have his day in court—his constitutional right—and he would not have Vasiliadis to represent him. The judge set the trial for the next day, giving Chester Reybitz, who was going to defend him, precious little time to prepare.

But when Reybitz, a tall, muscular bear of a man with a gruff though friendly manner, walked into court on Wednesday, he again asked for a continuance. He knew that he was dealing with a client who was not capable of thinking clearly from one minute to the next, yet he still hoped that Larry would see the wisdom of his argument. If Larry continued to insist the trial be held, there was the slim possibility, Reybitz had found out, that Dr. Sadoff might be able to get to Easton that afternoon. He was testifying in Philadelphia that morning, was uncertain he would be finished in time to make the ninety-minute journey, and was definitely unavailable the next two days.

Mark Refowich, the Assistant District Attorney, had not opposed the idea of a continuance on Tuesday, but he did now. If Larry wanted the trial to begin, the prosecutor was ready. He had already brought witnesses to Easton on short notice (he too had expected Larry to waive his right to a speedy trial), and was not about to send them home while

Larry played games with the court. Judge Robert Freedberg asked Larry what he wanted to do. First Larry said he'd waive the rule, then he said he wouldn't. And it went like that, back and forth, until everyone became completely exasperated with him. But when pressed for his final decision, it was the same as before—he wanted the trial to commence.

So at one-thirty that afternoon the bizarre trial of *Commonwealth of Pennsylvania* v. *Lawrence J. Bradshaw* began.

Tenacious and hard-nosed, Mark Refowich wasted little time in warming up the jury for the case they would ultimately have to decide. His first witness was Farid Salloum—and Larry came face to face with the reason why he had been in custody for the past six months.

Salloum told the jury that the last thing he remembered that night was leaving the library about midnight. The next thing he recalled was waking up in a Syracuse hospital (near his hometown of De Witt, New York) at the beginning of January. He said that he had had three operations—two on his skull, one on his jaw—and was scheduled to have a plate put in his skull in a month's time. When he first got out of the hospital, he said, he had had to learn how to use his right side again, which had become temporarily numb.

Asked if he had ever had any arguments with Larry, Salloum said there were two or three incidents, but hastened to add they weren't arguments but "just pretty much hysterics on his part." The prosecutor wasn't about to ask him to elaborate, because it would only open the door to the kind of details about Larry's behavior that he wanted to keep out.

"Did you date any of the same girls or take out the same girl?" Refowich asked, laying the groundwork to disprove Larry's claim, if it came up, that Fred had raped Kathy Van Tyne.

"No, not at all."

"You had your own social life?"

"Oh, definitely. It was completely different."

Refowich had no further questions on direct examination. He would let Reybitz, his former boss when Refowich was a Public Defender, have his turn.

* * *

"You mentioned that on several occasions he went into hysterics?" Reybitz asked, hoping Fred might unwittingly bolster Larry's defense of insanity.

"Yes."

"Could you explain that for the jury?"

Fred told the jury that Larry woke in the night, yelling at him and "blaming me for a couple of things," but was not specific. Refowich had prepared his witness well. Fred said Larry came into the room once and tried to convince him that the United States was going to war with Russia and that his behavior was "very sporadic," "very hyper," and "off-the-wall a little bit." Reybitz did not want to push Salloum very hard. He had suffered enough, and there was little point in trying to suggest that Fred might have provoked Larry into the assault. That tactic would only backfire with the jury. Reybitz's ultimate success in defending Larry would depend on Dr. Sadoff—if he ever appeared.

After a few more questions by both Reybitz and Refowich, the prosecutor called his next witness—Officer Pedro Torres, one of the two Lehigh policemen who had been summoned early that morning.

Following the officer's straightforward account—including the fact that the victim's blood and hair were on the pointed (as opposed to blunt) end of the stonemason's hammer—Tom Morog described to the jury how he had alerted the two female Gryphons that morning; had pounded on Larry and Fred's door for them to open up; had heard Larry say, "I'm trying to help this guy"; and then had captured Larry after he climbed out the window, bringing him back inside with the help of a friend.

No sooner had Refowich called his next witness, Kathy Ignar (one of the Gryphons), than a man suddenly entered the courtroom—a man whom Chester Reybitz had never spoken with in person, but was awfully glad to see.

Dr. Robert L. Sadoff had just arrived from Philadelphia. Reybitz asked the judge if the doctor could be called instead of Miss Ignar, and if he could have a few minutes to confer with him. After fifteen minutes, Dr. Sadoff was ready to take the stand.

* * *

273

Psychiatric testimony, generally used by the defense far more often than by the prosecution, has always been the subject of controversy. Can a psychiatrist determine what someone's state of mind was at the time he committed the offense for which he is charged? That is the key question, and there are probably as many opinions about it as there are psychiatrists willing to come into the courtroom and testify.

What Chester Reybitz initially needed to do was establish Sadoff as a figure of authority and eminence—a professional in whose hands even the most cynical Doubting Thomas could feel secure. Sadoff's credentials were indeed impressive: clinical professor of psychiatry at the University of Pennsylvania; lecturer in psychiatry and law at the Villanova University School of Law; former president of the American Academy of Psychiatry and the Law; an examiner on the American Board of Forensic Psychiatry; author of about sixty articles and three books; and, most significant, in terms of the jury's viewing him as unbiased, someone who had testified in many trials before, for the defense *and* the prosecution.

On direct examination, the doctor described all the things Larry claimed Fred was doing to him: drawing his emotions from him, taking his sex from him, making him feel girlish ("wet and warm and wushy"), trying to make him his wife, spying on him for the police. The jury was also informed of Larry's concerns about a war with Russia and his desire to drive to South Texas over the holidays just so he could get cheap gas. Asked his diagnosis of Larry, Sadoff told the jury exactly what he had told Stanley Vasiliadis—that Larry was suffering from paranoid schizophrenia. "I have got to explain that schizophrenia is a major mental illness, a psychosis where people are not in touch with reality. Paranoid means that he projects his feelings onto others . . . that it's *you* who are against *me,* not that I am against you; you who are trying to have sex with me, not that I am interested in you sexually.

"The diagnosis continues," Sadoff insisted. "It isn't just that he had it on that particular day. He has it even now."

Did he know right from wrong or realize the extent of his actions that day? Reybitz wanted to know.

No, the doctor said, Larry had been acting under the influence of his psychosis's delusional system and could not reasonably have known that what he was doing was wrong. He had believed he was in danger and was protecting himself.

"Doctor, have you ever examined other patients, persons who have suffered from paranoid schizophrenia, who, in fact, you found to understand the implications of their actions?"

Refowich objected, but was overruled. Yes, Sadoff said, he had seen people whom he had also diagnosed this way who *knew* what they were doing, *knew* it was wrong, and were *not* legally insane.

Asked if Larry was competent enough to attend his own trial, the doctor said that despite Larry's being psychotic and mentally ill, he did understand what was going on and could work with his lawyer.

Reybitz had what he needed—for now. But Refowich, no shy wallflower, was ready to try to bulldoze the edifice Reybitz had just erected.

The prosecutor's approach was to portray the doctor as a hired gun—a man who examined people for short periods of time, testified in a good number of cases, and was well paid for his services ($100 an hour). But Sadoff had heard it all before. He was cool and unshakable.

Refowich wanted to know how Larry could be competent to stand trial, yet not know the difference between right and wrong on the morning of December 20, 1979.

Sadoff, who earlier had admitted Larry's competency was "borderline," insisted he didn't say that. "I said when he hit the roommate over the head, he didn't know rationally, reasonably, that what he was doing was wrong, because he did it as part of his delusional system, which was part of his psychosis."

The prosecutor and the "expert witness" parried back and forth like two gladiators. Though it was impossible to tell what effect the doctor's testimony was having on the jury, his disturbing conclusion that Larry was still psychotic and mentally ill had to be damaging to any chance Larry might have for an outright acquittal.

The following morning, Lynne Andreach took the witness stand. The nineteen-year-old chemical engineering student told the jury how the entire girls' hall was "shaking from the force of the blows" that morning. She testified that Larry "appeared to be in shock. A person in shock appears very gray, and his cheeks sunken in, and almost in a delirious state, and that's what he looked like." Asked if, as a Gryphon, she had ever had to deal with Larry because of any problems he had caused, she said she had been told he was "harassing some girls in my hall."

The case against Larry continued to build. The medical records administrator of St. Luke's Hospital—the one that admitted Fred—testified. So did Kathy Ignar, Keith Conley, and the student trained in first aid who had helped out until the ambulance finally arrived. Sergeant Neil Schlottman said it appeared to him that Larry would have known the difference between right and wrong that morning. Officer Kinch said that Larry appeared normal at the dorm, but became glassy-eyed and started to hyperventilate at police headquarters. Investigator Ammend, who saw Larry only at police headquarters, concurred with his colleague, adding that Larry was nervous and fidgety after his preliminary arraignment in front of Magistrate Gombosi. He was "wringing his hands and just appeared to be staring," Ammend said, but also seemed to know what was going on.

Following Ammend's testimony, the two lawyers had a discussion with the judge that the jury could not hear. Refowich wanted to enter into evidence the Miranda warning card that Larry had signed, waiving his rights, before he spoke to Harold Smith and made his incriminatory admission of guilt. The prosecutor felt that it showed Larry knew exactly what he was doing—especially since he had refused to sign the same card two times earlier that morning. The judge agreed to enter it, and then Refowich called Harold Smith, who had been seated next to him throughout the trial, to the stand.

Refowich asked Smitty to read the Miranda warning card to the jury—the one they had seen and heard their favorite detectives read so often on television. But this wasn't television. Each member of that jury carried the considerable burden of ultimately deciding what Larry really felt and thought the morning he almost killed Fred Salloum.

Smitty told the jury that when Larry told him about Fred's alpha waves controlling him, "he got a look like I never saw, when he said about that change into a female. He was anywhere but in that room." Then, after a few more minutes, Smitty said what Larry told him: " 'I hit him and I hit him and I hit him.' "

The words echoed in the courtroom, just as they had in Smitty's mind from the time, six months before, when he first heard them.

With the testimony of Investigator Harold J. Smith, who told Reybitz on cross-examination that the police had not, to his knowledge, been spying on Larry nor did Larry claim to him that they had, the Commonwealth of Pennsylvania had called its last witness. It was five minutes before noon, and before the judge let the jury recess for lunch he agreed, over Chester Reybitz's objection, to the state's request that the hammer and the Miranda card circulate among them. Refowich was taking nothing for granted. He wanted them to hold the heavy Warren-Teed stonemason's hammer in their hands and see the blood and hair of Fred Salloum that was still on it. He wanted them to see the card that Larry had signed, indicating he understood what Smitty had read to him and was willing to talk anyway.

The jury (ten men and two women, and two male alternates) that filed out of the courtroom had been asked to absorb a great deal in the past twenty-four hours, and by the end of the afternoon they would be asked to render a verdict.

Before the jury returned to their seats at one-thirty, Chester Reybitz notified the judge that he wanted to approach the bench. He told Judge Freedberg that he had advised Larry to testify in his own behalf, but that Larry did not wish to. The judge assured Larry that if he did not testify, the prosecutor could not argue that it should be seen as a silent admission of guilt. It was the state's burden to prove its case—not the defense's—but the judge told him it was his right to testify if he wanted. "I would rather not," Larry said. "I think everything has been said already that is needed to be said."

But no sooner had he said that than Freedberg asked him once more, just to be certain, and this time Larry said, "Okay, I'll testify. I don't care."

On direct examination by Reybitz, Larry was a tight-lipped, frustrating witness. He was reluctant to say what had caused him to attack Fred and practically denied that Fred had any control over his mind and body or had done anything to him at all.

. Asked if he had known what he was doing at the time he assaulted Fred, he said that he had.

"Tell the jury, then," Reybitz urged him, "why you struck him over the head."

"Because I felt he was going to . . ." Larry said, then paused before continuing, ". . . get the hammer and hit me first, so I hit him before he hit me." At least he was still claiming self-defense.

"Was he standing when you struck him over the head?"

"Yeah, he was."

"Was he facing you?"

"No, he wasn't."

"What was he doing?"

"He was grabbing his books."

"And where were his books located with regard to his bed?"

"They were on his desk."

". . . How far away, may I ask you, from his desk was he?"

"Two feet."

"Two feet. And when you struck him, did he fall down?"

"Yeah."

". . . Where did he fall?"

"Well, he didn't fall down. He didn't fall down right away—or he didn't—"

"What did he do?"

"He started to kneel down."

"He started to kneel?"

"Well, he started to fall down, yes. He started to fall down."

"Did he ever attempt to turn around and face you?"

"Yeah. Well, at least I felt he was."

"Well, did he or did he not?"

Larry shrugged his shoulders. "Didn't give him a chance."

"So after you hit him, he began to fall, and he fell to his knees, and you kept hitting him?"

"Yes."

"That's where he fell, then: two feet from the desk; is that correct?"

"No. He fell lengthwise across, on the floor, around his bed—or something like that."

"And you are positive that your roommate, Fred Salloum, was not sleeping in his bed, sound asleep, when you first struck him over the head with the hammer . . . ?"

"Oh, I'm positive."

It was now the prosecutor's turn, and he was relentless. When he asked Larry about the hammer, Larry said he had bought it the day before the attack, put it in his car, and was going to use it for "protection" when he got to Mexico.

"Protection in Mexico?" Refowich asked, a bit incredulous.

"Well, it's—I shouldn't have bought the thing, but that's beside the point."

"Why shouldn't you have bought it?"

"Because it was a dumb thing that happened right afterwards . . . so I'm in here now. That's why I should not have bought it."

"You don't like being in here now, do you?"

"No."

". . . When you bought this Exhibit No. 1, did you plan to use it to hit Fred on the head?"

Larry paused before answering. "No."

"When did you decide to use this to hit Fred on the head?"

"When I was down in my car."

". . . How far was it from where your car was parked to the university?"

"About half a mile."

". . . What time did you leave the car to go to the university?"

"About three-thirty, three forty-five."

"Was that in the afternoon or morning?"

"Morning."

"Morning. And when you left the car, you took . . . Exhibit No. 1, didn't you?"

"Yep."

"Carried it with you all the way from that car up to your room and Fred's room, didn't you?"

"Yes."

"But you were going to take this with you to Mexico for self-defense, weren't you?"

"I was going to keep it in my car, yeah."

"But you didn't keep it in your car; you took it with you, didn't you?"

"Yeah."

"Felt you needed some protection?"

"Yeah, you could say that."

"Well, I would like you to tell me why did you take Exhibit No. 1 with you from the car that morning?"

"So the guy wouldn't bother me in my sleep, that's all. I didn't want to hit him, but he jumped up."

"Why didn't you want to hit him? Did you think that was something that was wrong?" Refowich asked, wanting to lead him into a trap.

"Yes, it's wrong. I did a wrong thing. I hit him over the head with a hammer, obviously."

"You realize what you did was wrong?"

"Yes."

"Are you sorry for what you did?"

"Yes."

"Did you realize when you did it that it was wrong?"

"Yes."

"Yet when you did it, and you realized it was wrong, you still did it, didn't you?"

"When I hit him first I couldn't stop, or else he would have turned around and got me."

"You hit him from behind, didn't you?"

"Yes."

"You didn't tell him you were going to hit him, did you?"

Larry said nothing.

"Did you?"

"I gave him warning."

"You what?"

"I warned him."

"What did you say to him?"

"Nothing."

"How did you warn him, if you didn't say anything to him?"

"I didn't."

"Did you warn him or didn't you?"

"No."

". . . Which hand did you hold this in?"

"The right."

"Your right hand?"

"Um-hum."

"Which part of it did you hit him with?"

"The blunt side of the hammer."

"The blunt, this side?" Refowich held it in front of him.

"Yes."

"Why did you use the blunt side instead of the pointed end?" he asked. The blood and hair were clearly on the pointed end.

"Because I didn't really want to hurt the guy. That's why."

". . . Because you didn't want to hurt him, you hit him with this blunt end?"

"There was no line of reasoning. I'm just saying when I hit him, it happened with the blunt side, and that's it."

"If you hit him with the blunt end, is the reason why you didn't hit him with the sharp end because you realized you might kill him, and that would be wrong?"

"Yes."

"Excuse me?"

"Yeah, you could say that."

". . . How many times did you hit him?"

"Six or seven."

"I think you said that the door was locked. Am I correct? The door to the room?"

"Apparently it was, yes."

"Who locked it?"

"I did, probably."

". . . Probably? When you came in the room, was Fred in bed asleep?"

"Yeah."

"No one came in the room after you, did they?"

"Nope."

"Did anybody go up to that door after you came in the room and touch the lock?"

"Nope."

"You locked the door; is that right?"

"Hmm. At some point I probably locked the door, yeah."

"After you hit Fred six or seven times with the blunt end of Exhibit No. 1 did anybody knock on the door?"

"Yes."

"Did anybody say anything?"

"Yeah."

"What did you hear said to you through the door?"

"What's going on inside the room?"

"And what did you say?"

"I said don't worry about it."

"Why did you say don't worry about it?"

"What else could I say?"

"Did you realize you had done wrong, and you didn't want anybody to see what you had done?"

"Obviously."

". . . Okay. Now, I think you said that you hadn't had any problems with Fred before this incident; is that correct?"

"Yeah."

"You got along?"

Larry gave another shrug of his shoulders.

"He didn't do anything to you, did he?"

"No."

"He never hit you, did he?"

"No."

"Never took anything from you, did he?"

"I don't think so, no."

"What?"

"No, no."

"Now, you saw Dr. Sadoff for about two hours; am I right?"

"No."

"That is not right?"

"No, it's not right."

"How long did the interview between you and the doctor take?"

"About forty-five minutes."

"About forty-five minutes?"

"Um-hum."

"So when the doctor said it was about two hours, he is mistaken?"

"Padding," Larry blurted out.

"What?"

"Padding."

"Padding what? The bill?"

"Yeah," Larry said, his response bringing a smile to the judge's face.

"Who is paying the doctor's bill at a hundred dollars an hour?"

"My grandmother."

After a few more minutes of testimony that served to reinforce the viciousness of the attack, Refowich pulled out one of the many letters Larry had sent to Lehigh's dean of students.

"Did you write in this letter," Refowich asked, "'I wish I had killed him instead of just injuring that faggot'?"

"That was a dumb comment, but—"

"Did you write it?"

"Yeah."

". . . Who is Kathy?"

"A girl I knew at M & M."

"Friend of yours?"

"Yeah."

"Just a friend?"

"Yeah."

"Did Fred Salloum have any control over what you did? Did he control you?"

"No, not that I was aware of."

"Did anybody control you? Did anybody tell you what to do that night or that morning?"

"No."

"You didn't hear voices telling you or animals telling you what to do, did you?"

"No."

Refowich sat down; he had succeeded in getting Larry to say all the things he would need to make a strong closing argument that Larry Bradshaw knew exactly what he was doing that cold December morning.

When Reybitz rose for re-direct, he was weary and annoyed. He had pinch-hit at the last second for Stanley Vasiliadis, but had gotten little cooperation from his client. In his hand he held one of the letters Larry had sent to the District Attorney's Office—a letter claiming (as did the letter to Dean Cohen) that Fred had raped Kathy Van Tyne. If Reybitz, who had the letter admitted into evidence, could show that Larry believed this, even though it had never happened, perhaps it would tip the scale back to the kind of argument that Sadoff had made in regard to Larry's delusional state. When he asked Larry if the statements he had made in his letter (which Reybitz did not specify, but which the jury would ultimately hear) were true and correct, Larry said they were.

But Refowich, convinced that Larry wasn't sure of *anything*, aside from his own name, had put Larry on the ropes during cross-examination, and was eager to deliver a knockout punch.

"Did your roommate rape your girlfriend?" he asked on re-cross.

"As far as I am aware of, no."

"But I thought you just said to your attorney that everything that was in that letter is true?"

"Yeah."

"Yet you now tell us that your roommate didn't rape your girlfriend?"

"I never said that."

"Well, read to us the first sentence."

"I said—"

"Of the third paragraph, please."

"I said in the letter he did rape my girlfriend, yes."

"Is that true or false?"

"True."

"It's true?"

"That's what it says in the letter."

"But did he rape your girlfriend?"

"I don't know."

"You don't know?"

"No."

"You do know whether or not you hit Fred on the head with a hammer seven times, don't you?"

"Yeah."

"And you do want the jury to believe that you are insane, don't you?"

"No."

* * *

Refowich sat down, triumphant. The young man for whom the insanity defense had been offered had just said he didn't want the jury to believe he was insane. How could the jury return a verdict other than guilty? Refowich wondered. Or had they been so persuaded by Dr. Sadoff's testimony that it would transcend anything Larry had said?

An officer of the court read to the jury the two letters that had been admitted into evidence. The judge told them that both sides would give closing arguments and he would then give them their instructions. Reybitz tried to stress the weight he felt they should give to Sadoff's testimony. Refowich not only attacked the psychiatrist, but tried some reverse psychology of his own. He told the jury that if any of them wanted Larry sitting next to their family that evening at McDonald's, then that person should by all means find Larry not guilty by reason of insanity.

In his instructions, Judge Freedberg reminded the jury that they were the sole judges of the facts and it was the state's burden to prove its case to them beyond a reasonable doubt. He told them not to be concerned with any penalty the defendant might get if he was found guilty, only with rendering a verdict, which had to be unanimous. He explained in great detail the charges against Larry and said that if he was found guilty of attempted criminal homicide, they must be satisfied that he did in fact commit the act; that he did it with the intent to commit the crime of homicide; and that the act constituted a substantial step toward the commission of the crime.

Since they were also being asked to decide Larry's plea of insanity, Freedberg stressed again that their judgment had to be based on what they felt his state of mind was at the time of the act. He told them that ordinarily a jury does not include reasons in its verdict, but since this was an insanity-defense case he was asking for a special form of verdict: they could either find him not guilty by reason of insanity (explaining that he could still be committed to a mental facility) or simply not guilty (if they couldn't agree on the insanity question).

At a few minutes before five that afternoon, less than half an hour after they had closed the door to deliberate, the jury had a verdict. *Guilty of an attempt to commit criminal homicide in the third degree* (acting with malice but without premeditation). *Guilty of aggravated assault. Guilty of reck-lessly endangering another person.*

Larry's two days in court were over, and no one from his family had come to be with him. (Frances was supposed to have been a witness, but told Reybitz the day before the trial she wasn't coming, and gave no reason.) Less than a month later, Larry was brought in front of Judge Freedberg again. But it was not for sentencing (which was being deferred pending the court's response to the defense's appeal motions). Larry's condition had deteriorated drastically. Once again, he was not eating and refusing to shower. The prison felt that another transfer to a state hospital was called for, and the judge concurred. But this time Larry wasn't being sent to the Allentown State Hospital. He was being transferred from the prison to the only maximum-security hospital in the state of Pennsylvania considered to be secure—the Fairview State Hospital for the Criminally Insane in Waymart—for another ninety-day commitment period.

30// Larry wasn't the only member of the family in 1980 who was getting used to new surroundings. In the spring, Frances, Marc and Lavinia moved to one of the most prestigious addresses in all of Manhattan—the moneyed world of 10 Gracie Square.

High above the East River, the building is a few blocks south of Gracie Mansion, the Mayor's residence. One of its two entrances is located on the south side of Carl Schurz Park—the park where Marc and Larry used to play as children and Lavinia did now—and is just east of East End Avenue, the street where Frances had had three apartments on different occasions.

But in New York a half block in either direction can suddenly take one from one world into quite another, and the world of East End Avenue, nice as it may be, and York Avenue (where she moved from) is not the world of 10 Gracie Square. And nobody was more aware of that distinction than

Frances Schreuder. She was entering a building whose occu-
pants, a doorman whispered curtly one day from behind an
electronically operated, cagelike garage door, were "the rich
beyond the rich"—Madame Chiang Kai-shek, Steve Ross
(the chief executive of Warner Communications), John Fairchild of Fairchild Publications, Gloria Vanderbilt (who
moved in after Frances) and a bevy of others—people whose
privacy and well-being the staff were well tipped to protect.
Frances had arrived and could, at last, begin living in the style
to which she had longed to be accustomed.

She moved into apartment 6A, but the "A" was misleading. The building has three lobbies, each with its own
elevator. Frances's apartment occupied the *entire* sixth floor
of her wing of the building and the floor above it—a
four-bedroom, twelve-room duplex that Berenice purchased
for well over $500,000. She wanted Frances to have a place
from which she would never again have to fear eviction.

At the New York City Ballet, George Balanchine was busy
choreographing a new work for the company's seventy-
second season, and Frances donated over $350,000 in order to
make the production possible. On June 19, "Robert Schu-
mann's 'Davidsbündlertänze'" had its premiere, and Frances
was in attendance. Shortly before that, she had been invited
to join the board of directors.

Not far from Lincoln Center, in her more modest cooperative apartment on West End Avenue, Marilyn Reagan was
becoming increasingly disturbed. She had heard from both
Joel Campbell and her mother what had happened with Larry
early that December morning at Lehigh, and it only served to
deepen her and Elaine's conviction that he had murdered
their father. Campbell told Marilyn he had been in touch with
the Bethlehem police and had requested a trip to Pennsylvania, but his superiors were reluctant. They still didn't feel
there was enough to go on. Marilyn and Elaine had been
disenchanted with the police right from the start, and their
decision to do nothing only added to the sisters' considerable
dissatisfaction. As she had in 1978, Marilyn offered once
more to finance a trip, but the department said no. So
obsessed was she with finding her father's killer that if she

could have had the entire Great Salt Lake dredged she would have, certain that a rusted gun would be brought up from its depths.

Though the police refused her offer, that didn't stop Marilyn from continuing her private detective work. She had gone to Salt Lake in April of 1980 to deal with some Bradshaw Investment business—Marilyn had managed to buy out the minority stockholders, and now, along with the bank, had the controlling shares—and had asked her mother, who was planning to be away, if she could stay at Gilmer Drive. It would not only save her the cost of a hotel, but would give her an opportunity to resume her search for the gun.

Knowing that Larry had been sleeping in the basement that summer, Marilyn had a flashlight with her as she walked down the steps one day. The basement had a dropped ceiling, and she thought maybe Larry had stashed the gun above it. She stood on a chair and shined the light above the one in Larry's room, but could see nothing. In the other bedroom there was a tiny opening in the ceiling by a heat duct. Standing on the chair once more, she gingerly slipped her hand through the gap and began to feel around. As she started to pull her hand back, she brushed up against something—something cold, like the barrel of a gun. But what she pulled down was not a gun but a set of keys.

Disappointed that she hadn't unearthed the murder weapon but feeling a small measure of elation nonetheless, she telephoned Joel Campbell's office, and an officer drove out to the house to pick them up.

Why were the keys hidden there? Marilyn wondered. And by whom? Were they the *new* keys that Don Bradshaw had brought up to the house that evening after Doug Steele had the locks changed, and that Larry had taken out of Berenice's hands? Or the ones from the summer of 1977 that Marc and Larry had used for their midnight raids? Or possibly the ones that fit the padlocks Doug had found undone that Sunday?

Prior to going out to Salt Lake, Marilyn received a phone call. The caller identified himself as a friend of Frances's and someone whom Marilyn had met on a couple of occasions years before. He wasn't a total stranger, but it was certainly odd that he was phoning her, and she asked him what he wanted.

He explained that he had opened a joint savings account with Frances a year before at the Chase Manhattan Bank. He had taken out a college loan for a master's degree in environmental studies, and was in the process of paying it back when he lost his job as a New York City public school teacher. Since he was unemployed, he was concerned that his various creditors (including the city's Parking Violations Bureau, to which he owed at least $3,000 in unpaid fines) would come to call, and knew that the only way he could "protect" his money was by having it in a *joint* account. He transferred his money from the Yorkville Savings and Loan and deposited $4,100 at Chase on April 18, 1979. Two days later he deposited another $400. Frances called him and asked if she could withdraw some money; he said she could, provided she replaced it. Frances withdrew $1,200 on April 30 and two weeks later deposited that amount back into the account. But by early September she had withdrawn a total of $3,688.43 and his efforts to recover it had been futile. He had written to her ("I was and am banking on these monies for my use in an era of hard times") without success, and had spoken with Marc about it. By chance he had bumped into her and Lavinia on the street in January. Frances had told him that she was going through a difficult period, needed the money for a "will fight," but fully intended to pay him back. Marc had told him things were "tight" and asked him not to put pressure on her. He had tried to be patient with Frances, he told Marilyn, but things were extremely tight for him as well and he needed the money.

What did he expect her to do? Marilyn wanted to know. If he knew her sister well enough, she said, he should know that money, no matter what the amount, was not safe with her. He knew the many years Frances had struggled over money with her "miserly" father, he said, and agreed there was no reason to think that his nest egg would have been secure. Marilyn said that if he expected her to cover his debt, she couldn't. He was at his wit's end, he said, and asked whom he might contact in Salt Lake with some connection to her father's estate. Perhaps he could get his money from them. Trying to

289

be helpful, Marilyn gave him the names of two people who could possibly help: Steve Swindle, the lawyer for Walker Bank who was dealing with the estate, and Lou Gerbig, a woman in the bank's trust department. He thanked her for the names and said that he would keep her apprised of his progress.

On May 21, he wrote a letter addressed to both Swindle and the bank outlining the situation. "When I asked for my own funds," he wrote, "I was treated by her as if I was doing something wrong. As a matter of fact, my own father was called and told that I was harassing her."

He told them about meeting her on the street with Lavinia and her assurance that "she would renew the balance on the account so that I could close it out in an equitable manner."

But since that accidental meeting, he said, "I have not had a cent restored to the account as far as I know at this date. I have written both regular and certified letters to her, her attorneys, and have had no response to any of them. I have called her law firm [the New York firm of Rogers & Wells] a few times and have been assured, as of this past Winter, that Mrs. Schreuder was going through a crisis and she would take care of the matter when she had settled more important affairs. . . .

"It seems that Mrs. Schreuder did have her problems and the request to wait with patience for forthcoming monies was a valid-enough request. However, I do think that this matter has been held in abeyance for an unnaturally long period and wish to have over with the situation. It is true that she apparently had a crisis with her son's behavior while at college [Marilyn was the one to tell him about Larry], enough apparently to cause her to make an attempt on her own life, according to her son. For these grave reasons I wish to appeal for my funds from you as I wonder why I haven't heard from her. She is either unwilling or unable to respond to my or her lawyers' appeals."

He attached the entire financial history of the transaction— all the withdrawal and deposit slips—and suggested that they contact the banks in question if they wanted to verify his claim. Knowing (again from Marilyn) that Frances had recently purchased a duplex and had rented a house the previous summer, he wrote, "I find this behavior strange in view of the fact that I have known her for over fifteen years, hence my appeal to your good offices for help in this eerie affair."

On May 29, Steve Swindle wrote him back, saying that Van Cott, Bagley did not represent Mrs. Schreuder and it was their opinion that this was a personal matter and had nothing to do with the estate. He suggested he write to Frances's lawyer in Salt Lake—Ron Madsen—and said he had already forwarded the material on to him.

As soon as he received Swindle's letter, the man fired one off to Madsen. Deciding to lay an official trail of paper and discontent, he sent copies to Swindle, Lou Gerbig, Peter Wallison (at Rogers & Wells) and Frances herself. Maybe Frances would be embarrassed enough to pay him his piddly amount and put an end to this nonsense. He understood, he wrote Madsen, that her allowance had been raised from $3,000 to $5,000 a month, and said that he would never have opened an account with her if he hadn't known and trusted her. Referring to himself as "some sort of family confidant," he said that he in fact knew her so well that he had lent her his American Express card once to take Marc on a college interview in Maine. ("Things like this are not entered into lightly. No one I know would lend their American Express Card to anyone.") He also said that he had lent her money "during her years of stress while going through some very harrowing and financially debilitating divorce actions first entered into back in 1963."

Saying that he did not want to stop payments on his college loan, he asked Madsen to view the situation seriously and to appreciate the fact that he was "hurt and poorer at this juncture for the experience. I look forward to hearing from you concerning this most pressing and disturbing affair and I expect a judicious decision to secure for me my missing funds through your access to available Estate funds."

The reply from Madsen was as discouraging as Swindle's had been. His client had not contacted him about this, he said, and he was not in a position to do anything unless authorized. Though these lawyers could not have known it at the time—especially Swindle—the man to whom they were writing was a persistent, embattled figure who was not about to fold his tent. He was an indefatigable letter writer and filer of lawsuits. The New York City Board of Education could attest to that. Often when he left a school because of an unsatisfactory performance rating, he filed suit against the school board but then failed to appear, as his own lawyer, in court. The case would be continued and, each time that happened, it cost the Board of Education both money and frustration. That was his intent. When he wrote letters of complaint about his dismissal, he would send copies to New York's two senators and his congressman, as well as to state politicians who represented his district.

He was fascinated by the legal process and had wanted to go to law school. So while his letters, on the one hand, gave him a vicarious chance to be lawyerlike in tone, the situation with Frances was genuinely beginning to anger him. Out of work and needing his money back, he decided to step up his attack.

On June 11—the same day that Larry went to trial—the man wrote Frances the kind of 1-2-3 businessman's letter she had often received from her father, a letter filled with misspellings and errors in punctuation that did not indicate a lack of knowledge so much as a lack of care. Get the letter written and make copies for the world—that was his view of progress.

To date you have, since last Fall stressed to me, at the time, that you were (1) short of funds (2) the manager (ass't) as the bank lost your own account (3) were moving (4) were going through a terrible time vis-a-vis your son, your sister, your mother, your own medical problems. I do not doubt any of these massive hemorhages. As you know, I have had some problems too in the past. However, before you toot off to South Hampton this Summer, I thought that you might make good on these missing funds though conceivably, one might think that a bank account such as this can be cleaned out in a more-equal-on-one-side-manner, than on-the-other-side-manner.

As you might well know, I have contacted your agents or lawyers here in NYC and also those in Salt Lake with no positive results so far. Positive Results is to be interpreted to mean, my money returned to me. I have been toying with the idea of having my Harvard-Berkeley lawyer nephew contact Peter Wallison, as they just might be class mates. I have also felt it incumbent to remind William Rogers [the former Secretary of State and the Rogers of Rogers & Wells] that he and my mother were old pals in Plattsburg, NY when she went to school there. I find all these facts interesting but of little use for this crazy affair.

Please try to settle this matter because in relation to the total of the monies you are wrestling over at present, this is carfare for your group for a month.

Throughout the summer there was no sign of progress. The man stayed in constant touch with Marilyn, often calling her from pay phones. Concerned that his phone might be tapped, he told her he did not want Frances (whose feelings about Marilyn he was keenly aware of) to know he was speaking with her. Marilyn had been the first to tell him what had happened to Larry, and he was stunned. Neither Frances nor Marc had mentioned it to him. He had tried to contact Larry at Lehigh once, was told he was no longer a student there, but nothing else. He knew that Frances could be very secretive when she wanted to be—especially about family matters—so he never asked.

During their conversations over the summer, Marilyn told him her theory that Larry had murdered her father and dropped the gun from his airplane into the Great Salt Lake, and that Frances was somehow behind it. The man said little. Frances had told him her father had been murdered, he said, and shown him some articles about it. Marilyn was both surprised at how much he seemed to know about the family and disturbed by the degree of sympathy he seemed to have for Frances's turbulent relationship with her parents—especially her father—over the years. Frances clearly had him brainwashed, Marilyn felt, so every time the man was critical of her father she defended him and the way he had treated Frances.

Did he know what had happened during the summer of 1977, Marilyn quizzed him, with the forgeries and the thefts? Yes, he did. In fact, he knew much more than Marilyn could have imagined.

* * *

By August he was still writing letters and getting nowhere. On the 12th, he wrote Frances again and suggested that she get the money to pay him from Berenice—"keeper of the keys to your main capital"—or by suing for past child support.

"I don't know why you think you can take these funds, use them and not replace them. I also don't understand how you appear to be taking advantage of a relationship of long standing by ignoring this most important matter. I would say that this amount is small in comparison to your allowance [$5,000 a month] and wonder why you would not negotiate in any manner. . . . As stated before, I find this behavior strange, illogical and irresponsible."

Having sent Berenice copies of his letters, he appealed to her directly in a letter on August 16. Surely, he thought, she would see how ludicrous the situation had become, and would want to straighten it out.

But like her daughter, Berenice was silent on the matter.

There was only one course of action left to him—one that he had hoped to avoid, but one whose procedures were familiar to him. He had been trying for nearly a year to recover his money; if he couldn't succeed by letter and phone call, he would have to take legal action.

Acting as his own lawyer, he filed suit in New York's Civil Court for $3,688.43. When he subsequently found out that Frances denied the charges—he had not come to court that day—he was livid. On the evening of Wednesday, October 15, he phoned Marilyn. His phone calls had become more frequent, and Bob Reagan had been urging Marilyn for a while to stop talking with him. Bob was not unsympathetic to the man's situation, but didn't see how Marilyn could help him. Marilyn paid no attention to her husband. In their last few phone conversations, whenever she repeated her theory about Larry, the man, who before had said nothing, hinted that Larry might not be the one. When she pressed him as to why he thought that, he offered nothing further.

But on this particular evening he seemed testier than usual. When Marilyn again brought up her favorite subject, there was a long silence on the other end of the line before he spoke.

"You're absolutely wrong, Marilyn. You've got the wrong boy."

"How can you say that?" she pressed, determined to pry it out of him if necessary. "How do you *know* that?"

"Because," he said. "Marc did it. He told me."

"Marc wasn't in Salt Lake," she insisted. "Larry was. What about the gun?" she asked, trying to contain her excitement. *"Where* is the gun?"

There was another long pause, as if the line had gone dead.

"I have the gun right here," he confessed. "Marc gave it to me."

Part Four//

We seek him here, we seek him there,
Those Frenchies seek him everywhere.
Is he in heaven?—Is he in hell?
That demmed, elusive Pimpernel?

—BARONESS ORCZY

31// The news was almost too incredible to be true. Amazed and delighted, Marilyn phoned Elaine to let her know. She still had to persuade Richard Behrens to part with the gun, but she was confident that she could. He had asked to remain anonymous—"at least until those boys [the police] do their homework" and confirmed that it was the murder weapon—and Marilyn agreed to protect his identity. Elaine and Mason told her to call Joel Campbell, and that under no circumstances should she allow Behrens to come into her apartment.

The next morning Marilyn called Salt Lake and spoke with Campbell, who had recently been transferred from homicide to sexual offenses against children. But this was still, at least in his mind, *his* case. If any warrant was to be drawn, he was going to issue it; and if any arrest was to be made, he was going to make damn sure he got credit for it. Marilyn told Campbell she thought she could persuade the man ("a longtime family friend") to give her the gun that evening. She had told Behrens to turn it in to the New York police himself, but he refused. She said she would send the police around to his apartment. If she did that, he said, the gun wouldn't be there and he would sue the police for false arrest. He would *only* give it directly to her. Campbell told her to take it to her local precinct and gave her a night number where he could be reached. That was it. No offer to alert the New York police ahead of time so they could plant a plain-clothes witness and protect Marilyn. No mention at all. It was a basic you're-doing-great-Marilyn-keep-on-truckin' response.

That evening—Thursday, October 16—Behrens phoned again, and Marilyn could tell that he would need to be dealt with carefully and cajoled into giving her what she wanted. She said that the $10,000 reward the family had offered two years before was still available. Knowing that he was unem-ployed, she felt this was the approach to take. But he said that if he gave her the gun and the police didn't "get their act together, I'll need a lot more than ten thousand dollars to get me out of the trouble Frances will put me in."

This came as no surprise to Marilyn, who had always assumed that her sister was involved in the murder. In fact, in one of their earlier conversations, Behrens had told her that during the summer of 1977 Marc and Larry were supposed to poison their grandfather's oatmeal with some pills that Frances had given them before they left for Salt Lake (the hope being, Behrens said, that it "would throw off his body chemistry one way or the other so he might have a heart attack or an overdose of something").

But there was more. He also told her that her sister had been looking for someone to kill her father in the fall of 1977, that *he* had introduced her to a man who had agreed to do it, and that the man was given "several thousand" dollars. But the man turned out to be a con artist, he said, and "beat her out of the money." Behrens had mentioned the man's first name and on more than one occasion, but Marilyn, oddly, neither wrote it down nor remembered it.

Campbell had told Marilyn to ask for the serial number of the gun, and Behrens promptly gave it to her: N281919. He mentioned that he also had a box of bullets Marc had given him and that he was extremely paranoid about both mother and son—afraid that they might find out what he had told her and suddenly appear on his doorstep. If that was the case, Marilyn said, all the more reason to get rid of the gun so they couldn't use it on him. Besides, she warned him, there was a new law that had just been passed in New York State that made it illegal for anyone to possess a gun without a license and carried a one-year jail term for the person foolish enough to do so.

Behrens listened to everything Marilyn had to say. But as she went on talking, he began to think about the past. He did not want it to come to this. He had known Frances for a long time, and had been a loyal friend. He had known her sons from the time they were toddlers, and Lavinia from the moment she was born. He had helped her spy on Vittorio and he had hidden documents for her when she was divorcing Frederick. She had even asked him to find someone to kill her father and he had done so. When that fell through, she had asked him to buy a gun for her and he searched for a hunting rifle in Virginia and New Jersey. But when he couldn't get any sort of weapon without signing for it, he refused to go further. Even he, loyal as he was, could see the potential problems in doing that.

Since he knew a good deal about ballistics from a previous job he had had, he suggested a shotgun—making it impossible, he felt, for a ballistics test to be done—but in the end that suggestion had not been taken. When Marc brought the gun back from Salt Lake that fourth Sunday in July and it was "dumped" on him, he did not refuse it. In fact, shortly after the murder, he and Marc drove Frances's Oldsmobile down to a gun shop in lower Manhattan, not far from the Brooklyn Bridge, and purchased a black vinyl cover for it. Behrens's father used to go hunting a lot (on one occasion, with Babe Ruth), and the importance of cleaning and taking care of a gun had been stressed to him from an early age. As he went into the shop to get both the cover and cleaning material for his newest possession, Marc took a picture of him. Like Larry photographing hundreds of highway signs on his cross-country trips, Marc wanted to record the event—to *prove* that it actually took place. Was it just another photograph to add to his collection—one that included all of those pictures of his grandfather's warehouse? Or was it a piece of evidence to use later, if necessary, against the family's loyal friend?

When Behrens got back to his apartment that day—an apartment crammed with all sorts of boxes and junk, decorated with model airplanes hanging from the ceiling, and inhabited by roaches scurrying up and down the walls—he slipped the gun into the cover and put it on a shelf. For more than two years the gun lay there, with the exception of the times he cleaned it. On occasion he thought about carrying it east a few blocks and dumping it into the East River, but he didn't. He had thought about going down to the South Street Seaport area and getting rid of it, but he never did. He had even thought about selling it, but made no inquiries. He had thought about doing all of those things, but from the night it had been brought over until now, the gun had never left his apartment.

No, he did not want to give it to Marilyn. Not really. But he was angry that his loyalty was being betrayed in this fashion. The amount of money—$3,688.43—might be "carfare" for Frances, but it was sorely needed by him.

On the other end of the line, Marilyn Reagan was waiting for his answer.

"I'll bring it over and call you when I get there." The "guy in compartment C" was about to emerge.

At about eight-thirty on that crisp October evening, Richard Behrens left his first-floor apartment at 326 East 89th Street, headed for the crosstown bus on 86th. In his right hand was an A&P shopping bag. The .357 Magnum he had held on to for almost twenty-seven months was in its black vinyl cover, inside a smaller paper bag. He could have been somebody's uncle, headed to a nephew or niece's birthday party, loaded down with presents. But he wasn't. He was an uncle of sorts, though, because not long after Frances had walked out on Vittorio and met Behrens at the Unitarian Church coffee hour he had become known as "Uncle George" to her sons.

When Behrens got off the bus at 86th and Broadway, he looked around to make sure no one was following him, and walked south four blocks, then west. From a pay phone on the northwest corner of 82nd and West End, he dialed Marilyn's number and said that he was across the street.

"Give the bag to the doorman," she suggested, hoping he would want to slip away quickly and she could secure a witness in the process.

"No way," he said firmly. "I will *only* give it to you."

Her husband had gone out for the evening. She said she'd

be right down. Even if Bob had been home and had tried, as a lawyer, to discourage her from taking possession of the gun, she would not have listened. Her mind was made up. She had to get that gun.

When she walked out the door of her building on the east side of the street, she saw somebody on the pay phone. She had met Behrens only twice before (at the same church Frances knew him from) and wasn't sure at first she would recognize him. But she did, wondering instantly whom he was speaking with, and worrying that maybe she was being set up.

It was too late to turn back, though, and she didn't really want to anyway. She began walking along 82nd Street toward Broadway (as she had said she would) and he followed behind her, close enough at one point to give her the bag. She turned right at the corner, and together they walked into a Burger King. Behrens bought a cup of hot chocolate for Marilyn and a coffee for himself. It was after nine-fifteen when they sat down, and Marilyn put the shopping bag under her seat, never checking to see if the gun was actually inside it. She wanted to get as many details as she could, but Behrens was reluctant to say much—at least not until the gun could be checked out. But he did tell her this: Marc had bought the gun from, of all people, a sheriff who liked to collect them; had arrived in Salt Lake the night before (by what means he was not sure); and had flown back to New York shortly after committing the murder that Sunday morning.

They finished their drinks, and once again Marilyn assured Behrens that he could remain anonymous for the time being. He promised to keep in touch and said he would call her; under no circumstances was she to call him.

As Marilyn crossed Broadway, continuing east on 82nd Street to the 20th Precinct between Amsterdam and Columbus avenues, Richard Behrens watched her until the darkness made her figure invisible. She had the gun, and nobody had seen him give it to her. He was not about to give it to a doorman—he could see through that suggestion just as he had seen through Frances's suggestion he *sign* for a gun. And when he had been on the pay phone earlier, he was not speaking to anyone but was merely pretending to as he "observed the street"—making certain there were no witnesses.

He knew that if for some reason the ballistics report (if there was one; he had been told that the bullets were smashed) did not check out and they could not confirm that it was the gun that killed Franklin Bradshaw, there was probably no case—and Marilyn would be walking into that precinct with a gun, but no real proof that anyone had given it to her. If it meant putting her, to whom he owed nothing, in jeopardy, so be it. He didn't necessarily want to do that, but as he boarded the bus that would carry him home, he certainly wanted to have that option.

"I'd like to see the highest-ranking officer on duty," Marilyn said, tense but excited as she stood before a glass window on the ground floor of the dimly lit precinct, clutching the shopping bag in her hand.

An officer looked up, his impassive face a sea of calm. "What is it, lady?" New York's Finest have seen it all, and they've heard it all.

"Here, you'll have to take this bag." The officer did not. "Please, take this bag," Marilyn said. "I was just handed it on the street and I believe it contains a gun." Getting a raised eyebrow but little more, she paused before continuing. "And I believe it's the gun that was used to kill my father in Salt Lake City, Utah, more than two years ago."

Three officers got up from their chairs at once. When one of them discovered that the bag did indeed contain a gun, a phone call was made upstairs. Within minutes a thin, dark-haired detective came down. His name was Ed Regan.

An Irish Catholic from the Bronx, Regan had been with the department since February of 1963, starting out as a patrolman not far from the place where he was born. He introduced himself to Marilyn, who showed him a business card. They walked upstairs, unzipped the black Weather Shield cover, and removed the gun. The handle was made of polished oak with delicately carved little ridges. It had a four-inch barrel with a blue finish, and the inscription on one side of the gun read: "HIGHWAY PATROLMAN, .357 CTG." Marilyn concluded that Behrens was probably right: he had said Marc had bought it from a "sheriff," and the gun she was looking at was a Smith & Wesson Highway Patrolman's Special. Asked for her story, she repeated what she had said earlier downstairs, adding that she had been in touch with Detective Joel Campbell, who had instructed her to turn the gun into the local precinct. Regan wanted to know the name of the person who had given her the gun, but she firmly said she didn't want to disclose his identity until it was established that this was the murder weapon. She would reveal his name at that time, she said, "if I have to."

As Regan vouchered the gun and invoiced it, he couldn't help thinking, We can't solve our own homicides, yet we're solving cases out of state. (A few weeks before Marilyn walked in off the street, a man had brought in a gun and admitted involvement in a crime in California.) The detective checked the computer to see if the .357 Magnum had been stolen (it hadn't been), put the gun in a property locker and forwarded it to Ballistics. At ten forty-six he sent Joel Campbell a teletype, confirming he had taken possession of the gun and asking Campbell to phone him the next day.

When the two detectives spoke, Campbell backed up Marilyn's statement and, more important, said that he had the two slugs from the body of Franklin Bradshaw. As soon as he organized a trip to New York, he said, he would be back in touch.

Marilyn and Bob had gone away for the weekend to their house in Dutchess County. When they arrived back at their apartment on Sunday night the phone was ringing. It was Richard Behrens. He said he had something that he should have given Marilyn on Thursday night—something that was in the bag Marc had given him the gun in.

It was a note, written on Kent School stationery with a name, address and phone number on it. Marilyn reached for a pen and a piece of paper and asked him to read it to her. The note—in Marc's handwriting—read as follows:

> DR. HERMAN CAVENAUGH
> 1805 MABERRY
> MIDLAND, TEXAS
> (915) 555-0700

He told her that he was fairly certain the gun had been purchased by Marc in Midland and that Marc had stayed with the Cavenaughs. Marilyn asked him to mail the note to her and he said he would. She relayed this information to Campbell, who already had contacted the Bureau of Alcohol, Tobacco and Firearms (ATF) in Washington with the serial number of the gun, hoping to find out to whom it belonged.

Marilyn knew that she would have to keep Behrens happy and did her best to do so. When she had told him about the existence of a reward, she had also offered to try to have any legal fees he might incur paid for by the estate. Jumping ahead in her mind to a trial and his role as a key witness, she spoke of the snow and the magnificent skiing he would find out in Utah, making it sound the most heavenly place on earth and implying she would gladly pay for any trips he might have to take.

But Behrens was not taken in by any of this. It was the ballistics report he most wanted to know about.

On Tuesday, October 21, Joel Campbell and Ed Regan spoke again on the phone. Campbell and another officer were planning to come to New York that Monday to have a ballistics test performed, and Regan promised to arrange for it. Now that a piece of physical evidence existed, the powers that be of the Salt Lake City Police Department saw the case as a "target of opportunity" and a chance, finally, to get what they loved most: some bang for their buck. Because Campbell was no longer officially in homicide, a huge, oxlike figure whose V-shaped torso made him look like a weightlifter was assigned to go with him. His name was John Johnson, a corporal who had been with the department sixteen years and in homicide for the last four.

The day after Campbell got the go-ahead to travel to New York he received some encouraging news from the ATF Trace Detail in Washington, D.C. The .357 Magnum had been sold by SArgent-SOwell Inc. of Grand Prairie, Texas, on July 21, 1977. The buyer had been a Sergeant Jerry A. Register of Colorado City, Texas. Campbell was astonished: it seemed Marilyn's source had been right. The gun had belonged to—and was probably sold by—a law-enforcement officer.

Campbell immediately phoned the police department in Colorado City and was told that Register had become the chief of police in the town of Stanton, which was about twenty miles from Midland—the city on the note. Campbell reached

Register that same day. The thirty-two-year-old Texan told him that at some point during the first two weeks of May in 1978, he and his wife, from whom he was now divorced, had gone to the Commercial Bank & Trust in Midland on a Saturday morning at about ten. They had been met by a young man in his late teens or early twenties, he said, and had sold the gun for around $175 to $200. He remembered that someone had "arranged" the sale, was vague about the details, and suggested that Campbell contact his ex-wife, who would probably recall things more clearly than he could.

Shara Vestal's initial recollection was fuzzy too, but she tried to remember the sequence of events as best she could. She had told a man named Fred Dillard that Jerry had a collection of guns and wanted to sell the .357. Dillard, she believed, informed an employee at the bank about the gun for sale, because within a week the employee called her, asking for a price. The next day the man called her again. He said he had a buyer for the gun, and instructed her to bring it to the bank that Saturday morning at ten. Like Register, she told Campbell that a young man in his late teens or early twenties drove up to the bank in a "yellow, newer sports car." Besides the three of them, she said, the bank employee (whose name "may have been Snow") was present during the transaction. She said that Jerry gave the buyer a receipt, but that the young man didn't reveal his name.

Campbell thanked her and said, as he had to Register, that he would most likely be traveling to Midland soon and would contact her again.

When Joel Campbell and John Johnson arrived in New York on Monday, October 27, Ed Regan had some bad news for them: the New York City Police Department no longer did ballistics comparison tests for outside authorities. But Regan's ex-partner said he would do an "unofficial" comparison as a favor. So the next day, Regan accompanied them to Ballistics, where Frank Nicolosi test-fired four shots from the gun into water. He put the specimens under his microscope, along with the two slugs the detectives had brought with them, and looked up a minute later.

"Gentlemen, you're in the ballpark," he said.

When they got back to their room at the Skyline Motor Inn

306

that evening, having also gone to see Marilyn, they made a decision. They would rent a car the next day and drive to the insurance capital of the country—Hartford, Connecticut. But they weren't going to investigate some financial scam or even to see the red-brick house where, far from the Mississippi, Mark Twain wrote *Huckleberry Finn*. They were going to see someone at Trinity College.

In the eighteenth century the area of Hartford that Trinity College would eventually occupy was known as Gallows Hill. In the late nineteenth, when teachers and students replaced hangmen and their victims, the college's trustees asked the English architect William Burges to design the new campus. With its striking Gothic chapel, archways, quadrangle and deep-green lawns, Trinity could be a credible understudy to a college at either Oxford or Cambridge—the models Burges was influenced by.

In September of 1980, after his year in exile—a year spent working as a security messenger for Mitsubishi Bank by day, playing video games late into the night, and helping his mother both take care of Lavinia and move to Gracie Square—Marc entered the class of 1984 at Trinity.

He stayed to himself a lot, took the bus home most weekends, and spent hours on end in the basement of the Mather Campus Center playing the pinball machines and video games he had grown to love. His reputation for this activity was so pervasive, in fact, that he acquired the nickname "Bee"—a reference to the sound the machines made.

The Wednesday in late October that Joel Campbell and John Johnson came to Trinity was a glorious autumn day in New England. Unlike many of the college's students, who wore blue blazers, bright crewneck sweaters, and walked hand in hand, Marc was dressed in a T-shirt, an old pair of corduroys that kept sliding down below his waist, and was alone as he entered the ivy-covered McCook Math-Physics Center for a class.

During the middle of it, a large man with jet-black hair and a tanned face walked in and told the professor that he wanted to talk with Marc. The man's name was Mike Schweighoffer, an ex-captain with the Hartford Police Department and the head of security for the college. He had been contacted by Joel Campbell earlier, told that Marc was a suspect in the murder of his grandfather and that they wanted to talk with him. Before giving his permission, Schweighoffer cleared the request with both the dean of students and the college vice-president and then alerted the Hartford police, who sent Detective Bob Beltrandi to pick up the Utah officers at the Hilton and escort them to Trinity.

When Marc came out of the classroom with Schweighoffer, he was introduced to Campbell, Johnson and Beltrandi and taken into another room. Schweighoffer, aware of the college's desire to be discreet and not alarm other students, wanted the discussion to be as unnoticed as possible. But there was little conversation at all. Contrary to what Campbell and Johnson had unrealistically hoped—that by flatly accusing Marc, they might provoke him into giving a full confession—Marc quietly said, "You'll have to prove these allegations in court," and walked out of the room.

But when he didn't go back to class, Campbell and Johnson were more than a little concerned that he might flee. They had taken a big gamble in coming to Trinity and confronting him in that fashion. If Marc thought they were only bluffing, in terms of proof, then he would probably stay at Trinity and act as if nothing had happened—innocent until *proven* guilty. But if he feared that they actually had something, then the detectives might have blown it.

By nightfall, word had spread slowly throughout the 1,700-member student body that some policemen had been on campus earlier that day and had questioned a freshman. About what, no one was sure. In Room 135 that evening in the North Campus Dormitory, Marc, shaken and surprised by the detectives' visit, told his roommate that he really needed to talk with somebody. But his roommate, who had gone to see Schweighoffer and been told in confidence that Marc was "under investigation," said that he would have to find someone else to discuss his problems.

There was always Mom.

32// Ernie Jones was thirty-three years old when he went to work in the Justice Division of the Salt Lake County Attorney's Office in August of 1980, but he had wanted to be a lawyer from the time he was a child. Six feet tall, 170 pounds and Boy Scout handsome, he had the wholesome, aw-shucks appearance of the farmboy that he used to be. The oldest of four boys, Ernie was born in Malad, Idaho, and moved, when his family decided to give up farming and he was about to enter fifth grade, to Ogden, Utah. His father eventually went to work at Hill Field, an Air Force base, and his mother became a junior high school teacher.

Since his father was a jack-Mormon and his mother a staunch Catholic, Catholicism was the religion in which he and his brothers were raised. Though Ernie was not a varsity athlete during his years at Weber High, he was just about everything else: vice-president of the student body as a senior; "The Happy Warrior" (the award for the most likable, all-around student); The Boy Most Likely to Succeed; a delegate to Boys State; and The Boy Most Likely to Be President. But what Ernie loved most of all was debating, and as a member of the school's team he traveled all over, earning a trip to San Francisco after he won the state's American Legion Oratorical Contest. When he graduated from Weber in 1965, twenty-fifth in a class of five hundred, he went to Weber State College on a debate scholarship.

After a year there, where he was president of his freshman class, Ernie transferred to the University of Utah and graduated in 1969. He began law school at the university that fall, married a girl he had known since high school, and went to Vietnam for a year as a legal clerk. In 1974, he took a job with the Weber County Attorney's Office; four years and a great deal of trial experience later, he went to work for the State Attorney General, dealing mostly with cases involving white-collar crime. Though he found the work challenging, he was extremely frustrated because very few of the cases ever came to trial. Ernie Jones was to the courtroom born, so when an opportunity came to join the Salt Lake County Attorney's Office, he grabbed it.

Jones was still the new kid on the block when the Bradshaw case was assigned to him shortly after Marilyn turned in the gun on October 16. Nobody in the office particularly wanted to issue on it, and even he, an obsessive worker eager to make his mark, was not thrilled about the assignment. It was an old case, people's memories would be fuzzy, there would be a lot of work to do, and he had no idea how strong or weak the evidence was going to be. All he knew was that a family friend had given a gun to Marilyn Reagan and said that Marc had admitted killing his grandfather; that the boy's mother might have been behind it; and that a lead would take them to Midland, Texas. When he went home that night, he brought a 1978 clipping on the murder from the paper and lamented to his wife what a weird and screwy case he had just gotten. Since he lived in the Ogden area, forty-five minutes from Salt Lake, he hadn't even read about the murder at the time it took place. But it wouldn't take him long to steep himself in a case that would take over his life and his dreams, that would take him in directions that he could hardly have imagined, and that would test every bit of his patience and knowledge of both law and people. Fiercely competitive below his easy-going surface, Ernie Jones loved challenges, and, as he soon found out, the Bradshaw case would be the biggest challenge of his young career.

On paper, Jones's client was the state of Utah, but, in a truer sense, it was really Franklin Bradshaw. And though Bradshaw hadn't liked lawyers, he would have found a lot to admire in Jones—his unswerving commitment to work, his penchant for simple brown-bag lunches (consisting, usually, of a bologna-and-cheese sandwich, potato chips, a banana and four cookies), his unpretentious manner, and his willingness to bed down in his office with a sleeping bag if necessary—and been pleased to know that he was in his corner.

Across the street from the County Attorney's Office, Joel Campbell had just returned from his trip. He filled Jones in on the details, and sent the two .38-caliber bullets recovered from Bradshaw's head and back, the four test specimens that Frank Nicolosi had fired in New York City, and the reddish-orange shirt Bradshaw was wearing the day he was shot to the ATF's regional laboratory in Treasure Island, California, for examination. He told Marilyn Reagan that he was planning to go to Midland, Texas, and wanted to have some pictures of Marc and Frances before he left. She didn't have any, she said, but promised to ask her contact for some.

Behrens was still phoning Marilyn, but his calls became less frequent. She told him that the ballistics situation appeared hopeful, and he told her that he was increasingly concerned about the intensive effort Frances and Marc were making to reach him. Since Behrens lived alone and had few close friends, he didn't doubt for a second who was pushing the buzzer to his apartment (located in the vestibule) with alarming frequency and calling him on the phone. The one time he did pick up it was Marc ("Well, I see that you and Marilyn have been busy,") and, he told Marilyn, he was getting "goosey." Marilyn told him about the photographs Campbell wanted for his trip to Texas, and he promised to send what he had. She received three pictures, sent Behrens $10 for his effort and expense in having them enlarged, but didn't hear from him again. After a week of phoning his apartment, leaving messages on his machine, and having, over the months, developed some of the same paranoia that he had, she was convinced that something had happened to him.

On Monday, November 17, Joel Campbell received two important pieces of information. The forensic chemist at the ATF lab in California told him that the bullet removed from Bradshaw's back matched the test specimens (the bullet from his head, however, could not be positively identified). Later that day, when Campbell phoned Marilyn to give her the good news, she said that she was prepared to reveal the identity of her informant—just in case someone had gotten to him.

Campbell wrote down his name, address and phone number, thanked her for the photographs she'd sent, and said that he'd contact her when he returned from Texas.

His case, at last, was starting to fall into place. Or so he thought.

Oil and guns.

Two things, more than any other, that a stranger can count on hearing about in the muscular West Texas city of Midland, midway between Dallas–Fort Worth and El Paso and right in the center of the oil-rich, pancake-flat Permian Basin.

One knows, of course, about the myths and legends—how *everything* is supposedly played out on a grand scale and larger than life itself; how the terms "laissez-faire" and "free enterprise" were invented with Texas in mind; how the people (whose attitudes are as wide open as the land itself) stubbornly, defiantly almost, consider themselves to be Texans first and Americans second and still lament the fact that the Republic of Texas ever became a state; and how, boom or bust, tomorrow, at least in Texas, will always be a brighter day, heavy with possibility.

A stranger can know all of those things, but knowing them does not prepare one for the reality—and two people who were not prepared for the reality that is Texas were Joel Campbell and Ron Nelson, the department's most decorated police officer, who had been asked to accompany Campbell on the trip and provide the "aggressive" element that some of their superiors felt Campbell lacked.

As their plane touched down at Midland Regional Airport and they drove east along Highway 80 toward town, the two detectives were entering a city that had more millionaires per capita than any in America, had the largest dealership of Rolls-Royces and Aston Martins in the country, and could probably boast—lest anyone think its citizens were *only* concerned with the making and spending of money—that well over half the population had a library card.

Whether Joel Campbell or Ron Nelson knew or cared about any of that was less important than the mission they were on—and the approach they brought to it. And one thing they learned very quickly is that no out-of-state police officer can shoulder his way into a place like Midland, Texas, imply that some of its citizens are outright criminals, and expect to be welcomed with open arms.

They went to the Midland Police Department, told the

local authorities why they were in town, and asked if they could interview some people there.

They went to the Commercial Bank & Trust and asked if a security guard named Snow—the name Shara Vestal had given them—worked there. Within minutes, a tall, white-haired man of sixty named John Snow ambled up the stairs. They explained who they were and why they were there and, after speaking with him for a few minutes, asked him to come to the police department later for a formal interview.

At the police department in Monahans, a town west of Midland, they interviewed Shara Vestal, who worked there as a dispatcher. A plain-looking woman of twenty-six, she had had nearly a month since her phone conversation with Campbell to think about the transaction.

Reluctant to cooperate, she nonetheless confirmed that Jerry Register had bought the gun from "SA-SO" (Sargent-Sowell Inc.) in 1977, and said he had decided to sell it because they were planning to go to El Paso and needed the money for their trip. She repeated what she had said on the phone—that she and Jerry took some guns from his collection over to Fred Dillard, whose carpet store was next to the General Finance Company where she worked, but that Dillard felt their asking price was too high. About a week later, she received a phone call from the bank security guard, who had heard she had some guns for sale. He said he was not in the market for a gun himself, but might know someone who was and asked for a price. They wanted $210 for it (the one they eventually decided to sell), she was fairly certain she told him, and he phoned back shortly thereafter to say he had a prospective buyer. Sometime in May of 1978, on a Saturday morning around ten, she met the security guard in the bank's lobby, and remembered a new-model sports car—either yellow or brown—pulling up. The driver was "very neatly dressed in a suit—a brown suit. He was about five feet ten, probably weighed about 165 or 170. His hair was sandy blond, a dark blond. A very intelligent young man, approximately eighteen to twenty-one years of age."

This could have been a rough description of Marc, except that Vestal then said that the young man and Jerry "had some friends in common." She said that she and Jerry gave him the gun, and he gave them cash. The gun was a Smith &

Wesson—a snub-nose, she thought. But she said they were selling so many at the time she wasn't sure. When they told her the gun they possessed had a four-inch barrel, she then remembered that the snub-nose (which had a two-inch barrel) had been sold to someone else..

"Do you know a man by the name of Malcolm McPhail?" they asked. John Snow had told them at the bank earlier that a man by that name had been involved in the transaction.

"McPhail's gas station," she said. "Yes, in Midland. I don't know of him personally, no. I heard of his reputation."

Did she know him by his nickname, Mac? No, she didn't; she just knew that he owned an Exxon station in Midland.

"Do you know a man named Bruce Stanley?" Another name that Snow had given them—someone else who might have been there that morning.

No, she didn't.

"Do you know a family by the name of Cavenaugh?" The name from the note on Kent stationery that Marilyn had gotten from Behrens and sent on to Campbell.

"In Midland, there's a Dr. Cavenaugh," she said, but added that she was not familiar with him or his family.

"Have you ever heard the name of Schreuder mentioned?"

"By you," she said, laughing, "that's all."

"You mentioned once before," she was told, "that that may have been the name that the person gave you at the bank."

It was a drop question, but she was not about to fall for it.

"Schreuder? No, that was a Mr. Snow—it wasn't Schreuder." And, she said, she wasn't even sure that his name was Snow.

Maybe she could remember Marc better if she saw some pictures, Campbell thought. So he flashed two in front of her: one of Marc and one of Larry (which Campbell had obtained shortly after Franklin's murder).

She looked at both carefully, but told the officers that she was sorry, neither person looked familiar to her.

The same day they interviewed Shara Vestal they spoke with Jerry Register at the Midland Police Department. Weighing about 275 pounds and looking as if he had just walked off the set of *The Dukes of Hazzard*, the Stanton police chief stuck to the story he had told Campbell on the phone in October. Like his ex-wife, he did not remember Malcolm McPhail's being at the bank that morning, nor could he identify the photos of Marc and Larry, though he did say that Bruce Stanley was someone with whom he had gone to high school.

Their trip was rapidly becoming a disaster. But they still had the murder weapon, and, because of that, they still had hope.

If Jerry Register is the kind of Texas lawman movies and television shows love to parody, Malcolm McPhail is the quintessential old-style Texan whom Lyndon Johnson would have been proud to know. In his sixties, McPhail is a large-featured, tough-talking, hard-drinking figure whom the Utah detectives made the mistake of confronting as if he had committed a crime by being involved in a gun transaction.

They had it "on very good authority," they said, that he had been involved in a gun transaction, a few years before, that resulted in murder. He didn't know what the hell they were talking about, he said. Didn't they know that guns are traded all the time in a place like Texas—that a gun transaction don't mean *nothing,* don't amount to a pile of shit? Why, he'd bought and sold hundreds over the years, he informed them. Every Texan he knew had a gun: they carried them in their cars, walked around Midland with them in shoulder holsters under their shirts, slept with them under their pillows at night. This was the most ridiculous thing he'd ever heard of—two detectives from Utah coming all the way to Midland to ask him about the equivalent of the weather.

They mentioned the Commercial Bank & Trust but they could have been asking him what he had eaten for dinner one night five years before. He did not remember.

But when they said the name John Snow, McPhail's expression changed. Slowly, he began to recall the day, indicating that he wanted to call John, "an old boy" he had known for years. After speaking with Snow for a few minutes, and also with one of the local policemen whom he knew well, he proceeded cautiously. He was offended by Campbell and Nelson and how they had had him come down to the police department as if he were a common criminal. He would tell them what he remembered—nothing more—and hoped they would be on the next plane out of town.

He had gone to the bank that Saturday morning, but could not recall the name of the young man who had gone with him. He said that the gun had been sold by a woman, whose name he did not know, but that Jerry Register was *not* there. Asked if he knew Dr. Herman Cavenaugh, McPhail said that his first name was *Herbert* (contrary to what the note said), but that it was really the doctor's eldest son, John, whom he knew best, explaining that John had worked for him when he had a service station. Could John Cavenaugh have been the boy with him that morning? He might have been, McPhail said, but could not say for sure.

The detectives then interviewed two young men who worked for McPhail—Roland Roballs and Nick Miller. Roballs recalled a conversation between McPhail and John Cavenaugh in which Cavenaugh asked him what was the best way to transport a pistol on an airplane. Nick Miller, who happened to be a good friend of Cavenaugh's, said that he remembered someone from out of town—a friend of John's—staying with the Cavenaughs during the period in question, but not his name. Maybe *he* could identify a picture, Campbell thought, pulling out the ones of Larry and Marc.

This is the boy, Miller said, pointing to the photograph on the left.

As the officers waited for John Snow to arrive at the police department, they sensed that Malcolm McPhail probably knew more than he was telling them. To make matters worse, neither Jerry Register nor Shara Vestal remembered McPhail's even being there, McPhail said that Register wasn't there, and nobody had been able to place Marc there. For all they knew, perhaps Marc had simply been visiting the Cavenaughs and had nothing to do with the transaction at all. Maybe Behrens had been lying to Marilyn. Somebody wasn't telling the truth—that was certain—and the detectives suspected that all of them had been talking with each other even before they arrived in Midland. John Cavenaugh and Bruce Stanley were out of town. If they could break John Snow down, they thought, maybe they could leave Midland with at least some of what they had come for.

No sooner had the interview begun than it seemed, to them, that Snow was holding back. They'd had "a gutful," they told him, and threatened him that if he didn't stop bullshitting them and start cooperating he'd end up in jail. Snow insisted that he was trying to help them and explained that after he learned Jerry Register had a gun for sale he phoned Bruce Stanley, who had a gun collection, and asked if he was interested. Stanley said he wasn't, but might know someone who was. The next thing he knew, Snow said, was that Stanley told him to set up the sale; McPhail and a young boy came down to the bank on a Saturday morning with an envelope stuffed with cash; and the woman from GFC came over and sold them the gun for, he thought, $175, of which he received a commission of $5 or $10.

Nelson was irritated. He had tried to tell all of these people, he explained later, that Campbell and he had not come all the way from Utah to collect on an unpaid parking ticket. They were investigating a murder, and he was not averse to throwing his weight around. He told Snow that he felt he was probably mistaken, and that McPhail probably wasn't there at all. Snow insisted that McPhail was there, but that Register wasn't—just McPhail, Vestal and "that boy" (who, Snow said, contradicting Vestal, was in blue jeans, not a brown suit). Said he'd stake his life on it, swear on a Bible, and take a polygraph test.

But when he was shown a picture of Marc and asked if he was "that boy," Snow said that he might be, but he wasn't sure.

If it had been up to Campbell and Nelson they would have flown home to Utah and never returned. Their feelings about Texas hospitality could best be summed up in the words of a Civil War general named Phil Sheridan, who, in speaking of Texas's brutal extremes in climate, once said: "If I owned Texas and all hell, I'd rent out Texas and live in hell."

But the two detectives didn't have that luxury. Once they got back to Salt Lake, Campbell knew, after speaking with Ernie Jones and his own superiors, that he and Nelson would have to go back to see Bruce Stanley and, more important, John Cavenaugh. Unless someone could positively identify Marc as having bought that gun, they had no chance of returning to Trinity College to arrest him. So on December 3, they flew back to Midland.

Bruce Wayne Stanley had had plenty of time to discuss things with his friend Malcolm McPhail, and he reluctantly told the detectives, whom he found just as offensive as McPhail did, what he knew. He had phoned McPhail after he told John Snow he was not interested in the gun Snow said was available. McPhail told Stanley that he also was not in the market for a gun, Stanley said, but that a boy who had worked for him in the past was. McPhail asked Stanley if he would go to the bank, see what condition the gun was in, and decide if it was worth the money being asked for it. After he examined the gun, he went home and called McPhail to tell him the gun was virtually new and that $165 or $175 for it would be a good buy. But, he said, he wasn't there when the gun was actually purchased; didn't know it was John Cavenaugh who had been with McPhail that day until recently; and, most significant, didn't know anything about a Marc Schreuder.

More than a half hour after Bruce Stanley left the police department, a blond-haired man of twenty-one arrived to be interviewed. As John Cavenaugh began responding to their questions, the detectives' spirits soared. He told them that his father mentioned there had been a homicide that a friend of his supposedly committed after John had gotten him a gun, which the friend had taken to Salt Lake City with him. He said that he had received a phone call from Marc Schreuder, who was a year younger than he and whom he knew from Kent School, some time during the summer of 1978. Schreuder was calling from New York, said that he was planning to do some camping out in Utah with his grandparents, wanted a gun for that purpose as well as for protection, and asked if he could get one in Texas. Cavenaugh said that wouldn't be a problem, and Schreuder told him that he might stop in Midland on his way out there.

Cavenaugh didn't think any more about it, he said, because Marc was "kind of a strange cookie" who was hyperactive and nervous and talked a lot of bullshit. Yet a couple of weeks later, John came home from work and there was Marc. He had arrived at the house by taxi while his parents, who had no idea that he was coming, or who he was, were having lunch.

He stayed at the house a couple of days, reaffirmed his interest in purchasing a gun, and, while John was at work, played Monopoly with John's two younger brothers. John phoned Malcolm McPhail and said that a friend of his needed a gun, and McPhail informed him not long afterward that a .357 Magnum was available. The three of them drove to the bank that day—John couldn't remember if they went with McPhail or took separate cars—and Schreuder was present when the gun was bought. Besides the three of them, there was another man and, perhaps, a woman present during the transaction—but he wasn't certain.

Schreuder had cash with him to buy the gun, most likely left for Salt Lake that day (which Cavenaugh knew was right near his own birthday, on July 24), and Cavenaugh hadn't seen him since. Cavenaugh was "ninety-five percent sure" that Marc had ammunition for the gun when he left, but couldn't recall if it came with the gun or if it had been bought by McPhail. He confirmed that the issue of how to transport the gun had come up, and that he had told him to put it in the suitcase he was checking through.

As Cavenaugh left the station, the detectives were relieved. Someone, finally, had been able to place Marc in Midland *and* identify him as the buyer of the gun. Wanting to corroborate Cavenaugh's story, however, they had asked Malcolm McPhail to return for a second interview. In the two weeks since they had last seen him, McPhail had remembered more about the transaction of two years before, but not as much as they would have liked.

When John Cavenaugh called him, McPhail said, he indicated his friend "wanted a heavy-caliber revolver." After he spoke with Bruce Stanley, McPhail said, he called Cavenaugh back and they went down to the bank—either in McPhail's car or separately—and were met by John Snow. But McPhail *insisted* that the friend was not present at the bank. He didn't rule out the possibility that he might have been in John's car—if they had taken separate cars—but if he was, Malcolm C. McPhail didn't see him. The only thing he knew for sure, he said, was that John Cavenaugh was trying to get the gun for his friend and had asked him what was the best way to take a gun on a plane.

319

What he remembered more than anything else, he told the detectives, was how pleased he was that he had been able to locate a gun that quickly and do John a favor. So pleased, he said later, that "I could have stomped my feet." Other than that, he attached no great importance to the whole incident.

There was more to be learned about Marc Schreuder's three days in Midland, Texas—three days, he later said, that were among the happiest of his life—but it would not be learned by Joel Campbell and Ron Nelson. They had a plane to catch and, before they went to sleep that night at the Mayflower Hotel in New York City, a man they wanted to see.

33// The buzzer to apartment 1W began ringing at about eleven-thirty that night, but the man inside, who had been in hiding for weeks, was not about to let anybody in. Suddenly, there was a pounding on his side of the door. Whoever was in the vestibule had somehow gotten in. On the other side of the door, the person who was knocking had seen a light on in the apartment and used a "loid"—a piece of venetian blind with tape on it—to open the locked security entrance. Detective Ed Regan identified himself and the two people with him—Joel Campbell and Ron Nelson (whose plane Regan had met at Newark an hour before). On the way in from the airport, Campbell had filled Regan in on more of the details of the case and he was becoming intrigued.

The door to the apartment opened slowly and there was Richard Behrens, dressed in baggy trousers and a tank top. In the dimly lit background the officers could see roaches playing tag on a cream-colored kitchen table and boxes of different shapes scattered around. Behrens asked Regan if he needed a lawyer, and the detective said he didn't feel one was necessary. So, at eleven forty-nine the interview with a surprised and shaken Richard Behrens began.

Behrens briefly outlined the chain of events that led to his admission to Marilyn that he had the gun and that Marc, not

Larry, had committed the murder. After he delivered the gun to Marilyn and she took it to the 20th Precinct, he said, he began to remember other things about the time the gun was "dumped" on him. "Now [Marc] either dumped it and I'm not sure myself but I have the impression that he had just arrived or maybe a relative was in the house and he wanted to get rid of the thing." He explained that in the past his apartment had been used as a dumping ground by Frances when she was going through her divorces: a place for her to hide her financial records. He found the note with the name Cavenaugh on it, he said, and told Marilyn that he imagined that it was either a kid Marc traveled with to Texas or visited there when he bought the gun from the sheriff.

He said that he was under the impression Marc and Frances had driven to Texas during the spring of 1978 and purchased the gun—and said that when Marc brought the gun back from Salt Lake he had told him how he had packed the gun into his luggage, rather than carrying it with him.

"Before Marc brought this gun to you," Campbell asked, "did he say anything to you about wanting to buy a gun or going to Salt Lake or anything?"

"They" had approached him, Behrens said, to get a gun in Virginia, where he had lived for ten years and where there was "a girl I know."

"Who's they, who approached you?"

"Mrs. Schreuder and her son Marc."

"When did they approach you?"

"Oh, Christ, way back, two or three—I don't know, I can't place it exactly, but I was approached way before this."

". . . When did he actually bring the gun to you?"

". . . It was the summer, I know that."

"Was it in 1978?"

"It was about two years ago."

"Do you remember what month?"

"My time—I can't remember exactly."

"Were you here at this address when he came to you?"

"Ya, ya—"

"And were you the only one here?"

"Ya, always been."

"Did he come by himself?"

"Can't even remember. I believe he did. I'm not sure."

"What did he say to you when he came in?"

"He said, 'Just get rid of this' and I said, 'What the hell do you want me to do with it?' and he started explaining what had happened."

"What did he say?"

"He said he'd been out there—"

"Out where?"

"To Salt Lake and he did his granddad in and all this kind of stuff."

"Did he say that he killed his granddad? What did he say? Be specific."

"He said that he had shot him, he really did, and this blew my mind."

"Did he say how or where or—"

"In the warehouse, the old man worked all the time, seven days a week, many, many hours a day, he's always there—"

"Did he tell you how many times he shot him?"

"No, Marilyn told me that."

"What did Marilyn say?"

"She said two times. Is it two times?"

"Did Marc say anything to you about how many times he was shot?"

"N—no."

". . . Did he say what day he shot him?"

"I'm sure he did, but . . . I can't really remember because it's fuzzy, it really is. It was early in the—it was in—oh, oh, the day? It was Sunday, that I do remember."

"Did Marc say that?"

"Yes. Yes."

"Did Marc say what time of the day?"

"Morning."

"Did he give you an hour?"

"Early morning, that's all I know."

"Now are you telling me this because Marc told you that or because Marilyn told you this? Or because you've read it in the newspaper?"

"Ah—he told me that it was a Sunday morning. I called Marilyn recently and I said when did this happen, the date, I really don't know, apparently it was in July she told me and . . . I said, 'Well, what about Larry? Wasn't he in Texas?'

and she said, 'No, you're off by a whole year.' . . . She said he was in Texas a year later, I said . . . maybe Marc bought this thing for Larry—"

That was certainly a possibility, but Campbell preferred to remain focused on Marc. "Okay, when Marc told you about shooting his grandfather, did he say why he did it?"

"Ah—no, I think the whole thing is money."

"Did he say anything about anyone else being involved?"

"I think he just played a hero and did it on his own—that impression I had very strongly, I had the distinctive feel—"

". . . Not on your feelings, but what did he say?"

"I could say he said it, but I'm not sure. I—I, it seems to me that he said he was alone, I had the distinct feeling he was alone."

"Did he say anything about . . . Larry knowing about it?"

"Ah—no, but I'm—I have a feeling that he did know, I know that."

"Did he tell you where he bought the handgun, where he got it?"

"He didn't name the town, but he just mentioned a sheriff."

"What did he say?"

"He said we bought it from a sheriff, I said that's great."

"Did he say *we* or *I*? Did you think somebody else was with him when he bought it?"

"I think—and I can only imagine that he went down there and he conned some people into saying he wanted a gun, maybe for target practice or whatever and he went step by step—I—I, obviously he had to know somebody."

"Did he say what town in Texas?"

"No, he did not—this address I just turned up a month or two ago, this paper—"

". . . Did you assume that he went directly to Salt Lake City from Texas?"

"No, there's a big gap there, because this is where Marilyn filled me in, to be honest. I say I had this address, this Cavenaugh, I have this thing I want you to find out, if it was really the one that did it, because the Salt Lake paper said that apparently there was a heavy weapon, a rifle or whatever, didn't know what it was, and I said please check it out. Then I started piecing it together on my own, I remember he did take a trip down to Texas and with a classmate . . . but I didn't know if it was Cavenaugh or not, apparently it was, and I told her, I said check this out. Now this whole thing about him suddenly appearing in July—he didn't tell me when he went down there, he just told me about a nice trip you know—"

". . . What part of July did he bring the gun?"

"I'm not that good, I can't really say, I remember it was the summer months, and that's how vague I am on this shit, I really am."

"I want to show you a picture. . . . Tell me whether or not you know this person, if this is the person that gave you the gun—"

"Yeah, he took that picture himself."

"Who is this person?"

"It's Marc Schreuder. . . ."

"Is this the kid that gave you the gun?"

"Yeah, sure is."

"Okay, tell me how you came into contact with the note that has Cavenaugh's name on it, where did that come from?"

"That's a good question, because the gun was dropped off and the note was with it?"

"Was it—"

"Now there was an address on it. . . . I don't know if this note was left through nervousness, carelessness . . . or what, but it was on Kent's stationery. . . ."

"Do you remember approximately what it said?"

"It gave . . . an address that said Dr. so and so Cavenaugh, so and so street—if you asked me to name the street I couldn't—Midland, Texas."

". . . Was the gun in a package? What kind of container was it in?"

"It was in a—this is where I blew it, I went down and I got him a package for it, this probably involved me, and then we went down to a store—"

"You and he together?"

"Downtown."

"You and Marc together?"

"Yeah, yeah."

". . . Was it the same day that he brought the gun to you?"

"No, it was afterwards."

"How much longer after?"

"I don't know."

"Weeks?"

"A week. . . ."

". . . Had you made arrangements to go buy a package for the gun?"

"No, he was—I drove down with he and his mother and they bought this. They said we're going to keep this thing and keep it right."

"Was she with—Frances Schreuder with you?"

"No, I can't remember, we went down by car, she must have been, she must have been."

"What kind of a package did you buy for it?"

"Well, he went in a store and got a cover for it, a black cover. . . ."

". . . When he gave you the gun, did he give you the bill of sale that he got for the gun or anything?" Shara Vestal had told the detectives that she and Jerry had given the buyer a receipt.

"No—Jesus Christ no, did he *get* a bill of sale—he got a bill of sale?"

"Yeah."

"You got to be kidding."

". . . When he told you that he had killed his grandfather, was he cocky or did he act like he was sad or—"

"He acted very, very goddam jumpy—"

". . . Why would he confide in you?"

"That's a very good question, because I was known as an uncle, he'd gone through so many fathers and everything that occasionally he'd come here. They dump things on me, they dump records . . . let's say if she was splitting with a husband, the last one, she split and dumped things and . . . I don't know why the hell he dumped [it] on me, this is the thing that I've been trying to figure out for the longest time—"

"Do you think that . . . his mother, Frances, knows about the homicide?"

"Oh yeah."

"Does she know that Marc committed it?"

"Yeah."

"How do you know that?"

". . . See, she wanted me to buy a gun, there's several things she wanted me to do for her . . . and when I see that they went ahead on it, apparently picked this thing up, because I wasn't about to buy a gun and I didn't and I was going down to Virginia. When she was asking for a gun, I don't know what the hell she was up to, because she's a very volatile person and I would say rather unpredictable."

"You say that she was with you and Marc when you went to buy the cover?"

"As I recall, yeah. I can't really remember, I might have gone down there alone with Marc, I really can't remember . . . I'm vague on it."

"Don't be afraid of involving her, okay? Just level with us, I mean you probably—"

"I'm trying to, I'm not holding out on you."

"She probably was talking to you, they were probably talking about the homicide that day, weren't they?"

"She has a way of blotting things out . . . she has a way of being very absolutely cold about things."

"Do you remember Marc talking about the homicide in front of her?"

"Yeah, yeah. She was a weird girl, she was weird. I don't know if she planned it or who planned—the kid's very headstrong, he could have been a—a—see, there's no father in the family and he's tried to assume an adult role and she put a lot of pressure on him."

"Did you keep the weapon here from the time Marc gave it to you until you turned it over to Marilyn Reagan?"

"Yeah, it just laid there in back with all that other junk."

"Did you say anything to anyone else about it?"

". . . No, no."

"About the homicide?"

"No, no. It's—it's too—"

"Why all of a sudden did you decide to tell Marilyn about it?"

"Well, Frances owed me money and a—all of a sudden she just decided she wanted to pay and a—"

"Decided she *didn't* want to pay?"

"She just held out on me on some money she owed me and I figured she was perhaps really flipping out bananas, crazy and a—there was a selfish motive in this . . . first of all, why I didn't throw it out, I can't figure out, maybe if I were smart I would have. On the other hand I was the only person, I started thinking, I was the only person that really knew about this and that isn't a very good position to be in, especially if suddenly somebody who has a record of turning on husbands, fathers, sisters and, you know, a really strange psychiatric record and you start thinking a—and I don't know why I did keep it, it was very crazy, a—"

". . . Since this occurred has Marilyn, or Frances rather, or Marc or anybody like that threatened you or told you not—"

"Oh, holy shit, boy you really hit a bomb when you went up there [to Trinity]. . . . You came here and confronted Marc and . . . this is not too smart, 'cause forewarned is forearmed and when I say forearmed I mean it, he buzzed down that next weekend, first I got on the phone—"

"Who's he?"

"Marc. He said, 'Well, you and Marilyn have been busy, haven't you?' and he said, 'By the way, how is Marilyn?' 'cause there's an unbelievable hatred between the two sisters. Apparently it's been going on for a long time, okay? And I said, 'Well, if you want to know how Marilyn is, why don't you call her?' and then I hung up and the reason I hung up, Mrs. Schreuder has gone through these divorces—I keep bringing this up, but she's got an education by using the best private detectives, she knows all about it, phone taps—I wouldn't say one word to her on the phone for the simple reason that she's coaching somebody and has got it tapped."

". . . Then he didn't come to your apartment, he just called you then?"

"No, after he called, then he came down and then the phone was ringing like crazy and I wouldn't pick it up, I haven't answered a phone since by the way. So . . . then there were a lot of rings on the bells and all this kind of stuff. . . ."

"So you never went out and talked to him then . . . ?"

"No, no, no. That's it."

"Has Frances called you or come down to see you?"

"I don't know, I don't pick up. I will not pick up."

The detectives left Behrens's apartment at about twelve-thirty and went to the bar at the Mayflower Hotel. Campbell

327

and Nelson had had a long day and were exhausted. But they weren't about to drift into a cynical place like New York City from a place like Mormon Utah and escape being peppered by the local bartender, who wanted to know how many wives they had and if they had horns that he somehow couldn't see. They were good-natured about the kidding and took it in stride. They could afford to be: Campbell, soft drink in hand, felt he had enough evidence at that point to confer with Salt Lake in the morning and get a warrant to arrest Marc. The situation with Frances, though, was much murkier: Behrens said she knew Marc had committed the murder, that she as well as Marc had asked him to get a gun, and that she might have come along with Marc and Behrens when they went to get a cover for it. But these were just the claims of one person. Campbell knew he would need far more than that. At least with Marc he had, among other things, the gun, John Cavenaugh's statement that Marc had bought it that day in Texas, and Behrens's claim that Marc had admitted the murder to him when he asked him to keep it.

But a puzzling question remained: if Marilyn had told Campbell about both the "hit man" whom Behrens claimed Frances had asked him to find and about the attempts to kill her father by putting things into his oatmeal, why hadn't the detective raised these issues with Behrens?

Mike Schweighoffer had a feeling they'd be back. As an ex-cop, he knew that two detectives don't come all the way from Utah just to ask a few questions and disappear forever. If seeing Joel Campbell again on the Trinity campus didn't surprise him, the fact that Marc, whom Schweighoffer had kept a discreet eye on for the past month, hadn't fled did.

Bob Beltrandi of the Hartford police had called Schweighoffer earlier in the day to say that he had received a teletype from Salt Lake City authorizing Marc's arrest on a fugitive-from-justice warrant. The charge: murder in the first degree —committed "for pecuniary or other personal gain." The teletype indicated they had a *juvenile* court order for Marc's detention—since Marc was under eighteen at the time of the murder, he was considered a juvenile in Utah—and that a certified copy of the warrant was enroute.

As he had in late October, Schweighoffer called both the

college vice-president and the dean of students to say that two Utah detectives—one who had been at Trinity before, and one who hadn't—were back, but that this time it was not to ask Marc some questions. Schweighoffer knew to proceed cautiously and first called to see if Marc was at his dorm. He wasn't. Schweighoffer looked for him on campus and was told that he was in the basement of the student center, playing his beloved video games. Schweighoffer told Campbell and Nelson to wait outside while he and Beltrandi went to get him.

Beltrandi stood by the glass doors to the game room and watched Schweighoffer speaking to Marc—almost like a father to a son. Marc was calm and unemotional as he walked outside on that cold, bright afternoon—the 5th of December. And when Joel Campbell said that he had a warrant for his arrest, read him his rights, handcuffed him and said they were going to police headquarters, Marc even acted a bit impatient about the whole thing. "Let's go," he urged them, "because I won't be there that long."

He knew somebody was going to do something for him, Bob Beltrandi recalled later. But even the cynical Beltrandi would be shocked to find out who that somebody was.

On the way to be booked at headquarters, Marc rode with Campbell and Nelson in the back seat of the unmarked Hartford police car and asked if they could stop along the way so he could buy some magazines.

"Hey," Nelson said in disbelief, "you're not going to a resort hotel, pal."

He certainly wasn't. He was going to spend the weekend at the old Morgan Street jail in cell B-7. Since it was Friday, Marc couldn't be arraigned until Monday, when he would be moved to the new facility on Weston Road. He would be confined to his seven-foot-long, five-foot-wide, eight-foot-high cell all weekend; his meals would be brought to him, and, because it was a short-term detention, he would not be permitted to shower. He tried to phone his mother, but he was unable to reach her. So he phoned the one person who he knew could get a message to her, the one person whose friendship and care for him he had always been able to count on.

*　*　*

329

When Susie Coleman, the young woman from the delicatessen on East End Avenue, received Marc's phone call, she was alarmed but not totally shocked. Ever since Campbell had made his initial trip to Trinity, Marc had told her, when she asked why he was coming home every weekend, that he was a suspect in his grandfather's murder and needed to discuss things with his mother. He told her that it was all a figment of somebody's imagination—somebody who wanted to get back at his mother, somebody who was trying to hurt her by hurting him.

"How could this be?" she asked him at the time. "Don't worry about it." She had known Marc since he was a child, and could not imagine him as a murderer.

"You don't know how these things can go," Marc said.

The whole thing seemed so unreal to Susie—yet now Marc was on the phone, calling from a Hartford jail. A freezing rain was falling outside as Susie pulled on her boots and walked around the corner to 10 Gracie Square. She gave the doorman a note she had written to Frances and told him that it was urgent.

At five minutes to eleven that night, Frances spoke with her younger son. Larry had been arrested the previous December, and now it was Marc's turn. But in his case there would be no question of whether to get him a private attorney. He would have some of the finest attorneys money could buy—and Berenice J. Bradshaw would be paying for them.

34// Within a week of Marc's arrest, his lawyers in Connecticut had not only gotten him out on $100,000 bail, but had, with the assistance of lawyers retained to represent him in Utah, discovered some legal issues that would greatly help his case. In order for Utah to extradite Marc and eventually try him for murder, they would need to have him certified as an adult. But in order to do that, the defense lawyers' argument went, he would have to be present for those proceedings. Since Marc had chosen to fight extradition and not return to the state that demanded him, Utah would have ninety days, under Connecticut law, to work out its problem or Connecticut would be obliged to throw out the case. It was a gap in the law that the esteemed Hartford firm of Robinson, Robinson & Cole was delighted to exploit.

Extraditing Marc was not the only problem facing Ernie Jones and Joel Campbell. Their star witness was not answering his phone. Campbell had received a letter from Richard Behrens—written on December 4, the day after Campbell and Nelson had interviewed him—requesting a tape of the interview, but since that time the detective had been unable to reach him. On December 16, Campbell wrote Behrens a letter, reminding him that he was "an essential witness in a serious criminal proceeding" and how important it was for them to stay in constant contact. The Salt Lake County Attorney's Office, he wrote, "is willing to overlook criminal violations on your part," provided Behrens continued to cooperate with them. They were concerned about his "safety and well-being," Campbell wrote, and suggested he "spend the remaining time until trial in Salt Lake City."

It was a very magnanimous offer on the detective's part, especially since neither he nor Ernie Jones had any idea when the trial was going to be—if ever. And quite apart from needing Behrens, the prosecutor knew he'd need something else: proof that Marc had actually been in Salt Lake City on the day of the shooting.

Since Campbell—and everyone else—had been looking at Larry as the leading suspect at the time, he had *not* checked cab, rental car, hotel or airline records. When he contacted the city's three major cab companies now, what he learned was not encouraging. The drivers maintain "trip sheets"—which record the location and destination of their fares—but those sheets are destroyed after two weeks. In addition, the drivers tell the dispatcher where their fare is going, but the dispatcher's record is kept for only about three months. Fares from the airport, Campbell was told, are usually reported in a general fashion—"cab 10 from airport to city with fare"—

and, more important, the turnover in drivers is enormous. But the company managers did offer to post a memorandum for all of their employees. Perhaps one of them would come forward and remember driving a stocky seventeen-year-old boy with dark-blond hair either to or from the airport—or somewhere in town—around Pioneer Day in 1978.

Campbell phoned the security personnel at Midland's airport and was told, according to his report, that the only two airlines that flew from Midland to Salt Lake at that time in 1978 were Frontier and Continental, both of which made stopovers in Denver. Continental, based in Los Angeles, checked all the available records and passenger lists it had for the name Marc Schreuder but could not find a thing. Frontier, based in Denver, did the same, telling Campbell that the majority of passenger lists from that period had been destroyed.

The situation with the rental-car agencies located at Salt Lake's airport was just as bleak: though some records were available, Campbell's report noted, the agencies said it was their opinion that records were kept with any degree of accuracy for only one year.

From the moment Joel Campbell drove to the Bradshaw warehouse that summer morning in 1978, his investigation had been marked more by problems and carelessness than by its few highlights. And though he didn't know it, things were about to get worse.

A few days after Marc's arrest in Connecticut, Frances and Richard Behrens were in a Second Avenue restaurant called the Midnight Express until the wee hours of the morning. Behrens had successfully managed to avoid Frances for the past month, but when he returned to his apartment with a pack of cigarettes he had gone out to buy Frances was inside waiting for him. She had managed to get in the security entrance, and he had carelessly left his apartment door open. She suggested that they go someplace to have some coffee and a little chat, and he agreed to join her.

"'For thirty-seven hundred dollars, how could you do that?'" Behrens recalled Frances asking him as they sat there. "'My God, I thought you threw that away long ago. You're the last person Marc ever expected.'" (Maybe so, Behrens thought, except he had reminded Marc earlier that year that he still had "something that belongs to you," and that Marc had nonchalantly said, "'Oh yeah, I should come by and get that.'")

Frances reached in her handbag and pulled out a note she had picked up in Behrens's apartment while she was waiting for him. The note had a name, address and phone number on it—Joel Campbell's. She said, according to Behrens, that she'd heard that someone, calling himself Uncle, had been talking, but at first she wasn't sure who it was. They discussed what Behrens had told Campbell on December 3 and she corrected something that he had said: "'Don't you remember? I was the one who gave you the gun.'"

Asked if *anyone* had seen him give it to Marilyn, Behrens said, "No, no one. I made sure of that."

By the time they left the Midnight Express—after Frances reminded him that he had kept the murder weapon in his apartment for more than two years, and, because of that, would probably be sent to prison for twenty years but certainly wouldn't last for more than twenty minutes—Richard Behrens was essentially back in Frances's camp. And she was back where she wanted to be—in control.

On Friday, December 12, Jim Conway phoned his wife from New York City. It was his sixtieth birthday and he was calling to say that he was about to leave for their home in Storrs, Connecticut.

"Jim," she said, "Ted Carey called and wants you to call him as soon as you can. It sounds important."

Ted Carey—whose real name is Hiram Bissell Carey III—was one of Marc's two Connecticut lawyers. Not quite thirty-seven, educated at the Taft School and at Yale, he looked as Waspish as his pedigree suggested, but in a refreshingly unstuffy way. Jim Conway, on the other hand, was a former New York flatfoot, a classic rough diamond whose attitude was "I do my job, get my money, and then the lawyers take over—which means it becomes a shithouse."

Conway phoned Carey, who said that he wanted him to go to New York right away. Conway said that he was still in New York, working on another case. Carey filled the old pro in on the few details that he knew—Marc had only gotten out of jail the day before and was offering little—and told him to go directly to 10 Gracie Square and meet with Frances, with whom he had been having long conversations throughout the week.

Frances was not home when Conway arrived. When she did get there she was startled to see him, and asked him to wait downstairs. Wanting to make sure he was who he said he was, Frances phoned Carey, who confirmed that Conway was working for them.

Frances and Conway talked for a while—mostly about Richard Behrens—and the detective was struck by how disoriented she seemed. Suddenly she suggested they go over and meet Behrens. He would probably be at a coffee shop on Lexington Avenue, she said, just across from Lenox Hill Hospital.

"We went over in her car," Conway said, recalling the cold December day, "and the little girl—a cute but very tragic figure—went with us. Frances said, 'He'll come in, he'll come in, he's spying on us.' Finally the door opens and he sidles in and sits next to us. He wanted to know who I was and she assured him four different times that I was on their side. I thought she was weird, but he's playing second fiddle to her, and the poor little girl is sitting there."

After initially sticking to his story, Behrens dropped a bombshell on Conway: what he had told the detectives from Utah—that Marc committed the murder and gave him the gun, and that he eventually gave it to Marilyn—was a lie.

Marilyn had threatened him and made him say that. She'd had the gun all along, he said, and she'd masterminded the murder.

As the four of them went back to Frances's apartment, Conway was baffled, but intrigued. Over the next few hours and days, he was told by Frances about the enmity that had existed for years between Marilyn and her, how Marilyn was jealous of her and the relationship she had with her mother, how Marilyn had always wanted to control things, like her father's estate planning, and take over his business with Doug Steele, whom Frances claimed her father had been afraid of and who, she said, had been stealing money from the business for years.

Conway took it all in, saying little. Frances wanted to know, he recalled later, "if I knew she was on the board of the New York City Ballet. She dropped names and told me about dinner parties. She'd even go so far as to say an Astor or a Rockefeller. If she had been in a 'Suzy' column, that would have been the ultimate." Conway did tell her that he knew Madame Chiang Kai-shek lived in the building, and she was upset to learn that he knew that, demanding to know how he had come to possess such privileged information.

As Conway sat there, he was trying to figure out the relationship between Frances and Behrens, and decided that in order to get more of a sense of him, he needed to see where Behrens lived. "I couldn't get a handle on these people," Conway said later, shaking his head, "they were so off the wall." When he suggested to Behrens that the two of them go to Behrens's apartment, the schoolteacher said he'd been staying away from there for a while because he didn't feel it was safe. There were two guys outside, he said, constantly watching the place.

"Look," Conway said, trying to ease Behrens's fears and amused by him at the same time, "if anybody bothers you, I'll blow his fucking head off."

"Are you packing?" Behrens wanted to know as they approached the entrance to his building.

"Sure," Conway lied, "I've got a .38 right in my pocket."

As they walked into the vestibule, Behrens opened his mailbox and took out a week's worth of mail. Once they got inside in the apartment, Conway was even more puzzled. He had just left a magnificent, though barely furnished duplex and was now sitting in "a disaster area," watching "the International Olympics of Cockroaches" run before his eyes.

Behrens told Conway that there would probably be a letter from Marilyn in the stack of mail. There was. Behrens ripped open the envelope; inside it were a $20 bill and the following note, written two days before:

DEAR DICK,

Haven't heard from you for several days? Please call and confirm that you are still around.

MBR

335

Maybe Behrens isn't so off the wall as I thought, the detective mused. He took the note with him and said that he'd be back in town soon.

35//

Throughout December, Behrens spent most of his time at Gracie Square—"my clubhouse." During the day he would discuss strategy with Frances and Marc, who had withdrawn from Trinity; at night he would either sleep there or return home well after midnight. He felt pretty sure that Marilyn would hire a private detective to keep an eye on him, and, as it turned out, he was right.

Frances and Marc wanted him to change his story completely, and officially turn everything against Marilyn. Frances would pay any legal bills he might incur. He was to type his recantation on *his* typewriter, have it notarized, and take it in person to Marc's lawyers in Hartford. That was the plan and he followed it to the letter.

On the day after Christmas, he and Marc found a notary who was open and had his eight-page, single-spaced document notarized. The following day, a Saturday, Behrens took the bus to Hartford and gave the document to Ted Carey, James Wade and Jim Conway.

Under the heading "Introduction to relationship with Marilyn Reagan," he explained the problems he had incurred with the joint bank account he shared with Frances. He was "vaguely aware" that her father's estate was still unsettled, and said that because of the strained relationship between Frances and Marilyn, he informed Frances before he contacted Marilyn about his dilemma. He said that Marilyn gave him the name of the Salt Lake lawyers and bank to write to, and that he kept her informed.

"It was painfully apparent from the beginning that Mrs. Reagan had little faith in her sister's word and assumed that her sister (Frances) would have to be sued for money. (Marilyn stated that 'she doesn't care.') Opinions of the rest of the family were equally negative. This included boys, daughter and mother. The feelings and expres-

336

sions of feeling were, indeed, quite hostile as far as I could tell. I began to feel quite uncomfortable in this realm of feelings being waxed against Frances and family and came to realize how deeply the hostility went within Marilyn's mind."

She had been working closely with the police in Salt Lake City, he wrote, and "seemed obsessed" with having Larry responsible for her father's death, while "he should have been viewed as a pitiful person instead of a person to be sneered at and attacked by attempts by agents of Marilyn to tie him into a tragedy at Salt Lake City."

Invective toward the family of Frances was unbounded, he said. While frustration was mounting on his part to recover his money, he became aware that Marilyn's thoughts and actions were "very bizarre and extreme in concept and conclusions reached," and listed some of them: Larry throwing the gun from an airplane into the Great Salt Lake; Marilyn's desire to "get into Frances's bank vault because she wished to get to mother's will"; her accusing Marc of visiting his grandfather's house a few months before in Salt Lake City, letting himself in with a key he found under a flower pot, and looking for his grandfather's will; her claim that Frances didn't really have an accident on the Triborough Bridge a few years before because she didn't follow up on a lawsuit she had filed; her reference to her mother and Frances as "those two"; her feeling that Marc "had it easy," even though he had worked during the past year; her wish that Frances be "cut off" from funds and her own desire "to take over the 'whole estate'"—which seemed "very outlandish to me because, as an outsider, I would have thought that others would have to be considered."

Early in the fall, he wrote, Marilyn asked him to have coffee with her at a place on Broadway and revealed that progress was being made in "her 'investigation.'" She apparently had come to believe that both boys were involved with the murder and "pressed this viewpoint whenever I had the ill fortune of hearing these tales of woe and weirdness. Apparently she had had the FBI in on this thing, or so she said. I had come to regard much in this area as very distasteful and not too enlightening."

She began to phone him quite a bit, he said, and he became

nervous "by her wishing for me to contact her favorite police types in Salt Lake City. . . . She opened with a sweet approach whereby she broached the subject of my involvement with her search for a person who could be connected with her father's tragic death because she indicated that she was a suspect in this whole affair." Even though she was convinced that Marc had purchased a gun in Texas and had used it "for her father's demise," he wrote, she indicated her belief that *she* had the weapon "through some mysterious method in her use of Utah Police." When he pressed her as to why she was convinced Marc and Larry were guilty, he wrote, she spoke in "hate-filled generalities" about their past and present behavior but was evasive about specifics.

She expressed a desire that he be filled in "on the 'facts'" so that he could substantiate her claims—a form of support she felt was necessary. "I balked at this strange situation and told her that I wanted nothing to do with cops per se and wondered aloud what she really meant by her leading lines."

". . . She, in effect, wished me to state that Marc had gone to Texas, somehow gotten to Utah, done his evil deed to his Grandfather and then dropped off the gun at my house. These thoughts were devastating to me and I balked badly at them. She indicated that I would have no real implication within the context of her scheme as presented to me at this time. She indicated that this only established a linking up of the gun with Marc into New York City. I continued to protest in further conversations with her via phone but was in a mood of what I would prefer to call one of desperation, anger, and extreme resentment toward Frances and family and was capable of such an act of desperation."

If he did all this, he said she told him, she would secure for him the family reward of $10,000 that had been offered at the time of her father's death, and pay for his legal expenses, his travel costs to Utah, and his lodging ("offered with the addendum that the Hotels in Salt Lake had skiing to a great degree at this time of year") while he was there.

He later found a note under his door, put there by New York City's 20th Precinct, he said, asking him to call Joel Campbell collect in Salt Lake City. He ignored the request,

but did ask Marilyn about it. She told him that they too
"wished to know the 'facts'" as she had outlined them to him.
She became more and more persistent, he said, and at the
same time he felt very betrayed by what he considered
Frances's indifference to his financial situation—ultimately
concluding that "the fat was on the fire and that things would
have to go forward as indicated. . . .

"She then gave me my lines which I was to relate to the
police which she claimed, I repeat, would get back at Frances
and family, give me a reward, give me a vacation in Salt Lake
as witness and do 'justice.' In my frame of mind of resentment, fear and ignorance, I went along with this seeming
bizaar scheme."

He said that he wished "to refute and to deny everything"
which he related to Joel Campbell in the conversation he
taped on December 3, because it was "false information."
Aside from the "inducements" Marilyn had offered him, he
said, he had agreed to do it with the assurance that he would
have no further legal involvement in it. He denied that Marc
had ever "frantically" called him after Campbell's "terror
raid" at Trinity, when the detective tried to "shake him
down"; denied that he had ever kept a gun in his apartment;
and said that his other statements were "equally erroneous"
and were given in a spirit of malice and revenge.

Over and over he repeated that all of the information on
the tape—"a legal fiction"—was fed to him by Marilyn and
that on certain questions Joel Campbell told him what to
respond.

Even though it arrived two days past Christmas and the
lawyers knew that Santa was bringing it, this astonishing
recantation was a wonderful present for Jim Wade and Ted
Carey. But they wanted to question Behrens closely
themselves—to depose him under oath—and so at four-
twelve that afternoon, Wade, the more senior of the two,
began.

Behrens told the lawyers and Conway how he had first met
Frances at the Unitarian Church and come to know the boys,
how she had drifted out of his life for the years when she was
in Europe, and how, when she returned, he had given

Frances advice on schools for Lavinia (he wrote a recommendation letter for her to a "preschool") and suggested that a boarding school for Marc would be better than a day school.

Having established his connection to the family, Wade asked him about the money Frances owed him, and his initial and subsequent contacts with Marilyn. Behrens stuck closely to what he had written. He then emphasized the tactics the police had used to gain entry to his apartment—his recollection that none of them produced a badge of identification, and his assurance by Regan that he didn't need an attorney present—and pointed out that his request for a tape of the interview had not been satisfied.

Wade asked if Behrens had, in his initial meeting with Jim Conway, told him all of the same things he was now saying in this interview.

No, he said, "I gave him a story to back up Marilyn's thesis, which was false."

"And why did you do that, why did you initially tell Mr. Conway one thing and then change your mind and decide to tell us what really had happened?"

"Well, I had several reasons. I felt that an innocent boy was being railroaded; I felt that I was doing it for reasons that were not honorable; and I felt that I had a lot of pressure and inducements put on me."

"By whom?"

"By Miss Marilyn Reagan. I was also told—I was led to believe that this affair wouldn't blow up into the monster that I consider it to be."

Did anyone threaten him or offer him any inducements to come to Hartford and make this statement? Wade asked.

No, he lied.

Was everything on his eight-page document in his own words and written in his own house?

Yes, he lied again.

Had he received any monies from Marilyn Reagan?

He had received some spending money—$40 in cash—which Marilyn had sent him because she knew of "my bad financial situation." Asked if Conway had been there the day he received a letter from Marilyn, Behrens said that he had and had given Conway the letter, but kept the $20 that came with it. He said he'd be willing to come back to Connecticut to testify, if necessary, and would do his best to let the lawyers know where he was at all times.

Wade asked about the letter Campbell had sent him on December 16 (which Behrens had given to the lawyers)—specifically about whether Behrens had promised to keep in touch with the police and if Campbell had mentioned any criminal violations to him at the time he interviewed him. Behrens said Campbell might have said he'd call him, and that no possible criminal violations on his part were ever mentioned.

Wade asked him to sign his name to the letters Marilyn and Campbell had sent him and to return to Hartford once the tape of the affidavit had been transcribed so that everything could be notarized.

Three days later, on December 30, Richard Rhodes Behrens did just that. But that only formalized what Spencer Austin, one of Marc's Salt Lake attorneys, had already let Ernie Jones know over the telephone in a New Year's greeting: if he was counting on Richard Behrens to be the state's key witness against Marc Schreuder, he could forget it. Behrens had recanted his entire story.

36// If anyone had a right to feel betrayed by Behrens's change of story it was Marilyn Reagan—but, oddly enough, she didn't. She figured that Frances had gotten to him, and was concerned only that he be turned back in the right direction. But her confidence in Joel Campbell, always shaky, was quickly disappearing. And the private detective agency she hired, for five days at a cost of $1,320, could not get to Behrens either; the closest they came was a failed attempt to sell him a magazine subscription.

If Marilyn was fairly nonplussed by all of this, Elaine and Mason Drukman were anything but. They had been concerned at the time Marilyn handed the gun in that the transaction had not been witnessed, and their fears had turned out to be genuine. "We didn't imagine that Campbell would tell her simply to get the gun from him—with no witness, nobody with a camera," Mason said later, still appalled at the way the detective had handled the whole business. "She was left totally vulnerable to any change of story Behrens might want to make—including implicating her, which they decided to do. It was a perfect setup."

Behrens's recantation was not the only thing that concerned the two sisters. Aware that Utah's attempts to extradite Marc were stalled, they retained an attorney in Hartford to offer advice on the thorny legal situation. Under normal circumstances, Marilyn and Elaine could be as frugal as their father. But these weren't normal circumstances. It had taken twenty-seven months—from the time of the murder until Richard Behrens gave Marilyn the gun on that evening in October—for the case to take any sort of shape, and they weren't about to let money or a careless detective (Campbell would later admit that he was more concerned with obtaining the gun than protecting Marilyn) prevent them from avenging their father's death.

While Marc's lawyers were thrilled to have his "uncle's" recantation, they knew that eventually they would need evidence to support it. Jim Conway was troubled by the relationship between Behrens and Frances—and his own inability to figure it out. The lawyers had a theory that Behrens, once they met him, might be Marc's father—the physical similarity between them, they felt, was remarkable—and that the idea of Frances's meeting him at a church social function was preposterous. But Conway did not buy that; he felt that Behrens's real object of desire was Marc. He saw Behrens as a sad and pathetic figure, but had worked in the city long enough to know "there were four million Behrenses walking around New York."

As for Marc, who told him that he had eaten out of garbage cans when he was eight but confided little else, Conway felt he "never reached him. I usually can establish a rapport with people, but I couldn't with him. I talked to him—when we talked about anything—about pinball machines. If you could talk intelligently about Pac Man, you were home free. I felt nothing for him, because he was so devoid of feeling for himself."

But if Marc was unwilling to say very much, his mother was

not. She not only attempted to sharpen the lawyers' and Conway's focus on Marilyn and Doug Steele as the true culprits, but her long, rambling discourses (Ted Carey would later say that to call them conversations was "a misnomer") ranged, Carey said, "practically through the universe of subjects that were tangentially connected to the criminal problem. Any number of diatribes or long, long, long, long explanations—none of which made any sense—with respect to the family background. She would spend hours pitting lawyer against lawyer"—complaining about the Utah lawyers to Carey and vice versa—"and was always looking for assurances I couldn't give her."

The only person whom both Carey and Conway felt they could rationally deal with was Berenice. In meetings in both Hartford and New York they realized very quickly that for her "there was no moral choice," Carey said, in paying Marc's legal bills. "She had a family and she was doing what she could to protect it." While it was clear to them that "Berenice and Franklin didn't exactly kiss over the boiled egg in the morning," they also realized that she had "demands from a child who took over her life to a large extent. The only thing that kept Frances alive was money," Carey said. "There was no other way to keep the woman alive and on this earth."

If Berenice was the only *person* they could count on, the only *thing* that the lawyer and the investigator could depend on was this: there was *nothing* to depend on, because, Carey said, "every two days the sands shifted."

Carey and Conway weren't the only ones for whom the sands were shifting. Ernie Jones and Joel Campbell were stunned by Behrens's recantation. "I felt sure that somebody had gotten to him," Jones said. "Either threatened him or paid him off, because it was such a phony story, we never believed it for a second." Jones might not have believed it, but as far as his floundering case was concerned, it meant two things: if the state didn't dismiss the case (which they considered doing), their only hope was that Behrens would change his mind and revert to his original story. But even if that were to occur, Jones knew that the legal damage was done: Behrens had already given two completely different stories, and the prosecutor would never be able to get a conviction—if and when he ever got Marc back to Utah—on the strength of Behrens's testimony alone.

The murder weapon and John Cavenaugh's placing of Marc in Texas would not be enough. The prosecutor was going to need a miracle.

Jim Conway is just the sort of brash Easterner most people in Utah find pushy and don't like. With Behrens's statement in his pocket, the private investigator arrived in Salt Lake in early January (before going on to Midland, Texas, where he got no cooperation from the local police and managed to get himself into—and promptly thrown out of—Dr. Herbert Cavenaugh's office, making an appointment as a patient and blowing his own cover soon after he arrived there).

The purpose of his trip to Salt Lake was to find whatever skeletons existed in Marilyn Reagan's and Doug Steele's closets, and to rattle them as noisily as he could.

He went to the offices of Parsons, Behle & Latimer, and met with Spencer Austin and another lawyer in the firm, David Dolowitz; they had been brought into the case by their colleague Ron Madsen (Berenice and Frances's lawyer), because of their experience in the criminal and juvenile areas respectively. Conway gave Austin a copy of Behrens's statement and a friendly piece of advice. He was just an old gray-haired cop who had been around a long time, he said, and had worked a lot of cases. "Don't assume anything logical about this one," Conway told him. "Proceed with a blank slate."

The old warhorse could have saved his breath. Austin already knew that. Somehow Frances had gotten his unlisted home number and had been bombarding him, usually on Sunday nights, with "wild tales of intrigue and conspiracy." But in a case in which, Austin said, "things were so amorphous that they would go up in granite and come back down in vapor I felt if I could throw that kind of fairy dust around [about Marilyn and Doug], I could get an acquittal."

Conway and Austin asked Nancy Jones to come to Austin's office for an interview; when she arrived, a colleague of Steve Swindle's was with her.

Conway wanted to know about the amendments to the will

that Nancy had typed, if and how Marilyn could have found out about them, and if the changes would have been detrimental to her.

No, they would not have been harmful to Marilyn, Nancy said, bristling at the investigator's aggressive manner and offering little else.

Did she feel more than one person was involved in the killing?

Yes, she certainly did.

Why had Mr. Bradshaw been so upset, and why had he made the changes?

Marc and Larry had stolen money from the business, she said.

Was Frances involved?

Yes, she was, Nancy said, and she was the one whom the changes would have disinherited.

Conway seemed surprised by this revelation and said the Hartford attorneys were not aware of that. Why, he asked, did she think Mrs. Bradshaw was willing to support Marc?

She didn't really know.

Did Mrs. Bradshaw have a copy or the original of the proposed amendment to the will?

No, she didn't.

Why wouldn't she at least have been shown them?

Because Mrs. Bradshaw was too close to Frances.

Was it possible that the police had copies of them?

She didn't know.

How might Frances have found out about them?

Mr. Bradshaw's filing system wasn't exactly confidential, she said. Anyone could have checked on anything if he wanted to, and Mrs. Bradshaw did work down there at that time on a regular basis.

Jim Conway was both frustrated and fascinated at the same time. While his hell-bent-for-leather approach hardly charmed the natives, he was picking up each crumb they threw him—learning that "there was a whole empire there to be grabbed" and feeling that there was no shortage of people who wanted a piece of it. "This case was like *As the World Turns,*" he said. "You had to watch every day."

One person that he watched very closely was Doug Steele.

"You go into this hovel, an old railroad site in the bad part of town," Conway recalled his visit to the warehouse, "and here is this guy in an old sweater, plaid shirt and denim pants, sitting in a dingy office. Steele says to me [imitating a down-home country accent], 'How ya doin' there, Jim, come on in.' All of a sudden the phone rings and he says to the guy on the other end, 'What did the ticker say at two o'clock? No, pick up that option. You better sell.' This is the little old country bumpkin selling carburetors and spark plugs one minute and then he's on the wire with some guy and he's into options, buying and selling, the whole thing. He played the part all right. He had everything on but the bib overalls. He gets off the phone and says, 'Oh, excuse me, Jim, a couple of the boys and I fool around with a few stocks. Mr. Bradshaw told me how to make a few dollars.'"

When Conway told Steele that the person who wound up with a smoking gun in her hand was Marilyn, Steele said he couldn't be more off base. He sang her praises and launched into a long diatribe about Frances and her two sons, reconstructing the summer of 1977 for Conway as if it were straight from a Stephen King novel and telling him about the memo Frank wrote after the boys left—the one he felt sure Frances had gotten word about. In Doug Steele, Jim Conway had met his match; he was not going to be able to push this "little old country bumpkin" around. He left Salt Lake with the feeling that "Marilyn and Steele were asshole buddies"—that she had probably learned about the memos from Steele. On the one hand, Marilyn and Doug had every reason to think Franklin followed through on his intentions and made them co-executors; but on the other, the thinking went, they'd have a perfectly good motive to kill him if they feared he might change his will yet again. This was the kind of fairy dust Spencer Austin was hoping to spread around—the kind that led Jim Conway to ultimately conclude that Marilyn was "a very able son of a bitch who was one of the main cogs in this whole thing" and Doug was "a devious bastard in her employ."

In late January, Allen F. Sullivan, an Assistant District Attorney in the Manhattan District Attorney's Office, received a letter from Ernie Jones, enclosing official papers requiring the attendance of a material witness—Richard Behrens—at a murder trial, soon to commence in Salt Lake City.

Sullivan, who had come to the D.A.'s Office in 1967, was regarded as one of its top prosecutors. Methodical in his approach, deliberate and low-key in his speech, Sullivan stood six foot two, had been a professional forester at one time, and was known to many people around the office as Smokey (after the well-known bear). With wire-rim glasses, soft facial features, and a rather formal, upright manner, the tall prosecutor looked more like a Catholic priest whom one would face on the other side of the confessional than the man who had been entrusted with the John Lennon murder case less than two months before.

In fact, as he sat in his office in lower Manhattan, looking at the documents in front of him, he felt sure that Jones must have seen his name in the papers in connection with that. Actually, Jones had simply phoned the D.A.'s Office, asked who handled the extradition of material witnesses in homicides, and, since Sullivan was the only attorney left from what had been the Homicide Bureau, was given his name.

"It seemed pretty cut and dried," Sullivan remembered. "It was a major homicide and I wanted to make sure it was handled correctly." He was the quintessential good soldier, always willing to lend a hand. The extradition of a material witness—or of a defendant, for that matter—was usually a straightforward business that required little time. But as Al Sullivan soon found out, *nothing* about this case was straightforward, and the time and effort it would require on his part would even try the patience of a priest.

On Monday, February 9, a little after eight in the evening, someone rang Frances's doorbell. When her French housekeeper opened the door, the figure standing there in a dark suede jacket and plaid shirt was not familiar to her. The visitor said who he was, and she told him to wait downstairs.

But the visitor followed her upstairs, taking in the apartment he had never seen, and when Frances saw him, she looked "as if I had come out of the grave."

"Hi!" Larry said. "I escaped." Indeed he had. At three-thirty that afternoon, he had phoned for a cab from the

Allentown State Hospital. He had been transferred back to Allentown from Farview in October; it had been decided that while he still was in need of mental health care and medication, he didn't necessarily need to remain in a maximum-security hospital. At Allentown, he had recently been allowed half-hour walks and had a job putting lamp parts together. He had been planning to escape for months. By February 20, he would have earned $20. But in the mail that morning, he got a birthday card (his birthday was the previous Friday, February 6) and $10 each from Granny and Marc. "So I decided," Larry said, "I might as well escape today. The cab came at four-fifteen—right in front of the hospital. The shift had changed at four and I was scared there would be a collision. The cabdriver took me to Bethlehem, but once I got out I couldn't find the bus station. So I called another cab and told the driver, 'Take me to the bus station,' which was in South Bethlehem. I waited about forty-five minutes and got on the bus to New York at five-thirty. The fare was only six-fifty one-way."

Larry had an uncanny memory for details like that. The two-hour bus ride gave him a chance to remember other things—especially the letter he had received from Ron Madsen the previous month, the letter that informed him that the Salt Lake police (despite Marc's arrest in Connecticut, which Larry had been told about) still had an interest in him as "either a principal or an accessory to this crime." But so did the lawyers.

Madsen explained that Jim Conway had been hired by the family and wanted to come to Pennsylvania to speak with him. Since Chester Reybitz had advised Larry that he did not have to speak with either Conway or Joel Campbell, Madsen decided to appeal to him directly, even going so far as to tell him that a few months before Campbell had asked his grandmother for pictures of him, "claiming that they wanted to present them to an eyewitness that would put you at the scene at the time of your grandfather's death. Of course we both know that you were in Utah at that time. . . ."

Larry disliked Madsen intensely, viewing him as a "shyster" who had prevented him from being released on bail before his trial and from having a private attorney, and who was, even now, telling him that it might be "a conflict of interest and impede our defense of Marc" if his firm were to appear on his behalf in regard to the murder. Larry might be a paranoid schizophrenic, but he was clear-headed enough to know that he was not about to cooperate with Ron Madsen.

If Larry's thoughts about this were sharp, being in prison apparently had caused him to forget that his mother's apartment was not a place where he could expect to be welcomed with open arms. And tonight was no different.

"My mother said, 'Go to the study,' and I talked with Marc and my grandmother for a few minutes. My mother came back in and said, 'You shouldn't have escaped.'" Four New York cops arrived and took him to Metropolitan Hospital, where he spent the night handcuffed to a bed. For the next two days he was in a holding cell in lower Manhattan, sleeping on the floor, before being taken to Rikers Island. He stayed at Rikers until February 18, when two detectives arrived from Pennsylvania with leg irons and a straitjacket. By that evening, nine days after he escaped, he was back in Northampton County Prison.

Was he angry at his mother for turning him in?

"No, I don't blame her. She didn't want to be accused of harboring a criminal."

But if he was planning to succeed in his effort to be free, why go home?

"I wanted to collect some checks and leave."

With some money and his car, which had been garaged in New York since shortly after his arrest, Larry could have done what he loved to do most: drive around America. He could have headed to Texas and to Mexico—as he had planned to do that December day more than a year before. The snow had stopped him then. If it hadn't, Larry would contend over and over, the attack on Fred Salloum would never have happened.

349

37// There was probably only one way to get Richard Behrens's attention, Ernie Jones finally realized, and that was "to slap him in jail." He had been patient long enough with the phantom schoolteacher; each time Ed Regan, who was overloaded with other cases, went over to pick him up as a material witness, Behrens was not there. When Campbell had interviewed Behrens in December he had had a warrant for his arrest on the charge of obstructing justice, but had planned to enforce it only if Behrens didn't cooperate. In retrospect, Jones wished he had.

On the night of February 25, Ed Regan and Ron Hoffman (a detective from the 20th Precinct who had arrested Mark David Chapman, the man who killed John Lennon) went over to Behrens's apartment, determined to find him. Regan used the same device to "loid" the security-entrance lock he had in December and began banging on the door to the apartment.

"He wouldn't open up," Regan remembered, tired of this cat-and-mouse game. "I said, 'Open up or I'll break it down. I have a warrant for your arrest as a material witness. You either stop this bullshit or I'll put you in cuffs.'"

Having failed to reach Ted Carey in Hartford, Behrens reluctantly went with the two officers back to the precinct, informing them that he had to have something to eat. Normally, Regan would have taken him to Central Booking, but he decided to keep Behrens overnight in the precinct's holding cell. He knew that "sometimes when you put certain people behind bars they have a strange reaction. He was a reluctant material witness, and I didn't feel he should be in with other criminals."

Despite all the trouble Behrens had caused Regan, the detective liked him because he was "a flake, a one-of-a-kind." The heat was off in the precinct that night as the detective and the gray-haired schoolteacher sat huddled in the lounge on the second floor, eating hamburgers, watching television, and "freezing our asses off." Despite saying over and over that "I'm not going to Salt Lake City, we'll straighten this out tomorrow," Behrens became less hostile and more genial as the evening wore on.

The following morning at ten-thirty, Regan and Allen Sullivan brought Behrens to Manhattan's State Supreme Court* to be arraigned before Acting Justice Herbert Altman. Behrens was assigned a court-appointed attorney named Fred Seligman, a former colleague of Sullivan's in the D.A.'s Office. Seligman and Behrens conferred, and Behrens made it clear that he did not want to go to Utah. The lawyer told the judge and prosecutor that instead of waiving the charge—Behrens would be immune from arrest under the law governing material witnesses—his client wanted to have a hearing, and he wanted some time to make a few phone calls.

While Seligman spoke with the people Behrens wanted him to—Spencer Austin, Marc and Ted Carey—Sullivan made a call to Ernie Jones to find out what the hell was going on. What he learned—as Seligman did—angered and embarrassed him: there was no trial about to begin in Utah that would require Behrens's attendance; in fact, the accused was not even in Utah, but in Connecticut, fighting extradition—a fight that he appeared to be winning.

Seligman's position was that the Utah papers were faulty: if Utah couldn't extradite Marc Schreuder, why should they be able to extradite Richard Behrens? Justice Altman was prepared to release Behrens until the following week. Regan warned Sullivan that if that happened, "he'll go with the wind." Sullivan phoned Jones again and asked him what he wanted to do. Earlier Jones had said that he wanted to have Behrens arrested on the charge of obstructing justice and Sullivan had talked him out of it. Was he sure that he wanted to arrest a witness? Sullivan asked. Yes, very sure, Jones said.

So late that afternoon, Behrens was paroled on the civil charge and, over Fred Seligman's strong objections, was arrested on criminal charges of obstructing justice and possession of a criminal weapon in New York. The next day, after another night in jail, he was brought back before Altman

---

*In the state of New York, the Supreme Court is the highest court of trial jurisdiction, while the Court of Appeals is the highest court.

again for arraignment on the new charges. This time the judge reversed himself, paroling Behrens on the criminal charges and sending him to jail on the original material-witness charge.

Over the next six days at the Queens House of Detention, Behrens stayed in close touch with Frances by phone, and Marc, in an effort to keep "Tricky" (as he called him) happy, dropped off a carton of Camels for him. By March 5, all three of them would have reason to celebrate.

Ernie Jones got the bad news all at once. Not only did the judge throw out Marc's case in Connecticut on that day—exactly ninety days from the time of his arrest—but he accused Utah of having "very little concern for the truth" in issuing its fugitive-from-justice warrant. If that wasn't enough to ruin Jones's day, Al Sullivan let him know from New York how displeased he was that Utah hadn't managed to get Marc certified and do their homework *before* asking his office to get involved in arresting Richard Behrens. Justice Altman was also annoyed, Sullivan said, and had mentioned, for the record, that any further motions brought to him involving the case would be presumed to be irregular and scrutinized carefully. Altman dismissed the civil charge against Behrens, but, Sullivan assured Jones, the criminal charges were still pending.

"This whole thing was *The Gang That Couldn't Shoot Straight,*" Sullivan remarked quietly in his office one day. "We could have walked away from it based on the argument of misinformation." But since it was a major homicide, his office continued the extradition procedure against Behrens, hoping he would start cooperating sooner or later.

As soon as word reached Marilyn that Marc's case had been dismissed, she decided to vent her frustration in a letter to Salt Lake City's two newspapers—the *Salt Lake Tribune* and the LDS-owned *Deseret News*—with copies to the Governor, the State Attorney General, the Salt Lake County Attorney (Jones's ultimate boss), and to the County Attorney's Office's Juvenile Division:

March 5, 1981

To the Editor

I congratulate Salt Lake City's police department and the U.S. Department of Justice on the expeditious handling to date of the "Sniper" case.* Let's hope the County Attorney can do as well on the murder charge.

However, the murder of a substantial Utah citizen, Franklin J. Bradshaw, seems to be more than they can handle. The murder weapon has been recovered and directly connected to the victim's grandson. Charges have been made. Unfortunately, badly bungled paperwork [in addition to the certification problems, the lawyers and police in both Connecticut and New York complained of various technical problems and errors in the documents themselves] from the County Attorney's office is no match for the thousands of inherited dollars that are being spent on the defense. As things stand now, this criminal matter may end with open charges and nothing being completed.

Why can't Utah get its act together for a white native son, Franklin J. Bradshaw.

Distressed,
Marilyn Bradshaw Reagan

Elaine decided to confront the situation in a different, more private way. In the middle of the night, she wrote this note:

Now I know everything.
I can't forget that you helped them murder Dad.

Elaine

It was to her mother. For days, Elaine waited and hoped for a response—*any* kind of response—but it never came.

---

*In August of 1980, an avowed racist named Joseph Paul Franklin shot and killed two black men who were jogging with two white women in Salt Lake's Liberty Park. The case came to trial in the summer of 1981 and received national attention.

38// The more Ernie Jones thought about it, the more he was convinced: it was time to make a change. He had nothing personal against Joel Campbell, but he felt that Joel was "an eight-to-four guy" who would do just so much and nothing more—a guy who would rather be deep into the Book of Mormon than obsessively working overtime on a frustrating case. In the five months since Jones had been working on the Bradshaw case, he had had a chance to read all the police reports and review the detective's work. He knew that within three days of the murder a number of people had suggested Frances and her two sons as strong suspects and Berenice as a possible one; yet when Campbell spoke with Frances on the day of her father's memorial service, "there were things in that interview," the prosecutor said, "I think he should have pursued, but just let trail off." An interview like that, he felt, was "a one-shot deal and I don't think Joel had any idea of what he was going to ask her. He needed to pin down dates, times and subjects and he just jumped into general questions. I can't imagine why Joel told her, at a certain point, 'This is confidential,' because people in law enforcement don't make promises like that." The fact that cab, rental car, hotel and airline reeords were not checked at the time; the unwitnessed delivery of the gun by Behrens to Marilyn; the interview with Behrens during which Campbell asked but didn't press him about Frances's knowledge or actual involvement—these were all "big, missed opportunities" and Jones, whose mild-mannered demeanor belied the gritty determination he had and felt Joel Campbell lacked, couldn't afford any more of them.

Michael George was in his office on the first day of April when the chief and lieutenant of the Salt Lake County Attorney's Investigative Agency knocked on his door.

"Mike, if a person was in Midland, Texas, how would he get to Salt Lake?"

On the wall, the athletic-looking twenty-nine-year-old investigator had a large map of the United States. Since September of 1980, when he joined the division from the Salt Lake County Sheriff's Office, George had been assigned to the Joseph Paul Franklin case. Franklin had used a rifle when he killed the two black joggers that day in Liberty Park, and George, in an effort to find it, was trying to trace Franklin's movements across the country.

"Midland to Denver to Salt Lake," George said, after taking a quick glance at the map.

Without even telling him why they wanted the information, they said thanks and walked out. But three weeks later they were back and told George that he was on the case.

From the time he had first entered high school, Mike George knew that police work was what he wanted to do. Born in Michigan, he had moved with his parents to the town of Hunter, Utah, when he was nine years old, the youngest of three children. His father had been working for the Hercules Powder Company and was transferred to Utah when the Michigan plant closed in 1961. Raised a Catholic, Mike George experienced, as Ernie Jones did, the difficulties and social isolation of growing up non-Mormon in Utah. Fortunately, Mike had a priest who helped organize a non-Mormon scouting and youth program, and through that, he would hear deputy sheriffs speak about their experiences in law enforcement.

When George graduated from the University of Utah in 1973, completing his major—criminology and corrections—in only two and a half years, he knew that he wanted to work for the Sheriff's Office.*

"To me, the Sheriff's Office was the class act in the county at the time. They had a lot of respect, I knew a lot of people in the department already, and was just always drawn to them." But there was one hitch—a requirement that a person be twenty-three to join, and George was only twenty-one. He

---

*Whereas the Salt Lake City Police Department is responsible for all that goes on in Salt Lake City, the Salt Lake County Sheriff's Office is responsible for crime in Salt Lake County. On occasion and in certain areas, the two entities join forces.

was about to take some graduate courses when he heard about an opening at the jail for a corrections officer. George took it for a year, and after an additional year working in communications, he became a regular deputy not long after his twenty-third birthday. From that moment until the time he left five years later, he worked in narcotics.

"If I could have worked narcotics for the rest of my career, I would have," he said. "To me it was the greatest thing I've done—or will ever do. I worked with the greatest bunch of guys in the world—we were really productive—but they only let you in for about five years and it was my turn to go."

Once he came to the County Attorney's Office, Mike George began experiencing the criminal justice system from a different perspective. As a cop it was his job to bring a case to the point of arrest; as an investigator, he was expected to work from the time of arrest until the guilt or innocence of the suspect was determined by a judge or jury. But even the most clearly defined areas of responsibility can occasionally become blurry, and the Bradshaw case was soon to be an example of that.

In bringing George into the case, a decision had been made that Joel Campbell did not have "enough time or resources available to him to push the case forward," said John T. Nielsen, the County Attorney Office's Justice Division head. Campbell was not "officially" being pushed out—he was merely being given some help; help, he would later say, he was grateful to have.

But at the time, Ernie Jones said, "he resented the fact that we got Mike into the case. I was never happy and I think Joel knows that. We didn't mean to show him up or take the case away or steal his thunder—but there were just some things I had to have."

During the next few days George was briefed by Jones and Campbell. One of the reasons he had been selected to work on the case was his experience in doing searches of airline records. As a narcotics detective, he had worked on the "Mexican Connection," a conspiracy to transport heroin from Mexico to California and Canada (passing through Utah on the way), and his ability to find certain records had helped to break the case. If Mike George knew nothing else, he knew the importance of getting records.

"Anytime you're doing *any* investigation, be it shoplifting or murder," he said, leaning forward to emphasize his point, "you gather *all* the records that are available to you. They're simply not around for a long time."

Airline tickets themselves are not kept at an airport longer than seven days, but some sort of record—either of passenger names or of billing—usually exists that would give a detective a place to begin. But at this point nearly three years had elapsed from the time of the murder, and Campbell assured Mike that he wouldn't find anything. But Campbell's assurance was only seen as a challenge by the dogged investigator. Having been told that money seemed to be the main motivation behind the murder, George was dismayed to find that neither Frank Bradshaw's nor Frances's phone or bank records had been obtained.

Shortly after issuing a subpoena for them, George received the telephone records from Mountain Bell for both the auto-parts warehouse and the house on Gilmer Drive for the years 1977 and 1978.* After looking at them carefully and noticing the extraordinary number of phone calls made to, and collect from, New York, he went to see Jones. "My God," George said, "it looks as if Frances is involved." Nobody had mentioned that possibility to him at first, and he hadn't yet read the police reports.

"I know," Jones told him, "But I don't think we're ever going to be able to put it on her." He was having a hard enough time getting Marc extradited, without worrying if his mother was behind it.

As George went home for the weekend, after less than a week on the case, he began to realize what Jones was reluctant to accept: they didn't really have a case. If Marc's

---

*Largely because of the Mormons' keen interest in genealogy, many records in Utah are kept for longer periods of time than in many other places. Whereas Mountain Bell in Utah keeps phone records for five years, New York Telephone, as George would soon find out to his dismay, keeps them for only six months.

lawyers stopped fighting his certification, brought Marc back to Utah immediately, and demanded their day in court, the case would probably be dismissed. Mike George didn't have to be a lawyer to know that—and he didn't miss the irony of the situation. The last thing a defense attorney usually wants to do is come to trial. The longer he can delay putting his client's fate into the hands of a judge or jury, the better. Time passes; people's memories fade. But George, who did not particularly like lawyers, sensed something else was at work here: "There was a deep pocket in this case, a lot of money to be made, and the attorneys realized that."

The old gravy train that Chester Reybitz had half joked about getting a seat on.

On Monday, April 27, after a weekend of reading the police reports, George interviewed Marilyn Reagan, in town on a ski vacation. Near the end of the interview, he asked her:

"Can you tell us anything else that would help our investigation?"

Marilyn had told him all that she knew—except for one thing. "Well," she said, "Dickie Boy [a nickname Behrens often used for himself] mentioned there was a hit man whom Frances had asked him to find and who had taken several thousand dollars from her."

George was floored. There was no mention of it in the police reports, nor had Campbell said anything to him—or to Jones—about it. Marilyn told George what she said she told Campbell: Behrens had mentioned his name but she had not written it down and did not remember it. When, at Campbell's urging, she had asked Behrens again about it, he would not reveal the man's identity. But she also said that she felt Behrens, who talked a great deal, was crazy and that it was difficult to know what was true and what was not.

George, who had read Campbell's interview with Behrens and felt it was "the biggest piece of shit on this earth," waited until Marilyn had left to ask him about this alleged hit man. Understandably edgy and defensive, Campbell challenged him with a rhetorical question of his own: How do you locate a hit man in New York City?

The answer, George said to himself, is, *You try*.

The main thing George felt, after speaking with Marilyn,

was that Larry was probably involved in some way—that he might have provided the transportation or, when he went to the warehouse to work that Saturday night, might have opened those doors so that Marc could sleep there—and he told Jones that Larry needed to be interviewed. When Campbell heard that, his eyes lit up. He had wanted to go east and interview Larry for some time.

"Let's go tomorrow," he suggested, as if he had just decided to fly to Puerto Rico with a lover.

If he wants to go tomorrow, George thought, he's going alone. When Jones asked George later why he wasn't going, George told him. "I'm not going to go back and make a fool of myself. They [Ron Nelson was going to accompany Joel] don't know what to ask, they don't have a plan, they don't know what the key questions are. I'm not going back."

The following day, Mike George did go east, but not to Pennsylvania. His father died in Michigan and he went back for the funeral.

In Easton, behind the sandstone walls of the Northampton County Prison, a thin and disheveled Larry Bradshaw told Joel Campbell and Ron Nelson that he had nothing to say. Nelson could see that he was "in bad shape—like a stand-in for a concentration-camp movie. His hair was matted as if he hadn't washed it for a while, and he looked like a guy who did a lot of acid—he knew you were there, but not really." Chester Reybitz, who was present, had advised Larry that it would be stupid to talk with anybody. He hadn't been officially sentenced yet, though Reybitz's motion for a new trial had been denied two days after Larry's February escape. "If they had evidence," Reybitz told Larry before they arrived, "you'd have been arrested."

If Larry Bradshaw was, in *any* way, connected to the murder of his grandfather, he was the last person about to say so.

39// The "cooperation" that the Manhattan D.A.'s Office had hoped for from Richard Behrens was not forthcoming. Behrens was fighting hard. He told his attorney, Fred Seligman, what he had told the Connecticut lawyers in December—he never had the gun—and said that if Utah claimed to have a positive on the ballistics, why weren't they giving Marc's lawyers a copy of the report? Seligman argued in legal motions that Behrens denied possession of the gun, and that the criminal charges against him were invalid because until Utah got Marc certified as an adult, the matter was still a civil one. On May 14, Behrens resorted to his favorite activity—filing suit. Charging the police department and the D.A.'s Office with "false arrest and malicious prosecution," Behrens claimed damages of $1,000,000.

But things were not as good for the embattled schoolteacher as they seemed. At some point, he feared, the game would end. He knew that Conway knew he had lied when he went to the law offices in Connecticut that day. He began to distrust Seligman, who he felt was, as a personal friend of Al Sullivan's, turning against him. Seligman had made a motion for discovery of the ballistics report. When Utah finally produced it—along with formal extradition papers charging Behrens with obstructing justice and tampering with evidence, both second-degree felonies—Seligman (informed that Utah was likely to win the certification battle) advised him that he had two choices: he could either go voluntarily or perhaps find himself going back in handcuffs. But one way or the other, he would eventually have to go. With rare exceptions, a person can fight extradition in a capital homicide case for only so long.

This is not what Behrens, nor Frances and Marc for that matter, wanted to hear. Ever in fear of tapped phone lines, Behrens began to meet with Marc in Carl Schurz Park. He told him that the net appeared to be closing; he had become suicidal, he said, and showed Marc where he had slit his wrists. He had taken Ortho, a poisonous weed killer, but instead of dying, he had merely been in the hospital for a few days with uncontrollable diarrhea. He asked Marc for some pills that might do the trick. But when Marc gave him a number of Quaaludes, Behrens, an admitted "wimpy guy," took only four or five and fell into a deep sleep. "I told Marc that the suicide thing was a bore," Behrens said, adding, "I've got to go out there—they have too much."

If that happened, he said both Marc and Frances had told him, they would somehow find a way to turn the whole thing around on him, and show that *he* had committed the murder; or, failing that, that the reason he had held the gun was so that *he* could use it to kill his stepmother, whom Frances knew Behrens hated. His stepmother, he felt, had been exerting "undue influence" over his father, and he was concerned she might by trying to persuade his father to cut him out of his will.

Before the extradition arrived, Behrens recalled, Marc told him that if they did, and Behrens had to go to Utah, Marc would be thousands of miles away in Brazil, dancing the samba.

During those clandestine meetings in the park, Marc gave Behrens more details about the murder—a reconfession of sorts—and, when Behrens asked, even reminded him of the name of the name of the hit man, which Behrens says he "blocked badly" on. "He said he told Behrens just about everything about the murder," a friend of Marc's recalled his describing those meetings, "and Behrens ate it up like candy. He wanted to hear about it. He was eager for it. He thought at first that Behrens was so fascinated because he liked the thought of murder. Later on he realized Behrens wanted to find out as much as he could about the case in order to protect himself. He said there were times when he wanted to kill Behrens— aside from when he found out Behrens turned the gun in. He was insanely jealous at times of his involvement with his mother. He said it was on a lover basis, yet of course Marc was *very* possessive of her."

When Mike George returned to Salt Lake in early May after a week in Michigan he got in touch with his contacts in the airline business and asked them to do some checking for him. One day, as he and Jones were discussing the airline problem, something occurred to him.

"Ernie," he said, "if we can't put Schreuder *into* Salt Lake City, let's see if we can show him leaving Salt Lake City." (Campbell had previously contacted Skyhawk Aviation, where Larry flew from that summer, and was told that Larry could not have landed at another airfield without filing the proper paperwork and flight plan. No record of any such plan could be found.)

George checked and found that American and United were the only two airlines that flew from Salt Lake to New York in July of 1978. He called a representative at American and explained the situation. After doing some checking, the representative called back a few days later with the bad news: there were no passenger name records available from that period. Though George had called United at the same time, they had not replied. He waited and hoped. After about a week, United phoned back: something had been found in the period he was looking for—a week before and after the murder. As the representative began to give George the information, the investigator's face lit up.

There was a Schreuder—an L. Schreuder—booked on United Airlines out of Salt Lake on July 23, the day of the murder, but the route was not direct to New York City: there were scheduled stops, and changes of plane, in Denver, Midland, and Dallas in between. George was confused. He was under the impression that was the way, in reverse, Marc would have flown *to* Salt Lake. For whatever reason, it seemed, he was flying back the same way.

But there was more, the representative said. The ticket was never picked up.

The investigator was suddenly back to square one, "because we thought that it *had* to be for Marc." George requested and obtained a passenger name record for Flight 726 at nine twenty-five on the morning of the murder—and, with United's help, was able to determine three important things: the flight was booked on July 13, the reservation was made *from* New York City, and the airline that accepted it was not United, but Continental.

George phoned Continental Airlines, whose records were

kept in Los Angeles, and explained his dilemma. When the Continental representative called him back, the message was this: all their records for 1978 were available on microfilm; there were thousands of them, but if he wanted to come out to Los Angeles and search through them himself he was more than welcome.

Uncertain he would find anything but determined to try, George planned a trip to Los Angeles with Joel Campell for May 28.

The Continental representative had not been kidding. As she began to pull, from the thousands of reels stored in the computer, the ones for all Continental flights from Midland to Denver to Salt Lake a week before and a week after the murder, Mike George could hardly blame the airline for saying he would have to scan through them. It was going to be monotonous and time-consuming, but he knew that from such tedious tasks minute mistakes could be uncovered and cases made.

Once the reels were pulled, he and Campbell started poring over the passenger name records for each flight. They were looking under Schreuder, Bradshaw, Jewett (Berenice's maiden name), Behrens, and Gentile.

The hours passed and they found nothing. Maybe he had missed something, George thought. As he began to run his eye down the reels again for the time period he was interested in, he noticed there were flights from Midland to Albuquerque, Midland to El Paso, Midland to Phoenix. He hadn't considered the possibility that Marc might have traveled to a particular destination and changed to a different airline.

George began scanning the Midland-to-Phoenix reel and thinking about the Dodgers game he was planning to go to that evening. At least the trip wouldn't be a total disaster. He had been at Continental the entire day and the task had been even more boring than he had anticipated.

But what a difference success can make. There, on the passenger name record for Flight 67, leaving Midland at three-fifteen in the afternoon on July 22—the day before the murder—was one of the names he had hoped to find: "GENTILE/L." The record showed not only that the passenger was planning to take Hughes Air West Flight 15 from Phoenix at seven thirty-five, arriving in Salt Lake at nine fifty-one, but that the ticket had been sold by American Airlines in New York City.

It was a chain reaction: American's computer had triggered Continental's, which in turn had triggered United's—the place where George had begun. While George, who tends to display his emotions, was jumping up and down, Joel Campbell was silently pleased.

"If United had sent us to American instead of Continental," George recalled, "we might not have found it." With the exception of their billing records, American had nothing available. "The whole thing was luck," he said. "I'd like to say I did a great job on it, but it was luck. I think somebody was looking out for us on that."

If luck and the perseverance of Mike George seemed to at least begin creating the miracle that Ernie Jones had been praying for, the prosecutor knew there was still a long way to go. The Bradshaw case had been a roller-coaster ride since he was first assigned to it, and when his excited investigator called from Los Angeles to give him the good news, Jones congratulated him, but quickly said: "Okay, you can put him into Midland and even into Phoenix, but not to Salt Lake City. You've got to get him the rest of the way."

That punctured George's balloon a bit, but as soon as he hung up the phone he called Republic Airlines (which had absorbed Hughes Air West the year before) in San Mateo. He spoke with a woman there who assured him that if he had the exact flight number she could pull the record within an hour.

As he was getting ready to leave for Dodgers Stadium, the phone rang. There was a ticket in the name of L. Gentile all right. But it had never been used.

On his way out of the hotel that warm, late-May evening, George realized that Jones had been right.

As he sat in his Salt Lake office reviewing the trip to Los Angeles in his mind, George wondered if the woman at Republic had possibly made a mistake. It was easy enough to do. He had thought that Denver was the only logical connecting place between Midland and Salt Lake and was delighted to find that he was wrong. So he picked up the phone and asked for the same woman he had spoken with from Los Angeles. Could she possibly check again? he asked. She promised to try, but held out little hope.

When she phoned back later that day, she had a confession to make: she had only found out half the story; that reservation had been canceled, but was later reconfirmed. If he wanted to research it further, she said, he would have to return to California; the airline could not do it for him.

On Monday, June 15, after months of legal wrangling, Marc Schreuder was finally certified to stand trial as an adult on charges of first-degee murder. His lawyers immediately asked for a stay of that ruling so that they could appeal to the Utah Supreme Court. But later that day, while the judge was considering their request, the prosecution moved to obtain a new warrant for Marc's arrest. The defense was furious and felt the state had behaved in a zealous and underhanded fashion. While the juvenile court judge eventually granted the stay, the district court judge who signed the warrant let it remain in effect.

Ernie Jones's feeling of elation, however, turned out to be fleeting. It was one thing to possess a warrant but quite another to make an arrest. For all that Ernie knew, Marc could be dancing the samba in Rio at that very moment.

40// Before Mike George went back to California with Joel Campbell, he arranged for John Cavenaugh, who had enlisted in the Navy and was based temporarily in San Diego, to fly to Salt Lake for an interview. After reviewing Campbell's reports on his two trips to Texas and reading the transcripts of the interviews he and Ron Nelson had conducted there, it occurred to George—as it had to Campbell and Nelson—that the people they had spoken with might have been withholding information. In order to see if that was true, the only person (aside from Nick Miller) who had positively identified Marc as being in Midland during that time seemed as good a place to begin as any.

Over and over, Cavenaugh identified himself as more of an "acquaintance" than a "friend"; he stressed to George, Ernie Jones and Joel Campbell that Marc was an "extremely excitable" kid who was a loner, and whom people made fun of and were amused by. Asked if Marc had ever talked about guns at Kent or what his interests were in general, Cavenaugh said he couldn't recall any discussions about guns but did know that Marc was interested in murder stories.

"Could you elaborate?" George asked him, keen to explore this sudden revelation. "Did he talk about planning them or plotting them?"

"Well, he read them," Cavenaugh offered.

"Constantly read murder stories?" the investigator pressed.

"I don't know if he did constantly, but I noticed that he read them." Cavenaugh, as it turned out, wasn't the only one to notice that. In the course of the interview, he told them that his younger brother recalled that Marc had a copy of Agatha Christie's *Death on the Nile* (a novel whose plot involves murder for inheritance) while he stayed with them in Midland, and was reading it. Cavenaugh's parents "loved him" he said, adding that Marc seemed very fond of them and his little brother, and was friendly, polite and cordial all the time he was there.

He said that he had gone over to McPhail's that Saturday morning and that McPhail had phoned Bruce Stanley (the fellow who went to check the gun out). At the bank early that afternoon, Marc gave McPhail the money ("Two hundred and some odd dollars, I believe. He was willing to pay any price") and McPhail gave it to the woman who was selling the gun. Back at McPhail's house, Marc asked how to use the gun, and though they didn't actually shoot any rounds, Cavenaugh said he did demonstrate how to load, fire and operate it. Marc had a plane to catch, Cavenaugh said, but he couldn't remember whether he or his mother took him to the airport.

"When he was packing his suitcase, did you see any camping gear?" George asked.

"None."

"Did you see a lot of clothes in his suitcase?"

Cavenaugh said it was "reasonably full" and did recall that he might have had a *Playboy* in it.

"Did Marc . . . ever use a different name than Marc Schreuder?" George asked. "Did you ever know him by Marc Gentile?"

"No."

George spelled out Gentile and asked Cavenaugh if he had ever seen it on anything—like Marc's plane ticket.

Cavenaugh had not seen it on anything, he said, nor did he ever see the plane ticket.

Shown a calendar of July 1978, Cavenaugh was asked to indicate when Marc would have arrived in Midland and when he would have left. Cavenaugh, who recalled that Marc came before his own birthday on the 24th, marked Thursday the 20th as his arrival date and the 22nd as his departure date—at approximately three to four in the afternoon. Since George already knew that the Continental flight to Phoenix was scheduled to depart at three-fifteen, he could barely contain his excitement.

Four days after the interview with John Cavenaugh, Mike George and Joel Campbell flew to San Francisco. They delivered the .357 Magnum to the ATF Lab on Treasure Island, and went to the Republic Airlines office in San Mateo. As they soon discovered, the information they had come to get could have been obtained by pushing one button on the computer and relayed to them over the phone: the passenger first made the reservation from Phoenix to Salt Lake for Saturday night, the 22nd, then changed it to Friday night, the 21st, and then switched it back again. In addition, Republic could confirm what Continental had said: the reservations had been made through American Airlines in New York City.

Back in Salt Lake, having interviewed Elaine and Mason Drukman in Berkeley before he left, George called American Airlines in Tulsa, Oklahoma. A woman in the revenue accounting office confirmed what George already knew (but still hoped was not the case): all they had was a billing record for 1978—nothing by name at all.

Since George had obtained a photostat of the Midland–Phoenix–Salt Lake ticket from Continental, he asked the

woman if she would research the ticket number before and
after the one he gave her.

A few days later she phoned back. The ticket preceding the
Midland–Phoenix–Salt Lake one was for an American flight
from New York to Dallas, connecting to a Texas International
flight to Midland; the day of departure was July 20—the
Thursday that Cavenaugh said Marc arrived at his parents'
house in a taxi. But there was a hitch: the Texas International
coupon was *never* received by American. Either the passenger didn't use it, she said, or Texas International, more likely,
simply didn't send it.

The ticket after the Midland–Phoenix–Salt Lake one was
for an American Airlines flight from Salt Lake to New York,
departing at nine twenty-five on July 23—roughly two hours
after the murder was committed that Sunday morning.

"Is there any way of determining who sold that ticket?"
George asked her.

Yes, she said, the die number on the ticket he was holding
would indicate that. George read off the information she
requested, and was told that the ticket had been sold at the
American Airlines office in the Plaza Hotel by Carolyn
Karoliszyn. He thanked her for her help and went to give
Jones the good news.

"We still can't show that that person was Marc." With one
astute comment, Ernie Jones, devil's advocate and ever
aware of what he eventually would have to prove in court,
managed both to dampen his investigator's enthusiasm (once
again) and make him even more determined.

When George reached Carolyn Karoliszyn on the phone
and briefly explained the situation, she said it was too bad he
hadn't bought the tickets from her partner. "She remembers
everybody and has testified at a lot of trials. I'm never able to
remember anybody."

They talked for a while longer, but Candy, as she calls
herself, could not recall the sale. If *anything* occurred to her,
he said dejectedly, giving her his work and home number, she
should call him collect, day or night.

Two weeks after the Governor of New York signed the
Utah extradition papers for Richard Behrens, Behrens re-

tained a private attorney. He first told Fred Seligman and Al Sullivan, whom he often dropped in to see without an appointment, that he would go to Utah, then he changed his mind. At Frances's suggestion, he had gone to see Norman Ostrow, a former partner in the firm of Rogers & Wells—Frances and Berenice's New York lawyers—and he in turn referred Behrens to Larry Goldman, a former Assistant District Attorney in the Manhattan D.A.'s Office.

Behrens and his father, a New Jersey physician who offered to pay his son's legal bills, met with the curly-haired, pipe-smoking Goldman on June 10, two days before Behrens was due to be extradited. When that day arrived, Goldman appeared in court and requested a month's continuance. Since he was new to the case—and Marc had not been arrested yet—his motion was granted.

His mother was urging him to flee. So was Granny. But Marc soon discovered that life as a fugitive in New York could be exciting. If he insisted on remaining in New York, then Frances did not want him to stay at Gracie Square any longer. After all, she could be charged with harboring a criminal. It had taken her years—and the murder of her father—to get to a place like Gracie Square, and she wasn't about to do anything that would jeopardize her existence there.

The message was clear, Marc told a friend: if he wanted to remain in *her* will, he would have to shoulder the guilt himself.

He lived under a variety of aliases in a variety of places, including the Sloane House YMCA on West 34th Street (where Larry had stayed over the Christmas holidays in 1978), the Midtown Motor Inn on Eighth Avenue and the Hotel Seville at 29th and Madison, just around the corner from the church where his mother had married Frederick Schreuder more than twelve years before.

His grandmother financed his life as a fugitive—$4,000 to $5,000 a month, he told his friend—and what she didn't give to him willingly, he stole. Theft, of course, was nothing new to Marc, and atfer all, he had had an excellent teacher. He took cash from Granny's purse and forged her checks—using the ones on the bottom first—and mostly invested the money in coins, his longtime passion.

369

As David Jablonski, an alias he had used once before, he walked the streets dressed like a bum, wearing stained old shirts, baggy trousers stuffed with gold coins, and carrying shopping bags to complement his appearance. He went to Times Square and watched X-rated movies for hours on end, then purchased the services of prostitutes in order to reenact what he had just seen. Sex would make him hungry, so he usually stopped at McDonald's to have some Big Macs before he went back to Room 727 at the Seville.

But as Alexander Bentley, he lived a different sort of life. Bentley was a name he had come across in a Dickens novel, a friend recalled Marc telling him, and Alexander seemed an appropriately Waspish first name to tack on to it. With an identification card listing that name, an address in the wealthy town of Greenwich, Connecticut, and his own picture, he would go to fancy Manhattan restaurants, alone and often in a rented tuxedo, and order lavish meals.

"He enjoyed life on the run," his friend remembered. "He felt it was like being a spy in a spy novel or the major suspect in a murder novel. He just loved the fact that he had no obligations—[that he was] able to go wandering around, walk into a bank, and get all the money he needed. He said it was the best time he'd ever had—he was independent and wasn't really lonely, though he wanted to go home at times."

Aside from his mother, his grandmother and his lawyers, he kept in touch with Susie Coleman, who knew he was a fugitive but believed in his innocence. She would occasionally visit him at the Seville or he would come to her apartment— not far from a private postal box on East 85th Street where he received money from Granny. In an oversized trenchcoat with no buttons and a hat pulled down low, he tried to be a Hitchcockian figure of mystery, often walking slowly past the window of Coleman's Delicatessen on East End Avenue. Five minutes later the phone in the deli would ring and Susie would answer.

"Did you see me?" Marc wanted to know.

"Yes, we all saw you," she said, wondering how he thought anybody could miss him.

With is odd, stumpy appearance, he might not have been the most ideal, inconspicuous recruit for the CIA, but at least he was receiving the attention he had so desperately sought throughout his life.

But life for Marc as a fugitive was not without its anxious moments. He also kept in touch with Bob Brown, his old friend from Allen-Stevenson, and was over at Brown's apartment one day that summer. While Brown knew that Marc had been arrested in Connecticut and the case had been dismissed, he did not know that the police might be looking for him.

"We went down to the street," Brown recalled. "Two policemen were talking to the doorman. I took my eyes off Marc for an instant and he was gone. A half hour later he called with some strange excuse about seeing policemen there and how he thought there was trouble and that we should get out of the way. I told him, 'You're being ridiculous. Come back.' He was apprehensive but he came back."

On another occasion that summer Berenice was planning to return to Salt Lake, and Marc, who was home briefly, offered to carry her bags downstairs. But once she got down there she discovered his as well.

"He said he was going with me," Berenice remembered. "We flew back to Salt Lake together and went to Evanston, Wyoming, early the next morning. I was going to get him a job in the oil fields. We thought he'd get a job and the whole thing would die down. But we couldn't find one. The next morning, a Sunday, we were going to Park City and tried to cross over to a gas station. I nicked the taillight of a Mercedes. Marc got out and left the car, left the scene. If the police saw him they would've put him in jail. He took off the next morning. His trip was supposed to be a secret."

41 // While Marc was enjoying a life of adventure tinged with just enough close calls to prevent complacency, Mike George continued to build his case against the young man he had never met.

On July 15, he and his supervisor, Don Harman, traveled to Midland, Texas, in order to "make amends." From speaking with John Cavenaugh, George knew that Joel Campbell and Ron Nelson had hardly forged lifelong friendships during their two trips there, but he was quite unprepared for the reception he got.

"I'd never been met by more hostile people in my life as an investigator," he recalled. "Our first interview was with Malcolm McPhail. We went to his office. He had an attorney there, the undersheriff on the phone, and said, 'You've got five minutes to talk to me, get your business said, and then I want you gone.' So I said, 'Fine, give me five minutes,' and I took that time to explain that he was an important cog in the case, an important witness for the state of Utah, and I apologized for the way he'd been treated. The next fifteen minutes were spent soothing him over. At the end of that time, he said, 'I'll help you any way I can.' "

McPhail said that when Campbell and Nelson talked with him he could not "remember" Marc Schreuder specifically—just that John Cavenaugh was getting a gun for his friend. But as soon as Mike George laid out a photo spread, McPhail picked one up and said, "I'll tell you right now. That's the boy I dealt with." He explained that he was not more forthcoming before because he felt "treated as if I were a criminal," then enlightened George and Harman in the same way he had tried to enlighten Campbell and Nelson: this wasn't Utah, gentlemen, this was Texas, and the buying and selling of guns was as natural for Texans as breathing, seeing oil spurt out of the ground, and counting money.

Once McPhail felt sure that they understood that, he remembered other things about Marc: his "suit or sport coat" was out of place for West Texas in July, and as soon as he had the gun and bullets (which McPhail sold him) he was "very anxious to get away." He confirmed what Cavenaugh had said the month before—that John had got in touch with him after Marc called from New York and before he came to Midland. Once Marc arrived, Cavenaugh brought him over, and that is when he phoned Bruce Stanley. To the best of his knowledge, he said, it was a Saturday morning, because that is when he cuts the lawn and does other chores. When they got to the bank to purchase the gun Stanley had checked out, he recalled handing over the $165 to $175 that Marc had given him to a woman, and that she either gave the gun to him or to Marc directly. Besides the three of them and Cavenaugh, he said, John Snow was the only other person present. After they got the gun (which was wrapped in brown paper in a new Smith & Wesson box and may have been in a paper sack), he recalled asking Marc what it was to be used for and was told that he was traveling to Utah or Colorado to visit his grandfather and go backpacking; he needed a weapon for "protection"—a "powerful" weapon.

What McPhail didn't say that day, but recalled more than two years later to a visitor, is that when John Cavenaugh first told him that he needed "a heavy-caliber handgun, a .38 Special or a Magnum" for his friend and why, McPhail said that a Ruger .22—a much less powerful gun—would be more than enough protection on a camping trip. And for all his talk about the insignificance of gun transactions in the Lone Star State, he was troubled when Marc asked him what kind of bullets he needed for the gun. "I started wondering right then why he was wondering what he would need if he was going backpacking." McPhail told Marc that he usually bought the highest-velocity bullet he could get, but that all he needed was .38 Specials if he was going backpacking. But McPhail also remembered saying, "If you want to use the gun for maximum protection, these .357 Remingtons* will blow your antagonist away.

"I felt he had never even shot a gun before or had one in his

---

*The difference in impact between ".357 Remingtons" and ".38 Specials"—both of which can be used in a .357 Magnum, the weapon in question—is comparable to being hit with a hardball or a softball.

hand," McPhail said. "This really stuck in my mind. I think he was determined—that he had a positive direction of travel."

By the time George and Harman went to sleep that night, after dinner with McPhail and Bruce Stanley at the Blue Star Inn, McPhail's favorite restaurant, they knew their public-relations effort had succeeded: McPhail and Stanley—who identified the gun from a photograph—were allies now, not enemies.

Over the next two days George and Harman interviewed Jerry Register and Shara Vestal, John Cavenaugh's parents, and John Snow. Since Register and Vestal lived on opposite sides of Midland, George arranged a meeting at a place convenient for both of them—a café in Odessa called the Kettle. Though the issue of whether Register was even present during the gun transaction was still unresolved—Vestal was the only person who said he was—the police chief certainly held forth as if he had been. He now recalled that the sale did not take place during May (as he and Vestal had previously said), but occurred between Old Settler's Day (held the second Saturday in July every year in Stanton, where he was chief) and August 4 (the day that his eleven-year-old son from his first marriage, who had been visiting them from Louisiana, was accidentally shot and paralyzed from the neck down). They used the cash—$175, he was "fairly sure"—to buy the boy some back-to-school clothes. It was probably the 22nd, he said, because that was a Saturday and Shara had to work across the street. At the bank, Register said, Marc (whose photograph, according to George, he was now able to identify, but couldn't when it was shown to him by Campbell and Nelson) was "kind of fidgeting around" as Register took the money from McPhail, and acting as if he was not interested in the transaction. Register did remember there was mention about "going to Colorado and going hiking or camping and, you know, backpacking and this kind of thing." After he and Shara left the building, he said, he began "aggravating her" about Marc, saying that he should have checked his age and wasn't really sure "who was purchasing the gun the way the deal went down."

* * *

When the two investigators went to interview the Cavenaughs at their large two-story red-brick house with a lovely pecan tree out front, an attorney was present as well. After the doctor's experience with Jim Conway masquerading as a patient, he was taking no chances.

The Cavenaughs identified Marc's picture and confirmed that he "probably" arrived on Thursday, July 20, at their house in a taxi at about twelve-thirty or one. He said he was going to visit his grandparents in Salt Lake City, Mrs. Cavenaugh recalled, and had lived with them for several years. "I remember saying, 'Well, you must be very close to them,' or something like that, and he looked at me sort of funny."

When he told them why he had come to Midland, "I was concerned because he was underage," she said. ". . . I talked to him about calling his mother and he assured me that that would be fine, his parents knew he was purchasing a gun and that there would be no problem if I called his mother and he would have been happy for me to have done so." He was so disarming and nonchalant about it, she said, that she never made the call.

Dr. Cavenaugh recalled Marc's sport coat, and his wife remembered that Marc was reading *Death on the Nile*—"his favorite," she said. "Agatha Christie was his favorite author and he had read it several times." They both recalled that Marc had to change his plane reservations—he was not able to get the gun through McPhail that Friday—and that his connection to Salt Lake was through either Phoenix or Tucson. "Phoenix sticks in my mind," Mrs. Cavenaugh said, "but I'm certainly not one hundred percent positive." Dr. Cavenaugh was able to confirm that Saturday, July 22, was the day Marc left—he worked only one Saturday a month and a check of his records showed the 22nd to be the particular one in July—but Mrs. Cavenaugh, like her son, could not recall how Marc got to the airport.

George and Harman had gone to Texas, George said, to "make amends." By the time they got back to Salt Lake they had achieved considerably more than that: they could place Marc in Midland from the 20th to the 22nd, show that he purchased a gun on that Saturday, and confirm that he went from there to Salt Lake. Now, if they could only find him.

When Ed Regan picked up his phone at the 20th Precinct on August 18, he was hardly pleased to hear Joel Campbell's voice. It had been ten months since Marilyn Reagan first strolled into the precinct that October evening and asked if someone would take her shopping bag. Regan did, never guessing at the time the continual involvement he would have in the case. Like Al Sullivan, Regan was understandably wary of any further cries from Utah for help; in trying to be accommodating, their respective offices had wound up frustrated—and sued by Richard Behrens—instead.

Even though Utah had held a valid warrant for Marc's arrest since the middle of June, Ernie Jones had been trying to cut a deal with Marc's lawyers that would bring Marc back, but his efforts had failed. Regan assured Campbell that he would do his best to find the boy, but was not about to get mired in quicksand again until he had their warrant in hand.

On August 31 he did, and drove over to 10 Gracie Square. He spoke with the building's manager, Gary Perman, who told him that he had not seen Marc for two months and that Frances was in the Hamptons for the summer. Regan gave Perman his card and the manager said that he would call him if Marc came around; but Regan had been a New York cop long enough to know one thing about the people who work in an exclusive building: "If the tenants take care of them, they're not too quick to give up information." Before driving back to the West Side, he stopped at Coleman's Delicatessen —a favorite hangout of Marc's, he had been told.

Like Perman, they said they hadn't seen Marc either.

That same day, Larry Goldman sent a letter and a copy of Richard Behrens's papers to Norman Ostrow. Ostrow, who had referred Behrens to Goldman in June, was now repre- senting Marc. But Ostrow was not the only one interested in Richard Behrens's extradition situation. Frances had been seeing Behrens's papers ever since Fred Seligman was ap- pointed to represent him in February—but of late they had been arriving in "anonymous" manila envelopes. On one occasion she received an unsigned, typewritten note urging

1 Franklin James Bradshaw

2 Berenice Harriet Jewett

3 The first Bradshaw Auto Parts store, 333 West
Center Street, Provo, Utah

4 Marilyn, Robert and Elaine Bradshaw

5 The Bradshaws (clockwise, from back left):
Berenice, Robert, Franklin, Marilyn, Elaine

Franklin and Berenice

7 Frances with Franklin on her fifteenth birthday

8 Vittorio and Frances Gentile, January 9, 1959

9 Frances with Lorenzo Gentile, her first son

10 Marco Gentile, Frances's second son

11 Marc Schreuder (center, back row), student at the Allen-Stevenson School, New York City

12 Frederick and Frances Schreuder, February 2, 1969

13 Franklin, carrying his "briefcase"

14 The Bradshaws' home, 1327 Gilmer Drive, Salt Lake City

15 Berenice

16 The Bradshaw Auto Parts warehouse,
337 Pierpont Avenue, Salt Lake City

17 Frances on the Staten
Island Ferry—a picture
later identified by
Myles Manning

18 Lavinia Schreuder

19 Marc, at Gilmer Drive, the summer of 1977

20 Marc, taking a picture of Franklin opening the warehouse—photograph by Larry Schreuder

21 Joel Campbell

22 Doug Steele

23 Clive Davis

24 Frances and Berenice at Salt Lake City airport, July 25, 1978, two days after the murder

25 Marc, at Kent School in 1979

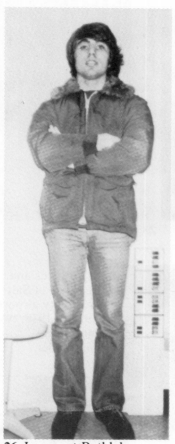

26 Larry, at Bethlehem
Police Department,
December 20, 1979

27 Richard Behrens

28 Myles Manning, at
Culver Lake, New Jersey
—picture taken by
Richard Behrens

29 Stephen Klein

30 Michael George

31 Marc Schreuder, March 3, 1982

32 Stephen Klein helping Frances Schreuder into car, March 22, 1982

33 Judge James S. Sawaya

34 Ernie Jones

35 Joe Tesch

36 Stephen Swindle, explaining estate of Franklin J. Bradshaw

37 Marc Schreuder, Paul Van Dam, Joe Tesch

38 David Frankel

39 Dr. Louis G. Moench

40 Michael Rosen, holding the murder weapon—a .357 Magnum

41 Ernie Jones

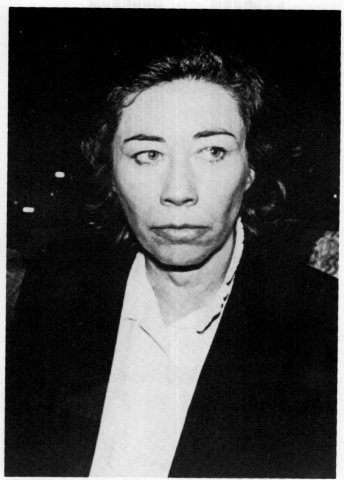

42 Frances, September 27, 1983

her to persuade Marc to flee and reinforcing the importance of that with a slightly altered quote from Baroness Orczy's *The Scarlet Pimpernel:* "They seek him here, they seek him there."

In the midst of everything, Richard Behrens, it seemed, had lost neither his sense of humor nor his love of adventure —nor, for that matter, his fear of what might happen to him.

One month later, after the police in Salt Lake made a formal complaint that New York was not doing enough to find and arrest Marc, Ed Regan and another detective drove back to Gracie Square. They took the elevator to the sixth floor and rang the buzzer to Frances's apartment.

When the housekeeper answered, they identified themselves and asked to speak with Frances. After a few minutes she appeared.

Regan told her that he had a warrant for her son's arrest. She said that he wasn't there and she didn't want to be bothered anymore. The door abruptly closed (Regan had not brought the search warrant he would have needed), leaving them in a dark hallway and fumbling for a lighter in order to find the button to the elevator.

On September 30, the day before Regan went over to Gracie Square, Ernie Jones and Mike George had a meeting out in Salt Lake. They had been told that the New York police were actively looking for Marc, but they had also been told that it might be impossible to find him in New York—that he could be anywhere.

"Mike, do you think you can find him in thirty days?" Jones asked.

"I think so," said the investigator, never lacking in confidence. "I'd sure love to try."

"Because if you can't," he continued, "I think I'll start bargaining with Van Dam and Tesch to get him here." (A few weeks earlier, Paul Van Dam and Joe Tesch had replaced Spencer Austin and David Dolowitz as Marc's Utah attorneys.)

This was exactly the kind of deadline and challenge Mike George loved. This was the reason he had become a cop. He went to speak with Don Harman and explained the situation.

George had worked closely with the Cincinnati police on the Joseph Paul Franklin case, and he told Harman that one member of that department, who was familiar with the New York City police, had advised him: "If you need something from New York City, they *won't* give it to you. Their police department is virtually uncooperative because they have too much crime of their own."

While that might have been one person's opinion it was enough to persuade Harman, who said he'd call his opposite number in the Manhattan D.A.'s Office and see if they would assign an investigator to it. Harman spoke with the head of the Investigation Bureau that same day and, two days later, sent him a probable cause statement, copies of the arrest warrant, Marc's NCIC (National Crime Information Center) entry that listed his arrest at Kent School as well as his arrest in Hartford, and pictures of both him and Frances.

"It is our hope," Harman wrote, "to track the suspect down by use of the phone records of the numbers listed in the probable cause statement." The three numbers listed were all billed to 10 Gracie Square: a regular service number, a credit card number, a number for outgoing calls only. Salt Lake had information, the statement indicated, that "the suspect receives phone contact from his mother on a regular basis," and that he used several different names—including Marc Bradshaw, Marc Gentile, L. Gentile, and James Davis.

Within a few days, Mike George received a telephone call from Stephen Klein.

Before joining the Manhattan D.A.'s Office in 1977, Steve Klein had worked for the securities firm of Bache, Halsey, Stuart and Shields. Every bit as intense as George, the bearded, thirty-five-year-old investigator had a great ability to remember details and focused mainly on investigations in the lucrative area of white-collar crime. From his Salt Lake counterpart, Klein learned that Marc might be homosexual—a theory that originated with Jim Conway; from Bob Beltrandi of the Hartford police, he discovered that Marc loved to play video games and was "a professional student," probably hanging out at a college somewhere. Getting no cooperation whatsoever from the people who worked at Gracie Square, Klein decided to begin his search around

New York University in Greenwich Village and the many gay bars in that area.

Back in Salt Lake, many things were going through Mike George's mind, but one in particular inescapably stood out: the whole case kept circling back to the question of money. A headline in the *Salt Lake Tribune* on October 12 asked: "Did Murder Victim's Estate Pay Fugitive's Lawyers?" George knew that a lot of money and stocks had been stolen in the summer of 1977, knew from that memo that Frank Bradshaw might have been intending to change his will and cut Frances out of it, knew that checks had been forged by both Frances and Berenice, and knew that money for Frances had been a constant source of friction in the family for years. He felt that if Marc was to be found, he would have to follow the money.

He issued an investigative subpoena for all of Berenice's bank accounts: after all, if she was paying Marc's legal bills, she might be financing his life as a fugitive. Once he had what he wanted, he began going through the bank's copies of each canceled check—the originals would have been returned to her—and came across one that said "re: Marc Schreuder," made out to what appeared to be MFB.

George went up to the University of Utah library and began going through the New York telephone directory. There was nothing under MFB. He drove back to the office and told the woman who was helping him VIA-chart* the case that he had struck out. She looked at the somewhat blurred photostat and said, "Maybe it's MTB." So they drove back to the library and looked again. There was one entry: MTB Interamerican Inc.

George phoned Klein in New York and asked him to check it out. What Klein had to say when he called back aroused George's greatest fear. MTB Interamerican Inc. was the

---

*VIA charting is a Visual Investigative Aid often used in complicated cases so that times, events, places or meetings can be quickly referred to. In this case, George had a continuous sheet of paper, circling a room, with squares, boxes and circles on it. The more he learned, the more he could fill in.

379

Latin American division of Manfra, Tordella & Brookes, Inc.—an internationally known company dealing in foreign currency, precious metals and coins.

"Motherfuck," George said. "He's out of the country." He could see it all: Marc had probably gone to a place like Bolivia (which does not have an extradition pact with the United States), and his grandmother was supporting him. Klein said that he would go to MTB at once.

MTB has two offices in New York City that are open to the public: one in the lobby of the imposing World Trade Center (the same building where Marc had worked for Mitsubishi Bank) and the other on two floors at Rockefeller Center. And it was on the mezzanine level of Rockefeller Center that Steve Klein met the person whom Marc Schreuder was buying gold coins from—Gerald Bauman, a husky man with bifocals who was one of the company's senior numismatists. At first, Bauman was reluctant to say anything; all he knew about Schreuder, he said, was that he was interested in collecting coins for a hobby, was reasonably astute about them, and dropped in periodically. As far as Bauman knew, Schreuder hadn't fled the country, because he had seen him recently.

The only address MTB had for Marc was at Trinity College. Klein asked Bob Beltrandi to check if Marc had been seen around the campus since the time of his arrest, and Beltrandi reported that he hadn't. Klein was in the process of getting MTB to bring Marc in under a ruse—if Marc called, Bauman was asked to tell him something special had arrived that he should come in to see—when Mike George phoned him again.

George had discovered another check—made out to Citipostal re: Suite 299 in the amount of $15—and told Klein he assumed Berenice was paying rent on a room or apartment for Marc.

"If it's fifteen dollars," Klein laughed, "he ain't paying rent in New York."

Citipostal, as Klein discovered, was a private post office with two locations in Manhattan. He and his partner, Frank Juliano, drove to the uptown location at 207 East 85th Street (not far from Gracie Square) and identified themselves to the manager. The manager told them that the post office had opened in July and that Marc, who used his own name and the address of Susie Coleman's apartment, had been one of its first customers. He was a nice kid who used to come in the evening (they were open till eight during the week) and talk with him and the other fellow who worked there about the stock market. But, he said, Marc was also "a little bit nuts"—especially when he looked through his mail. Whenever a certified letter arrived for him, that usually meant a check from "Granny" was inside. But when those certified letters didn't arrive in Suite 299 (his box number) he would start cursing and storm out of the narrow building.

Klein meanwhile had discovered that MTB was not the only coin dealer that Marc frequented, though it was the main one. He learned that a major gold coin auction had been held recently and that Marc had not only attended but made some purchases—purchases that he wanted sent to an address at 373 Fifth Avenue, Citipostal's other location where Marc had another box. Instead of having Marc come to MTB, Klein decided to set Marc up through Citipostal. The plan was this: when Marc came to the Fifth Avenue location, he would be told that his package had inadvertently been sent to East 85th Street.

On Thursday, October 22, Klein and Juliano (who had worked on the French Connection case, and had helped protect the narcotics detective later known to the public as "Prince of the City") set up their surveillance. Even though they had been told that Marc usually came in the evening, they arrived at about eleven in the morning. While one of them kept watch from the outside, the other stayed out of sight in the back.

But on that Thursday, Marc did not appear. On the following day they stayed until near closing time again and left in frustration. Maybe Marc had been tipped off, they wondered, or was suspicious as to why the box he wanted sent to Fifth Avenue was being held for him at 85th Street instead.

Before going to Citipostal on Monday morning, Klein and Juliano were told that if Marc did not appear by the end of the day they were to drop their surveillance. When the investigators arrived, they learned that Marc had come in on Friday just after they left. Klein spent most of Monday in the back while Juliano kept watch outside. Shortly before five-thirty, one boxholder came in, followed by another, dressed in a brown corduroy overcoat with a fake fur collar, jeans and a pullover terry-cloth shirt—the young man who paid rent on Suite 299. The manager walked in the back and quietly told Klein. By the time he emerged, Juliano was already behind Marc and in position. The other boxholder was discreetly asked to leave, and within seconds, Marc's life as a fugitive was over—at least for now.

He was searched for a weapon, read his rights, and placed in handcuffs. Though clearly afraid, he was also calm enough to ask if he could go outside and pay the cab driver who had driven him uptown and was parked down the street. The investigators told him to forget it. Once they took him back to their office for processing, Marc phoned Norman Ostrow and "Popo" (Frances's French housekeeper), and then was taken to Central Booking.

Ernie Jones had given Mike George thirty days to find Marc, and with the help of Steve Klein, he had. Though George was disappointed that he hadn't made the arrest himself, it really meant a lot to him, he would later say, that he had helped get Marc arrested in New York without ever going there.

About a month before his arrest that night, Marc had planned to leave the country. For $10,000, he told his grandmother, he had obtained a fake passport. Ostrow had discussed the possibility of his surrendering in a place where he might be able to get bail while fighting extradition, but Marc wasn't about to do that. Yet when he told his mother that he was thinking about leaving—the thing that she and his grandmother had been urging him to do all along—she talked him out of it, he later claimed to a friend, saying that the police had not been around for a while and even suggesting that he might be able to return home soon.

And home, ironically, was where he was thinking about going the night that Klein and Juliano surprised him on East 85th Street.

42// On November 13, less than three weeks after his arrest, Marc was released on $150,000 bail. His new team of New York lawyers—Michael Armstrong and David Frankel had replaced Norman Ostrow*—had virtually done the impossible: they began with a law that clearly states bail is not allowed when someone is being held for extradition on a capital offense—and found a way around it. Even Al Sullivan grudgingly conceded they did "a beautiful job of advancing strong arguments for a very weak position." But unless the defense could now prove—in this situation the burden was on them—that Marc was not in Utah at the time of the murder, Marc would be going out to Salt Lake sooner or later.

Four days after Marc was released on bail and took up residence at the Gracie Square Hotel, a place whose only link to luxury is embodied in its name and location on East 86th Street, Richard Behrens's day in court—at least in New York—appeared to be over. The warrant for his extradition was ordered to be executed. Larry Goldman, who had sensed for some time that the story Behrens had originally told Joel Campbell was more accurate than his recantation, bluntly told his client that the time had come for him to tell the truth. He could probably get him a grant of immunity, he said, but only if "we talk the facts and cut out the shit."

Behrens could see at this point that he'd have to protect himself. Marc hadn't left the country, as Behrens had hoped,

---

*Because Ostrow's law partner is the son-in-law of the Manhattan District Attorney, their firm does not accept any cases in New York County in which "a substantial matter of discretion is involved," so as to avoid any appearance of a conflict of interest. In October of 1984, Ostrow removed himself as attorney for John A. Zaccaro, husband of Geraldine Ferraro, when the D.A.'s Office began a formal investigation into Mr. Zaccaro's business dealings.

and the schoolteacher felt sure that Marc's extradition was imminent. Frances's threat—that if Behrens lost his extradition fight, she'd find a way to turn it on him—had never left his thoughts. After all, he had hardly been an innocent in this matter. He had been a silent conspirator throughout and, in crucial ways, an active one—finding her a hit man, searching for a gun, agreeing to keep the one that Marc brought back, and going so far as to buy a cover for it.

As much as Behrens enjoyed being contrary, he did not want to go to Utah in handcuffs. He trusted Larry Goldman; if Goldman said it was time to play ball, he meant it.

David Frankel was having problems. As he sat in his office at 26 Broadway in lower Manhattan, the twenty-eight-year-old defense attorney was experiencing the kind of empty feeling that usually comes to prosecutors who prepare for trial without the thing they need most—proof. Marc and Frances were telling him that Marc was home in New York that Sunday morning. Marc was also telling him something else—the thing that everyone initially thought at the time: Larry had committed the murder. While these might be elements to build on for Marc's trial, they were not going to prevent him from being extradited. There either had to be someone else who could provide a credible alibi as to where Marc was that morning—or there probably wasn't anybody.

Slowly, Marc began to trust Frankel. After all, Armstrong and he had performed one miracle; maybe they could pull another rabbit out of their legal bag of tricks. But Marc had an idea of his own—the old escape plan.

He was going to go to Argentina and travel "incognito," he told Frankel. Frankel just laughed at him and told him that he would need $50,000,000 if he expected to last in Argentina for more than six months. Still, "incognito" became a catch phrase between them and the idea of Marc's possibly escaping their "one moment of levity" in the midst of everything that was being discussed. From his own observations, his conversations with Frances, and other things he had managed to learn, David Frankel knew one thing probably more clearly than anything else: Marc was tremendously loyal to his mother. "He was really somebody who looked desperately for her approval," Frankel said. "She was something special to him, and he didn't want to face her wrath, which, at times, could be pretty terrible."

From the moment Marc was arrested at Citipostal, Mike George began preparing to go to New York. He hadn't pushed to go in October because he thought he'd have only one chance and wanted the trip to be as productive as possible. At the top of his priority list were Richard Behrens (who, he had heard, might revert to his original story if granted full immunity) and, through Behrens, the hit man Behrens had mentioned to Marilyn. He also wanted to reinterview Marilyn; to visit Candy Karoliszyn at American Airlines, the fellow from MTB who had sold coins to Marc, the people at Citipostal, the manager of the Hotel Seville (where Marc was staying when he was arrested), among others; and, if possible, to travel both to Kent School and Trinity College.

Since George had been to New York only once before, arriving late one evening and leaving early the next morning, he had no idea of what New York was, he said, or what he would find there when he and Don Harman arrived on a cold Wednesday night, the second of December.

The following morning they left the Ramada Inn and went downtown to the D.A.'s Office to meet Steve Klein and his boss. Once they got there, Mike George received his first lesson in one of the ways New York was different from the laid-back atmosphere of Salt Lake City: "Everything had to be just right in New York," George recalled. "Everybody has got to meet everybody and know what everybody's doing. It's almost like a class system."

When Harman and he traveled to the Upper East Side to begin finding out as much as they could about Marc and his family, George was amazed to learn something else—that New York was a city of neighborhoods. "One block does not know the next block. You get away from East End Avenue and other people know nothing about East End Avenue. Every area has its own culture. They've got their bar, their deli, their market, their tailor all on that block, and everybody knows everybody. People in Salt Lake don't understand that about New York." They spoke with the people at Citipostal on East 85th Street and found that Marc listed two names on his application as references: Vicky Brown (the mother of Marc's friend Bob) and Paulette Thuiller ("Popo," Frances's housekeeper). They went to 1675 York Avenue and spoke with the superintendent, Andrew Fuleki, and other building employees about the nearly six years the family had lived there. Fuleki couldn't show them apartment 18B—the apartment they had lived in—but produced a floor plan for them to see. They began talking to merchants along York and East End avenues, and they made a point of going into Coleman's Deli; Susie Coleman's name had appeared on the back of a number of checks George had seen. He began talking with someone in the back room of the deli who answered to that name, but didn't discover until later that it was not Susie but her protective mother with whom he had been speaking. Every merchant they talked with, George recalled, knew who Frances was and said that she had owed them money at one time or another. When a tailor was asked about the Schreuders, he pulled out a wad of slips within seconds, pointing out that they were still unpaid from years before. They went to 10 Gracie Square, took pictures of the family's apartment from the outside, and spoke with the building's manager. He said Frances was a terrible tenant who tended to be hysterical and was highly distrustful of workmen; she had bought three bathtubs, he pointed out, which had been sitting in the hall for months. Whereas Lavinia was well taken care of, Marc was not; he was unkempt and constantly played the Atari games in the basement that a tenant had put in as a goodwill gesture. He was "a different type of kid," George recalled the manager's telling him, then spoke of the tensions between Marc and Frances, Marc and Berenice, and Berenice and Frances. But Gary Perman did not want them to leave with the wrong impression: this was a classy building, and he proceeded to drop the names of some people who lived there in order to support his claim.

For George, the picture that emerged matched the one that he had been painting in Salt Lake: the family had been plagued by financial troubles, Marc was basically a loner who had not been allowed to have many friends, and nobody seemed to know, or admit to knowing, a great deal about Larry—still very much a suspect.

On Friday, December 4, Don Harman spoke with Larry Goldman on the phone about the possibility of meeting with Behrens. Two days earlier Goldman had long discussions with Ernie Jones and Al Sullivan about full immunity for his client, and had met with Behrens that night in front of Elaine's, a famous New York restaurant in Behrens's neighborhood. Behrens, ever paranoid about Frances and not eager to have his attorney see where he lived, insisted on meeting outside, despite the bitter cold.

Goldman told Jones that Behrens would tell the truth if given immunity. "There's a lot more here than you guys know," he said. But Jones wanted some assurances from Behrens that if the grant was issued, Behrens "wouldn't turn around and say he was in this up to his eyeballs"—that he in fact had committed the murder. (Jones knew of an instance where someone did just that, and though the immunity was ruled invalid, he knew that a prosecutor had to be extremely careful whom he issued a grant to—especially since the defense generally keys on that as an issue with a jury. But Jones also felt confident that most juries "realize that a lot of times, in order to solve a case, you get your foot in the door from someone who is an accomplice. That person tells you who else is involved.")

Though Goldman now told Harman he felt Behrens had essentially been telling the truth when he was interviewed by Joel Campbell a year before, he did not know for sure if Behrens would come around. In any case, they weren't going to meet with Behrens, Goldman said, unless they had an immunity grant or, at the very least, a certificate protecting him from arrest as a material witness.

As soon as Harman got off the phone, he called Jones and told him to make sure that the certificate, which was being signed that day, was sent by express mail.

George and Harman next went to see Carolyn Karoliszyn-Morris (she had gotten married since George first spoke with her) at the American Airlines ticket office on West 49th Street

in the Rockefeller Center complex. The American office at
the Plaza had closed in 1980 because of lack of business, and
Candy, who had begun working for the airline in 1966 as a
reservation sales agent in Los Angeles, had since been
transferred to this new location. Since she hadn't recalled
anything about the ticket transaction when he spoke with her
on the phone, the first thing George wanted to do was
somehow conjure up the Plaza location in her mind—by
mentioning that it would have been the summer and probably
very hot—in the hope that she would recall Marc that way.

It didn't work.

So he brought out the airline ticket he had—the one that
had her die number on it and showed the Continental flight
from Midland to Phoenix, connecting to the Hughes Air West
flight to Salt Lake. She identified the handwriting on it as
hers.

He then showed her a photo spread. The attractive thirty-
six-year-old woman with dark curly hair looked at the eight
pictures carefully. There were two that looked familiar, she
said, one in particular.

She had picked out a picture of Marc. But George,
knowing that he probably would bring her to Salt Lake to see
if she could identify Marc in a lineup (if they ever got him out
of New York), did not tell her that; he asked why she had
issued three separate tickets instead. It was easier to rewrite
one if you do it that way, she said, but couldn't remember if
Marc had requested it as well. She did remember that he had
paid cash, that he seemed young to have that much money on
him, and that he was planning to do a lot of traveling in a very
compressed period of time.

They thanked her for her help, and she invited them to
come back later for an office party to celebrate the annual
lighting of the huge Christmas tree they could see towering
above the skating rink across the street. They said they'd try
and left.

It wasn't until afterward that she remembered something
about his eyes.

Lifted by Candy's identification of Marc, George was a
man obsessed with accomplishing all that he had set out to do
by the following Thursday—the day they were scheduled to

leave. Outside the airlines office he and Harman split up, and George walked halfway down the block to visit Gerald Bauman at MTB, amused by how close together, in a city like New York, some of his destinations were. Though the investigator didn't have a subpoena for MTB's records, he was allowed to look at Marc's account and copy things down. By the time he walked back outside, he was caught up in a crush of people making their way to the tree lighting. Darkness and a freezing rain had descended as George found his way back downtown to the D.A.'s Office, before taking the wrong subway to the Ramada. He had been in town less than forty-eight hours and "had never seen that many people in all my life."

Ed Regan picked George up at the hotel and took him to the 20th Precinct. After he interviewed Regan and Ron Hoffman, he was given a Cook's tour of some of the "crime scenes" they had worked, including the Dakota on Central Park West, where Hoffman told him how the doorman had simply pointed to Mark David Chapman, who was standing out front reading *The Catcher in the Rye,* as the man who had killed John Lennon. They told him about the violinist who was murdered at the Metropolitan Opera House and how the case was known among the detectives as "Fiddler off the Roof." When they got back to the precinct, Regan offered George a drink.

"No," George said, "I know you guys are on duty."

That's okay, they said, and proceeded to take George in the back room—the same place where Regan and Behrens had sat huddled in the cold ten months before. What George found there, he later said, "was nothing like 'Barney Miller' or anything else I'd seen. There was the most hellacious party going on. Two detectives had just gotten their gold shields and I'd never seen a wilder party in all my life. I was flabbergasted."

But he joined in nonetheless—after all, it was the Christmas season—and later, after a careening drive through the snow to the Lone Star Cafe in Greenwich Village ("my fingerprints were imprinted on the armrest"), crawled into bed to sleep it off.

* * *

If there is one thing that Mike George likes as much as, if not more than, police work, it is sports. In the back of his mind, along with all the puzzle pieces of evidence he was trying to fit together on this trip, was a lifelong desire to see Yankee Stadium.

On Saturday he and Harman, knowing that Marc was a camera buff, went to practically every camera store on the Upper East Side to see if anyone could remember him from a photograph. No one could. George told one store owner that he wanted to go to the stadium, and asked directions.

"'You're fucking crazy,'" George recalled the merchant telling him. "'You're white, you don't go there.' But I persisted and he told me how to go. Boy, was he right. By the time we got there we were the last whites on the train. There was one guy who started coming down on us and I was never so close to thinking I was going to have to kill somebody in all my life. Don thought it was funny and I was scared. I was looking at my briefcase, which had my gun. You see, I still believed in horror stories in New York. As soon as we got off the train, we found the closest cop and identified ourselves. He got us in, even though it was closed."

The following day, after having seen Marilyn and Bob Regan on Saturday evening, the two investigators split up once more and Harman traveled to Hartford. George received the certificate that would protect Behrens from arrest and, first thing Monday morning, began to negotiate with his lawyer to interview him. He also arranged a trip for Wednesday to Rikers Island (where Marc had been in jail and where he hoped to find someone Marc might have confessed to), obtained copies of Marc's and Larry's birth certificates, and located Vittorio Gentile's business address.

When Harman returned to New York that night he told George that Trinity College's attorneys had given him a hard time about getting records, but that he had managed to speak with Marc's former roommate, who described the night Marc expressed a need to talk with somebody.

On Tuesday morning they went to the office of Borrelli Pearls at 608 Fifth Avenue. Vittorio hadn't arrived yet, so they waited for him. When he did, they said they were in New York investigating the death of Franklin Bradshaw.

"What do you mean?" he said. "What's wrong?"

"We're here to investigate his killing."

Frances had told him that her father had died—the night after it happened, he said—but not how. He thought it had been a heart attack. In any case, he wanted to know, what did all this have to do with him?

"Well, we're here to talk to you about your son," George began.

"Lorenzo?"

"No, Marc," George said. "He's been charged with the murder of his grandfather." Vittorio just "lost it," George recalled later. "I thought he was going to have a heart attack. It took us about a half hour to get him calmed down. We said, 'Well, Mr. Gentile, we need your help. I know that's hard because that's your son. All we want is the truth.'" They asked about friends and he mentioned Susie (Coleman) and Bob (Brown), but not their last names. "I tried to establish a bond with him," George said, by mentioning that his mother was Italian. "Told him I'd never lie to him: 'If you want to know an answer, you ask me and I'll tell you the truth.'"

"Well, there is one thing I need to know," Vittorio said.

"What's that?"

"I've been trying for two years to find Lorenzo. All his mother says is that he's away in college but not which one. I'd just like to call Lorenzo and talk to him."

"Don't you know what happened to him?"

No, he said. He'd heard Lorenzo had been in trouble but nothing more.

"He's in prison," George told him, watching the color go out of his face.

What for?

"Bludgeoned his roommate."

Did he kill him?

"No, but my understanding is that the boy is physically damaged. Your son is in prison in Pennsylvania."

Gentile, practically catatonic, said he was going to call his wife and asked if George would speak with her. George got on the phone and explained the situation—Marc was out on bail, living somewhere in New York; Larry was at the Northampton County Prison in Easton. He gave her all his

391

numbers. If they wanted to know anything else, he said, they should just pick up the phone and call him.

At one o'clock they went to Larry Goldman's office. (Goldman had not promised they could see Behrens, but had arranged with his client to arrive later, after he had a chance to speak with them.) George and Harman began to do their p.r. number on Goldman, and it was just as well they did, because the lawyer made it clear that he was not about to let them destroy the trust and confidence he had worked so hard to build.

Once he established that they weren't "badasses," George said later, Goldman informed them that Behrens was outside; he was going to let the investigators meet him, but not ask him any questions. So into the room the five-foot-eight-inch, 195-pound schoolteacher nervously made his way, dressed in black pants, a black sweater and an open-necked shirt and wearing a tattersall hat.

At last George was able to clap eyes on the figure he had heard so much about. Using a soft, straightforward approach, the investigator began to tell Behrens what he had told the people in Texas—that he was a witness for the state of Utah and that they needed him. He would be given full immunity, George said, but he had to tell the truth. Like a football coach giving a sales pitch to a potential recruit, George gently assured him he would be "a member of the team," working for them and with them.

After about an hour, Goldman took the investigators outside and said that they could go into some areas with him. George suggested that he ask Goldman the questions and if Behrens wanted to answer he could; if he didn't, fine. At first, the questioning proceeded in this formal manner; when the subject of Behrens's statement to Campbell came up, Goldman told the investigators there was one glaring thing wrong with what his client had said:

He didn't get the gun from Marc that night. He got it from Frances.

Behrens began talking and explained that his memory was refreshed by Frances herself the night he went for coffee with her to the Midnight Express. He had, at one point, really believed Marc had brought him the gun, he said; at the same time, he realized he had gotten in far deeper than he wanted to be, and knew that he didn't want to cross Frances, because she could be "ruthless."

He told them about the pressure that was put on him to recant his story and about his meetings with Marc in Carl Schurz Park—how Marc had essentially reconfessed the crime, describing, among other things, the noise of the gun, the blood on the floor, and the flight back to New York.

Everything was starting to come together, George thought. Frances was as deeply involved as he'd suspected and would be even more so if Behrens could tell them about this so-called hit man Frances had hired. By this point, George felt he had developed enough of a rapport with Behrens to ask him about it.

Frances was looking for someone to kill her father, he said, preferably a Mafia type. He had told her that it would be a mistake to get mixed up with that kind of person, and promised to try to introduce her to someone who might be interested. He had a neighbor, he told her not long after that, a local "yegg" named Manning whom he had spoken with and who was interested in meeting her. He put them together and walked away from it, he said, and the guy wound up taking several thousand dollars from her without pulling off the job.

Where could they find this Manning? George asked, eager for anything Behrens could offer.

He was a printer at the *News*, Behrens said, or at least was the last time he saw him.

George had a name, but "all that mattered," he said later, "was that Behrens was back on our team. He was in the fold. To me, that bought the trip."

George left Larry Goldman's fifty-fifth-floor office on Fifth Avenue with more than just Richard Behrens back on their team; he left with a tremendous amount of respect for Goldman himself—a lawyer who was unwilling, George said, "to perpetuate the lie."

43// By the time George and Harman arrived at Rikers Island on Wednesday, they knew two things: there was a good possibility they might be able to take Marc back to Salt Lake on Friday; and "Manning" turned out to be a Myles Manning, who worked the evening shift at New York's *Daily News*.

Though they were scheduled to fly back on Thursday and were almost out of money, those two little nuggets were worth more to them than any amount of cash could be, and they decided to stay as long as necessary.

The inmates housed in the homosexual wing at Rikers told the investigators Marc was "strange, but not gay." They claimed he was in that wing because he was young and needed protection, and that the officials knew that if he wasn't gay, he wouldn't be bothered. Unfortunately for the investigators, Marc told everyone he was in on a narcotics charge, and confided in no one. (As it turned out, it was protection he needed. Within a day or two of his arriving at Rikers, Marc's face was bruised. When one of his lawyers asked him about it, he said that he "didn't respond to a guard quickly enough.")

At eight that evening, after a battle to pierce the building's tight security, the investigators were allowed into the *Daily News* on East 42nd Street. They first spoke to Manning's foreman, who said Manning was on his dinner break and would be back at eight-thirty. They assured him that Manning was not in trouble—they just wanted to speak with him.

When the five-foot-six-inch, barrel-chested figure of Myles Manning appeared about a half hour later in the foreman's office, the investigators introduced themselves but did not say at first that they were from Utah.

"People say you are involved in a crime," George began. "I don't believe you are, other than in a peripheral way, which may have happened before the crime."

Manning said that he was clean and not involved in anything. All George knew was that he was talking with a guy named Myles Manning. He didn't know if he was the right guy, or even if what Behrens had told them the day before was the truth. If this *was* the right guy, a picture—as it had with the woman from American Airlines—would begin to tell the story.

"Tell me," George said, flashing a photograph of Frances in front of him, "that you've never been involved with this woman."

Manning's face and body movement instantly gave George his answer. He went pale, and started to shake and perspire.

He said that he did know her, and when George pressed him for specifics, the forty-one-year-old printer admitted she had hired him to kill her father.

"That's what I wanted to know," George said quickly. "Now we're going on tape." Al Sullivan had had a grand jury subpoena drawn up that morning—just in case Manning, if he was the right guy, refused to speak with them. George told him, as he had Behrens, that he would be given a grant of immunity in both Salt Lake and New York if he cooperated and told them the truth. Reluctantly, Manning agreed.

He said that he couldn't recall the name of the woman in the photograph nor the name of the man who first introduced them.

"You stated," George said, "that at the time he introduced you to her, you were drinking quite heavily?"

"Oh, yeah."

"And you stated that the man had an occupation?"

"Let me qualify that. It was during a period that I was drinking quite heavily. At that specific time I was not drinking."

How old would the man have been?

"Approximately my age. He had to be in his forties." (Behrens would have been fifty-one.)

"Forties? Okay, and his occupation?"

"Schoolteacher."

". . . Where was your first meeting with her?"

"In her apartment on York Avenue."

"Her apartment on York Avenue? You do not recall the exact address?"

"No, I could point it out. It is 80, 80 what, 88th Street, 89th Street, something like that."

"Okay, when this male introduced you to her, as you were going to her apartment, did he state the reason for introducing you to her?"

"Yeah."

"And what was the reason?"

"He said that she wanted her father done away with. I just went along with him."

". . . So there was just the three of you at that time?"

"He wasn't there."

"The man wasn't there? So there was just yourself and a person that you identified as Frances Schreuder."

"Right."

"Okay. Do you recall approximately the date of this meeting?"

"I'm trying to think of that. Shortly after I started working here, so it had to be '77, '78."

". . . Do you remember what part of the year—winter, fall, summer?"

"Early in the year. No jackets, so it had to be early in the year."

". . . So we are talking around spring?"

"Around spring."

"Do you recall it being spring and not fall?"

"No, it was spring. It was quite a while ago and it was a rather hazy period."

"I understand that, we just . . . need to zero the date in as best as possible. Do you recall if there was a holiday around there that we can tie this to?"

". . . It was just shortly after a restaurant called the Palace opened. Because I had been wanting to go to that."

"How long had the Palace been open?"

"The Palace had been open about four or five months."

"What is the address of the Palace?"

"I don't know. I could never afford to go there."

". . . Is it up in that area of the town?"

"No, it is on 57th Street or 59th Street, somewhere around there. About the most expensive restaurant in New York."

". . . All right. So you went up there, apparently this gentleman who introduced you to her left? Or just took you to the place?"

"He just gave me the address and I went."

". . . And the only thing that he told you at that time was that he knew a lady that wanted to have her husband—"

"Not her husband, her father."

"Excuse me, her father killed off and was maybe willing to pay money for it?"

"Oh, yeah, quite a bit."

"Quite a bit of money. So you went up there and you introduced yourself to her?"

"Ah, yeah, she already knew of me, though."

"She knew of you through the other gentleman, I take it?"

"Right."

"Okay, nobody else was present?"

"I think her daughter might have been, a little kid about that big."

"Tiny girl?"

"Yeah, a little blond-haired girl."

"Do you recall what her name is?"

"No."

"Was she of an age that she could have understood what was going on?"

"Yeah, but she wasn't there long enough."

". . . And where was this [conversation] taking place in the apartment?"

"In her living room."

". . . Why don't you tell me what she said and what you said?"

"Well, I don't know verbatim."

"I'm not saying verbatim. The gist of the conversation."

"Well, first she asked me where I worked and I told her. . . . And she said, 'Well, people that work for newspapers know people.' And I said, 'Yeah.' . . . She said that [that other guy] said that I could either do or have arranged to have . . . her father done away with. So I figured there was no harm in agreeing with it, so I said sure. She said, 'Well, people who work for the newspapers know a lot of people, so therefore I take you for your word,' and I said, 'Fine.' Then she offered me money and I said great."

"How much money did she offer you?"

"Five grand."

"Five thousand dollars?"

"Uh huh. And I said great. So about, I don't know, two or

three days later or something like that, she came up with this, I was laughing when she did it, I couldn't because it was worth five thousand dollars, but I almost did. She came up with a typed-up letter with directions on how to get to her father's place and his name, I don't remember what it is right now. . . . All I recall is that it was an elderly guy."

"Okay, a typed letter?"

"Yeah."

"Directions. Where did she say her father lived?"

"Ah, Utah."

"Do you recall the city?"

"No."

"The place, his name?"

"Yeah, what kind of truck he drove, a little pickup thing, and he owned a store."

"Do you recall what type of store?"

"No, I wasn't really paying that much attention."

"Mr. Manning, do you still have that letter?"

"No, I don't."

"Did you destroy it, or did she leave it with you?"

"She left it with me and she gave me a picture of him."

"Do you still have the picture?"

"I don't have any of it. I got rid of it, I wasn't going to use it anyhow."

"What was the picture of, just him or was it a family picture?"

"No, it was the picture of his store with the truck outside and him."

". . . Did she tell you how she wanted him done in?"

". . . No, she said she would leave that up to me, any way I chose to do it."

"Did she give you a time period?"

"Yeah, that she did, that she did."

"How long of a time period?"

"About one month."

". . . All right. Mr. Manning, did she ever pay you any money?"

"Yeah, she gave me five thousand dollars."

". . . Cash?"

"Yeah, there again I laughed about it, because she insisted on giving me everything in fives and tens."

"Did she say she had to go to the bank and take that money out?"

"Yes, she did."

"Do you recall what her bank was?"

"No."

". . . Okay, what was the money in when she gave it to you?"

"An envelope, a large envelope."

"And where did this meeting take place?"

"Right outside where I live."

"Outside on the street?"

"On the street."

". . . Mr. Manning, did she ever give you a reason as to why she wanted her father killed?"

"No, but I got the impression that she didn't like him too much."

"Any motive, any ulterior motive?"

"No, she never said."

"Did you ever ask her?"

"No, it wasn't really important because I knew I wasn't going to do it."

"Okay, so she gave you the money. What was your next contact with her?"

"About two weeks later. It had to be about two weeks later."

"And where did that contact take place?"

"The guy that I told you, I don't know his name."

"But you would recognize it?"

"Yes, I would know. . . . I met her right in front of his apartment and then I went into his apartment with her. That is when I told her that I got arrested in Salt Lake and forget about it, I ain't going there."

"Okay, just a minute now. You met in front of a friend's apartment and went inside?"

"Right."

"And the reason for the meeting was what?"

"She wanted to find out why it wasn't done."

"She wanted a progress report?"

"Right."

"Okay, and what did you tell her?"

". . . I said to her that I went to Salt Lake with a friend of mine. We spent the night in jail. Somebody turned us in, so therefore I ain't doing it. And she got very mad."

"What did she say to you?"

"Not too much, but she cried a lot."

"Did she try to impress you to have her father killed again?"

"Oh yeah. Yeah."

"At this time," George pressed again, needing evidence of motive, "did she mention why again? . . ."

"No, at no time did she ever mention why, just that she wanted it done. To tell you the truth, I had forgotten about it until you guys came today."

"Okay. What did she say about the money?"

"Well, she wanted it back and she said something similar to she is going to have to go on relief now because she couldn't afford it. . . . She was going to have to take her kid out of private school and go to public school and she gave me a whole song and dance."

"She said she had to go on relief because she couldn't afford anything?"

"Right."

"Said she had to take her kids out of private school?"

"Yeah, one kid, I didn't know about the other."

George asked again about the typed-up letter Manning said Frances had given him. It was unsigned, he said, and contained directions on how to get to where her father worked. In addition, she told him that she wanted her father's death to look like an accident, preferably involving his pickup truck on his way home. If he found any money on him, Manning claimed Frances told him, he could take it. "It probably couldn't have been too much anyhow," Manning said. "I mean if she is giving it away that free."

"Mr. Manning," George asked, "when you got the five thousand dollars, did you deposit any of it in the bank?"

"No, I just blew it."

"Any record of that money anywhere?"

"No."

"Where did you blow it at?"

"It took me a whole week. Ah, I spent quite a bit of time in a bar," he said, and, "just to make it look nice," he also spent a couple of days at the YMCA on 47th Street.

"That was just to make it look like you were what, out of town?" George asked.

"Right."

"And this would have been directly after she gave you the money?"

"Yeah."

"Then when you registered into the YMCA, did you register under your name?"

"Oh sure, I wasn't trying to hide anything."

". . . Okay, getting back to the time, what did you tell her about the five thousand dollars? Did you tell her she wasn't going to get it back or what?"

"Oh, no, she did not get it back. I told her I used it to get out there with. I used it for a lawyer out there to get me out of jail, and I used it to get back."

". . . Did she ever say that she was going to force you to pay it back?"

"Yeah, she said something about, I'm trying to think of the guy's name, a real prominent lawyer. He was in trouble in Washington, I can't remember his name."

"She dropped his name?"

"Oh, yeah, she dropped it very hard."

"The lawyer would be getting back to you?"

"No, no. A lawyer knew people who would be getting back to me."

"Did she threaten you with any type of physical—" Don Harman began.

"Sure, but I passed it off."

"—like she would hire a hit man?"

"Yeah, but I passed it off. . . . I thought it was a joke and a half. So I just responded there and told ˑr, 'You mess around, you mess around with a bent-nose crowd, forget about it.'"

Manning said that in addition to spending part of the $5,000 on booze, he also used it to pay some bills. But, he cautioned them, "the people I paid off, I couldn't go telling you." Asked how they could corroborate any of what Manning told them, the printer suggested they check the YMCA's records—and check with "the guy who introduced me . . . if I knew his name."

". . . Did he live in the area?"

"About four or five houses east of where I did. On the same side."

"Does he still live there?"

"I've seen him in the neighborhood, I really don't know."

"Have you ever seen Mrs. Schreuder in the neighborhood?"

"No, not since there."

". . . Did she ever tell you her name?"

"She told me the name, but I—"

"Does the name Frances Schreuder . . . ring a bell?"

"The name Frances rings a bell. The last name, I don't know."

"But you positively identified the picture?"

"Oh, I know definitely. Names I can't remember, faces I do."

The investigators brought out a photograph of Franklin. Manning said he didn't know his name, but when George mentioned it, the printer remembered that a name was listed on the letter Frances had given him, and that a picture of the man, standing on the sidewalk in front of a hardware store (Manning thought), was included with the material.

"Did it look like a picture that might have been taken by an *amateur* photographer?" Harman asked, thinking it was probably taken by Marc or Larry.

"Oh, definitely."

". . . How was he dressed in the picture?"

"Shirt and slacks."

"Not an executive?"

"Oh, no. I do remember asking her, come to think of it if she did mention something, she said that she was going to get an inheritance and when she showed me the picture of this guy, I said, 'How can this guy leave you money? He don't look like he has any.' You know, he wasn't in a suit and tie, and he wasn't, he didn't look like the executive type. She said, 'Oh, don't worry about that, I'm going to get an inheritance.' I said, 'All right, fine.'"

". . . When you were inside her apartment and you had gone upstairs and you were into the apartment, describe some of the furniture that was there."

"Let's see, I went into the apartment, go in a little ways

and on the left-hand side was a couch. The window was directly in front of you. . . . Just off the kitchen there was a table there."

"Describe the furniture. Was it expensive furniture?"

"It was good furniture. When I say good, I couldn't afford it."

"Were there any vases or antiques around that caught your eye?" (They had heard from Behrens that Frances had some expensive items.)

"Not that caught my eye, no."

". . . Mr. Manning," George asked, "from the first time that you met her to the last occasion, how long of a time period was it?"

"The first time I met her to the last occasion, not more than a month."

". . . Did she say that she was becoming destitute? That she was running out of money?"

"She did when I told her that I came back from Salt Lake," he said, pointing out that he didn't feel sorry for her "because anybody that wants to do that kind of thing should be taken."

Asked if he could show them the apartment building she had lived in, he said he could do even better: he could take them to the eighteenth floor.

Holy shit, George thought, *he remembered the floor.* "Do you remember what apartment number?" George pressed.

"No."

"Was it to the left or to the right when you got off the elevator?" Harman interjected.

"To the right."

"Was there a doorman?"

"Yes."

"What did he look like?"

"I think he was a Spanish guy."

"Did you talk to him?"

"I knew him."

"You *knew* him?"

"I knew him from the bar."

"Would he know that you were going up there?"

"Yeah, he would, because he had to ring her."

"What is his name?" George asked.

"I don't know."

"Could you point him out to us, if he is still there?" Harman asked.

"I—"

"You said you knew him from the bar?"

"Yeah, but you have to understand something," Manning said and went on to explain that he was not looking to involve anybody else in this. But they pressed him for more information, and he reluctantly gave it to them.

Before ending the interview, the investigators asked once more about the note of instructions Manning said he had received. But *this* time he said it was written, not typed, explaining she "scribbled it left-hand because she said she didn't want anything around that would tie her into it."

"Did you observe her write that note?" George asked.

"No."

"She just told you that about the note itself."

"She told me."

How would he describe her?

"Weird. . . . I know she hunched over whenever she was talking to me because she was taller than I am. I notice that about taller people; if they hunch over I don't trust them because they are trying to, they are phony. Anyhow, the guy that introduced me to her implied—he didn't come out and say so but he implied—that she was wealthy, that is why it didn't bother me about the money."

After a few more questions, the interview was over. Before leaving and letting Manning get back to work, George asked if there was anything else that stuck out in his mind about the whole incident, and the rotund printer said there was nothing he could think of.

Over the next few weeks and months, though, he would recall other things, and the things he recalled that night would come into sharper focus for him. Throughout the dramatic interview, George and Harman were completely "flabbergasted" by the fact that there really *was* a hit man, that they had found him, and that he was sitting there talking with them about what had happened. Manning had done more than identify Frances's photograph. He remembered where her apartment building was and the very floor she lived on; that

Lavinia had blond hair; that the man in the photograph Frances had given him was elderly, had a pickup truck, and clearly didn't look like an executive; that the man who introduced him to Frances was a schoolteacher who lived four or five doors to the east of him (Behrens was at 326 East 89th, Manning at 318 East 89th, four doors away); and, most important, that Frances had mentioned getting an inheritance if her father was killed. "It was unreal to us," George explained later, "that this was actually happening."

Like Manning, George had also been shaking—but for a different reason. He had been shaking with so much excitement that he kept his hands under the table and couldn't stop his voice from cracking.

When he went to bed that night, sleep would not come. He lay awake, reviewing the events of the last two days in his mind, and came to a conclusion: *he had enough evidence to charge Frances Schreuder with first-degree murder.*

44// Just as soon as Ernie Jones walked into his office the next morning, the phone rang. It was Mike George, eager to tell him about the interview with Manning the night before. From the time George had been assigned the case eight months earlier, Jones and he had developed a strong bond of respect for each other. Jones admired George's determination and perseverance—his go-anywhere-do-anything attitude that was so much a part of his own makeup. The investigator had been in New York only a week and Jones was impressed by how much he had accomplished. While Joel Campbell was still officially involved in the case, George had taken over right from the start. But even as George was describing his latest coup and Jones sat there, both stunned and delighted, he knew continued caution was the right approach.

He said that it would be a mistake to charge Frances with anything at that point—not until Behrens actually flew out to Salt Lake and testified under oath that Frances had given him the gun. They had to be sure that Behrens would really show up. As far as what Manning had to say, Jones was still uncertain how it all fit together, because Behrens hadn't told them enough about his own role in that triangular relationship. The link wasn't strong enough, he felt; they'd waited this long for things to fall together, and they could afford to wait a bit longer.

Once again, Jones had managed to prick the investigator's balloon of triumph. But George knew that the prosecutor had been right before—about having to prove it was Marc who actually used those plane tickets—and was willing to give him the benefit of the doubt.

The Vanderbilt branch of the YMCA is on East 47th Street in Manhattan, not far from the United Nations. Myles Manning said that he stayed there for a few days after receiving the $5,000 from Frances. Though he wanted to make it seem as if he had left town, he said, he used his own name when he registered. So the two Utah investigators and Ernie Cruz, another investigator from the Manhattan D.A.'s Office, went there that Thursday, hoping to find the receipt that would confirm both Manning's story and the exact time of his stay. Since Manning thought that it was the spring—a time when people weren't wearing jackets, he remembered—they began to look through all the receipts from April 1978 until the day of the murder in July. Separated into stacks of hundreds, the receipts were tucked away in a heatless storage room, the only warmth coming from a tiny lightbulb overhead; the kind of conditions under which Franklin Bradshaw would have felt right at home.

There was nothing under "Myles Manning" for that period. So they decided to backtrack—from December 1977 until April 1978. It was not just freezing in the room; it was monotonous work. But whether it was airline records or YMCA receipts, they were *records*—and records had been crucial to the case so far. But they struck out again. Maybe Manning was wrong about the time, George thought. People sometimes don't wear jackets until well into the autumn. So they started going through the receipts from June 1977 through November. Nothing in June. Or July. Or August or September. It was near the end of the day, and they were exhausted. They'd been there since the morning and had looked at nearly *seventeen thousand* receipts. Ernie Cruz wearily began to go through October, as George scrutinized November. If it wasn't in either of these months, they were going to call it a day. George finished his stacks, and Cruz was about to tackle the last one for October—the one that happened to contain it.

Cruz held it up to the light. Myles Manning. He had stayed in Room 435 for three nights. He had checked in on October 29, 1977, at twelve thirty-four p.m., having paid the princely sum of $11 a night.

Mike George emerged from the room, gripping the newest piece of his puzzle—a puzzle that was finally starting to take shape. It was "another high"—an early thirtieth-birthday present.

But on Friday he would not be able to depend on his own devices for another shot of adrenaline. That would have to come from the New York justice system.

The cast of characters assembled in Justice Harold Rothwax's courtroom: Marc, with his lawyers Mike Armstrong and David Frankel; Al Sullivan and Steve Klein; Mike George and Don Harman, ready and waiting with plane reservations to Salt Lake City from three different airports.

As Armstrong argued as passionately as he could, Mike George divided his attention between listening to the lawyer's speech, watching Marc, and feeling disappointed that Frances had not appeared. Never having seen her in person, he had wondered if she looked vastly different from the photographs Joel Campbell had gotten from Marilyn of her on the Staten Island Ferry—smoking a cigarette, getting a drink, sitting on a hard wooden bench while Lavinia played in the background. And, more important, he wondered if she had somehow found out what Richard Behrens had told him late Tuesday afternoon in Larry Goldman's office, learned that Myles Manning had been discovered the following night, and had decided not to come to court more out of fear than a lack of concern for Marc.

"Are the Utah authorities not here?" The judge's voice interrupted his thoughts.

"The Utah authorities are here," Al Sullivan answered the judge. Marc was going to Utah. No evidence had been put forward that Marc was *not* in Salt Lake City on the morning of July 23, 1978. If the defense attorneys had a case, it would have to be argued at a proper trial—a trial out there. Armstrong's request for a stay so that he could appeal was denied. Had George and Harman not been present, a stay would probably have been issued.

Armstrong and Frankel asked if they could sit and speak with Marc alone for a while. George, reluctantly, said yes. But as soon as he did he regretted it. George knew that Armstrong was a powerful lawyer, a man with friends in high places. What if one of those friends, he thought, happened to be over at the Appellate Division that very moment, somehow cutting a deal? He had had enough of New York justice and wanted to get his prisoner.

After nearly forty-five minutes, he knocked at the door. "We've got to go," George said. "We're going." He put handcuffs on Marc and began to hurry him out of the courtroom and down the steps to a waiting car. Asked his destination by the lawyers, George said "JFK." But once they got Marc inside the car, he said, "Get us across state lines. Once we're in another state, they can't touch us. Go to Newark."

It was already past four on a Friday afternoon—gridlock in the urban jungle. Steve Klein had recently gotten his driver's license—another lesson in the New York education of Mike George; many people who live in New York don't know how to drive—and refused to join the honking fray. So Harman took the wheel, with Klein directing him to the Holland Tunnel and the safe haven George felt New Jersey represented on the other side. What the investigators didn't know was that Marc and his lawyers had decided beforehand that if their *habeas corpus* motion was dismissed and their request for a stay denied, they wouldn't fight it any further.

As George sat with Marc in the back seat, he began to think how different he was from the impression he had formed of him. Earlier in the week he had trailed Marc one day as he left the D.A.'s Office, where he was required to report twice a week to Steve Klein. As he kept his distance, hoping Marc would lead him to something or someone that would help bolster the case, he was amazed by Marc's appearance. "I mean," he said later, "this kid's supposed to have money, and he looks like a frumpy, dumpy bum." Yet as George read him his rights and said that he would not ask him anything about the case (a promise he had made to the lawyers), he was impressed by how polite and articulate Marc was. George, who guessed that Marc was in a state of shock because "we just swooped him right off the streets, more or less," was hoping that Marc "might pop out with something," but he said little. As soon as his handcuffs were removed, though, he began to relax a bit.

Once they arrived at the airport, Marc asked if he could buy a book, and George said that would be fine. The three of them "sat there and bullshitted like three tourists waiting to board a plane." George was not informing anyone, he told Marc, that he was a prisoner, because the investigator had no desire to be stuck in the last seat of the airplane in the smoking section. Like a strict father, George said that if Marc "acted like a gentleman at all times" there wouldn't be any problems.

They had a smooth flight. As Don Harman began reading the book Marc had bought, Michael Crichton's *Congo* (when Harman got back to Salt Lake, he had become so engrossed in it that he purchased a copy), George began to talk with Marc about what was in the news, gold coins (which George knew nothing about) and photography—all this in order to establish a rapport with him. At one point George looked over and Marc was buying a mini bottle of vodka for a screwdriver. He told him that he couldn't have it, and the flight attendant, eager to make a sale, asked why not.

"Because I said he can't." Marc put it back on the tray, and the woman gave George a puzzled, who-is-this-guy kind of look.

"Why can't I have it?" Marc asked, turning to George.

"Because you're only twenty," said George, thinking of the minimum Utah drinking age. "You don't turn twenty-one for another week and a half. Besides, I won't let you drink anyway. You're a prisoner."

That was one thing George never lost sight of—that he was taking someone accused of committing a brutal murder back to the state that had wanted him badly for just over a year.

At eleven o'clock that evening, two weeks before Christmas, Marc Francis Schreuder was brought to the Salt Lake

County Sheriff's Office. After turning over $125.45, two identification cards (his own and the one for Alexander Bentley), two keys, a Visa card, two subway tokens, two books, three blank checks and a pack of Life Savers, he was booked into jail.

But like Houdini, he wouldn't be there for long.

45// At a time when the world seemed ready to fall apart, when facts of our life in alarming numbers were being reduced to a state of primitivism, Balanchine's creation of a classic ballet in all its well-ordered values was a reason for hope and joy.

Anatole Chujoy was writing about George Balanchine's choreography of *The Nutcracker* for the New York City Ballet (and the special meaning the famous production, composed by Tchaikovsky and based on E. T. A. Hoffmann's 1816 *The Nutcracker and the King of Mice,* has for so many people), but that December his words would have had a particularly poignant meaning for Frances Schreuder. Though both of her sons were in prison, her reason for hope and joy during the Christmas season was embodied in Lavinia, who had been chosen to dance in *The Nutcracker* for the first time.

Frances had tried to use her influence as a board member to make sure Lavinia was selected, but her daughter was chosen on her own merit. One Saturday afternoon, though, shortly before a matinee performance was about to begin, Frances made her presence felt. The performance was to begin at two, but there was no sign of Lavinia, who was one of the children in the party scene in Act I and one of the angels in Act II.

At one fifty-five David Richardson, a dancer with the company and the ballet master in charge of all the children in the production, had to make a decision. He told one little girl to get into a costume for the first act and phoned another, who lived in Brooklyn, to be there for the second.

Suddenly, Frances, with Lavinia in tow, rushed in, hysterical, out of breath, and crying that she had had to take her mother to the hospital and that's why they were late. Calmly,

Richardson told her that Lavinia would not be able to dance that afternoon. (*The Nutcracker* is performed throughout December, and each child generally appears in every other performance.)

Frances said that she *had* to perform, so Richardson, not wanting to upset the other children more than they were already, told Lavinia to get into her costume, but not to do any dancing.

Far from being appeased, Richardson recalled, "Frances was on a rampage, screaming that she was going to speak with my supervisors. When she later saw the girl that was going to take Lavinia's place in Act II she said, " 'I'm going to kill that little girl in Lavinia's costume.' "

Visibly shaken, the girl went over to Richardson and said, "That woman is crazy."

"Please don't worry about it," he comforted her. "It's only a figure of speech. I'll speak to her."

In remembering that day, twenty months later, he said, "In my heart of hearts, I wasn't nervous or scared. I'd never worried about the board or Lincoln [Kirstein, the cofounder of the company with George Balanchine] before. But for the first time, I worried that maybe she could cause trouble with Lincoln."

That evening, Richardson suggested to Frances, who was smoking and drinking heavily, that they go to the lobby and talk. Trying to be conciliatory, he gently proposed that she make a recommendation to the board that the dressing facilities be improved for the children performing in *The Nutcracker*. He tried to draw her out and see if she agreed with him. She promised to speak with the company's manager about it but offered little else.

Switching gears, he said, as diplomatically as possible, that he wished she wouldn't make any more scenes and try to push her weight around—that it only would be detrimental to Lavinia. "Lavinia can get the parts on her own," he assured her. "If she has any chances in the future, it's important that people not think it was because of your position."

Sadly, her "position" meant more to her than he could ever have imagined at that moment.

* * *

411

Three days after Marc left New York, Frances's name came out in court for the first time. Before Justice Eve Preminger in State Supreme Court—the judge who had ordered Behrens to be extradited in November—Larry Goldman and Al Sullivan were cutting a deal that would officially give Behrens his full immunity.

Having agreed that Behrens would not be prosecuted on the charge of possessing a weapon (which he kept, Sullivan *now* claimed, "pursuant to an agreement with Marc Schreuder *and* his mother, Frances") or for perjury (in regard to his recantation), the prosecutor mentioned "additional behavior" on Behrens's part he had learned about in the last few days. ". . . Mr. Behrens had certain dealings with others, among whom were Marc Schreuder and his mother, and possibly others, relating to arrangements which could be made, plans which could be effectuated in order to kill Franklin Bradshaw. It is my understanding that Mr. Behrens, other than giving certain advice and certain facilitation . . . for instance, putting Mrs. Schreuder in touch with a potential killer, who turned out not to be what he appeared to be, that Mr. Behrens really took no active role and at most added certain moral support. . . ."

Behrens would be held harmless for this too, Sullivan stressed, provided he continued to cooperate.

Back in Salt Lake, Mike George was getting reacquainted with his family after his exhausting but exhilarating trip. Just before Christmas, Vittorio Gentile phoned him to ask where Marc was; Frances had refused to tell him. Right here in Salt Lake, George said, in jail. He told George he'd been to see Larry and had sent away to both Utah and Pennsylvania for newspaper clips about his sons.

There was also something else—something that he had remembered after they left his office a few weeks before. At the time it happened—in the spring of 1978—he hadn't taken it seriously, but he felt that George should know about it now.

With Gentile's phone call, word from New York that Manning was cooperating with Al Sullivan and Steve Klein, and the prospect of a visit to Salt Lake by Behrens looming early in the new year, Mike George's spirits couldn't have been higher.

But cops are cynical, suspicious people. They often feel that their cases, no matter how strong, can fall apart as easily as a house of cards. If the defense doesn't do something to screw things up, the prosecutor or a judge probably will. When George was in narcotics, he had a hard time finding prosecutors who were willing to "make" his cases in court. He could rely on his informants with more confidence than he could on them. This time it was a judge who spoiled his New Year's celebration—and Ernie Jones's for a second straight year.

On December 28, Judge Peter Leary of the Third District Court decided to set bail for Marc at $100,000—an ironic and (to the state) insulting $50,000 less than the amount his grandmother had posted in New York. For the third time in little more than a year Marc would be free.

46// By his own admission, Ernie Jones is a terrible loser. His colleagues knew it, his tennis partners know it, and his wife knows it. "Ninety-nine percent of the time he is wonderful to be around," Mary Lyne Jones says. "But during that other one percent, you might as well just hit the trail."

And hitting the trail was exactly what Jones feared Marc would do when he was released from jail on Tuesday, January 12. While the prosecutor was publicly complaining to a reporter for the *Salt Lake Tribune* about how long it had taken the state to get Marc extradited in the first place and the irony of Berenice's once more posting the bail money for him, Mike George was following Marc to the Stratford Hotel, a glamourless, inexpensive walkup on Second South. Marc checked into Room 203 and George into the one right next to him. If Marc made a phone call, George would put a stethoscope-type device against the inside of his closet (on the other side of the wall from the pay phone) and listen in. On another occasion, he trailed him to an address on Ninth South, where Marc met an older, heavyset woman; together they traveled to a private residence and looked at a used car. Walking down the street, right next to them, was a man smoking a cigarette—a detective George had asked to help with the surveillance.

If Marc didn't use a car and drive straight to Canada or Mexico, he had more than enough money, George figured, to fly anywhere in the world. George had no idea what Marc might do—or where he might go—but he would continue trying to find out.

Three days after George began his tail, Marc, never having once detected it, took a cab to Salt Lake International Airport. George waited until Marc boarded a plane to New York, then called Jones from a pay phone.

"I want to take Marc off the plane," he said, "and have already threatened to seize it if they won't let me on board. Under the terms of Marc's bail, is he allowed to leave Salt Lake?"

Jones immediately called Judge Leary and explained the situation. The judge reminded the prosecutor that Marc was required only to contact Pretrial Services twice a week and give them his address and location. He neither had to appear there nor stay in Salt Lake City. As long as he followed the conditions of his bail and appeared in court when he was scheduled, the state could not legally hold him. When Jones phoned George back, the investigator grabbed the receiver on the first ring, then slowly hung it up.

As he watched helplessly through the large plate-glass window, Marc's plane pulled away from the gate and headed toward the runway. He wasn't just some relative left behind, after a final embrace, longing for the moment a loved one would return. No, his feelings burned deeper than that. Not only was he convinced that he would never see Marc again, but, as the plane lifted off and slowly ascended eastward into the Utah sky, he could see months and months of hard work disappear with it.

Al Sullivan was stunned that Marc was out on bail—"the crowning irony," he said, after all that New York had done on

Utah's behalf. And Steve Klein told Mike George that Marc could not be watched in New York. Klein's investigation of Frances's bank accounts—to see if he could isolate the $5,000 Myles Manning claimed she paid him—and into the con man's background was one thing. But a surveillance of Marc was out of the question. New York had no jurisdiction.

During his month in the Salt Lake City-County Jail, Marc had made the acquaintance of a man named Millard Kaiser. A former cabdriver, Kaiser was awaiting trial on charges of sodomy and told Marc that his wife, who was on welfare and supporting their nine-month-old daughter, was hoping to get enough money together to post bail for him. When Marc said that he was thinking of buying a car once he got out on bail, Kaiser said that if Marc bought it through a relative of his, he might have enough money to gain his temporary freedom too.

Thus was the moment that Marc Schreuder met Mary Lou Kaiser.

"I fell in love with him the first time I laid eyes on him," Mary Lou remembered with a smile. She was fifteen years older than he was—practically old enough to be his mother—weighed roughly 250 pounds, and loved his blue eyes. She was still married to Millard Kaiser at the time, but they had separated the previous August. Since she was a devout "Pentecostal Holy Roller," however, she told Kaiser he would have to divorce her and thereby "carry the sin."

She didn't read the newspaper, didn't have a television (it was against her religion), and thought that Marc was in jail on a drug rap—the line he had given Millard. When they met about the car, Marc mentioned that he was flying back to New York and she had no idea if she'd ever see him again. And though neither of them perhaps fully realized it at the time, each needed the other.

Mary Lou's maiden name was Garcia, and she was born in Torreón, Mexico, the fourth of six children. Her father had been a Pentecostal minister in Colorado before her birth, but by the time she arrived he was a "backslider." When she was five, he moved the family to Bingham, Utah, and worked as a miner at Kennecott Copper. In Bingham, she recalled, "everybody—all nationalities—lived in a lot of harmony. I didn't know what prejudice was until I left that town." In fact, she said, there were only two people in Bingham people were afraid of—"Mike, the town bully, and my father."

While her mother was an "angel incarnate," her father was "very strict, very mean, and very domineering." He didn't own a car until he was in his fifties, liked to walk everywhere, raise his own food, and work hard—a workaholic like Frank Bradshaw." But he was also something else: "a violent alcoholic—mostly with me, because I was a gutsy one. I used to tell him what I thought of him—that he was a dirty, drunken old man."

Forty-five when Mary Lou was born, he wouldn't let her date, drink or put on makeup. She had to wear her hair and her clothes long. "My father told me I was going to be an old maid," she recalled, "so the first dumb idiot that came along and asked me to marry him, I did."

She was twenty-five, he had been in a mental institution, and their marriage lasted six months. Her second husband was arrested for burglary; they were married for about a year, divorced, married again for four months, and divorced once more. Then, in 1980, she married Millard Kaiser, and the following year, in April, she gave birth to a lovely brown-haired girl with button eyes whom she named Monique.

Mary Lou and Monique were over at the jail, visiting Millard, when she accidentally bumped into Marc a few weeks after their first encounter. He had returned to Salt Lake after all. They began talking, and he wound up walking her and the little girl home. Mary Lou asked him to stay for a while, but he declined. She asked him to come back and see her sometime, and a few days later he did.

They talked about "everything and anything," and she asked him to move in. Just like that. He said he would—on one condition: she clean up her place and keep it that way. She asked for two hours and accomplished it in four, but as long as they lived there it was known as the "Roach Hilton."

During the day he would often see his grandmother, who was continuing to support him. Toward evening, he would either go back to Mary Lou's apartment for dinner or take her and Monique out for a meal. He did not move all of his belongings into her apartment immediately, and told her why. "I have a lot of morals, you know. You're still Millard's wife." But she assured him that things between her and Millard were over, and it wasn't long before they decided to move to a new place.

His grandmother thought that he was still at the Stratford, and he continued to keep some of his things there with the manager—especially some gold coins and cash. Knowing she would disapprove of his new "friend" and his living with her, Marc showed his grandmother a vacant apartment at 838 Roberta Street and said he wanted to move in on March 1. He didn't like the "sleazy" atmosphere of the Stratford any longer and Berenice didn't either, so she agreed to pay the rent for a place she thought he would be living in alone.

While his lawyers continued to work toward his preliminary hearing, Marc became more and more attached to his new family. He finally was having sex he didn't have to pay for—with a mother figure who doted on him and nuzzled him close to her breasts—and he began to think of Monique as his own child, a notion that Mary Lou did nothing to discourage. It wasn't long before he was referring to Monique as "Baby," and, once she could talk, she called him "Poppy."

Richard Behrens made his long-awaited appearance in Salt Lake City on February 11. Larry Goldman came with him, and for two solid days they worked with Mike George, Ernie Jones and Joel Campbell on the huge VIA chart that now circled the conference room a couple of times.

As Behrens began responding to their questions, Jones could hardly believe the schoolteacher was actually sitting there, *in Salt Lake,* revealing more and more of what he knew about the whole bizarre tale. And, like George, he couldn't get over his appearance; they had had this picture in their minds of a "little evil man" and he turned out to look, George said, "like a little grandpa."

During his visit, Behrens tried to explain more fully the extent of Frances's relationship with Marc—the kind of control she had over him that enabled Marc to carry out her plan. By the time Behrens left, George, once more, wanted to issue a warrant for Frances's arrest. But once again the prosecutor came up with a good reason to wait. Knowing that Behrens's recantation had probably damaged a certain degree of his credibility, Jones wanted to see how the "little grandpa" would survive the kind of white-hot cross-examination he was bound to receive at Marc's preliminary hearing in March.

Shortly after Marc was extradited to Salt Lake in December, his lawyers had requested a lineup in order to see if some of the state's witnesses could actually identify him. The lineup was set for Tuesday, March 2, at nine in the morning, and Mike George had arranged for three witnesses—Carolyn Karoliszyn-Morris from New York, and Jerry Register and Malcolm McPhail from Texas—to fly in the day before.

Paul Van Dam (the bearded, former Salt Lake County Attorney who, along with Joe Tesch, had become Marc's new Utah lawyer six months earlier) had told Marc to meet him at eight-thirty that morning, but when Tuesday arrived there was no sign of him. Van Dam knew that Marc was supposed to move into his new apartment the day before, but he did not know exactly which apartment in the small Roberta Street complex it was. So he drove over and began going door to door, knocking on each one. But none of the people who opened up even faintly resembled his client.

By nightfall, the news that Marc had jumped bail was on the radio and television and in the afternoon paper. A warrant was issued for his arrest. Ernie Jones told a reporter from the *Salt Lake Tribune,* "This doesn't surprise me in the least. I'm sure he's gone. . . . I'm afraid he may have left the country." Paul Van Dam told the same reporter that Marc had been "good about reporting to me and Pretrial Services up until now. The last time I heard from him was last week. Where he is now is a mystery. I have no idea."

On Wednesday morning Mary Lou turned the radio on shortly after seven. She and Marc had spent the last two days moving into apartment F on the second floor—using shopping carts to transport all their things from the Roach Hilton—and were preparing to spend their first full day together in their new home. But what they both then heard changed all that.

"God, I hate waking up to the news," Marc said.

"What's going on?" Mary Lou demanded to know. "What are you really wanted for?"

"I'm wanted for the murder of my grandfather."

"Did you do it?"

"No," he said, not about to jeopardize his relationship with her at this stage.

Since they didn't yet have a phone, they walked around the corner with Monique to the Royal Studios. Mary Lou worked there, booking appointments for people to get their pictures taken, and had a set of keys to the place. Marc realized that since he didn't have Van Dam's unlisted home number he had no way of reaching him. Van Dam had also been moving—to a new office—and hadn't gotten a phone yet. Marc tried to phone Frances in New York, but there was no answer. So they left Royal and began to walk back to their apartment.

They never got there.

"Hey, Marc, how are you doing?" It was Ron Nelson, offering a cold greeting to someone he hadn't seen since that December day at Trinity when Marc was arrested for the first time. "You're under arrest."

A phone call had come in to the police department that morning from the manager of the apartment complex. He had just seen the news on television, he said, and was certain that Marc Schreuder was the same person who had moved into apartment F two days before.

Nelson and another detective had arrived at the address within minutes of the call and began banging on the door of the second-floor apartment and peering through the window. No answer and no one seemed to be home. They were just about to leave when they saw Marc at the bottom of the steps.

By nine fifty-five that morning, a flustered Marc Schreuder was back in jail.

Mike George was elated. Like Ernie Jones, he had been certain Marc had fled for good. The two Texas witnesses who had flown in for the lineup had already left town, but a pregnant Candy Karoliszyn-Morris had not. So at one forty-five that day, seven individuals—including Marc—walked the lineup plank just for her. Of the seven, there were two whom she wanted to see repeat the procedure. On a piece of yellow legal paper she wrote, "I believe it to be 3."

Joe Tesch began asking her questions about number 3—Marc—and what she was doing when she saw him. She explained that she had sold him airline tickets in 1978 at the American Airlines office at the Plaza Hotel.

How was it that she was able to recall him?

It was an unusual transaction, she said—a series of tickets. Unusual for a younger person to come in with cash. Her typical customer was an adult who paid with a credit card. But there was something else. Something about his eyes. And his ruddy complexion.

Grasping for straws, Tesch zeroed in on the word "believe" that she had written and asked if she was sure. She was "ninety-nine percent sure," she said, admitting that she had been shown some photographs a few months before, but had *not* been told if the person she identified was the suspect.

Had she read any Salt Lake newspapers the last two days?

No, she hadn't. Mike George had specifically warned her against reading or watching anything.

Tesch again pressed her about the ticket sale and why she was able to remember the person she picked out.

Younger people usually went off on vacation, she said, and this was "such a quick trip." His hair—"kind of unkempt and flyaway type"—and his "stocky" build were also similar to what she remembered. And there was something about his eyes, something she couldn't quite articulate.

Marc's day was not over yet. He had to appear in front of Judge Leary and try to explain his whereabouts. He had known about the lineup, he said, but had "forgotten" exactly when it was. He had tried to phone Van Dam on Tuesday morning, but was told he was in the process of moving offices and didn't have a phone yet. Though Marc was speaking with Joe Tesch's secretary, he neither asked to talk with Tesch—Van Dam was the lawyer he was primarily dealing with, he said—nor left his name. He had "intended" to try to reach Van Dam later, but didn't. "As I was very busy moving and had lots of stuff to do I tended to put it off." He denied he had been in New York over the previous weekend and said the first time he knew he'd missed the lineup was that morning, when the news came over the radio.

Had he heard a knocking on his door on Tuesday morning? Van Dam asked.

Yes, he had. But he had been in the bathroom, and by the time he ran to answer it no one was there.

When Ernie Jones questioned him as to why he couldn't reach his attorneys earlier that day, he said he didn't have home phone numbers for either of them—that Van Dam wouldn't give him his unlisted number—and that he was planning to go to see Van Dam at the time he was arrested.

Later in the hearing, Van Dam told the court that while he never anticipated a problem about Marc's showing up, he was willing to shoulder some of the blame himself. If he had stayed longer at the door on Tuesday morning, he said, Marc would have been there. "If I could have got to a telephone," the amiable lawyer said in his calm, soft voice, "we would have had contact with him. I think a series of events unfortunately came together to prevent him being there."

Leary didn't buy it. Marc went back to jail, his failure to show up that morning a costly mistake. Berenice had to forfeit the $100,000 she had posted for him.*

That evening, Mike George went over to Roberta Street to interview Mary Lou. She hadn't known about the lineup, she said, or the real reason he had been arrested in the first place. Other than that, she had little to say. George searched the apartment thoroughly and found nothing.

Marc had never expected to be back in jail. At least not under these circumstances. A couple of days later he told Mary Lou, "I should have left the country. With you speaking Spanish and me speaking French, we could have traveled half the world. But they would have caught us—a young boy and a heavyset woman with a baby."

The longer Marc stayed in jail the more hopeless he felt his situation had become. His preliminary hearing was scheduled for Tuesday, March 16, and Mike George had good reason to be worried that Marc might not live to attend it.

---

*On April 6, the judge granted a motion returning all of the money to her except for $2,165.

He had received a tip from an old informant of his that Marc was considering suicide. George immediately went over to the jail and asked to see him.

"You don't have to talk to me," George told him. "I'm not going to ask you anything on the crime, but there's something I want to talk to you about."

Marc said he didn't mind talking with him and admitted that he'd thought about committing suicide. "I don't have anything to live for," George recalled Marc telling him, "and will ask for the death penalty if I'm convicted at trial."

"That's bullshit," George snapped. "If they give it to you they give it to you. But you're never going to be executed. Don't even think about it."

"Well, I don't want to go on living."

"You've got to realize we've got a pretty good prison out here," said George, referring to the Utah State Prison. "There are a lot of programs available to you. You're young, you're not going to spend the rest of your life in prison. Nobody in Utah does. You can either make something of your life in prison or you can become a bum."

"What do they have out there?" Marc wanted to know.

George told him about some of the programs the prison offered—especially one that would enable him to go to college—and he persuaded Marc to let some mental-health counselors begin talking with him.

"What he was trying to tell me that day," George said later, "was that he was not a deranged killer. I told him I knew that—that he had always been polite to me and that I'd tried to be polite to him. But I said that he had to go through his trial."

And the next step down the road to that was the preliminary hearing.

47 // In many ways a courthouse is like a racetrack. Every day, a potpourri of slick-talking touts, seedy hangers-on, old ladies carrying knitting baskets who are not afraid to swing them in disgust, and moneyed, fresh-faced figures in three-piece suits offer up the one thing they have in common—opinions. From those no one is spared: the judges, the prosecutors, the defense attorneys, the jury—and anything and anyone else imaginable.

Around the corridors of the Metropolitan Hall of Justice in Salt Lake—a building as neurotically spotless as the city itself—the "morning line" on one particular judge is this: if the state somehow loses its way in the dark, "ole Jay Elmer" will hold up a lantern and help them find it.

Jay Elmer is Third District Court Judge Jay Elmer Banks, a former Salt Lake County District Attorney who *never* lost a case; in 1972 alone, his fourteenth and last year in that position, he personally tried *thirty-three* murder cases. Won them all. A strong advocate of capital punishment, Banks is known to many as the Hanging Judge. When a big murder case comes along, it is no secret in places like the Manhattan Club, the Cabana, and Stanyon Street—private clubs near the courthouse along Fourth South where many lawyers, judges and other court personnel bend elbows at the end of a grueling, litigious day—that Jay Banks wants to preside over it.

The general purpose of a preliminary hearing is to determine whether a crime has been committed and whether there is reasonable and probable cause to believe that the defendant committed it. If the judge is satisfied of both these things, the defendant is bound over to stand trial.

As Marc's preliminary before Judge Banks began on Tuesday, March 16, Paul Van Dam asked if the hearing could be closed to the press and spectators and Banks agreed. Before the first witness was called, both sides argued their interpretation of an earlier ruling about what the County

423

Attorney's Office was required to supply to the defense: Jones made a distinction between police reports—which he turned over—and the "work product" of his office, which could include everything from legal strategy and impressions to, most important, the reports assembled by Mike George. Joe Tesch said he was not after their impressions and legal theories, but felt entitled, by law, to have George's reports because he was a "peace officer."

In reality, the true impact of a particular law—*any* law—is less in how it actually *reads* on the books than in the vastly different ways lawyers and judges *interpret* it. And at this stage of the perpetual cat-and-mouse game of discovery, Banks was inclined to side with the state and get on with the hearing.

The first person to be sworn in made her way slowly to the witness stand. Dressed in black and wearing a big hat of the same color, Berenice Bradshaw was nearly seventy-nine years old. She had just come out of the hospital—come to defend her grandson and her family from a prosecutor she felt was "so crooked he couldn't sleep in a roundhouse."

On direct examination, after identifying a photo of the man she had been married to for nearly fifty-four years and pointing out the boy who was accused of murdering him, she began to talk about that Sunday morning, the 23rd of July, 1978, as if it were yesterday. Her husband worked 365 days a year, and on that particular morning she heard him leave at quarter to seven—she heard the car start and looked at the clock—for the warehouse.

Where had Larry been?

He had been in bed asleep, she said, and hadn't gotten up until ten for a flying lesson. (On the day of the murder, she told Joel Campbell that Larry had gotten up at nine.) Shortly after he had left, three men had arrived to tell her what had happened.

Had she seen the defendant, Marc Schreuder, that morning?

No, he had been back in New York, with his mother.

Had his mother been working that summer?

No, she had been receiving money from her and her husband, but she had no idea how much.

424

Asked about the summer of 1977, she reluctantly admitted there had been "a lot of complications" when Marc and Larry worked at the warehouse and that the employees hadn't wanted them back the following year.

"Was there a conflict between Frances and your husband?"

"From time to time."

"Okay, and what was the source of that conflict?"

"Well, it just was mostly over financial assistance."

"Can you explain to us what the problem was?"

"Just living."

"And—" he began, but was cut off.

"Making ends meet, let's put it—"

"Can you explain the position that was taken concerning that conflict?"

"No," she snapped. "I don't know what to say. I used to help them . . . well, we both did. My husband and I both financed them a great deal."

Asked if Marc had been in Salt Lake on the day of the funeral, she said that his mother had him stay home and take care of his sister. When Jones asked her about her husband's will, she said that besides herself, the only three people receiving money from the estate were her three daughters.

"What about the defendant, Marc?" Jones asked, treading into the delicate area of the state's charge—that he had murdered his grandfather for "pecuniary or other personal gain."

"Not directly," Berenice said, "no."

On cross-examination, Paul Van Dam's strategy was clear: do everything possible to deflect attention from Marc. Hadn't it been Larry who had stolen some auto parts from her husband and Marc who had told them about it?

Yes.

Had she ever heard Marc threaten his grandfather or "make any physical moves toward him"?

No, not to her knowledge. She certainly wasn't going to mention the time she had found him standing over Franklin in the middle of the night, convinced he was trying to poison the air.

How would she describe the relationship between Marc and his grandfather "as far as their feelings for one another"?

"Well, I am sure that Marc thought—" She began to cry. "Marc thought a great deal of his grandfather and his grandfather did of him."

"Would you like a moment, Mrs. Bradshaw?"

"No." She had collected herself and was ready to go on.

". . . Isn't it true that Mr. Bradshaw was not as generous as you wanted him to be to Mrs. Schreuder?"

"Well, he did a great deal for them."

"Yes, but my question was, you wanted to do more for them than he did?"

"Yes, at times." But Frances wasn't the only one who received money from them. She said she had bought an apartment for Marilyn in New York City and the land north of the city she and her husband had built their cabin on. Marilyn was also the one, she stressed, most actively involved in the family business.

"Shortly after the death of Mr. Bradshaw, did you have any discussions with Marilyn regarding her taking over or doing the business of Mr. Bradshaw?"

"Well, on his death, she was—she wanted to take over everything, but I wouldn't permit it."

"And isn't it true, since that time, that there have been some rather unfortunate and bad feelings develop between Marilyn and yourself and Elaine?"

"Yes."

". . . What was the reason that they are not happy with you now . . . ?"

"There's been a feud always."

"What is the nature of that feud, Mrs. Bradshaw?"

"Bitterness and hate."

"Between what parties, which persons?"

"Marilyn and Elaine towards their younger sister, Frances."

"And has that gone on, you say, for a long time, all their life?"

"Yes, always."

"Is that still the case, to your knowledge?"

"Yes."

As Mike George sat next to Ernie Jones, listening intently, he knew that the situation had polarized dramatically. Two months earlier, Marilyn had written another letter to Salt Lake's two newspapers (which the *Deseret News* published), complaining about Judge Leary's granting of bail to Marc and the fact that "a lot of high-priced lawyers have been employed, with the deceased's money, and been able to show their influence. As things have been going, I do not believe this case will ever be brought to trial, because the dead man's money will be able to buy whatever is necessary to see to it that it doesn't."

In February, Elaine had written George a letter, implying her mother might have stolen her father's new will from the locked file cabinet that Nancy Jones had caught her in one day—the one to which Frank supposedly had the only key. She was "haunted," she wrote, despite the fact they didn't go, "by Mother's insistence that we [drive] to the warehouse the day after Dad's murder so that 'Larry could check out the keys.' Mother was adamant that she have this cabinet, which I thought strange at the time knowing that she was not motivated by sentiment." The letter continued:

Are you aware of what Behrens told Marilyn regarding Marc and Larry trying to poison Dad? This attempt was unsuccessful, they thought, because "he didn't eat enough." He ate only twice a day: He prepared oatmeal for himself in the morning and he took from home his late afternoon meal of meat loaf . . . made in advance by Mother. The horrible part is that I'm now wondering if Mother cooperated with this poisoning attempt. When I start thinking about that I also think about another curious thing: When we were in Salt Lake in June of 1978 Mother kept repeating that she thought that Dad looked terrible and that she thought he must be ill. Mason asked me at the time if this was a bit of wishful thinking and I allowed as how I had had that same thought because he seemed fit and hearty to me. (He always arose at 5:30 a.m. and did an hour's worth of calisthenics, including 100 push-ups and at least 15-minutes of jumping rope and it was this latter which awakened us every morning while we were there!)

After you questioned me regarding the disposition of Dad's bodily remains, several things flashed into my head: Mother was most insistent upon cremation and pleaded with Marilyn to help her out by dealing with family objections. Although we knew that Dad wished to be cremated, Marilyn and I have since concluded that respecting family beliefs is something which Dad would have been in accord with and we wish that we had tried to persuade Mother to allow them to bury his remains. But one might assume that evidence of poison would thus be destroyed, right? Is it possible to detect poison in ashes? In any case, it may be something you might want to ask Mother about.

All of this weighs very heavily upon me. I sure would like to believe that my Mother had nothing to do with my Father's murder, but the evidence to date suggests otherwise. I need for a trial to happen so that I can know one way or the other. Can you understand that? If it never happens I will be forever in purgatory, never knowing for sure, doubting my own sanity. I do know that Marc, Larry and Frances killed my father—about that I have no doubt whatsoever—but was my Mother an active or a passive participant? I have wanted to believe that Mother was a passive participant but the recent evidence tells me that I am a victim of wishful thinking. . . .

Though Mike George had not ruled out anything, he knew that in murder cases theories were never in short supply. Jones and he had discussed the possibility that Berneice Bradshaw might have been involved in—or at least knew about—the plans to murder her husband; but the "evidence" Elaine was talking about was not nearly strong enough to support a charge against the formidable matriarch of this torn and troubled family.

"Mrs. Bradshaw," asked Paul Van Dam, still cross-examining her, "would it be fair to say that by having spent the summer with your two grandsons, Marc and Larry, you got to know them rather well?"

"Yes."

"Would it also be fair to say that Larry was a more aggressive individual than Marc?"

"Yes."

"Did you see him as being . . . more violent than Marc at any time?"

"Yes, I would say so."

During the summer of 1978, she said, when Larry was the only one living with them, he and her husband did not see much of each other—Franklin was always at work and Larry was not permitted to go down there. On the morning of the murder, she went down to wake Larry up for his flying lesson, and he left "pretty much at ten," slightly revising what she had testified earlier—that he had gotten up at ten.

"I assume prior to that time you were not aware of your husband's death?"

"No."

Van Dam asked her if she knew where Larry was today, and she told the court that he had been committed to a hospital "for mental illness," and explained what he had done.

"Do you know, or were you aware of at some time in the past, a man by the name of Behrens?"

"I have just heard of him."

"Had you ever met him?"

"No."

"So you did not know him or meet him back in about 1963 in New York?"

"No."

"And you have had no contact with him since that time?"

"No."

". . . Were you aware at any time in 1978 that your husband might be drafting a new will?"

"I had heard sort of indirectly that . . . he was thinking of making a new will."

Doug Steele and Nancy Jones had felt fairly certain she had either seen that memo or heard about it—and now, to Ernie Jones's delight, she was admitting it under oath.

"And from whom did you hear that, Mrs. Bradshaw?"

"I don't know. I just—"

"Did you ever see that new will?"

"No."

"Did anyone ever tell you the terms of that new will?"

"No."

"You know who Nancy Jones is, correct?"

"Yes."

"Did you ever have any conversations with her regarding the new will?"

"No."

"Did you ever have personal knowledge of the fact that Mr. Bradshaw might be planning to disinherit Frances?"

"I had heard something to that effect, yes."

"And do you recall from whom you heard that?"

"No. I don't know."

Shifting back to Richard Behrens once more, Van Dam managed to elicit the fact that she knew Frances and he were having a conflict over money, because Frances had told her.

"Did she tell you a great deal about it?"

Jones objected that it was hearsay, Banks sustained it, and Van Dam indicated he was finished.

On re-direct, Jones knew he needed to get the spotlight back on Marc; if Van Dam could lead her down one avenue, he would try to take her down another. She admitted that Marc had been suspected of stealing money in the summer of 1977 and indicated that was why her husband had not allowed him to return in 1978. But when he asked if Marc had resented that, Van Dam objected that no foundation had been laid, and the judge agreed. So Jones tried a different tack.

"Do you know why it is that Larry came back to Salt Lake City in the summer of '78 and Marc did not?"

"Because Larry wanted to work," she said, unwilling to state the real reason: that Frances had thrown him out.

"Mrs. Bradshaw, is it true that your husband refused to finance or pay for any of Marc's schooling after the summer of 1977?"

"No. I don't recall such a thing." She might not "recall" it four and a half years later, but she had forged checks for Marc and Larry's schooling in September of that year—and the prosecutor knew it.

"Do you recall at any point in time your husband refusing to pay for Marc's education?"

"There was one year. I don't recall just which year it was that I paid for their schooling."

". . . Mrs. Bradshaw, you indicated that you were aware that a will was being prepared that would disinherit Frances Schreuder?"

"I had heard sort of whispers—nothing directly."

"Do you know why your husband would want to disinherit the defendant's mother from a will?"

"No, I don't."

Shortly before noon that Tuesday, Berenice Bradshaw finished testifying. Though she had been treated with deference, the experience had unsettled her. But what had occurred in Judge Banks's courtroom that day was mild compared to what lay ahead.

Dan Schindler, the former employee who had found Franklin's body, testified next, followed by the Medical Examiner who had performed the autopsy, Joel Campbell and Ed Peterson, the forensic chemist from California who had done the ballistics test. Joe Tesch asked that Peterson's testimony be stricken, because he had brought neither notes nor photographs for the defense to examine; but Judge Banks denied the motion.

No sooner had Jerry Austin Register lumbered into the courtroom and settled his wide frame into the witness box than he was shown the .357 Magnum that used to belong to him and identified Marc, wearing a white T-shirt, as the person who had bought it. (Earlier that day, he and John Cavenaugh had identified him in a lineup.) He said the sale took place about ten a.m. on July 22, 1978, and that Malcolm McPhail and John Cavenaugh had also been present. (When he had been asked about this in earlier interviews, he had either not remembered or not committed himself.) He explained how he was able to determine the day of the sale (between Old Settler's Day and the day his son was shot and left paralyzed) and recalled that Marc said he was going hiking and backpacking "I believe in Colorado."

On cross-examination, Register answered Paul Van Dam in the same easygoing, yes-sir-no-sir manner he had maintained with Jones. He described himself as a collector of guns who tended to "trade" far more guns than he sold; in fact, he'd been "trading firearms since I was fourteen years old." When Campbell first called him about this, he was confused and caught "off-guard"; the detective asked him about a .357 Magnum he had sold but did not mention what model. He had had three or four in his possession at the time and "could not distinguish which gun he was talking about." When he first met with Campbell at the Midland Police Department, he said he was not able to identify Marc from the pictures he was shown.

How was he able then to recall things today as well as he was?

"Well, sir, I think when a policeman or anyone calls you up and tells you something right offhand . . . your mind kind of starts rolling and you really can't put events together until you have had some time to think about it. . . . And it took me several weeks to put this thing together, to get it all worked out in my own mind."

When he said he didn't really remember things clearly until he had met with the County Attorney's investigators, Van Dam wanted to know if they had *told* him the date of the sale.

"No, sir," he shot back.

Register had said on direct examination that Marc seemed uninterested by the gun sale, and Van Dam now asked him to explain what he meant by that. The officer said that Marc was "trying to avoid looking at me and talking to me." Though he said he had been concerned about Marc's age at the time ("around eighteen years old, I would guess") and had thought he should ask for some identification, his wife had assured him that "if he is with Mr. McPhail, you know, he is okay."

". . . [Is it a] requirement under law you have to be a certain age to purchase a firearm?"

"As far as I know, it is not, sir, in the state of Texas."*

". . . Mr. Register, have you ever been charged of a crime for having sold this firearm to a minor?"

"No, sir, I was not."

"Were you aware at the time that it was actually against the law to do so?"

"I still don't know if it is against the law."

"In Texas?" Judge Banks asked.

"In Texas," Register finished his sentence.

When Van Dam asked him if he knew the gun's serial number, he said, "Yes, sir. It's N281919."

How was he able to recall that so quickly from memory?

---

*Under the Gun Control Act of 1968, which does *not* exclude the state of Texas, if this had been an "official," over-the-counter transaction, Marc would have had to be twenty-one to get a handgun. He was seventeen at the time.

When Don Harman showed him the paperwork from the company through which he had purchased it, he recalled the 1919.

"Do you customarily memorize or remember the serial number of the weapons?"

"No, but I usually don't get a serial number that repeats itself more or less and that one just being 1919 . . . that part just stuck."

In his sailor's uniform, John Cavenaugh looked quite impressive as he began answering Ernie Jones's questions on direct examination. His explanation of the events as he recalled them was consistent with what he had said in earlier interviews—including *his* recollection that Jerry Register was *not* present during the sale of the gun. The gun was bought from a woman, and the owner of it, he thought, was "the sheriff of Midland."

On cross, Van Dam asked him how well he knew Marc at Kent. He said he probably knew him "as good as anybody else," and thought of him as intelligent and a loner.

When he got Marc's phone call, did he recall "any voices in the background talking to him or hearing anything in the background"?

No.

"Just his voice?"

That's all he could recall.

Switching back to Kent—and away from the subject at issue—Van Dam established that people had made fun of Marc there. While Marc never reacted angrily or violently to this, Cavenaugh claimed, he was excitable. "You could tell when he was excited. He would talk faster than normal. His leg might shake a little bit."

But when Van Dam asked him if he had displayed any of these traits while in Midland, "not really" was his reply. They had discussed whether Marc, who was not familiar with guns, should buy "a rifle, shotgun or pistol," he said, "and we finally agreed that a pistol would be his best bet." While a rifle or shotgun is what you usually use when you go camping or hunting, he said, he had recommended a pistol because he knew it would be difficult for Marc to purchase a firearm in New York City. Because Malcolm McPhail was "a personal friend" as well as a gun collector, he had decided to contact him about obtaining one.

But there was still the mystery of whether Jerry Register was there that day which needed to be clarified.

"Have you had occasion today or in the past, Mr. Cavenaugh, to meet the deputy sheriff by the name of Jerry Register?"

"I met him yesterday."

"Did he look familiar to you?"

"No."

"You haven't met him before?"

"No. I don't remember meeting him before."

"He is a rather distinctive-looking gentleman, wouldn't you say?"

"Yes."

Van Dam asked him about the woman who he said actually sold the gun to McPhail. "You have given a statement earlier as to something she said. And I want to ask you about it. Do you recall a woman who sold the gun ever saying that the man who owned it could not be present for some reason?"

"I remember her saying something to that extent."

"Do you remember any reason that she gave that he could not be present?"

"I might not even be right about her saying that so—"

"But there is something—"

"Yes. Something that tells me that the old man couldn't be there and wasn't present and his wife made some explanation for it."

On re-direct, Jones asked if he recalled the woman's name, but he didn't. He did, however, remember the name of the murder mystery Marc was reading in Midland. *"Murder on the Nile,"* he said (stating the title incorrectly). "I think it was by Agatha Christie."

On that intriguing note the blond-haired Texan left the courtroom, and Mike George left his seat to get the state's last witness—the one whom the defense had long been waiting for.

Ernie Jones had hardly begun his questioning of Richard Behrens when Joe Tesch broke in. Unless the witness was going to say what he said in two sworn statements (the statement that was notarized in New York and the interview with the lawyers in Connecticut), Tesch told Judge Banks, he ought to be advised about perjury. Jones said that he would be referring to the *initial* statement Behrens made—the one to Joel Campbell—and that he had discussed "the penalties and the impact of his testimony" with both Behrens and Larry Goldman, who was present at the hearing. Once Behrens was warned by Judge Banks about the consequences of giving false testimony, the prosecutor wasted little time.

"Mr. Behrens, back in July of 1978, where were you living?"

"I was living in New York City."

"And were you aware of the death of Franklin Bradshaw here in Salt Lake City on or about the 23rd of July of 1978?"

"I became aware of it, yes."

"Did you have occasion to talk to Marc Schreuder about that death?"

"Yes, I did."

"When was the first time that you talked to him about the death of Franklin Bradshaw?"

"Probably, certainly, the 23rd or 24th."

"Where would you have been at the time of that conversation?"

"In my house."

"Okay. And was there anyone else present at that time?"

"Mrs. Schreuder."

"His mother?"

"Yes."

"Do you recall what he told you at that time concerning the death of Franklin Bradshaw?"

"I can't remember the exact words, but he indicated to me that he had shot his grandfather."

"Did he tell you why he shot his grandfather?"

"At that time, the strong indication was—message I got was that it was for money, for financial reasons."

". . . Did he tell you the type of gun that was used?"

"I can't remember exactly. Well, certainly, as I received it on the 23rd, I saw it and I knew what type it was because I looked at it. . . . It was a pistol . . . a .357 Magnum."

"Did he tell you the number of shots that were fired?"

"Initially, he didn't. I found out later how many shots were fired."

". . . Okay. Did he ever tell you the location of the wounds, where he had shot his grandfather?"

"Not initially, but much later. . . ."

"Do you remember when that took place?"

"Took place this last summer."

". . . Do you remember where that conversation took place?"

"Yes. It was in a park where we both lived. He lived within a block. I lived within three or four blocks of it."

"And was there anyone else present during that conversation?"

"No."

"What did he tell you concerning the location of the wounds?"

"In the head and in the chest. That's what he told me."

"Did the defendant tell you where the shooting took place?"

"Yes, within the—Mr. Bradshaw's working quarters or office."

". . . Did he tell you what time of the day the shooting occurred?"

"Early Sunday morning."

"Mr. Behrens, did the defendant tell you where he had obtained the murder weapon from?"

"In the first meeting, I had the message given to me by him that it was from a sheriff."

"Do you know where that sheriff was located?"

"Not initially. But there was an address given with the gun when the gun was given in haste. And when I examined it, I saw an address of a person named Cavenaugh. . . . It was Midland, Texas, and the gun was bought in that town as such."

". . . Did you ever have a conversation with the defendant in which he related to you when he purchased this gun?"

"Yes."

". . . My question is, when did you talk to him about that subject?"

"After he had dropped the gun off at my apartment."

". . . And do you remember if anyone else was present?"

"Mrs. Schreuder."

". . . How many conversations did you have with the defendant about the death of Franklin Bradshaw?"

"Many."

". . . In any of these conversations, was there a discussion about how he got to Salt Lake City?"

"Yes."

"And do you recall when that conversation took place?"

"Certainly when he dropped the gun off—after he dropped the gun off. The main conversations of how he got there, who he got it from and everything were certainly between the 23rd and before the funeral."

"Who would have been present during that conversation?"

"The one time Mrs. Bradshaw was present," he said, then corrected himself to say "Mrs. Schreuder." Marc told him he had flown to Salt Lake and that after he did the shooting, he "spirited out of Salt Lake" with the gun.

"Did he explain to you how he got it out of Salt Lake?"

"He took it back with him on . . . an airplane and he put it in luggage which was not inspected by the people who inspect for firearms. In other words, it wasn't on his person but . . . was put in the luggage compartment of the plane."

"Did he talk to you about what he did with the gun once he got out of Salt Lake City?"

"No. Well, I knew that it was brought to my house. What he did before that, I don't really know."

"Was there any discussion whether or not he gave the gun to anyone else?"

"He gave it to his mother."

". . . You say you received a firearm from somebody?"

"Yes."

"Who gave you that firearm?"

"As far as I remember, it was Mrs. Schreuder."

She made "the initial dropoff," he said, bringing the gun to his apartment on "the 23rd or the 24th." She had the gun in either her "bag or handbag" and it was "unceremoniously dropped on me." He placed it in "a second room to my dining room in a sort of shelf arrangement I have, in a box that was there"—and there it stayed until he and Marc, "at my suggestion," drove down to a gun shop to obtain a case and "a cleaning device" for it about a "day or so later, week or so later."

In addition to receiving the gun and the Cavenaugh address, he was given a box of cartridges that he later disposed of. He kept the gun in his apartment from the time he received it "until I gave the gun to Mrs. Marilyn Reagan" in October of 1980, explaining how he had taken it to West End Avenue one evening and recounting the conversation he had had with Marilyn prior to doing so.

Had he had any discussions with Marc prior to the homicide, Jones asked, about the purchase of a gun?

Yes, he had. He received a phone call in the spring of 1978, asking "if I could see about purchasing a weapon." He never did.

"Did anyone besides Marc ever ask you to obtain a gun?"

"Yes."

"Who was that?"

"Mrs. Schreuder."

Her request came before Marc's, he said. "The content of the conversation was that if I were going to travel, to try to look for a weapon."

For the time being the prosecutor essentially had what he wanted—Marc's admission to Behrens and Frances's involvement in terms of giving Behrens the gun. Jones knew that Joe Tesch would try to carve the schoolteacher into little pieces—and that all he could do was hope that Behrens would survive.

Before focusing in on the matter in question, Tesch asked Behrens to provide his biography to the court. He had taught a variety of subjects (general science, biology, economics, English, history, mathematics) in a number of places (Virginia, North Carolina, New Jersey and New York) in both public and private schools. Along the way he worked for the *Reader's Digest*, wrote advertising copy in Lynchburg, Virginia, worked for a microscope company, and edited textbooks for Prentice-Hall. During 1977 and 1978 he was taking courses toward a master's in environmental studies at City College in New York, and during the summer of 1978 at one point he traveled to Virginia.

Was it early or late in the summer? Tesch asked.

It was around July 13, he believed, and he stayed about a week, returning to New York on the 19th.

Had he ever had any psychiatric illnesses?

Back in the early fifties, he was "rather confused," and for about two to three years saw a psychiatrist, who diagnosed him as having anxiety.

Tesch wanted to know how and where he had met Frances, and Behrens explained they had met in about 1963 at a coffee hour at All Souls Unitarian Church in New York. He knew her "quite well," and met her sons at the same time. As she was going through her first divorce he tried to "lend her moral support," and allowed her to hide records at his apartment.

Ernie Jones objected that this was immaterial—he could see the picture of Behrens Tesch was trying to paint—and Judge Banks agreed, saying that "it's too damned remote" and urging the attorney to stick to the matter at hand.

But Tesch persisted.

"Is it not true you became emotionally and sexually involved with Frances Schreuder in the sixties?"

"I got to know her pretty well."

"Okay. Again, eventually, you had a love-hate relationship with her?"

"Did I eventually have a love-hate relationship?"

"Yes."

"I don't understand the question. Could you rephrase that?"

"I will withdraw the question."

"Thank you."

"Did Frances Schreuder, in fact, at times of your life provide support for you, provide money to help you meet bills and live?"

"No."

"Never?"

"Never."

"There came a time when you gave Frances Schreuder some money to hold; is that correct?"

Yes, it was, Behrens said, explaining the situation.

Had she ever told him what happened to the money in their joint account? Tesch asked.

Yes, she had. "Her explanation was there was a will fight and there were many holdups. She said that there were many facets to this. She was getting an allowance of five thousand dollars a month. But for one reason or another, she claimed that it was being held back. . . ."

Asked if he had known of her need for money, *prior* to her father's death, Behrens said that "there were times when she was in great financial straits. I got that message loud and clear."

". . . She told you those things?"

"Over the years, I heard this many times. She would be poor and then rich. Then she would be . . . cut off. Then she would get new allowances and she would be going through various crises, financial crises."

Had she told him during the first half of 1978 that "she was becoming deeper and deeper in financial problems"?

No, it was more like the fall of 1977, he said.

"Did she complain about it all that winter and into the spring and into the summer that she was not receiving enough money from her parents to keep going?"

"She did say that, but she always seemed to . . . sight a way to go to Southampton."

Hadn't she in fact confided in him that "she knew that if her father died, she would get part of the estate and that would solve her problems"?

"She didn't use those words, but I got that impression."

"When you say you got that impression, how did you get it?"

"From her?" the judge interjected.

"From her."

"What did she say or do to give you that impression?" Tesch resumed.

"She indicated that she would reach a point where she wished to do away with her father. She asked me if I could find someone who wouldn't help her along these lines. . . ."

"When did she do that?"

"I would say it was something like the summer of '78, '77, '78, early '77, middle of '77."

"And it was in that connection that she asked you to obtain a firearm; is that correct?"

"No. In spring of '78, she asked me to obtain a firearm in that connection."

"And she told you, did she not, that the reason she wanted that firearm was to do away with her father?"

"Yes. It was the spring of '78 that she told me that . . . actually her son called me up and asked me if I were traveling to Virginia or anywhere to see if I could obtain a firearm."

"Let's talk about Frances Schreuder," said Tesch, determined to steer things as far away from Marc as possible.

"All right."

"Did she ever ask you to get a firearm so it could be used in killing Franklin Bradshaw?"

"Yes. I don't remember the exact words. That's the problem. She did indicate that."

". . . She also . . . confided in you and planned with you concerning his murder; is that correct?"

"No. She planned with somebody else, asked me if I knew anyone who would commit a murder for her."

"And you gave her a name?"

"Yeah. At first, I indicated that I didn't know anybody. And then I indicated somebody, that I didn't really know his background all that well. I knew him as a person that lived nearby, and I really didn't know that much about him. I knew he worked for a newspaper and that's all."

"But you told her that you thought he was a hit man and he could do it; is that correct?"

"What's a hit man?" Behrens was toying with Tesch, whom he had begun to dislike intensely.

"Someone who would murder for money."

"I didn't say he was a hit man and I didn't know a—"

"You didn't know what a hit man was?"

"Yes. I knew what a hit man was. I didn't use that slang and she didn't either. [The term Behrens later said he both used and preferred was "button man."] The point is she wanted to talk about somebody who would help her along these lines. And I indicated that I really didn't know these type of persons. I read about them in the paper, [and] I am not saying I knew sterling characters, but I didn't know these people that really do this. Perhaps people talk about them, but I didn't know anyone actually doing it."

"The name, in fact, you gave her was Myles Manning, was it not?"

"It was."

"And you knew him to be involved or believed that he was involved in the profession of killing people for money; is that not true?"

"He is in the profession of being a man—as a printer. I didn't know him as a person that was involved in killing people."

"Did you not take ten thousand dollars cash from Frances Schreuder to Myles Manning?"

"No."

"Did you not tell Frances Schreuder that the ten thousand dollars she gave you was to pay Myles Manning to kill Franklin Bradshaw?"

"Absolutely not."

"Did you just keep the ten thousand dollars?"

"I never got ten thousand dollars from Frances Schreuder. I never got ten thousand dollars. I was never given ten thousand dollars. I never saw ten thousand dollars."

"What did you tell her about Myles Manning in the spring of 1978?"

"I said, 'This is Myles Manning. You speak with Myles Manning and don't tell me what you say to Myles Manning.'"

". . . Okay, did money change hands?"

"I was told that money changed hands."

"After you introduced Myles Manning to Frances Bradshaw, did, in fact, you come to learn from Frances that she had paid him ten thousand dollars?"

"I don't know where you get this ten-thousand-dollar figure from. I have never heard of it before except just now from you. Could you tell me where you got that figure?"

". . . . If I told you we got it from your bank records," Tesch resumed, "would that make you feel bad?"

"Would make me laugh."

"What kind of money did you hear was paid to Myles Manning by Frances Schreuder?"

"It was indicated between five and ten thousand. I was told seventy-six hundred, five thousand. I didn't know exactly."

"Who told you that?"

"She did."

"This was the spring of 1978?"

No, he said, it was the fall of 1977, around late September or October. She told him that Manning didn't do it, he said, and it was after that she asked him if he would get her a weapon. But when he found out he would have to sign for it, he "never got her one." They started talking, he admitted, about trying to mail-order one through a magazine, using "perhaps false names" and a post office box. "Many, many ideas were falling over the place," he said. (He had begun to cite Alexandria, Virginia, as one of them, but stopped himself. Marc had told him there was a large munitions depot in Alexandria where he could get a gun and have it mailed to a post office box in Fort Lee, New Jersey—just across the Hudson River from Manhattan.) He "listened to her discuss them. I acted more or less as a sounding board. . . . [They were] her ideas, not mine."

"From your knowledge of Frances Schreuder, can you tell us about her personality?"

"At what time period?"

"1978. Would you describe her as a headstrong woman?"

"Well, she . . . used to be a passive-aggressive personality. Passive-aggressive personality is the sort of person that is sometimes extremely passive then will flare up and be extremely aggressive."

"You have seen her on several occasions in that extremely aggressive personality?"

"Yes. At times, I have seen her in that other stage, the very passive."

"When she was in her aggressive mood, did you find her to be extremely persistent?"

"I believed her to be quite persistent, yes."

". . . How would you describe the relationship between Frances Schreuder and her son, Marc?"

"I would say they had a very, very close relationship."

"In fact, is it not true that Marc had almost no friends and that . . . his mother [was] perhaps his only close personal contact in the world?"

"I don't really know that."

Tesch had been working on Behrens for a while now, but

had been unable to shake him from what he had contended since the beginning of the hearing. Unless, of course, Behrens was lying about everything—and was more than just a "sounding board."

Hadn't Frances and he developed a plan in which Marc would "call a friend in Texas and obtain a weapon under the pretext of going camping"? Hadn't he been supposed to meet Marc in Phoenix after he obtained it? Hadn't he in fact gotten the gun from Marc in Phoenix, traveled to Salt Lake City, and killed Franklin Bradshaw? Hadn't *he,* not Marc, been the one who had brought the gun back to New York and used it to extort money from Frances? And when Frances would not pay him the money he had given her to hide, hadn't he then threatened to blame the murder on Marc?

To all of Tesch's imaginative scenarios, Behrens's answers were no. When asked why he had told Marilyn about the weapon, he stuck to his original story: he was concerned that everyone thought Larry had done it and he was "sore about the money" Frances owed him; the $10,000 reward, he said, had nothing to do with it.

"Now, from the beginning when you started talking to . . . Marilyn Reagan, after Frances Schreuder would not pay you the money, she told you immediately that she believed Frances committed the murder or had been indirectly involved?"

"She did not."

"Marilyn told you she had a grand dislike for Frances, did she not?"

"Not so much words. I picked up on it though. I had been told by Frances that she disliked Marilyn and I got the message that they didn't speak to each other. . . ."

"It may sound sharp, but in vernacular they hated each other, did they not?"

"I would say so. It appeared to me that way."

Tesch pulled out the eight-page statement Behrens had handed to Marc's lawyers in Hartford on December 27, 1980—the one that implicated Marilyn—and asked him about it. Behrens said that he had typed it at Frances's apartment that month; she and Marc had been there when he signed it; and Marc had driven him down to a notary in order to get it notarized.

In explaining why he had composed the statement he was now disavowing (and the oral one in Connecticut he had made and sworn to), he said there were two reasons: anger toward—and fear of—Marilyn ("promises were made to me that weren't true"); and "because Mrs. Schreuder told me I would get twenty years in jail and I was involved in this up to my eyeballs. . . ." She suggested, he said, that the only way for him to avoid that "was to turn the whole business around and say that Marilyn possessed the weapon initially."

But what about the note and money he received from Marilyn the day Jim Conway was at his apartment? He had been missing and she wanted to know where he had been. As far as the money—a $20 bill—he had written her many letters and "she claimed it was for stamps." He had earlier received another $20 bill. (Though he was not asked what it was for, Marilyn claimed it was $10 for the photos of Marc and Frances he had paid to have blown up.)

Once again Tesch asked him about the evening he received the gun. It was either the 23rd or the 24th, he said, probably the 23rd. Frances came first, around seven or eight. "She was very excited and she was gushing forth many things and indicating . . . that this was a murder weapon and she didn't know if Marc had been followed. She didn't want it on her own premises. . . . She was very conscious, very surveillance-conscious of who was following this weapon or Marc. . . ." She had given him the gun, a box of bullets, "an envelope with Cavenaugh's address," and, in substance, had told him Marc had just murdered her father.

What had he said?

"I was very excited," Behrens said. "I wanted to get her out of there and I said, 'Get the hell out of here. What the hell are you doing?' Words such as that. 'What do you want me to do with this?' Then she got out very fast. We didn't have any long conversation."

Later—either that night or the next day—Marc and she were at his apartment together. On this occasion, he recalled, Marc said that "he had seen a sheriff, that he had come back from Texas, that he had gotten this gun, that he had flown in, that the gun had been put in a suitcase in the baggage compartment. . . ."

Was there a discussion as to what to do with the weapon?

"Well, I said that if I wanted to turn you in I couldn't, because of this being on my property now. Then the offerings were made that I could sell the gun, I could throw it away, I could dispose of it or whatever I wanted to do with it." The next meeting was when he and Marc took Frances's car to get "a case" for the gun and a "gun cleaner kit."

"That, in fact, was done at your suggestion, was it not?"

"Yes, it was." Tesch had brought this up earlier. Why was he asking Behrens about it again?

"And the reason that was done," Tesch began, "was that now you had obtained a weapon without having to sign for it, you had hoped to use [it] against your own mother to get her estate?"

"No," Behrens said, knowing that this could only have been fed to Tesch by Marc and Frances and amused that Tesch had gotten it wrong: he was concerned that his *step-mother* was exerting such "undue influence" over his father that he would be cut out of his *father's* estate, but he was never thinking of using the gun to kill her.

"Right?" Tesch persisted. "Why then did you suggest that those items be procured?"

His father and grandfather were hunters, he said. In his father's summer house, there was always a shotgun and a Savage .30-30. He knew that anything made of metal needed to be cleaned "because within a week or so, it is going to rust if you don't do it." Behrens drove the car down to a gun shop whose name he couldn't remember; it was on Chambers Street between Church Street and Broadway. He went in alone and Marc stayed in the car. Either on his way in or out, he said, Marc took his picture—a picture, he said, that "his mother asked me to destroy"—and may have joined him in the store at one point. Once he got back to his apartment, he put "the paraphernalia" in the same place where the gun, bullets and envelope were.

Had he ever told either Marc or Frances that he was going to get rid of the gun?

Yes, he "certainly did somewhere along the line." And as everyone in that courtroom knew, if he had, they wouldn't be sitting there at that very moment—because the case, almost certainly, would never have been solved.

446

Never short of theories (and running out of time), Tesch came up with another one: one that had to do with the envelope Behrens had turned over to Marilyn Reagan.

Actually, Behrens said, it was the note inside the envelope that he had sent her. He had made a copy of it and burned the original; the first time he opened the envelope, he said, was just before he mailed it to Marilyn.

Wasn't it true, Tesch asked, that *he* had written the note on Kent stationery in order to frame Marc, and burned the original so that a handwriting analysis couldn't be done?

It was not true, Behrens said. He had burned the original and given her a copy so that she would have evidence—which she requested—and he could "stay in the background" and not have his fingerprints on it.

After a few more questions, Tesch threw in the towel.

On re-direct, having earlier heard Judge Banks (who had read all of Behrens's previous statements) express his feelings in open court that "I can't believe what he said either time. It's apparent he is a liar one time or the other," Jones led Behrens to the night he had had coffee with Frances at the Midnight Express in order to nail down the reasons he had recanted his original story.

On re-cross, Paul Van Dam stood up to do the questioning. In a tone of disbelief, he asked the fifty-five-year-old school-teacher if he was really telling the court that Frances Schreuder was able "to paint a scenario for you, an older man, well educated, who had lived longer than she in her life, and literally scare you" into doing the things he had described.

"I have had junior high students scare me who were sixteen. They have sometimes overwhelmed me."

"Would it be fair to say you are easily intimidated?"

". . . I am saying I can be intimidated, not whether it is easy or hard."

"Were you also afraid of Marc?"

"At one time I didn't know. I just really didn't know because if somebody commits a murder, you don't know what they are going to do. I didn't know really. Mostly, I wasn't afraid of Marc."

But if he had simply "walked out to a garbage can or a dumpster or the river" and dropped the gun in, wouldn't his involvement have been finished? Had he ever thought of that?

Yes, he had, but could give no real rational explanation why he hadn't done so.

He had said in his statement to Joel Campbell, Van Dam reminded him, that Frances had put a lot of pressure on Marc. What did he mean by that?

She would lock him out of the house if he didn't do what she wanted. She would "put pressure on him to do this act, put all kind of pressure." Locking him out would be one way, he said, screaming at him another.

Did he feel she was a person with "an unusual ability" to pressure people?

At times, he said; she made him "think quite a bit about twenty years in jail and I interpret that as pressure."

The three-day hearing was over. Behrens had been severely tested, but had not been broken.

Once Behrens left the courtroom, Banks informed Marc he could take the stand in his own defense—either under oath or not—but he declined. Despite the judge's lack of faith in Behrens's testimony, he felt that even *without* it, he had enough evidence to bind Marc over to stand trial. And in making his final remarks, he reiterated that point of view. "Under oath," began the judge, whose sideburns and chiseled face give him the appearance of a tough Western lawman, "he's given two entirely different stories. And although he gave a reason why there is a difference in the testimony, quite frankly I would throw the whole thing out except as it is corroborated by other evidence in the trial. That's why," he said, peering at Tesch and Van Dam, "I indicated my feeling before you completed cross-examination on him and certainly in your argument. I am rejecting his testimony as far as purposes of this hearing are concerned. It's something that the prosecutor has to struggle with and gives the defense a lot of ammunition at the time of trial. . . .

"Mr. Schreuder," he continued, looking right at Marc, "you are bound over to stand trial in the Third Judicial

District Court of the State of Utah . . . on the charge of criminal homicide, murder in the first degree."

As Marc left the courtroom in his green felt slippers and returned to jail, he had no idea of the forces that had already been set into motion.

48// When Steve Klein received the teletype just before one-thirty that Thursday afternoon, the investigator was not totally surprised by what it said, but he wanted to make sure. The message had come from Joel Campbell, but since Klein's dealings had been with Mike George and Don Harman, he spoke with Harman on the phone. Harman confirmed it: they had a warrant for Frances's arrest, and it was being sent by express mail.

Klein, along with two other investigators, arrived at 10 Gracie Square shortly after two. A doorman told them that Frances had left the building not long before. Klein asked to see the manager, Gary Perman, whom he had met when he was inquiring about Marc five months earlier. If she was out—and Klein had some doubt that she was—they wanted to be waiting for her when she got back. But when Perman contacted the housekeeper she told him that Mrs. Schreuder was at Lincoln Center and probably wouldn't be back until much later. Nevertheless, the investigators set up a surveillance on the north end of the building and waited.

Hours passed with no sign of Frances. Perhaps she had been tipped off. Security was especially heavy that day and evening at the exclusive address. Aside from Madame Chiang Kai-shek's bodyguards, who maintain a constant vigil, a number of New York City police officers were on duty to protect the Turkish Ambassador to the United Nations from possible attack (a fellow Turkish ambassador had recently been assassinated in Europe); in addition, Steve Ross was throwing a huge party and the gates to the building were in constant motion as limousines came and went.

At ten, under instructions from his office, Klein terminated the surveillance and planned to return early the next morning.

For a young associate in a high-powered New York law firm, five in the afternoon rarely represents the end of a working day. But for six weeks David Frankel had been toiling on a tender-offer case, often staying at the office until well past midnight. When the case was finally settled around five that Thursday afternoon, Frankel left work for the unfamiliar environment of his apartment and what he hoped would be his first good night's sleep in a while. He turned in about ten and was fast asleep when the phone rang an hour later.

"Frances," he said, recognizing her voice immediately, "how did you possibly get my home phone number?"

"I looked it up," she said, sounding hysterical.

"What's the problem?" he asked, none too pleased to be woken.

The police were at her door, she said, with a warrant for her arrest. He *had* to come and represent her.

"I'll try to find you another lawyer," he said, not knowing that Norman Ostrow (Marc's former lawyer, who stopped representing him after his arrest) was in contact with her. "But if the police have a valid warrant for your arrest, I suggest you let them in."

No, she was not about to do that.

"Then they'll break down your door."

No, she assured him, they're not allowed.

"They most certainly are," he said. He told her that he would call her back and immediately phoned Mike Armstrong to discuss the situation.

Throughout the long night—almost every half hour, Frankel said—Frances continued to phone him, claiming that the police had "come back" and asking him what she should do. By seven on Friday morning, he was in his office, trying to reach Mike Shaw, a prominent attorney and close friend of Armstrong's from their days in the U.S. Attorney's Office together.

* * *

Steve Klein and Ernie Cruz returned to 10 Gracie Square at about the same time that Frankel was getting to his office. Two doormen assured the investigators that Frances had neither entered nor left the building since the previous evening—and were reluctant to let them in. Just as Klein and Cruz began explaining that they had a warrant, one of the building's tenants opened the door on his way out. Klein grabbed hold of it and they let themselves in, first going to see Perman and then proceeding to Frances's apartment.

Klein rang the doorbell of 6A and Paulette asked who it was. Identifying himself as Cruz, he asked her to open up. She said she wouldn't, but he could hear her "talking to another female in whispered conversation." So he rang the bell again, officially informing her that he had a warrant for Frances's arrest. It made no difference.

While Klein continued ringing the bell and pounding on the door, Cruz went back downstairs to get Perman. But he too was unsuccessful.

They had been there about a half hour before Klein, who could no longer hear any movement on the other side of the door, decided to solicit help from the 19th Precinct. Aside from realizing he would need assistance in all the exits to the apartment, he hoped that "the uniforms would do it. Very often people see a uniform and they realize that it really is the police and they open up." But, alas, this didn't work either.

Klein tried to phone Frances from Perman's office. No answer. At about eight-thirty—roughly ninety minutes from when they first arrived—a note was slipped under the door and into the hall. As Ernie Cruz picked it up and read it, Paulette instructed them to "call Ostrow," the man whose name and home number were on it. When Klein phoned him, Norman Ostrow said that he had spoken with Paulette *and* Frances, and that Frances was "agitated." If Klein could please give her some additional time, he felt sure he could persuade her to open up and surrender. Klein reluctantly agreed and went back upstairs. But when he heard the phone continue to ring and not be picked up, he began shouting through the door to Frances that her attorney was trying to reach her.

Getting no response, Klein again went downstairs and

phoned Ostrow. The lawyer pleaded for more time and said that Frances's mother was trying to reach her from Salt Lake. Shuttling back and forth like Henry Kissinger on a peace mission to the Mideast, Klein decided he would write a note. He informed Frances what he had said earlier—that Ostrow was trying to phone her—and that her mother was as well.

But all Klein could hear was a ringing phone. He went back to Perman's office once more and phoned Ostrow for the third time. For nearly two hours Klein had tried to be patient and make the arrest as discreetly as he could. But there was a limit, and the investigator had just about reached it. He told Ostrow that if Frances did not open the door, they would have to force it open.

While Ostrow said that he wanted to keep trying, he also told Klein that he was "very concerned" about Mrs. Schreuder's "emotional state," that she sounded "suicidal" to him when they originally spoke, and that she was "potentially a threat" to her daughter, who was in the apartment with her.

"That triggered it," Klein recalled later. "I said, 'Well then I'll *have* to go into the apartment. . . . You've told me she's in there, that she's hysterical—possibly suicidal—and that her eight-year-old daughter is in there. I have an obligation to at least protect the little girl's life, if not Frances's.'"

They broke the door down. As Klein went searching throughout the first floor of the duplex, the three police officers went upstairs to the second and found Frances in a nightgown and in bed with Lavinia. The moment Klein got into the room, he told her that she was under arrest and began to read her her rights. She and Lavinia were "crying and hysterical," Klein said, recalling that she neither acknowledged the arrest nor gave any "outward" sign of understanding what he had read to her.

At nine twenty-two the phone rang and Klein answered it. It was David Frankel. While neither he (because he was still Marc's attorney) nor Ostrow (for the same conflict-of-interest reasons that had prevented him from continuing as Marc's attorney in October) could represent Frances, Frankel told Klein he would assist her until she retained somebody for her who could. Frances was undressed, Klein told Frankel, and was not cooperating with a policewoman who had just arrived.

Thinking how "incredibly patient" the police were being, Frankel got on the phone with Frances and persuaded her to get dressed. On the other line he was speaking with Mike Shaw, who had agreed to represent her. Frances told Frankel she would get dressed, but couldn't leave until she finished writing her poetry and didn't want to leave until he and Shaw got there. Frankel asked Klein if that would be okay and he agreed. Since Frances had calmed down, Klein decided once more to advise her of her rights, and, this time, she was able to acknowledge each question.

As Frances began to get dressed, Klein was on the phone outside her bedroom, asking his bureau to send a female investigator who could help accompany her to Central Booking.

"Mommy, Mommy, don't," Klein heard Lavinia scream and dropped the phone, rushing into the room with Ernie Cruz. Frances was trying to get out the window, but was struggling with Lavinia, who was holding on to her left thigh. Klein grabbed Frances by her shoulders, while Cruz pried Lavinia loose. As soon as she let go, Klein pulled Frances back in, put her on the bed, cuffed her and took her to the precinct.

From the 19th Precinct on East 67th Street, Klein phoned the Emergency Medical Service and asked that some paramedics be sent to examine Frances. David Frankel arrived at the precinct in a siren-wailing squad car, having been told at Gracie Square, "Counselor, I'm sorry, we had to take the alleged perpetrator away" and assured that "it will all be explained to you down at the precinct." While not unmindful of how "Kojakian" it all seemed, Frankel was angry that Klein had promised to wait for him and then broken his word. He went rushing into the precinct and confronted the investigator, who asked him to calm down while he explained what happened.

Frankel went and sat with Frances, who was "absolutely hysterical" and handcuffed to a chair. "I mean," he said later, "here was this woman from 10 Gracie Square, obviously out of her element. I just felt this compassion for her and I was the only face that she knew. I reluctantly signed in as her attorney—Shaw had not yet arrived—but decided I didn't care. Here was this hysterical woman whom I could help for a little while."

He told her not to say *anything* to him; she told him that she just wanted to hold his hand. For more than five minutes the two of them sat there together, until the six-foot-five-inch patrician figure of Mike Shaw appeared. Shaw asked Frankel to brief him about the case and go over some of its legal issues. As Marc's attorney, Frankel had to be very circumspect, and he was.

The paramedic who examined Frances told Klein that while she was physically sound, he was concerned about her emotional stability. He recommended that she be taken to the psychiatric emergency room at Bellevue Hospital. After Frances spent more than two hours at Bellevue, which did not have facilities for women prisoners, a staff psychiatrist concluded that she was in further need of care. So Klein took Frances to the City Hospital Center at Elmhurst, a half hour away in Queens, arriving there about three in the afternoon. After an initial examination, a psychiatrist was inclined to release her; but when Klein informed the doctor that Frances had tried to jump out a sixth-floor window earlier in the day, she was admitted for further observation and tests.

Earlier that day, beginning with accounts in the *New York Post* ("POLICE: HEIRESS TOLD SON TO KILL GRANDDAD") and Salt Lake's *Deseret News* ("Daughter accused of plotting '78 death"), the newspapers and wire services began to cover the story. Over the next two days, while the *New York Times* was restrained in its coverage, the *Daily News* (which had run only a small story at the time of Marc's arrest in New York) ran the story as its lead headline on page one: "NAB MOM & SON IN DEATH PLOT" was followed—based on an interview with Joel Campbell about Larry Bradshaw—by "2ND SON IN SLAY PLOT? Mom's rich dad was victim."

Campbell was telling the media he'd heard "a rumor" that the Bradshaw estate was worth between $400,000,000 and $700,000,000; Steve Swindle, the estate's lawyer, would only say that it was "very substantial." The stories told of how "tight" Bradshaw was and of the feuding that was going on in the family at the time he was killed; they said that Frances had ordered the killing out of fear she and Marc would be cut out of her father's will or, according to one account, that they already had been. Myles Manning was referred to as "an acquaintance" who had been paid $5,000 to kill Bradshaw and "apparently never came to Salt Lake City"; Richard Behrens as "a friend and former business associate" whom Frances had first asked to get, then to hold, the murder weapon. No details were given about where the gun was obtained—only that Frances's sister Marilyn Reagan had received it from Behrens and turned it in to New York City police in October of 1980.

The detective who received the gun that night couldn't quite believe the news when he saw it on television. Ed Regan simply hadn't thought the case would ever reach this point. Even the normally unruffled Al Sullivan was stirred by the press reaction and told Ernie Jones at the beginning of the following week that "there are guys in New York who would give their right arm to have their case on the front page of the *Daily News*." Mike George, while delighted by the arrest and disappointed once more he couldn't be there to make it, was amazed by the patience Steve Klein had shown. "If I would have had *any* inkling she was in that apartment, the door would have come off in five seconds. Apparently in New York, you don't do that in Gracie Square. But that doesn't mean anything to me. I could give a shit less. If it was Spencer W. Kimball [the President and Prophet of the Mormon Church] and he's in that place and I've got a warrant, the door comes off and that's all there is to it."

But as Klein explained later, "the whole point of the 'negotiations' was to protect her privacy and to prevent the little girl from being traumatized by the arrest of her mother."

The New York legal community is, in many ways, a small and tight-knit world; not only were Mike Shaw and Mike Armstrong good friends and former colleagues, but earlier that week Shaw had received a long-distance phone call from a lawyer who represented a prospective codefendant in a matter on which they had both been working. Larry Goldman was calling from Salt Lake to discuss the case, mentioned why he was out there, and said he would be back in his New York office on Friday. When he arrived, there was a message waiting for him. Shaw had called to say they now had two cases in common: he was representing Frances Schreuder.

Mike Shaw had his work cut out for him. Since he would be facing some of the same legal issues in terms of bail and extradition that Armstrong and Frankel had with Marc, he obtained copies of their briefs and spoke with Paul Van Dam in Utah. As soon as Frances was declared fit to leave Elmhurst she would be arraigned, and Shaw wanted to be prepared.

On Monday, the *New York Times* carried a story in which Doug Steele talked about the memo Bradshaw had written—the one indicating that Frances was to be cut from his will—but pointed out that since it wasn't notarized and a new will had never surfaced, he didn't feel his boss really intended to change it. He only wanted his daughter to hear of it, Steele felt, and "be frightened" into changing her ways. "But the memo backfired," he concluded. "In essence he shot himself. He pulled the trigger."

In the same article, Marilyn denied any kind of feud existed among the sisters. "But there was a lot of friction between our parents," she admitted, "over our sister demanding a lot of money that my mother wanted to give her and my father did not. . . ."

Around midday Steve Klein got word from Elmhurst that Frances was ready to be released and he drove out to the hospital to pick her up. The hospital's report said she had "calmed down a great deal," was fully aware she had to face arraignment, and had discussed her case with her attorney.

The following day, after Frances spent the night in jail, Mike Shaw argued in State Supreme Court that Frances should be entitled to bail. Referring in his papers to this "bizarre and tragic situation," he argued that the "integrity" of the warrant against Frances "plainly must stand or fall on Richard Behrens's testimony"—testimony, he pointed out, that a Utah judge had found to be "wholly incredible" the week before. Not only had her son been released on bail the previous November, but the case against him was far stronger because *no one* was claiming that Frances had even been in Utah at the time of the murder—one of the main arguments he would use in helping her fight extradition. Besides, Shaw said, she was a "good bail risk": there was "not a shred of criminal allegation or charge in her past" (he was not aware of her 1964 conviction on the charge of third-degree assault); she was on the board of the New York City Ballet; and she had complete responsibility for her young daughter.

A winning argument before one judge, however, does not necessarily guarantee success in front of another. Though his colleague Milton Williams had been persuaded to allow Marc to be released on bail in November of 1981, Benjamin Altman was not prepared to do the same for Frances. But he did allow her to spend a few minutes with the person who had flown two thousand miles to be by her side.

Berenice embraced her youngest daughter. With their heads on each other's shoulders, they cried for five minutes before Frances was led away and eventually taken to Rikers Island.

"It's all been such a horrible nightmare. I can't take it any more," Frances said, pleading with Berenice, "Please help me, get me out of here."

Berenice had responded to her daughter's cries for help in the past and she wasn't going to let her down. Two of her grandsons were in jail and now Frances was; her oldest daughter had not only turned in the gun but was telling the press that her own mother was partly to blame for what had happened. Berenice's world was caving in; she had more money than she could ever spend in her remaining years, but it was neither bringing her peace nor buying her happiness. As she left the courtroom, on her way to Gracie Square to take care of her only granddaughter (who had been told that "her mommy was in the hospital"), Berenice snapped: "How can they put her on trial for this?"

Frances spent her forty-fourth birthday, on April 6, at Rikers Island. She had been there for two weeks, and when her mother came to visit, Frances told her that two black inmates had pinned her down and "slashed" her ears. Though

Berenice sometimes had to wait two hours to see her daughter, she still trooped out there three times a week; and once Lavinia figured out that her mother was not in the hospital, she went a few times as well.

For Easter, Paulette took Lavinia to a store on East End Avenue and bought her a ballerina bunny. Few merchants in the neighborhood, if any, were unaware of what had happened, and the owner of this particular store saw Lavinia often.

"She's a sad little creature," the owner was saying a month after Frances's arrest, recalling how Lavinia came to the store once with a baby carriage and a doll inside it. "Most little girls hug and kiss their dolls, but for her it was a kind of object that she directed no affection toward." On another occasion, she came in to buy some Smurfs. She had $30 with her, and when the owner asked if her mother knew she was about to spend all of that, Lavinia suggested the owner could call her and find out. When she did, Paulette answered and told her that Lavinia could have whatever she wanted.

In Salt Lake City, Ernie Jones began preparing to go to trial as the case continued to attract national attention. In *Newsweek*, a piece entitled "Who Killed Grandfather?" played on Marc's "passion for Agatha Christie murder mysteries" and said that he seemed to be "starring in one." The *National Enquirer* told readers, in its purple-prose lead, that "Naked greed was the demon that whispered murder to heiress Frances Schreuder."

While the prosecutor was publicly expressing the hope that mother and son could be tried together and Marc's lawyers were saying they would actively oppose that, Jones knew that Frances would fight extradition as long as possible. And as he sat in his office sifting through the evidence, the thorough prosecutor also knew something else: Richard Behren's credibility as a witness was so shaky that unless it could be shown that he was nowhere near Salt Lake on the day of the murder, the defense would only step up, at trial, the kind of battering-ram attack they leveled at him during Marc's preliminary.

So on April 21, exactly one year from the time he first took over the investigation, Mike George embarked on another trip. Along with Neil Boswell, a fellow investigator, he flew to

Washington, D.C., rented a car and drove south to the town of Lynchburg, Virginia. Behrens had testified that Lynchburg was not only a place where he used to work but where he visited for about a week in July of 1978, from the 13th to the 19th. It was also the place where he had looked to buy a gun for Frances on an earlier visit. Behrens told George that he usually stayed with an old friend of his, a woman named Dorothy Ferguson, and that he had stayed with Ferguson that July.

Ferguson told George she would talk to them, but only in her lawyer's office. After they spent nearly three hours with her there, Ferguson relaxed enough to invite them to her house. She not only confirmed what Behrens had told George (though Behrens didn't tell her whom he wanted to buy a gun for, she said), but recalled that she had made some phone calls to Behrens *after* he left, and probably still had the old bill to prove it.

While she went hunting for the month and year in question, George knew that this kind of information could possibly derail the defense's best-laid plans. When she reappeared and gave the receipt to him, George was pleased by what he saw: phone calls to Richard Behrens on July 20 and July 22—the day before the murder. Unless Behrens could establish his exact whereabouts on that Sunday, this would probably have to do.

Before leaving Lynchburg, George and Boswell went to see the two people whom Behrens had said he had asked about a gun. The more people who could corroborate Behrens, the better. One of them, a friend of Ferguson's who worked at an Army-Navy store, was recuperating at home after a series of heart attacks and was in no condition to recall or identify anybody. But the other, who worked in a candy store, was: he picked the schoolteacher out of a photo lineup and confirmed that he had been looking for a weapon to buy.

From Lynchburg the investigators drove back to Washington and flew on to New York. Mike George had another laundry list of things he wanted to do and wasted little time in getting started. He and Boswell had dinner with Vittorio Gentile and his family, went to see Marilyn and Bob Reagan, and paid a visit to Carolyn Karoliszyn-Morris. George knew from experience that prospective witnesses can become quite nervous close to the time of trial and that keeping them calm was important.

They went to see the "real" Susie Coleman at the delicatessen on East End Avenue—George having seen her mother in December—and, aside from saying that Marc was a momma's boy and had told her *before* his arrest in Connecticut that he was a suspect in his grandfather's murder, she offered little else. They went around the corner to Gracie Square and met Paulette. She showed them the first floor of Frances's duplex, but not the second; Berenice was upstairs in one of the bedrooms. Aside from its spaciousness, George was not impressed; in fact, he said later, he would much rather have a place in Queens, looking across the river at Manhattan, than live in Gracie Square and wake up each morning to the sight of Queens.

On Sunday, the 25th, having searched through Richard Behrens's apartment the night before "for anything negative on him that we should know and that he wouldn't tell us," George drove to Pennsylvania to see Larry. Having no idea whether Larry, whom he'd not met before, would speak with him, he just showed up at Northampton County Prison unannounced. Larry had been given a sentence the previous May of two years five months to four years eleven months; with credit for time served, he was eligible for parole in a month's time. As Larry was brought to the room where George and Boswell were waiting, George could tell right away that "he was a sick kid. His fingernails were extremely long, he was filthy, and all of his gums were bleeding. When he first walked in, I told him who we were and he turned around and started to walk out. I said, 'Wait a minute, just hear me out.'"

George gave him his pitch and Larry agreed to stay and talk, shaking and grinning the whole time. Amazed by Larry's "unbelievable recall," the investigators listened to him describe his bus trip from New York to Salt Lake in the summer of 1978 and all the highways, towns and places he stayed along the way. He said how happy his grandfather was that he had come down to help him the late afternoon and evening before the murder; how he and his grandmother had invited him to join them for dinner but he wouldn't; and how he had woke up the next morning to go flying and, while up in the air, saw cars parked around the house and eventually came home.

Since Larry would answer no specific questions about the murder itself, George tried to goad him. He pointed out the airline tickets with L. Schreuder and L. Gentile on them, saying that Marc and Frances had tried to frame him, that his mother really hated him, and that he and his brother never really got on all that well.

Larry's initial reaction to the airline tickets was one of total amazement and laughter (later he would say that it didn't surprise him at all). He wouldn't talk about his own crime to George and Boswell, but did tell them that he now realized that the things he believed were happening at that time really weren't. He opened up about his childhood—about how his mother constantly locked him out and always favored Marc—and it was from this that George felt he gleaned a great deal.

"It enabled us," he said later, "to focus in on Marc's fear—what really pushed him into committing the murder—of being locked out. We didn't know Larry had been locked out until we talked to him. He was always the odd man out in that threesome. Marc wanted Frances's acceptance—and if that meant alienating himself from his brother, he would do that. Marc always wanted to be on the inner fold."

Before they left that day, George pressed Larry for his opinion on whether his mother and brother had committed the murder. "His impressions were that they had done it," George said. "He didn't come right out and say it, but didn't deny it either. I was left with the impression that he knew all that had happened with them."

Looking wan and depressed, Frances appeared in court the next day wearing the same burgundy suit she had left Gracie Square in five weeks before. But by the end of the day, she had reason to feel better: a different judge from the one she had been arraigned before decided to let her out on bail, essentially accepting the same argument that Michael Armstrong had made on behalf of Marc: that once the Governor's extradition warrant arrived, a judge had the power to grant bail if he so chose. For George it was "a double whammy": not only could he not escort Frances back to Utah, but Joel

Campbell's haste had come back to haunt him. In his eagerness to have the warrant signed, Campbell had taken it to a circuit court judge who crossed out the stipulation for "no bail" and wrote in the amount of $500,000—the same amount that was now being set for her in New York.

When Frances was released from Rikers Island the next day, her departure caused a stir. The certified check that gained her freedom, a Department of Correction spokesman told the *New York Post,* was the most money his department had seen "since the day [multimillionaire drug kingpin] Nicky Barnes showed up with his $1 million bail in cash."

49// Before leaving New York to fly back to Utah, George wanted to see Myles Manning. Once Manning's name had been brought out by Joe Tesch at the preliminary hearing, Jones and George were determined to show at Marc's trial that Marc knew all about Manning—that one of the reasons *he* had to kill his grandfather was that Manning had not.

But the situation with Manning had changed since George saw him in December. For one thing, George had not been able to find the doorman who Manning said could confirm that he had gone to Frances's apartment. For another, neither Utah nor New York had direct access to him any longer. Four days after Frances's arrest—and two days after his name appeared in all the papers, including the one he worked for—Manning retained a large, big-talking attorney from Brooklyn named Edward ("just call me Eddie") P. Dean. A Fighting Irishman from Notre Dame, Dean informed Al Sullivan and Ernie Jones that all future contact with Manning had to go through him. Manning had been promised immunity but he hadn't received the grant in writing; he not only wanted Dean to get him that, but decided if he was going to have to testify in Utah, he wanted a New York attorney with him. They had become a package deal. Utah couldn't have one without the other.

George and Boswell had arranged to meet the duo for

lunch at an Italian restaurant not far from the District Attorney's Office. When the lawyer and his client were fifteen minutes late, George walked to the bar and there they were.

"We knew we were in trouble right from the outset with Dean," George said later, trying to explain his frustration. "He was a Utahn's image of a New York person: he was pushy, ignorant, and we did not like him at all."

But they needed Manning and, three days after the lunch, the immunity grant was signed. Four and a half years after he claimed he had first been asked, Myles Manning would be going out to Salt Lake after all.

Not long after that lunch, Manning was food shopping in a D'Agostino's on the Upper East Side and "bumped into the little namby-pamby who likes to wear Bermuda shorts." When they first met, Manning and Richard Behrens had been neighbors, a printer and a schoolteacher, leading lives of anonymity in a city that usually ensures that. Now they were men on whom a large spotlight was shining—men whose names had been in *Newsweek* and the *New York Times,* men who, despite their cloaks of immunity, were going to continue finding out just how hot and uncomfortable that spotlight of notoriety could be.

Each spring, the School of American Ballet has a workshop dinner, and the surprise appearance at 1982's event was made by Frances. She came alone and was invited by David Richardson to sit at his table. Many of the people present were uncomfortable and few wanted to speak with her. Though she was innocent until proven otherwise, what she was accused of doing hardly had created the kind of publicity either the school or the New York City Ballet delighted in. Yet one board member—who described Frances as "very emotionally driven, very intense, neurotic and strange"—said that he didn't believe she was guilty: anyone with the kind of strong interest in dance that she clearly had, he suggested, couldn't possibly do something like this. And Frances herself told David Richardson how supportive everyone in the company had been—especially Lincoln Kirstein, who had sent her a number of letters, she said, and was completely behind her.

"Did Lavinia know that you were in jail?" Richardson asked.

Lavinia had originally been told she was sick, she said, and was relieved to find out that she was not.

Richardson remarked on how thin she looked, and asked what her chances were. She couldn't talk about it, she said, but felt her chances for acquittal were very good.

In court earlier that day, one week after Mike George had left town and unbeknownst to Richardson, the judge had ordered Frances to go to Utah. But he agreed to stay that order so that Mike Shaw could appeal.

As Marc's trial date got closer, Joe Tesch and Paul Van Dam began filing loads of defense motions—for everything from a change of venue because of pretrial publicity to the prohibiting of testimony by the former Medical Examiner because of controversy surrounding his academic qualifications. Ernie Jones, meanwhile, was telling the press that the state was going to push for the death penalty. "I think most people have a hard time believing that a grandson could ever kill his grandfather—or that his mother could ever put him up to it." Because of the planning involved, Jones said, "to me, this is the type of offense where the death penalty should be asked for."

Berenice Bradshaw had left Salt Lake and Mike George couldn't find her.

He wanted to subpoena her as a witness for Marc's trial and was disturbed to find out she wasn't in New York either. When he finally learned that she had gone to Cape Elizabeth, Maine, to visit some relatives, the local police wouldn't cooperate with his request to serve her, nor would the relatives even acknowledge knowing anyone by the name of Bradshaw.

Ernie Jones got a telephone call from Kevin Kurumada, a handsome thirty-one-year-old attorney who had formerly been in the Legal Defender's Office and was now in private practice. Kurumada had just been hired to represent Mrs. Bradshaw, he said, and told Jones that he wanted a grant of immunity for his client before she would consent to testify.

(Kurumada, whose father is a dentist whom Berenice used

to see as a patient until Franklin decided his fees were too expensive, had been recommended to Berenice by the law firm of Watkiss & Watkiss, which had begun serving as local counsel for Frances at the request of a firm in Washington. Though Mike Shaw had gotten Frances released on bail, and was continuing to fight her extradition battle, it had been decided that if or when her case came to trial, the Washington firm of Williams & Connolly—whose leading light was Edward Bennett Williams, one of the top attorneys in the country—would represent her. With word spreading throughout the Salt Lake legal community and around the courthouse that Williams & Connolly had come on board, strong speculation began that Frances would plead insanity: after all, Vincent Fuller of that firm was using that defense for John Hinckley at that moment.)

Jones told Kurumada that he didn't think a grant of immunity was necessary. But Kurumada insisted. Statements had been made about her forging checks, and once her daughter was arrested and sent to jail, she was concerned that the same thing could happen to her. She had checked into a Maine hospital, and there she would remain unless Kurumada could get that grant.

While Jones assured Kurumada that the state was not going to prosecute her for forgery, he decided to play ball anyway—under one condition: the grant would not include *any* participation she might have had in the murder. If they were able to uncover any evidence along those lines, they would still be able to charge her.

Once Kurumada agreed to that, Jones told him to go ahead and draw it up. For Jones, this was just one more curious incident in a case that had had its share of them. Normally, the widow of a man who was murdered would be the state's very best friend. But he had long ago accepted the fact that *nothing* about this case had—or probably ever would—run true to form.

Marc's lawyers, increasingly nervous about the prospect of the Hanging Judge presiding over his trial, were trying to buy as much time as they could. The trial had been postponed from June 7 to the 14th. But their motion—that Jay Banks should be disqualified as the trial judge because he had also been the committing magistrate and because of comments he later made about the strength of the evidence—had been rejected.

While Marc's fate would ultimately lie in the hands of a jury, the two attorneys knew full well that a judge is like the captain of a ship: not only do most jurors respect his authority, but he can affect the mood of a trial in many ways—by the evidence he allows or disallows and the comments he makes during the course of it.

They also made a motion requiring Frances to attend the trial, arguing that her testimony would be crucial to Marc's defense in regard to Richard Behrens, whom they considered the state's key witness. At first Banks granted that motion—which also would have given her a temporary immunity from extradition—but then vacated it a day later, saying that she could not be compelled to testify and possibly incriminate herself.

Of the many other motions the defense filed, one in particular hinted at the kind of strategy they might have in mind: a request for more time in which to enter a possible insanity plea for Marc—a motion Banks took under advisement, then rejected. As far as he was concerned, these boys had had plenty of time to prepare themselves for trial. Eighty prospective jurors were being called for that Monday morning, and Jay Elmer Banks was ready to go.

On the third floor of the jail, in cell 3B16, Marc Schreuder waited. In the three months since his arrest in March for missing the lineup, he had developed a reputation for being a quiet, cooperative prisoner who borrowed a lot of books from the jail's makeshift library, ate an inordinate number of candy bars and played a solid though conservative game of chess. ("He played chess," one inmate said, "like a Jewish mother cooks dinner—risk-free.") Mary Lou came to visit him regularly (as did Berenice, when she was in town), and while he forged friendships with some inmates in his tier, two others threatened to take his life. In a prison's harsh, unwritten code, killing someone in your family is generally understood to be nearly as unacceptable to other prisoners as being a snitch or a spy or a child molester. One of the prisoners who threatened him was willing to spare his life if

Marc allowed him to charge a certain amount in the jail's commissary on his account; but the other one warned Marc that if he so much as talked to him, "he wouldn't live to see the next day."

When he was not reading and playing chess, Marc would use the phone as often as possible. Even though two times a week was supposed to be the maximum, Marc would bribe guards with candy bars and that would do the trick. Contact with his mother was virtually nonexistent at this point; so when Marc was not on the phone with Mary Lou, he was often speaking with his stockbroker back in New York. Even from jail, where he was being given Thorazine as a tranquilizer, his interest in the market was as strong as ever—something that would have made his grandfather extremely proud.

On Sunday, June 13, the day before the trial was to begin, Ernie Jones was in his office going over last-minute strategy with Dave Walsh, a fellow Deputy County Attorney who had been assigned two weeks earlier to help Jones with the case. What was considered an undesirable case in October of 1980 when Jones first began working on it was clearly more than that now, and Walsh was pleased to be asked. Members of the Army Reserve, they had been drilling together earlier that day and had come to the office in order to meet with Ted Cannon, the County Attorney.

Jones had gotten a phone call the night before from Marc's lawyers. In a pretrial hearing on Friday, they had accused Jones of withholding evidence from them and making misleading statements; now they were calling to make one last stab at a deal. If Jones would agree to a lesser charge of manslaughter, the state could save itself a lot of time and money. As he had before when they had raised this, Jones told them to forget it, but did not reject the idea of a plea bargain entirely. He slept on it that night and decided to discuss a counterproposal with Ted Cannon that afternoon: an offer to reduce the charge to second-degree murder in exchange for the one thing Jones felt he would eventually need—Marc's testimony against his mother.

But when Jones called that Sunday with his offer—one he had mentioned before, but never formally extended—it was promptly rejected: second-degree didn't interest them, and

Marc was not prepared to testify against Frances. They had one card left to play, and if their client would let them, they were inclined to use it.

Nobody saw it coming—and by midday on Monday, word had spread as quickly as if a Mormon missionary had converted a band of heathens. Paul Van Dam and Joe Tesch had surprised everybody by making a motion to waive a trial by jury and let a judge decide Marc's fate—any judge but Jay Elmer Banks.

The statement Banks had made during a hearing on March 30—that he felt there was sufficient evidence to convict Marc beyond a reasonable doubt—had scared the hell out of Van Dam at the time. When the defense lost its motion to have Banks disqualified, Van Dam asked Banks if he would ever consider disqualifying himself were the defense to waive a jury trial. At the time, Banks said that he would, and it was that very promise that Van Dam was asking his former boss to make good on now.

With eighty potential jurors waiting patiently, Jay Banks retired to his chambers to do some "soul searching." After an hour, he took the bench. There was no doubt in his mind that he could preside fairly over this trial, he said; but as "a man of my word," he was going to step aside.

The strategy had worked—but only partly. The defense had succeeded in removing Banks, but not in gaining the one other thing—a long delay—they had hoped might follow as a result. On Tuesday, the Utah Supreme Court not only rejected another series of defense motions but the presiding judge of the district court immediately appointed James S. Sawaya to hear the case. If the defense had surprised everyone by waiving a jury, Sawaya had a surprise for the defense: he was not going to require weeks of preparation; in fact, he was ready to hear the case at ten o'clock the next morning.

Part Five//

This is a boy on something like a runaway boxcar or a ship in a typhoon.

—JOE TESCH

50// Under normal circumstances, the twenty-eight seats in Judge Sawaya's oval, windowless courtroom on the fourth floor of Salt Lake's Metropolitan Hall of Justice are never filled to capacity. But these weren't normal circumstances. This was a murder trial—one that had not only been the focus of considerable publicity, but carried with it the possibility that Marc could face the same Utah firing squad that Gary Gilmore had more than five years before. And there is nothing like a murder trial—the murder of a Mormon, no less—to bring out the public and the press in a law-and-order state like Utah. Long before ten that Wednesday morning, people were pressed against the door of the courtroom, waiting for the bailiff to let them in.

It had been nearly four years since Franklin James Bradshaw had been murdered, and Ernie Jones had been rehearsing his opening statement in the same exacting way he had once prepared for championship debates. He knew that Joe Tesch and Paul Van Dam would probably be challenging *every* piece of evidence and *every* witness. If Jones was to get the conviction he believed to be proper, he would have to earn it. There were advantages and disadvantages to not having a jury; and one of the big advantages, Jones felt, was that the judge, being the sole trier of fact, would be inclined to let a great deal of testimony and exhibits into evidence so that he would have a more solid basis for making his ultimate decision.

In a passionate, hour-long opening argument, Jones did his best to portray the man for whose death he was ultimately seeking justice and to lay out the case the state would attempt to prove. Calm, emotionless, and dressed like the prep-school student he once was, Marc sat next to his lawyers and listened to the prosecutor describe his grandfather as if he had been the embodiment of the American Dream.

At the time of his death, Jones said, Franklin Bradshaw could not be considered a typical man of seventy-six. He was a man of ingenuity and ambition who became a millionaire and worked at an incredible pace up until the day he died. While he had four children and provided for all of them, Bradshaw was a "strong believer in the work ethic" who felt that no one should get "a free ticket or a free ride." It was this belief that caused friction and constant turmoil between him and his youngest daughter, Frances. He did not like her life-style in New York and tried to use his financial control over her to bring her and her family back to Salt Lake to live. This desire of his not only strained the relationship between father and daughter, but also caused a certain amount of friction with his wife, who sided with Frances. The evidence would show, Jones assured the judge, that Bradshaw had started to prepare a new will—one that would have excluded Frances—and made a number of copies of an outline for it which he left lying around.

Jones described how Franklin left for work early on the morning he was murdered and how, when Dan Schindler found his body in a pool of blood nearly two hours later, it was made to appear like a robbery. Two slugs were recovered from his body, the family offered $10,000 to anyone who would provide information that might lead to an arrest, but there were "no leads" (Jones said, not wanting to reveal the true story) and the investigation came to a virtual halt until October of 1980. It was then, Jones said, that a man named Richard Behrens, who had been owed money by Frances and was holding the murder weapon, gave it to another of

471

Bradshaw's daughters, Marilyn Reagan, who in turn handed it in to New York police. Once ballistics tests confirmed it to be the gun, Jones said, Joel Campbell flew to New York on December 3, 1980, and met with Behrens. Behrens was someone Frances had known since the 1960s when they met at a church in New York City, Jones said; he had been given the gun and told by Marc that he had traveled to Salt Lake to kill his grandfather and that the reason "had to do with the fact that Franklin Bradshaw controlled the money."

After Marc's arrest in Connecticut and his release on bail a few days later, he and his mother threatened Behrens that unless he recanted his story and said that Marilyn had had the gun all along, he would be charged as well. So on December 27, 1980, Behrens traveled by bus to the office of Marc's lawyers and told them that he had lied to Campbell a few weeks before—and that Marilyn had told him to make up the story.

In an attempt to determine which of Behrens's stories was true, investigators not only discovered airline tickets—tickets which showed that someone using the name Gentile had traveled from New York to Dallas to Midland to Phoenix to Salt Lake City just before Bradshaw was killed—but found that the woman who sold the tickets could identify Marc as the person who bought them. Gentile was the name Schreuder was born with, Jones pointed out, then went on to say that Midland was the place where the gun was bought the day before the murder, and that the state's witnesses would include both the person whom Marc bought it from and the person whom Marc had phoned a couple of weeks before his arrival there on July 20 and stayed with until he left.

The evidence would show, Jones went on, that in October of 1977 Richard Behrens had introduced Frances to a man named Myles Manning—a man whom she met with several times, paid $5,000 to kill her father, but who never carried out the plan.

"The state's theory," Jones explained, "is that Frances Schreuder wanted her inheritance. She wanted money from Franklin Bradshaw and she wanted it now. . . . She needed somebody to carry out this dirty plan but she couldn't find anybody to do it. So," he paused, wanting to underscore the full impact of what he was about to say, "she turns to her own son, her own flesh and blood, to kill her father."

As soon as Jones finished, Paul Van Dam informed the judge that the defense would not make its opening statement until after the state had rested its entire case—an indication to Jones that the lawyers wanted to see how well the state could survive the artillery fire that doubtless awaited each witness who ventured forth to take the stand.

Dan Schindler was the first and he held up nicely, describing the scene that Sunday morning and remembering the time of his arrival more accurately than he had at the preliminary hearing exactly three months earlier. Larry Stott, the first police officer to arrive at the warehouse, said that when he found Bradshaw's body "the back of his head was gone" and that he couldn't tell at first whether "an ax or a bullet" had killed him. Donald Aldous, the officer who photographed the crime scene and checked for fingerprints, couldn't recall the partial palm print he reported he found on the front, inside left door. In any case, the now-retired officer said, it was impossible to check out a palm print without having a suspect's to compare it against. And from the time of the murder until he left the department in May of 1981, he had never been given any suspects. Following the testimony of Carl Voyles, the officer who initially headed the investigation with Joel Campbell, the prosecutor felt he had painted enough of the crime scene—in words, photographs and diagrams—and the autopsy that followed to persuade any doubter that it was a brutal murder. He was now ready to bring on the first person—and last witness of the day—who could begin to address the motive for it.

Doug Steele really hadn't been the same since Frank died. The auto-parts business had been sold to some people in Orem in 1980, and even though Doug had stayed on and still put in long hours, he still felt as he had the morning he got the phone call from Dan Schindler—that his world had been destroyed. It had been five years since the summer of 1977 when Marc and Larry worked at the warehouse, but the memories were still agonizingly fresh for Steele—and, a month before the trial, he was saying (in reference to Marc and Frances) that he wanted "to see the sons of bitches hung."

Doug told the court he "was with Frank for thirty-two years" and that Frank was "good to his employees and treated them fine." In 1977, he explained, Frank told him that two of his grandsons were coming out to work for the summer and "instructed me to treat them as I would any other employee, that I would be in charge of them."

"Did you experience any problems at all with the defendant that summer?" Jones asked.

"From day one," Steele snapped, and went on to explain about the shortage his daughter discovered that afternoon at the bank. Tesch objected—it was hearsay, his daughter wasn't here to testify, and besides, there was no way to prove Marc stole the money—and the judge sustained it. It was the relationship between Marc and his grandfather that Sawaya most wanted to hear about.

"Frank had a lot of compassion," Steele continued, "and he had a lot of patience with them. He was greatly disappointed in their work habits and how they performed at the warehouse." Suddenly, Van Dam broke in, asking that Steele confine his statements *just* to Marc. That would be difficult for Doug—the two of them were inseparable in his mind—but he tried.

Terrible. Disrespectful. Dishonest. Arrogant attitude. Each thing he said to describe Marc was objected to—and stricken. It was too general. What about *specific* conversations between them that he was present at?

This was just the opening Steele needed. He described the morning in August when the two $10,000 checks came through and Frank accused Marc of breaking into his file and stealing his stock certificates; how Frank had asked him to take Marc upstairs and "see if I can talk some reason into him"—but that after almost an hour of pleading with Marc to confess and assuring him that his grandfather would forgive him, he had gotten nowhere.

But when the prosecutor attempted to establish Steele's knowledge of conflict in the Bradshaw family, the judge sustained Tesch's objections. So Jones went directly to the controversial "morning memo"—the one that excluded

Frances, State's Exhibit 22—and showed the barely legible photocopy to Sawaya and then to Steele. Steele identified it, saying that Frank had shown it to him at the warehouse in either December of 1977 or January of 1978, had run off a number of copies of it, and given him one. Tesch objected that it was irrelevant unless it proved actual knowledge on Marc's part, but was overruled. Steele then mentioned there was a second memo Frank gave him—one that Bradshaw signed in the afternoon—that stated the *same* information on it. (This of course was not true—the second memo did *not* indicate the one-third split and the exclusion of Frances.)

Asked if he was aware of Bradshaw's original will, Steele began to say that he was and that Frank had mentioned "numerous times" that he didn't like it. But once again Tesch objected and it was sustained. So Jones moved on to Berenice and why she was working at the warehouse in the months preceding his death.

"For money," Steele said in his matter-of-fact way.

"And for what reason?" Jones wanted him to go further.

"She was broke," Steele said, later adding that she was practically Frances's sole source of income during that time.

During a ten-minute recess, Dave Walsh came up with a possible solution to the considerable problems Jones was having with the hearsay rule: a legal exception to it that dealt with "state of mind"—and might permit Steele to testify to some of the things Bradshaw had told him about his family. When court resumed, Jones cited the exception and, over Tesch's objections, the judge agreed.

Unshackled, Steele said that Frank was proud of his family and proud of his grandsons. He showed him their report cards—"how they got straight A's and how they got top of their class"—and would have done anything for them. But the problem was this: it was "all long-distance. Frank had no physical contact with them. They were in New York and Frank was in Salt Lake." In January or February of 1978, *after* Frank had showed him those memos, Frank was telling him that "he wanted Frances, with the children, to come back to Salt Lake to live. He was willing to give up their home on Gilmer Drive and that him and Berenice could take an apartment or condo. He told me he didn't like the New York atmosphere and the conditions the kids were being brought up under and that . . . she had no visible means of income and that he was tired of supporting her and that he wanted her to come home. Frank told me that Berenice had finally exhausted all of her financial means of support for Frances and that she was dead broke. . . . He wasn't going to come forward with any more money for Frances and that her only out would be to come home and live. . . . Being the grandfather, maybe he could have some influence on the grandchildren and bring them up in his own image, which is the Bradshaw clan. . . . He wasn't going to support her any longer. He said, 'I have to make a stand.' "

The following morning Doug was back on the witness stand, and this time the distinction between the two memos became clear: after showing him the morning memo, Bradshaw asked Steele for a ride to Second South and Main, where "he was going to see his lawyer." But late that afternoon, Steele admitted, he was surprised when Bradshaw gave him a signed memo (the one that had *no* mention of excluding Frances), had wondered why it was different, but said they never talked about it. When the issue of the two $10,000 checks made out to cash (as well as the others that Nancy Jones received that morning) came up again, Steele said the checks were forged by Frances and deposited in a New York bank, and that Bradshaw "was convinced it was the two boys in conjunction with Frances." Asked why the police weren't notified, he explained that Frank didn't want them involved because "this was family." He said that Berenice told him the reason Larry worked the night before the murder was a desire "to earn some extra money"; he elaborated on Berenice's coming to work at the warehouse; and he claimed that Frank told him, "I am cutting off all the funds for Frances and she [Berenice] knows it, and if she is going to earn any money, let her do what she wants with it and send it back to her." Berenice kept asking him, Steele said, how much "we" were worth. "I told her I think we're worth all kinds of money," he said, but was careful not to "give her any dollar-and-cent figures."

Was she in the warehouse the day those copies of the

morning memo were left lying around? the prosecutor wanted to know on re-direct.

Yes, she was.

Mary Jane Cavenaugh took the stand next and told of her and her husband's surprise when Marc—"a rather well-dressed young man"—arrived by taxi at their home that Thursday afternoon. She said Marc seemed surprised that her son John had not told them he was coming, and she invited him in: it wasn't until later that day that she found out why Marc had come to Midland. She expressed her concern to Marc about his purchasing a gun, she said, and suggested that perhaps she should call his mother and clear it with her. "I really should have called her," Mrs. Cavenaugh said in a motherly tone of regret, "but Marc was very open and disarming about it." He had no objection to her calling, she said, and told her, " 'No, that would be fine. . . . She did not mind, she wanted me to have it for protection.' "

Marc had wanted to leave for Salt Lake that Friday, she recalled, but the gun couldn't be purchased until the following day, so he had to change his reservations. "I know there was some question about going either through Phoenix or Albuquerque."

On cross-examination, in the first lighthearted exchange of the trial, Van Dam asked Mrs. Cavenaugh about the peculiar relationship Texans had with guns.

"Don't y'all wear one on your hip?"

"I have one on my hip now," she shot back with a smile, telling him that they had guns in their house and that her twelve- and fourteen-year-old sons both had .22s.

Before leaving the stand, she said that Marc was well behaved, open, and relaxed the whole time he stayed at their home. Her son Jim, whom Marc played Monopoly with, probably spent more time with him than anyone else, and was the one who remembered his reading *Death on the Nile*.

In response to the defense's objection, Jones told the judge he had asked her about this seemingly irrelevant detail because the book "is similar to the case we have before us."

Mary Jane Cavenaugh had no sooner left the witness box than her son John, practically saluting as he took the oath, filled her seat. The only significant change in his testimony from what he had said at Marc's preliminary—and in earlier interviews—was this: he was the one who drove Marc to the Midland airport that Saturday afternoon for his flight to Salt Lake and the "camping trip" he said awaited him there.

The last witness of the day was Nancy Jones. She had stayed on for two years after her employer's death, helping the bank sort out his estate, and was now working for an oil and gas company in town ("Everything I know about the oil and gas business I learned from Frank Bradshaw," she will proudly tell anyone who asks). Like Doug Steele, Nancy was expected to testify about the financial battles in the family and the controversial memos. Describing herself as someone who "just did everything" in the seven and a half years she worked for Bradshaw, she explained that she would draw up rent checks for Frances, birthday checks for her and her children, and checks for Marc and Larry's private schools. But when he refused to pay for their schooling after the summer of 1977, Berenice did, forging two checks and being called (by Nancy) to come down to the warehouse and explain her actions. Frances, meanwhile, was "asking for money all the time. She was just asking and asking for money. Mrs. Bradshaw was giving her money all the time she was requesting it."

Nancy told the court about the phone call she received ten days before the murder—the one in which Marc was phoning collect to speak with Berenice and that resulted in Nancy's drawing up a check for $3,000; the check, payable to Lavinia, her boss told her would be the last one they would ever have to send.

She described the day she discovered the two $10,000 checks—he *never* made out checks payable to "Cash"—and how Frank started crying and screaming, "Oh, my God," telling her to stop payment on all checks coming from New York. As far as the memos were concerned, she said, *she* typed the top part of the memo—which is the same on both copies—but *he* typed the part on the unsigned, morning memo that excluded Frances. Though he had asked her not to talk about the memos, she said, she was able to corroborate Steele's story that there were copies "laying around on his desk and around the warehouse."

After two days of testimony, the state's case appeared to be headed in the right direction; but the smart money said that Jones, as the defense's continuing objections and the judge's warnings reminded him, would have to prove eventually that Marc was aware of his grandfather's intentions to change his will—and that any change would adversely affect *him*—if he hoped to get a first-degree conviction on the charge of murder for pecuniary or other personal gain.

On Friday morning, a transportation officer for the jail (who was also a notary) testified about a document she had notarized in late April; it was a note from Marc, authorizing a $2,700 check to be given to a fellow inmate's girlfriend and containing his signature. The handwriting on the note had been compared, by a document examiner who testified next, with the note on Kent stationery that contained Dr. Cavenaugh's name, address and phone number—the one Behrens claimed Marc had written. Since the note Behrens mailed to Marilyn was a Xeroxed copy, the examiner said he was only 70 percent sure that Marc's handwriting was on both copies.

As soon as the supervisor of customer services for SArgent-SOwell confirmed that her company had sold Jerry Register the murder weapon in question, the public and press got their first look at the immense figure they had heard, read or written about. No longer a police chief but a mere patrolman now, Jerry Register was not the best witness in the world—though his good-ole-boy persona provided a certain degree of humor to all assembled. Joe Tesch pointed out certain discrepancies in his testimony from what he had said both at Marc's preliminary and in previous interviews, sneered at his "still improving" memory, and indirectly accused the County Attorney's Office of feeding him information. But Register clung to his story: that Marc was in the bank lobby that Saturday, "dressed a little funny for West Texas" and was told, by either Malcolm McPhail or John Cavenaugh, that the gun Register had just handed over "will take care of anything you run across while you are back-packing."

The world of wills, estates and trusts can seem extraordinarily complicated and mystifying to an outsider, and nobody knows that better than an attorney who specializes in that area. So in preparing to testify at Marc's trial, Steve Swindle made up a chart that he hoped would help answer some of the questions surrounding the Bradshaw estate.

Swindle's chart showed that at the time of Bradshaw's death his estate was valued at $10,460,288.71. Another $5,000,000 to $10,000,000, he pointed out, had been realized from the sale of various assets—and he left no one in doubt that the final value of the estate could be much higher than that.* He explained that the original signed copy of his 1970 will had never been found and that an unsigned copy had been admitted into probate. He showed how the will was divided into two trusts, marital and family; how the marital part was worth more (71.629 percent) than the family, which had the taxes taken from it; and he told of the family turmoil that led to Berenice's disclaimer, less than four months after the murder, of the family trust—the one under which both children *and* grandchildren were listed as beneficiaries. But while the three daughters began benefiting immediately, the grandchildren would not be entitled to any income until they were at least twenty-one *and* survived their mothers. Asked by Jones if Frances would have known about the contents of her father's original will before he died, Swindle referred to the July 3, 1976, letter she wrote to his colleague Dave Salisbury that indicated she did.

But if Marc wasn't benefiting directly from his grandfather's will, and had no knowledge of its contents, or any intent on his grandfather's part to change it that could be tangibly proven, it seemed that Jones was still faced with the thorny problem of persuading Sawaya that Frances's pecuniary gain would be Marc's as well—and that anything Frances might have known he would have been told.

Malcolm C. McPhail took the witness stand first thing Monday morning, the 21st, and fixed his eyes on Marc. "He

---

*Because of Bradshaw's considerable oil and gas holdings—and their fluctuating prices—it is practically impossible, Steve Swindle said in 1985, to arrive at a precise figure. The most precise thing that can be said is that the estate's value is "open ended."

looked me straight in the eyes," the Texan recalled. "I could have hugged him. I felt so sorry for that little man. He looked like a little nephew of mine in his blue blazer and gray pants. But goddammit, I had to do it. Damn, I hated it." McPhail did his best to enlighten the gathering about guns in Texas ("It is easier than not to deal outside of the license requirements in the state of Texas") and explained the transporting of them as if everybody automatically carried one when he traveled. He said he told Marc to do "the same thing I guess we all do—box the shells separately and tape them, both the shells and the gun. If you got two cases, separate them. Put one in one and one in the other so that the gun will be empty and then transport it by checking it through." McPhail should know. He had brought a gun to Salt Lake City with him—just in case.

But for all his boldness, he would not admit he had actually inspected the gun and handled the transaction at the bank (though he said he looked at it carefully back at his house and would say later that if he had known he could have gotten it for $175 or $180 he would have bought it for himself).

But why did he even go to the transaction? Van Dam wanted to know. If everything was all arranged, "it seems like John Cavenaugh could have simply gone down and picked that thing up."

"Well," McPhail began in his thick accent, slowly drawing the word out, "you reach a point where you got training years, and I knew John Snow [the bank security guard]. I knew the reputation of the gun [from Bruce Stanley]. I knew Marc Schreuder. I knew John [Cavenaugh]. My purpose was to assist them to the point of transfer of the gun and I guess just to smooth it over because none of them knew the others."

By the time Richard Behrens took the stand on the afternoon of the next day, six more witnesses had come forth to tell what they knew. A Continental Airlines representative, looking at a blowup of the second ticket of the three Marc had allegedly used (the one from Midland to Phoenix to Salt Lake on Saturday, July 22) confirmed that the ticket had not only been purchased through American Airlines in New York but in fact had been used; he admitted, however, that he

481

could not say if "GENTILE/L" —or Marc for that matter—was the person who had used it.

Shara Vestal, Jerry Register's ex-wife, offered a physical description of the young man she recalled being present when the gun was sold, but could not say for sure that Marc, sitting across from her, was that person.

Ed Peterson, the ballistics expert, barely survived a blistering two-hour cross-examination by Joe Tesch, but Carolyn Karoliszyn-Morris of American Airlines not only identified Marc, as she had in March, but was, finally, able to articulate what it was about his eyes that stuck with her ("they were just piercing . . . looking through you almost"). Asked how she was able to sell a ticket on an airline other than American, she said that normally she couldn't—unless the person was paying in cash (he was) and there was a ticket on American preceding it (which there was—New York to Dallas). And since he was paying in cash, she said in response to another question, she would not have asked him to verify that he was—or wasn't—"L. Gentile."

After the former keeper of records for Hughes Air West testified and the passenger name record for Flight 15—the one from Phoenix to Salt Lake—was entered into evidence, another representative from American took the stand and completed the intricate picture. Explaining American's microfiche record, she said they had received a copy of all of the used flight coupons except the one from Texas International; either it was billed under an incorrect number, or the passenger didn't make the trip from Dallas to Midland, or Texas International never sent it to them.

If an ideal witness, from the prosecution's point of view, is one who simply answers questions, never volunteers, and produces no unwanted surprises, Richard Behrens is not that person. But for a defense team struggling to find the perfect figure on whom to cast a long shadow of doubt, Behrens seemed made to order. Joe Tesch and Paul Van Dam had worked Behrens over during Marc's preliminary hearing and they had been looking forward to the schoolteacher's return.

Right from the start, Ernie Jones knew he was in for a long afternoon. Behrens (whose father had died the day before) was in terrible shape: he was mumbling, speaking with his hand in front of his face, and having all sorts of difficulty with the microphone; if he wasn't about to swallow it one moment, he acted as if it were about to bite him the next, sitting as far back in the witness box as he could. Though Judge Sawaya had a reputation for being unperturbed on the bench, he was exasperated by Behrens and later said he was "the most frustrating witness I have ever had."

Nonetheless, the judge heard Behrens testify, on direct examination, that Marc told him the reasons he killed his grandfather were that "he was hounded very hard by his mother, because they were afraid of being cut off from monies and they didn't want to be out on the street." Now that was more like it, Jones thought, exactly the kind of testimony the state needed the judge to hear.

"And do you recall what Marc told you about working here in the summer of 1977?"

"Yeah," Behrens said. "He had worked in the parts warehouse and he had mentioned some of the adventures he had had in that summer. And among them were putting stimulants into the grandfather's oatmeal and similar food that he ate."

Tesch shot out of his chair like a human cannonball.

"Object. Irrelevant. I also have this problem, Judge. We have made demands for every statement of this witness and we have received a couple. But nothing like this has ever been included in any of that. And I think that it ought to be inadmissible as violation of disclosure, a ruling of Judge Banks'."

"No, I will hear it," Sawaya said. "Overruled."

"Did he indicate the purpose of the stimulants?" Jones knew he was pulling a surprise and savored it. Behrens had told Marilyn about this before he turned the gun in, and Elaine had reminded Mike George about it in her letter four months earlier.

"Yes. Mr. Bradshaw was very old and I had been told previously by [Marc], by his mother, that heart failure, early deaths seemed to go along the family lines, very hard-driving family, executives, et cetera. And they were attempting to—he was attempting to kill his grandfather by over-stimulating him, hoping he would have heart failure, and he also indicated that he just got sick. It didn't really work."

"Did he tell you when he attempted to do that?"

"Several times during the summer. . . ."

"Did he describe to you the type of stimulants?"

"I don't know the exact type. They were stimulants, however, excessive amounts."

By the time Jones finished on direct, Behrens had added some other interesting details: Frances had wanted him to have his recantation notarized for "insurance reasons"—that she "would have to give it to Mrs. Bradshaw to convince [her] to pay the legal fees"; Marc was just as involved in threatening him to change his story in December of 1980 as Frances was. Marc told him that Larry and he had stolen, in the summer of 1977, "some kind of bond" worth $150,000—but that he had blamed it on Larry. And then of course there was the will—the will that Behrens claimed "the whole family was conscious of" and that he heard Marc and Frances discussing at the end of the summer of 1977, not long before he introduced her to Myles Manning.

On cross-examination, Tesch began in the same way he had during Marc's preliminary—addressing the issue of Behrens's grant of immunity, getting him to recount his career, and portraying him as a close friend of Frances's.

Did he recall having conversations with Frances Schreuder in the fall of 1977 to the effect "that both of you could use a hit man"?

"No," Behrens said without hesitation. Tesch had raised this issue at the preliminary—Behrens's concern about his father's marriage to his stepmother, and how that might have affected Behrens's share of his father's estate if they had divorced. "When I spoke to Frances Schreuder about my father's wife," he went on, "I talked to her about legality because she was an experienced person in the ideas of divorce." *She* was the person who wanted a gun, he insisted. *He* did not.

Why had he picked Myles Manning as a potential hit man for Frances? Tesch asked. "Maybe things are different in New York than in Utah, but what made you think that he might be a hit man?"

Having earlier said he was "a casual acquaintance" whom he had known for "several years," Behrens pointed out that "he was in the printer's union and the union people in New York and perhaps other places, I believe, enjoy an unsavory reputation . . . and he was a union type."

Was Manning the only union type that he knew?

"No," said Behrens matter-of-factly. "I belong to a union too."

But wasn't it true that in addition to speaking to Manning about Frances, he had spoken to him about his stepmother?

Yes, he had. He told Manning that he wanted "a witness" and took him to his father's summer house at a lake in New Jersey. His father had asked him not to come around anymore, he said, and he felt that his stepmother's "ill-felt undue influence" was to blame for his request.

"You took a ride up there with Myles Manning to case your parents' house, did you not?"

"No," Behrens insisted. "I knew the house pretty well. I didn't have to case it."

But wasn't it true that in his conversations with Myles Manning, the printer "told you in fact that for an amount of money he would kill Joan [his stepmother] for you"?

"No."

"And is that not also why you and he went up to your father's house?"

No, that was not true.

But his admission that, like Frances, he too was concerned about a will—his father's—and the possibility of being cut out of it was an undeniably intriguing parallel to a story that was holding both the judge and the spectators in thrall.

It had been nearly fifteen years since Marilyn Reagan had seen Marc, and the image she still held in her mind was of "a little, clean-cut boy in the best of clothes—little short pants and knee socks." But that was a long time ago; the nephew she now saw sitting across from her in the courtroom was the person, she felt certain, who had murdered her father. As Ernie Jones began to question her, he knew that the worst was yet to come: that her degree of "involvement" throughout the entire investigation was the kind of thing that would come back to haunt him when it came time for the ruthless cross-examination that surely awaited her.

Once Behrens recanted his story and Jim Conway began

485

asking questions about her, Marilyn herself knew that if and when Marc ever came to trial, the lawyers would try to portray her as someone who was as keenly interested in her father's will—and what she might get out of it—as her youngest sister; in essence, someone who also might have wanted her father dead. She was determined to be as circumspect as possible.

It would take more hours than anyone in that courtroom had to spare for her to reveal her complete feelings about her parents and her youngest sister, but even her terse responses told a lot. Asked to describe her relationship with her father, she said: "Dad was busy a lot, working a lot. But I felt in the time we had together we understood each other." With her mother: "It *was* very good." With Frances: "Distant. We lived different kinds of lives." Her father's attitude toward money: "He was very frugal. Money to him was what he needed to run his business and he had several businesses." Her mother's attitude toward it was different, she said. "One statement she made was, 'If he has all this money, why can't we spend it?'"

But when asked about her father's will and her knowledge of it, she told both Jones and Van Dam that all she knew was that he had a will, she had seen it once, but didn't know what it actually contained until *after* he died. (She was not telling the truth about this, but the defense was not able to prove that; asked about this later, she said she had "honestly forgotten" she had actually seen the will until "I reviewed my notes.")

"When did you become aware of what you have termed in the past as 'another will'?" Van Dam asked, in the midst of an increasingly acrimonious exchange.

"After my father died," she said, corroborating what Steele had said earlier—that he hadn't told Marilyn or Elaine about the memos until they arrived in town for the funeral. "Are you talking about the half-page outline?"

"Yes. Did you consider that to be a will?"

"No, an intent to write a will."

Then why did she tell the police that she thought it was a will?

"I thought he had written a will, using that outline [naming

486

her and Doug Steele as co-executors of the estate] and using the 1970 will as his guide." While she admitted that a "second will" had never been found, she distinctly recalled Doug Steele saying "that it was his understanding Dad had rewritten his will, giving Frances fifteen dollars as an intentional disinheritance." (She had mentioned this in her interview with Joel Campbell two days after the murder, but Steele was not asked about this at trial nor recalls it to this day.)

She gave her account of her dealings with Richard Behrens, admitted she had sent him $30 as "a reimbursement" for the pictures of Marc and Frances he had sent, the stamps he had bought and the many pay-phone calls he made—but flatly denied she had ever asked him to "make up" a story about who was involved in her father's murder.

She confirmed that Behrens had told her about Marc and Larry's attempts to poison her father's oatmeal before he gave her the gun, but told Van Dam that she didn't inform the police about it because "it had no relevancy to the murder."

"Do I understand you to say," he asked, more than a little bit incredulous, "that an attempt on your father's life the summer before he was actually killed . . . had no relevance?"

Of course it did, she said, but there was no way to prove it.

"Well, I am not suggesting you were proving anything. But it seems to me a piece of information that you might pass on to the police."

"Mr. Van Dam, I was not in constant contact with the police after every telephone conversation with Mr. Behrens."

"I don't believe I have suggested you were, but this seems to be an unusually good piece of information. My question was, did you pass it on? You said no and I am asking you why not."

"I didn't pass on the fact that Frances stole a hundred and fifty thousand dollars I have never been able to trace either."

"How do you know she did it?"

"Because Mr. Behrens told me she did."

"What else did Mr. Behrens tell you about Frances?"

"He told me about them spending some time out in Long Island. The family had rented a house out there. He told me about Frances and he sneaking around trying to get divorce material on Vittorio, just general items like that."

"And at least as far as these items, which are apparently clearly major violations of law, you did not pass these on to the police at the time?"

"Objection," Jones said. "That's been asked and answered, Your Honor."

"She just told me of another one," Van Dam countered.

"She may answer," the judge said.

"A hundred-and-fifty-thousand-dollar theft you didn't pass on; is that your testimony?" Van Dam resumed.

"That is correct."

"Did you ever check with your father—or did you ever check with your mother regarding this attempted poisoning?"

"My father was dead when I found out about it."

"Your mother?"

"My mother was not in communication with me."

"Isn't the reason you didn't pass this information on, Mrs. Reagan, simply you didn't believe it?"

". . . I did believe it."

"You did believe it?"

"I did, but the oatmeal had all been thrown away."

"Did he give you the details of how this was done?"

"No."

There was also the troubling issue of the hit man and why she hadn't informed the police about that. After initially testifying that Behrens had mentioned a hit man—again, like the oatmeal, prior to his giving her the gun—but that she had not heard his name "until now," she admitted, on cross, that he had mentioned it once but she neither remembered it nor wrote it down. It wasn't until *after* she had received the gun that she told Campbell about it, and when she asked Behrens for the name again, "he wouldn't give it to me."

She denied she had ever taunted Frances, locked her in closets or scared her ("it's not my style"); denied she ever tried to take over her father's auto-parts or oil-lease business (claiming she had no knowledge of either); and said she was "not after involvement in this crime."

Marilyn was under siege and she did her best to ward off every blow and insinuation. "She didn't want it to leak out that she had really horrible feelings toward Frances," the court reporter opined later. "She was trying to protect her testimony from being vicious toward her." But under Van

488

Dam's constant pressure, Marilyn did drop her guard long enough over the two days she was on the witness stand to say two things that captured her feelings of resentment as well as any other: she did not like the way Frances "was always pitting my mother against my father to get more money," and she thought that it was "very unfair not to have a mother when she is living."

That mother, whom she insisted she was still open to, was very much alive and would be testifying later that afternoon. But before Berenice Bradshaw was called to the stand, two new characters walked on stage—two characters who would be remembered in Salt Lake City for some time to come.

Throughout the trial, Mike George had taken full responsibility for every witness the state had called—especially the ones who had come from out of town. He picked them up at the airport and took them to their hotels, carefully deciding ahead of time who would stay where, trying to make sure that none of them spoke to the press or, in most instances, to each other, and warning Richard Behrens not to offend *every person* he met by asking if he was Mormon. George thought of them as the members of "his team"—each with a role to play—and he was prepared to do just about anything to make sure they were happy, content and relaxed; he knew from experience how some witnesses could seem calm and forthcoming during "rehearsals" with the prosecutor, then tense up and self-destruct once they were under oath before an unfriendly defense attorney.

Normally, responsibility for witnesses is someone else's job in the County Attorney's Office, but Mike George had become particularly protective of this case and was perfectly happy in his role of chauffeur, bodyguard and camp counselor. There was one witness, though, that he wanted Ernie Jones to see for himself—a witness whom he had purposely never described.

"Wait till you see this guy, Ernie," George said as they waited at the airport together earlier in the week. "I can't describe him. You just watch people get off and *you* tell *me* who Myles Manning is."

"Here he comes," said Jones, breaking into a smile. "That little guy there." And as soon as Jones saw him, he felt certain of one thing: that just having Manning walk into the courtroom would speak volumes "because he's the kind of guy I think you would go to—as a hit man or a con man or whatever you want to call him."

The courtroom was filled to capacity as Manning was sworn in and Eddie Dean squeezed himself into a chair right behind Jones and George. It's not every day that a hit man testifies in Salt Lake City, and the assembled gathering was hanging on every word.

Not long after Mike George and Don Harman surprised Myles Manning at the *Daily News* that December evening, Manning remembered more about his encounters with Frances Schreuder—information that he relayed to Al Sullivan and Steve Klein. He had had four meetings with her—not three. The first (beginning in "late summer" of 1977) was not at her apartment, as he had previously said, but in front of his house on East 89th Street. Behrens, who lived four doors down, had arranged it, but was not present when they actually talked. Manning said he was sitting on the fender of his car in his dungarees, waiting for her to show up, and was surprised that she did. Behrens introduced them and left. They spoke for five minutes, he said, and during that time she asked if "I was the person that Behrens had suggested to her and if I was willing to do it. And I said, 'No, I would have somebody do it.'" She didn't mention whom she wanted killed at that point, he said, nor did she commit herself to any sort of arrangement. The second meeting, "about a week, week and a half later," was also arranged by Behrens. He and Frances met again in front of his apartment, he recalled, and went on to a restaurant by the name of Dresner's.

"Do you recall what she said to you at that time?" Jones asked.

"Yes. She asked me if I would do it and how much it would cost."

"I said, 'No, I won't do it, but I will have it done and it will cost you five thousand dollars.'"

"Where did you come up with the figure of five thousand dollars?" Jones asked, aware that Manning had originally said *she* suggested the amount.

"That's basically what I owed out," Manning explained.

". . . Owed out?" The prosecutor wanted him to clarify that.

"In different bills," he said, explaining that the figure seemed fair to her.

The third meeting, about two weeks later, was at her apartment. Behrens walked him over to the building, but did not come upstairs with him. And it was at this meeting, he said, that she gave him a hand-drawn map, written instructions, a picture of the man he was supposed to kill ("an elderly man, kind of thin, gray hair, white hair"), a picture of his warehouse, and the $5,000 in "fives, tens and twenties in a large manila envelope." She asked him how it was going to be done, he said, and he told her "it was none of her business. She was just paying for it. Then she said it had to be done quickly and it had to look like an accident or a holdup."

What else had she told him about this man?

"Well, that's when I found out it was her father."

Had she told him why she wanted him killed?

"She didn't come right out and say it, but she implied because of an inheritance."

Since Manning had earlier told George "she *said* that she was going to get an inheritance," Jones pressed him as to how he had reached that conclusion.

"Well, I'm trying to remember the words she used. Basically because it was her father; secondly, because she was saying that she needed money. I just put two and two together."

When he left the apartment, he explained, he went to the YMCA "to kill a couple of days."

Did he have the $5,000 with him?

"Sure did," he said without hesitation, then recounted his fourth and final meeting with Frances in Behrens's apartment, where he lied about the "problems" he had run into in Salt Lake ("we came out here, got picked up, and I went back") and she began crying and telling him she would have to take her kids out of school and go on welfare. That was the last time, he said, he had ever seen or heard from her.

As Joe Tesch prepared to cross-examine him, he reiterated to the judge the defense's continuing objection to *any* testimony that could not ultimately be connected to Marc. Sawaya acknowledged that but also said that the state was "entitled to the reasonable inferences that any of this evidence may warrant." That was music to Jones's ears and confirmed what he had earlier suspected: the judge wanted as much information as possible before making his decision.

Tesch quickly established that Manning had never seen or spoken with Marc before. Frances told him she had a son; that was all he knew. (In December, all he remembered her mentioning was a daughter.) Behrens was someone he had known for six or seven months (Behrens had said two or three years) who used to come up to him on the street and try to pet his dog. He admitted that he and Behrens had once gone to the lake where the schoolteacher's father and stepmother lived, but said it was "a social encounter." At least for him it was; he simply wanted to go to the lake, but conceded that Behrens had gone there "to spy."

"Is it not true that in fact he tried to hire you to dispose of his stepmother?" Tesch asked.

"No, he did not." Nor did he ever pay him any money to spy on his stepmother, nor be a witness to anything. Tesch decided not to push it further.

Didn't he remember, Tesch asked (expressing Behrens's recollection), that the first meeting with Frances was in front of Behrens's apartment, and that he and Frances went into the apartment to get off the street?

No, he did not, sticking to his story that he had met her in front of his own apartment.

"What was said at the first meeting?" Tesch asked, wanting to hear him repeat what he had said on direct examination.

"She asked me something about 'Am I the person that Behrens knew and was going to introduce her to?' and I said, 'Yes.'"

"Putting on your best Jimmy Cagney act at this point?" Tesch said, knowing Jones would probably object and it would be sustained.

He explained that when she started asking him *who* he knew "I just named a few names, knowing she wouldn't know any of them."

"Okay," Tesch said, "Harry the Spike, things like that, or what were you saying to her?"

"Not quite that way, no," Manning said, unbothered by Tesch's barely hidden contempt.

492

Which way then?

"Just names."

"A lot of guys with crooked noses, crooked-nose names?"

"Well, they were mostly Italian names, yeah." Names he had made up right on the spot. Manning corroborated Behrens's story that Behrens was merely the person who brought them together, was not privy to any of their meetings, did not receive any money, and was unaware that Manning was not planning to carry out the murder. When Manning left the courtroom, there was a distinct feeling that the defense hadn't been able to do all of what perhaps they had hoped: to somehow show that Manning and Behrens were conspirators in the whole thing.

Throughout his testimony he was unflappable, answering each question as if he were being asked about a lazy summer day he had spent at the beach. He did not try to dodge the fact that he and his brother had been thrown out of a few apartments in New York or that he had had a drinking problem—though he did claim that it had begun "tapering off . . . three or four months" before his meetings with Frances.

"He didn't try to be more than he is or less than he is," Jones said later. Just plain old Myles, who had flown from New York to tell an astonished group of Utahns how he had conned Frances out of $5,000 and paid off some outstanding bills. The "knockaround guy"—as Eddie Dean called him— who took the money and ran to the Y.

Before Berenice Bradshaw took the witness stand at three-forty on the seventh day of the trial, there was a five-minute discussion in Judge Sawaya's chambers about her grant of immunity. Van Dam expressed his opinion that while she had no personal need of the grant, he felt that her possession of it should not be made public. "Mrs. Bradshaw is old . . . and we would like to spare her any embarrassment or any problem in the community" that she intends to go on living in, he said. A lawyer from Portland, Maine, who had met with her in the hospital there, warned the judge that the whole matter had put her "under tremendous strain." Sawaya said the grant could be held in confidence and that he hoped the questioning of her wouldn't have to be too lengthy.

493

Though helping the state of Utah successfully prosecute her grandson was the last thing Berenice Bradshaw wanted to do, she provided, on direct and re-direct examination, many of the answers Ernie Jones wanted the judge to hear: her husband ate oatmeal for breakfast every morning for years; Marc had never called her in July of 1978 to say he was coming to Salt Lake to do any backpacking or camping; her husband was upset with Marc and Larry during the summer of 1977 about cash and checks that were missing—but she denied she had ever seen those checks or had them brought to her attention. After initially denying any recollection of a call from Marc on July 13, ten days before the murder, asking for $3,000 ("these things happened so frequently that I cannot pinpoint them"), she did, after some considerable pressing by Jones, admit to remembering it "vaguely"—the call in which Marc said this would be the *last* money they would ever ask for.

On cross-examination, Paul Van Dam—as he had during the preliminary hearing—tried to move the spotlight of suspicion away from Marc and onto Larry and Marilyn. But Berenice was holding firm: she didn't recall telling Elaine or Marilyn that Larry left the house shortly after Franklin that morning; she did recall Larry's working at the warehouse the day before the murder, but said that it was in the morning and that she wasn't there (contradicting Larry's recollection—and an earlier version of her own—that it was in the early evening and they both were present).

But did she have any occasion to check and see if Larry was in the house that Sunday morning before she went down to wake him up?

No.

Did she check to see if his automobile was anywhere around?

No.

When he left to go flying, did she have any recollection as to where his car was or having heard it leave?

No.

Did she recall, the night before the death, that she or Larry received any phone calls that evening?

"I wouldn't remember."

His line of questioning going nowhere, Van Dam asked about Marilyn. As she had at the preliminary, she said their relationship had changed and she was disturbed that Marilyn, after her husband's death, had "wanted to take over and I didn't want any of my family to take over." She claimed Marilyn walked into the warehouse and said, "'I am taking over,' and the manager said, 'No, you are not.'" She admitted that she went along with Marilyn's rental of an office at first, but then canceled the lease and sent the furniture back.

Yet when Van Dam probed into the relationship between Marilyn and Franklin, she said they were "very devoted to each other." She said that she didn't think Marilyn knew what was in his will, and that she had never discussed her own with her. She denied any knowledge of whether her husband had actually made a new will—only that she heard someone in the office say he was planning to.

"Did you ever have any knowledge as to whether or not Mr. Bradshaw intended to disinherit Frances and her children?"

"I heard him say once that he was going to disinherit Frances," she admitted, having said three months earlier that she didn't know who told her.

"When was that?"

"But I never told *anyone*," she interjected quickly, determined to protect her youngest daughter and family.

Why did her husband say that?

"Well, I don't really know," she said, not about to rise from her chair and string a clothesline of soiled family linen from one side of the courtroom to the other. "I don't think I could pin that down."

And what about the relationship between Marc and Franklin?

They got along fine, she said, ironically telling the court before she left that Franklin didn't want either Marc or Larry to return to Salt Lake in the summer of 1978.

If ever there was a trial to explode the idea that consistent, black-and-white testimony is possible, and to illustrate the treacherous waters of family relationships, this was surely it. It wasn't just that different witnesses remember things differently; the passage of time can partly be blamed for that. It's just that they remember them the way *they* want to. And no amount of swearing to tell the whole truth and nothing but is ever likely to change that.

Ernie Jones was sitting in his office later that afternoon when the phone rang. He was tired, hadn't seen much of his family—one of his daughters rationalized that "at least we see Daddy on television"—and was eager to get home. Eddie Dean was on the line, calling from the Holiday Inn where he and Manning were staying.

They hadn't flown out on the same plane because Dean's father had died and Dean hadn't arrived in Salt Lake until a day later. He hadn't had a chance to get to the bank before going to Kennedy Airport, so he left New York with only $100 in his pocket; by the time Mike George met him on the other end that figure had been reduced by the number of drinks he'd had.

A few weeks earlier he had asked Jones and George to upgrade his and Myles's plane tickets to first-class and, while they were at it, to book them into the finest hotel. Jones and George told him they would have to settle for the same coach seats and hotel accommodations that everyone else had; if they wanted first-class tickets so badly, they would have to pay the difference.

Now Dean was calling with a new request—a cash advance of $300. He'd been with a hooker the night before and he had given his last bit of money to her. *No way,* Jones said, outraged. His room, meals and transportation were covered. That was it. Anything extra was his problem.

Dean was angry and hung up. His client had delivered and Dean was determined not to be "a prisoner in a goddam Holiday Inn."

A few minutes later, Jones's phone rang again. The woman on the other end identified herself as the manager of the Holiday Inn. She said that Mr. Edward P. Dean was at the desk, claiming that the County Attorney's Office had authorized a cash advance in the amount of $300. She wanted to clear it with him, she said, before giving him the money.

Practically speechless, Jones told her to keep Mr. Dean occupied and he would send someone out to clear everything up. As he hung up the phone, Jones knew there were only two ways to deal with the problem: "take a hard stand or try to soft-sell it." Since he knew that he was going to need Manning if he was able to bring Frances to trial, he decided on the latter approach. And there was no one better to do the "soft sell" than Don Harman—"our p.r. man," as Mike George called him.

So Harman drove out to the Holiday Inn on North Temple, not far from the airport, packed Dean and Manning into his car, and took them on a tour of the Great Salt Lake.

Though Dean never got his "advance," Jones agreed to authorize the hotel to cash a check for him. As for the story about the hooker, Dean laughingly denied it, but not without saying this: "If I had tried to get a hooker, I sure would have tried to get them to pay for it."

The following morning, Ernie Jones resumed his questioning of Mike George that had begun the day before. Close to resting his case, the prosecutor felt that George could tie up some loose ends, attempt to clarify some mysteries—and attest to the hard work, luck and perseverance that had gone into the investigation. The kind of effort that would not have been lost on Franklin Bradshaw.

In a detached way that revealed neither the excitement nor the dismay that he had experienced in the fourteen months since he had been working on the case, George explained that he had initially been asked to do an investigation into airlines records. From the moment he began answering questions, the difference between his testimony and that given by Joel Campbell on the third day of the trial was apparent. Where Campbell had been rather vague and forgetful, George was precise and confident as he told of the step-by-step procedures he had followed in piecing together the records he had found, and told of the information he had learned from the witnesses he had interviewed on his various trips.

On cross-examination, though, Paul Van Dam was able to point out the kind of things that could keep alive the idea that either Behrens or Manning or Harry the Spike, for that matter, might have committed the murder: George had not checked to see if either of them had flown from Phoenix to New York—the implication being that one or both could have come into Salt Lake by another means of travel, left for

Phoenix after the murder, and flown home from there; there was no passenger name record or ticket still in existence to confirm that L. Gentile had taken that American flight on Sunday morning back to New York (though the airline had received a ticket indicating it had been used); and while the YMCA receipt showed Manning had stayed there in late October of 1977, George admitted he had not checked to see if anyone there remembered him (he did not have a picture of Manning at the time, he explained) or whether Manning's identification would have been required.

"Mr. George," Van Dam said, "I know that you have spent a fair amount of time with or around Marc Schreuder. Would you describe him for us, please?"

"Very intelligent, calculating individual."

And did he view what happened in Texas as something done by that sort of person?

Yes, he did.

"Using his own name, going to a friend's house who knew him well, buying a gun in the presence of many people?" Van Dam asked, his incredulous tone unmistakable.

Yes, the investigator insisted. Going to a place miles removed from New York, "with at that point no traceable means of following him . . . then committing a murder approximately two thousand miles away from Midland, Texas. I consider that very intelligent and very calculating."

"Would you use your name in doing that?" he was asked.

"If I was not able to get a gun by any other name and I had a friend in Texas where it is very loose to get a gun, I certainly couldn't go to my friend's home and tell them I am Joe Blow."

On Monday morning, June 28, Ernie Jones called his last witness, a woman who had ridden the rails across the country to help out an old friend. Identifying herself as a writer, Dorothy Ferguson verified that Richard Behrens had stayed with her in Lynchburg in July of 1978 and that she had phoned his apartment in New York and spoken with him on both the 20th and the 22nd. She told the court that in 1977 Behrens had talked with her and said "he believed that Mrs. Schreuder was planning to do away with her father." She said she had told him if he thought she was serious about this, he should contact the Salt Lake City police—warning him that "if you don't, then I will."

But he had a warning for her, she explained: "It will be very, very dangerous. You could be killed if you do." She heeded his advice at the time and said that Behrens called her sometime later to say that "Mr. Bradshaw had died." He didn't say it was by "foul means" but before long "he began to drop hints that the family was involved. . . ."

On cross-examination, she confirmed that Behrens was looking for a gun in Lynchburg but "I was not aware he was trying to obtain it on behalf of any family." In her deep Southern voice she offered that she was very much in favor of gun control, and had even given Behrens "a little speech" about it.

On re-direct, Jones prodded her to be more specific about the hints Behrens had dropped and she tried to accommodate him. "He indicated to me that it had been engineered by Mrs. Schreuder but he never came out and said it. . . . As time went on he began to say . . . a 'male' and maybe 'he' and I got the impression that he was referring to one of the sons."

At ten forty-five, after Doug Steele was recalled to say he never remembered Marilyn coming into the warehouse and announcing her desire to take over the auto-parts business, the state rested its case. The defense asked for a recess until two and the judge granted it. Over the next three hours, speculation and rumors were rampant as to what their strategy would be or who, if anybody, they would call. They had raised the possibility the previous Friday that Frances, protected by temporary immunity from her ongoing extradition battle, might appear and testify about Behrens. The fact that her local attorney was seen conferring with Tesch and Van Dam only served to support that notion. But Ernie Jones, as much in the dark as anybody, had not been contacted about issuing such a grant. So like everybody else, the prosecutor just waited, wondering what would happen next.

51 // David Frankel and Ted Carey had each received a phone call over the weekend—a phone call that contained a disturbing request.

Frankel boarded a plane in New York at about the same time Carey was boarding one in Windsor Locks, Connecticut, just north of Hartford. They had decided to meet in Chicago and fly on to Salt Lake from there. Van Dam and Tesch had asked them to arrive by Sunday evening so that the four of them could discuss a strategy—one, Frankel and Carey worried, that could have a potentially destructive impact on their own careers.

They had become good friends since they met the previous October in New York. Aside from being savvy lawyers, they loved sports and were avid golfers. Frankel thought it a bit ludicrous when Carey suggested they bring their clubs. After all, they weren't likely to be in Salt Lake longer than two days, and they certainly weren't going there for a vacation. But given what was being asked of them, they figured that they might as well have some fun at the same time. They had been in close contact with Tesch and Van Dam while the two were preparing for trial. But since they had not been present during any of the proceedings, they were eager to get as much background on what had been said as they possibly could. Tesch and Van Dam said it was unlikely Judge Sawaya would give Marc murder one; the state's case looked pretty strong but it seemed to them the judge was looking for a way to compromise. Marc had spent four hours with a local psychiatrist—two two-hour sessions before the trial began— and the doctor's testimony, they felt, could make a very persuasive argument for a verdict of manslaughter. But before putting him on, a certain amount of foundation would need to be laid—and that's where Frankel and Carey came in. The four of them agreed that having Marc testify would not be a good idea. That left one other alternative—have the two of them testify in Marc's behalf.

What Tesch and Van Dam were asking them to do—break

the sacred bond of confidentiality between attorney and client—was bad enough. But in Frankel's case, the request was even worse: *he was being asked to take the stand on Monday afternoon and admit that Marc did in fact kill his grandfather*—a confession Marc had made to him the previous November.

From late that Sunday night until three the next morning, the four of them sat in the Salt Lake Hilton discussing the pros and cons of the strategy. Even though the Utah lawyers were confident that Marc would take their advice and agree to waive the attorney-client privilege, Frankel and Carey said they wanted to sleep on it and discuss it with Mike Armstrong and Jim Wade in a few hours' time.

When Tesch and Van Dam left, the two friends just sat there, staring at each other, unable to move. "One of us said," Carey recalled, " 'How in the hell am I going to sleep with this goddam decision on my mind?' This was revolutionary what we were thinking of doing. To our knowledge this was the first time this had ever happened. What we were being asked to do was essentially contrary to every piece of training we'd ever had. You *don't* do that kind of thing. Even if the guy *wants* you to do it, you resist it. You can just see it now: 'Carey squeals on client.' How was the bar going to react? What about other clients? Quite frankly, it had dawned on us that this was a reasonable way to handle the situation in terms of *Marc's* well-being. As far as ours, that was a problem. We were faced with this situation: Who's Number One here? Were we going to put our careers on the line? Who was going to take the knife for him in the *hope* that he could get a manslaughter?"

Not only could they not sleep, but it was too early to call Armstrong in New York and Wade in Hartford. Frankel got up, went over to his set of golf clubs and pulled out his putter and a ball. Carey did the same and suggested they play a round of miniature golf. "So we open up the door to our rooms at three-thirty a.m.," Carey carefully explained, "go out into the hall, which is dark, and turn the hall lights on. You know, this is Salt Lake City. They roll up the sidewalks. We started off gently. We're betting a dollar a hole. Things start getting more and more revolutionary. We start teeing off from the top of the bed with wedges. The crowning blow—which did it for Frankel as far as his getting some sleep—was when I set up this hole and we were teeing off from the top of a table, at one end of the room. We had a great dogleg and I had created a number of hazards—one of which was one of my white woolen socks. Frankel tees off and is in a great position to make the dogleg. I tee off and my ball rolls right into the sock. I was hung by my own petard. Frankel is catatonic at this point, then laughing. I asked him for a rule interpretation: Could I play an unplayable lie? He said no. So I bashed at the thing and both the sock and the ball go flying and punch a hole into the wall of an adjoining room. Frankel, at this point, says, 'I quit. I'm too weak from laughing.' "

They managed to get an hour and a half of sleep before receiving a wake-up call from the front desk at six. When they finally reached Armstrong and Wade the advice they got was the same: You've got to do what you've got to do. It may be revolutionary and unheard-of, but once the facts are known in the legal community it will be no problem, though you may run into unjustified criticism.

A few hours later the four lawyers met with Marc, who said that this was what he wanted. Frankel asked Van Dam, Tesch and Carey to leave the room while he and Marc spoke alone. Frankel then asked Carey to come back in and the three of them spoke some more—"so that together," Frankel said, "we could evaluate if this was what Marc *really* wanted." It isn't that Frankel didn't trust the two Utah lawyers. But they had lived through the trial and were understandably caught up in it; Frankel felt he had to determine, both as an outsider and as an interested party, if this was the right thing to do. He told Marc that he hadn't followed the trial and could only give him "gut instincts." After a half hour, the decision was the same: Frankel and Carey were going to take the stand. The two lawyers met with the psychiatrist whose testimony would follow theirs—unless the prosecution objected that their testimony was hearsay and inadmissible, which was a distinct possibility—and read his report, then Frankel requested an in-chambers conference with the judge.

The discussion in Judge Sawaya's chambers had all the tension of a high-powered summit meeting. Aside from Marc,

Carey, Frankel, the defense and the prosecution, Kevin Kurumada was present on behalf of Berenice and David Watkiss, Jr., on behalf of Frances. Outside in the courtroom, every seat was filled, the doors were locked, but even though it was two p.m. no one had any idea what was going on or when the afternoon session would begin.

The defense gave no indication of what the two lawyers would say. Nervous and uncomfortable, Frankel pointed out how crucial it was that the record show Marc was *voluntarily* waiving the attorney-client privilege—and that the press understand that as well. Watkiss immediately raised the question of Frankel's similar relationship with Frances, obviously concerned as to what the curly-haired attorney might say about his client. Neither Frankel nor his firm represented Frances, he said. Both she and Mrs. Bradshaw had been told that from the moment his firm took on the case. The only time there was ever a problem with that understanding, he said, was when Frances was arrested and he explained the circumstances—from the time she first called him that Thursday night until he was required to sign in as her attorney at the 19th Precinct the next day. But Watkiss was not satisfied. He said that Frankel had spoken with her between sixty and seventy times; he was concerned that the attorney would be unable to avoid "revealing insights" from his conversations with her. Of all the conversations he had with her, Frankel snapped, "only three were substantial" and the others consisted of her phoning hysterically and his trying to get her off the phone.

As Ernie Jones listened to all of this, there were a number of things going through his mind. Should he object on the basis of hearsay and try to force them to put Marc on? Or should he sit back and wait to hear what Frankel had to say—and avoid the risk of not having Marc *or* Frankel testify at all? As far as what might come out about Frances, he was concerned that the defense would try to blame everything on her in an attempt to get Marc acquitted or have his charge reduced. Or that just the opposite might happen: that Frankel might take the stand and say she had nothing to do with it. But he also was thinking that "maybe something will come out that will give us a stronger case against her. You just weren't sure what you were going to hear."

He might not have been sure, but he decided to listen anyway.

At five minutes to three, a grim-faced Paul Van Dam stood up to give his opening statement in the hushed courtroom. It would be brief, he said, because he wanted to introduce three witnesses who would explain how Marc was "a young man who found himself in an extremely strange and extremely pressing and overwhelming circumstance in his life. . . . We believe, Your Honor, that though Mr. Schreuder is going to admit the responsibility for this act that the explanation, the fullness of the explanation, fits an appropriate category in law in this state which we will also argue to the court at the appropriate time."

It was, as someone said later, "an incredible bombshell, a page right out of Perry Mason," and the press were dying to get out and call in the story. But the courtroom door had been locked for more than an hour, so they—and everyone else—were held captive as the tale unfolded.

The defense had a tape and transcript they wanted to have admitted into evidence. A few seconds of the tape were played in court, and Ted Carey, the first witness, identified the two voices on it as being those of Frances and Lavinia. No further explanation was given about the tape (which David Watkiss had earlier tried—and failed—in chambers to prevent from being introduced), but that too would come. Carey told the court that he had spoken with Frances many times over the phone, had met her twice in New York (Lavinia was present both times), and that in his opinion she was "the most difficult individual" he had ever had to deal with in his professional or personal life.

That said, David Frankel took the stand and Joe Tesch wasted little time. Over a two-week period, beginning about the time Marc was released on bail in mid-November of 1981, he and Marc had met between eight and ten times (roughly fifty hours in all) in his law office in lower Manhattan.

"Did there come a time in those conversations when Mr. Schreuder admitted to you direct involvement in the death of his grandfather?"

"Yes, sir."

"And approximately how far into your conversations did that occur?"

"It was after about four or five conversations." Keenly aware that every eye was on him, he was determined to be deliberate in his answers, and he was.

"And at that conversation," Tesch asked, "what did he admit to you concerning his involvement in this crime?"

"Marc said that he and his brother, Larry, had murdered their grandfather."

Ernie Jones and Mike George were spellbound. While the press were scribbling furiously into their notebooks behind them, mentally composing their leads for the television broadcasts that night and the next morning's papers, the prosecutor and investigator were kicking themselves: they had not been able to find one solid piece of evidence—other than Larry's failed answer on the polygraph test—to link Larry to the murder, and it certainly seemed as if Berenice had given him a perfect alibi.

"Did he tell you why?" Tesch pressed.

Yes, he did. "The gist of the explanation was that he was terrified that his mother was going to commit suicide and because, over the past year to year and a half, she had hysterically warned both he and his brother about the possibility that Mr. Bradshaw was going to disinherit Mrs. Schreuder and he was worried that if they didn't get—retract that. Worry is perhaps not a strong enough statement. Between the two of them, they felt this act was necessary for the protection of their mother."

"Did he state to you at the time whether or not his mother was involved?"

"Yes, sir. He said she was not."

"Did he state to you whether or not she knew about the plot?"

"Yes, sir. He said she did not."

Jones could hardly believe what he was hearing and could see the case against Frances embarrassingly slipping away. He should have tried to stop this when he had the chance in chambers, but he would now have to wait until cross-examination.

"Did he say or can you remember anything more about the

505

phrase that you had just used, that he said it was necessary for the protection of his mother?"

"By the time this conversation came up, I had already spent approximately twenty to thirty hours with Marc. We had developed a relationship based on perhaps just that longevity, but also on my constant harping at him that the only way I could help him was to get the truth. He had expressed on any number of occasions his devotion and loyalty to his mother. So that when he told me this story, I was not particularly surprised."

"Did he relate, in using the word 'protection,' did he reference that to any matter of pending danger to her?"

"He felt sure she was suicidal. He had told me that she had already tried to commit suicide on two other occasions, one of which he told me that he found her lying on the floor, as I recall, having taken some pills, and called the paramedics. He said she had constantly expressed to him the fear of being poor and that this was his way of assuring that that would never happen."

"Did there come a time when Marc Schreuder admitted to you involvement of his mother in the death of his grandfather?"

"Yes, sir."

There it was. Jones and George were breathing easier, but the prosecutor was now convinced that Tesch would try to tip the scales too far to the other side.

Frankel explained that he was not satisfied with the details Marc had given him. "I pressed him for more in clearer detail. His story changed from time to time. The meetings that we had were at times very emotional. I was not easy on him. . . . On many occasions, in order to try and find out to my satisfaction what the truth was, I indicated to Marc that I thought one or another person might have been involved, that his story didn't jell . . . and one of the people whom I constantly pressed him on was his mother."

Marc consistently denied her involvement, the lawyer recalled, but when the admission came—either on the 27th or 28th of November—Marc had been in his office for about three or four hours and "I had spent probably the last hour leading up to this, telling him that I felt that his mother was involved, that he was trying to protect her. He constantly shook his head. I yelled at him any number of times. We went over and over the same material many many times. I am sure at many times during these few hours I told him that I simply couldn't help him unless he told me the truth and he hadn't done so. And while I don't recall the exact question that I asked him, what he said to lead up to that question, there came a time where I again asked him if his mother was involved and he looked at me and said, 'Yes.' "

"How did he say yes? In what manner did it come from?"

"He put his head down and simply said, 'Yes,' very quietly."

"And what happened for the next few moments?"

"I simply watched as Marc tried to gain control of himself. He was shaking. And for about two or three minutes nothing was said between the two of us. I then told him how I thought I understood how difficult it was for him—how difficult I thought it was for him to tell me that. He nodded his head and for about, as I recall, ten or fifteen minutes, there was no conversation of any substance that we had. And then after that, I pressed him for details of how he and his mother were involved."

For the next few hours, Frankel "just sapped everything out of me," Marc later told a friend—hours in which Marc would cry, laugh, almost become delirious and, finally, feel relieved that he had confessed. As he sat in the courtroom now, those hours came flooding back to him. Throughout the trial, he had shown little emotion: he and Mary Lou, who had been in court every day, had smiled at each other a few times, and he had grinned when John Cavenaugh described him at Kent. But this was different, and even before Frankel began to recall how he shook that day, Marc put down a book he was reading, laid his head on the desk, and started to cry.

"He told me that for about the year or year and a half prior to the murder," the lawyer went on, "his mother had told him that his grandfather had to be killed because he was going to disinherit them and they were going to be thrown out on the street with nothing to eat, that she had persisted in this over that period of time on frequent occasions. That at one point,

Mrs. Schreuder had attempted to hire what Marc called a hit man to murder Mr. Bradshaw and that she paid him five thousand dollars to do it and that, apparently, this hit man, whose name Marc told me was Myles Manning, said he would do it but simply took the money and was never seen from again. At that point, and I am not certain exactly what point this is in time, but Mrs. Brad—excuse me, Mrs. Schreuder told Marc that he was going to have to do it and they were going to have a plan, a way that Marc could murder his grandfather. . . . Marc told me that his mother suggested a number of scenarios for how this might be done and eventually it was decided that Marc or she would have to get a gun and Marc would have to go up to Utah and shoot his grandfather."

". . . What did he tell you about those particular facts?"

"He told me that his mother had tried to purchase a gun, as I recall now, either by herself or through Mr. Richard Behrens. That they had not been successful and that she was sure that Marc had some school friends who could help Marc buy a gun. Marc said that he didn't want to do this. He said to me that his mother had told him that it had to be done. Marc said that finally he just came to the conclusion that he simply had to do it if he was going to be able to live with his mother. He said that his mother told him the best time to do it was on a Sunday because Mr. Bradshaw was generally in his warehouse early in the morning by himself. That they planned to do it on a Sunday, that Marc called a school friend of his named John Cavenaugh who . . . lived in Texas and had always bragged about guns in the state of Texas. That he had told his mother this and Mrs. Schreuder suggested that this would be the way where Marc could get a gun. That it was decided that Marc would go down to Mr. Cavenaugh's home, which was in Midland, Texas, and try to purchase a gun; and that if he was successful, he was going to go to Salt Lake City and shoot his grandfather."

He flew on to Salt Lake, Frankel said, registered in a hotel, and called his mother. They spoke for "an hour to an hour and a half" and he "told her that he didn't want to do it. He was crying. He couldn't do it. Mrs. Schreuder told him that it had to be done, that there was no getting around it, that he had to be a man. And Marc told me that he felt at that point if he didn't go through with it, he would never see his mother again."

While Marc was out on bail, Frankel explained, Frances didn't want him living at home, because she was afraid "of what the neighbors and what the cooperative board would think." So Berenice had rented a small hotel room a few blocks away (the Gracie Square Hotel) and Marc was only allowed to come home for meals.

Had Marc ever told him about what had happened between Larry and his mother?

"Well, he had told me numerous stories about Larry being locked out of the house on many occasions, forced to sleep in the corridor or on the street. . . . He was terribly afraid that it was going to happen to him if he didn't go through with the shooting of his grandfather." From what Marc told him, Frankel said, it was clear that he "had no friends whom he could turn to" and that on one occasion he said "his mother was the only friend that he had."

Asked about the tape that Ted Carey had earlier identified, Frankel said that Marc had given it to him; he had heard parts of it, kept it in an office drawer, and eventually gave it to Paul Van Dam.

What about the gun? Had Marc ever told him what he had done with that?

"He told me that he flew back from Salt Lake City to New York that morning, that he put the gun in his luggage, that his mother had insisted that he bring the gun back with him. That he had told her that he had thought that they should get rid of the gun but that she said no, that he came back to New York and his mother asked him for the gun, which I think was in a paper bag. And he gave the gun to his mother. He told her he thought that they should get rid of the gun, again, but his mother said no. Then his mother gave the gun to Mr. Behrens."

It was about four-thirty when Ernie Jones stood to confront David Frankel. There had been a fifteen-minute recess during the defense's direct examination, but it had taken only fifteen seconds for word to spread to news desks and around the courthouse of what had just happened. In one hour, Frankel had corroborated what the state had been saying in nine days of trial. Jones was quietly pleased, but he was not about to let the attorney pull Marc off the hook of murder one so quickly; he felt Marc was more than just a tool of his mother's desires and was determined to show that. If Tesch could use Frankel as part of his strategy to get manslaughter, Jones would try to use him both to confirm other elements in the state's case (maybe picking up some interesting nuggets along the way) and to reveal a number of things that Marc perhaps *hadn't* told him. According to Frankel, Marc had told him about the cash and blank checks he and Larry had stolen in 1977 and how upset their grandfather had been. He had told him his grandfather was making a new will that would exclude his mother, because *she* had told him about it. He said he'd learned about Manning from his mother (and the $5,000 she had left under a pillow on their living-room couch); and that he had purchased an airline ticket at the Plaza, flown to Texas under the name of L. Gentile, gone to a closed bank that Saturday with Cavenaugh and his friend, and bought the gun from "a deputy sheriff or his wife" (Frankel couldn't recall which one).

Had Marc told him how he had gotten into the warehouse on Sunday morning? Jones asked.

"Yes."

"How was that?"

"Told me he walked in through a side door."

"And how did he get through the side door?"

"I presume he opened it."

"What time did he arrive at the warehouse on the morning of the 23rd?"

"To the best of my recollection, he said somewhere between six-thirty and seven."

"Before or after Mr. Bradshaw had arrived?"

"Before."

"And did he tell you where he hid in the warehouse?"

"As I recall, Marc told me he waited outside until Mr. Bradshaw arrived."

"Then what did he do?"

"He went in the warehouse."

"And once he got in the warehouse, what did he do? Where did he go?"

"Mr. Bradshaw was standing in front of the counter. As I recall, Marc told me he went up to him and that he shot him."

"Where did he shoot him?"

"In the back."

"Did he fire more than one shot?"

"Told me he fired two shots."

"When did the second shot occur?"

"Shortly after the first."

"Where did he shoot his grandfather?"

"I don't remember Marc telling me."

"Was there any conversation before he shot his grandfather?"

"No."

"He just walked into the store and shot his grandfather?"

"He told me that his grandfather's back was to him and that he walked up to him and stopped for a few seconds and hoped that his grandfather wasn't going to turn around."

"And did he?"

"No."

Frankel recalled that Marc had taken a taxi from the airport when he arrived from Texas, but could not remember how he said he had gotten back to the airport that Sunday morning.

So where did Larry fit in to all this?

Marc's initial story, Frankel reiterated, was that Larry and he had planned and carried out the murder—that Larry had reserved his hotel room and phoned their mother to confirm that their grandfather would be at the warehouse that Sunday. But "later on," Frankel said, "he told me that his brother had nothing to do with it."

Had Marc ever told him that Larry had unlocked or left unlocked any of the doors in the warehouse the night before?

No, he hadn't. He knew that Marc had used Larry's name to travel under (but could not remember why) and he said that Marc had never told him about an airline ticket in the name of L. Schreuder that had been ordered from New York for use on the day of the murder.

Jones asked him about a number of other things—all of which the lawyer said Marc had never told him about: *Death on the Nile;* his asking Richard Behrens for a gun (Frankel said he knew Behrens was asked, but had not obtained one);

attempts to kill his grandfather in the summer of 1977; the phone call requesting $3,000 and whether that money had been used to purchase the airline tickets and the gun; Marc's recounting of the murder to Behrens; the pressure he and Frances had exerted on Behrens to change his story (though Frankel pointed out he had never asked him about it).

Had Marc ever told him that the reason his mother insisted he bring the gun back from Salt Lake was so that it could be used against Myles Manning? (Behrens had told the state that revenge against Manning had been mentioned at one point.) No. Had Marc ever told him that as recently as February he had stolen $40,000 in jewelry from his mother? No. Was he aware that Frances had filed a complaint in New York about this? No. Had Marc ever told him that he forged his grandmother's signature on checks "to the tune of almost $300,000"? No. Well, then, what money had Marc admitted stealing? As he recalled, Marc had forged his grandmother's checks for about $40,000 the year before and used it to purchase coins.

Jones was bothered by Frankel's earlier suggestion that Marc had no friends, and the lawyer, who said he couldn't recall saying that, admitted "there was at least one friend that he told me he had."

"His name?"

"It was her. Her name was Susan Coleman."

Pleased that Frankel confirmed what they already knew, he pressed his luck. "Did he also mention the name of Bob Brown?"

Yes, he had, but Frankel added that, in his opinion, "when Marc talked about these people there was a difference between 'they were friends' or people he knew."

But of all the points Jones wanted to make during his cross-examination, the key one was that Marc had not always told the truth.

"How many times did he lie to you, Mr. Frankel?"

"Many."

"In fact, for all you know, he may not have given you *all* the details to this murder, even now?"

"That is correct."

* * *

On re-direct, Tesch immediately shifted to Frances. Jones had pointed out that Frances was not at Kent or Trinity or in Salt Lake during the summer of 1977, and Tesch wanted to make sure the judge understood her control over Marc was as strong as if she had been. Frankel explained why Marc and Larry had stolen from their grandfather and told of their mother's complaints that they weren't sending back enough money. One of the reasons Marc stole from his grandmother, Frankel said, was "to finance his getaway"—an escape that Marc said his mother was encouraging. "He told me that she said to him the best thing for everybody would be if he just disappeared."

Before Frankel left the stand, he said that his firm insisted (in November of 1981) that a number of coins Marc had purchased with the money he stole from his grandmother be returned to her. But just to prove Marc wasn't cured—and to get in his last dig—the prosecutor waved a check for $20,000 in front of Frankel and asked if Marc had told him he had forged this in February of 1982.

"I have no knowledge from what Marc told me." That was Frankel's careful, lawyerly way of saying that he knew from other sources.

David Frankel's day in court was over. Paul Van Dam repeated to the press what they had been told by Sawaya: it had been Marc's decision for Frankel to testify. "It's got to be," he explained. "It's his life. He wanted to get it all out."

He looked as impressive as his credentials. A tall, lean, white-haired figure in his sixties, Dr. Louis Moench, the physician who had been called to testify that Tuesday morning, had been a practicing psychiatrist for nearly forty years and taught at the University of Utah's medical school. In his long career, he had treated thousands of patients and had been asked to testify—by both the defense and the prosecution—as an expert witness about two hundred times. He was clearly a man to be reckoned with.

Moench had seen Marc once in May and once in June—the day before the trial. He was the key to the defense's chances for manslaughter and he quickly eased into a calm and confident narrative of what he had learned from his roughly four hours with Marc, and from listening to the Frances-Lavinia tape that the defense had given him.

He told the court of Marc's family background, of Larry's emotional problems and the reason why he had been sent to prison, of how Marc felt he had—and had to—become his mother's psychiatrist, of what happened during the summer of 1977, of how, after it, his mother's insistence that Gramps had to be killed because he was in the process of writing her out of his will became "one of the major issues in the household," and of how this idea involved Richard Behrens and Myles Manning as well.

During the spring of 1978, Moench explained, Marc and Frances "spent a great deal of time talking about a scenario or script for the killing of the grandfather and they talked about who would do it. . . . The mother decided that someone in the family would have to do it and that Marc was the one."

"By April she was broke," Marc said, according to Moench's written report that had been admitted into evidence, *"and became obsessed with bumping off Gramps, the only thing that would save our family—'I'll have to move to Harlem with Lavinia [he quotes his mother saying] and lock the door on you if you don't do it. Look, Marc, it is not really killing, it is the right thing to do for us. Gramps is old, and he doesn't care about people and he won't help us. I wouldn't live with Granny and Gramps, would rather die.'"* Granny and Gramps had invited them to come to Salt Lake and live with them, and Marc says he wouldn't mind, he liked them. *"Granny gave all she had to mother, but mother was never satisfied."*

Marc thought the mother should sell some of [her] jewelry but she wouldn't. She said they were near eviction. "'We've got to pull it off now. Look, Marc, it has to be done. . . . You can use Myles' plan.'"

"Marc said he pled against the idea," the psychiatrist said, but was unsuccessful. He explained how Marc had gotten in touch with John Cavenaugh, flown to Texas, and stayed with John's family. "[Marc] said that they treated him so well there that he wondered if there wasn't some way he could stay there with the family and not proceed with this plan. I don't recall the number of times he talked to his mother, but during that time of purchasing the gun and coming to Salt Lake, he had talked to his mother, tried to dissuade her from this plan. And she had insisted that this was the only solution to the problem. It was the right thing, that Gramps was an old miser, that he was a Howard Hughes, that he was destroying their family." That if Marc didn't do this, "she would never speak to him again. He flew to Salt Lake City, said he stayed in a hotel overnight and, as I recall, one of his phone conversations to his mother was after he arrived in Salt Lake City that evening."

*Told her he had a gun—she was pleased—"If you want me to do something else"—she said (very emotional) "There is no other way, we've discussed this before and I'm not going to discuss it with you—a sicko—a psychotic"—(would call him that whenever angry with him)—"You've got to do it for Lavinia"—argued with her about his childhood—extremely bitter about it but she insisted there was no other choice. He stayed up most of the night . . . —thinking of way out—excuses or lies—but "I can't lie to her—she always knows and if I come back with any excuse, I'd get locked out permanently, she'd commit suicide, or threaten—if I told her I failed, she'd lock me out permanently—like Larry—so I thought I'd have to get it over with."**

The following morning, Moench said, Marc went over to the warehouse and "waited for Gramps to come in his little green pickup truck. He said he hoped that somebody else would come so that that would interfere with this. And he said that he asked Gramps why Gramps didn't send them the money that they needed and that Gramps didn't give a satisfactory reply. He said he hoped that Gramps wouldn't stay in the position of looking at him because he would be unable to shoot him if he were looking at him. . . ."

"It had to be done. I couldn't go back to N.Y. and face Mom. Why don't I just walk out and go to Granny's for summer. Was really waiting for someone to come in—I couldn't face him—I shot him in the

---

*Additional notes of Dr. Moench's from which report is drawn and which accompanied it.

back. I wasn't going to get anything out of it—I wasn't in his will—he was going to pay for my school."

"Said he then went back to the hotel. He said he was very upset, just about missed his flight. That he was on the flight back to New York, concerned that hopefully Gramps was not dead but then what would Mother do? Mother would never accept him if Gramps were not dead. . . .

On plane—obsessed with idea he was only injured and he might be alive—if he was alive, "Mom would be angry—messed it up as usual . . . he was a great man and not an evil old miser like Mom said. I really liked him. I've done my best and if she didn't like it—too bad." Asked mother to do it herself—but she called him a coward and she couldn't leave Lavinia; he offered to tend Lavinia. . . .

Couldn't believe he'd done it—just wanted to get home and tell Mom and hoping she would approve—he had done something right for once. She was at beach with Mr. Baron's [sic] all day long.

"When he arrived at the apartment, Mother and Lavinia were not there. He said he stayed in the deli until they did return and that Mother . . . embraced him and kissed him and hugged him for about ten minutes while he was sobbing. And he said she had never done anything like this before in his life."

" 'Where is the gun?' " [Marc said she asked] —gave it to her, she gave it to Barrons [sic]. . . . "something horrible had been done"—mo. reassured "it was the only way. I believed her then, but that's nuts. Granny called with news . . . Mom cried, 'Oh, my God, what happened.' " pt. talked to Granny—"60 seconds"—then to Mom for hour.

Having received this information, Van Dam asked, could he characterize or explain to the court the nature of the relationship that existed between the mother and son?

"It was my opinion," Moench slowly began, "from these two two-hour interviews and discussions, that there was an extremely pathological relationship between Marc and his mother, that this was characterized by Marc going through a relationship that was inappropriate for his age in the sense that he had not resolved—forgive the jargon—the Oedipus situation [which Moench refers to in his report as "extremely severe"] in which a little boy is usually closely attached to his mother until he gets past Cub Scout age,* then comes to the conclusion that his father is the model that he wants to follow and becomes then attached more to his father and imitates his father and in a way moves his mother to a more peripheral relationship. This is what ordinarily happens in a normal family. This did not happen in Marc's situation. There was no male figure. Very obviously, his father was gone before he was aware. Frederick was not an ideal figure for him. Gramps was one of the figures, but Marc had not gone through a stage in his emotional development in which he detached himself from his mother. He, in essence, became his mother's best friend and confidant and adviser. And I have thought it an extremely pathological way since he described her in extremely dramatic terms, shall we say."

"Can you describe for us just a moment the use of the term 'pathological'?"

"This is just an indication that the relationship was not normal, that it was, in essence, a sick relationship."

"Can you describe for us, Doctor, your opinion regarding the strength of the relationship in regards to the amount of sway or influence this mother would hold over this child?"

"It was my opinion, at least from Marc's discussion of his relationship with his mother and her behavior, that she was an extremely controlling person, that she insisted that she have her way on everything, that she was always right, that if he or Lavinia didn't do exactly as she said or Larry didn't do exactly as she said, that she would threaten suicide or make a suicide attempt . . . would threaten locking him out, would threaten disowning him. And he found this extremely terrifying. This was, I think, by far the strongest influence in his emotional development."

"Doctor, you have listened to the tape that has been referred to and identified as Defendant's Exhibit 92, which is an interchange between Frances Schreuder and her daughter, Lavinia, and that, I believe, has been your only actual contact with the mother in any sense; is that true?"

---

*"Cub Scout age" is between eight and ten. The age for "resolving" the complex, some professionals say, may begin as early as four.

"That is true."

"You listened to that tape. Can you draw any conclusion or can you enlighten the court regarding the personality of the mother and the effect of the kind of technique, language that was used in that conversation with this young daughter?"

"I am not sure I can always separate what Marc told me about his mother and what I heard on the tape, but the tape, as I recall, was an interchange between Frances and Lavinia, lasting approximately an hour . . . in which Frances is asking this little girl essentially what is a sentence and just drumming and drumming and drumming into this little girl this question, what is a sentence, and saying it starts with a capital and that usually it is more than one word and it ends with what? What does it end with? And what are the exceptions? And the little girl usually crying with this, 'Mama, Mama,' and not being able beyond to say a sentence begins with a capital letter and when what does it end with? she is unable to say. The mother in this tape is berating this little girl for talking in class. And she said you will never be invited to any of those beautiful parties. All you will do is talk to those little Jew girls there. You are going to be sent to a mental hospital . . . and you will never get out, if you don't learn what this sentence is. And I will never come and see you. She goes on and on in this regard."

The tape, which Marc recorded in October of 1979, is in fact even more horrific and disturbing than the doctor suggests. On it, Frances employs the same divide-and-conquer tactics that Berenice had used with her as a child. She tells Lavinia, who was all of six, that Berenice "wants you sick and under her thumb and she's not your mother. She has ruined you. She is not a good mother. She is bad. And she's not a good grandmother." She reminds Lavinia how much she hates "West Side girls" and that unless she pulls her grades up and learns to read she'll have to keep going to St. Hilda's & St. Hugh's (on the Upper West Side; the same Episcopal school where Marc and Larry had gone years before). She "can never go to pretty-girl schools," Frances shrieks, "go to pretty-girl parties on the East Side. . . . You will never have all the pretty things that all the girls on the East Side do."

On the second side of the tape, when Frances continually

asks her what a sentence is and she is not able to respond, Frances tells her, "You'll never get married, you'll never see boys, you'll never go out and work. You'll never see your mother again. . . . You'll never see your house again. Nobody. . . . You'll live in the hospital. They have special hospitals for children who are disturbed. . . . And they stay there the rest of their lives. They are not permitted to go out ever."

For one brief period, when Lavinia is able to say, under Frances's prompting, that a sentence begins with a capital letter and ends with a period, Frances tells her that she wishes Lavinia could learn at home and reminds her that during the previous school year they used to laugh together over stories Lavinia would tell her. "You learned not to be afraid of Mom," Frances says, "and not to be afraid to make mistakes and not to cry. I'm not a fearful person, Lavinia."

"I know," Lavinia says.

"I get angry when you are afraid, afraid to learn and afraid of me."

But this calm moment quickly ends as Lavinia, once more, is unsure of what a sentence is.

"What is a sentence?" Frances asks. "You have it in all those books. Don't you remember? I showed you tonight. I showed you six times. I've explained it to you. I've had you repeat it to me. . . . And five minutes ago you finally said it is—said correctly what a sentence is. . . . What is a sentence?"

"A sentence is—"

"Shut up and tell me. I don't want to see you stall for time anymore. You sit and repeat words over again. Just tell me what a sentence is . . . and stop crying and stop shivering. What is a sentence, you coward? You belong in a zoo with the animals."

After "four solid hours," Lavinia finally gives her, in fragments, the answer she wants. A sentence begins with a capital letter, contains a complete thought, and ends with a period, question mark or exclamation point.

"I consider this child abuse," Moench was saying, "and extreme pressure of the worst form. I would much prefer hearing about a parent spanking a little child. I think this is outrageously abusive. And this pretty well confirms the way Marc describes how she put pressure on him and on Larry to do what she wants."

"Doctor, assuming, if I may, that this sort of behavior actually went on with Marc from an early age until the time that he committed this act, what kind of psychological effect would this have on him?"

"I am not sure I know whether this is just Marc's view of his mother, but I think he reacts to the mother as he sees her and describes her. But I think it has a profound effect, that his first priority is always to please Mother and to prevent her from doing something dangerous to herself or rejecting or throwing him out of the household."

"Doctor, were you able to form an opinion or do you have an opinion regarding Marc's propensity to violence? This was a horrendous act on his part. How was this able to be accomplished under the circumstances, as you know Marc?"

"I don't see any other evidence in Marc of any propensity for violence. I think he was always trying to be the peacemaker in the family. And while I appreciate there may be information I don't know, I see no propensity for violence. But I think his efforts to please his mother and to prevent rejection transcended any judgment about [the] right or welfare or well-being of another person. That his mother's influence was so strong that nothing else mattered that much."

". . . How would you characterize, in medical terms, the mother's personality?"

"I appreciate the problems of trying to make a diagnosis from the information given, but there was enough information given and the confirmation of this opinion by the tape . . . to use two different diagnoses to satisfy my mind about her character: *narcissistic personality disorder,* which essentially means I want what I want when I want it and if I don't get it, there is going to be trouble. The narcissistic character disorder is a pathological disorder in the sense that the first-person pronoun is the most important part of the alphabet. Other persons' welfare or well-being or comfort or even life may not be that important.

"The other included a *histrionic personality* and that describes a person being on a stage all the time, being the center of attention, feeling entitled to everything, feeling entitled to all of the attention, all of the influence, always the center of the stage all the time and that everyone else then has to play roles around this person."

". . . Doctor," Van Dam asked, "do you have an opinion as to what Marc believed would happen if he didn't obey the demands of his mother regarding the killing of his grandfather?"

"Yes, sir, I do."

"And what is that?"

"It was my opinion that Marc felt that if he did not carry out his mother's orders, that they might well indeed be evicted from the apartment, as his mother had repeatedly stressed, and wind up in Harlem in the gutter. He also was quite frightened that his mother would attempt or actually commit suicide if he failed. And he was terrified that he would be locked out of the apartment and banished from his mother's presence."

"Doctor, what do these symptoms add up to? I mean, how do you describe the nature of Marc's personality? Is he mentally ill?"

"I don't see him as mentally ill. I see him as—at the time of the alleged event and much of the time subsequently—as operating under extreme emotional turmoil. But I don't see him as psychiatrically ill."

"Let me ask you this, Doctor, in the words of a statute, would you say that he—"

Jones shot up to object. Van Dam was asking Moench to make a legal conclusion. The judge said that the statute (for manslaughter) states "that if he is acting under the influence of extreme mental or emotional disturbance, and I see that as probably a factual issue." Jones argued but lost, so Van Dam rephrased the question with the correct wording and got the answer he wanted.

Before leaving Dr. Moench at the mercy of the prosecutor, there were two more issues Van Dam hoped to resolve: whether there was a reasonable explanation for Marc's "emotional disturbance" and whether he could have responded any differently.

Marc's "indoctrination or brainwashing," Moench said, had been going on throughout his life. "The pathological

521

relationship with the mother and her demands on him constituted the explanation." As for the second question: "I don't think he had the capacity or the coping skills to deal with this in any other way."

It had been decided ahead of time that Dave Walsh would cross-examine. There are some lawyers whose entire personalities change once they step into the courtroom and Walsh is one of them. The friendly, almost meek nature and wry sense of humor he displays on the streets of Salt Lake dissolve into all business when he begins bearing down on a witness. But with the distinguished-looking psychiatrist, he had to be careful: if he appeared to be riding him too hard, he might dilute whatever he was able to achieve.

As it turned out, Walsh threw up almost everything imaginable. Things Marc didn't tell him about: traveling under a false name; going to the deli on his return in order to have an alibi (according to Behrens's testimony); hiding the gun in Behrens's apartment; concealing it in a suitcase; attempts to poison the oatmeal and joking and laughing about it; telling Behrens (according to Marilyn's testimony) that killing his grandfather was "easy"—as opposed to what he told Moench (that he was nervous and upset); that no one else was on the phone when he called Cavenaugh (according to Cavenaugh) —as opposed to Marc's telling Moench Frances was on the extension; checks of Berenice's that Marc had forged; other friends that he had.

Moench's response was essentially the same: any of that would be important to know, but it would probably only be confirmatory of the opinion he had reached. The examination of Marc was the crucial thing.

"Doctor," Walsh asked, "how certain are you of your conclusion?"

"I am comfortable with my conclusion," he said, adding, "I don't think there is any certainty." He said that in his thirty-five to forty years of practice, he had diagnosed "around twenty or so" people in the same way he had diagnosed Marc. Asked to define "comfortable," Moench said, "I have no question in my mind that the diagnosis and interpretation I have made is consistent with the facts and that if there are minor details, or even important details, I will still feel that this is the interpretation of what happened and what went on in his mind."

If Frances had told him to kill himself, Walsh asked, would he have done that?

"I don't know how I could answer that. But I think he would very seriously consider doing it."

"Would he do it in fact?"

"If I could guess that far ahead, I would play the stock market," Moench said, breaking the tension slightly in their increasingly testy exchange.

The ironic thing was that the state didn't really disagree with Moench's professional opinion of the relationship between Marc and Frances; they simply didn't feel that he was in a position to make a legal judgment. They wanted it both ways and were determined to try to have it. Marc had told Frankel one thing about the shooting—that his grandfather's back was always facing him and they had *no* conversation—and Moench just the opposite. That bothered Walsh, so he decided to ask Moench about it. But Moench replied that he "didn't pass judgment" on whether Marc was telling him the truth. He said earlier that he had had "thirty-eight years of experience talking to people and I think I can tell usually when they are *not* telling me the truth. . . . I formed the general opinion that most of what he told me was true, but I didn't think all of it was true."

Asked to reconfirm that Marc told him he hoped, after the shooting, that his grandfather was still alive, Moench said that was true.

"Did he tell you that after he shot him in the back, he placed the .357 Magnum up against his skull and pulled the trigger?"

Tesch objected on the grounds of no foundation but was overruled.

"He didn't tell me any of the details of the actual shooting," Moench said, but then corrected himself a moment later: "I think he told me he shot his grandfather when his back was turned."

"And hoped that he would live through those two types of wounds?" Walsh asked in a skeptical voice.

"Well, I think this was fantasy that he went through while he was on the airplane, hoping that what he had done had really not resulted in the death of his grandfather."

"He hoped he would live?"

"Yes." The doctor was holding firm. "He was going through what I think is a denial and a state of fantasy at the same time."

Throughout the grueling cross-examination, Moench pointed out other things: he didn't think, as Walsh suggested, that Marc "was trying to blame somebody else for what he had done"; on the contrary, he thought that "he was still defending her" during their sessions. Not only did Marc weep when Frankel testified the day before, but he wept several times in Moench's office—an indication, Moench said, "that we had touched on sensitive issues and he was emotionally upset" because of it. When the judge asked him whether his diagnosis of Marc at present was different from what he said Marc's state of mind was at the time, Moench replied he thought "there's been a significant change. . . . I think he has resolved part of the Oedipus complex. He's no longer feeling that he has to do everything exactly as his mother said or that his mother is always right."

"If it were a fact," Sawaya asked, "that he did steal forty thousand dollars' worth of jewelry from her, would that be evidence of a change in his mental attitude about her?"

"Yes, sir. I think he is changing and I think that would be evidence of a change."

Bothered by the fact that Moench's conclusions were drawn primarily from Marc and the tape (a psychologist had previously tested Marc and Moench had also spoken with him), the state asked Sawaya if they could have their *own* psychiatrist examine Marc in order to present a possible rebuttal testimony. Tesch objected to this—by law, this is granted only when an insanity defense has been offered—but Sawaya decided that determining Marc's "state of mind" at the time was critical, and he wanted at least one more opinion.

The following morning, though, having considered the defense's further argument that it would be a violation of Marc's Fifth Amendment rights protecting him from self-incrimination, the judge altered his decision slightly. He still wanted a second opinion, but the state's expert witness would have to testify without examining Marc.

As soon as Ernie Jones and Dave Walsh came back to the office, they got busy. The judge had adjourned court for two days, until Friday morning, and they had little time to waste. But when they started phoning around, they learned that no local psychiatrist really wanted to get into "a pissing contest" with Moench—with or without examining Marc. So they decided to try to get someone in California.

The first person they thought of was Seymour Pollack. Walsh had alluded to Pollack in his cross-examination of Moench the day before, and Moench had called him "one of the outstanding authorities on forensic psychology." But when they phoned Pollack's office, they found out that he had died recently, and were told to try Jay Ziskin. He was unavailable.

If they didn't find somebody quickly, they could see an unwanted verdict of manslaughter coming their way. John Nielsen, their immediate boss, suggested they call the Los Angeles County District Attorney's Office, which recommended two people: one of them was at UCLA and the other was a man in private practice in Berkeley. The man from UCLA not only wanted "an awful lot of money," Nielsen recalled, but he was "a bit equivocal." Walsh meanwhile was speaking with Lee Coleman. After the psychiatrist said he would be available, Walsh burst into Nielsen's office and said, "John, he's not your ordinary shrink. He's a debunker. He's going to tell us that psychiatric testimony is a bunch of hooey—especially since the crime occurred four years ago."

They had their man.

52// Lee Coleman arrived in Salt Lake in the late afternoon of the following day. Ernie Jones was waiting for the bearded psychiatrist with a stack of material for him to pore over; in addition to Dr. Moench's testimony, his report, notes and the tape, Jones supplied him with police reports, interviews with various witnesses, and the testimony of David Frankel and others. Over the next several hours, Coleman reviewed the material and discussed it with Jones. By the time they were finished, it was past midnight and pointless for Jones to make the forty-five-minutes drive home. Coleman went to his hotel and Jones simply unrolled his sleeping bag and curled up inside it. As he lay there, he felt sure the psychiatrist's testimony would repair whatever legal damage Moench may have inflicted on his case. But Lee Coleman wasn't the only reason Jones was pleased.

Earlier that day he received word from New York. Frances's appeal of the extradition order had been unanimously rejected by the Appellate Division. She had one avenue left—the Court of Appeals in Albany.

Lee Coleman turned out to be everything the prosecutor had hoped for—and more. Cool and self-assured, he repeatedly delivered the message that he said he would. A psychiatrist was no better prepared to determine a defendant's state of mind four years after an incident—or right after it, for that matter—than a lay person. He had no place in the courtroom. Psychiatry was an art, Coleman said, not a science like medicine, which could *prove* things with blood tests and x-rays. Psychiatrists could form opinions and sometimes provide a valuable therapeutic service to their patients, but it was wrong to call them as expert witnesses. They could be as easily fooled as anybody else—if not more so. "There isn't a shred of evidence," he said, "to indicate that they have any such tools [to determine state of mind] and there is mountains of evidence to indicate they don't have any of those tools."

For Moench to say that Marc suffered from an "unresolved Oedipus complex," the doctor contended, was "storytelling. There is no scientific way that Dr. Moench can determine that." Based only on two interviews with a man who was on trial for murder, Coleman said, "there is not even general agreement about whether the Oedipus complex is very important." Of even more concern, he said, was the conclusion that Marc "lost his free will [Coleman's term, not Moench's] as a result of his mother's influence. Free will is not something that psychiatrists know how to determine."

There were many things about Moench's testimony that

bothered Coleman—things that he found more significant than Moench had—and the prosecutor was eager to bring them out: Marc's not telling Moench about the second shot to the head and going through his grandfather's pockets; his opinion that Marc didn't have a propensity for violence at this time—something that psychiatrists, Coleman said, were also unable to determine; his diagnosis of Frances based on a tape recording, with no knowledge of why it was made or any ability to determine its authenticity; his flip-flop as to whether Marc was lying to him, first saying he thought he could tell (which Coleman insisted he couldn't), then conceding that Marc probably wasn't being truthful at all times (indicating to Coleman that Marc had the capacity to lie); his saying that even if he had received additional information about the murder his conclusion would probably not change—it was those very facts, Coleman said, that a case should be decided on, not a psychiatrist's "hunch."

On cross-examination, Coleman conceded that he belonged to a *minority* of psychiatrists (Thomas Szasz being the best-known) who believed as he did—that "psychiatry has absolutely no legitimacy in the courtroom"—but that a *majority* felt that psychiatric testimony was "misused" by the courts. Try as he might, Paul Van Dam was not able to shake the doctor from a testimony so adamant and unhesitant that, one person said later, it almost seemed "canned."

Salesmen are fond of saying that "if you can't close, you can't sell." And with the departure of Lee Coleman, it was time for Ernie Jones and Joe Tesch to make their closing arguments—their final push to the man whose burden it would be to pass judgment on Marc Francis Schreuder.

Calling the case "a rather bizarre and rather unique fact situation," Jones quietly but firmly reminded the judge that David Frankel had essentially confirmed everything the state had set out to prove—"all of our suspicions, all of our hunches, probably most important, all of the evidence which this court had heard": Marc had killed at his mother's request, and the motive behind the murder was money.

From the evidence presented, he said, it was apparent "that Franklin Bradshaw wanted his children to understand something, I guess, about the rules of life, about the values of life, and, I suppose, the message was that money wasn't everything or at least it shouldn't be everything. But to his daughter, Frances Schreuder, money meant everything. It was the driving force in her life. . . ."

Pointing out that the murder was "a planned execution," Jones said that it fit "the definition of premeditation" for first-degree murder. "[They] were clever, cunning and calculated. They are cold-blooded killers. . . ." He talked about the oatmeal and Behrens's contention that Marc and Larry had joked about it afterward. He spoke of the thefts in 1977 and his feeling that Marc's grandparents "meant nothing to him." He talked about the plan to use a hit man; Frances's asking Behrens to get a gun, followed by Marc's request; and Marc's phone call to Berenice, ten days before the murder, pleading for $3,000.

"Your Honor," Jones said, hitting the right note of incredulity, "could it be that that three thousand dollars . . . was the money he used to buy the airline ticket and . . . firearm to kill his grandfather?"

Carefully touching each base, Jones insisted that Marc had plenty of time—from the day he left New York until the morning in the warehouse—to think about what he was doing. "There was no one here in Salt Lake City putting pressure on Marc Schreuder to pull the trigger," he said, adding that he didn't believe Marc and his grandfather ever had a conversation before he shot him, or that his grandfather was ever facing him. In opting to believe Marc's story to Frankel, Jones said that Marc was "at least composed enough at this time that he doesn't just run out of the warehouse. He carries out the plan to its ultimate. He walks over, with his grandfather lying on the ground in a pool of blood, with the entire back half of his grandfather's head missing, and he turns his grandfather's pockets inside out, throwing change on the floor. He then removes his grandfather's wallet and takes the credit cards out and throws those around. . . . Certainly a very clever, a very devious act on the part of Marc Schreuder."

It was clever to give the gun to Richard Behrens, he said. After all, he would then become an accomplice to the crime. He had hidden things for Frances in the past, why not give him this? "But there is something else also clever about what

[they] did," the prosecutor said. "They gave it to Richard Behrens because they know Richard Behrens. They know what he is like and everyone in this courtroom heard him and he is a rambler. He makes disjointed statements. Even if Richard Behrens went to the police, who on earth would ever believe a single thing he had to say? . . . There wouldn't be one person in this courtroom that would have convicted Marc Schreuder on the testimony of Richard Behrens. But we know from all of the . . . corroborating testimony offered . . . that really what Richard Behrens told this court is the truth. He may not know how to say it, and he may not know when to stop saying it, but what he said was true."

This was *not* a manslaughter case, Jones told Sawaya. "This is not like the man in the barroom brawl who comes out on the short end of a fist fight and goes home and gets a firearm and comes back and then kills his assailant. This is not like a man who is baby-sitting a two-month-old child and becomes angry and upset at the baby crying and hauls off in a moment of anger and kills that child. Those are manslaughter cases, but this case, these facts do not constitute manslaughter.

"I suppose the defense is telling us that Marc Schreuder was so tied to his mother's apron strings that he couldn't do anything, that he virtually was a puppet. Whatever Mama wants, Mama gets. According to Mr. Frankel, one of the reasons that Marc did this is because he was afraid of being kicked out of the house. . . . It is a little difficult to believe that his mother has so much control and exerts that much pressure on him that even when he is here in Salt Lake [in the summer of 1977] or up in Connecticut [at Kent and Trinity], she can control his every action. To hear the defense's theory of this case, they suggest that the only way Marc would have pulled that trigger is because his mother made him do it."

And yet when she told him to leave the country, Jones said, he hadn't. Didn't that indicate his mother didn't have quite the control over him that the defense was suggesting? And if Marc was so loyal to her, why was he implicating her in the murder at all? From David Frankel, the prosecutor said, the court now knew that Marc was a liar (he had given Frankel different stories) and a thief; in addition to the thefts in 1977, he had stolen $40,000 from his grandmother. "And why did Marc steal that forty thousand dollars?" Jones asked. "Was it because Mama made him do it? No. The reason that Mr. Frankel gave us was he needed money to buy rare coins. He needed money so he could run away. And he needed money for his old age. Sure doesn't sound to me, Your Honor, like the defendant was under the stress and pressure of his mother in that situation."

Jones reinforced Lee Coleman's skepticism about the four hours Dr. Moench had spent with Marc and the absence of any corroboration—except the tape of Frances and Lavinia. "We don't know if this is a typical conversation by the mother," he said. ". . . We don't know why this tape was made. Does Marc just sit around in the house and flip the tape recorder on and record his mother from time to time? . . . We know, Your Honor, from the testimony that the doctor's examination is only as good as the information he receives. And Dr. Moench told the defendant, 'I want the truth.' And yet on cross-examination at one point he said, 'It doesn't really matter whether I have all the facts or whether everything he's told me is the truth.' In fact, at one point he said, 'I am sure he may have been lying to me.' There is something missing in that analysis. If he wants the truth, then why is it that the truth doesn't matter? How do you make any kind of evaluation or diagnosis if the individual you are talking to isn't telling the truth? . . . One of the questions that was asked Dr. Moench, 'Wouldn't this young man have a motive or a reason for lying to you?' And Dr. Moench said, 'No. Maybe quite the contrary. I think he may be more truthful because he is in a first-degree murder case.' Compared it, I think, to a deathbed situation or a gallows concept. But of course the other side of that coin is that Marc Schreuder knows if he can convince Dr. Moench that he was acting under an extreme emotional disturbance, he has a good chance of reducing this case from capital homicide to manslaughter. And I submit to the court that if he had any reason to lie, that was it.

". . . Marc Schreuder had four years to think about his defense. And what he does in this case is continue to blame other people for his actions and his conduct. . . . First of all, make it look like a robbery, blame somebody else. Can you imagine if somebody had been picked up and charged with this robbery because they just happened to be outside the

Bradshaw Auto Parts store on that morning? That's exactly what Marc and Frances wanted. . . . But then if for some reason the police can start this case, maybe we should blame Larry. After all, he's the black sheep in the family. He has every opportunity. He is right here in Salt Lake City on the day of the murder. He had gone down to the store the night before with his grandfather. He had been involved with the thefts the year before. It's perfect. . . . And so Marc picks up an airline ticket and uses Larry's first initial. Incredible, blame somebody else. Don't accept any responsibility for it, Marc. Blame your own brother for this murder.

"Finally, if that doesn't work, we will blame Marilyn Reagan or Richard Behrens. Then finally, when we get right down to the end of this case, it's the old, 'Yes, I did it. I am responsible, but Mama made me do it.'

". . . Your Honor, I submit to this court that this was a defense that was raised in despair and desperation," Jones continued. Because of the strength of the evidence, he implied, the defense had "no choice but to come up with this defense, to try to fit it in in hopes of reducing the case to manslaughter.

"Dr. Moench says that he classifies the defendant's relationship with the mother as being a sick relationship. And I couldn't agree more . . . that this young man would kill his grandfather at his mother's request and blame his brother, his aunt, and a man he considered to be the same as an uncle. There has to be something sick about people who do what Marc Schreuder did in this case. But being sick, as Dr. Coleman said today, is not the same as being in a diminished capacity or suffering from an extreme emotional disturbance. There is no mental illness or disease for Marc Schreuder. What you have in this case is a young man who is extremely obedient, who listens to his mother and follows her instructions, and that is not a defense to first-degree murder."

The figure who now rose to address the court that Friday afternoon, just before the beginning of the long Fourth of July weekend, was no longer the feisty defense lawyer, challenging the credibility of nearly every state witness he cross-examined. Joe Tesch's purpose was different now—he was planning to ask for justice tempered with mercy—and he proceeded to give as eloquent a closing as many courtroom aficionados could ever remember.

He said that he had spent the previous day with his wife and children and that it had given him a chance to reflect "on what children are for me." It was only this morning, he said, that he recalled "what we mean by a normal life and how bizarre in truth this whole matter is.

"This is not a traditional first-degree murder case in any sense. While it may be professionally stimulative for all of us lawyers involved to have a case that raised such spectacular facts and such spectacular legal issues, we are now at the moment of truth, and what a moment it is. This is not a boy on a mission to kill. This is a boy on something like a runaway boxcar or a ship in a typhoon. I say that because in looking at him and seeing he is a boy and was a boy of seventeen at the time of this commission and in reflecting on the question we, as fathers and adults, know about the care it takes to raise children, who understand the world and their responsibilities in it, can understand all too well what a storm he was in. That from the day of birth, with the exception of four days we will talk about, through to the day of arrest, he had never known normal life and never had guidance and was instead intertwined in the web of events of which he had little or no control. . . .

"I think to characterize the victim in this case—and I start here because I think we have to, to understand what this family is all about—as a man to whom money meant very little is wrong. In fact, he, as we now know, became a person to whom money was not any longer a means but an end. And we know that from his wife's letter to him in 1975 complaining that although she was in her seventies, she was still required to work for room and board at the auto-parts store. Her insistence that that not continue, her requests to him that they use their vast wealth, in fact, to help their children and their grandchildren, which she . . . understands he will not do. Although it may be said that he was attempting to teach his children and his grandchildren something about values in life . . . the fact, as we all know, is what he was doing was shouting to his children . . . that there was nothing important *except* money, seven days a week, all of your working hours, all of your awake hours, spent in the pursuit of money."

This was the legacy he left to his three daughters, Tesch said, pointing out that for the one who testified, "money meant a great deal. [Marilyn] was her father's daughter and we get those indications in the sense that, in spite of having a home and summer home . . . she was unwilling to spend the money to make long-distance phone calls."

But this was all window dressing for the main focus of his remarks—Frances. Though they had tried to produce her as a witness but couldn't, he said, "we do know her from a tape recording," which he felt could not be staged and was an indication of "the severity of the storm within which Marc Francis Schreuder was surviving or not surviving very well. . . .

"It is, I think, difficult for us as parents and human beings to perceive in a realistic sense the strength of that. We did not grow up in a storm. We did not grow up in the legacy. We did not grow up with a mother who, I am sure, we will come to know when she is returned here, to be everything that she's been described as. It is difficult to imagine, as lay people, what the strength of that connection might be. We are, for sure, all junior psychiatrists. We are salesmen, we are debaters, we are people who for a living, as lawyers, argue and try to do it effectively, and in doing so, we watch the other person's eyes. We tend to try to figure out what they are thinking and why, where they want to go and when, what will be effective and what will not. But to suggest that we are, therefore, as expert in determining the state of mind of a person suffering from such a characteristic disorder four years ago as is a person like Dr. Moench is incorrect. . . .

"No one who has been in this court saw Marc the day of the crime, at least not at the crime scene or at the hotel before. No one who is in this courtroom saw Marc immediately after the crime. It is suggested that because he was relaxed in Midland, Texas, that he felt no pressure, that he was acting as a seventeen-year-old cold-blooded killer, and that is proof of it. I would submit to you that what Midland, Texas, was in his whole life was the eye of the storm, having lived a life in the hurricane of Frances and having to move from there to criminal activity. There was only one repose, perhaps only one time in his life ever that he knew normal family life as you and I know it. That was Midland, Texas.

"It is clear from what we saw of Mrs. Cavenaugh and John Cavenaugh that they are well-adjusted people, that they had family life, that they interacted in a normal, loving sense. Marc Schreuder had never seen that before, ever. And when we think of seventeen years without that, it becomes quite easy to understand why Marc did not want to leave . . . that he would react favorably to a home environment that included love and normal interaction among adult people, that was not consumed by Grandfather's legacy and the pursuit of money. It appears, however . . . that Frances's consumption was, of course, greater than her father's."

Tesch reminded the court that Marc was a juvenile at the time of the murder and that juveniles are "subject to pressures from adults" and can be convinced to do things without benefit of the kind of full maturity needed to resist. "There is without doubt," he said, "a person involved in this case upon whom the full weight of the law should fall. She is not here; the full weight of the law on this boy must be tempered. That is what we, as a society, are all about."

In his own words he passionately reiterated what Dr. Moench had said and insisted that personal gain was *not* Marc's motive: "Feeding the lion" was. "Feeding Frances . . . meeting her desires and avoiding being cut off from her. . . .

"As children, I think we can all remember the sort of terror that goes through a child's mind when he believes his parents are fighting . . . [and] can remember experiencing what a grand and great and serious and severe threat it was that if ever a parent would say, 'If you don't behave, I'll send you to an orphanage,' [or] 'If you don't behave, I'll send you to live with grandmother.' And I think if we take this boy, having had no parents really, but having the natural tendency of a child to need parents, and finding himself in the position of being the male in the family and yet still, I think, having the needs of a child, we can begin to feel what he was feeling. And I think only if we put ourselves in those shoes can we begin to determine whether or not this was an extreme mental or emotional disturbance for which there is a reasonable explanation.

"I think the case is done and I am glad it is your decision

534

and not mine. I would ask only that the court keep in mind that we do not ask from a boy a life for a life, and that he has had no chance. We see progress; Dr. Moench sees progress. David Frankel sees progress, and we have glimpses that underneath he's a pretty good boy. We all know that we all have breaking points. We all have been involved in frustrating or aggravating or persistent emotional relationships where the encounter was such that, some time in our minds, we have contemplated violence on ourselves or others, and that's coming from strong people.

"But if we take a boy who, in his seventeen years, had nothing of the love and the care that we have had and put him in that same situation . . . with the unresolved emotional and growing-up psychological problems that he had at that time, then I think we see that this is clearly a manslaughter case. It is more that than anything else, and I would request that the court make that finding."

Judge Sawaya thanked both sides and said that he wanted the holiday weekend to consider his decision. Immensely likable and soft-spoken, he had been a judge for twenty-three of his fifty-five years—but this was the first capital homicide case in which the decision was solely his. And for this native of Wyoming—the son of a shoe-store owner, a Navy veteran, a father of seven and a grandfather of ten—it would not be made lightly.

53// On Tuesday, July 6, at ten in the morning, it was the judge's turn to speak: ". . . And based upon the facts as determined from the evidence, the court is prepared to find beyond a reasonable doubt . . . that the defendant intentionally and knowingly caused the death of Franklin Bradshaw on July 23, 1978, in Salt Lake County, State of Utah."

Ernie Jones and Mike George were home free. Or so they thought.

"The court feels," Sawaya continued, "that there is some reasonable doubt with regard to the reason for the killing [and] is therefore prepared to find that the defendant did not cause the death . . . while engaged in the commission of, or attempt to commit, an aggravated robbery, or for pecuniary or other personal gain. I think the evidence would support the reasonable doubt finding that the defendant caused the death . . . based upon the desires or wishes of another person.

"The court finds that the defendant did not cause the death . . . while under the influence of extreme mental or emotional disturbance for which there is a reasonable explanation or excuse. . . .

"The court will therefore rule that the defendant, Marc Schreuder, is guilty of the lesser but included offense of criminal homicide, murder in the second degree."

For the lawyers it was an unsatisfying Mexican standoff, a kiss from their sisters. Marc reacted to the verdict without emotion, but left the courtroom with a slight grin on his face. Tesch and Van Dam had no comment for the press and Ernie Jones remained in his seat long after the room had emptied out. Stunned and angry, he too refused to talk with reporters, but Ted Cannon, the Salt Lake County Attorney, did. "If this wasn't a first-degree murder case," he snapped, "we don't know anymore what is."

The judge had been prepared to pass sentence, but at Van Dam's request, he agreed to wait until Friday morning.

That night, Marc had a visitor.

"How do you feel?" Mike George asked him.

"You know," Marc said, "the funniest part of this trial was looking at the expression on your faces when the judge said second. You guys were *really* disappointed."

"How did *you* feel?"

"Well, I evaluated it over the weekend and decided I was sure I was going to get a second."

"You know," George reminded him, "this is the first day of a whole new life for you," then discussed with him again the same sort of things he had when he had heard Marc was considering suicide—what prison would mean and how Marc could affect the kind of life he would have there. "You're no longer under the control of your mother. You've got to go out there and stand up for yourself. Prison is going to *force* you to mature and to stand up for your rights."

The courting of Marc Schreuder had begun.

Part Six//

He has an almost spooky attachment
to her . . . like a lover talking about an
old lover.

—BRYAN BAIRD

54// By Friday morning, the armchair quarterbacks had analyzed the trial and weighed in with their own carefully reasoned "verdicts." "Shit, first they ran a defense of whodunit then they practically pled insanity." "They could have sold manslaughter a helluva lot easier to a jury than to a judge." "No judge or jury is going to go for a psychiatric defense in this state after that damn Hinckley decision." "They should have put the kid on instead of that shrink and those Eastern lawyers. He should have had enough guts to take the stand." "Sawaya copped out. It was murder one or manslaughter."

And manslaughter was what the defense was *still* pushing for when court convened at nine. In a shortened version, Paul Van Dam delivered the same kind of deeply felt pitch that Joe Tesch had three days earlier, reiterating that it was "a true defense." Having asked Marc to approach the bench, the judge told him that he appreciated his attorney's remarks but that the nature of his offense was such "that I can show no leniency in this matter and I am going to impose the sentence to the full measure of the law. . . . You face a possible life sentence in this matter and you may very well spend the rest of your life in the Utah State Prison. I can only suggest to you that you make the most of it, that you not be a troublemaker. That you go out there and try to get an education that the

540

state will offer to give you. . . . The conditions aren't the best out there, but they aren't so bad that you can't make the most of it and perhaps someday come out a better man than you are today. You will be a much older person when you come out because my recommendation to the Board of Pardons is that they keep you there for a good length of time. But regardless of the length of your time that you serve at the state prison, you can use it productively and fruitfully, if you have a mind to do it. I don't know how remorseful you are about this whole affair. But I . . . haven't seen a great deal of evidence of remorse in this matter. A higher judge than I will someday determine whether you have been pardoned because of it. I have no inclination to do that. You committed a cruel and heinous crime. Besides the fact that you have taken the life of a human being, that human being was your own grandfather and I find that inexcusable."

Whereupon Marc, his head bowed, received an indeterminate sentence of five years to life, an additional six years for the use of a firearm (to be served consecutively) and a fine of $10,000.

For Paul Van Dam and Joe Tesch there would be an appeal to the Utah Supreme Court—a body that stood somewhere to the right of Attila the Hun—provided Berenice was willing to pay for it. But for Ernie Jones and Mike George, their battle was only half over. And they knew that bringing Frances Schreuder to trial, let alone convicting her, was not going to be easy.

When they got back to the office, a detective was waiting for them with a letter. Written in a childlike scrawl, it had been sent to no one in particular at the police department. And so they began to read.

6/22/82

DEAR SIR:

A reference is being made to a middle-aged woman of Salt Lake City, anent a conversation I had with her in regard to another person she wanted killed.

I am presently residing at the U.S. Penitentiary in Terre Haute, Indiana, serving a 10-year sentence for unarmed bank robbery. I am staying here temporarily as a hold-over prisoner, en route to my final destination, Federal Correctional Institution, Oxford, Wisconsin. In March, I became eligible for parole and am scheduled to be released this December. When I am released, I will establish residency in Hopkins, Minnesota.

In January, 1978, I was released from the Hennepin County Adult Correctional Facility in Plymouth, Minnesota, where I served 10 months for a felony conviction, for attempted theft over $2500. Shortly thereafter, I received a long-distance telephone call from a woman named Francis, who told me that she had learned I was an arsonist and that she wanted an establishment set afire. I told her that I'd be willing to arrange an appointment with her in the metropolitan area of Minneapolis. She said she'd be willing to fly into Minnesota. I gave her the name of the place where to meet me—at a restaurant in Bloomington, Minnesota, nearby the airport. . . . I cannot recall the name of this restaurant, although I could identify its structure, located on Hwy. 494. She told me that when she arrives in Minnesota she will contact me. A few weeks later, I received a call from her, wherein she explained she had just arrived and was ready to converse with me. I told her how I would be attired and then drove to this restaurant.

When I arrived at this restaurant, she recognized me immediately. We sat down together at a booth and began confabulating. After our waitress took our orders and served us coffee, we then directed our conversation to the arson. She inquired what experiences I have had in arson, and I told her that I had set some businesses afire in the metropolitan area, but never outside of Minnesota. She, also, inquired what I charged for my services, and I told her 10 percent off the top of the insurance premiums. After exchanging some more words, she finally conceded that she really didn't want me to carry out an arson, but that she wanted me to kill somebody for her and that she would pay me 10 percent of whatever she inherits from his death, saying, "I heard you are also crazy and smart enough to kill somebody." I asked her who this person is and how much he is worth. She explained that he "is my stepfather and is worth several millions of dollars." I explained to her that I was not skilled to carry out a contract and I was therefore not interested, but she insisted, explaining she was having trouble finding a hit man. She then suggested having me make his death appear as an accident by setting him or—causing him to die from smoke inhalation—his house afire. Adamant in my refusal to kill her stepfather, I told her I was not interested. She then stated that she will probably have one of her sons kill him. I asked her how she learned of me, and she said that she obtained my name from a person (she refused to name) who is acquainted with some truck drivers.

From 1974 to '76, when working temporarily on truck docks, I gave my name to several truck drivers, explaining I was an arsonist, purposefully to have my name spread throughout the country. Apparently this is how she learned of me. Detective David Teclaw, of the Hopkins Police Department, can confirm my alleged involvement in arson.

The reason I did not bring this to anybody's attention earlier is that I did not want to jeopardize my chance for receiving a parole prior to making my initial appearance before the parole commission which was held this last May.

Now that I am scheduled to be released, I have no reluctance to bring this to your attention, as a good citizen.

Thank you for your moments.

Respectfully,
JEFF MORRIS
24099-175

On the afternoon of July 13, Marc arrived at Utah State Prison. Often referred to as "the Point" because of its location—Point of the Mountain—the prison is about thirty minutes south of Salt Lake on Interstate 15, a drive that takes one past food warehouses, lumber yards, mobile and split-level homes, new buildings going up, and the Mormon Temple in West Jordan, white and gleaming in the distance, before opening out to a landscape of rich farmland, dotted with horses and tractors.

Of all the prisons in the country, it is one of the best known. Gary Gilmore was shot to death in the cannery there on a cold January morning in 1977. Ted Bundy had spent time there. So had Jack Henry Abbott, who wrote about the prison and others in his book *In the Belly of the Beast*.

New inmates are known as "fishes," and once they walk past the flower-lined entrance of purple petunias and yellow marigolds, they are placed into "the fishtank" of "R&O" (reception and orientation) for a period of time. Marc was to be housed in medium security, in cell D-104 of "Dog Block." Because of the notoriety and nature of his crime, the prison

543

anticipated that he wouldn't be popular with his fellow inmates. By putting him in a cell that was close to the block officer's station and keeping him on the first tier (where "escape risks" and inmates who "might have problems" are generally housed), the prison was doing what it could to ensure his safety.

At about the same time Marc was being issued his prison clothing and locked into his new "house," Richard Behrens was leaving his apartment to go to a coffee shop at the corner of 86th Street and First Avenue. Two men were waiting for him. They identified themselves as Frances's lawyers from Washington and asked if he would be willing to have a drink with them. He said he'd rather have coffee instead. Bill McDaniel, Jr., and Aubrey Daniel III (who had been the Army's prosecutor in the case against Lieutenant William Calley for his actions in the My Lai massacre) had a lot of questions for the suddenly popular schoolteacher, and they fired away: *Did Marc really do it?* Yes. *Is Larry really crazy?* Yes. *Did Frances really indicate that she killed her father or wanted it done?* Yes. *Did he know that if Frances was found guilty she could be shot?* He didn't believe that. *Was he currently working as a teacher?* No comment. *Is Marilyn crazy?* According to Frances. *Is Frances crazy?* Yes, and is at times normal. She said she would either blame the murder on him or plead insanity. *Did she kick Marc out?* Yes, she kicked out anybody when she flew into rages. *Did he really think Marc could be forced into killing his grandfather by threats?* Yes. Either he would be thrown out or she would commit suicide. He had no choice. She went into tirades—"super tirades that lasted for days or longer. I have witnessed these tirades many times." Behrens said he was sure prosecution had many witnesses, including Vittorio, who could attest to this, though he was labeled a drunk during their divorce proceedings. *Did he get violent with her and the boys?* According to Frances. *What did he know about their marriage?* She married him to escape from home; Marilyn claimed she had a "nervous condition" in college. *What about her second husband?* Never met Schreuder. Frances reappeared in his life by calling and slowly revealing that she "was splitting with number two." *What should their case be?* "Tell your client to flee with anyone she wishes to Brazil or any other place as she is as guilty as hell. Or better use the insanity plea as she said she would excepting that the Hinckley thing is trying at times like these." *What people might know of these alleged meetings with Manning?* There were no doubt some. *Had he spoken with Frances recently?* No. *What about Frances's brother who died in an institution?* Died back in the sixties. "Probably could not compete in family due to non-father or inherited craziness which was not curable apparently."

They asked about his stepmother and why he had taken Manning to the lake in New Jersey that day. It was just as he stated in court, he said: "to be witness to my father's wishing me to stay away." They asked if he and Frances had any mutual friends. He said that she kept her life "compartmentalized," but was certain that the prosecution would be interviewing the ones she did have to prove her "nuttiness and outlandish scenemaking." The ones that he knew about he would mention at trial.

Behrens asked them how Frances was faring and they said she was under strain, in town and planning to appeal further. He wanted them to know how intelligent a person Frances was; that when she rented a place on Long Island she had considered working in real estate, and had also thought about the law. He felt she would have done well in both, if it weren't for the fact she had a daughter to raise. "I thought that her paranoia would stead her well in law . . . as good lawyers have to have lots of that."

When the three of them left the coffee shop, who should come walking in but Myles Manning. Behrens identified him to the lawyers and they followed him back inside. Behrens did not; he walked home and wrote to Larry Goldman that night: "I find these chance meetings with Myles Manning very coincidental and timed . . . like a bad movie."

55// In the midst of all the crises that had befallen the family, it was not surprising that "the black sheep of the family"—as Ernie Jones had referred to him in court—had been somewhat forgotten. Larry was to have been paroled in late May. He had requested a transfer of his parole to New York but therein lay the problem. Thirty days was usually the maximum amount of time a person stayed in jail in Pennsylvania past his parole date; Larry had been stuck for nearly two months. Vittorio and his wife very much wanted to help him, but they didn't have enough room for Larry to live with them. Larry had a grand idea of going to live at Gracie Square, but that was clearly out of the question. Berenice and Frances agreed they did not want Vittorio to be involved, but they could not agree on what would be the best solution. The only thing that everyone seemed to agree on was that Larry had to either be in a strictly supervised environment, or in a private institution.

James Onembo, the director of treatment at the Northampton County Prison, took an active role in trying to resolve the situation. He knew that Larry "needed some sort of workshop at a sheltered residence" and "couldn't exist in a regular job." He met with Vittorio. He spoke with Berenice on the phone and Frances would get on the other end. "I always sensed the motherly instinct on the part of [Mrs. Bradshaw] to comply with the wishes of her daughter," he recalled. But he sensed from his conversations with Frances that "she seemed irrational and tended to push her irrational, dominant personality." He soon began to realize that Larry—who was becoming more and more edgy the longer he was in prison—was "exactly where everybody wants him."

To say that Mike George and Ernie Jones were amazed by the letter they received from Jeff Morris was putting it mildly. As things stood, Richard Behrens and Myles Manning were their key witnesses against Frances. It was highly unlikely that the state would be able to present testimony by Dr. Moench and David Frankel—Frances's lawyers would argue strenuously that it was hearsay. And they knew that their chances of persuading Marc to take the stand—their main hope—were virtually nil. Marc told Moench before the trial that while he had not heard from his mother, he still loved her; more important, he had said that he would rather commit suicide than accept the state's offer, made *before* the trial, to testify against her in exchange for second degree.

But instead of being excited by this letter—this possibility of a *second* hit man—Jones and George were uneasy from the moment they read it. "You get a letter, unsolicited, out of the blue," George explained, "and you are immediately skeptical—even before you sit down and talk to the guy." Once they began to do a little bit of checking, they found that Jeffrey Charles Morris, an adopted, twenty-nine-year-old native of Minnesota, had a fairly extensive psychiatric history (with diagnoses ranging, at different times, from "paranoid schizophrenia" to "borderline personality"), an acknowledged dependency on alcohol from the time he was seventeen, a reputation for being a con man, a history of trying to "inform" the police as "a responsible citizen" on other occasions—and was someone who had an inordinate interest in court proceedings and had begun attending trials in Minneapolis as a teenager.

But with *this* case, Mike George knew, every lead, no matter how flimsy, *had* to be followed up—and, he rationalized, if a person was looking for a hit man, "you don't go to your parish priest to find one."

George reached Jeffrey Morris by phone at the federal prison in Oxford, Wisconsin, and said he wanted to come talk with him. Morris said that instead of being kept at Oxford, he was being transferred to a prison in Bastrop, Texas. George asked for a physical description of Frances over the phone and said he would be in touch with him at Bastrop in August.

But shortly after their phone conversation, George received another letter from Morris.

7/28/82

DEAR SERGEANT GEORGE:

I am writing to make it very clear and precise that I do not want to make myself involved any further in the homicide case of a gal named Francis.

In our previously held telephone conference anent Francis, you told me that you were intent on visiting me at my next designation and asked me if I'd be willing to testify against this person at her trial.

I would appreciate it very much if you would not visit me. If you decide to do so, I will decline to accept your visit. Furthermore, I do not want to be subpoenaed. If I am, I will comply with the subpoena, but given an ineloquent testimony, even though whatever statements I relate to the court will be of full veracity.

I am fully aware of what's expected of every respectable and law-abiding citizen to perform. But, given my present situation in light of the enormous notoriety surrounding this case, I will have to permit my own person interests be the over-riding factor against the commonwealth.

If I projected too much candidness in this letter, will you please accept my apology. But, as explained in our conference, I never would have known that Francis had her father killed (whom she referred to as her step father) after she asked me to kill him if it hadn't been for your telling me this.

Thank you for your moments.

> Truly yours,
> JEFF MORRIS
> 24099-175

Jeff Morris would learn very quickly that Mike George was not a man who took kindly to receiving a "Dear John" letter.

56// Mary Lou Kaiser didn't drive, but that wasn't going to stop her from getting to the Point to see "my honey" on the three days a week Marc was allowed visitors, and from bringing him a fresh supply of chicken empañadas and blueberry nut bread. Since the prison was concerned that inmates would try to shake Marc down for protection money, whatever Mary Lou deposited in his account was monitored carefully. During one of their visits, a phone rang in the large visiting room and the officer in charge picked it up. In prison, one inmate said, "the walls have ears," and the prisoner on the other end of the phone had a complaint. Millard Kaiser, who had also been transferred to the Point, was upset that Mary Lou was bringing their daughter to the prison but not to see him.

"If that's what it takes to see Marc," she told the officer, "I'll let him see Monique."

Mary Lou was not Marc's only visitor. Every two weeks or so, Mike George came as well. "What I needed to do," he recalled, "what was foremost at this point was to get Marc on *our* team. That was undoubtedly a primary goal and objective of mine, because I thought his testifying against his mother was a possibility. I couldn't say I had a rapport with him, but at least he was talking to me, and a lot of defendants won't talk to the arresting officer.

"I don't know if it was so much sympathy as a greater understanding—after seeing and hearing his defense—of his situation that I was feeling about him at this point. How these kids grew up, the environment they grew up in, of Lavinia and what her mother may make *her* do at some point in her life that won't be good for her. . . .

"As far as I know, Tesch and Van Dam did not know I was going out there. And as far as I was concerned, this case was over as far as my being allowed to see him. I told him several times, 'If you *want* your attorneys present or *don't* want to talk with me, just tell me.' He said, 'I don't want them present and don't want them to know that I'm talking to you.'

"The first couple of times I was there he was really apprehensive. He didn't know what prison was like. He received a lot of threats from people who called him 'Grandpa Killer.' He told me he was amazed he hadn't had any sexual problems. I think he's been hit on, but he says he's never been forced into a sexual act. When people went to him and offered protection for money, as soon as they realized he didn't have any they backed off him. . . .

"To me, he was not the hard-ass criminal who hates cops

that we usually deal with. He takes responsibility for what he did. . . . I was spending a lot of time talking to Moench and reviewing the prison psychological reports so I wasn't completely shooting in the dark. I knew what I had to do, but didn't know whether I could do it or not. I *had* to be his friend and that's a tough decision for a cop to make. Do you want to put yourself into that situation? And it's difficult to do.

"Marc had *no* friends. He was reestablishing a relationship with his father, but they were two thousand miles apart. He was beginning a relationship with Mary, but he's on the inside and she's on the outside. He was receiving letters from Susie Coleman, of whom he said, 'We're really good friends. We can understand each other and talk to each other.' "

Mike George was a smart enough cop to know that it would be a mistake to press Marc too hard about anything right away—or to expect Marc to trust him. He had testified that Marc was not a very intelligent and calculating individual, and he meant it: Marc was not so naive that he wouldn't realize immediately one of the main reasons George was coming to see him. But there was one thing George *had* to know: was there *anybody* else who might have been involved?

"Boy," Marc said, "the only thing I can think of is Mom mentioned another hit man. All I know is that he was from out of state and that it was after Christmas of 1977—maybe February or March of 1978."

Without letting Marc know why he had asked, George could barely contain the elation he felt. February or March of 1978 was consistent with what Morris had written in his first letter: *In January, 1978, I was released. . . . Shortly thereafter, I received a long-distance telephone call from a woman named Francis. . . .*

Once again, Mike George was bound for the Lone Star State.

57// After first telling prison officials at Bastrop, located about thirty miles southeast of Austin, that he did not want to see Mike George, Jeff Morris finally agreed to the investigator's visit. George arrived at the prison with a colleague, who was going to give Morris a polygraph test. While George was not a big advocate of these tests, he knew they were still an indicator, however flawed, of whether or not a person was telling the truth.

More than anything else, George wanted to know if Morris (who stood five feet eleven inches tall, weighed 185 pounds, and had brown hair, gray eyes, and scars on both wrists) had read about the case anywhere, heard about it on the radio, or seen anything on television. After all, there had been articles in *Newsweek*, the *New York Times*, the *National Enquirer*, and the *Globe*, many newspapers around the country had carried wire stories, and the letter Morris wrote was sent on June 22, right in the middle of Marc's trial.

Puffing on a cigarette, Morris replied that he had not seen, heard or read anything.

Did the meeting with Frances really occur as he'd described it?

Yes.

Why had he waited more than four years after this alleged meeting to contact the authorities?

It was as he explained in his letter, he said. He did not want to jeopardize his chance for receiving a parole prior to his initial appearance before the parole board in May of 1982.

Did she ever inquire where she could get a gun or a person to do this, after he said he was only interested in arson for profit—not in committing murder?

He told her that she could find either in North Minneapolis.

Was he withholding any information—or making any of this up for personal gain?

No, he was not.

551

George brought a photo lineup with him and Morris selected *two* pictures. One was of a secretary in George's office; the other was the one of Frances on the Staten Island Ferry—the same photo that had turned Myles Manning's face white that December night eight months before. Morris also drew a map for them, indicating the location of the restaurant on Highway 494 in Bloomington where he said he had met with Frances, but he was still unable to remember its name. He reiterated what he said in his second letter—that he *didn't* know she had gone through with the murder when he wrote to Salt Lake in June. And then he came out with something that persuaded the investigators Morris might really be telling the truth—something that George was fairly certain had never appeared in any press account: Frances had mentioned that she had a daughter in the ballet.

Morris had not only passed the polygraph test, but had told them more than they expected to hear. As they left Bastrop, George—who had confirmed with the Hopkins Police Department that Morris had indeed advertised himself to truck drivers as an arsonist for hire—said he'd stay in contact. Frances was close to being extradited, he felt, and he told Morris that when she was, there was a strong possibility Utah might want him to testify at her preliminary hearing. Jeff Morris had made Mike George's team. For now.

Berenice Bradshaw had a difficult decision to make. Having told people that she believed in Marc's innocence until she heard about his confession to David Frankel and Louis Moench, she was now faced with deciding whether to finance his appeal. After initially saying she would, she then decided she wouldn't, and Paul Van Dam was informed of this in an August 16 letter from Kevin Kurumada, asking that he and Joe Tesch turn all their materials over to the Legal Defender's Office.

But by the following week, Berenice seemed to be undecided once more. Marc was brought in from prison for a hearing in front of Judge Sawaya, because the defense, prior to being fired, had requested one more stab at getting Sawaya to reduce the sentence he had given Marc—an effort that failed. Berenice came to the hearing and she and Marc were allowed a few minutes together in the hall outside the judge's office.

It was a teary, emotionally charged reunion. They hugged each other and Marc kept saying, over and over, "Granny, oh Granny." But when she told him that the three bathtubs his mother had bought were *still* in the front hall, he laughed. When he told her how excited he was that he could go to college at the prison, she said he should make the most of it.

Once Marc left, she and Paul Van Dam discussed the situation. She asked if he *really* thought Marc did it. Van Dam assured her that he had. In terms of the appeal, she said that what she really wanted to know was if it would do any good. "I'm not going to pay any more money if it's not going to do any good."

Van Dam told her that he felt they had some valid issues to raise—centering mainly around the preliminary hearing and some others of a more technical nature—but there were no guarantees.

She listened, then left without committing herself. Unless she changed her mind, they were still off the case.

Paul Van Dam and Joe Tesch were not the only two lawyers to be canned. Frances had become disenchanted with the firm of Williams & Connolly and had started canvassing in August for new attorneys. She sought out two men who had been her attorneys in the past. Howard Cerny, who had represented her in her marital proceedings against Gentile, told her that he thought it would be a mistake to keep switching attorneys. That was not what she wanted to hear. So she went to see Irving Erdheim, who had represented her when she got her divorce from Schreuder (and who had earlier represented Gentile against her). Defending someone for murder was not in Irving's line of work, but he made a recommendation and said she should feel free to use his name.

By the end of August, Erdheim received a letter from Frances. She thanked him for referring her to Roy Cohn— former counsel to Senator Joseph McCarthy during the 1950s and one of Robert F. Kennedy's principal *bêtes noires*—and said that his firm, Saxe, Bacon & Bolan, was going to represent her. Though Cohn—like Edward Bennett Williams, one of the select group of attorneys who are known throughout the country—would not be actively involved on a day-to-day basis, she would be dealing with two of his top colleagues, Michael Rosen and John Lang.

Once Williams & Connolly was officially notified of Frances's decision, they were actually relieved. Frances had made it increasingly difficult for them to communicate with her, and in acknowledging their dismissal, they wrote to say that her allegations that they were trying to hurt her were "totally unfounded" and "so preposterous as to not warrant a response." As had initially been speculated, there had been strong consideration given to running an insanity defense, and those discussions, an attorney for the firm said later, "may have accentuated her disillusionment with us."

As she had done so many times over the years when Frances seemed to be reeling from crisis to crisis, Berenice took a trip. She went to San Francisco for about ten days with a man named "Chips" Smallwood whom she had met a few years before. He had gone on other vacations with her, loved to dance and have a good time, and shared her interest in genealogy.

While out in San Francisco, Berenice had an idea. She had had no contact with Elaine for quite some time and was perfectly aware of how her daughter felt—Elaine suspected her involvement in the murder and disapproved of her paying of Marc's and Frances's legal bills. But that did not stop Berenice from being curious about the new house Elaine and Mason had bought in Berkeley. Knowing that they would still be at their summer home on the Oregon coast, she and Chips decided to take a taxi out to the house.

Anyone who might have seen her that early September day, standing at a distance, camera poised, could have thought she was a spy for the CIA or a would-be burglar. But she wasn't. She was a distressed seventy-nine-year-old mother of a family that was torn apart, trying to get a photograph for her scrapbook. As Berenice began to snap the picture, she saw someone in the window and began to run.

She never got her picture of the lovely house on Park Hills Road, but an unwanted shot of the garage instead.

On Tuesday, September 14, Frances's extradition battle of nearly six months came to an end. She had to surrender and, three days later in Salt Lake City, she did. It had been decided that Kevin Kurumada, who had been Berenice's lawyer, would become her local counsel and represent her at an arraignment in circuit court that afternoon. (Ernie Jones would later argue that it was a conflict of interest for Kurumada to now be representing Frances. Though Jones lost his motion to have Kurumada disqualified, he did succeed in getting Kurumada to have Frances sign a waiver of any conflict. After all, Kurumada said, "Frances's interests were Berenice's interests.")

Frances stood silently in front of Judge Floyd H. Gowans as he arraigned her on the charge of first-degree murder, set her preliminary hearing for November 15, and allowed her to remain out on bail. At three-thirty she was "officially" arrested and taken to the county jail, where she was booked, fingerprinted, photographed and released. She gave no home address and no Social Security number, and listed her occupation as being a director of the New York City Ballet. The person she told them to notify in case of emergency was not her mother, but an old friend from high school who lived in Oakland, California.

For years, Franklin Bradshaw had wanted his youngest daughter to come home, to come back to the Salt Lake Valley to live. But this was not the sort of homecoming he had had in mind.

58// When Mike George first began visiting Marc in prison, Marc viewed the investigator's courting of him with amusement. After all, George was one of the people who had helped convict him of second-degree murder, and now he wanted him to testify against his mother. Though

George did not press the subject at first, Marc would either manage to change it, whenever it did come up, or say that he could sure think a whole lot better if he had some Chicken McNuggets. And the next time George came to visit, Marc would get his wish. It wasn't long before Marc began referring to George as "my little contact with the world."

Frances's preliminary hearing was rescheduled for December 6, and on November 23 the executive secretary of the state's Board of Pardons wrote Paul Van Dam a letter. Once it became clear that Frances was likely to stand trial, Berenice had "reconsidered" her decision to have Marc with a public defender. Van Dam not only would continue on with his appeal, but would advise Marc in dealing with the state's efforts to obtain his testimony against his mother.

The board's letter said that on November 3 four of its members had met with some representatives of the County Attorney's Office to discuss this "extremely serious matter." The state was asking the board for "some oral or written assurance . . . of special consideration," should Marc decide to testify. The board declined to take any formal position, the letter said, and would not until Marc's first hearing before the board in July of 1983. (In Utah, prisoners receive an automatic hearing one year after they are sentenced.) But, the letter went on, "any truthful testimony consistent with Mr. Schreuder's admissions in his own trial would in my estimation be viewed . . . as information mitigating on his behalf. Likewise, no testimony or testimony at variance with his admissions . . . would be viewed by the Board as aggravating." The letter concluded by saying that the state informed the board they would be "most willing to speak favorably toward Mr. Schreuder should he cooperate and will appear at any future Board hearings in his behalf, either at his request or at their own initiative."

Shortly after this, word leaked out that Marc was possibly planning to testify at Frances's preliminary.

It had been nearly three years since that snowy December morning at Lehigh when Tom Morog heard the cries of Fred Salloum coming from room B-225. Pat Naylor, the residence area coordinator that year, not only remembered what happened, she also remembered that Larry still had a trunk in a storage room in Rathbone Hall. She had written to Frances about the trunk shortly after Larry's arrest, but had never received a reply. (Larry had two trunks: the one that the police had looked through in McClintic-Marshall a few hours after the attack, and this one.) The storage room was in the process of being cleared out, and Naylor wanted to make sure that the trunk wasn't discarded by mistake.

As she opened the lid that Wednesday afternoon, the day before Thanksgiving, and looked through the trunk's contents, she found two Cessna receipts from Skyhawk Aviation on the day of the murder, a telephone directory from a hotel, fifty-five packets of photo negatives, fifty-eight letters, a Utah license plate (which Larry said he had gone back to retrieve when he attacked Salloum), a savings slip and canceled check from Citibank in New York, seventeen job applications, and seven legal papers relating to his change of name, But there was something else—something that sent her scurrying to a phone to call Mark Refowich, the attorney who had prosecuted Larry.

When Refowich received Pat Naylor's call, he told her to do nothing until he had phoned Harold Smith at the Bethlehem Police Department. Refowich told Smitty what had happened, that Naylor could be at headquarters at half past five, and that he would meet them there.

As Refowich looked carefully at the *original* 1970 wills of Franklin and Berenice Bradshaw later that day, he noticed that there were some notations and question marks in the margin of Franklin's will (but, as it turned out, nothing that specifically mentioned Frances). All Refowich knew was that Bradshaw's death had to do with money, that the person he prosecuted had been a key suspect at one time, and that he'd better call Salt Lake.

Jones and George asked that *everything* be held for them, because the investigator was planning another trip to New York in a few weeks. Since Naylor hadn't found a *new* will, they were more excited by the possibility of what the letters she found might reveal about the plotting of the murder. They had pretty much dismissed Larry as a suspect at this point—after all, he was the one who had been set up to take the fall—but this one phone call had changed that.

Mike George flew to Minneapolis to collect Jeffrey Morris and bring him back to Salt Lake for Frances's hearing. Morris had been released from prison in Texas and was now on parole, staying at a boarding house.

Knowing that he would need to try to place Frances in Minneapolis during the time of this alleged meeting with Morris, George had asked Marc about some of his mother's habits when she traveled. Marc told him that she paid cash, liked to fly American or United, and preferred Sheraton or Marriott hotels.

Once he picked Morris up, George drove to a Howard Johnson's in Bloomington, located at the intersection of highways 494 and 100. From the map Morris had drawn in Bastrop and his verbal description of the restaurant, George had determined that this was where Morris claimed he had met Frances.

Morris showed George the booth they had sat in and said that when they had finished their business, Frances had left the restaurant and walked around back to the parking lot. She was either staying at the Howard Johnson's or, since she made a phone call, possibly waiting for a cab.

As George soon discovered, records at Howard Johnson's were kept for only one year. He checked with the four Sheratons and one Marriott in the area, but found nothing. He knew from his investigation of Marc that American would no longer have any passenger name records or tickets—just a billing record—but he thought that United might. After all, it had been United's unused ticket for "L. Schreuder" on July 23, 1978, that had started him off. United said they only had records available from May 1, 1978, on; but since Morris was now revising his initial story—that he had met with Frances in February or March of 1978—to say that there was no snow on the ground (a condition that often doesn't exist in Minnesota until April or May), George decided he had nothing to lose by stopping at United in Chicago on the way back from his trip east to collect Larry's things. George checked with Northwest Airlines—the principal carrier between New York and Minneapolis—but they had nothing. And, as George knew all too well, New York Telephone would not have anything either. If there was one thing that kept coming back to haunt him, it was Joel Campbell's failure to get Frances's telephone records shortly after the murder in 1978. If that had been done, George felt, the phone call to John Cavenaugh would be on there, the phone call that Marc said he made to Frances the night before the murder probably would be on there, and, if Frances had contacted Morris, that call might be on there as well.

But as things stood, there was no way for George to corroborate Morris's story.

The first thing one notices is the lions.

White in color and made of stone, two lions greet a visitor to the offices of Saxe, Bacon & Bolan, tucked away in an unpretentious brownstone on East 68th Street in Manhattan. But the lions are more than the centerpiece of the dimly lit reception area, which often looks more like a loading dock than the passageway to a law firm whose clients have included, and include, everyone from Aristotle Onassis and Carmine Galante to George Steinbrenner, Donald Trump and Martina Navratilova.

The lions symbolize the nature of this aggressive firm—and one of its leading lions is Mike Rosen. Boyishly handsome, with silver, slightly shaggy hair dropping down over his forehead and darting, fiery brown eyes, he was forty-one years old when he first met Frances Schreuder and began working on her case. Born in the Flatbush section of Brooklyn, he grew up across the street from Barbra Streisand on Ocean Parkway. His father owned a restaurant in Manhattan called El Borracho, part of the city's café society for many years—along with such places as the Stork Club and El Morocco—and famous for its Kiss Room, where women pursed their lips and left their colorful signatures on the walls.

Rosen had had what he calls "a Duddy Kravitz life," working as a busboy and a waiter in the Catskills during summers and on weekends, from the age of fifteen, when he started at the Commodore in Swan Lake, right through his graduation from Brooklyn Law School in 1964. That experience, he said—waiting on people, seeing them at their best, and often at their worst, and still having to cater to them—

had, more than anything else, helped shape his understanding of the world. Before joining Saxe, Bacon in 1972 he had worked, from 1964 until early 1968, as an Assistant U.S. Attorney for the Eastern District of New York. He was in charge of the Selective Service program and "vigorously prosecuted draft evaders so that those who *were* going [to Vietnam] did not resent it." Feeling that his time in that office represented "the finest training ground for a trial lawyer that exists today;" he went to work for Joseph E. Brill in February of 1969, and it was through him, a legal hero of Rosen's, that he met Roy Cohn, whom Brill was representing at the time.

When he met Frances, Rosen had been preparing to go to trial in the case of Robyn Arnold and Robert Ferrara—a case that *New York* magazine called "one of the most bizarre criminal cases that New York has seen in years." A woman named Diane Delia had been murdered, but she hadn't always been Diane Delia. She used to be John Delia and had been engaged to Robyn Arnold, Rosen's client. When Delia decided to have a sex change, Arnold paid for the operation. When Delia was found murdered, Arnold was indicted for it, along with Ferrara, who had been dating Diane. But when the jury returned its verdict, Robyn Arnold was acquitted, and Robert Ferrara went to jail.

With that case behind him now and with the help of investigators and his good friend and colleague, John Lang, Rosen was prepared to go to Salt Lake for Frances's preliminary. But was Salt Lake prepared for this hard-nosed kid from Brooklyn?

On Monday morning, December 6, Mike Rosen, John Lang and Kevin Kurumada appeared in Judge Paul Grant's courtroom, but Frances did not.

She had been admitted to the Westchester County Medical Center on Saturday for "severe internal bleeding." According to an affidavit, which she had signed and Lang had notarized the day before, she was voluntarily waiving her appearance.

Ernie Jones had been afraid of this. He pointed out to the court that first he had been told, the previous week, that she "did not want to appear" because she needed to be in New

York with Lavinia, who was in *The Nutcracker* for the second straight year. (Jones spoke with someone at the ballet and learned that *The Nutcracker* was performed throughout December, and that Frances did not *have* to be there.) "And now," he said, "we receive information that it is not the ballet that prevents her from coming, but this surgery [she had been given a "d & c" that morning] and certainly that series or chain of events, I think, is rather suspect."

John Lang rose from his seat. It was "outrageous," the tall, fifty-two-year-old, ex-FBI agent said, for Jones to say that. "She didn't plan it this way. It is something that happens. And it is brought on by pressure. And there is a lot of pressure in this matter."

The fireworks had begun, but Paul Grant's cool head prevailed. He decided that he would hold the hearing without Frances, but that she would have to come to Salt Lake as soon as possible to formally waive her appearance at a proceeding that had gone on without her. Grant's concern was the record; if he bound Frances over to stand trial, he didn't want a judicial mistake on his part to taint the process.

Jones called his first three witnesses—Dan Schindler, Joel Campbell and Ed Peterson—and then told the court that Serge Moore, the former Medical Examiner, couldn't appear until the afternoon and that Jerry Register's plane from Texas was just landing.

"Are we going to have Marc Schreuder?" Rosen asked, telling the judge that Jones had been noncommittal about it in a previous phone conversation. He couldn't care less about Serge Moore and Jerry Register. They had nothing to do with his client. Marc was the one who had pulled the trigger and bought the gun.

"We anticipate calling him," the prosecutor said. Then everyone broke for lunch.

When the afternoon session began, Lang said that he had spoken with Frances's doctor, who had informed him that she could be ready to travel by Friday. Serge Moore and Jerry Register testified but were not cross-examined, and then the duo of Myles Manning and Eddie Dean made their way into the courtroom.

561

"Is there a need to be nervous," the judge asked, "when there is an equal number of New York attorneys [to Utah attorneys] in the courtroom?"

"Does this break the record, sir?" Rosen asked good-naturedly, as he, Dean and the judge bantered for a few minutes before Ernie Jones began his direct examination.

The prosecutor methodically established Manning's part in the drama, then it was Rosen's turn. He wanted to know where Manning, who had left the *Daily News* a week after he testified in Marc's trial, was currently living.

"I'd rather not say," he said, "because it can lead to somebody getting hurt."

"Who?"

"Me."

"Who is going to hurt you?"

"I have no idea. That is the trouble."

The judge said that he did not have to reveal his address, and Rosen moved on to point out a number of contradictions between Manning's testimony at Marc's trial and the interview he had given to George and Harman one year before. Manning denied ever being an alcoholic (just "a heavy drinker") and said that he had not stopped off at any of the three bars Rosen mentioned on his way back to the newspaper the night he was interviewed. In a constant effort to impeach Manning's credibility, Rosen kept echoing the notion that even though the detectives offered Manning immunity in exchange for *truthful* answers, the printer either failed in numerous instances to be truthful (about the chronology and location of his meetings with Frances, for example; or by saying he had met her "shortly after" beginning work at the *Daily News*, which was in 1973, and then saying he met with her in 1977; or in saying she had suggested the amount of $5,000 and later saying he had)—or in saying he didn't remember something (like Frances's or Richard Behrens's name) and later recalling it. Rosen was a master at this sort of cross-examination, carefully scrutinizing earlier statements that a witness had made and then throwing them back at him in court. Before sitting down, Rosen brought up the trip Manning and Behrens had taken to the lake together—which, Manning admitted, had occurred around the same time he was meeting with Frances. Asked when he had last met

Behrens, Manning, having apparently blocked out the chance encounter with him and the two Washington lawyers on the night of July 13, said it was in a supermarket.

"You guys go shopping together?"

No, Manning said, they had talked for about five minutes. It had been before Marc's trial and the conversation had to do with the fact they would both be witnesses. This was the first time he had met with him, he claimed, since that fourth and last meeting with Frances in Behrens's apartment in the fall of 1977.

Earlier, Rosen had asked him if he had been working in 1977, and Manning said he had.

"Did you file an income tax return?"

"Yes, I did."

"Did you declare any of that [$5,000] in your tax return?"

"No, I didn't." Of course he hadn't. He had paid off those bills he said he had accumulated to some people whom he refused to name.

If Rosen had achieved nothing else with Manning, he gave the stocky printer—and the state—a brief preview of what they could expect in the future.

At ten the next morning, Mike Rosen had his first crack at Richard Behrens.

As he had with Manning, Rosen deftly established contradictions between certain things Manning and Behrens had said—not only about the meetings with Frances but when the two of them first got to know each other. And he was particularly interested in knowing how they had met and what Behrens remembered about Manning's little dog—the thing that ostensibly brought them together.

"His 'little dog' was walked every day," Behrens told the court. "And if he happened to be out in the street I would see his dog. . . ." But Behrens wanted to set the record straight about Manning's Samoyed. "It wasn't a little dog. It was a very big dog, which I think he may have had to have destroyed."

"Was that before or after you tried to pet him?" Rosen sneered, then withdrew the question. "Did there come a point in time when you went over to Mr. Manning and tried to strike up a little acquaintanceship because of his dog?"

"His dog was very outstanding, because you would see him with the dog all the time. And one of the occasions when I first met him, the dog was very vicious and you couldn't help but notice that."

"That's why you started talking to him?" Rosen asked in disbelief.

"One of the reasons why," Behrens maintained. "He was a person on the street."

Rosen showed Behrens a business card and asked him to identify the man whose name was on it. Behrens said he was the lawyer for his father's estate. Rosen pressed Behrens about the trip he and Manning had taken to his father's house on the lake, but Behrens remained firm in his denial that he had ever wanted Manning to kill his stepmother. However, he was smart enough to realize that Rosen was not likely to let that trip—and the reason why he and Manning had gone there—be buried along with his father.

Behrens was the state's last witness. Marc Schreuder did not appear after all. Nor, for that matter, did Jeffrey Morris, whom the defense knew nothing about. Jones was confident that the judge would feel reasonable and probable cause had been shown.

As is customary, Rosen moved to have the charges dismissed. In a sharp and perceptive argument, he pointed out a number of telling details. When Joel Campbell first interviewed Richard Behrens, Campbell had told him not to be reluctant about involving Frances, and Behrens had said he wasn't holding out on him. (But what Rosen didn't say was that Behrens had in fact implicated her. He had told Campbell he had asked him to get her a gun, but the detective hadn't pressed the issue at the time.)

Nowhere in that interview, Rosen said, did Behrens mention Myles Manning. Manning had admitted lying to the court, Rosen said, and he urged the judge to weigh both his and Behrens's testimony with "the greatest, greatest scrutiny."

It was strange, Rosen said, that Behrens was "familiar with two of the three watering holes that Mr. Manning probably drowns in as well as the YMCA that he was supposedly holed up in while he was supposedly doing this murder"—and yet it was "totally incredible" that Manning did not know from Behrens that Bradshaw was murdered, but from the investigators, who told him the night they came to the *Daily News*.

There was no credible proof offered by this "odd couple," as Rosen called them, that Frances had had pecuniary gain in mind as a motive to kill her father—and no proof that she "had anything in the world to do with the shooting of Franklin Bradshaw." For Behrens, who Rosen claimed would "say anything to help himself or benefit himself," to testify that Frances refreshed his memory the night they went to the Midnight Express that she had given him the gun was "a lot of nonsense." All he would have had to do, Rosen suggested, during the time he was trying to collect his money from her was say: "'Frances, remember the package of July 23, 1978? This little gun that you gave me?' She not only would have given him thirty-seven hundred dollars, she would have given him thirty-seven thousand or three hundred and seventy thousand. . . ."

"Don't you think," he asked rhetorically, "there's enough money in that estate to warrant Frances's coming up with the thirty-seven hundred dollars to stop him from doing something? If she gave him that gun, she'd let him write all over the place and go to court? . . ."

If you believed a guy like Behrens, Rosen had said earlier, you'd buy the Brooklyn Bridge eventually.

The judge didn't quite see it that way. He informed both sides the next day that the state had successfully carried its burden, and when Frances appeared in Salt Lake the following week, dressed in a calf-length black mink coat, she was officially bound over to stand trial.

59// Berenice had gone to New York to see Lavinia dance in *The Nutcracker*, and was amazed at how well she seemed to be coping, both with the strain of her mother's situation and her own disappointment at not getting the lead part of Marie.

"Lavinia had been promised the lead* and then this scandal broke out just about the time they were about to announce the lead and they couldn't," Berenice explained, then began to cry. "Every time I went and saw *The Nutcracker* I just sat and cried because *she* should have had the lead. Every time I saw that little girl in the lead I could picture Lavinia there— where she wanted to be, was supposed to be, but couldn't be. So I just sat and cried.

"I think she knows why she didn't get the lead. Frances doesn't keep anything from her. You can't. You *think* you're keeping something from her, but she's very, very wise."

Mike George left Salt Lake the day after Frances's preliminary and flew Jeff Morris back to Minneapolis, before going on to New York. From seeing Mike Rosen in action, George knew that his efforts to persuade Marc to testify would have to be stepped up—Marc had initially given him the impression that he would testify at the preliminary, but as the day of the hearing grew near, "he was totally losing it"—and that if there was any way of obtaining proof that Jeffrey Morris had met with Frances, he would have to find it.

Don Harman met George in New York, and together they went to 1675 York Avenue to see the superintendent, Andrew Fuleki, whom they had visited a year before. Frances had been living there during the time when she would have flown to Minneapolis, and they wondered if she might have signed out in a book—indicating she was going out of town—or told a doorman. Nobody remembered anything. George asked if anybody knew the maid who would have been working for Frances at the time—thinking that she might recall such a trip—but nobody did. In an attempt to

---

*According to David Richardson, she had been seriously considered for the part, but never actually promised it. While the ballet company was concerned about the bad publicity that might have resulted had Lavinia been chosen for the part—one that guarantees a certain amount of media exposure to the two girls who alternate in the role—Richardson maintains that the other two girls were chosen on the basis of ability.

find that person, he researched the car accident Frances and Lavinia had had on the Triborough Bridge just before Christmas in 1977. He thought that her name might appear on a police report, but it didn't. Aside from Morris himself, George's only source seemed to be Marc; and his knowledge had come from the long phone calls he and Frances would have while he was away at Kent.

They once again went to see Susie Coleman at the delicatessen, the one Marc went to when he came back that Sunday. Through his sources at the prison, George discovered that they sent "notes in code" to each other. In one of them, George recalled, Susie had written to "Dear Mr. So-and-So: This is the dental office of Dr. Munchenburger. You are due in for a check-up. Doesn't the world think we're all crazy?" At first, George thought the note was from Frances, "trying to psyche him out" by playing on Louis Moench's name, and George got the warden to agree not to deliver the card. A few days later, George said, "I go down, ask him about Susie and if he gets any cards from her, and he says, 'It's funny. I talked to her the other day. I've been expecting a card from her, but haven't received it.' 'What kind?' 'Oh, they're just funny cards. We call each other different names.'"

But as George realized, knowing about their friendship was one thing, persuading her to open up to him quite another.

On Monday, December 13, the investigators went to Pennsylvania. Mark Refowich assisted them in getting a search warrant for all the material that was found in Larry's trunk and then they went to see Larry. He was *still* in prison, but James Onembo, the official who was trying to help him, had found a suitable halfway house in Reading that could probably take him.

Though Larry did not know that his trunk had been discovered, he did not hesitate when George nonchalantly asked him where his grandparents' original wills were. Once he said he had them and they said that they now did, Larry revealed that he had "found" both wills in the summer of 1978, not long before the murder, in his grandfather's study in the basement. He knew he had the originals all along, he said later. "I just smiled when people asked me about it. It was a little secret I kept to myself. The bank said they had copies of Grandpa's, so I didn't think it was any big deal."

Asked why he had stolen them, he said, "Don't call it 'stealing.' I 'took them into my possession' when I was looking for hidden cash in his study."

What about a *new* will his grandfather might have had?

He smiled and said that he didn't know anything about that.

George felt that Larry looked much better and seemed more coherent than the last time he had seen him in April. Even though the discovery of the wills and the testimony Frankel had given at Marc's trial—first that Larry was involved in the murder, according to Marc, and then that he wasn't—had made George consider him again as a suspect, he was more interested in finding out how Larry felt about possibly testifying. Larry, whose bitterness toward his mother had only continued to grow, said that he loved Salt Lake, would come if the state paid his way, and wouldn't lie if he was called to the stand.

"That surprised me," George said later, "because I thought he'd want nothing to do with it. But you can't, from a practical legal standpoint, put a witness on the stand and *not* know what they're going to say."

Larry could say he was going to tell the truth, but it was more likely he would turn out to be a loose cannon on the deck—the kind that could sink their case.

60// 1983 didn't start off very well for a man named Allen Arbesfeld. Two days after New Year's, he walked into the men's room of a restaurant in Minneapolis called the Blue Ox. Someone followed him in, struck him over the head with a ball peen hammer, and took more than $500 from his wallet. Besides leaving the hammer behind, Arbesfeld's assailant carelessly left a towel on the floor—a towel with the name Andrew and the number 2 on it.

The manager of the restaurant had seen Arbesfeld and the other person enter the restroom but noticed that only one person had come out. He walked in to investigate, and found Arbesfeld lying in a pool of blood.

While Arbesfeld was rushed to the hospital with a fractured skull, two Minneapolis police officers, called to the scene, took the towel to the Andrew Board and Care Home at 1215 South Ninth Street. An employee at the residence identified the towel as being one of theirs and said that the 2 indicated it came from the second floor. From the description that the restaurant manager had given to the officers, the employee told them that the person they were looking for was Jeffrey Charles Morris.

Morris was arrested and charged with attempted murder, aggravated robbery and assault. The same person who had said he told Frances Schreuder nearly five years before that murder was not in his line of work had apparently just tried to commit one.

On January 11, Ernie Jones and Mike Rosen had a pretrial hearing in front of Third District Court Judge Ernest F. Baldwin, the judge who would eventually preside over Frances's trial. A trial date was set for May 2, and the defense was given until February 18 to file preliminary motions. Curious to know what some of them might be, the judge was told by Rosen that he was going to ask the court to reduce Frances's charge to second-degree, arguing that *if* Frances was found guilty, she should not be convicted on a stiffer charge than "the actual killer" was. Rosen also said that research was currently being done into the amount of publicity both cases had received—and that another motion might be for a change of venue.

But most of the half-hour hearing centered upon Ernie Jones's continuing efforts to have Frances's bail revoked—an effort that Rosen felt was "purely vindictive" on the part of the state.

Ernie Jones was not the only one concerned about Frances's being free on bail. Elaine and Mason Drukman were as well, but for a different reason.

On February 24, their oldest son, Sam, noticed a woman,

standing next to a silver Mercedes, taking pictures of the house in Berkeley in which he lived. Other than thinking she might be a real-estate agent, he gave it no further thought.

Two days later, he was doing some painting on the first floor. Through the small glass window in the front door, he happened to see another woman going through the mailbox outside. He had picked up his mail earlier that Saturday, but had left some junk mail in the box. As he opened the door to question the woman, she was already headed across the street—to the same silver Mercedes he had seen on Thursday.

Sam Drukman hadn't seen his Aunt Frances since the day of his grandfather's memorial service. He demanded that she give back what she had taken, and the driver, the same woman who had been taking the photographs and whose daughter was in the back seat with Lavinia, told her that she should. Sam grabbed the mail out of Frances's hands and the Mercedes sped away.

Upset and startled by this, Sam immediately called his mother and told her what had happened. Elaine picked up the phone, called Berenice in Salt Lake, and demanded to have Frances's Bay Area phone number.

"I cannot give out that information," she recalled her mother saying, before abruptly hanging up.

Elaine was not about to let the matter drop. She eventually reached Frances in New York. When Elaine told her who was calling, "Frances said, 'I used to have a couple of sisters, but I don't anymore,' and began ranting and raving. I said, 'Look, you bitch, just leave my kids alone,' and that brought her to a halt."

But Elaine went further. She informed the Berkeley police and postal inspector what had happened—as well as Mike George and Ernie Jones. She said that her family was frightened and wanted Frances's bail revoked. "If Frances gave pictures [of Franklin and his warehouse] to Myles Manning," Elaine said later, "why did she want pictures of Sam's house and my house? To kill us?" (She had learned that someone had been outside her house with a camera the previous September, but did not know that it had been her mother.)

"I'm more worried about my sons than myself," she

continued. "If they're knocked off, everything goes to Lavinia and Larry," referring to the fact that Marc could never benefit from his grandfather's will by law, and that Frances's share was being held back until the final outcome of her trial.

On March 17, Ernie Jones filed an affidavit about the incident with the court. Shortly afterward, though, he and Mike Rosen had a telephone conversation in which Jones agreed to allow Frances to remain out on bail provided she not communicate with any of the people on the list of witnesses the state might call, except for her mother, her two sons, and the lawyer Ron Madsen. What persuaded Jones to compromise was Rosen's argument that if Frances was in jail in Salt Lake, not able to work with him in New York preparing her defense, the trial might be delayed well beyond May—something that the prosecutor did not want. He had been living with the Bradshaw case for nearly two and a half years and was longing to be done with it.

Aware that his decision would displease the Drukmans, he said, "With any other judge, I might have pushed for it. But I was not convinced Baldwin would consider the incident significant enough. All I had was her going through the mailbox and pulling mail out, but didn't know *what* she was after. There were all kinds of theories, but I couldn't prove anything."

61 // Earlier in March, on the 14th, Larry was finally released from Northampton County Prison, nearly ten months after he first became eligible for parole. He had been accepted to the Threshold mental health program in Reading, and Berenice was going to pay for it. As part of the terms of his parole—his status until November 29, 1984—he was prohibited from going anywhere near the campus of Lehigh University and, specifically, from having any communication with Kathy Van Tyne. He was also required to continue taking Prolixin, a powerful antipsychotic drug he had first received at Farview in the summer of 1980 and which had been part of his regular medication for the past fifteen

months. Though he was given Cogentin to counteract its effects, the Prolixin still caused Larry's hands to tremble and he gained a great deal of weight.

But he was leaving prison, and that was a drug he would gladly take.

Marc was leaving too. Two days after Larry went to Threshold, Marc was moved from his cell in D Block to the Special Services Dormitory (SSD) and into the Young Adult Offenders Program there—a move that marked one more step in Mike George's plan to obtain Marc's testimony at his mother's trial.

Marc had applied twice for a transfer to SSD—viewed by general-population inmates in the "Big House," the main building of the prison, as a country club—but had been rejected both times because of the nature of his offense. But on this particular Wednesday, at the instruction of the warden, he was told to "roll it up" and off to SSD he went.

During the eight months he had been on Dog Block, he had stayed pretty much to himself. Aside from one fight he was in when someone poured water on his television, he directed most of his energy toward his studies and to playing chess with two inmates (not on Dog Block) who had been in the Salt Lake jail with him before his trial. Whenever Dan Shaffer or Michael Moore would defeat him, Shaffer recalled, he would go into "a complete depression." But chess was not the only thing Marc felt competitive about. When Moore became the first person to get an electric typewriter at the prison, Marc was on the phone to Paul Van Dam the next day for an IBM Selectric—and Berenice wound up getting billed for it. When Moore got himself a Sony stereo, Marc got a more expensive Pioneer unit. "Marc always has to be one step ahead," Moore said. "He wants to be part of the team," Shaffer added, "but he wants to be in charge."

One of the first people Marc met and became friendly with at SSD was Bryan Baird, a native of Salt Lake who was about eight months younger than Marc and was in prison for a bank robbery he had pulled in the summer of 1981. Under the influence of cocaine and responding to a dare, Baird told a teller he had a gun (but actually didn't), made off with $7,000, but turned himself in to the police shortly after he got away. Sentenced to one to fifteen years, he had come to the Point in January, after some time at a drug-rehabilitation center.

Like Marc, Baird was in the college program and had come from a background of some affluence. While Marc and he "basically hit it right off at SSD," he was unaware of the main reason Marc had been transferred from the Big House: if word got out that Marc might be thinking of testifying in May, the warden and the prosecution knew he would get a "snitch jacket" (or "collar") and that his life would be in danger. If he was at SSD, the thinking went, he would be relatively safe. Not only do inmates despise people who kill someone in their family but they don't like snitches of any kind—especially family snitches. Baird explained part of the prisoners' code: "Family is Number One. You should protect your family. You don't say anything—even if they are the ones who put you in."

The state meanwhile continued to work on Marc. As his mother's May 2 trial date loomed closer, he was occasionally taken from the prison to the County Attorney's Office to meet with Ernie Jones. "There was no way we could interview him out at the prison," he said. "So we made arrangements to take him out. I don't think people really realize what goes on behind the scenes and what work goes into a case. Nobody could realistically expect we could go out to the prison and say, 'Marc, we want you to testify against your mother.' That by itself is an incredible task—asking somebody to testify whom you've just spent the last year convicting. On the other hand, I don't think we were wooing him by holding out anything terrific by saying we'd go to the Board of Pardons for him. Maybe it sounds corny but we just tried to be upfront and honest with him: 'Look, whether you testify or not,'" Jones said they told Marc, "'your mother is going to blame you for the murder of your grandfather. You might as well let the people know what *really* happened. And why should you want to sit in a cell and take all the blame for this? You have all along.'"

The state wasn't alone in its efforts. Mary Lou had been assiduously courted for Mike George's "team," and was urging him as well. Marc said he wanted to see her on his trips to Salt Lake and George arranged that. Marc's father was in constant contact with Marc and was also planning to testify. After all the years of virtually no relationship at all between father and son, it had taken the murder to bring the two of them back together. "I want you to testify against your mother," Vittorio recalled telling Marc. " 'Papa, how can I do that to my own mother?' " Because, Vittorio said, "you have to look out for your own life. The decision is yours only. But you have to tell the truth."

Yet all of the prosecution's strategy and all of their enlisting of allies—their intense playing of the deadly game of divide and conquer that this family knew well—did not change the unmistakable message that the prison psychological reports and Louis Moench were giving them: Marc wanted to testify, but probably wouldn't. He had not had enough time to break the bond that held mother and son together. "Moench said at one point," George recalled, " 'The biggest ally you've got is time. The longer he goes *without* seeing his mother, having to stand up and fight in prison, being himself, becoming his own man . . . will help you. But I still don't think he will.' "

If Marc needed time, so did the defense. During another pretrial conference on April 6, in which Rosen argued—and the state responded to—twenty motions the defense had filed, Rosen asked for a continuance of six months; the judge gave him two weeks—until May 16. But on May 6, the lawyers came before Judge Baldwin once more. When a defense team has the kind of deep and seemingly bottomless well of riches that Mike Rosen *et al.* were able to draw on in preparing for Frances's trial, it is not unusual—it is fashionable even—to ask a professional firm to do exhaustive research into the area of juror prejudice and pretrial publicity with an eye toward jury selection. Rosen told Judge Baldwin in April that he had hired "a walking computer" to do just that. The "walking computer" was Jay Schulman, whose work in this field included such high-profile cases as Claus von Bülow, the Brink's robberies north of New York City (involving Kathy Boudin) and the Hyatt Regency Hotel disaster in Kansas City.

Schulman had hired a Utah firm to assist him, and by the time of the May 6 hearing, based on phone interviews with

634 out of 1,000 registered Salt Lake County voters,* he had discovered the following things:

—96.4 percent had read or heard about Frances and Marc Schreuder. Asked what they remembered reading or hearing, their responses ranged from "He was a kid, his mother put him up to it. The kid didn't do too bad of a defense. The state had a hell of a time getting the mother back" and "He was so brainwashed to the point he was minding his mother. . . . It was really the mother in him. She's sick," to "He did the job. Whether his mother told him to or not, he was old enough to know better," and "I just heard the basics—that mother and son murdered the father for inheritance purposes."

—80.2 percent had already formed an opinion that she was—or probably was—guilty. ("She is the culprit. She put him up to it. She cooked up the murder scheme so she is definitely guilty." "It's hard to say without all the facts. . . . The son claims she is guilty. Most kids wouldn't just go and indict their mother." "Premeditated first-degree murder for money. She is one hundred percent guilty of manipulating her son into committing murder." "A mother has an awful lot of influence on a child. The mother was definitely guilty." "She's been too evasive, she's trying to hide something. She didn't want to come back from New York.")

—61.5 percent "strongly" favored and 25.1 percent "somewhat" favored the death penalty for persons convicted of first-degree murder. If the crime was killing a relative for money, 74.2 percent "strongly" favored it, though only 13.2 percent "strongly" favored it if a person was party to a murder but did not actually commit it.

"Almost everyone remembers one or more facts," Schulman wrote in his affidavit. "The great majority remember two or more facts. The single notorious fact is not a fact at all but a perception. Namely, that Frances Schreuder 'directed' her son Marc to kill her father. . . .

"Given the saliency of the Schreuder matter in Salt Lake

---

*Though the remaining 366 interviews were not completed until May 9, 1983, Schulman said in an affidavit that the results would not vary even 1 percent. The overall survey would have a sampling error of + or − 3 percent.

County," he concluded, "it will take a continuance of at least a year to begin to dispel the rampant prejudices concerning Mrs. Schreuder."

The conference before Baldwin that Friday was almost a carbon copy of the one in April. At first.

In addition to asking for another continuance, citing everything from the "devastating" Schulman findings to the notion that Lavinia, who was about to dance in *Coppélia* with the New York City Ballet, would be "thrown out" and have her dance career destroyed if the publicity of the trial surfaced in New York at that time, Rosen argued other issues—from whether Frances was technically in her father's will in the first place to whether Dr. Moench should be allowed to testify. But of all the things that concerned Mike Rosen ten days before his client went on trial for her life, he was especially troubled by his inability to find out who one witness was on the list of seventy-two that the state might call: Jeff Morris.

Rosen told the judge that the only address for him was a federal parole officer in Minneapolis and the only thing the defense had on him was a "yellow" (or "rap") sheet that showed he was a bank robber. When they asked the parole officer if they could speak to him, Rosen said, they were told that no information could be given out. The parole officer said to write a letter; when they did, they were informed that Morris didn't want to speak with them.

"Do you have any statement from him, Mr. Jones?" Baldwin asked.

"No, Your Honor." Jones felt fairly sure the letters they had received from Morris were *not* exculpatory and that, by law, the defense was not entitled to them. He also felt that they did not constitute a witness statement because they had not been solicited by the state. He had raised a general concern about this in April, without directly alluding to Morris, and Rosen had specifically asked that if there was anything the state wasn't sure of in the way of discovery, and that might be exculpatory, the issue should be raised with the judge "so we don't get caught later." But Jones was not prepared to disclose anything he didn't have to—especially about Jeff Morris.

"Well, who is he?" Rosen demanded to know.

"Can you tell him," the judge asked, "who he is, what he is going to testify about?"

"Well, I would prefer not to, Your Honor. I think we have given everything we have in writing."

"Did you give them an address?" Baldwin said.

"Yes, I have," Jones said. "That is the same address I have got." The address he gave them was "110 South 4th Street. Room 426."

"It is the federal courthouse," Rosen offered.

"How do you get ahold of him?" Baldwin, a man with a short fuse, was beginning to get impatient.

"That address that we gave the defense. That is the way we have—"

"But you are the prosecutor," Baldwin reminded him. "They will give it to you."

But when Jones stuck to his story—one the judge clearly didn't believe—Baldwin demanded to know the subject of Morris's testimony.

"Well, let's put it this way, his testimony is similar to Myles Manning's."

"I don't know what that means," said Rosen.

"You know exactly what it means," said Jones. "You know what Myles Manning testified to."

"That he is a hit man?" Rosen was stunned. "That Frances Schreuder hired him to kill her father? Is that what you are representing, Mr. Jones?"

"That is right," Jones said.

The judge warned Jones that the prosecution had "a continuing duty to make disclosure," just as the defense had to disclose "alibi or insanity matters" to them—and that if it turned out he was lying and the state could have gotten another address for Morris, he might very well ban his testimony.

By now Rosen was seething. Like the judge, he had the kind of volatile nature that could erupt on a second's notice. This was the *first* time this had ever come up, he told Baldwin, and he wanted to know how he could give the judge an "alibi" for Frances if he didn't have enough time to find out who Morris was. "I don't see why they can't give us the details. This isn't a game. This isn't football or hockey. . . . A woman is on trial for her life."

577

Baldwin seemed to agree, telling Jones he thought something had been "hidden in the bushes." Rosen said that Kevin Kurumada had asked Jones about Morris, but all they got was a rap sheet (an incomplete rap sheet, it turned out, that indicated "Jeff Morris" from the state's potential witness list was really Jeffrey Charles Morris and, because it stopped in 1980, made no mention of what had happened at the Blue Ox just four months before).

Instead of caving in, Jones defended himself. The defense had had Morris's name for two months. They were given a rap sheet on him. Whatever the state handed over, Jones complained, the defense "always want more. They always want us to tell them something else about the case."

Rosen said that until they found Morris he didn't feel they could go forward. He said that federal parole regulations require a parolee to report once a month to his probation officer. "I will have somebody outside that office every day for the next x-number of months and we will ask everybody who walks in if he is the fellow. . . . We have been prejudiced by this situation and it is not just a transactional witness of little moment. This is an alleged hit man."

Baldwin said he would sign an order for the parole officer in Minneapolis, asking him to make Morris available, but warned Rosen that Morris "can tell you to go to the devil." Rosen said he knew that. All he wanted was time—the one thing Baldwin wouldn't commit himself, at that point, to giving him.

Six days later, on May 12, Mike Rosen and Ernie Jones appeared before the Utah Supreme Court. Baldwin had decided not to allow for a continuance and the defense had filed a petition against him, claiming "abuse of discretion" and enabling them to go before the state's highest court.

Rosen carefully laid out the scenario in front of the five justices. He told how Jones had "successfully camouflaged and hidden from us . . . this key witness." He explained that Morris's name was "conveniently sandwiched" between two other witnesses from Minneapolis who were connected with the airlines; that the name itself, Jeff Morris, was wrong, his real name being Jeffrey Charles Morris; and that his rap sheet showed him to be not only a convicted bank robber, but someone who had been committed to psychiatric evaluation and incarcerated in five different prisons over a period of two years. He said how reluctant Jones was to tell both the defense and Judge Baldwin what the gist of Morris's testimony would be. Once he did, Rosen said, he then showed the judge a letter from Morris—"outlining his entire testimony," placing Frances somewhere in 1978, and he said that the defense had just learned of it. He had heard there was a second letter—one in which Morris said he *didn't* want to testify—but he was not certain about that. He said in the last few days, through a Minneapolis investigator, he had discovered—but could not yet verify—that Morris had "a long extensive history of mental disease," that he had other arrests and convictions besides the bank robbery, that he had used "numerous aliases" and had "impersonated several officers." It would take time to subpoena all of Morris's various records—and time to prepare an adequate cross-examination. If the state wanted to use him, he should be required to have a psychiatric evaluation. If they wanted to go to trial this Monday, he said, then let them go without Morris.

Ernie Jones essentially repeated the argument he had made to Baldwin earlier: the defense was claiming surprise when in fact they'd had Morris's name for two months. He admitted that he was concerned whether the letter Rosen mentioned could be considered a "witness statement"—something he would be required to turn over as part of discovery—because the state had not solicited it. And that is why he had gone to Baldwin with it, he said, pointing out Baldwin's feelings that the defense probably wasn't entitled to it, but he was going to let them see it anyway.

Asked by one of the justices if the state was definitely going to call Morris to testify, Jones said there was "a good chance" but wouldn't commit himself. "A lot of it depends on the testimony and the way that testimony is presented to the jury. . . . I don't think we will know until we get there."

But the justices seemed persuaded by the arguments Rosen had made and reminded Jones that the defense was not asking the state to do their work for them—only for the time in which to do it themselves.

Sensing the judicial wind was blowing in his direction, Rosen was ready for his final push. Morris described himself as an arsonist in the letter, Rosen informed them. If that wasn't evidence that might impeach Morris, Rosen implied, he didn't know what was. "I think I'm entitled to have that information [including a complete rap sheet and psychiatric history] before he gets up on the stand and says, 'That lady hired me to kill her father,' in a circumstantial-evidence case, which is all they have. I think I have a right to ask every doctor who ever examined that man, every prison official—he was in five different prisons—why he was transferred from prison to prison. . . . We didn't have the rap sheet March 3rd [when they received the state's list of potential witnesses]. How am I going to cross-examine this man? . . . I don't have anything. They knew about this fellow. And maybe I let her down because there was seventy-two witnesses. And maybe I was fully thinking to put him with the other . . . Minneapolis fellows. He was in the airlines. He was an airline employee. So, maybe I was a fool. But don't take it out on Frances Schreuder. She didn't get fooled about this. Maybe I should have banged the doors down. But when the prosecutor goes to the federal probation office, they gave him that information. When I go there, I have to write letters and I have to make formal requests under the federal rules to get information. I don't think Mr. Jones had to do that. They turned me down cold. I had to start dictating letters to get information just before a murder trial. I'm sorry."

"Mr. Rosen," one of the justices said, "could I ask you a question? Assuming the state calls this witness, how important will the testimony of this witness be in the overall case? Would you classify him as the state's key main witness?"

"I say he's devastating for the following reasons. The state has another alleged hit man who was allegedly hired by Mrs. Schreuder in New York. He's a New York hit man. Personally, I think I can very easily destroy that man's testimony as well as [their] other witnesses." But if they could bring Morris in, he said, somebody who was not involved with all the people in New York who were trying to frame Mrs. Schreuder and he said that she "hired me too, you're looking at murder one. You're looking at that from the penalty phase as well. Whether she carefully, in advance, planned this horrible act. That's the death penalty right there. . . .

"We should have a chance to really go into this guy and take this guy apart molecule by molecule."

Late that afternoon, the Court reached a decision. Rosen had won. The following day, after Judge Baldwin set a new trial date for September 6, Ernie Jones still couldn't quite believe it. "Rosen's the best I've ever seen," said Jones, shaking his head. "There's not a lawyer in the state of Utah who could've gotten that continuance from the Utah Supreme Court."

Once confident about his case, Jones was now admitting that he felt the state only had "a fifty-fifty chance" of winning it. In the opinion of one local lawyer, "Ernie had set himself up with other prosecutors and defense lawyers for gracefully losing—if that's what it came down to—by saying how much he respected Rosen and what a good attorney he was."

The prosecutor had good reason to worry. His case *was* circumstantial, just as Rosen had said. That didn't mean it couldn't be won, but it would be far more difficult than putting the murder weapon into Marc's hands.

The situation with Morris could blow up in his face at any second. It wasn't just that Morris didn't want to speak with the defense; Jones wanted to prevent him from speaking with the defense by keeping Morris's exact location hidden. It would have been simple to tell the defense about the attack on Allen Arbesfeld—but the state chose not to: the less the defense could find out about Morris, the better. But now that Rosen had a continuance, Jones had no doubt that he would have people combing the flatlands of Minnesota to find him.

Before Rosen got the continuance, Mike George had brought Marc up to Salt Lake for "a dry run." But just as Marc found himself unable to testify in December, George said he "lost it again. He psychologically fell apart—couldn't sleep, talking to himself, pacing."

At the prison, his caseworker, Mona Ladue, had been discussing with him what his testimony might mean and the state's efforts to extract it. She told him that he would have "to live with his conscience for the rest of his life. If they're trying to buy you, then you're selling yourself."

Marc was working as Ladue's clerk in SSD, and though she found him "very trying at times," she also felt he "had really grown up on the blocks" and was gaining in self-esteem, strength of mind and self-confidence. "Marc's scars go back a long way," she said. "It's a shame this crime had to happen and he had to come here to find out who he was and that he's a separate entity from his mother."

When he wasn't working as a clerk, he was helping out in the kitchen, lifting weights, and spending a lot of time with Bryan Baird. "Marc is very intelligent and likable," Baird said, "but also very headstrong and more than a little bit narcissistic. He likes the world to revolve around him. He has a tendency to go into tirades. If something doesn't go right for him, he will launch into a string of obscenities and wave his hands. Almost anything can touch him off. He has tirades about papers. He will sit and *iron* articles from the *Wall Street Journal,* so that the paper isn't wrinkled. He subscribes and is in the financial pages at *all* times. If you pick up the paper without his permission, it is like you have hit someone in his family: 'How dare you do this? How could you do this?' Money is his bitch-goddess. He adores making money, gloats over it, and is always looking for new ways to make it. He's somewhat of a loner who talks more at people than *with* them in a sort of condescending way. I think he basically wants to be accepted by everybody, wants to be a friend to everybody —but he also rejects everybody. He wants the friendship on *his* terms. I may have been an exception. He feels himself to be of superior intelligence and is perfectly willing to let you know that."

One day, not long before Frances's scheduled May trial, Bryan saw that Marc had some court transcripts and was looking over them. Bryan asked him why he was doing that and Marc said he was preparing to go back to the Board of Pardons in July.

Over the next three to four days, walking around the yard of SSD, Marc began to open up to Bryan. Bryan was not a lawyer or a psychiatrist or a police investigator or a reporter. He was in no position to be of any tangible help—or harm—to Marc, nor was he being paid to do so. He was, perhaps, in the best and purest position of all. He was Marc's friend. He lived with him every day, he cared about him, and he told him that whatever Marc wanted to tell him, he would not stand in judgment of him.

"At times he would get very emotional and cry in telling me about it," Bryan recalled. From the way Marc talked about "Mom," Bryan could tell "he has an almost spooky attachment to her . . . like a lover talking about an old lover. Whenever he talks about 'going back to her,' it's how somebody would talk about going back to an old lover. 'If I didn't do exactly what she wanted me to do,' " Marc told him, " 'she'd threaten to cut me out of her will or say that she didn't love me anymore.' "

Bryan could tell "he really believed that—that she would hate him and that he wouldn't have anybody to love him. Marc is a person who needs to have someone caring for him. I think he was deathly afraid of not being loved by her. And I think that's why he did what he did—being at her beck and call, sitting in her room for hours just listening to her tell him about all the rotten things that were going on, the rotten things her family were doing to her. I was very convinced. Normally, I'm a very mistrustful person but I could tell he was very sincere about it and telling the truth. . . . There was a hell of a lot of pain behind all the things he had to do for her—and all the rejection he felt from her."

Marc talked about Larry and how he always saw him as a rival for their mother's attention. "He mentioned Larry's going to a special school—for psychiatric reasons—because Larry was having trouble coping with problems at school and at home. He said he never really liked him until Larry got arrested and he felt sorry for him." But over the past few months they had grown close, Bryan explained, and that Marc said, " 'I used to think of Larry as a psychotic—a crazy man, beating up his roommate—and didn't want anything to do with him.' " But as his own prison sentence went on, Bryan said, "he realized that everybody is capable of that."

Marc said he'd never really liked his father before—before all this happened; that his mother would tell him "hands off, he's bad news," and that he had seen his father, whom he characterized as "a problem drinker" but not an alcoholic, hit her a few times. But "since he has been in prison," Bryan said, "he has just clung on to him. He really idolizes him now. Whenever he talks about his father it's like he's talking about

God. He thinks his father could do just about anything. I feel he really needs the relationship with his father and brother to take the place of the one with his mother."

Marc talked about his childhood, Bryan said, "like he is free *now,* and was in prison *then.* He really resents his mother for putting him in that black-and-white position—you either love me or you're out in the street. It almost gets to the point of such intense hate that he can't even speak about it, he's so angry. I'd had a strange childhood too, but I didn't think parents would do that."

Bryan read the court transcripts Marc had and the transcript of the conversation between Frances and Lavinia. But from Marc himself, Bryan learned things that hadn't come out at his trial—things that further persuaded him Marc felt "there was no way out for him."

In the summer of 1977, Marc told Bryan, the murder attempts with the oatmeal were more like a game to him than real. He said that he and Larry had "developed that. That his mother sent them out with these amphetamines and that they had tried to poison him. He said it was quite frustrating to have to go through all the rigmarole they did before they did kill him. He said at the time he was *more* pissed off at [his lack of success] than the fact he had to kill his grandfather. Marc was fascinated by the prospect of killing someone—a morbid curiosity of what it would be like. He related the killing of his grandfather to 'like being in a murder novel.' I think for him it was like the American soldier in Vietnam who went there wondering what it would be like to shoot and kill somebody.

"But in 1978," Bryan said, "he didn't want to do it—until it was accomplished." When the deal with Manning fell through in the fall of 1977, he told Bryan, he was " 'pissed off to the point where I had thought about finding Manning and killing him.' In retrospect, though, he was happy and felt 'Mom deserved it.' " When he arrived in Salt Lake that Saturday night, having wanted to stay on with the Cavenaughs, he took a cab to the Hotel Utah, the finest in town and located directly across from the Mormon Temple. He checked in under the name of David Jablonski—the same name he used three years later at the Hotel Seville. After the phone call to his mother and a fairly sleepless night, he took about three different cabs from the hotel to the warehouse so that he could remain anonymous. Marc told Bryan that "Mom" had instructed him to wear "something nondescript like Levi's and a T-shirt but he ended up wearing a blue blazer"—like the prep school student he was—"a yellow shirt, blue baggy pants." He said it was his last act of defiance. He wanted to look very dapper—like a CIA agent—instead of some hobo off the street. He waited outside the warehouse "on pins and needles, kind of delirious almost. He wanted to back out a couple of times but she had reinforced it all in his mind— starving to death, eviction, she and Lavinia having to live in Harlem. He thought his grandfather was a miser, didn't like him, but didn't think he should die."

When he slowly opened the door and walked inside the warehouse, Gramps was surprised to see him. Contrary to what Marc had told Frankel (but did tell Moench), they had a conversation. Marc asked why he wasn't giving Mom any money and Gramps said, "I'm tired of giving your mother money. She knows the reason why. She doesn't deserve it. I'm tired of throwing money out into the streets." "That's *no* answer," Marc told him, repeating his question. Perhaps it was something in Marc's voice—or in Franklin's memory of Marc standing over him in the middle of the night the summer before—but it made him "a little bit nervous," Marc told Bryan. "It was like out of a movie. He sensed what was about to happen." Marc kept on talking to him, waiting and praying for him to turn around, and when he did, he shot him.

Marc saw the "look of shock" on his grandfather's face before he died—and then, when he was down on the ground, he shot him again. Shot him a second time "to make sure he was dead. I didn't want to have to go through it again."

The first thing he felt was relief, he told Bryan, as he scattered the contents of his grandfather's wallet around the floor to make it look like a robbery. He was shocked at "how quickly the life went out of his body." The impact of the gun had made his arm numb all the way up to his shoulder. There was blood everywhere, and, along with the relief he felt, was the feeling of "how easy it was, that it happened so quickly. I thought there would be the agonizing death scene, but he just died, almost as if he were asleep."

In a daze, he took a number of cabs back to the hotel, his hand clutching the gun in his pocket. "It was just like a part of me," he told Bryan. "I never took my hand off it. Didn't want to let it go. If somebody had come and tried to pry it out with a crowbar, they couldn't have done it, because my hand was so attached to it."

Once back in the hotel room, even as he began vomiting, even as he put on the clothes Mom had wanted him to wear, he never took his hand off the gun until he was ready to close his suitcase and pack it inside.

Once he was back in New York, having barely made the plane in Salt Lake, his mother told him, "'Thank God, it's finally over.' She just hugged me as if I'd been away for thousands of years. I had never experienced that and Mom was almost dizzy with joy. I was crying, walking around blathering for a while, just talking about it to myself, 'Grandfather is dead, Grandfather is dead.'"

Having told Moench that at first he "wanted to be caught" and told Mike George that if he had been caught within the first year, he would have "folded like a ton of bricks," Marc told Bryan he just went numb after the initial shock of what happened, that "it really didn't affect me at all. I just started going on about my business. But after a few months, it started to hit me hard." Back at Kent for his senior year, "the remorse would come in really heavy at times and then just be gone—as if nothing had happened." And by the time he got to Trinity—a lonely experience for him, he said, like being "in the middle of a crowd in New York and not knowing anyone"—he felt certain that he would never get caught, that "my name would go back into anonymity, that no one would ever hear of me again, no one would care, and all the heat would die off."

As Bryan listened to Marc reveal these and other details, he felt both shock and sorrow—shock at what he was hearing, sorrow for Marc. While Marc told Bryan he deserved to spend time in prison, Bryan felt that Marc had not yet come to terms with the fact he'd killed somebody. "I feel sorry that he doesn't really feel he did anything wrong. It's a heinous crime he did—and he deserves to pay for it. I don't think he sees that. He feels he should do a minimum amount of time."

And, Bryan soon realized, he didn't feel he should do it alone.

Around the same time Marc was opening himself up to Bryan Baird, his grandmother was reaching out to her sister-in-law and occasional nemesis, Bertha Beck. In a letter on May 18, Berenice told Bertha that there was "no need for this trial." She and Frances were happy that it had been rescheduled, she wrote, "because we can plan our summer. However, I wish it were over. I can't see how Frances is going to survive this ordeal." She told Bertha she was going to New York about the end of June and that Lavinia was currently dancing at Lincoln Center in *Coppélia*. "She is a beautiful, intelligent dancer. All this family scandal is going *very* hard on her." She wrote that her heart "bleeds for both of them. It is all so unnecessary, drummed up by hate and jealousy.

"We have suffered," she closed, "and the worst is yet to come."

In order to do what she could to prevent that, Berenice had paid a little visit to the warehouse to see Doug Steele. She had been down to see Doug after Marc was convicted, and at the time, Doug had said to her: "You told me that Frances went down to the deli that Sunday morning to tell Marc and that he was all upset about Grandpa's death. That would have been impossible. If that was the case, why didn't they produce some witnesses that Marc was at the deli?"

"We did have a witness who was going to testify," Berenice snapped, "but she changed her mind. Her father talked her out of it." That wasn't true. Frances had asked Susie Coleman to alibi for Marc, but she wouldn't.

Since Mike George had told Doug that Frances had gone out of town that day, he wondered "why Berenice would weave such a story." Unless, of course, that was the story Frances had told her.

He knew that Berenice felt he and Nancy Jones were "paid off" to testify at Marc's trial, so he was surprised by her visit this year. "I have a lot of money," Berenice reminded him, "and I'm going to leave it to whomever I want. In the next few weeks [this was prior to the original May trial date] I guess I'll find out who my friends are."

Doug instantly saw it for what it was and had a reminder for her: "Berenice, I got the subpoena just like you. When I raise my hand to God, I'm going to tell them the truth. I can do no less and no more." Frank Bradshaw had been like a father to Doug Steele and no amount of money was going to change that. Not now. Not ever.

62// Once Mike Rosen hired a private investigator in Minneapolis, it hadn't taken long to get a better idea who Jeffrey Charles Morris was. Rosen had retained Paula Giese on April 20, three weeks before he appeared in front of the Utah Supreme Court. A former assistant professor at the University of Minnesota, Giese quickly learned that Morris had been in the Hennepin County jail since January, had pled guilty on April 1 to the charges of aggravated robbery and assault (the attempted murder charge was dropped, even though Morris said he "may or may not" have been hired to kill Arbesfeld), and had been sentenced, on April 19, to serve seventy-six months. At the jail, she learned that he "was supposed to be at Stillwater"—a state prison east of Minneapolis—and that he had been in touch by phone with the Utah authorities since shortly after his arrest. When she phoned Stillwater, she said, they were non-committal as to whether Morris was there or not, but she soon found out that he was supposed to be picked up on May 13 and taken to Utah for Frances's trial three days later.

She relayed all of this information to Mike Rosen before the May 6 conference with Judge Baldwin—Rosen's "best recollection" is that she hadn't—though Rosen did not know what connection Morris allegedly had to Frances until Ernie Jones was forced by the judge to reveal it. If Jones had been less than open with Baldwin and the Utah Supreme Court, so, to some extent, had Rosen. Notwithstanding the prosecutor's clear reluctance to disclose Morris's true whereabouts, there was always the possibility that if Rosen had let on that he knew more about Morris than he had revealed, he might not have gotten the continuance he had argued for so brilliantly.

Giese, meanwhile, finally established that Morris was at Oak Park Heights, a new facility near the one at Stillwater. But when she tried to see him on June 21, she was told that he was on the phone to Utah. "Morris sent word refusing an interview," read an affidavit that she filed, "with the message that any interviews would have to be arranged through Sergeant Michael George, the Salt Lake County Attorney's investigator, who had instructed him to do it that way."

Nine days later, on June 30, Mike George picked Morris up in Minnesota and flew him to Salt Lake "so we'd be able to control him better." But from the moment Morris arrived at the Point—having been explicitly told by George "not to tell *anyone* why he was there"—they weren't able to do that. Even protective custody didn't prevent Morris from letting people know how important he was to the state of Utah and earning himself the snitch jacket that George was afraid he might get. Morris had a different story: he told George that people at the prison were on to *him,* somehow *knew* why he was there, and that's why he was having such a hard time. Though George still believed that Morris had probably met with Frances, he didn't believe that.

Less than a month after Morris entered the Utah State Prison, having nightly paced his cell and enthusiastically sung the praises of Hitler and angrily complained that his towels weren't white enough, "the most difficult prisoner to manage" the warden had ever seen was transferred to the Tooele County Jail and booked under a different name. But life in Tooele was no easier for him—or anyone else. He got a letter one day with his real name on it, became "crazy" and "paranoid," according to George, that people knew who he was, and wound up threatening a guard and eating toilet paper before being moved again.

After a short stay—and more trouble—at the jail in Summit County, Morris was booked into the Salt Lake City-County Jail on August 13. If he was just across the street from the County Attorney's Office, the thinking went, the state would finally be able to control him.

But as they soon discovered, Morris was like a bull running through the streets of Pamplona.

If Jeffrey Morris couldn't resist telling the world why he had come to the land of Zion, Marc couldn't resist telling Bryan Baird, Michael Moore and Dan Shaffer where he had been. While his forays out of the prison were a closely guarded secret from the local media, they were a growing source of resentment on the inside. At first, most inmates were under the impression that Marc's leaving had something to do with his hearing before the Board of Pardons. But that impression was shattered one day in May when Moore, Shaffer and other inmates watched with amazement as Marc, in street clothes, walked right out the front door of the Big House and into his father's waiting car. Though it had been cleared with the warden, Baird said, "other inmates wanted to kill Marc because of that" and "a lot of the officers didn't like it at all. They couldn't believe that a murderer was being let out the way he was."

In July, Marc went before the board and instead of receiving a rehearing date in five to seven years—the normal period for someone convicted of second-degree murder—he was given one in three. But "the straw that broke the camel's back"—as Baird called it—came not long afterward. On his way back to SSD, Marc walked into the medium-security culinary, a vast area whose walls have brilliant murals, painted by inmates, of deer, bears and Indians. He spotted Moore and Shaffer and went over to talk with them.

"What brings you into the medium culinary?" Moore asked, noticing the "glisten" in Marc's eye and his "wily" grin.

"I just got back from *Return of the Jedi*," he told them, pleased with himself. He had gone to the movie with Mike George and Mary Lou.

It had been quite some time since Moore or Shaffer had seen a movie, other than the ones that were shown in prison, and they hardly knew what to say.

Asked if he liked it, Marc said how disappointed he was by the movie's anticlimactic ending. He explained that Darth Vader, the villain, was unmasked at the end and shown to be frail, old, soft and innocent. He was surprised that a villain—who he imagined would be strong, masculine, and "not the kind who gave up," he later told Baird—would look like that.

Shaffer, sensing that the movie had made quite an impression on Marc, prodded him to be even more specific about Vader's appearance.

"You know," Marc said, slowly and reflectively, "he was almost grandfatherly."

63// Frances spent part of July in Saratoga Springs, New York, where the New York City Ballet performs each summer and where Lavinia was attending a ballet camp. Some parents had decided not to allow their children to attend the camp because of concern that Frances might be there; while one father conceded that he didn't know if she was innocent or guilty, he was not taking the chance that his child would be in "an unchaperoned situation."

Before Frances went to Saratoga, she allowed Larry to come and stay at Gracie Square over the long Fourth of July weekend. Provided he cleared it with his parole officer in Reading, Larry was free to travel within a certain area. He had driven to New York two weekends earlier and stayed with his father, but when he asked his mother if he could stop by, she had refused and told him she was too busy. Berenice was in town that weekend too, having come to New York earlier than she had planned; but when he asked his mother if he could possibly see *her,* away from the apartment, the answer was again no.

Over the holiday weekend, Larry said, he had to wait on his mother hand and foot. Documents were spread all over the apartment. She told him he would never get anywhere in the "social circles" of New York with the name Bradshaw—a "farmer's name, a hick's name"—ironically forgetting that a colleague of hers on the board of the ballet was Mrs. Thornton F. Bradshaw, wife of the head of RCA.

But she also told him something else—told *him* because,

591

with Marc gone and their relationship severed, there was no one else, other than Berenice, perhaps, in whom to confide. She said that while she had confidence in the lawyers she had, she was still worried that "I'll get killed or go to jail"; worried that Vittorio was going to tell Marilyn that "I had confessed the whole thing to him," in order to get some money from Marilyn; and, most of all, worried that Marc would come forward and testify against her, his own mother, in order to get a lighter sentence.

What Larry didn't tell her was that he had been encouraging Marc to do just that.

64// Ernie Jones wasn't quite sure what they were. Neither was Judge Baldwin. In any case, when Mike Rosen's letter arrived, citing them as his reason for requesting another continuance, the judge quickly phoned "a Jewish friend of mine" to find out about Rosh Hashanah and Yom Kippur.

Informed of their significance, Baldwin agreed to compromise. He still wanted to see the lawyers in court on September 6 and 7 to hear some further defense motions, but he would allow Rosen to return to New York after that to spend Rosh Hashanah with his family. Jury selection would begin on Monday, September 12, and would probably be concluded by that Thursday so that the lawyer could return to New York once more, for Yom Kippur, before the beginning of the trial on the following Monday.

Since taking on the Schreuder case, Mike Rosen had tried to learn as much about Utah and the Mormons as he possibly could. When he first appeared out there in December, he had noticed a Star of David and the Ten Commandments not far from the steps of the courthouse. A good sign. Mormons identified with Jews because they had both suffered from persecution, yet they were the only people alive who called Jews "Gentiles." So as he prepared for trial, it really wasn't his being Jewish that concerned Mike Rosen so much; it was how a lawyer from New York, with an unmistakable accent, was going to play in front of a Utah jury. Warned by Jay Schulman that "the carpetbag" issue might hurt, he had decided that this whole subject of New York was one that he planned to raise during jury selection.

Sitting in his office in early August, wearing jeans, sneakers and an open-necked beige shirt, he was saying how "playing away from home makes you even more cautious. It's not my ballpark. It's a different society. I'm not only defending my client but I have to take different factors into account—the society, myself. I'll have to feel it as I go along. It's a total unknown, which I don't even have to bother with in New York."

But if he was cautious, he was also brash—confident that he could destroy people like Manning ("I'll pin his ass. He'll never want to hear of Utah again"), Behrens ("he has had little boys in his bed" and tried to get Manning to kill his stepmother), Gentile (a "suave, diminutive Continental greaser"), Marilyn ("This really comes down to Marilyn vs. Frances. Marilyn only gets an allowance at this point but stands to get a lot") and, if the state was foolish enough to use him, Jeff Morris. He was so confident that he even phoned Ernie Jones later that month and told him that he was going to blow him and his case right out of the courtroom.

He was going to use the same words Jones had used to convict Marc and turn them against him. He was going to show the jury that the state could not flip-flop. He was going to continue to fight to keep Moench off the stand; he didn't want his medical opinion or anything else. He felt sure the state would try to introduce "the tape," but felt equally sure he could keep it out; something like that could be lethal in the hands of a jury. He would show that Frances was *not* in the will and that trying her for murder one on pecuniary gain was all wrong. He believed totally in her innocence, he said, and would prove that she was being framed by people. He knew that Williams & Connolly had suggested an insanity defense to Frances, but said that it would have been "a dishonest way to go" and that they had been on "a Hinckley high." As any responsible lawyer would, Rosen had also explored the insanity defense with Frances—"to see whether or not she felt it would be an easy way out. It was bait. She wanted no part of it and has never wavered from her innocence."

But the one thing he was less sure about was Marc.

Paul Van Dam and Kevin Kurumada drove out to see Marc and he told them that he probably wouldn't testify. He told Berenice that he definitely wouldn't. But Marc was telling Ernie Jones (whom he called Bud) and Mike George that he would, though they didn't know whether to believe him. Marc was right where his mother always liked to be—in charge. He might have been going through pain in trying to make his decision, but he had not lost his sense of drama.

Marc was not the only person causing Jones and George to have sleepless nights and to wearily say to each other that "this trial has *got* to go in September—win, lose, or draw." Jeff Morris had asked a Catholic priest to bring him newspaper accounts of the case. And Fast Eddie Dean was threatening, he wrote Jones, that "in view of our past experiences" he couldn't guarantee Myles Manning would appear in Utah unless he received "five hundred ($500) dollars against my and Myles's expenses." Dean was tired, he said later of their two previous trips to Salt Lake, of "dancing on basketballs" out there and being squeezed so tightly into tourist class that by the time Myles arrived in Utah "he was stuck to his seat." After Frances's preliminary hearing, Dean had submitted "a bill for my time—aiding and abetting the good people of the state of Utah." The bill was for $1,100—two days out of the office for Dean at $500 per day, plus $100 for meals and booze (which, he pointed out, was $25–35 less than the actual amount). Even though Jones had explained to him that the state did not pay for such things, and had made a "special effort" by paying for Dean at all, Dean had submitted the bill in December—and kept resubmitting it. (The County Attorney's Office, faced with the reality that they needed Manning, finally paid.) While Jones and Dean were going back and forth about Dean's new request, who should call but Richard Behrens. He had once again "bumped into" Manning—this time near a roofer's store on East 90th Street—and had gotten the distinct impression that Manning didn't know

594

when the trial was supposed to start and might not show up for it. Once Jones heard that, he got in touch with Al Sullivan, apprised him of the situation, and asked if he could force Dean and Manning (whose place of residence Jones truly did not know) into court and make them comply with the subpoena. Always willing to help, Sullivan said he would try.

If Manning could not be located, if Marc didn't testify, if Moench wasn't allowed to offer his diagnosis, if Morris self-destructed, and if Behrens was ripped apart on the stand, the odds against the state's winning would be a lot longer than the fifty-fifty Jones had cautiously expressed in May.

The last judge that most lawyers want to ply their trade in front of in the Third District Court of the State of Utah is Ernest F. Baldwin. "There are no cherries in his courtroom," his bailiff warned a stranger, pointing out that "he's bit everybody in the ass" at one time or another. He insists the attorneys who come before him be properly dressed in coat and tie, and if he feels that a lawyer is not asking the right questions of a witness, he will.

In his office one late August afternoon, listening to Fats Waller and Art Tatum and smoking a Players cigarette, the crusty, sixty-six-year-old former football player was happy to talk about anything except the case he was soon to preside over. Born a Mormon in the Utah mining town of Silver City, where his father ran the mining company's store, he moved to Salt Lake at the age of two. An avid reader of comic strips ("Momma" is his favorite), he attributes his high blood pressure to being a judge, is not averse to phoning the local newspapers if he feels they have been "too unrestrained" in their coverage, and often relaxes after work at the Ambassador Club, where he plays gin with Jay Elmer Banks and drinks Jack Daniel's. Asked how his wife would describe him, he said, without hesitation, "She'd tell you that I was a son of a bitch," before adding that they had recently been divorced.

As he stared at the three volumes of *The State of Utah* v. *Frances Bernice Schreuder* sitting on the corner of his desk, he said that he had been preparing very hard for this trial, and then pulled out a sheet of paper containing a quote from his judicial hero, former United States Supreme Court Justice

Robert H. Jackson, that reflected Baldwin's view of his role:
". . . the trial judge sits alone and does most of his work with
the public looking on. He cannot lean on advice of associates
or help from a law clerk. He works in an atmosphere of strife,
with counsel, litigants and often witnesses and spectators
bitter, biased and partisan. . . ."

If that was to be the atmosphere of Frances's trial, Ernest
Baldwin would be in control: nobody was about to turn *his*
courtroom into a circus.

65// For a man worried about being seen as a carpet-
bagger, Michael Rosen certainly brought a lot of
baggage to court on the sparkling morning of Tuesday,
September 6.

Dressed in a gray pinstripe suit and a solid red tie, Rosen
had the smile of a man with a secret up his sleeve. As he and
his two colleagues, John Lang and Kevin Kurumada, began
unloading their papers, Rosen looked up for a second and
said, "They didn't tell me in law school that I'd have to schlep
so many bags." Like Willy Loman, Mike Rosen had arrived,
bringing his roots—and Steve Swindle—with him. The only
person not with him was Frances. She would not be coming to
Salt Lake until Sunday—the day before jury selection.

Across the aisle, Ernie Jones, Mike George and Dave
Walsh wore the faces of pallbearers at a funeral. Wearing a
light blue suit and a dark blue tie, Jones had also asked Steve
Swindle to come to court, a clear indication that the issue of
the will, and what each side felt it said, had not been settled.

At twenty minutes to ten, a local lawyer named Ron
Yengich walked into the courtroom. He had recently begun
representing Berenice and, as her subpoena required, he had
brought her to court. Steve Swindle went over to greet her
and say how well she looked. From behind tinted glasses she
simply said, "I'm dreading what's ahead of me."

The judge told her that she did not need to stay, but had to
be available if called as a witness. As for Steve Swindle, the

judge was sure he could find his way back to his office and would be available in the unlikely event he was needed. As Judge Baldwin had told both sides a number of times, *he* would decide what the will said.

When Mike Rosen stood to address the court, he not only picked up where he left off in May but set the tenor for the weeks ahead: Jeff Morris. "This phantom." Any money paid to him by the prosecution? Did they buy him cheeseburgers? Take him to the movies? These were the kinds of things he wanted to know in preparing for cross-examination.

Concerned that the judge had fallen under Rosen's spell, Jones reminded Baldwin that the court had "bent over backwards for the defense in this case," forcing the state to turn over far more information than was required by law and opening a Pandora's box in the process.

"I don't want to be facetious," the judge said, "but when Pandora opened her box, what did she find?"

Jones said he didn't know, but before the noon recess he would see Mike Rosen holding one open—just for him. After some thrust and parry about Dr. Moench (the judge said he wouldn't decide until Moench took the stand exactly what he would be permitted to say), the admissibility of Bradshaw's memos, the will, and some other matters, Rosen stood to make a motion—a motion "made in all candor with a distressed heart"—to dismiss the charges on the basis of "prosecutorial misconduct."

On Monday, August 22, at one-thirty in the afternoon, Rosen said, he had received a collect phone call in his New York office. The caller identified himself as Sergeant Morris Anderson of the St. Paul Police Department in Minnesota. Anderson not only began volunteering information about Jeffrey Morris, Rosen told a silent courtroom, but was asking whom Rosen had spoken with and the kind of defense he was planning. Believing it to be a phony call, he contacted Anderson in St. Paul as soon as he hung up and was told that the sergeant had not phoned him. That same week, he learned that Morris, from Utah, "had been making telephone calls throughout the country . . . *shopping* cases," trying to convince law-enforcement people that he was a participant in a crime when he wasn't.

Convinced that it was Morris who made the call, he asked the judge to hold a special hearing, with "the phantom" present, to determine if he made the call; if so, where he made it from; and if it was made "with the knowledge and acquiescence" of the prosecution.

With all eyes focused on Ernie Jones, Rosen said he also learned Morris had been in Salt Lake during Frances's preliminary hearing and, "for all I know," was sitting in the courtroom. Though the state gave them an address for Morris in March at the federal building in Minneapolis—and Jones, he said, denied to the Utah Supreme Court that he knew how to reach him in any other way—Rosen told Judge Baldwin that they had learned of two other addresses the state had for Morris: a halfway house in Minneapolis in October of 1982 was given as an address on Morris's subpoena for the preliminary, and a writ that the state had the judge sign on April 1 listed Morris at the Hennepin County Adult Detention Center.

Rosen told the judge that he had written to Jones on August 8 (asking for *all* information—either exculpatory or which might be used to impeach or discredit a witness—that he was entitled to by law, including corroboration as to when exactly Morris allegedly met with Frances) and that Jones had written back that Morris could not be specific on the date, placing it between "winter of 1977 and spring of 1978." The prosecutor's letter was "carefully worded," Rosen said, because Morris's original letter said "it happened in January or February" (actually, Morris wrote that he received a phone call from Frances "shortly" after his release from jail in January and that he met with her a few weeks after that) and the defense had learned in July (*before* Jones wrote his letter to Rosen) that Morris was now saying the meeting took place in late April or early May. Why would the prosecutor do that, he asked, especially since the defense had a transcript of an interview that took place in Mike George's office on July 21? And if the prosecutor had, as he implied he did, a way of "corroborating" Frances's presence in Minneapolis, why couldn't the defense see that evidence?

What's going on here? Rosen asked the judge, reminding him that his client's life was at stake.

That's what Baldwin wanted to know. Staring icily at Jones, he said this seemed serious, and he wanted his answer after lunch.

What had begun as a routine pretrial hearing had turned into a landmine—the kind Rosen had warned Jones about.

As Jones, George and Walsh left the courtroom they now wore the poker faces of men whose reactions were impossible to fathom. They had found out about the call to Rosen shortly after Morris placed it. George had returned from a brief vacation and had gone over to the jail to "chew his ass out" for all the trouble he had caused at the different jails he'd been in since coming to Utah. Morris knew that *he* was the reason the trial had been delayed. Not only was he now asking for more and more details about the case in order to "sugar-coat" his story and make himself "the star witness" of the trial, but George felt that if they did use Morris, he might be so unpredictable on the witness stand that a mistrial could easily result. While George still had a cop's instinct that Morris had met with Frances, he didn't think Jones should put him on.

"And so I'm screaming at Morris, doing my Gestapo act," the investigator recalled, "and then, right out of the blue, he says, 'I've done something you're either going to punch me in the mouth for or shake my hand.'"

When told what it was, George didn't believe him—didn't believe anybody could be that stupid. Morris said he would deny it on the stand—that it was his word against Rosen's—and George told him that he would do nothing of the kind. Besides, he said, the call had probably been taped (it had been). But Morris had an answer for that: there were people who were adept at "voice impressions." Morris had an answer for everything, it seemed, as George had him transferred to Behavior Modification—a more polite term for solitary confinement—and away from the telephones he loved to use.

After Jones found out about the phone call, he thought about calling Rosen, but didn't. "I may have made a bad decision on that," he admitted. "I didn't know how to handle it. We just weren't sure with Morris. He said he made the phone call, but he was such a b.s.er that we thought maybe he was playing games with us. And I didn't want to call Rosen and give him some ammunition if we didn't need to. That's why I was frankly relieved to hear Rosen say it in court and I thought, Okay, he really did do it."

As the afternoon session opened, everyone was waiting to see how the state would reply. In an attempt to ease the tension, Judge Baldwin playfully informed the prosecutor that the press had helped him find out what was in Pandora's box. "Worries, trials, tribulations, and you know what the very last thing was at the bottom? Hope. So when we open Pandora's box, why, we can always find some hope."

Jones needed hope. Yes, he sheepishly admitted, they knew about the phone call, but not until *after* it was made. He stuck to his story that at no time were they ever trying to hide Morris from the defense and that his probation officer was their *sole* source of contact—even while Morris was in jail. Morris had been moved "several times," he said, and had told them he did not want to speak with the defense. As soon as Morris was transferred to Utah, Kurumada was notified, and was notified again when he was moved to the county jail. In fact, he said, the state made Morris available so that he could personally tell Kurumada that he didn't want to speak with him. As far as the July 21 meeting in Mike George's office that Rosen referred to, Jones said that it was an interview between Morris and a Sergeant Brown from Minneapolis (Brown had flown to Salt Lake to discuss *another* case that Morris said he had knowledge of) and had nothing to do with this case. No one from his office was present, Jones said, and they had never heard the tape of that conversation nor seen the transcript. (Rosen had obtained it, along with other records he had subpoenaed in Minnesota.)

Before he sat down, he told the judge that the defense's allegations of wrongdoing and deception were "incredible."

The prosecutor's speech made Mike Rosen bristle. Writing notes to himself in large letters on a yellow legal pad, he now rose to suggest that if he hadn't brought up the phone call, the state, whose "actions speak louder than words," never would have. If the state had addresses for Morris, he asked, why were they referred to some federal building "where we ran around for five days knocking on every single door. . . . What is the point to this, Judge?"

The point Baldwin wanted to know was this: did the prosecutor have "some other witness" besides Morris who could place Frances in Minnesota? Jones did not want to answer that, but the judge, losing his patience, asked him again. As he'd explained to the defense, Jones said, there were no airline tickets placing her there; he might have a witness who could say that she was out of New York City during that time, but could not say for sure she was in Minnesota.

But of all the things that had been raised that Tuesday, Baldwin was most perturbed by the fact that Morris could have such access to a phone at all. "This mollycoddling . . . of these prisoners down in this county jail is beyond belief. . . . I am bothered all day every day with crooks," he said, warning that "the day one calls a juror after they have been put down there, I am requesting that the County Attorney make a formal investigation. . . ."

While he was not going to dismiss the charges, he said, he would consider granting the defense's request for a special hearing with Morris.

Floors below, in the bowels of "the hole," Jeffrey Charles Morris—alias Robert Michaelson and Jeff Nelson—paced. Had he been able to read a newspaper or speak on the phone, he would have been delighted to learn how much time and attention was continuing to be lavished on him.

66 // "They made me feel like Queen for a Day."
Jeff Morris wasn't the only one in the limelight. Berenice Bradshaw was too. On Friday, September 9, she had been feted by Westminster (her old high school where she had spent eleventh and twelfth grades and which was now a

four-year college) in appreciation of a huge donation, and she was describing the experience to a visitor the following day. Sitting outside behind 1327 Gilmer Drive on that warm Saturday afternoon, she was as groomed and immaculate as the house she lived in. She had a huge photo album out, and as she took it into her hands and began to turn the pages, one could not help noticing that each of her fingernails was bitten deep to the quick.

In "Epilogue," one of Robert Lowell's last and best poems, he wrote:

> We are poor passing facts,
> warned by that to give
> each figure in the photograph
> his living name.

Berenice, in her way, tried to do that. As the matriarch, she so would have liked to rewrite the tragic history of her family—especially now, the day before her youngest daughter was coming home to stand trial for her life. But it was impossible. Nearly every time she looked at a picture and began to speak of the distant past, it was the inescapable present that she wound up talking about.

She would see pictures of Marilyn and say she was the easiest of her four children to raise, "always the best one to me," but the one who, along with Elaine, was now trying to destroy the family. According to Frances, she said, Marilyn had been "bankrolling" Gentile and might have paid for a few of his trips to Utah in order to persuade Marc to testify against his mother.

Pictures of Bob: "If he had been well," she said, "*he* would have been my best child." She said she recalled the time the V.A. hospital called her and said they were thinking of putting him in an apartment. "That's like putting a baby in the gutter," she said she told them. "Going to put a mentally ill man in an apartment by himself. Oh my God. Can you imagine that kind of reasoning. . . . They're always trying to put them out, put them somewhere, put them in a home, put them *someplace*. That's the strategy up there."

Pictures of Frances with Franklin: "I think they loved each other. It was a perfectly normal relationship as far as I was concerned. But the kids didn't see much of him. That's for sure. Why, he didn't eat dinner at home for thirty-five years. He tried to do his best, but he didn't have the understanding some people have. She's got the same characteristic as her father: she can't face reality. Most everybody tries to fit in. Life is compromise all the way through. You adjust to things. Frances can't. When she wants to do something, all hell can't stop her."

Pictures of Franklin and herself: "He was the first fellow I'd met that I could just sit and talk with. That's what attracted me to him." She told how the neighbor's son had once said, "'Mr. Bradshaw is a fine man, but he never should have married.' He was right. He was married to his work. What are you going to do with a man who from early in the morning till late in the evening wasn't here? However, he loved his family. I feel very sure of that. I think he admired me. I have no reason to think anything else. But we were not affectionate, not the kind who were kissing and hugging and that sort of thing." Her life now, she said, a life that "has been tragic for thirty years—ever since Bob started going in and out of hospitals," was much the same as it was before, except she had a chance to travel more, and there were hundreds of pictures to attest to that. "I felt like I was always living alone. I certainly wanted to get divorced a lot of the time, but what are you going to do with four kids? I had a sense of obligation and duty—it was permanent. Today people walk out on each other all the time."

Pictures of Marc and Larry: During the summer of 1977, or shortly after that, she said she recalled thinking that, sooner or later, "both those kids would wind up in prison. Both of them were awful to live with. They're both very headstrong, uncooperative—the type who think the world owes them a living. You can't dent them, you can't reason with them. *Nothing* reasons with them.

"Marc is a terrific liar—you cannot believe *anything* he says. I didn't always feel that—until he became a teenager. He was *always* driving a wedge between his mother and me. He'd tell me he would go and tell his mother lies. And Frances would get all upset thinking I'd said this or that and she'd be mad at me."

Asked how responsible she felt Frances was for what happened in 1977, the album practically fell off her lap as she rushed to her daughter's defense and raised her voice, her hands clawing the air: "How could she be responsible for the way those boys acted when they were carrying on the way they'd *always* acted? They always acted that way. Always. How can *she* be responsible for what happened in '77? That's nonsense. We had them here time and time again—one full summer [1968], Larry for one full year—and they had carried on from the time they could walk. She could never do anything with them. No. She was not responsible for what they did." She paused for a long moment and then went on: "Only to this extent will I say this. They did not have a normal family life. It was not normal in any sense of the word. A woman trying to manage these two kids and wondering how the rent is going to get paid. That's *not* normal. I don't know how she could have done it differently. It is absolutely impossible to portray those boys as they were. No one will *believe,*" she said, stretching out the word and repeating again, "No one will believe what we went through. Had they had a normal life, with a father—" she said, then stopped. "But I don't think with Frances's temperament there could have been a normal life. Ever. I don't think any man could have put up with it. Not really.

"She and her family seemed like they could never get enough. Franklin was paying their rent and board for a long time—and Frances said he'd often send her checks. They seemed to have very rich appetites. They're *not* the sort of people who believe in getting along with what you have, and making what you have do."

But as the afternoon wore on—as she talked about everything from her romance with her first love, Arthur Tuck, to her elopement and hobo trip with Franklin to the hardships her children suffered growing up among the Mormons, warning her guest not to be fooled by them ("they will vow and declare and try to give *everybody* the impression that they are *so* liberal, and *so* friendly. You should live among them. That's how you really get to know them. It's one of the reasons my kids left Utah. They hate the place")—it was what lay ahead that consumed her.

Though Marc had told her he was not going to testify, it was clear that she wasn't sure what he might do. She was sick and tired of paying lawyers and had recently fired Paul Van Dam for the second time. She said that when Marc got a typewriter—"the most expensive one there is"—Van Dam had sent her a bill plus a "search fee." When she refused to pay for the stereo he wanted ("he must really be living some country-club life out there") and eventually paid for himself, she still got a bill for a "search fee." She'd had thirty lawyers, she said, and had written as many of their names down as she could remember. Some of them were so "pesty," she said, and one "wanted to live the rest of his life off my money." *Thirty* lawyers, she emphasized, "and there's not a Good Samaritan among them. I like Rosen and company [despite its costing her "five hundred thousand before they would even speak to us"], but can't understand why they haven't approached Marilyn. They seem to be afraid of her."

She couldn't understand why *anybody* would believe Richard Behrens: "He testified for four hours [at Marc's preliminary] and the judge said, 'I don't believe this man.' And still, by God, they're accepting his testimony. Why should they accept his testimony if they don't believe him?" Or Jeffrey Morris: "Frances says he keeps changing his story too. I think it shows the corruption of our public officials. None of us ever heard of him. Why would Salt Lake do such a gag as that? That's just corrupt. How corrupt can you get? Bringing a phantom in here that nobody's heard of? Whoever—what kind of deeds is that? God." Or Myles Manning: "Frances said she *never* heard of a man by that name. He alleges she gave him five thousand dollars in five-dollar bills. Why she never had five thousand in the first place. I can't conceive of such a thing, I just can't. I think that's a made-up story. She didn't have that amount of money to begin with."

Nor could she completely understand, she said, why Marilyn and Elaine felt Frances had inserted herself as a wedge between her and them. While not denying one existed, she said: "Don't ask me to unravel that. They are all *so* bitter and *so* violent, I will not attempt to unravel that. Who's to blame for that is beyond all reckoning. *Nobody* can establish that."

Maybe not, but as the afternoon ended and Berenice looked forward to an evening of dancing with Chips at the annual Greek Festival, she did want to reestablish this: "The main reason I stick by Frances is that she *needs* me. She's the only one who doesn't have a husband. . . . It isn't that I want to favor her over the other two, but they don't need me, so I will stick by her through thick and thin—regardless of what they say, think or do. Regardless. That's up to them."

The following morning, the *New York Times* ran a curtain-raising story on the trial with the headline "NEW YORKER TO GO ON TRIAL IN MURDER OF HER FATHER." Later that day, Mike Rosen and Frances boarded a plane at Kennedy Airport for the nearly five-hour flight to Salt Lake. While Rosen had been back in New York for Rosh Hashanah, John Lang, Kevin Kurumada and Jay Schulman had been busy poring over the list of a hundred prospective jurors who had been asked to appear on Monday morning. They had pinned a large map of Salt Lake County on the wall of their suite at the Marriott, where Frances would also be staying, and were locating the jurors on it by zip code.

Kurumada and Berenice drove separate cars out to the airport that Sunday evening to meet the plane. Frances had fallen into such a deep slumber on the flight that by the time it arrived Rosen had a hard time waking her—and when she saw her mother, she barely acknowledged her. Back at the hotel, Berenice said, Rosen was "reading the riot act to her," and reminding her of the importance of "selling herself to the jury."

67// *The State of Utah* v. *Frances Bernice Schreuder* was not the only first-degree murder trial beginning in the Metropolitan Hall of Justice that week. Jay Elmer Banks had one too, and while he and Judge Baldwin had barred all television cameras from the building, that didn't stop the three local stations from setting up early on the clear Monday morning to get footage of "the New York heiress"—as the local papers called her—and her team of lawyers for their broadcasts later that day.

In a sensible beige suit and black patent-leather shoes, Frances looked a model of restraint as she ascended the steps of the courthouse. Between Rosen and John Lang, Lang was the one with whom she felt most comfortable. He was eight years older than Frances, and had a kind-uncle appearance and soothing bedside manner that his more flamboyant and short-fused colleague lacked. Keeping Frances under control was an important part of his job. This was Mormon Utah, not 100 Centre Street in Manhattan, and the slightest display of hysterical behavior on her part could destroy, in an instant, all they had worked for.

When Frances was a freshman at Bryn Mawr and living in East House, one of the games that she and her housemates would play was "Murder in the Dark." It originated in England as the "Murder Game" and was written about in Ngaio Marsh's novel *A Man Lay Dead*. In the Bryn Mawr version, the number of people who played determined the number of cards that were picked from a deck—one of which had to be the ace of spades. The woman who picked that was the murderess. The lights were then turned off for two minutes, during which time the murderess chose her victim, whispering to that unlucky person that she was the corpse. A scream was then heard, followed by a thud. Everyone was required to freeze *except* the murderess, who could assume any position she wanted before the lights came back on. An investigation was then held, followed by a trial. The game was said to be not only fun, but wonderful preparation for a career as a detective or a lawyer—two areas Frances had had some experience with since leaving college.

As she sat at the defense table with her glasses on, intently scribbling notes on yellow foolscap while the process of selecting a jury began, she looked, for a second, more like a successful lawyer who had distinguished herself at Bryn Mawr—more like the daughter her father had hoped she would become—than a forty-five-year-old woman charged with murder, fighting desperately for her life in a state to which she had vowed never to return.

Over the next few days, both in open court and in the closed-door, individual *voir dire* Rosen had pushed hard for, the judge, state and defense heard a panoply of reasons why people didn't feel they could serve. Despite the judge's joking that the only "legitimate" instance he knew of when a juror was excused from duty was the postmaster—and *only* postal employee—in the town of Henefer who was released because of citizen outcry over not receiving their mail, the excuses ranged from high blood pressure, impending senility, and a first-grade teacher who felt her students would be "completely lost" if she were away for the four weeks the trial was expected to run . . . to a woman who had gone to see her priest and said she felt emotionally incapable of serving in a death-penalty case.

By late Thursday morning, after the judge roughly outlined the case and after all the questions were asked and answered, a jury of seven women and five men—plus two women alternates—was impaneled. Among them were a truck driver for the United Parcel Service, a retired foreman whose son had once worked in the Sheriff's Office, a retired Army RN, a government accountant, a construction worker, a housewife, a teacher (and former psychology major), a restaurant manager who said she had a seventeen-year-old with a mind of his own, a widow, and a middle-aged student. All except one had children. All were white. All except one had heard of the case. Two smoked. Only one had prior jury experience. One had lived in New York State for three years. Another had a sister there. Many had said they were nervous, but one declared that it was a privilege to be chosen.

Admonishing them "to speak to no one and let no one speak to you," and to avoid what he earlier called the "half-truths" of newspaper, television and radio accounts of the case, Judge Baldwin said they were dismissed until ten on Monday morning.

Once the jurors had filed out of the courtroom, Ernie Jones told the judge he had one other matter he wanted to bring up. He had received a phone call the previous Friday from New York, he said, his voice heavy with concern. The caller informed him that the New York City Ballet was leaving for Paris next week, and that Mrs. Schreuder had made application to go with them.

Even before the judge could finish assuring the prosecutor that she wasn't going anywhere, Rosen shot up like a man who had just discovered his suit had caught fire. "Mrs. Schreuder has not left this country," he railed, "and will not leave this country and where I am, she is."

Baldwin said that he didn't give a damn about the New York City Ballet—or [the Salt Lake–based] Ballet West for that matter. He didn't even care if they disbanded. He didn't anticipate any problem, he said, and was certain there would be none.

But the prosecutor's tactic had worked. He managed not only to get in a well-timed dig at Rosen, but to completely unsettle Frances, who flew back to New York with Rosen later that day.

"They can't think of enough things to do to Frances," Berenice shouted down the phone that evening, enraged by what she heard Jones had said. "Mr. Jones is inhuman. I think he's horrible. He is out to destroy Frances. He is a horrible species of humanity."

Had it been up to Berenice Bradshaw, she would have taken on the whole state of Utah if necessary. There was more she wanted to say—much more—but couldn't. She had "proof," she claimed, that her phone was being tapped.

When Berenice fired Paul Van Dam as Marc's lawyer in August, she retained, on Kevin Kurumada's suggestion, a former colleague of his from the Legal Defender's Office who was now in private practice. His name was Wally Bugden.

Knowing that Bugden and Kurumada were good friends, Ernie Jones felt certain that Bugden was no more than "a plant," his sole purpose being to dissuade Marc from testifying. On September 16, three days before the trial, Bugden went to the prison to find out what Marc was planning to do. At the end of their visit, Bugden had his answer and Marc had $300—compliments of Berenice—for a correspondence course he had told Bugden he wanted to take.

When Jones heard from Bugden later in the day that Marc

was not going to testify, he "accepted it for what it was worth. I didn't know one way or the other." Neither did Bugden. Not really. He only knew what Marc was telling him.

"I've finally come to a place where I know where I'm going—and what I have to do."

"Well, I hope you feel good about it."

"I don't feel good about it, but it's something I should have done a long time ago."

About a month before his mother's trial, Marc and Bryan Baird had this conversation. But as the trial loomed closer—especially during jury selection, when he saw his mother on television each night—he began floundering, Bryan said. "He was nervous. He didn't want to go back to the county jail"—where Mike George was planning to take him temporarily, in order to protect him from the potentially dangerous atmosphere at the prison. "He didn't want to go anywhere. He was fluctuating between not wanting to do it to being damn sure he was going to do it. He went through a lot of hell that week."

Marc had other "family tapes" at the prison, besides the one he had recorded of Frances and Lavinia, and as he tried to decide what he was going to do, he listened to them with his headphones and sought courage from what he heard.

68// On Sundays in the autumn, Mike George usually watches professional football on television. But his plans for Sunday, September 18, were different. Vittorio Gentile was arriving from New York that day and George rolled out a red carpet at the airport and took him to his hotel. He explained to Marc's father that he was going out to the prison to collect Marc and that they would join him later. (The state had told Judge Baldwin and the defense that Marc would be brought to the judge's chambers at one-thirty on Monday, during the lunch recess, to reveal his decision.)

But when George arrived at the prison, he discovered that

Wally Bugden had gotten there before him. Bugden had been trying to see Marc and was told that Marc was allowed to see no one *except* Mike George. Incensed by this, Bugden kicked up such a fuss that he had been ordered to leave the grounds. Just as he was about to depart, he saw George.

"You won't let me see my client," Bugden complained.

"Settle down," George said. "I'm going to have him here in a minute."

When they all arrived back at the County Attorney's Office, Bugden and Marc spent the next hour talking by themselves. By the time Bugden emerged from the office they had been sitting in, his demeanor was entirely different from earlier in the afternoon. The word he got, he told George and Ernie Jones, was the same as on Friday: Marc was not going to testify.

Once Bugden left—Marc having said he did not want him present when he talked with the state—Marc spoke some more with the two men who had doggedly courted him for more than a year. At the end of this discussion, he said he didn't really know what he was going to do.

As they had from the beginning, the sands just kept on shifting.

When George and Marc finally arrived at Vittorio's hotel, they found the little jeweler with his bags packed.

"I'm going back to New York," he said, angry because they were so late. "I don't like being treated this way."

When George tried to explain what had happened, Vittorio said, "I've got a phone and you could have called me."

"Yeah," the investigator conceded, thinking that a day he had planned so carefully was becoming a nightmare, "you're right. I apologize."

He couldn't afford to lose Vittorio. Not now. If he lost him, he'd lose Marc. Feeling that a nice dinner might relax all three of them, George drove Vittorio and Marc to Le Parisien, located right across from the courthouse.

In apartment F at 838 Roberta Street that Sunday evening, the smell of chicken empañadas and blueberry nut bread permeated the air. As Mary Lou was preparing these for Marc, she was telling a reporter of her and Monique's love for her honey and just how vulnerable and easily influenced he was. "Had it not been for his mother," she said, "that kid would have gone far."

Pinned to the refrigerator was a note to Monique—

> I LOVE YOU BABY
> POPPY
> Marc F. Schreuder

—and in the living room, newspaper accounts of the case were strewn about. As she sat in the apartment she and Marc had moved into together, flanked by a painting of the Last Supper on the wall and a copy of the Ten Commandments attached to the door leading into the hall, Mary Lou was certain that Frances would get convicted. It wasn't just her ESP that convinced her of that, she said. It was the state she lived in. "This is Utah. You *got* to remember this is Mormon Country."

Because she was getting her hair done early the next morning before the trial began, she had to clean up the Royal Studios that evening (in order to supplement the welfare money she now received, Mary Lou usually worked there an hour every morning) and her visitor went with her.

Just before eight, there was a knock on the glass door. "Marc," she beamed, her face bright with love as he and Mike George walked in. Whatever their dinner had achieved in calming his nerves, its effect was ruined now. Neither of them expected to see Mary Lou with a reporter—especially not the night before trial when she knew that they were coming by to pick up some T-shirts and underwear—and Marc told her how displeased he was.

"At that point," George said later, "we no longer had any bearing on the situation. He was as high-strung as a banjo wire. I was in turmoil, my stomach was just turning somersaults. It was a shitty day and I'd had it so well planned and it turned into shit."

When George got home late that evening, he phoned Ernie Jones. It was near midnight, but it didn't matter. Jones had not been able to sleep and had spoken with a distressed Bugden earlier that evening. Bugden had tried to phone Marc both at the prison and at the county jail to find out if anything had changed after he left the County Attorney's Office, but was told that he was not at either place. Jones said that he was surprised Marc was not at the prison, and as for what Marc was planning to do, he had no idea.

As George related all that had happened, there was only one thing the prosecutor wanted to know.

"Do you think he's going to testify, Mike?"

"Boy, he's too uptight, Ernie. I can see him falling apart. I don't think so. I think you better be prepared to go without him."

North of Salt Lake City that night, in the Davis County Jail in Farmington, Marc lay awake, thinking about Mom.

Part Seven//

About suffering they were never
  wrong,
The Old Masters: how well they un-
  derstood
Its human position; how it takes place
While someone else is eating or open-
  ing a window or just walking dully
  along;
. . . .
They never forgot
That even the dreadful martyrdom
  must run its course
—W. H. AUDEN

69// After days and days of brilliant sunshine and temperatures in the eighties and low nineties, cool air and rain-threatening skies greeted Mike Rosen and John Lang on Monday morning as they left the Marriott to play an early game of tennis. After Rosen and Frances arrived back from New York the night before, he had stayed up late working on his opening statement and had had only a few hours' sleep.

Whatever he may have been spouting publicly about the "horrible" publicity he felt the case was receiving, a big trial was the lifeblood of a courtroom lawyer and Mike Rosen had been directing all of his energy toward this moment. Like a surgeon preparing for a complex life-or-death operation, he knew that he could afford no mistakes. His skill and his ego were on the line. Somewhere among those Utah jurors he would find the ones who could persuade the others to set Frances free.

The first figure to arrive outside Judge Baldwin's courtroom and take a seat on the hard wooden bench was Berenice Bradshaw, wearing a yellow-and-green dress and a straw hat with a rope band. She soon found out that a potential witness could not attend the proceedings. As other people began to line up outside in the hope of getting a seat (including Mason Drukman, who had flown in from California), Harry Klekas

—the judge's fifty-year-old bailiff who favored black shirts and used to be Jack Webb's bodyguard on the set of *Dragnet*—reminded the throng of press and spectators that the press would be seated first and that a seat for the morning session did not guarantee one for the afternoon.

Once every seat was filled and a goodly number of people were sent away disappointed, everyone's eyes seemed to focus on Frances, visibly nervous in a navy-blue suit and pale yellow turtleneck.

Before Ernie Jones moved to the lectern to face a jury whose composition he was reasonably happy with and to make his opening statement, Judge Baldwin reminded the jurors that whatever they heard from either lawyer was *not* to be taken as fact (unless stipulated by mutual agreement) but their *interpretation* of the facts. The facts would come from the evidence—be it physical or circumstantial—and they were to be the sole judges of that.

Hunched over the lectern, the gray-suited prosecutor gave an opening statement that was a virtual carbon copy of the one he had directed to Judge Sawaya fifteen months before. But this time, he said, the evidence would focus not on the person who killed Franklin Bradshaw but on the person who had ordered his execution—"a woman who was driven by greed and power and a desire for money . . . who would destroy virtually anyone who got in her road, who blocked her access to money . . . a woman who ordered her own son, her own flesh and blood, to kill her own father."

Mike Rosen was all charm as he approached the lectern. Ever conscious of being an outsider and how it might work against him, he reminded the jury that the reason he was there was that Frances lived a few blocks from his office in New York. Moving to a spot behind her chair and putting his hands on her shoulders, he said, "I represent this human being, this lady, Frances Schreuder," and no one else. He was going to try to scare them, he admitted, because what they were about to do would be one of the most serious things they would ever do in their lives. This was a death-penalty case, he said, but before the state "can put Frances's life on the line," they would have to convince each of them that they had met *their* burden—a burden that never shifts. Her presumption of innocence was like a protective coat around her shoulders—"it protects us from people saying we are guilty and goodbye"—and he was there to suggest that it would never be removed.

Be patient with me, he pleaded to the jurors, it was going to take time. If Mr. Jones wasn't going to focus on "the shooter," he certainly was. The prosecutor was correct in saying there were tensions and problems in the Bradshaw family, he went on, but he was not going to stand up there and insult their intelligence by saying a family with sisters and with wealth had no problems. Would they be human if they didn't? he asked. But that wasn't what this case was about, he said, bobbing and weaving around the room like a well-trained middleweight who could easily go the distance. This case was about a "cunning, clever, headstrong, intelligent, independent, 'A' student" who tried to kill his grandfather by poisoning him the year before he actually succeeded in murdering him, who abused both his grandparents, and whose method of killing his grandfather displayed "a viciousness you can't transmit from anybody."

Aside from being about "a kid out of control," he told the jury, the case was also about Richard Behrens, "a family hanger-on, a man in the neighborhood, a friend of Frances's . . . 'Uncle Dickie' to Marc and Larry." If the architect of this courtroom, he said, had built a window, the jury would have to decide whether to throw his testimony through it. The proof would show that he was "concerned and frightened" about being disinherited by *his* father ("What a coincidence!") and "shifts what he says when it suits his convenience."

The case was also about Myles Manning, "an admitted drunk and alcoholic," who would testify to Behrens's fears about being disinherited by describing "a trip that this odd couple takes . . . a mysterious trip in the woods . . . snakes-in-the-grass kind of stuff at the *same* time that these witnesses are saying Frances Schreuder was plotting and passing money. . . . And you will hear why they were up in the woods. And you will decide whether this is just a coincidence or a big smoke screen.

"You will hear it. It will give you the opportunity. I don't want to spoil it for you. This opening statement is kind of like coming attractions. When we used to go to the movies and used to . . . have songs and balls that keep bouncing, we used to sing with the ball. Keep your eye on the ball. Don't let them smoke you out of here. . . .

"Now, Mr. Jones says you will hear from a lot of people about Frances wanting to kill her father. He didn't mention them but I think . . . that a former husband of Frances's—Marc's father, Larry's father—a guy named Vittorio Gentile will be here. The proof will show that besides beating up Frances, he just ran out on everybody and took off to Italy. That's the kind of proof they are going to start giving you.

"There are other witnesses. He didn't mention too many, so I am going to quit while I am ahead, but watch if he calls them. Watch the cross-examination. Watch it. Watch the way they testify. Watch how Behrens talks and Manning talks and how they do and watch if I find they said something else on other occasions. . . .

"We are not looking for edges. We don't have to prove a thing. . . . Be fair and let's begin a search for the truth. That is what this is a search for, the truth. Yes, what I say is not evidence either, but hold me to it. Give me some time, I will bring it out . . . and when I come back to you in summation, I again will be able to look you straight in the eye and say, 'Bring back a verdict loud and clear and firm that Frances Schreuder is not guilty.'"

As soon as Rosen was finished, the court took a brief recess and Wally Bugden slipped across the street to the County Attorney's Office. He was not interested in hearing the testimony of Dan Schindler and the former Medical Examiner. He was waiting to see Marc. Ernie Jones and Mike George had told him before court began that Marc spent the night in Davis County, and would be brought to the office by noon. Bugden was concerned that the state was keeping Marc from him, and when there was no sign of his client at twelve, twelve-thirty or one o'clock he became more and more convinced of that.

Next door at Hardee's, during the lunch hour, the first reviews on Michael Rosen's performance were being filed over hamburgers and coffee. Two elderly women who had spent a good portion of their lives attending murder trials and had sat through Marc's the year before shared their opinions. The New Yorker's hard-driving style was off-putting to people out here, the one reckoned, and probably would be to the jury. "Sir," began the other, clutching a knitting basket, "I will tell you this: Sarah Bernhardt will never be dead as long as Mr. Michael Rosen of New York is alive and in a courtroom."

At about one forty-five, Marc finally arrived. He had been having lunch with his father and Neil Boswell, the investigator who was "late" in bringing him in from Davis County. Instead of being brought to Jones's office, he had been taken through the entrance that led from the jail to right outside the judge's chambers—a route that he had traveled during his own trial and one that was off limits to the press. Bugden was furious. Surely Boswell could have been reached by a beeper, he felt, and told that Marc's lawyer was waiting to see him. As it stood, he had less than five minutes to speak with Marc in the court reporter's office before Marc would tell the judge what he was planning to do.

Outside in the courtroom, it was nearly two. Every seat was filled except for the jurors'. When Judge Baldwin reappeared to take the bench, he told Ernie Jones to call his next witness.

"We would call Marc Schreuder, Your Honor."

Marc walked into the hushed courtroom through its north entrance, wearing his light blue prison shirt, jeans and a pair of sneakers. He did not look at his mother as he sat in the witness box. Rosen asked to see the judge at the bench, and while that conference was going on, John Lang was speaking quietly with Frances, who was glaring at the son she hadn't seen for more than eighteen months.

"Mr. Schreuder," Judge Baldwin began, "are you the gentleman who was heretofore before the court and was convicted of the crime of homicide in the killing of Frank Bradshaw?"

"Yes, I was."

Told by Bugden that Marc's case was on appeal to the Utah

620

Supreme Court, Baldwin informed Marc that he was under no obligation to answer *any* questions, on the grounds that it could incriminate him, and asked him if he had had the advantage of a lawyer's advice.

Marc said he had talked with several lawyers and their advice had been mixed. "Mr. Bugden has not given me advice yet because he feels I haven't had adequate information. However, I have discussed the matter extensively with my two former attorneys, Joe Tesch and Paul Van Dam, over a period of several months . . . and I have come to a decision."

"And what is that?"

"And that decision is to testify at this time."

Baldwin said that he was going to authorize Marc to speak with Bugden once more, but an impatient Jones interrupted and asked Marc if he felt he *needed* that additional time. He didn't, he said, because "I don't think anything Mr. Bugden can say will give me any more information than I already have."

The judge, however, was determined that Marc speak with Bugden again. And Jones was equally determined that he not, eliciting from Marc the fact that he not only had met and discussed this with Bugden the day before, but four or five times before that—and that Bugden had been retained by his grandmother, not by him.

It didn't matter. Baldwin wanted the two of them to talk, and Marc shuffled out of the courtroom to do so. Back in the court reporter's office, Marc loudly reiterated what he had said to Bugden earlier: "I'm doing this for Lavinia," he said. "Someone should care about Lavinia. I care about Lavinia." When Bugden said it could affect his appeal, Marc snapped that he didn't care. Mom had ruined everybody's life and she *had* to be stopped.

She had to be stopped. Twenty-five years earlier a psychiatrist had told Elaine the same thing about Frances. And as Frances now waited in the courtroom, her own son, for so many years an extension of herself, was on his way to do just that.

While Marc was away, Rosen was asking that his testimony be postponed until Tuesday because the state had told him before lunch that Dr. Moench and Vittorio Gentile would be

621

the only two witnesses in the afternoon. Baldwin said he was going to allow Marc to testify and hoped that it would help the court over "a very substantial hurdle" in regard to the psychiatrist's testimony, which Baldwin said gave him "grave problems." The two sides compromised: Marc could testify now and Rosen would cross-examine him in the morning. From Rosen's point of view it wasn't ideal, but it might cause Marc to have some serious second thoughts; and it would give the defense an opportunity not only to scour the transcript (which the court reporter promised to get to them as quickly as possible), but to face a jury fresh from a good night's sleep.

When Marc reappeared, he emphatically informed the judge that his decision was the same. Bugden announced that while he had told Marc not to testify until the prosecution put into writing what they had promised Marc they would do for him in exchange for his testimony, Marc was not prepared to take his advice. Upon hearing that, the judge asked that the jurors be brought back.

And so it began.

Jones led Marc through some preliminary questions in order to relax him—his age, who Franklin Bradshaw was, who Frances Schreuder is, his willingness to testify and his awareness that he didn't have to, etc.—before pushing closer and closer to the heart.

"Mr. Schreuder, who killed Franklin Bradshaw?"

"I did."

"And do you recall how you killed him?"

"Yes, I shot him."

"Do you recall what you used to shoot your grandfather with?"

"A gun."

"Do you recall the type of gun?"

"It was a .357 gun."

Once Jones had showed it to him and he said it looked "pretty much" like the one he had bought, the prosecutor asked him to tell the jury *why* he had killed his grandfather.

Rosen objected and the judge told Jones to rephrase his question and lay the proper foundation.

"What is it that led you to kill your grandfather?"

"Well," he paused, "my mother asked me to."

"And for what reason, Marc?"

"For two reasons. I think the first reason was that she hoped to inherit a great deal of money very quickly as soon as he died, and she was also afraid that at some point in time he might cut her out of his will."

This was exactly the kind of testimony Jones had longed to hear and had feared that he never would. It was one thing to hear it from Richard Behrens, or even a David Frankel or Louis Moench, but quite another to hear it from Marc. Whatever the ultimate impact of his testimony would be in terms of substance, it would be far surpassed by the sheer emotion of the drama that was unfolding. Mike George had told Marc, over and over, that he did not have to look at his mother, and he didn't. Turned slightly toward the jury—they were the ones, George told him, he had to convince—Marc continued to respond to the prosecutor's questions the way a man might confess to an incestuous relationship he had kept secret for years, while his mother frantically wrote notes on legal paper to remind Rosen what a liar Marc was.

"Marc, was there a plan as far as how you were to kill your grandfather?"

"Yes, there was."

"What was the plan?"

"That I was to come out to Salt Lake City, shoot him and return."

"And where did you get the information as far as how you were to carry out the murder?"

"From my mother."

"And can you explain the details how you were to carry out that murder?"

Yes, he could. She had discussed it with him "numerous" times at 1675 York Avenue, the last meeting taking place on the day he left for Midland. Richard Behrens was present, and Lavinia probably was too—though, he added, "I think she was too young to participate in the discussions."

The first time his mother had ever made the suggestion that his grandfather had to be killed was in late 1975 or perhaps 1976, and Larry was possibly present. "In a joking sort of way she said that we were broke and we had no means of income and that killing Grandfather is the only way of assuring we would have funds to sustain the family through the years."

"Were you in fact broke at that time?"

Yes, he said, "except for funds given to us by Grandmother."

Asked about the summer of 1977 and why he and Larry had come to Salt Lake, Marc said they had come "to steal some money for Mom and at the same time we were supposed to kill Grandfather."

Who had told them to come out and steal?

"My mother."

And who had told them to come out and kill their grandfather?

"My mother."

How were they supposed to accomplish that?

"Well, we were supposed to put amphetamines in his oatmeal and make him have a heart attack, induce a heart attack."

Did he bring those amphetamines with him to Salt Lake?

"Yes, I did."

"Where did you get the amphetamines?"

"My mother got them. I got them from my mother."

But when Jones asked him if he had attempted to kill his grandfather in the summer of 1977, Marc said he had not—an answer, Mike Rosen noted with a smile, directly in opposition to what Richard Behrens had said at Marc's trial.

"Marc, were there any other plans . . . to kill your grandfather in the summer of 1977 . . . ?"

"Yes, there were."

"What were some of the other plans?"

"I think there were two other ones that I can remember. One involved burning down the warehouse, knocking him out and . . . leaving him inside. Another one involved throwing some kind of electrical appliance in the bathtub while he was taking his morning bath or something like that."

"Did you ever attempt either one of those plans?"

"I did not."

"Who gave you those ideas about burning the warehouse or electrocuting your grandfather?"

"My mother did."

As far as the thefts were concerned, Marc said they involved stocks, checks and cash and estimated their total to be about $200,000. Except for "a little bit of the cash," he sent everything to his mother and said that when his grandfather discovered some of the thefts "he was very angry." Marc identified three checks Jones showed him—including the two for $10,000 each—as ones he had sent to her, and he unhesitatingly identified the signature on the back of them as belonging to her as well. During that summer, he or Larry usually called their mother once, sometimes twice a day— "from Granny's house or mostly from pay booths or sometimes from the warehouse"—and talked for as little as ten minutes and as long as three hours. Most of the calls were collect ("she told not to charge things to the warehouse because it would look bad"), and one of the subjects of discussion was the death of his grandfather.

Asked if he had a camera with him that summer, Marc said that he had and went on to say that he had taken pictures of a number of things, including the warehouse, and that when he returned home to New York, he had given his mother some of the photographs "because she asked me to."

"Do you know what she was going to use the photographs for?"

"Yes."

"What?"

"She said she wanted to give them to a hit man so he could carry out the murder." In addition to the outside of the warehouse, the pictures were of his grandfather, the area around the warehouse, and the inside of the warehouse.

"Are you familiar with the name of Myles Manning?"

"Yes, I am."

"Who is Myles Manning?"

He was the person his mother had told him ("in about September of 1977") she was going "to use to kill Grandfather." She had first mentioned his name at Dragon Hall ("a large mansion in Southampton") and said that he was "a hit man who was connected with the Mafia, who knew the Dons," whom she had met through Richard Behrens, and to whom, she told him, she had given $5,000 as a partial payment to carry out the murder.

Here was another contradiction for Rosen's list: Manning had testified both at Marc's trial and at Frances's preliminary that the $5,000 was the *only* payment that had been discussed.

Besides Manning, Jones asked, "are you aware of any other attempts by your mother to hire someone to kill your grandfather?"

"Yes, I am."

"How did you learn about anyone else being hired?"

"Through a phone call." It was late February or early March of 1978, he was at Kent, and his mother told him she was going to hire someone "from out of state." But where out of state he did not know.

It was an unconvincing effort on the prosecutor's part to establish Jeffrey Morris. Jones had not alluded to him in his opening statement, or even asked Marc if he knew that name. For anyone who had been following the case and had read about Morris in the newspaper accounts, it was a subtle confirmation that "the phantom" would probably not get his big chance to shine after all.

Jones quickly moved on to higher and safer ground, having Marc describe to the jury the various efforts his mother had made to obtain a gun before his own successful phone call to John Cavenaugh. He told of going with Mom to a gun store in midtown Manhattan, her telling the salespeople that she wanted a rifle for him to go hunting with and being told that "all kinds of papers" had to be filed and that it could take as long as a year before she could get one. She also went to a magazine store, he said, and "purchased stacks of gun magazines," hoping to get one by mail. He recounted Richard Behrens's unsuccessful efforts to get one in Virginia and New Jersey. When all else failed, he called Cavenaugh. Mom had phoned Kent, gotten Cavenaugh's father's name and address, and Marc had made the call from the foyer of their apartment on York Avenue.

"What was your mother doing while you were talking to John Cavenaugh on the telephone?"

"Well, my mother had one of those yellow legal tablets and she had written some notes on what to say during the call, okay, and during—"

"Like one of these?" Jones held his own up to the jury to enliven the scenario.

"Yes, one of those exactly."

"Do you recall what she was writing on the tablet?"

"Well, as the conversation was going on, she would write

little things about what I was to say or [if] she thought I wasn't asking enough questions in one area, she would write down questions I was supposed to ask him and to try to help me get a gun from him."

Then there was the phone call to Granny—the one that Mom had asked him to make shortly before the murder—and the request for money, the last money they would ever ask for.

"We didn't have any way of paying the rent, telephone, electric or stuff, and we were going to get evicted and cut off and everything, so I asked Granny if she could send Mom . . . a few thousand dollars, enough to pay the rent and some phone bills, just to get us going for another month. . . ."

But, as Marc admitted, that wasn't all the money would be used for: some of it went for his plane tickets under the name Lorenzo Gentile.

"Why did you use the name Gentile?"

"Well," he said, looking at the plane ticket Mike George had retrieved more than two years before, "because Mom didn't want my name on the ticket so if the police found out anything . . . suspicion would be cast on Larry instead of me." Mom had "insisted" Larry's name be used, she made the reservations, and he went and picked the tickets up from a lady whom he never saw again until she testified at his trial.

On that note, after an hour in which many of the twelve jurors and two alternates kept shifting their eyes from Marc to Frances and back again as if they were at a tennis match, Jones suggested a brief recess. He was only halfway through, but he knew that even the most explosive testimony could lose its impact after a while. And so the curtain came down on Act One of a tragic play that could just as easily have traced its roots to Greece, centuries before, as to the house on Gilmer Drive, ten minutes from the courthouse, where Berenice Bradshaw would soon get word of the "horrible" thing her grandson had done.

At twenty minutes past three, Ernie Jones began again, no longer the awkward farmboy whom the city bully practically rode out of Salt Lake on a rail two weeks earlier when the embarrassing subject of Jeffrey Morris was raised. Marc's decision to testify had changed the prosecutor into a picture of tranquility.

Marc told the jury how he had purchased the gun, flown to Salt Lake, taken a cab to a hotel—whose name he did not recall—and phoned Mom to say he didn't want to do it.

"And, Marc," Jones said, "do you recall what your mother said to you when you told her you couldn't go through with it?"

"Yes," he said, his head bowed.

"What did she say?"

"Basically she said that, well, she said a lot of things to me. One of the things she said was, 'Well, if you don't do it, don't come home again.' She made it clear to me, you know, and she was determined I was going to go through with it, you know. We said a lot of stuff. It was a long conversation, a lot of arguing, I don't remember all of it."

"How long would you have talked to your mother on the phone?"

"An hour, hour and a half at least."

"Marc, in the course of that conversation with your mother, did you start to cry?"

"Yes."

"Why were you crying?"

"Because I didn't want to go through with it. That's all. I just didn't want to do it."

As he began to describe the next morning—how he arrived at the warehouse by taxi and hid out until his grandfather arrived in his little green truck—Frances closed her eyes.

"And what did you do?" Jones asked, continuing to guide him through it.

"I think I waited three or four minutes. Then went in the warehouse."

"Did you talk to your grandfather?"

"Yes, I did."

"How long did you talk to him?"

"Twenty minutes, maybe fifteen minutes."

"Marc, do you remember what you said to your grandfather?"

"Object, Your Honor, please." Mike Rosen's voice had

barely been heard all afternoon. Since the conversation was out of the presence of the defendant, he said it was hearsay.

The judge said Marc could reveal the general subject of the conversation, but not its specifics.

"About Grandfather sending money to Mom," Marc resumed.

". . . Then what happened, Marc?"

"After the conversation, I shot him."

". . . Do you recall where you would have shot him, as far as the location on his body?"

"Just remember two shots. I don't remember a whole lot."

"Was he facing you as I am?"

"I think I—I think his back was to me. I waited until he turned his back because I couldn't shoot him when his face was to me."

". . . And where was the second shot?"

"I think it was to the head."

"Marc, do you recall what you did to your grandfather after you shot him?"

"I pulled out his pockets and stuff and, you know, took out his wallet and took his money out of his wallet and stuff. Scattered the credit cards around."

"And why did you do that?"

"Because Mom said that's what I had to do, make it look like a robbery."

Taking "seven or eight dollars in dollar bills" from his grandfather's wallet, Marc said he went over to the Ute Cab stand, got a taxi back to the hotel and then another one to the airport for the flight home, and he described the emotional scene when his mother saw him soon after he arrived.

"Marc, when you went back to New York City, did you take the gun with you?"

"Yes."

"Why did you take the gun back?"

"Because Mom told me to."

"And what did you do with the gun?"

"Gave it to Mom."

"Do you know what she did with the gun?"

Yes, he said. She first tried to give it to Richard Behrens, who didn't want to take it, so she locked it in "her little white desk." She wanted Behrens to take it (which he ultimately did) "because Mom was afraid they were going to have a search warrant for her house." The reason she confided in Behrens, Marc said, was that she always had "for that kind of stuff, hid stuff there," recalling the "reams and reams of paperwork" he had hidden for her during her legal battles with Frederick.

Both he and his mother had discussed the murder with Behrens, he said, but some of what they told him after it happened was misleading (saying that Marc had *driven* to Midland, for example, or that he had bought the gun in Virginia).

"What was the reason for doing that?" Jones asked.

"Well, Mom felt that it was a mistake to confide in Mr. Behrens in the first place. I guess she had misgivings about it later, I mean after the funeral and stuff, and so she, I guess, she was covering up and angry at me for talking to Mr. Behrens, so she felt that . . . if he ever told anybody, he would tell them crazy information or something."

Moving ahead to the joint bank account Behrens and Frances shared, Jones asked if Marc knew about the account and had ever spoken with Behrens about it.

Yes, he had; Behrens had called to ask what had happened to his money, and his mother had instructed him to say that she wasn't home. His mother had the money to pay him back, but didn't "because she was always broke."

But wasn't he aware that Behrens was holding the .357 Magnum?

"Yes, I was."

"Couldn't Behrens have simply said to your mother, 'Hey, I have got this .357 Magnum. Just pay me thirty-seven hundred dollars or I am going to turn this over to the police'?"

Marc explained that *he* was the intermediary between his mother and Behrens: he would tell Behrens, if he called to speak with her, that she wasn't home and didn't know anything about the money; later, he altered the story to say that Mom was trying to get it, but had recommended that *he* try to get it himself, through the various places he wound up writing to.

After his arrest and his release on bail in Connecticut, he said, he was present at Gracie Square when his mother was "instructing Mr. Behrens" how to change the story he had given Joel Campbell and to turn everything around on Marilyn—and he was present when Behrens prepared the statement which did.

He told about the places he had stayed as a fugitive in New York and the aliases he had used (he had invented the name of David Jablonski, he said, and his mother, driving him to the Hotel Seville one day, had said she liked it because it "sounded like a lower-class Jewish name" and was in keeping with the "sleazy" kind of place the hotel was) and said that while he had never considered leaving the country, his mother had suggested he do so.

He had received no money as a result of killing his grandfather, he said, but his mother had. She told him she was going to get $3,000 a month immediately and "then she was going to lie" to get it doubled to $6,000; "then, if she waited long enough, that the large chunks of money distributions from the oil and gas—"

Baldwin cut him off. He wanted the jury to understand that the money Marc was talking about did *not* come from the will of Franklin Bradshaw—a statement that Mike Rosen was, at that point, grateful to hear.

A few minutes later, when Rosen saw what Jones was holding in his hand, he inched forward in his chair. It was the Frances-Lavinia tape, and the prosecutor had been building everything toward this moment. Rosen had made a motion two weeks earlier to prevent it from even being raised—but the judge had not ruled. If the judge allowed it in now—as Sawaya had—the case could be over.

No sooner had Marc identified it as "one of my tapes" than Rosen sprang up to say he objected to this whole line of questioning on this "proffered" exhibit. Baldwin said he would allow Jones to lay a foundation for it. Over repeated, vehement objections, Jones was finally able to establish whose voices were on the tape, but he was not—no matter what he tried, and he tried everything—able to have Marc say *why* he made the tape. So he asked Marc if *he* had been subjected to any kind of pressure from his mother as a child.

"Yes, I was."

". . . What kind of pressure did she put on you?"

"Well," he said, talking at a more accelerated rate than he

had before, "if she wanted you to do something, it was very difficult to say no. It was impossible to say no because she's very persistent and she just keeps harping on you and harping on you until she gets you to do anything, doesn't matter what it is. You just don't tell Mom no. . . ."

"Can you give us an example of the types of pressures that she imposed on you?"

". . . Well, she often, you know, if you said no, she would scream or yell or go into hysterics, then threaten to—a lot of times she locked me out of the house and she did on a lot of occasions, too. . . . I would ring my doorbell maybe a couple of hours later or the next day and then . . . I would do it, because I didn't want to get locked out."

"Did your mother actually lock you out of the house?"

"Sure she did."

"How old would you have been when that happened?"

"About thirteen or fourteen."

"Did your mother ever hit you?"

"Yes."

"How old would you have been when that started?"

"Thirteen or fourteen."

"Do you recall some of the threats she made to you as a child?"

"Judge," Rosen said, knowing he had to break the momentum of this, "I am going to object to this whole child psychology." The judge agreed. It was assuming facts not in evidence.

"How often would this occur, Marc, this kind of pressure?"

"All the time."

"Were you afraid of your mother?"

Again Rosen objected, and the judge sustained it. The prosecutor could pursue the subject but had to reframe the question.

"Marc, what is it then that led you to kill your grandfather, Franklin Bradshaw?"

"My mother ordered me to."

"Were you just willing to follow whatever she said?"

"Pretty much. I didn't really have a choice even if I wasn't, you know, eventually I would at some point in time, you know."

"If you hadn't carried out the murder, what were you concerned about?"

Another objection, but this time it was overruled.

"Go ahead, Marc."

"Can you repeat the question, please?"

"If you hadn't carried out the murder of your grandfather, what was your biggest concern?"

"My biggest concern was, God, Mom would hate me forever. She would never let me back in the house and she said that in the telephone conversation the night before I did that, you know, if I don't do it, just don't come home again, the door will be locked. . . . Doors can be opened, doors can be locked, you know."

Jones could have stopped there but didn't. He had to try once more.

". . . You mentioned this tape. What is the purpose of your making that tape, Marc?"

Rosen was livid as he objected once more, and Baldwin agreed that no foundation had been laid.

"Marc, has the decision to testify in this case been a difficult one for you?"

Objection. Sustained.

"Have you had second thoughts about testifying in the case?"

Objection. Overruled.

"Yes, I have."

"Would you explain to the jury some of your concerns?"

Objection. Sustained.

"Do you still love your mother?"

Objection. Sustained.

"Marc, why have you been willing to testify in the case?"

Objection. Sustained.

"Have there been any promises made to you in exchange for your testimony?"

"No, there haven't."

It had gone on for two hours and it was over—at least until Rosen had his crack at him the next morning. Near the end, Mary Lou was crying, and Mason Drukman, so shaken by what he'd heard, had thought of asking the judge to be released from the locked courtroom.

Frances had told Larry during the summer how afraid she was Marc might do this, and now he had. And so, in a few minutes, would Vittorio Gentile, the last witness of the day.

In his thick Italian accent, beads of perspiration forming on his brow, the pearl merchant carried the jury back in time, back to 1959 and his marriage to Frances in St. Patrick's Cathedral and to the day, more than four years later, when he came home to find her and his two sons gone. He tried to reconcile with her, he said, but "the situation became so tragic for me because I was completely destroyed"—monetarily, physically and emotionally—"that I had to move back to Italy."

But he said that when he came to the States for a visit in 1973 (despite their being divorced and his being remarried) he was "her guest for a month during the weekdays." And once he returned to the States permanently in 1975, he told the jury, they would have lunch "many times."

"Who would initiate the conversations or suggest that you go to lunch?" Jones asked.

"Sometimes it was on my side, sometime it was on her side."

"Do you recall ever meeting with her sometime in the spring of 1978 to go to lunch?"

"Yes, that was one of the lunches we had."

"Do you remember where that lunch took place?"

"I believe that the particular lunch was at a place where we used to go very often, Gino's Restaurant."

". . . Just the two of you?"

"Just the two of us."

"Was there some discussion at that lunch about her father, Franklin Bradshaw?"

"There was only one discussion after we finished lunch that was talked about. Something she mentioned, something . . . to put a contract on her father."

"Mr. Gentile, do you recall how that statement came about or how—"

"No, it was just out of the blue sky." He said that he was "astonished" and couldn't believe that she would say something like that.

"Did you say anything to her?"

634

"I said—" he began, then stopped short. "I was speech-less." They were leaving the restaurant, he recalled, when she said it and she might have repeated it. He said he didn't know what she meant by it, nor did she elaborate. That was the last time he'd had lunch with her, he said, but he had seen her as recently as nine or ten months ago.

Mike Rosen had been waiting for this chance to tear into Vittorio Gentile. Long before the trial, he had known what Gentile was coming to say. It had been intriguingly alluded to in a backhanded manner at Marc's trial by Paul Van Dam, but never expounded upon. Mike George had learned about the lunch from Gentile shortly after he first met him; this and Marc's telling him that arson was another method his mother suggested he and Larry might use to kill their grandfather in 1977 were two more factors in the investigator's willingness to believe Jeff Morris.

Gentile had not wanted to testify at Marc's trial (he didn't trust Marc's lawyers, because Berenice was paying the bills) and he had not wanted to testify against Frances, whom, in his own peculiar way, he still loved. But he did want Marc to testify, and his own decision to take the stand had helped his son to reach his.

"You said something in passing," Rosen began, "you think a discussion took place at a restaurant called Gino's, a place you *used* to go to. That is what you told me, you *used* to go to Gino's?"

"Yes."

"You don't go to Gino's anymore?"

"Oh, yes, I go definitely."

"You go there every day, don't you, practically?"

"Of course."

"Sure. That is on Lexington right near Bloomingdale's, right?"

"Correct."

"You walk past the window, [people] will see you sitting at the bar every afternoon, won't they?"

"Yes."

"While you were married to Frances, did you ever beat her up?"

"No."

"On November 8, 1982, do you remember being interviewed by an investigator named John McGrath from my office?"

Yes, he remembered.

Did he admit to Mr. McGrath that he had beaten Frances?

"No, I did not admit to beating Frances. I admit slapping when she had a crisis. I don't call hitting on the face once to stop her crisis beating. She was never hospitalized."

"She wasn't hospitalized," Rosen said, summoning every ounce of scorn and contempt from his repertoire. "*That* is what you are saying—after you hit her, she wasn't hospitalized?"

"No beating," Gentile said, then explained his view of the matter: "A slapping on the face is one thing, a beating is another."

Establishing that Gentile had tried—but failed—to gain custody of his children, Rosen asked if he had been speaking with Marc lately.

"No," Gentile lied.

When was the *last* time? Rosen wanted to know.

"I spoke to Marc about . . . three or four months ago."

"That was out here in jail in Salt Lake, right?"

"Yes," Gentile said, but when pressed, he admitted that the meeting was not in jail but at a motel where he was staying.

"Four months ago your son was in a motel?" Rosen asked, knowing all about it.

Actually, it was just before Rosen's investigator came to see him in New York, he said. He had asked Mike George if he could see Marc privately and George had brought him.

Did he happen to tell Marc recently over the phone not to worry because he would be home in a few months?

"No, never," he insisted.

Under Rosen's skillful prodding, Gentile admitted that a New York court had taken his name away from his children, that he had no contact with his sons while he was in Italy, that he didn't know Larry had been certified as a handicapped child at the age of four, and that he had been held in contempt of court and ordered arrested on a number of occasions.

Those orders had been given, he said, because of back

alimony, and "I am in the business which I need liquid money, and I could not pay all that amount of money."

"You need liquid money?"

"Yes, to do my business."

". . . Oh. And you couldn't take some of that money in the bank and give it to your kids?"

"Not when I was overwhelmed with payments."

"But the court ordered you to pay it, did they not?"

"So I went [into] bankruptcy, that is why I moved back to Italy."

"You went to Italy when the court did that, right?"

"Of course. I couldn't pay. I couldn't pay. What could I do? I had to close my business, I had to do everything. There was nothing else. She was spending like a maniac."

Reminding Rosen that he was getting off the point, Baldwin suggested he ask another question.

"I sure will, Your Honor. Now, Mr. Gentile, you have told His Honor and this jury under oath, sir, that at a luncheon at Gino's Restaurant in the spring of 1978, Frances told you she was going to put a contract out on her father . . . ?"

"Yes, sir."

". . . You didn't call the police, did you, Mr. Gentile?"

"No, I didn't."

"You didn't call out to Salt Lake City saying, 'Oh, there is a contract on Mr. Bradshaw'?"

"No, I didn't."

". . . And this [lunch] was how many years after this bitter, bitter divorce, some almost eight, nine years later she is telling you this?"

"Yes. We went to lunch at least twice a month."

"Mr. Gentile, are you telling His Honor and this jury that after the history you have had with Mrs. Schreuder she would tell you something like this? That is what you want us to believe?"

"Exactly."

On re-direct, knowing that Gentile had wilted under Rosen's barrage, Jones did what he could to redress the balance. He gave Gentile another opportunity to explain his hitting of Frances ("Sometimes she had hysterical convulsions and [this] was one way to bring her out") and to explain how the bitterness of their divorce had lessened as time went on ("She was abroad, and I was in Rome. And occasionally she was calling from Belgium on the phone for a couple of hours") and their relationship had become "friendly" once more.

Whether the jury believed it or not, Jones didn't know. It had been a long day for everybody, and the judge, sensing the jury's fatigue, told them that he was going home to watch Monday Night Football and suggested that they might do the same. The defense had a long night ahead of them. It would be a few hours at least before the court reporter could rush a transcript of Marc's testimony over to them at the Marriott and they could fully prepare the kind of cross-examination that would "water down" (in Kurumada's words) the undeniable impact of what had transpired. While they had never ruled out the possibility that Marc might testify, they, like the state, had not really believed he would be gutsy enough to do so. They were in a deep hole with a short ladder. But it was only the first day of trial; they had at least managed to keep the tape out, and there was a long way to go.

Nobody was more aware of that than Ernie Jones. If he had known for sure that Marc was going to testify, he would have saved him until the end, built up to his testimony climactically, and made sure that the last image burned into the minds of the jury was the one they had witnessed that afternoon. But he couldn't afford to take that chance. The courting of Marc Schreuder had, from the start, been like a roulette wheel, spinning round and round. So when it stopped, with Marc's having the final encouragement of a lunch with his father and deciding to go forward, the prosecutor had no choice but to put him on. He *was* the state's case. Everyone else was needed to corroborate him.

Jones and Mike George were surprised that he had held up as well as he did. They thought he might break down and cry if he looked over at his mother, or say that it had been *his* idea and that Mom had *nothing* to do with it. It wasn't until he said that she had asked him to commit the murder that they had begun to relax. They had done everything they could to prepare Marc for his day in court. They had told him he had to stop tugging at his lip when he talked, because it might be distracting to the jury. Since he also had a habit of fiddling with the part of his hair that swooped down over his forehead, George had taken him for a haircut less than two weeks before.

"At the end of Monday," George said, "we're standing tall, we're looking good. But once you've climbed to the top of the mountain, we have nowhere to go but down."

70// "Mr. Schreuder, my name is Michael Rosen. I represent Mom."

Marc and his father had been to Don Harman's house for an Italian dinner the night before, but he was about to find the next two hours a great deal less pleasurable than that evening had been. Rosen, Lang and Kurumada had been up most of the night and they were ready to go. Jones had recalled Marc in order to reinforce that his mother had discussed his grandfather's will with him a number of times, and now it was Rosen's turn.

"Now," Rosen said, "you told His Honor and this jury yesterday under oath, sir, that there is no deal, no promises . . . in exchange for your testimony. Do you remember that testimony here yesterday under oath?"

"I don't recall it, no."

But once Rosen pointed out the page in the transcript where the question and answer appeared, Marc said that he did.

"Hasn't the prosecutor promised to communicate on your behalf to the parole board, sir?"

"Yes, they have."

". . . You don't consider that some sort of a promise?"

"I don't know what to consider it."

". . . As you sit here today, sir, do you have an expectation that maybe the prosecutor's communication to the parole board will get you out of jail a little earlier than they're going to let you out?"

"Perhaps."

Through Marc's continuing response to his questions, Rosen was cleverly able to remind the jury that Marc's manslaughter defense at his own trial "wasn't bought" and that the prosecutor had gone over all the questions he had asked Marc on Monday *prior* to trial. It didn't matter that no prosecutor—or defense lawyer, for that matter—puts on a witness without doing the same thing; what mattered was that Rosen had an amazing knack of making even the most ordinary practice seem illicit and conspiratorial.

"Did you ever go to the movies with Sergeant George?" Rosen asked, plunging into the area of Marc's trips outside the prison.

"Yes."

"When did you go to the movies with Sergeant George?"

"I believe it was sometime in June or July of this year."

". . . Go out for hamburgers, something like that?"

"No, we did not go out for hamburgers."

"Was it just you and Sergeant George who went to the movies?"

"No, it was not."

"A lot of armed guards with you, I guess?"

"No."

". . . Who else went to the movies with you and Sergeant George?"

"Mr. George, myself, my girlfriend."

"Your girlfriend in Salt Lake City."

"That's correct."

"What did you go to see, *Fantasy Island?*"

Jones objected, the judge struck the question, and Rosen apologized.

"What else did you do on the evening that you were out with Sergeant George and your girlfriend besides go to the movies?"

"On that day? I believe that's all we did."

"Is there another day you and Sergeant George may have been out together?"

"Oh, yes."

"Tell me about it."

"Well, there were a number of occasions. I can't recall any of them offhand. I think there was one where I went up to the

University of Utah to get an award in which Mr. George accompanied me."

"What was the award?" he sneered. "Prisoner of the Year?"

Once more, Jones objected and Rosen withdrew it. Baldwin warned Rosen "to stay within the rules." This was exactly the kind of sarcasm that could turn off a jury and defeat everything he was trying to achieve. Taking a slightly more conciliatory approach, Rosen let Marc explain that he was taken to the university for a banquet in which he was inducted into the academic honor society of Phi Beta Sigma.

Asked about his testimony the day before—that Richard Behrens was at what Rosen called a "preflight meeting" with him and Mom—Marc said he couldn't remember exactly what he had said. When Rosen read the testimony back to him, Marc altered his answer to say he was "fairly sure" of what he told the jury; however, there were so many meetings "between Mom and Mr. Behrens" prior to his leaving that "a lot of it gets foggy."

"Now, you told Your Honor and the jury yesterday that . . . Mom gave you some amphetamines. Do you recall that, sir?"

"Yes, I do."

"And . . . that your instructions were to go out to Salt Lake City and poison your grandfather with the amphetamines or put it in his food or something like that? Do you remember that testimony you gave us yesterday?"

"Yes, I do."

". . . But you told us also, did you not, Mr. Schreuder, that you did not attempt to kill your grandfather in 1977?"

"That's correct."

"But you told us you were calling your mother one or two times a day from Salt Lake City during the summer of 1977, remember that testimony?"

"Yes, I do."

"Notwithstanding your mother's direction, sir, supply of drugs and telephone calls, you still came home without doing what you said she instructed you to do; isn't that a fact, sir?"

"That's correct, yes."

Jones could see exactly where Rosen was heading and he

was powerless to stop him. When Behrens testified, Rosen would bring out that Marc had told him that he *had* tried to kill his grandfather. Or, worse still, if the jury could be shown that Marc had come out to Salt Lake, *not* followed his mother's instructions, and was still allowed to come home, then they could perhaps be persuaded that Marc either did not have to do what he was allegedly asked to do in 1978 or that he could easily have done this on his own. Rosen didn't have to *prove* anything. That wasn't his job. He just needed to create enough reasonable doubt to give Frances a one-way ticket home.

In a calculated effort to get Marc to look at his mother, Rosen moved away from the lectern and walked in her direction, asking him about Myles Manning and whether he was *certain* she had first mentioned his name at Dragon Hall in Southampton in September of 1977.

"I believe so. There is a question whether she actually mentioned the name of the hit man at that point in time or if she mentioned the fact she was just going to hire a hit man, but I am pretty sure she mentioned the name in September at Dragon Hall in 1977, yes."

"Pretty sure or are you positive as you sit here testifying against your mother?"

"I am pretty sure."

"You also told us that your mother supposedly said she made a five-thousand-dollar down payment to this supposed hit man, correct?"

Yes, it was. And it was also correct when he said it was Mom's idea to travel in Larry's name. But when asked about Dr. Moench—which Rosen pronounced "munch"—he seemed fuzzy as to what year he had seen him and admitted, when asked, that he occasionally had a problem "remembering exact dates and times and stuff like that."

Determined to paint a picture for the jury of Marc as a bright, independent individual and investor with a mind of his own, Rosen brought out the fact that he had graduated with honors from Allen-Stevenson and was credited with being "a man of persistence with powers of organization and self-confidence" (though Marc did not recall that, Rosen had the school record to prove it); that he had been an honors student at Kent, separated from his mother by *one hundred miles,* who had scored 1210 on his college-entrance Scholastic Aptitude Tests *before* he shot his grandfather and 1320 *afterward,* and who was characterized as having both "a sharp mind" and "an unfortunate tendency to overlook directions."

Marc admitted that he had had a stockbroker in Manhattan, that the account had not been shared jointly with Mom, and that the money he had used to purchase nearly $20,000 of stocks had not been given to him by her. Asked if he had dealt in rare coins, he said that he had, and confirmed that he had made a purchase once of approximately $17,000 and that Mom hadn't shared in or given him the money for those activities either.

But when asked if he had ever stolen $40,000 in jewelry or money from Mom, he said that he had never stolen *anything* from her.

"How about Granny? Ever steal some money from Granny?"

"Yes, I did."

"Forty thousand dollars?"

"No." Actually, he admitted, "a very rough estimate" would be more like $70,000 or $80,000.

Asked if he remembered the photography lab at Allen-Stevenson, Marc said that he did.

"And did you not proceed to destroy that photography lab?"

"No, I did not."

". . . Did you steal anything from there?"

"No, I did not."

"Did you . . . do anything in that photography lab other than be a photographer?"

"No, I did not."

"Now, you were supposed to graduate Kent School in 1979, correct?"

"That's correct."

"And you had already been accepted to college in May, had you not?"

". . . Yes, I believe I had."

"And that is when you broke into the school's store a couple of times, right after that in about May of 1979 . . . ?"

"I believe so, yes. I didn't know exactly May, I am not sure."

". . . And you stole some money and you stole some keys, did you not?"

"I stole some money, yes."

"And you had keys to other boys' rooms?"

"I don't remember that, no."

"You don't remember you had some other property that didn't belong to you in your possession . . . ?"

"I am not sure."

"How about sneakers and other guys' possessions, their pens and stuff? You don't remember any of that?"

"No, I do not."

"Moms tell you to do that?"

"No, she did not."

". . . And you tried to blame this whole thing on another kid; isn't that true?"

"No, I did not try to blame a kid. I told the truth as I am now."

Turning to the summer of 1977, Rosen asked if Marc had gotten along with everybody at the warehouse. No, he had not. People were upset with him, he conceded, but he denied ever defecating in the ladies'-room washbasin or going to pornographic movies when he was supposed to be working. He admitted that his grandparents were upset with him, but denied he had treated his grandfather terribly or had used "bad language" to him.

"Didn't Doug Steele . . . call you aside that summer like a Dutch uncle and try to tell you to be nice to your grandparents?"

"I believe he said something of the substance, yes."

Unable to get Marc's answer to his question of whether Doug Steele had also told him that his grandfather was afraid of him (the judge sustained Jones's objection that it was hearsay), Rosen asked if he had told Richard Behrens that he had tried to kill his grandfather that summer.

"That's right."

"You told that to Uncle Dickie, didn't you?"

"I told it to Richard Behrens, yes."

"Was he known to you as Uncle Dick?"

"No, he was not. He was known to us as Uncle George."

". . . When did you tell him that you tried to kill your grandfather in 1977?"

"I don't remember exactly. Probably after the summer was over at some point."

"You weren't telling the truth then, I take it?"

"Yes, I was telling the truth."

"Did you try to kill your grandfather in the summer of 1977?"

"Well, we were sent out there to *try* to kill him, yes, we were."

"But you didn't attempt to kill him, did you?"

"No, we did not."

"Still were allowed home?"

"Well, yes."

After a few other questions, Rosen returned to Behrens—one of his favorite subjects—and Marc's relationship with him.

"Now, you told us yesterday that Richard Behrens was Mom's friend, correct?"

"That's correct."

"You were pretty close to Richard Behrens, weren't you?"

"Yes, I am."

"As a matter of fact, you shared a lot of private thoughts, did you not?"

"Not really, no."

"Did you ever, for example, Mr. Schreuder, take pictures of Richard Behrens in your bed?"

"In my bed? I don't remember."

"I show you what has been marked Defendant's Exhibit 47. Take a look at that, Mr. Schreuder. Tell me if you recognize that picture."

"Yes, I do. I recognize who is in it and everything."

"Recognize the room?"

"Yes, I do."

"Your room?"

"Right. Well, it's my half of the room, because me and my brother shared it."

"Is he in your bed?"

". . . He's *on* my bed. I don't know if he's in it or not."

But when Rosen tried to have the photograph admitted into evidence in order "to show the relationship," the judge sustained Jones's objection that a proper foundation had not been laid.

Undaunted, Rosen asked Marc if he ever told Behrens he had acted *alone* in the killing of his grandfather.

"I don't believe so, no."

"Why don't you think about it for a second?"

"Well, I told him a lot of stories Mom wanted me to tell him. Phony stories. I am not sure I—I told him a lot of stuff, so I am not sure what I told him and what I didn't, sir."

"Now, I am going to ask you again. Do you recall telling Richard Behrens that you acted alone?"

"I don't think so, no."

"How many times did you meet with Richard Behrens after the murder?"

"Many times."

"Fifteen, twenty times?"

"I don't know. I can't put an exact figure on it. It was a lot of times, though."

"I want to know what a lot is. Give me an estimate, your best estimate, sir."

From 1978 until now, Marc said, thirty-five or forty times.

"Did you ever tell anybody your brother, Larry, was involved in the murder of Gramps?"

"Yes, I did."

"As a matter of fact, didn't you snitch on [him] at the end of 1977 . . . about him stealing some auto parts?"

"Yes, I did."

The longer Rosen kept trying to crack Marc's cool resolve and polite demeanor, the stronger Marc seemed to get. If Rosen was going to lose this case, lose it because of Marc, he was going to make damn sure Marc relived that Saturday night and Sunday morning in Salt Lake five years before— relived it with Mike Rosen as his tour guide.

"You arrived here in Salt Lake City on Saturday night, July 22, 1978?"

"That's correct."

"And you took a cab, you say, to a hotel?"

"That's correct."

"Were you wearing a disguise or anything?"

"No, I was not."

"What is the name of the hotel again?"

"I don't remember."

"And the next morning you leave the hotel at seven in the morning?"

"That's correct."

Rosen went over and picked up the .357 Magnum from the clerk's desk. "Where did you have this when you left the hotel?" he asked, brandishing it right in front of Marc.

"In my . . ." He paused, then said: "I had a blazer on like you do and I put it in the pocket."

When Rosen opened his suit coat and began to put it in his left inside pocket Marc said that was exactly where it was. As Rosen continued on, Frances, shaking, clutched John Lang's arm.

"And this is about seven in the morning?"

"About, yes."

"Give or take. Did you make a call, reserve a cab, 'Hello, pick me up at the hotel'?"

No, he said, he just caught one that was out front.

"Big hotel?"

"It was pretty big, yes."

"I mean like the Marriott and the Sheraton and all this?"

"I am not really sure. It was late at night and I don't have a lot of recollection of it."

After he did the killing, Rosen wanted to know, did he have the cab wait for him?

"No, I didn't."

"So after you did the killing, you told His Honor and the jury, you went and hailed another cab?"

"I did not hail a cab, no, I did not."

"You went to some cab stop?"

"The Ute Cab stop is about half a block down from the warehouse."

"And there was a cab waiting there?"

"There usually is, yes."

"At seven-thirty . . . on a Sunday morning, there is a cab there?"

"That's correct."

"Let me ask you: Did you get any blood on your clothes after you shot your grandfather in the head?"

"No, I did not."

"Not a drop of blood got on you, right?"

"That's correct."

"[After] you left that warehouse, what did you do with the gun after you shot it?"

"I put it back in my pocket."

After a number of questions about the mechanics of getting back to New York, Rosen returned to the killing itself, determined to leave no doubt in the jurors' minds how vicious it had been.

"Now, Mr. Schreuder, you had approximately a twenty-minute conversation with Gramps before you shot him in the back, isn't that correct?"

"That's correct."

"And then how much of a period of time elapsed before you shot him in the head?"

"Between when and when?"

"Between the time you shot him in the back and the time you shot him in the head, how much time elapsed?"

"I am not sure, just a couple of seconds."

"Did you shoot him in the head as he was going down?"

"No, I did not."

"Shoot him in the head after he was down?"

"Yes, I did."

"I take it, Mr. Schreuder, that there was quite an amount of blood on the floor after you shot your grandfather, wouldn't that be fair to say?"

"I am not really sure. I didn't see any when I did."

"And when Gramps was on the floor, did you take stuff out of his pocket?"

"Yes, I did."

". . . Actually put your hands in his pocket, didn't you?"

"Excuse me?"

"You put your hands in his pocket, didn't you?"

"Yes, I did."

"Did you ever tell Richard Behrens that it was easy to kill Gramps?"

"No, I never did."

Rosen sat down and Jones leaped up to begin his re-direct examination, determined to explain some potentially fatal areas of Marc's character that Rosen had managed to expose.

Asked about the money he said he had taken from his grandmother, Marc told the jury it was checks he had stolen and forged while she was in New York at Gracie Square. The reason he did it, he claimed, was so that he would have "getaway money." He was hoping not to be extradited, he was scared, and "I just thought running away was the answer." (Rosen had asked Marc on cross-examination if he had any idea of what he had said under oath the day before and Marc had said no. That comment was less flip and more truthful than it seemed, because on Monday he said he had *never* thought of leaving the country, even though his mother had urged him to.) He said he told his mother that he was stealing from his grandmother and that her response was "it was fine as long as I didn't get caught."

The reason Marc couldn't recall what teachers at Allen-Stevenson and Kent had said about him, he claimed, was that his mother would receive his report cards and wouldn't always show them to him. ("She would summon me in the room and tell me what I got and let me read one or two selected report cards, but I wasn't allowed to see a lot of them, no.")

But he didn't always get good grades, he told the jury. In sixth and seventh grade at Allen-Stevenson he got "a lot of C's" and his mother told him about them.

"What was her reaction?"

"Oh, she—at that point in time she flew into a rage and would take a belt out and start beating me."

"How many times did that happen in connection with bad grades?"

"I think it was three or four times."

After a few more questions, it was finished. Nearly noon and time for lunch. It was hard to read anything of import in the jurors' faces as they somberly filed out—except, perhaps, the relief from concentrating that the next two hours would bring. Marc's two days in court were over, but the potential for physical harm that awaited him back at the Point was not. Frances had stared at him throughout his testimony with a mixture of iciness, tears when Rosen was reliving the day of the murder, and incomprehension; and even now, long after he left the witness stand and the courtroom, she continued to stare at the spot from which he had betrayed her—and from which he seemed to hold, yet one more time, her fate in his hands.

During the course of a big murder trial, often the dramas unfolding offstage—the ones that a jury never sees and may never hear about—can have as much impact on the ultimate verdict as anything else. The courting of Marc Schreuder and his decision to testify was clearly one. The deal that was cut to bring that testimony about was another. On the day before, at the end of Jones's direct examination, Marc had said that no promises had been made to him in exchange for his testimony. A few hours earlier, when Rosen refreshed his memory on cross-examination, he told the jury that the County Attorney's Office had promised to appear on his behalf before the Board of Pardons—an offer made to Marc nearly a year before. But there was more to the deal. Wally Bugden had asked that if Marc's appeal before the Utah Supreme Court was successful and he was granted a new trial, his testimony—and anything he might have said to the state in preparation for that testimony—could not be used against him. The state had agreed to Bugden's request that everything be in writing, but Marc had said nothing about this other part of the deal. During the midmorning recess, Bugden spoke with Marc and informed him that he *had* to reveal it; otherwise, it could be seen as perpetrating a fraud on the court. But when Jones, on re-direct examination, asked him an hour later, just before the end of his testimony, about any deals, he once again mentioned the first part of the deal but not the second.

As "surprised" as Bugden was by Marc's failure to do that, he was even more surprised that Ernie Jones hadn't asked Marc a leading question to clarify the deal. If Marc "honestly forgot," Bugden felt, "there is no way Ernie Jones could have forgotten. He's the prosecutor. He knows what he's promised. I felt [his failure to do that] was to not water down what the jury had just heard."

During the lunch recess, while Bugden went back to his office and drew up the agreement for the state to sign, Rob Denton, an attorney who had been helping Paul Van Dam on Marc's appeal, met with Marc in the County Attorney's

Office. He too had been disturbed by Marc's failure to disclose *all* parts of the deal and wanted to find out why. Marc repeatedly told Denton that he had forgotten and that the pressure of being on the stand had been "one of the factors" which had caused him to forget. Denton said that it was "absolutely imperative" he return to the witness stand and let the prosecutor know of his desire to do so.

Ernie Jones happened to walk in at this point and Denton told him of his concern. While Jones did not seem to share Denton's consternation, Denton left the office with the impression that Marc would be recalled to the stand that afternoon.

The jury was not in the courtroom when the afternoon session began at two. Nor was Marc. Mike Rosen had told the judge he wanted to make a motion without the jury present. He moved that the judge declare a mistrial—or, at the very least, declare that Marc's *entire* testimony be deleted from the record—and cited his reason in the form of a question: how could Mr. Jones say he was "surprised" that Marc testified when the state had been working with Marc for months, the prosecutor had "whipped out ten to twelve pages of questions," and Marc seemed so "well-prepared"?

No longer amazed by *anything* Rosen came up with, Jones calmly said that the state, while indeed prepared, was as surprised by Marc's ultimate decision as anybody else.

The judge denied the motion but not before saying something that had been festering in him since the morning: "It is incomprehensible to this court," he said, looking straight at Jones, "that people serving time in Utah State Prison are running around town. The corrections system in this state is beyond comprehension. . . . I am appalled, absolutely appalled at what I heard today."

Once the judge was done venting his spleen, Dr. Louis G. Moench was called to the stand, and Baldwin warned the prosecutor that he could ask Moench only about his diagnosis of Marc—not about what Marc had told him.

But no sooner had the psychiatrist (whose connection to Marc Jones had mentioned briefly when Marc was on the stand) begun testifying than that warning seemed meaningless. Over Rosen's vehement objections, the judge allowed

Moench to relate much of the family background he had learned from Marc, and to put forth the notion that the tape—which was still not in evidence—had contributed to his diagnosis. He essentially told the jury what he had told Judge Sawaya—that Marc, "the junior partner" in the murder plan, was "operating under extreme pressure and domination from his mother and suffered from a pathological Oedipus complex." Without becoming too technical, he explained that it was a "sick" relationship.

On cross-examination, Rosen did everything he could to portray Moench as someone was "bought" by Marc's lawyers, whose only verification for his findings was Marc (Rosen, of course, made no reference to the tape), and who was now testifying for the same side that had brought in a psychiatrist the year before to say that Moench was storytelling.

While Lee Coleman had managed to upset him, Mike Rosen did not: Moench was unflappable throughout.

Carrying a stack of papers and dressed in an electric-green polyester suit and red sweater, Richard Behrens walked forward as the state's last witness that day.

While this was the fourth and perhaps final time be would be testifying, it was the first time he had actually seen his friend of twenty years sitting across from him. What effect that might have on the heavyset schoolteacher remained to be seen.

Once Behrens got comfortable with the microphone—overcoming this problem more easily than he had at Marc's trial—Ernie Jones was like a cockswain as he took Behrens through the entire story. He might have told it three times before, but this jury was hearing it for the first time, and the prosecutor made sure to touch all the bases. For the most part, Behrens held up well, corroborating much of what the jury had heard from Marc. As for the papers he had lugged to court, he wouldn't need them until the next morning, when Rosen would get his chance at him. They were all the statements he had ever made—all the truths, lies, and contradictions that reflected his deep involvement in the whole affair. Even the best witness, the state's thinking went, couldn't remember *everything* he said and how he said it on previous occasions—and Richard Behrens, who was far from being that, would need all the help he could get with Mike Rosen.

So back to the Holiday Inn he went, where he was booked under the name of Mike George.

As the trial entered its third day, the strain on Frances was beginning to show. She had been in tears at different points during Marc's testimony, though seemed heavily sedated throughout Tuesday afternoon. But waiting for the jury to be brought in on Wednesday morning and for Richard Behrens to resume the stand, she was again near tears as she glared at the prosecution and gesticulated to her lawyers the points she wanted them to make.

It had been nine months since Mike Rosen had last questioned Behrens, and during that time he had subpoenaed a good number of his records. Rosen was on a search-and-destroy mission and Behrens was his next target.

He asked Behrens if he recalled teaching at the Kew Forest School in Forest Hills, New York, in 1972, and Behrens said he did.

"And you taught there for about a year, did you not?"

"I certainly did."

"And they wouldn't renew your contract for the second year, remember that, sir?"

"I certainly do."

"And that was because you couldn't keep your hands off the kids, remember that, Mr. Behrens?"

"No, I don't."

"Remember that you were discharged from Kew Forest because you couldn't maintain order in the class without resorting to physical punishment, remember that, sir?"

"Yes."

From there, Rosen moved quickly to the period of 1977 and 1978. "Wouldn't it be fair to say, Mr. Behrens, that your contact with Frances in the fall of 1977 was occasional?"

"No, it wouldn't be fair at all."

So Rosen immediately cited an answer Behrens had given to a similar question at Marc's trial *("I was going to school. I was in touch occasionally.")* and asked him if he recalled giving that answer under oath. Yes, he did, but when he tried to elaborate, Rosen cut him off. He wanted yes-or-no answers, not long-winded explanations.

"Did you ever tell Officer Joel Campbell on December 3, 1980, that Marc was very headstrong?"

"Yes, when he was seventeen."

"Isn't it true, Mr. Behrens, based on your knowledge and observation of the Schreuder family, that during the late 1970s and before July of 1978, Mrs. Schreuder was a hard disciplinarian with Marc?"

"She was and sometimes she wasn't, but mostly she was."

"But you didn't know what she did with Marc, did you? You didn't—"

". . . I knew her twenty years. I certainly had a pretty good idea."

". . . Were you asked this question and did you give this answer under oath on March 17, 1982, to Judge Banks at Marc's—"

"What day was that?"

"Would you let me finish my question?"

"I would like to follow you."

"I will let you follow me. Let me finish my question. At Marc's preliminary hearing, page 42."

"All right."

"*Question:* 'Is it not true that during the late seventies, prior to July of 1978, in fact Frances Schreuder was an extremely hard disciplinarian with Marc?' *Answer:* 'I don't know what she did with Marc.' Did you give that answer under oath, sir?"

"Yes."

"Now, you knew, did you not, that Marc put a lot of blame on his brother and other people . . . for things he might have done?"

"He put the blame of stealing a one-hundred-and-fifty-thousand-dollar bond and auto parts on Larry."

"He put a lot of blame on Larry, didn't he, for a lot of things, to your knowledge?"

"Those are two things I am aware of."

"Did you ever tell anybody that Marc put a lot of blame on Larry?"

"I might have."

In response to Rosen's questions, designed to show more of

a closeness between Behrens and Marc than between Behrens and Frances, Behrens testified that Marc often stored photographs at his house (including the one Behrens gave to Marilyn of Frances on the Staten Island Ferry); that Marc gave him the box of bullets; that Marc told him that he *had* put stimulants in his grandfather's oatmeal; that Marc went with him to the gunshop to get a cover; that Marc called to arrange the 1981 summer meetings in Carl Schurz Park where Behrens learned more about the murder and Frances wasn't present.

"And isn't it a fact," Rosen asked, "that Marc, at the end of the summer of '77, said *he* was concerned about being cut off financially?"

"Yes."

Continuing to show the jury the sterling sort of character he felt Behrens was—the character that the state was asking them to believe—Rosen brought out his two unsatisfactory performance ratings from two New York schools; his desperate need for money; his dealings with Marilyn and knowledge of a reward; his concern over possibly being cut out of *his* father's estate and, Rosen suggested, his thoughts of killing his stepmother to prevent that from happening; his arrest in New York and the $1,000,000 lawsuit he filed as a result of it ("under Frances's urging," Behrens contended); and the immunity deal he was able to cut—a deal that included protection from charges of illegally possessing a gun that he oiled, cleaned and carefully removed his fingerprints from . . . a gun that, depending on one's belief in the different stories Behrens had given, he might or might not have been asked to dispose of.

As Ernie Jones took it all in, not only was he unsure where Rosen was ultimately going, but he had the uneasy sense that Rosen did—that *every* question he asked had a purpose. In Marc's trial, without a jury, Jones had had a clearer idea of the impact his evidence was having. As a judge, Sawaya had heard and seen it all before, and was not afraid to let in practically everything. And even though Jones was disappointed in what he felt to be a compromise verdict, the elements of that trial looked wonderful and safe to him now. He'd been able to get the tape in; he couldn't with Baldwin.

He'd been able to get Behrens's letters to the world in; he couldn't with Baldwin. "You don't know in a trial," he said later. "You don't know how the evidence is going—how the jury perceives it. And all you do is play it from one witness to the next. It can be some little thing in the case that ultimately turns the tide; sometimes it can come early in the trial, or late. Maybe it's not *what* is said, but the *way* it's said or the way it's asked, or the pause between question and answer and the next question."

Jones did his best on re-direct to bolster Richard Behrens, to fill in things that Behrens said about Frances on previous occasions but that Rosen had carefully left out, and to swing the momentum back to the state's side of the courtroom. But it was Mike Rosen's three questions and Behrens's three responses on re-cross that left the last—and perhaps lasting—impression the people in Utah would have of the schoolteacher from East 89th Street.

"What did you do to save Franklin Bradshaw's life?"

"What could I do?"

Rosen moved closer to Behrens and raised his voice. "What did *you* do to save Franklin Bradshaw's life?"

"What could I do?"

"Did you do *anything?*"

"I did nothing."

71 // Well, they finally made it. When the courtroom door was opened to let Richard Behrens out, Myles Manning and Eddie Dean, without the cash advance he had zealously sought, walked in. Eight days before, after Steve Klein found Manning at the address he did not want to reveal at Frances's preliminary hearing, Manning and Dean appeared, as ordered, in State Supreme Court to assure Allen Sullivan that they would go to Utah. Ernie Jones had been prepared to proceed without Manning, and had even marked up Manning's testimony at the preliminary in the event he needed to present it.

Dressed in a gray suit that made him look more like a portly banker than the bartender he currently was, Manning took the stand, no doubt giving the God-fearing members of the jury the first glimpse in person they had ever had of a hit man, real or otherwise. Like Behrens, Manning had his previous testimony with him. In addition, Jones and George had prepped Manning extensively. They knew he had a tendency to answer questions before he thought about what he was saying. Rosen had caught him in a number of contradictions at Frances's preliminary, and the prosecution warned him against calling Behrens a liar (Rosen will attempt to pit you against him, they said) and against getting angry. If you don't recall something, they told him, just say so; when a contradiction comes up, admit you were wrong. Just tell the truth. They had a lot riding on Manning's testimony and they were praying he would come through—that the jury would begin to believe him from the moment they saw him.

Manning began well enough, transporting the jury to East 89th Street in Manhattan, describing it as a residential area of five-story walkups, and recalling his first meeting with Richard Behrens on the street. But when Jones asked him if he could point out the woman Behrens introduced him to, he motioned to Frances and said, "That lady over there looks similar, but 1977 is a long time." When the judge was asked if the record could reflect his identification of her, Rosen interrupted to say he would not consent to it. If part of his master plan was to suggest Frances and Manning had *never* met, this lack of certainty could only help ensure its success.

Behrens had only told him her first name, he said, but he did recall that she was taller than he was (Frances is five-seven, Manning five-six) and about in her early thirties (she would have been thirty-nine in the fall of 1977). He told the jury about their first three meetings, Behrens's role as matchmaker, his going to the Y (and identifying the receipt to prove it), what he had done with the money, and his fourth and final meeting in Behrens's apartment when he "explained" to her what had happened when he and his buddy got to Salt Lake, and her reaction.

Before Jones sat down, he asked Manning if he had recalled *all* of the details about this when Mike George and Don

Harman first interviewed him. No, he admitted, he hadn't. But he had let Allen Sullivan know that he wanted to make some changes in what he had told the two investigators.

Rosen wasted no time in resuming the attack he had launched at Manning the previous December. Yes, Manning admitted, he was drinking quite heavily during the time he said he met with Mrs. Schreuder and had, in Rosen's words, "a pretty extensive drinking problem" then. Yes, he had been thrown out of an apartment on East 87th Street because of it. When Manning said that he had known Behrens for only a few months at the time of his meetings with Frances, Rosen asked if Behrens had been lying when he said they had known each other for a few years. Jones objected that it was argumentative, and the judge sustained his objection, warning Rosen that he would not let one witness testify to the credibility of another. But it didn't matter: Rosen had made his point, and even if he hadn't, the jury had heard the other half of the odd couple not long before.

So on Rosen went. Yes, George and Harman had gone through the whole story with him before they put it on tape. No, they didn't say they had spoken to their attorney about immunity for him (Rosen immediately pointing out, from the transcript of Frances's preliminary, that Manning had said they had—a fact borne out by the interview itself). No, he didn't recall Frances's or Behrens's name until the investigators reminded him. Yes, he did tell them he thought the meetings with her had taken place in the spring and agreed that, again in Rosen's words, "this whole thing occurred in a rather hazy period." Yes, he did say at the time that the first meeting had been in her apartment and that she had offered him $5,000 (though he later said this was the site of the third meeting and that *he* had come up with the figure at their second meeting).

"At the time?" Rosen said. "At the time you talked to the police was closer in time to the alleged event than now, isn't that correct?"

"Yes."

"Is your memory now, here in 1983, better than it was in 1981?"

"No."

Well, hadn't he told the police that her daughter might have been present at that meeting and that she might have been of an age that she could understand what was going on? Yes, he had. And hadn't he testified at the preliminary that she was either nine or ten? Yes. Did he know now that at the time he claimed he saw her she was only *four* years old? Yes, he did. And hadn't he told the police that Mrs. Schreuder had allegedly told him at the time he received her written instructions—what Rosen called "a road map to murder"—that he was to commit the murder *during the week* and while the man was on his way home? Yes, he had.

Did it make sense, Rosen implied before he sat down, that Behrens had arranged all those meetings with Frances and Manning; that Manning had agreed to go along with Behrens to his father's lake house in New Jersey (knowing of Behrens's fears of being cut out of his father's estate and the purpose of the trip) at the *same* time the meetings were allegedly taking place; and that Manning was now telling the court that, from the fall of 1977 until the night in December 1981 when the Salt Lake City investigators greeted him, he did *not* know that the Bradshaw murder had occurred and did *not* remember the name of the man who had allegedly set up those meetings in the first place?

In the course of a few hours, having brought out nearly every contradictory statement Manning had ever made, plus the ones where his version of things differed from Behrens's, Rosen had not only given the jury a lot to think about but left the state wondering what lasting effect his efforts might have.

On their way out of the courtroom, Fast Eddie informed the press that he and Myles would be across the street, having a few drinks. When court was in recess for the day, he magnanimously offered, why didn't they come over and join them.

As Ernie Jones took a break by letting Dave Walsh question the last two witnesses, the jury got one too, in the form of comic relief. It had been a day for large men, and Jerry Register's three-piece brown suit fit so tightly on his mammoth body that he looked as if he had been poured into it. Though his testimony was brief, the baby-faced officer brought a nervous smile to the faces of some of the jurors when he lovingly held up the .357 Magnum he used to own and explained that "this is the gun that lied to me." The reason it lied, he said in his Texas drawl, was that its serial number—N281919—always confused him. It was a Smith & Wesson N28, but Smith & Wesson also had a model 19, "and I always thought about the 19 as belonging to a different weapon." If he was confused about that, he was not confused about the boy who wound up with it.

While Ed Peterson, the ballistics expert, droned on about lands and grooves and other related matters—things that Behrens claimed Frances once said the police would never be able to prove—Frances seemed far removed from Ernie Baldwin's courtroom. And wherever she was, as someone said of Larry once, no one was there with her.

Later that evening, Bob Lewis, the court reporter, was sitting in the bar of the Marriott, having just delivered that day's transcripts to Mike Rosen's suite. He was just beginning to wind down and rest his fingers when whom should he spot wandering around but Eddie Dean. Lewis, who had become totally absorbed in the drama that he was recording each day, invited Dean to join him. Dean offered to buy and promptly announced that he would be sending the County Attorney's Office "a big bill." Asked about his law practice, Dean said, over a glass of Chivas, that he was "a little one-man band" and wasted no time in giving Lewis his card and an if - you're ever - in - New - York - and - in - trouble - give - me - a - call - you - never - know pitch.

"He made comments," Lewis recalled, "about what a chintzy deal it was—how tight the County Attorney's Office was—this was a real raw deal to have to come out and do this and he thought there should have been something extra. I asked him if he wanted a copy of his client's testimony and he said no, but asked what I charged. I said, 'What the statute says I can.' He said, 'Well, aren't you getting anything under the table for this? Aren't they making it worthwhile?'

"He seemed surprised that I wasn't, and said that back in New York there is always an extra dollar sign, here or there, floating around on this kind of deal." Then Lewis broke into a big smile. "I think Eddie might have been worried that my palm was getting greased and his wasn't."

72// Not only was Frances's trial at the top of the news on television each night, but Judge Baldwin's outrage at Marc's "running around town" had prompted KUTV, the NBC affiliate, to do a story about it, interviewing everyone from the State Corrections Director (who, with the backing of the Governor, had ordered a full investigation) to Mary Lou Kaiser. While the defense had been concerned about the amount of publicity the case had received before the trial began, this was precisely the kind of sidebar stuff (even though the jurors had been warned not to read, listen to, or watch anything) that might work in Frances's favor. As for the trial itself, the headline in Thursday morning's *Salt Lake Tribune*—

> Lawyer Gets
> Tough on
> 2 Witnesses

> Inconsistencies Jar
> Schreuder Trial

—unnecessarily reminded Ernie Jones of what he already knew: it wasn't over until it's over.

The first witness called to the stand on Thursday was Joel Campbell. Before a group of spectators that now included Frank Bradshaw's sister Bertha, who had come from California, the officer began recounting his investigation to the jury—until he got to the sensitive area of his interview with Frances on the day of her father's memorial service. The judge excused the jury so that Rosen could question Campbell and the judge could resolve a matter the defense had hoped he would have ruled on by now. During that July 26, 1978, interview at a certain point, Campbell had asked Frances about her sons' activities in the summer of 1977. He told her that what she said to him would be "strictly confidential," but she responded, "I don't care, they're my sons," and continued on. A few minutes later, the detective raised the question of a new will and Frances said there was one. Rosen's argument was that the confidentiality Campbell promised her extended to *everything* after that point *except* the part about her sons. Jones, still mystified that Campbell had even uttered it, said it didn't, pointing out to the judge that she had been under no obligation to reveal what she knew about her father's estate.

The judge disappeared into chambers to read the transcript of the interview. Five minutes later, he reemerged with his decision: Campbell could testify and the defense would be allowed a continuing objection.

So the jury heard about a new will, and about the man who Frances thought had prepared it—Herman Wood, the accountant who had set up F & B. Asked if he had spoken with Mr. Wood, Campbell said that Wood had died. But what the jury didn't hear was that Wood was alive at the time of Franklin Bradshaw's death and that neither he nor any lawyer in Salt Lake City had a copy of what had become the most famous missing will in the state of Utah. Assuming there even was one.

On cross-examination, Rosen instantly zeroed in on one of the many reasons Ernie Jones had sent out a cry of help in April of 1981 for Mike George. Richard Behrens had testified that he told Marilyn Reagan about a hit man named Myles. But when Rosen asked Campbell if she had mentioned that to him in an interview on October 27, 1980, he said he couldn't recall whether she had or not. Nor, when he looked, could he find it anywhere in his police reports. But wasn't he working very closely with Marilyn? Rosen probed. Yes, he was. He received photos of Marc and Frances from her (the ones he took to Midland, Texas) and a set of keys she had found at Gilmer Drive—keys that fit not only one of the padlocks Doug Steele found unlocked that Sunday morning, but Bradshaw's file cabinet as well. He spoke with Marilyn thirty to forty times, he admitted, but did not recall her telling him about a hit man.

Though Rosen was not able to prevent Frances's statement about a new will from coming out, he had at least managed to start another fire of doubt—and to arouse the jury's curiosity for Marilyn's appearance later that day.

Dave Salisbury took the witness stand next, telling the jury that he was the lawyer who had prepared Franklin Bradshaw's 1970 will and trusts; that he had had at least one "fairly lengthy" phone conversation with Frances about her parents' estate planning (but none with either of her sisters); and that he had received a letter from her after that—the one dated July 3, 1976, which Jones asked him to identify. But when the prosecutor moved to admit it into evidence, the judge and Rosen blocked his path. Baldwin wanted to examine it first and Rosen felt that would be a splendid idea.

The next lawyer to walk into the courtroom had not wanted to appear at all. His name was not on the original list of potential witnesses but had been added during the summer, added after Jones persuaded him, with case law, that the attorney-client privilege didn't necessarily exist after the client had died. But the prosecutor would still have to convince the judge that Alma Boyce could tell the court about the visit Frank Bradshaw had made to his office on a hot August day in 1977.

Married to a Bradshaw, the seventy-year-old, silver-haired attorney looked like an eminent head of state. Speaking in a measured, lawyerlike way, he told the jury that he had known Bradshaw for thirty-five years—as his client and someone he saw at family gatherings. Rosen had informed the judge long before that anything Boyce might testify to would be hearsay, and he now rose to object vehemently to every question Jones asked. The judge allowed Boyce to reveal that Bradshaw had come by to discuss his estate and will. Asked if he had made any suggestions to his client about making changes in that will, Boyce said that *he* had not; the *only* suggestion he had made was that Bradshaw, because of the size and nature of his estate, needed "real expertise" in this area.

"Was there any discussion with him about the changes that he wanted to make . . . ?"

"Yes, at the very beginning of our conversation he named some specific changes that he wanted or specific terms that he wanted in a new will."

But when Jones asked him what those changes were and if

they affected any of the beneficiaries, Baldwin drew the hard line Rosen had hoped he would take. Boyce could not answer that; and, as far as the judge was concerned, the *only* two beneficiaries in that will were Berenice Bradshaw and the Walker Bank and Trust Company. Period. Over and out. Jones had run into a brick wall. Baldwin had heard the prosecutor's argument before—that it went to "state of mind" and that the change of a will was an exception to hearsay; the judge had rejected it then and was rejecting it now.

After Rosen offered no cross-examination, Jones, helpless in his desire to have the jury hear that Bradshaw had told Boyce he wanted to cut Frances out of the family trust, did manage to elicit this: upon hearing Boyce's recommendation that he see someone else, Bradshaw had said that he would see Herman Wood.

Before the afternoon session began, the jury was, as they had been on Tuesday, kept out of the courtroom at the defense's request. Before Nancy Jones and Doug Steele took the stand, Rosen wanted to get some idea of the judge's position on the two memos he knew the prosecutor would seek to introduce into evidence. Baldwin said that he would expect the state first to lay the kind of foundation that showed Frances *knew* about them. Jones said he couldn't do that in any direct way, but insisted there was strong circumstantial evidence already offered—by Marc and Behrens—that implied she knew about the changes her father intended to make. Besides, he said, the "state of mind" exception to hearsay (which had worked at Marc's trial) did not say anything about *proving* the defendant knew about the changes. But once again the judge fell on the side of the defense: if she wasn't in the will to begin with, how could she be cut out of it?

Jones shook his head dejectedly as the jury returned and Nancy Jones was called.

On direct examination, in her plain-spoken style, Nancy told the jury everything she had told Judge Sawaya the year before; but when the prosecutor asked her about State's Exhibits 15 and 16 she might as well have been talking

Serbo-Croatian for all that the jury learned about the content of those memos.

Doug Steele followed Nancy into the courtroom and confirmed Ernie Jones's opening-statement description of Bradshaw as a man who worked seven days a week and as much as fifteen hours a day. But, Steele said, to many a raised eyebrow, "sometimes on Sunday he would knock off and go home early—at seven or six-thirty."

Like Nancy, Steele recited much of the same chapter and verse he had at Marc's trial about the summer of 1977. He described the relationship between Frances and her father as "very strained" and said that in the last few months before he died they weren't speaking at all. In approaching the memos with Steele, Jones cleverly asked if Steele had ever seen Bradshaw working on a will. Yes, he had. And while Jones was not able to have Steele explain what the memos were, Steele was able to say he had been given copies of them at the warehouse and that Bradshaw had asked him for a ride downtown that same day.

"Did you take him to see an attorney named Alma Boyce?"

"He didn't tell me the attorney's name."

"Objection. I move to strike that kind of question," Rosen seethed. "Mr. Jones is really putting some testimony in evidence there about Alma Boyce. That is just not fair, Your Honor. I move to strike the answer."

"We have the answer," Judge Baldwin said. "He does not have any idea and I told the jury before and I will tell you again—what lawyers state are *not* facts."

But Jones was like a wild stallion who had bolted from the barn. He had to get something—*anything*—in about Steele's conversation with Bradshaw to enlighten the jury.

"Do you remember what you would have said to him about the documents?"

"You really mean it, don't you?" Steele reported to the perplexed jury, before court adjourned for a short recess.

Before Doug Steele left the stand and went out in the hall, Ernie Jones and Mike George huddled with him in animated conversation. Ten minutes later, with everyone back in his seat, Jones told the judge he had one more question before cross-examination.

"Mr. Steele, you mentioned before we broke that you had had a conversation or a meeting with Frank Bradshaw concerning State's Exhibits 15 and 16."

"Yes."

"You recall what your first comment to him was concerning those documents?"

Rosen said it had been asked and answered and the judge agreed.

"My question is," Jones said without breaking stride, "was there *another* statement that you made after that initial statement?"

"Yes. I asked him, 'Are you really going to cut her out of your will? Do you really mean it?'"

Rosen could hardly get the words "We move to strike, Judge" out of his mouth he was so enraged by the state's tactics. And though the answer was stricken, the question Rosen asked later, on his way out of the courtroom, perfectly characterized the helpless feeling any lawyer would have had in that situation: "How do you unring a bell?"

If a smart prosecutor often thinks of himself as a stage director of a repertory company as well as an actor, it's because, in a sense, he is. The success of his case can depend on the order in which his witnesses appear. Marc's decision to testify and Jones's to put him on immediately had caused the prosecutor to shuffle his lineup. So it wasn't until Wednesday that Marilyn Reagan found out that she was to fly to Salt Lake on Thursday morning and testify on Friday. But when she arrived—without her suitcase—the state had decided to put her on the stand Thursday afternoon.

By the time Marilyn walked into the courtroom, wearing a pair of white earrings she had borrowed from a cousin, the jury had heard all about her, as if she had been a play or movie that had received controversial reviews and that they were finally getting a chance to see.

As Jones took Marilyn through the paces, continuing to fit the pieces of his intricate puzzle together, Frances fixed a stony glare on her oldest sister and kept it there. At Marc's trial, Marilyn had said she *hadn't* known the content of her father's will before he died, but she now admitted she did. Of

State's Exhibits 15 and 16, which Jones shamelessly refused to give up on, she said—as she had the year before—that she hadn't seen 15 (the one that cut Frances out) until *after* her father died, when she was at the warehouse with Elaine sorting through his papers. She corroborated Behrens's testimony that he had originally told her *Frances* gave him the gun (before he told Joel Campbell otherwise) and said that she had asked him, when they had a hot drink at the Burger King on the night of October 16, if Marc had said anything about killing her father and that Behrens had said, "Yes. He said he did it, and it was easy." As far as learning about a hit man, Marilyn's story changed slightly from the year before: At Marc's trial, she said that while the subject had come up *before* she got the gun from Behrens, she had not told Campbell about it until afterward and that when she tried to get the name out of Behrens (she had not written it down when he first mentioned it), he wouldn't give it to her; she now said that she learned about the hit man *after* she got the gun, and couldn't remember whether it was Joel Campbell or Mike George who had asked her to try to get his name.

As years go by, memories fade, naturally or purposefully, and no one was better equipped to exploit a witness's "loss" of that faculty than Mike Rosen. Like a spurned lover seeking revenge, he had been lying in wait for Marilyn for quite some time.

After establishing that she too had received financial help from her father over the years (for her education), Rosen asked if she recalled testifying on her sister's behalf while Frances was going through her divorce with Vittorio Gentile. Yes, she did. And had she described to the court that he had beat her. Yes, she had.

Given her familiarity with legal matters, estates and trusts, had she ever discussed various financial arrangements with her father? No, she hadn't. His insurance policies with him? No. Had she ever *written* to him about estate planning and insurance programs? She didn't remember.

That's why Rosen was there, bringing out a letter she had written which asked who the beneficiaries of his life-insurance policy were. But this was mere window dressing for the main subject on Mike Rosen's mind—her father's will: what exactly she had known about it, and when.

As she had to Jones a few moments before, she admitted that she knew the contents of the will and understood "most of it." She had discussed its terms with her mother and father, but didn't remember the details of her discussion with him.

Rosen promptly turned to testimony she had given at Marc's trial, where she had been asked if there had been any discussion concerning the terms of his will and had replied, "That was his business"; and if she wasn't concerned with what those terms might be and had answered, "I was sure he was going to leave everything to Mother, which is what he did." Had she given those answers? he wanted to know. Yes, she had. And had there been any discussions with anyone about the *changing* of her father's will? Yes, there had. But Rosen once more went back to her previous testimony and showed the jury that her answer had been just the opposite.

He then brought out a letter Marilyn had written in April of 1976 to Frances and Elaine, telling them of a trip she had made to Salt Lake and her feeling she was in a good position to offer their parents advice about taxes and estate planning. As for the lease she had taken out on office space, she said, it had been "for the purpose of helping Mother manage her affairs"—not because she wanted to take things over.

This wasn't the only side of Marilyn that Rosen wanted the jury to see: there was the Marilyn in frequent contact with Behrens and Joel Campbell; the persistent go-between who had given the detective the serial number of the gun, the note on Kent stationery with Dr. Cavenaugh's name and address, and the pictures of Marc and Frances—yet who inexplicably had *not* given Campbell the information about Frances's alleged attempt to hire a hit man until much later, even though she admitted Behrens had mentioned it several times *before* he gave her the gun. (On direct, she said she hadn't learned about a hit man until afterward, but returned to her original story now.) And there was also the Marilyn who said she didn't remember complaining in March of 1981 about the state's handling of her father's murder—until Rosen pulled out a copy of the letter she had sent to the two newspapers (with copies to various authorities) and the judge read out the line that said, "The murder weapon has been recovered and directly connected to the victim's grandson."

When Rosen sat down, his cross-examination had left two more things for the jury to grapple with: If Marilyn had heard about a hit man from Behrens, why hadn't she told Campbell right away? And if (as she said on direct and Behrens testified) Behrens had told her Frances gave him the gun, why was there no mention of her sister in her letter of complaint?

On re-direct, Jones quickly brought out that Marilyn's knowledge of Frances's "beatings" had come from Frances and that "the only time I ever saw any indication of physical abuse was one time when she came to my house she had a red mark on her cheek and a red mark on her arm" (a statement she altered later in an interview). And then he tried to puncture one of those mystery balloons that Rosen had deliberately left hanging in the air.

"When Mr. Behrens first told you about a possible hit man, did you take that statement seriously?"

She had earlier mentioned what a chatterbox he was, and now, over Rosen's objection, she answered no.

"Well, when did you first start to take Mr. Behrens's comments about the murder seriously?"

"When I found out he had the gun," she calmly replied.

If this was the first and last time Mike Rosen and Marilyn Reagan would ever meet, he was going to make certain that she wouldn't forget him.

"You told Mr. Jones about seeing some red marks on Frances and *that* is how you knew she was in some kind of difficulty with Gentile," he asked on re-cross. "Remember telling him that a few minutes ago?"

"That and what she told me, yes."

"Didn't you tell the Supreme Court, New York County"—he stepped closer, waving the 1963 affidavit in front of her—"that your sister appeared at your home severely beaten and her face disfigured?"

Instead of her answer came something between a laugh and a strange cackle.

"I don't know what is so funny, Mrs. Reagan. *Didn't* you?"

"The semantics," she said, in answering his first question.

"Mrs. Reagan, I show you what the court has allowed to be marked as Defendant's Exhibit 53 and I ask you whether that is your signature on that affidavit."

"Yes, it is."

As Rosen angrily packed his briefcases and everyone began to quietly file out, Frances remained in her seat, shaking and crying. Through four days of testimony she had seen her son, her ex-husband, her friend, and now her hated sister parading past her. There had been photographs of her murdered father, checks that the state said she had forged, memos they implied she had known about, a letter she had written, and much more. Putting his hand on her back, John Lang did what he could to comfort her—and so, that evening, would somebody else.

73// When Frances was at East High School one of her closest friends was Monika Weber, who moved with her parents to Salt Lake City in 1954 and later became Monika Clyde, a professor at Mills College in Oakland, California, the woman whom Frances had listed at the Salt Lake jail the year before as the one to notify in case of emergency, and the driver of the silver Mercedes that day in February when it stopped in front of Sam Drukman's house in Berkeley. Monika's father, Fred Weber, was a German POW who was held in Utah from 1943 to 1946 and decided that he liked the state so much he came back with his family eight years later and became a Mormon—a decision that changed his life. "Before converting," he said with a rich German accent and winning smile, "the only thing I believed for sure was that three pounds of meat made a good broth."

Tragedy was not unknown to Fred Weber—he had a daughter die of diphtheria at nineteen months—and one of the many things he now believed was that if someone cried out for help, it was his duty "to stretch my hand out" to that person.

So when Monika phoned her father to say that Frances had

called her and said she was feeling "all alone," Fred Weber had no hesitation about rushing down to the Marriott to see what he could do. He hadn't seen Frances since she and Monika were teenagers at East High together, and the middle-aged woman he now saw was "scared to death."

He invited Frances to his home for dinner that Thursday night and she accepted. She ate well and talked nonstop for nearly four hours. She told the Webers that she was innocent, that she had never wanted her father killed ("I couldn't be that stupid to expose myself to this sort of thing," she said), and that one of her sisters had said that she was the ugliest girl she had ever seen.

When Weber drove her back to the hotel late that evening, Frances asked if he could stop while she bought some cigarettes. He did, and moments later she came out of Albertson's with four cartons.

"If the state rests today, we're going to rest," Mike Rosen said on his way into court the next morning, implying that he was not going to put Frances on the stand nor call any witnesses. As far as the buoyant attorney was concerned, the state had not proved its case—and he was not alone in that conviction.

Instead of beginning at ten in open court, the morning's proceedings started in the privacy of Judge Baldwin's chambers. Ernie Jones wanted to call Steve Klein to the stand and Mike Rosen was citing all of the reasons the judge shouldn't allow that to happen. If Klein had been flown out here just to tell the jury that Mrs. Schreuder had tried to throw herself out a window, he said, *none* of what he would say was probative of what she was charged with and was highly inflammatory and prejudicial besides. Jones argued there was case law that supported the theory that a defendant's actions at the time of arrest "may be relevant to the question of consciousness of guilt." After a few more minutes of listening to their highly charged exchange, the judge said he would let Klein testify.

The second matter to be dealt with was Berenice Bradshaw. Her lawyer informed the judge that both sides had agreed that she need not appear as a witness and that the only testimony to be offered would be her recollection—excerpted from her testimony at Marc's trial—of what time both she and Larry got up that Sunday morning.

In open court, the judge read aloud the testimony of Berenice Bradshaw, and then Ernie Jones called Steve Klein to the stand. With a stern preface by Rosen that he was objecting to Klein's entire testimony, the jury heard the bearded investigator proceed, step by step, through Frances's dramatic arrest, telling them that once he heard Lavinia yell, "I ran into the room with my partner, past Officer Cimler, and observed Mrs. Schreuder attempting to jump out of the window of her bedroom. Lavinia was holding on to her one leg. The other leg and a portion of her torso and arms were out the window. I grabbed Mrs. Schreuder and my partner, Cruz, grabbed Lavinia and we pulled [Frances] back into the room, put her on the bed and handcuffed her. That was at about ten-twenty a.m."

Rosen wasted little time in trying to fill in what he felt the investigator had left out of his story.

"Did you see with your own eyes police officers in Mrs. Schreuder's bedroom with guns on her and Lavinia . . . ?"

"No, sir."

"Are you telling us that didn't happen?"

"Yes, sir."

Three more times, louder each time, Rosen asked in his most disbelieving voice if that was the investigator's testimony to the judge and the jury under oath. Yes, it was, Klein said testily. After a few questions about whether he knew the housekeeper was French and might not have understood the meaning of the word "detective," Rosen asked him if he carried a gun.

"At this moment?"

"Not at this moment. In your official duties."

"Yes, I do."

"You carry a gun?"

"Yes, sir. I am a police officer."

"Well, that is what I asked you. As a police officer, New York City police officer, is there not a regulation that when police officers enter an area to effectuate a felony arrest that they have their weapons drawn?"

He wasn't a New York City police officer, he told the jury,

but an investigator with the Manhattan District Attorney's Office. He didn't know what the police department's regulations were. Though he and the other officers were carrying weapons that morning, *no* weapons were drawn, he said on re-direct, because he didn't see any reason to do so.

Perhaps it was fitting that Ernie Jones's last witness was the thirty-one-year-old investigator who had lived with this case nearly as long as he had—and without whom there might never have been a case at all. Mike George had shaved off his beard for the trial—when he worked narcotics he used to wear his hair nearly to his shoulders—and as he took the witness stand now he was prepared to give the jury the big picture, to tie together whatever loose strands of evidence still remained, and to corroborate, if possible, what other witnesses had said. He especially tried to clear up the confusion about Myles Manning, explaining that Manning's recollection he had gone to the YMCA—and George's finding of that receipt—helped Manning remember the meetings had taken place in the fall, not in the spring as he had originally said.

On cross-examination, after Jones introduced bank records that Mike George had found to show Frances's deposit of the forged 1977 checks into her account, Rosen wanted to continue about Manning. Hadn't Manning told him he could pinpoint his meetings with Frances to the opening of the Palace restaurant in New York four or five months earlier? Yes, he had. As soon as George acknowledged that, Rosen held two pieces of paper triumphantly in the air and asked Judge Baldwin to take judicial notice of them: an article in the *New York Times* on June 8, 1975, and one in *New York* magazine on April 20, 1975, about the Palace, *more than two years before* Manning was now saying he had met with Frances.

But Rosen wasn't through.

"Sergeant, remember talking to Mr. Manning about some money that he said he got from Mrs. Schreuder?"

"Yes, sir."

Money in small bills? Yes. Had he heard Mr. Manning testify in court? Yes. Had Manning ever told him that the money he supposedly got from Mrs. Schreuder he took to the

673

bank? No. So once more, Rosen reached into his bag and showed Mike George what he had found: the investigator's notes, obtained through discovery, that showed the words "Took money to the bank" right after he wrote down about the $5,000 in fives and tens. George said it was *not* in reference to that (*if only it were,* he thought, *because they had not been able to isolate the $5,000 Frances had given Manning from other withdrawals she made*) and that it was a mistake on his part.

On re-direct, George explained that the reason his notes were in error was that Manning was talking about *Mrs. Schreuder* going to the bank and that he had recorded it incorrectly. "At no time did Mr. Manning tell me he had taken the money to the bank."

On re-cross, in his best Mike Wallace style, Rosen asked, "Are you telling us, Sergeant George, that the note you made that read 'five thousand dollars cash, fives and tens—took money to the bank' really means *Frances* took money *from* the bank? Is that what you are telling us?"

"That is correct," George said without hesitation, "and it refers to the statement [transcript of Manning's interview] which will bear it out."

With that ball (and others, Rosen hoped) perhaps still in the air, there was no further testimony to be heard.

Before the jury was excused until the following Tuesday morning at nine, when they would hear closing arguments and be asked to render a verdict, Judge Baldwin had some things he wanted to say. At the request of the defense, he revealed the additional part of the agreement Marc had made with the County Attorney's Office. He admonished them once more to turn the other cheek to any press accounts of the case ("they are not trained as lawyers and I don't understand the press"). And he promised them they wouldn't have "to brown-bag it" on Tuesday. They would be given "one good meal," if not two.

After lunch on Friday, the lawyers gathered again to resolve some things before each side submitted a list of jury instructions. Baldwin had told them before lunch that he was

674

thoroughly exhausted—"I have been working without purse or script"—and he looked it.

Jones wanted certain materials admitted into evidence and Rosen fought him tooth and nail: phone records in 1977 from the warehouse to Frances's number in New York, corroborating Marc's testimony that he was in touch with his mother regularly (admitted); Behrens's lawsuit against Frances (just the joint bank account attached to it); some of Frances's petitions for a family allowance that stated her complete dependence on her father for financial support (admitted); and the fifteen-page letter Frances had written to Dave Salisbury in 1976 that showed her knowledge of the 1970 will and her concern that Marilyn would convince him to change it (Baldwin reiterated that he wanted to read the letter and then decide).

And the day wouldn't be complete if Jones didn't try, once more, to slip those memos past a tired judge. But Baldwin's fatigue did not prevent him from telling the prosecutor, "I haven't one scintilla of evidence that any reasonable person could believe that she knew *anything* about those two pieces of paper." And try as he might—repeating his argument that even if she didn't *know* of them directly, she certainly *thought*, based on what Marc and Behrens had testified, she was to be disinherited—Jones could not persuade the judge to let them in. Once Ernie Baldwin dug in his heels, very little under heaven was going to move him.

When it was Rosen's turn to speak, he asked that the charges against Frances be dismissed for the following reason. Citing a 1978 Utah law that said one accomplice could not corroborate the testimony of another, Rosen argued that both Behrens and Manning fit into that category and could not corroborate Marc. At this stage of the proceedings, he said, the proof of guilt must be beyond a reasonable doubt, "independent of accomplice testimony."

Jones's argument—aside from his uncertainty whether the 1978 law or the one that replaced it a year later, which said a conviction *could* be obtained with the *uncorroborated* testimony of an accomplice, was applicable—was this: Behrens was *not* an accomplice. What Utah had granted him immunity for was hiding the murder weapon—not the things he had done before the murder. Simply knowing a murder was about to be committed, he said, did *not* make him an accomplice. While he had introduced Frances to Manning, Manning had never carried out the crime, nor had Behrens gotten any of the $5,000; nor, for that matter, had Behrens been successful in obtaining a gun for Frances. But even if the judge found that Behrens was an accomplice, Jones went on, there was the evidence of Manning and Gentile which "tends to connect her to the crime."

And that, it so happened, was Baldwin's feeling, though he qualified his opinion about Behrens by saying it *appeared* he was an accomplice without actually committing himself.

Having failed in that effort, Rosen ended everyone's afternoon by climbing aboard his favorite hobbyhorse: "pecuniary gain" and his desire to have it dropped from the charge. Since the judge had already found that Frances was not an immediate beneficiary of the will and Jones's position was that even if she wasn't she was afraid of being cut off from funds, Rosen said "it defies all logic" that she would kill the very person who would send her that money.

Jones countered that the evidence showed Frances knew that it was much easier to get money from her mother—and that by killing her father, even if *everything* went to Berenice, "she knew her chances of inheriting part of that fortune were much better . . ."

Rosen could barely contain himself from laughing at the state's "new theory"—that Frances hadn't killed for *her* pecuniary gain, but for her mother's—and saying how absurd it was. "Her mother already had money and was supporting her for years, according to Mr. Jones, so how can we have four sides to the same coin?"

Baldwin said they couldn't. "I have not one shred of evidence," he told an astonished Jones, "that she had the ability to manipulate her mother that you seem to indicate is your theory." If Mrs. Bradshaw had wanted to, he said, she could have given all her money to "some guru sitting on a mountain in Egypt"—a remark that made Frances laugh.

He said he would drop the word "pecuniary" from the charge and submit the case to the jury on personal gain alone—with this caveat: he felt pecuniary and personal gain were one and the same.

After a denial of two more motions for mistrial, based on the comments by Alma Boyce and Doug Steele which Rosen felt were improperly elicited, Baldwin said he would see the lawyers privately on Monday to go over the final instructions.

74// Nobody raced to the courthouse on Tuesday morning faster than Berenice did. Since the trial began she had sat, with the blinds drawn, in her little house on the East Bench, reading the local papers, watching the news on television, and getting telephone bulletins at the end of the day on who had said what about Frances—and about her. She had been frustrated by not being allowed to attend; no such barrier remained to her on judgment day, and she wanted to find out if these New York lawyers had been worth the money she had paid them.

Outside the courtroom she was approached by Bertha Beck. Bertha had been in Salt Lake for nearly a week and had not been able to decide whether to phone the woman she had known for sixty years. But she had dialed Berenice's number by mistake the night before, and as soon as Berenice realized it was Bertha, she said, "You weren't going to call me, were you?" Bertha said that was true, because she didn't know what to say.

As they stood there now, joined by Bertha's daughter and another Bradshaw woman by marriage, Berenice was holding forth about the trial (and the coverage it was receiving all across the country), Frances's lawyers ("they have cost me a million") and lawyers in general (pointing out that there were so many in America, "surely a couple will starve to death").

As the million-dollar defense team walked into court, John Lang was not with them. His daughter had suddenly become ill and he had to fly back to New York to be by her side. Without the one lawyer who was able to comfort her, Frances grimly asked her mother, who was dressed in black, to sit right behind the defense table, and then tried to make eye contact with each juror as he or she took his seat.

For Ernie Jones and Mike Rosen, wearing the same gray suits they had worn on the first day of testimony, the spotlight was on them, on their final opportunity to persuade the jury of Frances's guilt or innocence. Day after day, the two lawyers had scrapped like alley cats—the lanky farmboy from Idaho and the streetwise kid from Brooklyn, a long way from home—and if there was only *one* thing they could both agree upon it was this: their affection for each other had done anything but grow in the ten months since they had first met at Frances's preliminary hearing.

As Judge Baldwin solemnly read the thirty-nine instructions to the jury—a copy of which each member had—he told them that they must return with a unanimous verdict and offered three options: *guilty of murder in the first degree* (that Frances Bernice Schreuder, intentionally or knowingly, solicited, requested, commanded, encouraged, or aided Marc Schreuder to cause the death of Franklin Bradshaw for pecuniary or other personal gain—the judge having decided, finally, to leave "pecuniary" in, but saying that the defendant's hope for such must be the *cause,* not the *result,* of the murder); *guilty of murder in the second degree* (if the jury found the aggravating circumstance of pecuniary or other personal gain did not exist); and *not guilty.* The instructions explained, among other things, about accomplices (it did not state Behrens was one, because Baldwin had told Rosen the day before that his comment on Friday about Behrens was not a ruling), and weight of testimony, and that no prejudice could be shown toward Frances just because she had exercised her right not to take the stand, and, finally and definitively, that she did not inherit from the will.

Ernie Jones would address the jury first, then Rosen, and then, because it was the state's burden, Jones would speak to them once more before they, the sole and final judges of the facts, would be locked in a room in order to decide Frances's fate.

Before a packed courtroom that included not only his wife, who had attended each day, but his mother as well, Ernie Jones approached the jury—that jury (except one) of fathers and mothers, grandfathers and grandmothers—as a father himself, as a neighborly Utahn, as someone who wanted them to think long and hard about *why* a seventeen-year-old boy would kill his grandfather. Because that was *the* issue in the case, he said. They had heard so much about the background of the Bradshaw family and the friction that was always there—there because of Frances. "Frances, Frances, Frances," he repeated, as if the jury could possibly forget, "did not get along with her father.... The topic or the subject of that friction was always the same thing: money. Money for Frances Schreuder." They had heard about it from Marilyn, from Marc, from Nancy Jones, and Doug Steele; "all of these people gave you the same story and the same information." They had heard "about the problems and the turmoil" Marc experienced growing up—not only from Marc himself but from Dr. Moench (a man, he stressed, with *forty years'* experience): being locked out, beaten with a belt for bad grades, "having her thumb on him day and night," and dealing with his mother's suicide threats and hysterical behavior. "Can *you* imagine," he asked them, "the turmoil and the trauma in a young boy seeing his mother try to commit suicide because things aren't going her way? This was something that Marc Schreuder had to live with as a child. *This* kind of family. *This* kind of background." He stressed Moench's comments about Marc being "the junior partner" in the murder and his diagnosis of Marc as someone suffering from an Oedipus complex and involved in a "sick" relationship with his mother—one that had gone on with "tremendous intensity" (Jones's words) for far too long and was far too "distorted" for a seventeen-year-old boy.

He meticulously went through nearly every reason, nearly everything they'd heard, as to why they should see, beyond a reasonable doubt, that money—Frances's fear of not having it, her desire to obtain it, her hope that she would inherit, as Marc had said, a great deal of it—was the motive behind the murder. "Was there a new will?" he asked, reminding them that Frances had told Joel Campbell that. "Or was this simply a figment of her own imagination? You know that in this case there has been no evidence that an actual new will has been prepared—at least none has been offered in evidence—but Frances thought ... her father had written a new will and that is important because we are talking about her intentions."

He recreated the summer of 1977—Marc and Larry's thefts totaling $200,000, her instructions to them to kill, the blank checks she'd forged and deposited (and the bank records to prove it), her sons' frequent contact with her by phone (and the phone records from the warehouse to prove it), the photographs Marc took that his mother later gave to Manning, Bradshaw's anger at all that happened—and took them chronologically from there up to the day of the murder itself; the stashing of the gun with Behrens ("a man she could trust"); their joint bank account and her withdrawals from it; Behrens's conversations with Marilyn and his ultimately turning the gun over to her on the night of October 16; Behrens's statement to Campbell on December 3, 1980, and why his fear of involving Frances had prevented him from saying she, not Marc, had given him the gun (even though he did tell Campbell that she and Marc had asked him about obtaining one); her insistence that Behrens change his statement to Marc's Connecticut lawyers; his ultimately telling Mike George about Frances's giving him the gun and about Manning; Manning's identification of her photograph and his description of their meetings; and, finally, her dramatic arrest three months later.

It had been a difficult case to solve, he assured them, especially since "Frances was so successful in manipulating people, so successful in hiding the evidence. But she had one flaw. She double-crossed Richard Behrens over thirty-seven hundred dollars. Marc said she could have paid him back. She had the money to pay him back but she wouldn't, because that's the way Frances is. Behrens struck back. He couldn't get his money so finally he started to leak information and finally he turned over the gun. But by then it was too late. Richard Behrens was trying to give us just a little information, but he went too far . . . to turn back. He tried to change his story, he tried to hold back, but it was too late. Once he gave us the gun, our foot was in the door and we knew that some of the things he told us were true. And we knew some of the things he said were not true.

"Members of the jury, I submit to you that after hearing all of the evidence and all of the testimony, that the evidence is there, that Frances Schreuder did mastermind this murder. I'm not asking you to rest your verdict on the testimony of

Marc Schreuder. Judge Baldwin told you that you cannot convict in a case like this on the testimony of an accomplice. But the instruction says that if there is other evidence, evidence that tends to corroborate, evidence which tends to connect the defendant to the crime, then you can convict. You cannot convict on the testimony of Marc alone, but there is so much evidence in this case that tells you that Marc Schreuder is telling the truth.

"When he walked into this court last Monday and took the stand . . . how difficult it must have been to testify against his own mother, how hard it was. But he told you, 'I killed Franklin Bradshaw. But I did it because my mother told me to.' He said, 'You just don't tell my mother no.' "

Jones was finished—for now. Before Mike Rosen began, Frances went over to Berenice, who began to cry as she reached up to hold her daughter's head in her hands. All of their hopes for an acquittal, for a chance to end their long nightmare, rested on the shoulders of Michael Rosen and in the expectation he would give the closing argument of his life.

Like a genial master of ceremonies, Rosen began by thanking the jury—and practically everyone else—for being as attentive as they had been. But that was where the pleasantries stopped. The last thing he remembered the prosecutor telling them was that "you can't say no to Frances." Well, didn't Marc say no in the summer of 1977 when he was sent out to Salt Lake supposedly to kill his grandfather? If he could kill his grandfather, Rosen suggested, he could kill his mother. Did they remember his asking them, during jury selection, if they believed that a seventeen-year-old boy could do something like this on his own? And that each of them had said he would keep an open mind that such a thing was possible, and had taken "a very serious oath" to come back with a verdict consistent with the evidence?

He had asked them to be patient at the beginning of the trial and, because "this is my last chance, and more important," he said, gesturing toward Frances, "this is Frances's last chance," he was asking them to be patient now. Holding up a stack of transcripts in each hand, he emphatically reminded them that *this* is the record in this case. . . . This is what this trial is all about . . . not what is in Ernie Jones's theories or Mike Rosen's theories"—but what the proof showed or did not show. If he had offended anybody by jumping up and down or yelling, he wanted to apologize. "If you want to take it out on me later, fine. Don't take it out on Frances. And I also want to apologize if, during the trial, Frances has been mumbling and saying things to John Lang or Kevin and myself and maybe the whispers carry too far, you can imagine the pressure she's sitting under there right now. Don't take it out on her."

Highly intelligent. Calculating. Headstrong. Didn't have an ounce of compassion. As cold as could be. Said it was *easy* to kill his grandfather. These were the things *witnesses* had revealed about Marc, Rosen reminded them—not him, not Ernie Jones—and they were still being asked to believe he had *cried* the night he said he called his mother from Salt Lake? Was this "some little robot" who went off to Kent School, a hundred miles from Frances, an honor student during 1977 and 1978 and before that at Allen-Stevenson, and then came out to Salt Lake to kill because his mother told him to? Was this what the state was asking them to believe, that he was "some little jerk who just obeys his mother's order to pull the trigger"? For someone with a stock brokerage account where he bought and sold securities ("ten thousand dollars at a clip"), a guy who dealt in rare coins ("at seventeen thousand dollars a pop") and had safe-deposit boxes and joint accounts (none of which were with his mother), were they really being asked to think of him, "as we call them on the East Coast," as "some little nebbish"?

"After Frances probably beat him for four years until he got accepted to college," Rosen said sarcastically, look what he had done. He had broken into the Kent School store "twice, not once . . . and he busts up the place," stealing "pens and sneakers and things like that." So he had had to sit out a year. "You don't think his mother would be mad? Hey, he blew his chance to go to college. . . . Self-destructive, irrational, and very, very bright. This is the little dummy that walks around with a pistol and blows his grandfather away because 'My mommy told me to do it.' Everything he said here, 'My mommy told me to do it. My mommy got the plane reservations, she gave me the name of a hotel.' *If he could kill his grandfather, he could kill his mother.*"

Didn't it just "knock the hat right out of [Mr. Jones's] argument that he obeys his mother," when he and Larry had supposedly been sent out in the summer of 1977 with instructions to kill and hadn't? "I mean, why didn't he kill in '77? You mean the amphetamines weren't strong enough?. . . What you have to do is crack one open, put it in the oatmeal, there goes Grandpa. He was afraid of not being able to come home? 'Oh my God, I better put the amphetamines in the oatmeal or I can't go home.'"

So where was he at the end of that summer? "He was at Dragon Hall, at home, at the beach. He was home with his mother. *Grounds for reasonable doubt,*" he intoned, a refrain the jury would hear over and over, *"grounds for reasonable doubt."*

But then he asked them to consider another of the state's theories—that Frances was so afraid of losing her inheritance she told her boys that if they couldn't kill their grandfather they should steal from him. "Wouldn't Frances Schreuder tell these boys, 'Look, fellows, you go out to Utah and just be so nice to Grandma and Grandpa because that's where it's all going to come from,' because if Frances tells them to come out here and act like the animals that they are, she knows for sure she's out of the ballgame." *Grounds for reasonable doubt.*

Like a traveling clothing salesman showing his fall line, Rosen asked them to consider these possibilities from his display case: since Frances knew her father, maybe she sent her sons out to Salt Lake with the idea that "a little hard work and a little more reality would straighten these kids out. Not a bad place to send some kids from New York. . . . Is that being a terrible mother?"

The $10,000 checks: Marc said they were sent to his mother blank, but why didn't the state say they had done a handwriting analysis that could prove the signature on the *front* was Frances's? Maybe it was Berenice's?

Marc and Myles Manning: Marc said he heard about Manning from his mother at Dragon Hall in late August or early September (he had said September), but everyone else had testified "this Manning thing" was in October, early November. "Don't you see they need somebody? They need somebody to back up Marc and . . . they are going to need somebody to back up Behrens and that is Manning. . . . It's an attempt to link Frances into this and that is what Mr. Jones did."

The phone call Marc said he made to his mother the night before the murder: if Mike George was able to obtain a 1977 phone bill from the warehouse to New York, where was the phone bill showing the collect call Marc said he made? "See," he told the jury, *"that* is corroboration and that is what they don't have. . . . Show me the call and I will sit down."

Behrens as accomplice: Rosen recited all the reasons he felt "Uncle Dickie" fit that definition and reminded them that if they viewed him that way, "then he can't back up Marc and Marc can't back up him."

The plane ticket for L. Gentile: Why would Frances put Larry's name on the plane ticket "if she wants to avoid, as Mr. Jones said, all connections with the crime? . . . Put Mike Rosen. Put Joe Blow. . . . Oh, I know it was Gentile, but you mean no one has ever heard of Gentile, Vittorio Gentile? This wouldn't come back to Frances Schreuder? . . . *That* is the mastermind we have here?" Jones was asking them to believe Marc, he said, when it had been *Marc's* idea—Marc, who had turned in his brother for stealing auto parts and who resented Larry's being back in Salt Lake in 1978 and getting flying lessons—"Marc's way of sticking it to Larry." *Grounds for reasonable doubt.*

Marc's "forgetting" the name of the hotel where he stayed: Jones couldn't take a chance, he said, that Marc, who knew his way around Salt Lake from the summer before, might make any decision on his own. If Marc remembered that his mother gave him the name of the hotel, wouldn't it be important enough to him to remember it now?

The day of the murder: if it happened the way Marc said it happened and he didn't have a disguise, could they imagine cab drivers not coming forward to claim the reward? Why didn't the state offer proof that he flew back that Sunday morning? Did Marc get Larry to take him in his plane and fly him to another airport? Or use Larry to open that back door when Larry was at the warehouse the night before? What corroboration was there to Marc's story about talking to his grandfather about money? "I am sure they did talk about money. I am sure Marc told him, 'Hey, Gramps . . . what is this nonsense going on, Larry getting flying lessons? I can't do this, I can't do that.'" Did anyone on the jury recall him saying he was sorry for what he did? Picking up the .357 Magnum, he needlessly refreshed their memories that there had been two shots, at close range, and that Marc had then gone through his grandfather's pants while he was lying in a pool of blood. "And they want you to believe that somebody else can transmit that kind of viciousness? *Grounds for reasonable doubt.*"

After a break for lunch, a break in which even some people who intensely disliked Rosen's slashing, sarcastic style were grudgingly admitting that it was the most brilliant closing argument they had ever heard, the attorney seemed even more possessed than he was before. He was fighting for Frances's life and he was earning his keep. With all due respect to Dr. Moench, Rosen said, he not only had *no* corroboration for what Marc had told him, but the man-slaughter defense offered at Marc's trial hadn't worked. If the judge hadn't told them last Friday the *full* details of the deal Marc had made with the state, he said, they never would have heard about it. Prompted perhaps by the *Salt Lake Tribune*'s editorial three days before, which said that "all the consternation is justified. . . . If one convict can deal his help for movies and restaurant meetings with relatives, the next may demand a day of fishing at Strawberry Reservoir and some nightclubbing," Rosen reviewed all the privileges Marc had received and said, "That's what this is all about. . . . Blew his grandfather into the grave and they took him to the movies with his girlfriend."

He moved on to Richard Behrens and said that *if* Frances had given him the gun, why would he have written all the letters he had to collect his money? Wouldn't he have just shown her the gun and said, "'Frances, come on. You remember this? Can I have my thirty-seven hundred dollars, please,' and . . . you know what she would have said? 'Thirty-seven hundred dollars? How about thirty-seven thousand dollars, Richard? Here, give me the gun. Here is your money.' . . . That's all Behrens had to do. . . . Baloney. She never gave him the gun.''

All of a sudden, he said, out of the blue, came Marilyn, who had all of these conversations with Campbell but didn't tell him about a hit man. The same woman who "was smiling every time she looked over at her sister fighting for her life." Wouldn't she have "picked up the phone the minute Richard Behrens told her about a hit man with Frances or getting the gun from Frances and said, 'Joel, you can't believe what I just heard.' . . . She writes everything else down *except* the name of a hit man. Things don't happen like that in real life. Don't check your common sense when you go in to deliberate this case." And even *after* Behrens gave her the gun, he said, she didn't tell Campbell about these things. "Doesn't that speak louder than my words or Mr. Jones's words?"

And what about Behrens's saying now that he had been afraid to involve Frances when he spoke to Campbell initially and she then forced him to change his statement? "We ought to put her in the UN," he suggested. "Maybe she can clean up some of the problems in Russia she can control so much." But he, like Marilyn, hadn't told Campbell about Manning. That's because Manning had never existed as a hit man for Frances. It was only when the heat was on, in November of 1981, when Marc and Behrens were fighting extradition, that Marc mentioned Manning to David Frankel and Behrens, in order to get immunity, mentioned him to Mike George. Behrens then had "a package" to sell, Rosen said: Frances gave him the gun and tried to hire a hit man. Since "no one is going to believe Behrens alone," Behrens got to Manning before George did, showed him Frances's picture and mentioned her name. After all, Rosen said, the picture of Frances that George later showed Manning originally came from Behrens.

Rosen forged on, reiterating every inconsistency he could think of: assuring them that Richard Behrens would apply for the reward when the case was over; reminding them how obsessed Marilyn was with knowing about her father's finances; suggesting that "a little sideshow" existed between Marilyn and Gentile—that Marilyn knew Gentile would be questioned about his marriage to Frances and she tried to downplay his treatment of her sister by saying she only had a red mark on her cheek, when the affidavit she had sworn to at the time said otherwise. "Why the lie? Why the lie? She said, 'Oh, that's semantics, Mr. Rosen.' Sure, a lot of semantics between a red mark on one's cheek and looking like a meatball."

And what about Gentile? "This guy is so bad that the court took away his name from his children. He has absolutely no contact with his sons for eight and a half years." After all that went on between Vittorio and Frances, "as bloody a physical and legal battle as you have ever heard, do you think Frances would confide in him something that could put her subject to the death penalty? . . . He denies beating Frances because his interpretation of beating is it's only a beating if you wind up in a hospital. . . . That's what kind of guy Vittorio Gentile is. He forgot that Marilyn put in an affidavit that he beat her like a sausage. He could have killed her then, but don't let him kill her now. Not on the word of Vittorio Gentile." *Grounds for reasonable doubt.*

Rosen had been pumping for nearly three hours and was almost through, he told them. "I know that won't disappoint a lot of you, but I am getting to the end." Not only was there no new will, he insisted time and again, but Herman Wood was a CPA—a man to give tax advice, not write or change wills. Besides, they hadn't heard anything about Franklin Bradshaw's coming back to see Alma Boyce after that, did they?

And what about Steve Klein, "who is a police officer but isn't a police officer"? From their own common sense and experience, he said, "what police officer makes a forced entry in a murder case and doesn't have a weapon out to protect himself"? And what was all this nonsense about her trying "to escape"? Was she going to fly to Argentina from "seven floors in the sky"? And what was policewoman Cimler doing while Klein was supposedly running into the room to "save" Frances? If they could bring Klein out from New York, couldn't they have brought Cimler? And if Frances had wanted to escape, he said, she could have done that the night before, when she and Lavinia came home and found out the police had been there.

For the finale he saved his "favorite person"—Myles

Manning, "who magically is drunk prior to October of 1977 and drunk after October of 1977 but he is not drunk during October of 1977." Manning was at the YMCA for three days for "a very perfect reason"—he had either been tossed out of one of the apartments he lived in with his brother or he was "drying out" before his next binge. A guy who looked at a photograph of Frances and said "she looks *similar* to the lady" he met? "That's a lady he supposedly met four times, took five thousand dollars from to kill her father, and she looks similar? *Grounds for reasonable doubt.*"

A guy who testified that Mike George gave him Frances's name and that he didn't remember the name of the person who introduced them? A guy who told George that Frances's daughter was nine or ten when these meetings were supposedly going on, when she was actually four and a half? That was Behrens's fault, Rosen said. He "messed up. He gave Manning the information but he forgot there was a four-year gap. He gave the age of Lavinia closer to when the cops were coming, not back in '77." But what Rosen found most incredible of all was Manning's saying that after Frances allegedly gave him his "road map to murder" and they met for the last time—the meeting where Manning explained how he got arrested, and so forth—she didn't ask him if the police had found all that material in his possession. "Wouldn't *you* ask that?" he said, putting his hands on his head, scanning each face. "That's when you would go out the window." And if Frances really did give him $5,000, where was the bank record to prove it? They had been shown bank records from 1977 to corroborate deposit of those checks, but no records to show a withdrawal of that amount. As he had offered to a number of times, he would take his seat immediately if they had that proof.

"Now, let me try to end the discussion of this record with something that if it is coincidence, it's the greatest coincidence in the history of mankind. And I suggest that it is not coincidence and betrays the fabric of Manning and Behrens's testimony. It's a place called Culver Lake, New Jersey."

He thought this case had to do with *Frances's* being worried about losing an estate. But lo and behold, the record said Richard Behrens feared the same thing at the same time. "You mean it's a coincidence that Behrens had the exact same fear at the same time? Baloney. . . . Manning says to you under oath Richard Behrens goes to the country house. He gets up to the house, Manning is waiting down by the lake. Richard Behrens says, 'Oh, I never got to the house. We bumped into my dad, Dr. Behrens, in the village.' *Obviously* they were up to no good and *obviously* by bumping into Dr. Behrens, whatever they were planning had to be aborted— but they were both up there . . . at the same time they were supposedly dealing with Frances."

So what they did, according to Rosen, was shift their "treachery" onto Frances, reminding the jury one last time that the heat was on, Behrens was about to be extradited, and knew that no one would believe him on his own. "Shift it to Frances and what a package they have." Perhaps Behrens promised Manning a cut of the reward? He didn't know, he said; *he* wasn't there and *they* both had grants of immunity. "You can't tell me that Myles Manning and Richard Behrens are talking about Behrens's being cut out of a father's will when at the same time Frances has the same motive for murder? That's incredible and an insult to your intelligence. Absolutely an insult. . . .

"Don't compromise," he pleaded with them, "you promised. If you have a belief one way or the other, stick to that belief. Don't give in, even if you're outnumbered. . . . Mr. Jones and I took you based on those promises and His Honor did as well. You can't make a mistake. There is no way back if you make a mistake. Stick to your beliefs. . . . A trial is something like a jigsaw puzzle. If you picture the wall with a beautiful frame and a jigsaw puzzle, it's all a beautiful picture when you first see it. Then what happens? Some of those pieces start falling out, the picture gets blurry, very blurry, and then more and more pieces start falling out and you start even losing the picture and then if all the pieces, all the critical pieces fall out, as I submit they have here, what are you left with? You are left with a frame.

"That's what we have got here. That's what you're left with, a frame, and the pieces have been coming out. I hope I have been taking the pieces out. I know it has been a long haul, but that's what I have been doing and I am showing you the frame.

"The state never loses a case, the government, the prosecution never loses a case, because when justice is done and if justice means not guilty, then the people win. And the state wins when justice is done. Do justice. I ask you to return this lady right here, this human being, this American who has gone through this trial, I ask you to return a verdict of not guilty loud and clear and I thank you for your patience and indulgence and attention."

For a few seconds, no one moved. Back in Mike Rosen's office in Manhattan, there is a red-and-yellow sign on the wall that reads: "If you can't dazzle 'em with brilliance, baffle 'em with bullshit." And true to that teaching, he had done his share of both. For three hours he had held everyone in thrall like an evangelistic preacher with the power to heal. Ernie Jones's mother turned to her daughter-in-law and shook her head. She didn't see how her Ernie was going to recover from this. On his way out of the courtroom to get some air, Rosen said, to no one in particular, "There must be an easier way to make a living," and Berenice, wiping tears from her eyes, told her million-dollar man that he had done just fine. But she had lost all feeling, she said, and wondered why the court didn't have the sense to provide a bar for a woman in need. And, as he had done each chance he got since arriving in court that morning, Fred Weber put his arms around Frances and gave her the kind of hug that that classmate from Bryn Mawr had felt she so desperately needed all those years ago.

Mike Rosen had told the jury it was only fair that the state have the last chance to address them, and Ernie Jones couldn't have agreed more.

"You know," he began in his down-home, we'll - all - be - seeing - each - other - again - long - after - this - brash - carpet- bagger - has - left - the - land - of - Zion voice, "I suppose it's a good idea the court gives you an instruction in a case like this that you are not to regard the statement of counsel as being evidence in the case, because I submit to you that after hearing the closing arguments of counsel, I certainly would take issue with his interpretation of the evidence." Was the defense really asking them to believe that Marc, Marilyn, Behrens, Manning and Gentile were *all* liars, *all* accomplices, and part of some conspiracy against Frances? "What is the motive . . . what prompts Marc Schreuder, the son of Frances, to walk into this courtroom and testify that she put him up to the murder?"

If *they* were witnesses, he suggested, they too would have a difficult time recalling the exact details of incidents occurring years before, and he asked they consider that in weighing the credibility of each person's testimony. There was a lot of pressure on a witness when he walked into a courtroom, Jones reasoned, noting that some of them might have experienced that feeling during jury selection. But if every witness took the stand and gave the *same* story, wouldn't they start to wonder about the candor of those statements and whether two witnesses might have gotten together and rehearsed what they were planning to say? The state knew about the discrepancies, he said, and never tried to hide them.

The "great deal" the defense implied Marc got, Jones said, might have been that, had Marc been promised a reduction in his sentence or been paid for his testimony. If he were to get a new trial, Jones said, the state could convict him again—with or without his testimony against his mother. He didn't *have* to testify, but he did. "This isn't a young man who just went out to the prison and is on his butt out there watching television for ten hours a day. At least he has got the gall to get up and go to school, to try to make something of his life after being convicted of murder. . . . I mean, you hate to say it, but maybe it was the best thing that ever happened to Marc, to be convicted of second-degree murder to get him out of that environment in New York City."

What the defense was trying to do, he warned them, was get them to listen to the question long enough that they would think it was the answer. If Marilyn and Behrens were part of this "so-called conspiracy," then why did Behrens turn on Marilyn and say she had the gun? If Vittorio Gentile wanted to make up a story about Frances, wouldn't he have come up with an even more incriminating one?

As Jones looked at the jurors, he could tell their concentration was on the wane. He appreciated their time, he said, and knew it had been a long day. But he wanted them to consider a few final things before they went about the business they had been chosen to do.

"Frances Schreuder," he said, a name that would forever

be linked to his own. "You ask yourself what kind of a daughter would order the execution of her own father. You ask yourself what kind of a mother would ask her own son to carry out that murder. You ask yourself what kind of a human being are we talking about . . . that makes it appear as though her own son Larry is the prime suspect? . . . What kind of a human being would then convince Richard Behrens that he should blame her sister Marilyn Reagan for the murder? . . .

"Frances Schreuder almost pulled off the perfect crime. Almost. There was only one flaw. She crossed up Richard Behrens for thirty-seven hundred dollars. The defense said the crime doesn't make sense. It's not logical. Murder never is logical. This isn't a logical woman. . . . That's why she tells her own son on the night before the murder, 'Don't come home if you don't kill Franklin Bradshaw.'"

She had tried to destroy everyone who got in her road, he said, and "there is only one thing standing in the road at this point in time, and that is a verdict in this case."

He thanked them and sat down. It was nearly five-thirty and he had done his best, but he had no idea if it had been good enough.

The jury, their faces even whiter than normal, was put into Harry Klekas's capable hands and told that if they were still deliberating by seven, he would take them out for a meal. If there were any messages they needed to relay to loved ones, the time to put them on a piece of paper was now. As for the two alternates, Judge Baldwin thanked them for their efforts and said they were free to go or could stay and chat with him. He advised them not to discuss the case with anybody, but knew that he could no longer prevent anyone from approaching them.

So it was hardly surprising when, a few minutes later, the two women were seated on a bench outside the courtroom and Mike Rosen ambled over like a shy teenager at a dance.

"Now, at least, I can say hello," Rosen said, adding that he was sure this had been an experience they would never forget.

"Well, it sure opened my eyes," one of them began, "and made me realize that the first opinion you have is not always the right one."

Rosen brightened. If she felt that way, maybe somebody in that locked jury room was saying the same thing. "Generally, the system works," he told them. "Sometimes it breaks down, but it's better than any system anywhere else."

"At first I was relieved I wasn't picked," the other alternate said. "But now I wish I could see it through."

No sooner had Rosen walked away and rejoined Frances than Dave Walsh huddled with them for a few minutes and then left, unsmiling, to go back across the street to the County Attorney's Office.

Mike George had brought in a television, and he and Ernie Jones (as well as Ernie's wife and mother) were about to watch the six o'clock news. All three local stations had their equipment on the lawn in front of the courthouse, and the top of each broadcast was going to come from there. George wasn't sure that turning on the news was such a good idea, but he couldn't resist.

The reporter for Channel 4, the ABC station, said that the general consensus among the press corps and the people he had spoken with was that Frances Schreuder would walk away, free and alive.

They felt as if someone had just clubbed them over the head with a sledgehammer. Jones, head in hands, almost passed out. George immediately switched off the set. "Geez," Jones said, barely able to speak, "are we up in the dark here on this case if the news media thinks this? Boy, have I missed the boat." Walsh pulled George aside and delivered the news he had been sent to get: the two alternates had given him the impression that they would have voted for acquittal. "Whatever you do," George told him, "don't tell Ernie. The man is going through too much."

On the fourth floor of the courthouse, Mike Rosen was smoking one cigarette after another. When he wasn't checking on Frances, who had sought refuge in a stairwell with Fred Weber and Berenice, he was beginning to talk about the case and about Mike Rosen.

"We did all we could," he said, standing near the plate-glass window that looked onto Fourth South and to the mountains beyond on the clear, still-light September evening.

"Who knows what this jury will bring back? I hear they cut you up pretty quickly out here, and that trying to win a murder case in Utah is like trying to climb that mountain there with Vaseline on your shoes. If I were back at 100 Centre Street, I'd have a better feel for how it might go. I'd have a couple of kids from the Village on that jury that would understand where I was coming from. I told them when I took the case that I had to be myself, a Jewish kid from Brooklyn. I can't pass myself off as Harvard or Brigham Young. When Jimmy LaRossa [a top defense lawyer in New York] first began, he tried to be Harvard with a three-piece suit and gold pocket watch and didn't get past his opening statement. He quickly realized that he was much better off just being Jimmy LaRossa.

"We tried to bring out every inconsistency we could. To open with Marc was a bombshell because there had been no previous testimony." They had considered putting Frances on before the trial began, but decided that cross-examination of the state's witnesses was their best defense. The judge had ruled Frances wasn't in the will; he had not allowed those memos in; and, most important, he had kept that tape out. Those were three of Rosen's key goals and he'd managed to attain them. Told that he hardly seemed winded after his three-hour final argument, Rosen said, "If you can't pump, you shouldn't be a lawyer. You *got* to be able to pump. If not, you ought to be closing houses instead. I could have gone a few more hours." When this was over, he said, he'd like some nice, dull extortion case or bank job. Chided that something like that might not be notorious enough for the firm of Saxe, Bacon, he laughed. "Ninety-nine percent of the people I defend are guilty. As long as they sign the retainer, I'm on board." Except for rapists, molesters and drug pushers, he insisted. They were out of the question.

At a few minutes past seven, the door of the jury room opened. They had been deliberating for an hour and a half and it was time for the bailiff to take them to the China Village restaurant on South Main for dinner. As they waited for the elevator, their faces gave nothing away.

* * *

694

Not long after they left, Frances, who had been chain-smoking, drinking Tab and speaking on the phone, walked with her mother and Fred Weber to Le Parisien. On the way there, Weber, his arm linked with Frances's, felt her "slipping away." Once they got inside the restaurant and were told they would have to wait a few minutes for a table, Frances broke into uncontrollable sobs. She was "kaput," the kindly German said later, simply kaput.

The prosecution had gone over to Crown Burgers on Second South and were back in their office before eight-thirty. Mike George called his wife on the office's direct outside line and asked her to phone back to make sure it was working. There was nothing to do—nothing they could do. They were captives, waiting for a phone to ring, feeling defeated. Walsh predicted the jury would be out two to three hours, Jones said six to eight, and George figured two to three days.

Back in the courthouse, Frances had fallen asleep on Fred Weber's shoulder. Berenice was sitting with a neighbor nearby, her voice rising above the milling crowd, outrage toward the cruelty of Ernie Jones lacing the smoky air.

By ten, hardly able to keep her eyes open, she walked into the courtroom and fell asleep.

Eight minutes later, there was a rap on the inside of the jury-room door. The judge had told the jury that if they had any questions or points of confusion to let the bailiff know. They had none. They had a verdict.

The phone rang across the street and Mike George knew immediately what it meant. "It's too damn quick," he said, certain that the jury had just thrown their hands in the air and said not guilty. Whatever color had returned to Ernie Jones's face since the six-o'clock news faded once more as he and Walsh started to leave. George could not face hearing the verdict and stayed behind, phoning his old partner in narcotics and then his wife to relay his gloomy prediction.

Half awake, her hair pulled back, Frances sat between Kurumada and Rosen as the jury filed in at ten-twelve. One juror smiled nervously as he took his seat. Maybe George was right. Rosen kept his head down. He never looks at his jurors and, like George, always expects the worst.

"Mr. Dawson," Judge Baldwin said, "you appear to be the foreman. Is that correct?"

Harmel Dawson, who had been selected as foreperson because he was the only one who had served on a jury before, told the judge that he was.

"Would you please hand the verdict to the bailiff?" Harry Klekas took the piece of paper from Dawson and solemnly walked it over to the judge. Baldwin looked at it for a second and then gave it to his clerk, instructing him to read it aloud.

"We, the Jurors impaneled in the above case, find the defendant, Frances Bernice Schreuder, Guilty of Criminal Homicide, Murder in the First Degree, a Capital Offense, as charged in the Information."

Judge Baldwin said that he was going to poll them one by one and ask a single question: "Was this and is this your verdict?" And one by one, each of them answered that it was.

They cut you up pretty quickly out here, Rosen had been told, and they had. Frances stared straight ahead, speechless, as Jones moved quickly to ask that her bail be revoked immediately. Rosen argued against that, and the judge, to Jones's utter astonishment, allowed her to remain free until the following Monday, provided she stay in Utah and Kevin Kurumada be responsible for her.

And come Monday, barring some unforeseen circumstance, Frances would be sentenced either to life imprisonment—or to death.

On his way out of the courthouse, Ernie Jones said he was "extremely pleased" and nothing more. As Rosen, Frances and Kurumada were preparing to avoid the press by going down to the basement of the building and out through a garage, Berenice Bradshaw was not trying to hide from anybody. With one person on each side of her, she walked out the same front door she had come in that morning, her head held high, and into a sea of cameras, klieg lights and reporters. Making no comment of any kind, she barreled through them like Moses dividing the Red Sea. She'd been living in this town for more than sixty years, and nobody was about to run her out of it.

As her mother disappeared into the night, Frances and her lawyers emerged and were instantly pursued. As they walked east on Fourth South toward Kurumada's office, the lights surrounding Frances illuminated her as if she were royalty, turning night into day at the very same moment a bolt of lightning flashed angrily across the vast Utah sky.

75// The following morning, *Today, Good Morning, America* and the *CBS Morning News* all reported the verdict, as did newspapers across the country. The *Salt Lake Tribune*, which, as a general rule, has only national and international news on its front page, ran it as the lead story, with the headline "Frances Schreuder Guilty" across the top.

Ernie Jones took the day off, Mike Rosen flew back to New York, but Mike George came to work and found a message waiting for him when he got there. While the prosecution had been out the night before celebrating its victory, Marc had been up all night with the caseworkers at the prison. From the moment he had arrived back at the Point a week before, he was, for his own safety, confined to the area of SSD and informed that he could not attend college that quarter, because classes were held in the Big House. But that didn't prevent a number of inmates from wandering down to SSD, asking through the window if it wasn't enough that he killed his grandfather without trying to kill his mother too, and threatening his life if he so much as stepped foot into the Big House.

Mike George went to see Marc the next day and Marc told him that "this is what should have happened. This is why I testified, but boy it hurts. She deserved to be convicted— somebody needed to stop her. Nobody talked to her all her life. But it does not feel good."

Bryan Baird had seen Marc as soon as he'd gotten back from testifying and recalled that he was "almost literally crushed. He was visibly shaken. He really loves his mom and when he went there to testify it was like him cutting the umbilical cord." When Marc realized that she could get the death penalty, Bryan said, he just sat on his bed, not talking to anybody and just staring, "unable to handle the fact he might lose her."

Back in Salt Lake, Bertha Beck, feeling vindicated by the verdict, was doing her best to reason with Berenice. Despite the uneasiness that had always marked their relationship, Bertha felt she had nothing to lose by offering her advice. She told her sister-in-law that it would be "very, very foolish" to continue fighting. "You won't get anywhere," she said. "Let it be where it is. Let it stand." She reminded her how Franklin had always talked about people leaving their money for lawyers to fight over and asked her to think carefully before "she put out another million." Prison hadn't been too bad for Marc, she rationalized, and maybe it wouldn't be for Frances. As for Rosen, she told Berenice he had made "a fool of himself" and that she might have done better with a local man. If she was going to continue handing out money, Bertha said, she might start with Franklin's half sister from Tooele, Sylvia Jean Christensen, who had a flock of children and was married to a schoolteacher.

Berenice acknowledged that an appeal might not stand much of a chance, but said they were planning to fight on. Rosen was going to bring back a crowd of character witnesses for the penalty phase of the trial, she said: Lavinia was flying out from New York (with the young woman who was taking care of her) and might be called; Lincoln Kirstein, the legendary cofounder of the New York City Ballet, had agreed to come (at Berenice's expense) from Paris, where the company was performing, and testify in Frances's behalf; and if George Balanchine were still alive, she assured Bertha, he would have come too. Money was no object. She had nineteen new oil wells, she said, they were all pumping, and one of them, in Wyoming, was even named after her. Though Frances could no longer benefit from the family trust (unless her appeal was successful), Berenice said she was going to set up a separate trust fund for her and see to it that Marilyn and Elaine didn't get a dime from her will.

76// Frances was only the fourth woman ever to be convicted of first-degree murder in the state of Utah. None of the others had been given the death penalty, and one had her conviction overturned by a higher court.

For Frances to receive it, the state would have to prove beyond a reasonable doubt that the aggravating factors of her crime outweighed the mitigating ones and that the death penalty was the *only* appropriate sentence in light of those circumstances. If that happened and the order was later enforced, she would have the grim choice of a firing squad or lethal injection.

Shortly after the verdict, Ernie Jones had indicated that the maximum was what the state had in mind, and on Monday morning, October 3, a somber Mike Rosen (then Frances, in a quavering voice) officially told Judge Baldwin what had been intimated to him on Friday: Frances wanted to exercise her legal right to have her sentence decided by him, not the jury which had convicted her.

Having settled that, Rosen tried to have the verdict set aside or at least reduced to second-degree; he claimed that he had "scoured" the record and that "absent Marc Schreuder's self-serving statements," there was *nothing* to corroborate the idea Frances had ordered this murder or that she had acted in the hope of pecuniary or personal gain.

Denying both motions, Baldwin told the court that he had received a letter that morning and was inclined to allow it into evidence. Though he did not read it aloud, the letter—marked as Defendant's Exhibit 65 and mailed from Puerto Rico by Federal Express—read as follows:

September 28, 1983

DEAR JUDGE BALDWIN,

My name is Marilyn Reagan and I testified before your honor in the case of my sister, Frances Schreuder. I wanted her convicted because I believe she caused the death of my Father through her son Marc.

When she was suspended from Bryn Mawr in her junior year, I was told by the school officials that she would not be considered for readmission without intensive psychiatric care. She has not had such care, I believe she is mentally and emotionally ill.

Even though she caused the death of my Father, I do not wish her death. The purpose of this letter is to ask you to consider some kind of psychiatric care for her rather than the death penalty.

Sincerely,
MARILYN REAGAN

Marilyn was spoken for, but there was still the question of Berenice. The state had told the defense and her lawyer *they* were planning to call her as their only witness—to help the court know something about Frances's "background" and "character," Jones said—and Rosen pleaded to the judge that not only could she offer nothing "in aggravation," but "with all the tragedy she has suffered," it would be wrong to force her to the stand. The judge agreed, so Jones offered six letters Berenice had written to Frances, Larry and Marc in the first half of 1978 (letters, written after she had gone to work at the warehouse, which told of her efforts to send all the money she earned to Frances and which complained bitterly of the treatment she was receiving in return). The judge accepted those but rebuffed, once more, Jones's persistent effort to have the Frances-Lavinia tape admitted—or even a transcript of it. While the tape fell into the admissible category of "character," Judge Baldwin continued to insist that Jones had never laid the proper foundation for it (despite Marc's testimony, the judge felt it wasn't clear how it was made or what may have been done to alter it), that it was apparently made *after* the murder, and that it had *nothing* to do with either the crime or Frances's relationship to her father.

While Berenice was spared being called to the stand, this was the written testimony she wanted to read if she had been:

I can not think clearly in these surroundings, your Honor may I read my testimony?

My daughter, Frances Schreuder, who I love very much, has been unjustly convicted of a crime which she had no part in, she has done nothing wrong. She has been a fine, devoted mother. She never neglected her children, she gave her children all the love, care and devotion a mother could possibly give.

I do not know of a young woman who has had the horrible life she has had. Two brutely, violent, alcoholic husbands who beat her and her children daily. She put up with inhuman treatment to protect two boys who were impossible to discipline and raise. She could have left these two boys with their brute father, gone off and had a good life for herself. But no, she stuck it out far longer than their health and minds could endure. A social worker who had been seeing this family told me had Frances stayed with Vittorio Gentile another year they would all end up in a mental institution.

This cruelty left permanent scars on these boys and ruined Frances's health. Larry was sent to a school for disturbed children and Marc had to have psychiatric treatment. These two boys became totally uncontrollable. Frances went thru years of total hell. . . .

Marc Schreuder is a terrific liar, a born thief, and a maniac for destruction. Richard Behrens belongs in prison alongside of Marc. Behrens was unjustly given immunity so he could lie, lie, lie and not get the punishment he deserves. Why hasn't Richard Behrens been sentenced for his part in this crime? The prosecution has protected Behrens, promised Marc Schreuder early parole for their lies, deceit and sculdugery.

The last time I talked with Marc he told me: "I will not testify against my mother." What happened to cause him to change his mind? On several occasions the prosecution took Marc out of prison, where he is serving time for the Murder of my husband, his grandfather, wined, dined and entertained him and promised him early parole if he would testify against his own mother.

. . . Where is the justice in this bizzare tragedy? And why is Frances Schreuder supposed to give her life for something she did not do?

BERENICE BRADSHAW

It was marked as Defendant's Exhibit 66, and shortly thereafter Mike Rosen called the first of his four character witnesses to the stand.

Fred Weber's daughter, Monika Clyde, had flown in from Oakland, California, over the weekend with her husband and their daughter, Melissa, who was the same age as Lavinia. She told the court she had known Frances since 1954, when they were juniors at East High together, and that in the nearly thirty years since then, Frances had been "a very loyal, good friend to me, a decent human being, very supportive of me when I was in trouble and always available when I needed her." Asked if she felt the death penalty would be appropriate, Mrs. Clyde said "absolutely not."

She told Ernie Jones on cross-examination that she did know Frances had been "taken out" of Bryn Mawr, but said she was not aware of her getting into trouble with law enforcement and insisted that no one had ever told her Frances had been stealing. "I was under the impression that college regulations at that time were very tough—like overnight, one could not stay out—and that she disobeyed some of the rather strict rules which were in effect in colleges at that time."

Mrs. Clyde showed great poise on the stand—until Jones asked if she was familiar with Sam Drukman and had gone with Frances the previous February to pick up some mail that belonged to him.

"Absolutely not," she said, offended he would even insinuate that she was a thief.

"You didn't do that, then?"

"Absolutely not," she repeated under oath, her face beginning to redden slightly.

So she wasn't aware, then, that his parents had filed a complaint, charging Frances with trying to take mail out of his mailbox? Yes, she was, she said. Frances's attorney had told her about it. "To my knowledge," she explained, "no mail was taken. I was with her at *all* times. She was at my house in my company at all times."

Unwilling to let it drop, Jones asked what kind of car she would have been driving at the time. When she said a Mercedes—the car Sam Drukman reported seeing—Jones pressed her once more, got nowhere, and then switched to Lavinia. If he couldn't get the tape in, he could at least ask if she had ever heard Frances yelling at Lavinia or threatening to put her into a mental institution. No, never, the matronly German professor said, and left the stand.

Blond-haired and oozing with Eastern sophistication, Mary Porter, the director of development for the School of American Ballet, swept into the courtroom and told the natives how

702

Frances had underwritten two student scholarships for the last four years. She had done so anonymously, Miss Porter said. "She did not want any recognition and she did not want to be praised and have a plaque on the wall or anything like that." And no, she said, the death penalty would not be appropriate for her.

On cross, Jones asked if she knew *why* Frances had been invited to join the board of the New York City Ballet. She could only offer an opinion, she said, having made it clear she was connected only with the school. Frances was very interested in the ballet—and not just because of her patronage, she said. She believed in it as an art form, in the work of the company, and wanted to be associated with it.

But wasn't it really more than just interest? Jones probed, wanting to get down to dollars and cents.

Well, it depended, Miss Porter said. Some members were invited to join because of their interest, some because of their ability to raise money, and, of course, some because of their ability to *give* money. As far as how much money Mrs. Schreuder had given the company, she did not know. But she did know that the school had received roughly $80,000 for the two scholarships ($10,000 a year for each student for the past four years); a $400,000 endowment for the George Balanchine Memorial Scholarship (set up by her and Berenice in July 1983, shortly after Balanchine's death); and about $20,000 to mount an exhibition—a historical retrospective of the school's first fifty years—at Lincoln Center.

What about Lavinia? Jones asked. Would she have been admitted to the school if the defendant had *not* been donating money?

"Absolutely," Miss Porter said huffily, elevating her head ever so slightly. "Our school," as I said, "has a reputation for being the best of its kind in the country, and actually I thought I might be asked this question and I was thinking you might be interested to hear, which is a fact, that we turned down Caroline Kennedy as one of our students. It doesn't matter *who* you are. It has to do with your ability."

At the conclusion of Miss Porter's testimony and before Rosen's third witness took the stand, Judge Baldwin had something to say. Since his daughter-in-law had given him hell for his comments about the New York City Ballet and

Ballet West at the end of jury selection, he vowed that he wouldn't, in future, be making any more remarks of that kind.

The next witness was the urbane W. McNeil Lowry. The former Ford Foundation executive (from 1953 to 1976, "I held every post there was") identified himself as a writer, lecturer and consultant, mostly about education and the arts. He had first met Mrs. Schreuder at Lincoln Kirstein's house in 1979, and aside from their interest in the ballet and their being colleagues on the company's board of directors, they had become fast friends, had had "long, long talks about anything and everything under the sun," and (he cleverly dropped in) knew people in common, like William Christensen, the head of Ballet West (who, the judge then revealed, was an old friend of his too).

Asked by Rosen if he would describe Frances as a socialite, he said "not at all," adding that he only knew "a few socialites" in New York and that his friends generally weren't in that category. In all the time he'd known Frances, he said, he found her to be "very humane," "very sympathetic and compassionate," "extremely sensitive" and "highly intelligent." The prospect of her receiving the death penalty, he said, was "incredible" to him.

As Ernie Jones and Mike George sat there listening to this glowing assessment of Frances, they practically had to pinch themselves to make sure this was the same woman they had just helped to convict. If McNeil Lowry had had all these discussions with her, Jones asked on cross-examination, had Frances ever told him anything about Larry and Marc?

"Frances was obviously—and we knew this—very much, of course, involved emotionally, every other way with events here in Utah," he said as carefully as he could. "These would, as you are aware, sometimes be covered in the press in New York. My interest in Frances Schreuder as a human being and my compassion for her did not lead me to probe about her two sons or any of the circumstances alleged in the death of her father. . . . I could see in this lady a great deal of tension and suffering at many times. I knew what some of those stories in the press could mean to her as she read them and I chose not to dig into those things."

Finding Lowry even more unshakable than Monika Clyde, Jones reminded him of his description of Frances as very humane and sensitive—words the prosecutor nearly choked on—and asked if he felt a woman who threw and locked her children out of the house possessed those qualities. The judge sustained Rosen's objection, but Jones plowed on. Would he say that someone who ordered the execution of her father was sensitive and humane? Objection. Sustained. And would he say that someone who refused to let her son back into the house after he was released from prison was sensitive and humane?

Mr. Lowry did not have to answer any of those questions, and was soon excused.

Mike Rosen initially had said he had *four* witnesses, but now told the judge he had nothing further. The possibility of calling Lavinia to the stand had been discussed, but Frances did not want her subjected to the press (which now included an ABC correspondent from Los Angeles and a reporter for the *Boston Globe*) or an insensitive photographer. The judge said he could control the situation *in* the courtroom, but not beyond it, so Lavinia, on perhaps the last day the ten-year-old girl would ever see her mother outside of prison for quite some time, remained at the Marriott with Melissa Clyde. When the courtroom door opened for the lunch recess, Mike Rosen's last witness—the one he felt he didn't need to call—filled the doorway, looming over everyone as he paced back and forth in his traditional black suit. Though few recognized him, Lincoln Kirstein had been waiting—waiting to speak against death.

As Kirstein, McNeil Lowry and Mary Porter walked with Frances out of the courthouse, trailed by television cameras, Mike George watched them go. He had been outraged by Lowry's and Porter's testimony and had been furiously scribbling notes on his pad all morning. "I was so pissed," he said. "I wanted to pick up my note pad and throw it at them. I wanted to holler at the judge, 'Hey, is *this* the pecuniary gain you kept saying she didn't get—or *wasn't* involved in this case?'" During lunch George told Jones, "Dammit, Ernie, she deserves the death penalty, because Frank Bradshaw died

705

just so these people could get up on the stand and testify that they could take *blood money*—and that's exactly what they're being funded with. If art means that a man has to die so that somebody can go to ballet school, or that a ballet production can be put on, or that a guy from the Ford Foundation can testify about all the good humanity this woman has, with *all* that's gone on behind the scenes in this case, that is *offensive.*"

Though they both knew it was highly unlikely that the judge would sentence Frances to death, Jones put the finishing touches on his final argument.

At ten minutes past two, Ernie Jones stood before Judge Baldwin and said he realized the death penalty was not appropriate to every case. But the United States Supreme Court, in *Greg* v. *Georgia,* had called it "an expression of society's outrage at particularly offensive conduct," and Frances Schreuder's conduct, he insisted, "constitutes an outrage to society." He touched on all the aggravating factors he felt existed in the record—ordering the execution of her father, ordering her own son to do it, and then trying to blame Marilyn for it—and said that "the hatred this woman exhibits for others in the family is amazing": pitting her father against her mother, her sister against her mother, her sons against each other (and teaching them both to hate their grandparents).

"What I cannot comprehend is that money in this case meant more than her own father, her own mother, and her own children. Money really meant more to Frances than anyone else, than anything else.

"Your Honor, I recently heard a statement and I think it's appropriate in this case. The statement goes like this: 'Don't tell me who you are, don't tell me what you will do, show me what you have done and I will know you.'

"Frances Schreuder," he said, turning slightly to look at her, "don't tell me who you are, don't tell me what you will do, show me what you have done, *then* I will know you.

"I submit that what Frances Schreuder has done in this case is to manipulate, to lie, to deceive, to plan, to contrive, to order, to solicit, request, demand and execute. Your Honor, I submit that Frances Schreuder's conduct in this case is in fact so vile and so treacherous that the death penalty . . . is appropriate and I would ask the court to so find."

At first Mike Rosen said he wanted to speak in terms of law rather than emotion, and at first he did. But what he really wanted to say, apart from what the people had said in the morning session, was what he had conceded all along: yes, there was friction, yes, there were problems, yes, things did indeed go wrong. But here was a woman who was "beaten to a pulp" by Gentile, who was "locked out" by Frederick Schreuder, and yet she tried, he said the record showed, to give her children the best education she possibly could. If it wasn't for her support of students at the School of American Ballet, "their careers or futures would have been nothing. . . ."

"I submit to Your Honor that the suffering here has been intense. Mrs. Bradshaw continues to suffer. There is a young child who suffers and could suffer immeasurably. There is good that you have heard in this record. Yes, there is always two sides of the story, but yet when two lawyers sometimes disagree on the emphasis or the facts, it's left to the court to look at the law. . . . " He said that the judge had before him "a record of troubled people and troubled times"—that not only had the state not carried its burden in terms of the death penalty but no member of the Bradshaw family had come forward to say that it was appropriate. "I ask Your Honor to consider all that we have put before you and your own perspective on this and ask you not to impose such a penalty."

It was the state's right to conclude and the prosecutor chose to do so. He wanted to make sure the judge realized that it was *money* which had gotten Frances involved with the two ballet organizations he had heard about that morning. More important, it was Frank Bradshaw's "*blood* money" and it proved what the state had been saying all along—that money meant everything to Frances. While the people who testified might have been sincere and honest in their opinions, he said, "they do not know the real Frances Schreuder"—the one whose cruelty her mother wrote about in those 1978 letters. And it was Berenice Bradshaw herself, he said before sitting down, who had told Joel Campbell on the day her husband

707

was murdered that whoever was responsible deserved the death penalty.

It was up to Judge Baldwin now. He saw no need to retire to make his decision; ever since the defense had told him the previous Friday it would probably be "placed in my hands, on my conscience, and in my guts," he had been "wrestling" with it and was ready to rule. The "true victims" in the case, he felt, were Berenice Bradshaw and Frances's two sisters. There were some "substantial" aggravating factors as well as "some" mitigating ones, and while the aggravating ones "may outweigh" the mitigating ones, the state had not satisfied him that the death penalty was the only appropriate and just way to go.

"As required by the statutes of the State of Utah," he said, fixing his eyes on Frances, "the laws as composed by the legislature and by which I am bound, it's my only obligation to find a judgment that would be life imprisonment."

Rosen asked the judge if they could submit a presentence report (his hope being that a psychological assessment of Frances might persuade the judge to reduce the sentence). While Baldwin said that "absent the most exceptional circumstances," he didn't see what good it would do, he granted Rosen's request. But he denied his next one—to allow Frances to remain on bail pending appeal—and said he would have to take that "to the gentlemen on the hill," the Utah Supreme Court.

With Frances's formal sentencing set for October 31, the judge said that she would be remanded forthwith to the sheriff of Salt Lake County and the court was adjourned.

As the courtroom slowly emptied, Frances burst into tears and began angrily pointing at Ernie Jones. The bailiff and a matron from the jail moved toward her with handcuffs. She held out a brass crucifix that was hanging around her neck, and warned them not to come closer. She had constitutional rights, she said, and one of them was her freedom of religious expression. She had been touching the large object all day, often displaying it in front of her white blouse in the hope, perhaps, it would send a plea for mercy to the judge. She did not want to part with her crucifix, she informed them. The man who had given it to her said she was to wear it against her chest—*always*.

On the way downstairs to the jail, just after three o'clock, the matron explained that *all* her property would have to be taken and that she would have to undergo a body search. Frances asked if she could keep her cigarettes—Carlton Menthols were the only kind she could smoke, she claimed— but was told they would have to be handed over too and that she could buy some from the machine. The machine didn't have Carltons, so she bought ten packs of Merit 100s (Menthol) to tide her over until the commissary opened the next day. In addition to her crucifix and Carltons, she surrendered a bottle of nitroglycerin pills (with a part of Lavinia's tooth inside it) she took for angina, $1,426, a white lighter, a silver barrette, a watch, her black patent-leather shoes, her navy-blue suit and her white blouse. She listed her occupation as a trustee of the New York City Ballet, which she still was, and the person to phone in case of emergency as McNeil Lowry. A year before, when she was booked into the jail, it had been a mere formality. Now she would be a prisoner there— #124863—until October 31. Two hours earlier, she had been having lunch in the Salt Lake Roasting Company with Lowry, Lincoln Kirstein and Mary Porter. Now she was being handed blue prison garb, white socks, and told that dinner would be at four and lights were turned out at eleven on weekdays. She said that she would "eat later" and, through tears, asked to see the medic.

She tried to explain to the medic what her needs were but was so "traumatized" that she couldn't remember dates or anything. The medic, a firm but gentle woman from Massachusetts whose grandfather had run a jail there for thirty-five years, gave her some nitroglycerin pills and said that psychiatric help could be made available to her, but Frances was not interested. She had questions and fears and the medic tried to give her answers and advice. Frances said she was afraid of being beaten up and "left to die." The medic told her that the inmates in the tier (an open-dorm arrangement in which each woman's area is her "condo") were "pretty nice" and that *she* wouldn't be frightened to sleep overnight there. She told Frances that she was no different from the others and that if she approached them in that way she would get along fine.

709

"I've left a ten-and-a-half-year-old daughter behind," Frances said.

"Well," the medic said, "the other women have left their families too."

"And what do I do if I have to cry?"

"You just sit on your bed and cry your heart out."

The last thing Frances wanted the medic to know was this: she would rather have had the death penalty than been sentenced to life in jail.

77// On the courthouse steps that day, Ernie Jones told the press that in his opinion torture killings and the murder of children were the only crimes likely to get the death penalty. A subdued Mike Rosen said that Frances had never once wavered from her claim of innocence and that the trial should never have been a death-penalty case to begin with. He expressed confidence in their chances on appeal, hope that he could win her release pending it, and said that the jury simply did not find the facts that were in the record.

Then what exactly did the jury find? For Kathleen Rachel Napier—forty years old, a housewife, a Mormon, a "middle-class" mother of six, and a woman who the state categorized as a "nice lady, soft, clean" during jury selection—there were a number of things. She was juror number four, and when she was first called for jury selection, she wanted to be picked; but after she was, she was "scared to death," and realized that it "wasn't a game or tv" but a human being's life she would be passing judgment on. The night before the trial began, her husband gave her "a husband's blessing" and prayed that she would have "courage and discernment" for what she was about to do. On the day before the verdict, she fasted and prayed and her husband blessed her again.

For her, Marc's testimony was the most damning. She felt that his feelings toward his mother now were ones of both love and hate, and that he "relived" everything in the courtroom. But when she first walked into the jury room to deliberate, her mind was not made up, unlike some of the others. It took five ballots for everyone to agree on Frances's involvement, but "the hardest thing," Napier said, "was deciding whether she *forced* Marc into it." While she thought Rosen had been unnecessarily theatrical—and some of the other jurors thought he was too sarcastic and rude—she also felt he was extremely good and persuasive, but unable, finally, to substantiate his insinuations, his "grasping-at-straws" argument that everyone was lying. "That Frances was the little innocent in this whole mess unbelievable, because everyone seemed to be describing the same person." She was not bothered by conflicts in people's recollections of times, dates and places, and said there had been important things in her life about which she was hazy. If everyone's story "had been one hundred percent with everyone else's," she said, "that would have seemed screwy." While she would have preferred a second opinion to Dr. Moench's, she was certain that he'd "been around long enough that he would have recognized it as a snow job on Marc's part."

She was frustrated at not knowing exactly what the tape was that Ernie Jones kept talking about, but she had no trouble realizing that even if Frances did not benefit directly from her father's will, money and hate were what the case was all about. After the verdict was delivered, she left the courthouse and cried all night long and the next day—not because she doubted her decision, but "because this little girl will lose her mommy." After a few days, though, she decided that Lavinia would now have more of a chance in this life. She was both surprised and relieved that the jury was waived for the penalty phase of the trial, and was angered by the character witnesses from New York. All the money that Frances had donated to the ballet only proved to Napier the kind of control she had over Berenice—and reminded her of something else. "Hitler liked Wagner's music, you know. Just because you have culture doesn't mean you can't do evil things. I can't enjoy Wagner's music because he was anti-Semitic. Culture does *not* make you humane."

When the state first considered Marilyn Facer for the jury, they thought she was a "sharp lady," but worried that she might be "too fair." In her late thirties and a mother of two,

Facer worked for H & R Block, was a nonactive Mormon, and described her family as being "everything" to her. Of all the testimony she'd heard, nothing appalled her more than learning of Berenice's reason for going to work at the warehouse. "This is *unbelievable*," she said. "How could Frances let her mother work to support her? You've got to be your own person. Before I would starve or mooch off of my family, I would get out there and work."

Facer was far less impressed with Marc's testimony than Napier, but when it was corroborated, she said, "it weighed heavy." While she felt sorry for Marc ("it must have been hard for him to do it") and was shocked when she first saw him take the stand, she said that a lot of the other jurors were concerned that he showed no emotion and that he didn't look at his mother. But Facer felt "his conscience was clear, and he had accepted everything and was doing his time to society."

If what she'd heard about Berenice appalled her, what she'd heard from Louis Moench convinced her. "I bought Moench one hundred percent. I've personally witnessed an Oedipus complex, but didn't know what it was called. I had seen a mother threaten suicide if her son didn't do what she wanted. She sent him out to steal for her. *Just as long as you don't get caught*. This was so real to me. I had seen all of this before. The boy was caught and went to jail, but he never turned on her."

Once the jury reached its verdict and before they left to go back into the courtroom, some of the jurors remarked about something they had witnessed earlier in the day. According to Facer, they were on their way to lunch and happened to hear Frances say, to herself, "Oh my God, I'm sorry. God, please forgive me."

At first, the women in Frances's tier were a bit awed by having "a celebrity" in their midst and tried to accord her the proper treatment. They brought her coffee, lit her cigarettes, and even helped her on with her shoes. But in jail novelty wears off quickly, and gestures like these are not made without the expectation of something in return. So when Frances (lacking Marc's "generosity" during his tenure at the jail) did not treat her "slaves" to items from the commissary, the royal treatment stopped. One of the trusties (prisoners with special privileges and responsibilities) threatened her that if she didn't start helping to clean she'd be sorry—and another warned her that if her "special visits" ("contact" visits with her mother that were often not during normal visiting hours) didn't stop she would meet a bad end. The inmates got together and filed a complaint with the jail administration; in addition to these two grievances, they claimed she was not taking showers, and was receiving perfume (though they couldn't find any), sleeping in her clothes, and monopolizing the telephone.

"I wanted to see her mop," Kristen Edwards said. "I never saw a rich person mop before. We were told she had a heart condition and couldn't." But eventually not only did Edwards (a pert eighteen-year-old who, with her boyfriend, had robbed a Salt Lake department store of $22,000) get her wish, but she (and another inmate) got to know Frances. "She can convince you that she didn't do it," Edwards said. "We kept pressing her to tell us what happened, but she would avoid it." She told them Marc was crazy and the reason she was in jail. She had sent him to tennis camp and put him through private school—and this was the gratitude she received in return. She told them how her first husband drank too much and beat her, Marc and Larry, and she insisted that sending the boys to Salt Lake in 1977 was not her idea but her mother's. She had mixed feelings about her mother, she told them, but left them in no doubt that she could get anything she wanted from her.

Once Frances became more comfortable with Kristen Edwards and Laura Williams, she played canasta and rummy with them and warmed up to her favorite subject—Lavinia. She showed them pictures of her and said that she would be dancing in *The Nutcracker* for the third consecutive year. One morning Frances did not get up on time, and had her phone and visiting privileges taken away. Since she had been phoning Lavinia every night since she had been in jail, she now asked Kristen if she would call Jeanie (the twenty-eight-year-old woman who was taking care of Lavinia and whom Frances had first met at Lincoln Center, where Jeanie worked as an usher) and find out how Lavinia was. When Kristen did, Jeanie told her that Berenice (who had flown back to New York to be with Lavinia) was driving them both crazy, and that she could now understand why Frances was the way that she was.

But as the day of Frances's formal sentencing drew near, it was Marc that Frances most wanted to know about: specifically whether Kristen or Laura had any information if his life at the prison was in danger as a result of what he'd done to her.

78// The warden of the Utah State Prison holds one of the most powerful positions in the state and the forty-year-old man who assumed it in September of 1982 was a broad-shouldered, Phil Donahue look-alike named Ken Shulsen. With a sense of humor as big as he is, Shulsen started working at the prison in 1968 as a guard on death row and was the person whose duty it was, nine years later, to tell the press—and the country—that Gary Gilmore was dead.

Sitting in his office in October of 1983, Shulsen anticipated Frances's arrival at the prison and the situation he would probably have to deal with when she got there. It was the first time, he said, that a son had incriminated a mother (the prison had housed brothers who had turned on each other before), and though they would be in separate facilities, he felt there was a possibility they would see each other. "We'll sit down with them," he explained, "either independently or together, though her legal situation may dictate what happens. Chances are probably quite great they may want to have contact, because time has a way of healing some wounds. It's still blood, it's still family."

When it was suggested to Shulsen that Marc had come to regard prison as a more hospitable home than he had ever known, Shulsen said if that was true it was "sad and pathetic. I don't think we need to lock people up for their rehabilitation. Marc was fearful when he first came here. You kill your grandfather and testify against your mother—that has to create confusion and anxiety. The environment here may have accelerated his maturity, but I don't have a lot of faith in what it has done beyond that. I was impressed with the way he handled himself in court. Most prisoners change after they come here for the better—but not a whole lot better. It's a minuscule difference."

Despite all the negative publicity Marc's trips out of prison had caused, Shulsen insisted he would continue to release inmates to "responsible" law-enforcement agencies. He assumed Marc would be eating in public restaurants, but felt that taking him to the movies "went too far." In future, he was going to require those agencies to "declare upfront what they are planning to do."

In the women's facility at the prison, some of the inmates were preparing to welcome Frances. Though the corrections officers had told them it would be a waste of time to "strong-arm her for money," they were planning to do just that. During the trial, they had watched the news and were surprised that she wasn't as classy-looking as they had imagined; in fact, they were quite disappointed that she appeared to be a "typical, neurotic person."

Of the thirty-odd women doing time in October, a few had a special interest in Frances: they had gotten to know Marc through college courses, and were eager to hear her side of the story, should she choose to tell it. One of them, Claudia Schauerhamer, was saying over dinner that if Frances was expecting prison life to be "cushy" because she had money, she would be disabused of that notion quickly. "Money won't do her a flip of good in here. She'll sit at the 'reject table.' She'll have to make her way with no help. I feel Marc is in here because of her. She had her thumb on him. He's brilliant, but so easily swayed and confused. If he changes his life-style when he gets out, he'll be the most successful person on earth."

While Claudia resented Marc's being wined and dined, she was even more resentful of the fact that certain inmates "can't do their *own* time." She had heard of the harassment Marc had been getting since testifying, missed seeing him at college, and had just received a letter from him.

DEAR CLAUDIA:

So far, I'm doing okay. These past several weeks have been devastating to me, probably the hardest on me. But things are looking up, and slowly but surely getting a little brighter. Unfortunately, there is no way I will be able to go to college this quarter as much as I wanted to because first of all, the captain down here has restricted me to the compound "for my safety." I agree. . . . There are a lot of hostile people in Medium Security who . . . do not understand all the facts.

So, I will not be lurking up to college this quarter. In a way I'm glad, because right now I am going through a lot of emotional turmoil, as I'm sure you know, but it isn't something I cannot handle. It is just something I must endure and which time will heal.

How are you and the kids? You sound great, and I hope you never get too upset over this situation. Tell Dan Shaffer hi for me, will you? At least poor Dan won't have to compete with me this quarter.

See you next quarter (hopefully) and in one piece—
MARC THE MAGICIAN

The emotional turmoil Marc said he was going through was not eased by Bryan Baird's leaving prison for a halfway house in Salt Lake. For someone who considered himself the brightest inmate at Utah State Prison, Marc had surprising difficulty understanding why Bryan wanted to leave. "He thought I should stay until I was officially paroled [in July of 1984]," Baird said, shaking his head in amusement. "At first, he'd say, 'Gosh, Bryan, I don't know why you have to go.' Then he would immediately not talk to me for a few hours. Wouldn't even look at me." While Bryan could partly understand Marc's feelings—he too had experienced that sinking feeling of abandonment and envy when a fellow prisoner was released—he knew in Marc's case it had a special poignancy. Bryan was the only person at the prison who had penetrated Marc's "protective shell," and what he now saw disturbed him. On the one hand, Bryan was proud of Marc for testifying, but he was also worried that if his testimony resulted in an earlier release date (which Marc was certain it would), "it would be detrimental, because he'd start living in that fantasy world of his again." And standing in the center of that world was the only woman he'd ever really loved—Mom. He was torn between wanting her to be sent to a different prison, Baird said, and wistfully talking about "going back to her." While he felt intense anger toward her on the one hand, that "spooky attachment" was still there. "Marc is *always* going to be open to her, *unless* he can come to terms with himself. I think he'd like to patch things up with her and go back to the same relationship with her that he had before—even though it caused him to do this."

But what worried Bryan more than the prospect that Frances might draw Marc back into her control was the anger he had witnessed during the seven months they had known each other: the tirades Marc went into when someone touched his *Wall Street Journal* (even though he felt no reluctance to touch or take something that belonged to another) or the rage he exhibited when one of his stockbrokers decided to drop him as a client. It was displays like these that made Bryan wonder seriously if Marc could ever murder again.

"I would say," Bryan began, drawing a long breath, "that given the *right* circumstance—something that threatened *his* monetary welfare—Marc is capable of it. I am confident he would not kill for money that wasn't his. But if his own financial situation were in jeopardy and he could fix that by murdering somebody, he would." You've got to understand, Bryan said: "He is a *very* cold person when he is angry. I think he knows, deep inside, he might be sick, but doesn't recognize it."

As Bryan got ready to leave on October 24, the last image he had of Marc Schreuder was this: they were standing outside on a glorious autumn day, near the spot where Marc had first begun to tell Bryan his story. "He said," Bryan recalled, "'I'm really going to miss you—I don't know why you have to go. But that's the way it is, I guess.' And he walked off. I tried to stop him and tell him goodbye, but he wouldn't stop. I decided to follow him back inside and say we'll keep in contact." When Bryan did, he found Marc sitting on his bed with his headphones on. But he was not listening to music. He was once again listening to the family tapes he had drawn on for a strange mix of courage and inspiration before he testified. He was "chortling gleefully," said Bryan, the picture burned into his mind, "kind of like a crazy person."

At first, Marc didn't look at Bryan. Then "he just stared blankly, as if to say, 'It's time for you to leave.'" And so Bryan did.

79// The day before Bryan Baird left Utah State Prison,
Elaine Drukman was sitting in her living room on
an overcast Sunday in Berkeley, California. She had gone to
Spain during her sister's trial and was relieved that she had
not been needed to testify. But that small measure of relief
was about all that she felt as she began talking of the
past—and the future. She had been thinking over the previous few months what tragic figures both her parents were—
two people, with little in common, who had been involved in
the wrong marriage. She had felt for a long time that her
mother was someone who would have been happier as "a
grand lady having parties," without the responsibilities of
children. Elaine loved both of her parents and had tried to
accept them for what they were, but that had not been easy. It
had not been easy to be bedridden and ignored as a child, her
parents convinced she wouldn't live past the age of twenty-
one. It had not been easy to accept their deep distrust of
doctors and psychiatrists and to see how that had prevented
them from seeking help for Robert for quite some time. She
had loved her brother so much, and still remembered how
brilliant he was, the "nocturnal walks" they had taken
together, and how she had taught him to dance; but, most of
all, how her father's lack of time with him and her mother's
drawing him into her deadly game of divide and conquer had,
especially after his lobotomy, essentially destroyed him, even
though he was still alive.

She had lived through his seizures, her mother's breakdown not long after Frances was born, her father's never
coming home for dinner, and the social ostracism of growing
up non-Mormon in Utah. She resisted (and resented) her
mother's attempt to turn her against her father, and she
tolerated his considerable weakness. And though she had
some pleasant memories—"wiggling" into his lap when the
family lived above the store in Provo and having an apricot
tree in the backyard of Gilmer Drive she could call her own

(until her mother had it cut down)—they were few and far between.

When she left home in the early 1950s, the migraine headaches she had so often did not go away. So she sought psychiatric help for them, and, eventually, they stopped. But whenever her mother came to visit, seeking solace from her and relief from Frances, it would take Elaine (and her family) weeks to recover. She had answered her parents' cry for help when Frances was suspended from Bryn Mawr, but had flown back to California, frustrated and angry. If they had been unwilling to take the Salt Lake psychiatrist's advice and turn their backs on Frances, she had tried to follow it. Since she couldn't put Frances into jail or into a hospital at that point, it had been her only way of expressing her disapproval, even if it meant being labeled a "bad sister."

Having lived through Frances's thefts, forgeries, lies and deceptions, she had wound up with her father murdered and her mother cut off from her. And even though Frances was in jail, Elaine felt that only a small measure of justice had been done. In the letter she had written to Mike George in February of 1982, a month before Frances was arrested, she said that she had "no doubt" that Marc, Larry and Frances had killed her father. But unless she found out whether her mother was "an active or a passive participant," she wrote, "I will be forever in purgatory, never knowing for sure, doubting my own sanity." Twenty months later, she still felt the same way. She blamed her mother for "fueling" Frances's hatred toward her father, and felt that the reason her mother had gone with Larry to the warehouse the night before the murder was to try to find her father's new will. After all, she reasoned, her mother had been discovered looking through his file cabinet months before, had seen the memo that her father had left lying around, and had told Frances about it. Elaine never bought the story that her father had asked Larry to come down and work that night and felt that Larry had picked Marc up at the airport, unlocked the doors of the warehouse so that Marc could sleep in "the nest" they had made for themselves the previous summer, and taken him back to the airport after the murder. She was impressed that Marc hadn't, in the end, said that Larry was involved, but it also occurred to her that perhaps they had made "a deal": Marc's "silence" in exchange for Larry's agreeing to give Marc some of the estate money that Larry would share with Lavinia if Frances's appeal failed.

Not only did Elaine feel that her mother had probably stolen the new will, but she still felt her mother might have been trying to poison her father's oatmeal in 1978, carrying on where Marc and Larry had left off the summer before. The memory of her mother's "wishful thinking" that Franklin looked terrible and worn out the month before his death (as opposed to her own feeling that he looked fine) still haunted her, as did her mother's change of stories about when Larry left the house that Sunday morning, her suggestion that Larry drive by the warehouse (after picking Elaine and Marilyn up at the airport) the day after the murder so that he could "check out the keys," and her story that another reason she and Larry had gone to the warehouse that Saturday evening was to take Franklin out for a meal when she knew full well that he didn't eat anything but jello past four o'clock.

It was these reasons—more than her mother's paying for Marc's legal bills, and her own belief that she had ESP (she was in San Francisco and knew the *exact* moment, she claimed, when her ex-boyfriend jumped off the Staten Island Ferry)—that had prompted her to write that note to her mother: *Now I know everything. I can't forget that you helped them to murder Dad.*

"I didn't think I had to go into any detail," Elaine said. "I had hoped she'd respond, but she didn't. I suppose I wanted her to say, 'You're off-base,' and then have a chance to talk about it." Elaine was disappointed that the police didn't do enough to rule out her mother's involvement—an involvement that Berenice has consistently denied. "They see an eighty-year-old lady who insists she and Larry were invited down for inventory and that's the end of it. To a large extent, I think they were very gentle with her."

That aside, what about the future for Elaine Drukman? "I need a mother and I need a mother desperately. I'm not the beauty she was, but I look in the mirror and say, 'There's my mother.' I fantasize taking care of her, but there's no way she'll let me in. I wish that she could find her own life, spend

720

her last years with some kind of peace of mind, but I don't think she will. Not as long as she is married to Frances."

In order for her and her mother to have any sort of rapprochement, Elaine said, her mother would have to make the approach. "I can't," she explained softly. "I don't share exactly the same feelings as Marilyn. Marilyn has more need of approval from Mother. What I need is very different. I *need* to love my mother. I need to have a mother who cares about me, but I'm never going to have that. So the next best thing is to be able to care about her. It's just made very difficult, because there's something in the way of that, something in the way of an honest relationship. I worked very hard to try and have that with her—one based on whatever mutuality we could find, and on affection, if there was any; certainly I felt very affectionate toward her. But I *can't* be dishonest, I can't do that. If I get back together with Mother, we have to have it out. . . .

"If *I* made that approach I'd say, 'Look, Mother, I want to love you. I want to take care of you, I do love you, but I *must* have honesty from you.' And if I didn't get it, to me it would be devastating. . . . But there is no indication to me she wants to resolve all this. If I saw *any* indication, I might be willing to venture out and confront it. But dealing with her in the current situation is dealing with Frances. If she gets a divorce from Frances, then I'm dealing with Mother. And with Frances, there is *no* honesty, there's only manipulation and exploitation. I can't deal with Frances. No one can deal with Frances. Mother has only used and exploited me since Dad's death and I finally reached a point where I said, 'No, I can't take it any more'—the constant anguish of trying to deal with her honestly. As soon as Dad was gone, Frances just grabbed Mother and that was the end.

"One of the things I've never played is the Female Game—stab each other in the back. Sisters play—and women in offices. I always thought it was the most awful game. My feeling about Frances is that if you let her, you too can become one of her victims. The more Mother is abused by Frances, the more Mother wants her back, and the more Frances says no. It's a really sadomasochistic thing, almost, going on. Somebody has to quit playing, because as long as this game is going on, I can't get in there, because I have to play the game too. It is a very deadly game and Frances is playing for keeps. And Frances *always* gets what she wants. Always has. Always will. . . .

"So I don't have a mother," she said longingly. "The mother I knew and loved is somewhere else."

As for Frances and any benefit she might get from being in prison, Elaine was skeptical. "Frances is capable of doing anything, but I doubt she's going to have any incentive at all. She doesn't want to take care of herself—she doesn't want to take responsibility for herself; it's much more fun to get somebody to do it for you, because then you're doing them in. . . . She doesn't think normally. If you try to figure it out in normal, rational ways of dealing with things, you can't, because it isn't. . . . I have a feeling that I'm *never* going to get rid of Frances. Somehow, even in prison, she's always going to be there. I can't see any reason why she shouldn't be out of my life. I've tried very hard and yet she keeps coming back into it."

Before her visitor left, there was one last thing Elaine wanted to say about Marilyn. "Frances has used and abused Marilyn something terrible. Marilyn is more innocent than I am. She doesn't have the street smarts or the cynicism that I do. She has always been more generous and kindhearted. I sometimes wish she had just a little more cynicism, because I think she could save herself a lot of hurt if she had.

"Marilyn needs to feel important and loved. I just cried over her position in all of this. I mean, Marilyn hasn't really done anything. I have done things that Mother could say, 'You're a shit.' Either writing that note or saying that Frances had to give that stock back. But Marilyn hasn't done any-thing."

When Marilyn Reagan mailed the special-delivery letter to Judge Baldwin from Puerto Rico, asking that her sister's life be spared, she did so for two reasons: for the reason she stated in the letter and because she hoped it would help her and her mother reunite. She knew that her mother blamed her and Elaine for *everything*—she had even begun calling herself "the whipping girl"—but that didn't dampen her desire to reopen the lines of communication, or prevent her from laying herself open to the kind of devastating rejection Elaine so feared. She didn't have children to fall back on for love and support in the way Elaine did. She had a husband, and while Berenice would perversely rationalize that that was enough, it could never replace, for Marilyn, her mother's love. While she did not feel her mother was as actively involved in her father's murder as Elaine did, she certainly felt Berenice "set up the psychological climate for it" and that her mother "never loved her husband as much as I loved my father." She was not surprised in the least that her mother was continuing to declare Frances's innocence—"she would rather not know than think it was Frances"—but that didn't matter now. Even though she recognized that "Mother is with the one who needs her the most, the one who will not let her be mother to all three of us"; and even though she, like Elaine, felt she would never see her mother again—she even asked someone who was in contact with her mother to tell her that she still remembered the last time she had seen her, at a lunch in New York about a month before she turned the gun in, and how beautiful she had looked that day in her yellow organdy dress—Marilyn was determined to keep trying.

On the same day that Elaine Drukman was sharing her thoughts in California, Berenice was sitting down to write a letter to Marilyn, who had written to her expressing her desire "to break this wall of silence between us."

Not long before Marilyn's letter arrived, Berenice had an unexpected visitor. It was her ninety-year-old neighbor Claire Flandro. The Flandros were Mormon and had moved next door to the Bradshaws in 1938, less than a year after Franklin and Berenice moved the family from Provo, and some of the Flandros' children had been the same age as Robert, Marilyn, Elaine and Frances. Berenice and Mrs. Flandro had had their share of disputes from time to time, but those—and the screaming and yelling she had had to endure during the summer of 1977—did not prevent Mrs. Flandro from feeling sympathetic to the woman she had known for forty-five years. As a Mormon, she felt that Franklin should have followed the tenets by which he'd been raised and been more than just the financial provider for his family. She hardly ever saw him and when she did it was usually in the middle of the night; he would be sitting at a table, bent over some work he had brought home, and the light that enabled him to do it would shine into the Flandros' bedroom and awaken her. Though the Flandros had little money in those days (during World War II), they saved up enough to buy some heavy curtains and ensure their rest.

In November of 1982, Berenice had received an invitation to Mrs. Flandro's ninetieth birthday party. She had lost her husband in an automobile accident a number of years before, and since then she had relied, more than ever, on the love and closeness of her family, who were planning the party. Berenice had not responded to the invitation, but did happen to bump into Mrs. Flandro at a 7-Eleven in their neighborhood. She thanked Mrs. Flandro for thinking of her, but said she couldn't attend; she was going back to New York to see her beautiful granddaughter dance in *The Nutcracker*. In an equally proud voice, Mrs. Flandro (who had been ill) told Berenice that her family had planned the whole party without even telling her.

"I envy you," Berenice said, then walked away.

Claire Flandro never doubted the sincerity of those three words and now, nearly a year later, she wanted to see if there was anything she could do.

After a few minutes, the door to 1327 Gilmer Drive slowly opened in response to her ringing of the bell. From the guarded look on Berenice's face, Claire Flandro could tell she was surprised to see her.

"I came by," Mrs. Flandro said, "because you are someone who has had a terrible heartbreak." She reached out to Berenice, and Berenice "practically melted in my arms." They went inside and began to talk, one old woman trying to comfort another—any differences, religious or otherwise, of no significance now. Mrs. Flandro listened to Berenice tell her, among other things, that she had "no grandsons" (saying that Elaine's sons were just ski bums who were "milking the trust" for their education), that Elaine still felt she had had something to do with her husband's murder, and that all Elaine and Marilyn really wanted from her was her money. Mrs. Flandro listened patiently, then offered Berenice this advice: if either Marilyn or Elaine reach out to you, accept it.

724

You're all alone now. Do whatever you can to salvage what's left of your family.

Bertha had told her the same thing. And so did a woman who had known Berenice and Franklin in Provo, during happier times. "Life is short," the woman wrote Berenice, "and no day ever comes back."

Berenice must have given some of this advice careful thought—or else she would not have written Marilyn this letter.

October 23, 1983

DEAR MARILYN:

I appreciated hearing from you & your attitude for "breaking the silence" between us. As I have said previously, I hoped when everything is "settled down" my family can be brought together. However much bitterness and hate has gone into this horrible ordeal, some of this can never be erased.

Only time can heal the broken heart & I'm suffering deeply from a broken heart. It is painful. Death is easy compared to the grief I'm going thru at this time. I'm suffering a living hell.

Give us more time. A true mother can not give up her children, no matter what they do. I'll go to my grave suffering for my family. I'm needed, so I'm holding on to what little strength I have left.

Lovingly,
MOTHER

Salt Lake had been enjoying a glorious Indian summer, and the last day of October—Halloween—seemed to belong more to July than to the carved-out pumpkins, fallen leaves, and mountains ablaze with color.

On the same Halloween Day fifty-nine years before, Franklin Bradshaw and Berenice Jewett had rendezvoused in front of a drinking fountain on the University of Utah campus and run off to Ogden to be married. She had worn a black velvet dress and a matching hat that day, and though she later felt "tricked" when she found out a Mormon had married them, she had been happy at the time.

As she sat in Judge Ernest F. Baldwin's courtroom on her wedding anniversary—on the day Frances would be formally sentenced—she was dressed in black once more and had begun to cry even before the matron brought her daughter upstairs from the jail.

The sentencing had been set for nine o'clock, but Mike Rosen, who had arrived only the night before, had asked that it be delayed an hour so that he could meet with Frances. He had been (for him) fairly low-key on the day of the penalty phase, but had now reverted to form. From the moment he had taken on the case, he had been bullishly confident about winning, but he had also left no one in doubt that if he lost, he would go down in flames and make sure that Salt Lake City never forgot him. If he had done the impossible once—gone to the Utah Supreme Court and gotten a delay in the trial—he could do it again and prevail on appeal. To the people of Utah he might have been too sarcastic, too theatrical, and, at times, downright rude, but he had worked hard for his client, was continuing to do so, and that had not been lost on those who had watched his performance and marveled at his ability. The state may have won the case, but there were still some people who felt they hadn't proved it—who felt that Rosen's closing argument had created enough reasonable doubt. But the jury hadn't bought it—hadn't, it must be said, ever come close to buying it—and, legally, that was all that mattered.

With Frances standing by his side in her blue jail uniform, white socks and sandals, Rosen informed Judge Baldwin that he wanted to read part of the psychological assessment of Frances that was included in the confidential presentence report: *"It is unlikely that Mrs. Schreuder would be a cunning mastermind behind any activity requiring patience and diligence. Finally, she is not capable of sustaining any emotion, including anger or hatred, over an extended period of time."*

As Rosen went on to tell the judge that this "critical finding" not only corroborated what the defense had been saying all along—that Frances was not guilty and the state had not proved its case—but that it "must have a very significant bearing on whatever penalty is imposed," Ernie Jones sat there, amused. Once again, he thought to himself, Rosen was taking things out of context, letting the court hear what he wanted them to hear. Jones and the judge had seen the presentence report, and what it also essentially said, according to Jones, was that Frances was capable of ordering the murder of her father one day and buying Lavinia a dress the next.

The judge had indicated Frances could speak, if she so desired, and in a low, barely audible voice, she did: *"I am innocent of the charges, Your Honor, and I intend to vindicate myself."*

Aside from telling the judge four weeks before that she wanted to waive the jury for the penalty phase, this was her only public utterance throughout the trial. After Jones made a few comments, Judge Baldwin formally sentenced Frances to life imprisonment.

As Frances slowly took her seat, Rosen told the judge he wanted him to consider "several salient points" that were part of the defense's request for a certificate of probable cause (which, if granted, could help in their efforts to win an appeal) and their request, once more, that he allow Frances out on bail.

What had gone on in this courtroom, Rosen said indignantly, was "a trial by ambush." The ambush began with the state's hiding of Jeffrey Charles Morris, yet he was never called to the stand. It continued with the state's saying they didn't know if Marc was going to testify and Marc's then saying there were no promises made in exchange for his decision to do so. And when the deal he had made had finally come out, it hadn't been because *Marc* "was struck with a light on the road to Damascus and wanted to cleanse his soul," but because his *lawyers* brought it to the attention of the court. Had the jury known this, Rosen argued, "it could have made a tremendous difference on his credibility."

On September 19, Rosen had asked the jury to pretend they were at the movies and that his opening statement was just a preview of coming attractions. Now he was giving the judge a preview of some of the things (in addition to the ones he had already mentioned) he would almost certainly raise on appeal: Moench should have been allowed to testify only in the event Marc didn't and should not have been allowed to "bolster" him; the comments by Alma Boyce and Doug Steele—more "trial by ambush" tactics—had been prompted by Jones, even though he knew the judge's feelings about the will; Stephen Klein should not have been allowed to testify (the state never even asked for "an escape charge" and only called him "to poison" the jury); and withholding of evidence (they had only seen two of the six Berenice Bradshaw letters the state introduced at the penalty phase; had they seen the one that complained about Marc's behavior during 1977, they would never have agreed to Berenice's not having to testify).

As far as his request for bail, Rosen said Frances had "a track record" unprecedented in forty-eight of America's fifty states: based on his research, there had *never* been a person convicted of murder one who was released on bail after the verdict and showed up for the penalty hearing. "Her presence speaks louder than anything I can say." But what he didn't say was that *no one* had ever been released on bail after that kind of conviction or even why the research didn't cover all fifty states. But that was Mike Rosen, throwing it up anyway, hoping it would stick.

Ernie Jones calmly defended himself against nearly all of Rosen's accusations, but it was his response to the issue of Jeffrey Charles Morris that raised the most eyebrows. ". . . After looking into his background and after working on him for three or four months, it was our position that Mr. Morris was *not* telling the truth and, therefore, we decided not to call him."

The judge denied both defense motions, but said that if there was a possible problem of mother and son being at the same prison, he would allow Frances to remain in the county jail (the maximum stay there being one year) if she so desired. He also said that he would allow her a few minutes with her mother, before the matron took her back downstairs.

During those few minutes, which Berenice had requested, the old lady's tears and embracing of her daughter were met with little emotion at all, as if Berenice were no more than a rejected lover whom Frances unhappily tolerated. This was all Marc's fault, Frances said, assuring her mother that she hadn't done anything. Over and over Berenice had vowed to the world that she would stick by Frances through thick and thin, no matter what *anybody* thought, said, or did. And she had. But over and over she had posed this question: "Why? Why does my daughter treat me the way that she does?"

She had been asking that question years before her husband was murdered and her grandson and daughter were convicted of it. And she was asking it still. But even if she knew the answer—and there were many—it was unlikely she would accept it.

At one forty-five that afternoon, after Mike Rosen assured the press that "the ambush continues" and Laura Williams had given her the hug she asked for, Frances left the Salt Lake City-County Jail for the Utah State Prison. Marc had made this trip, south on Interstate 15, for the first time fifteen months before, and now it was her turn—to travel the route her father had so often, on his way to the little town of Lehi. With more than $1,300 in her purse—and the knowledge that Berenice would see to it that she never ran short—Frances could easily keep her end of the "business deal" she had arranged with Kristen Edwards: Frances would buy a large-screen television and a video cassette recorder, and Kristen (who would soon follow Frances to prison and become her roommate) would charge their fellow inmates an admission fee.

On the way down to prison, Frances said little to the matron who accompanied her. She did say how pleased she was to have her brass crucifix back and told the heavyset woman of its importance. It had been twenty-seven years since Frances had left Utah for Bryn Mawr College in the autumn of 1956, and now, barring a miracle, she would be back home for quite some time. That had been her father's hope, and she had, finally, fulfilled it.

Conclusion//

The weight of this sad time we must
   obey,
Speak what we feel, not what we
   ought to say.
The oldest hath borne most: we that
   are young
Shall never see so much, nor live so
   long.

           —King Lear, V.iii.325

In the year of Franklin Bradshaw's death, according to the FBI, nearly one of every five persons murdered in the United States was related to his assailant. Some of the homicides were blamed on a "romantic triangle," some on an "argument over money or property," and some fell into the category of "unable to determine." While statistics and categories often serve as useful barometers, they can't begin to reveal, in the case of murder, the immeasurable destruction, pain and suffering that lie behind them.

When Marc fired two shots at close range into his grandfather's back and skull that Sunday morning in Salt Lake City, not only was he killing his grandfather but, in a way, he and his mother were killing the entire Bradshaw family and everything—both good *and* bad—that Franklin Bradshaw stood for.

"Society moves by some degree of parricide, by which the children, on the whole, kill, if not their fathers, at least the beliefs of their fathers, and arrive at new beliefs. This is what progress is." Sir Isaiah Berlin made this ironic comment in London about six months before Franklin Bradshaw was murdered. While Frances had managed to do both, it was impossible to see, in human terms, what progress had been made. But it was more possible to understand, if not accept, *why* she had done it—and why, in the end, Marc felt he had no choice but to carry out her ultimate request.

"Look, Marc, it is not really killing, it is the right thing to do

732

for us, Gramps is old, and he doesn't care about people and he won't help us. I wouldn't live with Gramps and Granny, would rather die." This is part of what Marc told Dr. Moench his mother had said to him, and it rings true. From the moment Frances began stealing, forging, passing bad checks, and selling stock certificates that did not belong to her, she was not doing this merely because she needed the funds. In fact, most of the time she didn't. She had arrived at Bryn Mawr with as many clothes as any woman in the school and with more than enough money to spend. But whenever Frances was faced with a choice at college (or throughout her life, for that matter) between abiding by the rules (either the school's or society's) or breaking them, she *always* chose the second alternative, a classmate said, "for the same reason most people eat a potato chip: she couldn't resist."

Frances was not stealing for the sake of stealing. As "the child no one wanted—ever," she was, in the words of the psychoanalyst Louise J. Kaplan, "stealing for love."

During Frances's trial Bertha Beck asked, "What does Frances have on Berenice that Berenice caters to her the way that she does?" The short answer is that Frances learned early on that her birth had been a mistake, that her mother had had a breakdown shortly after it, and that Marilyn (and to a lesser extent Elaine) had been "mother" to her for a crucial period of time. Whatever guilt Berenice felt about that—and it seems overwhelmingly clear that she felt a great deal—Frances knew how to exploit it and, as Elaine said, "orchestrate it from day one": to make her mother pay, literally and emotionally, for that transgression for the rest of her life.

In the opening soliloquy to Shakespeare's *Richard III*, the hunchbacked Richard, Duke of Gloucester (who later becomes king), says:

> But I, that am not shaped for sportive tricks,
> Nor made to court an amorous looking glass;
> I, that am rudely stamped, and want love's majesty
> To strut before a wanton ambling nymph;
> I, that am curtailed of this fair proportion,
> Cheated of feature by dissembling Nature,

> Deformed, unfinished, sent before my time
> Into this breathing world scarce half made up,
> And that so lamely and unfashionable
> That dogs bark at me as I halt by them;
> . . . .
> And therefore, since I cannot prove a lover
> To entertain these fair well-spoken days,
> I am determined to prove a villain,
> And hate the idle pleasures of these days.

In 1916, in "The Exceptions" (the first of three essays Sigmund Freud wrote under the heading "Some Character-Types Met with in Psycho-Analytic Work"), Freud discussed what he saw as the meaning of Richard's soliloquy: " 'Nature has done me a grievous wrong in denying me the beauty of form which wins human love. Life owes me a reparation for this, and I will see that I get it. I have a right to be an exception, to disregard the scruples by which others let themselves be held back. I may do wrong myself, since wrong has been done to me.'

"And now we feel," Freud continued, "that we ourselves might become like Richard, that on a small scale, indeed, we are already like him. . . . We all think we have reason to reproach Nature and our destiny for congenital and infantile disadvantages; we all demand reparation for early wounds to our narcissism, our self-love. Why did not Nature give us the golden curls of Balder or the strength of Siegfried or the lofty brow of genius or the noble profile of aristocracy? Why were we born in a middle-class home instead of in a royal palace? . . ."

Frances could not be the dancer her mother wanted. But neither could Marilyn or Elaine. Frances did not possess her mother's beauty. But neither did Marilyn or Elaine. Frances told her mother in a letter how lonely she felt growing up. But so, too, did Marilyn and Elaine. According to Berenice, Frances said she couldn't understand why her daddy didn't come home for dinner like other daddies. Marilyn and Elaine said they wished he would have, but that they understood why he didn't. All three sisters saw what happened to their brother (even Berenice admitted, in describing her and Franklin's efforts to toilet-train Robert, "When I think of all of the cruel things we did to that boy . . . I just shudder"), but it was Frances who vehemently accused her mother of forever treating him like a baby and turning him into a vegetable. All four Bradshaw children were, to use a professional term, "narcissistically deprived," and all four displayed their frustration, their "rage" about that, in different ways. Robert wanted, more than anything, to follow in his father's footsteps, to "be the 100% partsman Dad can be proud of," to carry on the Bradshaw name. When he saw that was unlikely, he even asked his father to set him up in a modest business somewhere, promising to call it anything but the last name with which he was born. It wasn't just the toilet training or Berenice's tying him to a rope, when they lived in Provo, so he wouldn't run away. Franklin simply had little time for him, and much of the time Berenice spent with him was devoted to enlisting him as an ally against Franklin. Berenice had no one—and nowhere—else to turn to express her deep unhappiness. When she verbally attacked Franklin, he would run back to the warehouse, unable and unwilling to endure the barrage. So she turned to her children, and Robert, in particular, used to get so worked up that he and his father would fight. Robert's epileptic seizures began at about the same time Frances was born, and neither Berenice nor Franklin wanted to face the reality that anything could be wrong with their only son. So they sent Marilyn down to the basement to live next to him, to take care of him—and swore to each other that there was no history of this behavior in either of their families.

In Freud's essay "Dostoevsky and Parricide" he wrote that while epileptic attacks are "as a rule determined, in a way we do not understand, by purely physical causes, [they] may nevertheless owe their first appearance to some purely mental cause (a fright, for instance) or may react in other respects to mental excitations." In the essay, Freud wrote of Dostoevsky and his "epilepsy" (which Freud uneasily classified as "hystero-epilepsy—that is, as severe hysteria"); of the murder of Dostoevsky's own father when the writer was eighteen; and of the murder of the father that occurs in *The Brothers Karamazov*. Freud saw a connection between these things and contended that these "deathlike," epileptic attacks "signify an identification with someone who is really dead or with someone who is still alive and whom the subject wishes dead. The attack then has the value of a punishment. One has wished another person dead, and now one *is* this other person and is dead oneself. At this point psycho-analytical theory brings in the assertion that for a boy this other person is usually his father and that the attack . . . is thus a self-punishment for a death-wish against a hated father."

If Robert's attacks, his physical fights with his father, and his verbal battles with his mother were the only weapons he possessed in an effort to express his rage toward both his parents—and his hope that he, like his siblings, could ensure a permanent place in their lives—they were not enough. It's not that Franklin and Berenice didn't love him. They loved him to the extent they were capable. Even when they finally sought the medical help he needed, Franklin sent Doug Steele up to Ogden with Robert instead of going himself. The doctors were appalled, Steele has not forgotten it to this day, and it is doubtful Robert ever did. They had the money to put Robert into a private hospital, but (aside from the lobotomy operation in Ogden and some time in a nursing home in Salt Lake) he spent the last fifteen years of his life in the state hospital in Provo and the V.A. hospital in Salt Lake. And when he finally died, Franklin's first instinct was not to tell anyone.

They didn't mean to destroy him, but they had helped.

Marilyn looks back on her years at Wasatch Academy—her opportunity to "escape" from home—as the best thing that could have happened to her. At a certain point, when she found the situation between her parents to be so unbearable, she pleaded with her father, "I don't care what you do, Dad, but please do *something.*" So he sent her and (for one year) Robert away to Wasatch, but he was never able to improve—or end—his marriage. His philosophy was always that if something's troubling you, you just get it out of your mind by sheer willpower. For a while, it seemed, he was able to do that through his work, but his children and his wife couldn't, and in the end, neither could he.

Marilyn left Utah for good in 1950, "to seek her fortune" in

New York, but she continued trying to be the "good daughter" her parents could count on, and, she now feels, her mother wound up resenting her for it, resenting the fact she couldn't succeed in turning Marilyn against her father. After all, Berenice and Marilyn are similar in a number of ways. Aside from their both being strong and forthright, Marilyn fulfilled the same role for Berenice that Berenice did for her mother; when Berenice's mother went to work full-time, Berenice resented having to do all the dishes and take care of her brother. In writing of how she was "robbed of my girlhood," and felt her mother always protected her brother "and wouldn't let my father administer the discipline he needed," Berenice was expressing sentiments that Marilyn (particularly in terms of herself and Frances) would later echo. Berenice felt deserted by her mother, and Berenice's children, in many ways, felt deserted by her. But as long as Berenice could be the all-powerful matriarch, she could exert—or at least try to exert—the kind of control over them that would ensure they wouldn't abandon her in the way she once had felt abandoned. Just because Marilyn had her own life did not mean she didn't need her mother or no longer wanted her love. But Berenice could not entirely understand that—that nothing could replace a mother's love.

In trying to find her niche in her parents' lives, Marilyn never refused their requests to help them with Frances—both in Salt Lake and in New York. But she quickly realized that all of the trouble Frances kept getting herself into—and her parents' reluctance and inability to turn their backs on her—only meant that Frances would be the one, time and again, to have their full attention. So she went to school in New York in order both to learn about business and to be, on some level, her father's daughter—to fill a void that her brother could not. But instead of admiring her efforts, her mother saw it as a devious attempt to control the empire, and so she blocked her path. Frances tried, through Behrens, to blame her for the murder, and her mother still holds her accountable for destroying the family. And yet, despite everything, Marilyn continues reaching out for Berenice's love.

* * *

Elaine's form of rebellion was to flee Salt Lake also, marry exactly the kind of man she knew her mother would not approve of—someone poor and Jewish—and transform herself from Young Republican to political liberal. As the "middle sister" she had been the mediator, but had resigned that thankless position long before. The game was too deadly, and Frances was playing for keeps. So the solace Elaine said her mother always found in her she finds in Mason and their two sons. For all her parents' shortcomings, she had tried to love and accept them for what they were, but she knew that in order to survive she had to escape.

Nonetheless, neither time nor distance nor her own family can ever erase the memories for Elaine. The bitterness is still there. The concern that something still might happen to her children in the way of physical harm. The sadness of knowing she has her mother's features and her deep-throated laugh, but does not have her.

So, for Elaine, there are still questions—especially about her mother's complicity—and there is still Frances.

Frances is "Berenice's baby." Frances is "her golden idol." Frances was "schooled" and "indoctrinated" by her mother. Berenice is "emotionally addicted" to Frances. "Mother and Frances have a symbiotic relationship." Over and over, these were the kind of opinions that had been passionately expressed by people who were close to them.

"It is the specific unconscious need of the mother," writes Margaret Mahler, "that activates, out of the infant's infinite potentialities, those in particular that create for each mother 'the child' who reflects her own unique and individual needs." In including Mahler's passage in her book *Prisoners of Childhood*, a book that focuses on the ways parents form and deform the emotional lives of their children, fellow psychoanalyst Alice Miller goes on to say that "if the mother's primary occupation with her child—her mirroring function during the period of early childhood—is unpredictable, insecure, anxiety-ridden, or hostile, or if her confidence in herself as a mother is shaken, then the child has to face the period of individuation without having a reliable framework for emotional checking back to his symbiotic partner." The child, who is "at the mother's disposal," often faces a situation in which the parent, Miller says, "unconsciously uses his new-born child to lay out for himself the tragedy of his own fate."

Berenice had not wanted to have Frances. She admitted it in her autobiography, joked (in response to why she had had any children at all) that she was "too tired to resist" and "I had four children before I realized what was causing it," and later told Don Bradshaw that "if abortions had been legal, she wouldn't have had any of her children." But it was Frances's birth in particular, coming seven years after Elaine's, that she chose to single out. It did not take Frances long to realize it—and to use that knowledge to her advantage—nor did it take Berenice long to try to make it up to her. And the vehicle for doing that was Franklin. Frances became a foot soldier in her mother's war of divide and conquer. Marilyn remembers that her mother's saying "If your father has all this money, why can't we spend it?" soon became "The only way you can get money from your father is to take it." Berenice had felt her own father was "stingy" and remembered how her mother used to pull "sneaky tricks" by going through his pockets, and on one occasion—the one she'll never forget—going through Arthur Tuck's pockets and finding the letter that broke her heart. She might have known she was marrying, in Franklin, a man who was bound to succeed, but she was "a play gal" (as she called herself) who did not know the effects—or, most of all, the loneliness—his ambition would have on her. He sought to control his money—to make sure neither she nor anybody else ever knew his worth—and she sought to control her children and express her rage and hostility toward Franklin through them. If Robert was the first casualty and Marilyn and Elaine refused to take sides, Frances was *her* recruit—the child who could not run from her the way her mother once had.

Elaine spoke of how Frances never wanted to take responsibility for herself—of how it was easier to let others do it for you—and she was right. Frances knew that her mother would *always* come to her rescue, no matter *what* she did, and she too was right. If Berenice could steal, Frances could steal. If Berenice could forge checks, Frances could forge checks. (When Joel Campbell asked Frances, three days after the murder, about the forgeries during the summer of 1977, she declined to talk about it, but did say that "my mother has done it for years.") If Berenice could lie, Frances could lie. *I have been wronged, therefore I am entitled to do wrong.* If that is the message of the opening soliloquy of *Richard III,* it is no less true in the relationship of Berenice and Frances—and no less true in the legacy Frances passed to Marc and Larry. When testifying about the checks he had stolen from his grandmother and forged, Marc said that Mom had told him it was fine, just as long as he didn't get caught. Yet when he, Larry and Frances did get caught in the summer of 1977 (and Frances had been caught many times before and after), Franklin never took any sort of action against them. Perhaps it was, as Doug Steele felt, his stubborn pride in the Brad-shaw name and his sense of privacy. But perhaps, on a deeper level, it was a result of his own guilt at not having been around more when his children were growing up—a realiza-tion that while he had shone brilliantly as an entrepreneur, he had failed as a father. He told Bertha once that the main reason he didn't leave Berenice was that he felt the children were *his* responsibility. And yet he didn't go to his daughters' weddings. He didn't take Robert to Ogden. He wrote count-less letters to Frances when she was going through her troubles with Gentile, but they were filled with opinions that the reason she was nervous and high-strung was because Berenice was; that if Frances got a divorce, it wouldn't be her father's fault but her own. He was not as cheap as everyone made him out to be, but he used his checkbook as a substitute for contact. He had planned to go to New York in April of 1965, had even told Frances what he was going to do when he got there, but he never did. It wasn't just that Frances threatened to have him put in jail or Marilyn advised him that his coming would probably do no good. He simply didn't make the time. He hated confrontation of any kind, but if had to confront something he found it easier to wage war on his old typewriter than to do it in person.

His whole world revolved around money and it is a bitter irony that he was killed because of it, and that Frances was tripped up because of it as well. While his letters over the years admit little wrongdoing on his part in what was happen-ing with Frances, there is evidence to suggest he felt responsi-ble. When Larry lived in Salt Lake for a whole year—one of the few periods in Larry's life he remembers with fondness—

and Marc for a summer, Franklin tried to be a father to them, spending more time with them than he had spent with his children. He had wrestled on the floor with them and told them stories. He was getting a second chance. Robert had died two years before and that still hung over him, no matter how hard Franklin might have tried to dismiss it from his mind. And when it was decided Marc and Larry would come to Salt Lake for the fateful summer of 1977, Franklin let the whole world know how eagerly he awaited the arrival of the boys who would someday take over the empire. He was going to tell them all about the Bradshaw heritage, take them to his different stores and show them off, and make sure that they didn't leave town without a full understanding and appreciation of the work ethic and the values he lived by.

But as Doug Steele so aptly put it, "they were long gone by the time they got to Frank." Even once the nightmare began, Franklin at first refused to believe that they were responsible. He did refuse to pay for their schooling that year, but Berenice forged some checks and took care of that. Even if she hadn't, he would have paid eventually, or Berenice, who grudgingly admitted that "he probably did more for Frances and her family [in the way of money] than I knew about," would have seen to it that he did. In the end, she usually prevailed over his weakness and his guilt. He might not have wanted to give Frances all that she desired; and Berenice might have been forced to go to work at the warehouse and punch a time clock; but the money, however delayed it might have been, kept flowing from west to east.

The irony, though, is that whatever he sent or she sent would never have been enough. The $200,000 Marc and Larry took in 1977, Marc had discovered to his dismay, was not enough either. Nor was the $3,000 check that Nancy Jones wrote out to Lavinia ten days before the murder—the money Marc said would be the last they would ever ask for; the money that was used to buy the plane tickets and the gun that killed Franklin Bradshaw. It was, as it had always been for Frances, more than just money. It was her way of ensuring that they never forgot what she felt they had done to her. To Frances, their money was her money. She felt entitled to it. (". . . [Marc and Larry] came to Salt Lake to find and send back to her the money that she felt she was entitled to," Dr.

Moench testified at Marc's trial.) She was dependent on them and hated them because of it. Even when she threatened them that this letter or that letter would be the last one she'd ever write, or that Berenice would never be allowed to see her or the children again, it never was, and Berenice always did. Her father had begged her to get a job, yet when she finally did, for a brief period in 1968, he reminded her that because she had no college degree, she probably would never get a better one—and her mother flew to New York and kidnapped her children, certain that she couldn't work and be a mother at the same time. If she couldn't make them proud of her through positive accomplishments, she could try to guarantee her place in their lives through negative acts. If Berenice wanted Frances to always remain "her child" ("I know what your psychiatrist means," Frances wrote Berenice, "when he says 'you want a baby.' You want a helpless baby of any age to gratify your needs"), then Berenice and Franklin would have to take full responsibility for whatever Frances did. That was the ultimate message Frances had tried to convey to them in letter after letter—letters filled with rage and hostility as well as (when necessary) charm and pleas for forgiveness. And that was the kind of message Frances gave to Marc when she told him that "it's not really killing, it is the right thing to do for us, Gramps is old, and he doesn't care about people and he won't help us." In her view of the world, she was entitled to steal, she was entitled to forge and, in the end, she was entitled to kill.

"Children begin by loving their parents," Oscar Wilde wrote. "After a time they judge them. Rarely, if ever, do they forgive them." Frances never forgave her father and she has never forgiven her mother. There was, to quote Alice Miller, a "vicious circle of contempt" between the three of them, a kind of Oedipus complex in reverse, in which Frances had to kill her father in order to safeguard her uneasy marriage to Berenice. But Frances was no longer Berenice's foot soldier. She had learned the game well and she was now in charge, making sure that the war her parents fought while she was growing up would continue. If she was miserably unhappy, she would see to it that they were.

Franklin was far from being the best father in the world,

but in his own peculiar and imperfect way he tried—and he did not deserve to die.

From Salt Lake to Bryn Mawr to New York, Frances carried all her antisocial behavior, hurt, loneliness and rage into her marriages with Gentile and Schreuder and into the kind of relationships she had with her children—relationships frighteningly similar to the kind she had, and continued to have, with her mother. If it is true, as Alice Miller writes, that "a child can never see through *unconscious manipulation*"; that "it's like the air he breathes; he knows no other, and it appears to him to be the only normal possibility"; that "the tragedy is that the parents too have no defense against it, since they do not know what is happening, and even if they have some inkling can do nothing to change it"; and that "unconsciously the parents' childhood tragedy is continued in their children"—if all this is true, it might partly explain Frances's unhealthy need to exert a Svengali-like control over her children, but it can never excuse her outrageous abuse of them.

Dr. Moench spoke of Marc's having suffered from an extremely severe, unresolved Oedipus complex, but his father was gone from the home before Marc in theory could have viewed him as a rival for his mother and before it could have been resolved. Larry was Marc's "rival" for a while (and so was "Uncle George," Richard Behrens), but once Frances saw that Larry was both unwilling and unable to be controlled, he was thrown out, time after time—and made to understand that he didn't exist, that Marc was better than he was. But no matter how often that happened, Larry's desire to feel wanted by her never waned. He happily went along with Frances's script for the summer of 1977—still calls it one of the greatest summers of his life—but was told he would not be allowed back home after it. While Larry says he was never part of any plan to murder his grandfather—"she knew that I wouldn't want to go along with that stuff"—he is not entirely convincing on that point. He admits that he knew about the oatmeal, admits that he and Marc would laugh as they watched Gramps running around the warehouse, red-faced and faster than usual, the amphetamine-laced oatmeal inside him, but denies *he* ever spiked it and that (as Marc told Bryan Baird) the idea of killing his grandfather by throwing an electric appliance into the bathtub was his. Larry, however, turns red-faced himself and flashes his "inappropriate" grin (the term used in his psychiatric reports) when asked if he knew *when* the murder was going to happen, if he unlocked those doors that Saturday night, if he hid the keys in the basement that Marilyn eventually found, and if he provided Marc with transportation from and back to the airport.

He says he didn't know anything, scoffs at the polygraph test he took which indicated that he did, and insists that Marc had a set of keys to the warehouse from the summer before (a contention that supports what Richard Behrens said). The only thing that sticks in his mind from that Saturday night is that his grandfather still owes him $12 for the work he did, but that it will be difficult to collect it from him now. As far as the next morning is concerned, he did happen to hear his grandfather doing his exercises on the floor above him, but insists he did not get out of bed until he got up to go flying. When it was pointed out to him that his receipt from Skyhawk Aviation for that day listed Los Angeles, Albuquerque and El Paso on it and he was asked if he flew Marc to any of those places so that his brother could fly home from a different city, Larry said he couldn't explain why those cities were listed there, that he had not taken Marc anywhere, that he had flown to Nevada and California on occasion, but not that day. He insisted that he never saw or stole a new will—only the original 1970 one he "took possession of"; that he didn't know anything about the "new" set of keys Don Bradshaw claimed Larry took from his hands that Sunday afternoon; and that he never had any desire to drive by the warehouse the following day, after picking up Elaine and Marilyn at the airport, to check the new locks Doug Steele had installed.

He was pleased that his mother was convicted—"she got what she deserved"—and seemed more amused than angry that she had tried to frame him with the airline tickets. "I hadn't done anything," he said. "That was typical Mom, always trying to throw dirt on me." In January of 1983, two months before Larry was released from prison, his psychiatric report at the time said he had "an excessive control of underlying feelings"; yet throughout the hours and hours of discussing the tragedy of his family, his matter-of-fact attitude on the surface slowly gave way to the resentment underneath: resentment that Marc had always been "her star, her pet"; that Frances had forced him to go to a military school rather than "an ordinary American high school where I would have met girls"; that she hadn't cared about his accomplishments there or come to his graduation; that she hadn't let him come home (except for one brief period) during his senior year on weekends; that he had had to spend Christmas of 1977 by himself and the following one at a YMCA. He said he'd never forget his "first memory of life"—the time she slammed him and Marc onto the floor after they spilled perfume on her bed; or how he begged and pleaded that she not sell his collection of wheatback pennies, which she did not once, but twice; or how she wouldn't post bail for him or get him a private attorney—an opportunity for Frances finally to control him—while at the same time she was moving into Gracie Square and contributing thousands of dollars to the New York City Ballet.

As much as he would like to, there are many, many painful things that Lorenzo Gentile/Larry Schreuder/Larry Bradshaw will never forget—including the night he took a hammer to Fred Salloum—as he attempts to gather together the pieces of his life and go on. And while the question of his complicity in the murder of Franklin Bradshaw may forever remain open (of all the answers Larry gave in response to this, none was more revealing than his vow that "no one is ever going to send me back to jail"), the question of whether he was a victim from the time he was born will not.

Despite having his own apartment now and nearly everything else that money can buy, nothing in reality has significantly changed for Larry. He is still on the outside, looking in. Berenice wants nothing to do with him, prefers that he have nothing to do with Lavinia, and wouldn't mind if he changed his name back to Schreuder, or to anything else he chose. He and his father are in contact with each other, but Larry sees little importance in that. In fact, he sadly does not attach much importance to anything—other than his financial welfare, the fluctuating price of gasoline, the country's continuing need for a strong defense, his slavish love of Chevrolets (in 1984, at one point, he had seven) and their slogan,

"Taking Charge," and his constant hope of meeting "a nice, skinny, American girl" he could one day marry.

What he places no importance on whatsoever is this: when his mother arrived at the Utah State Prison she filled out a form that stated she had only one son. Him. That made Larry laugh—the kind of laugh that could make one cry.

With Larry effectively vanquished as a rival (and Lavinia not yet born), Marc had his mother all to himself—and she had him all to herself. He was at her disposal in the same way she had been at Berenice's. Marc told Dr. Moench of becoming his mother's best friend, of staying up till all hours to listen to her problems, and of spending a year in her bed after they returned from Europe. When he did something that enraged her, he was often beaten or locked out, deciding that he preferred the former because he didn't think he could fend for himself as well as Larry could—and because he didn't want to lose her. He (and Larry) had seen her anger expressed toward others as well. They were present that Sunday afternoon in August of 1964 when she attacked the teenage babysitter. He and Larry had witnessed her fights with both Vittorio and Frederick; he and Larry had felt her brush on their bodies more times than they care to remember, and then had seen that brush applied to Lavinia's as well. They learned quickly to be charmed by her smile and devastated by her frown—and Marc, in particular, soon realized that you didn't say no to Mom. It was easier and safer to absorb her view of the world—and of her parents and his grandparents—than to risk losing her. So he became her trusted foot soldier in the same way she had been Berenice's. Any other friends were seen as threats. She had great plans for him (Yale and so forth), and "exalted masculine ideal," Louise Kaplan writes in *Adolescence,* which she would have transmitted to him during infancy and which he would do his best to fulfill. But the paradoxical nature of ideals is that they can *never* be satisfied, can never be adequately reached. That didn't stop Marc from trying—trying to be everything his mother didn't become and, as a result, enabling her to live vicariously through his accomplishments—and it later didn't stop Lavinia from becoming the dancer that Frances had once tried to be (in an effort to please *her* mother), as well as a pawn that Frances could use against Berenice.

In writing about the character of "the impostor," Louise Kaplan refers to a character disorder that reaches fruition in puberty, "a form of criminality that is typical of males." The prominent features of this disorder are "a kind of mirroring relationship to the mother and an absentee or emotionally unavailable father," the person being expected "to mirror the exalted ideal" of the parent who is present. The impostor is "a person who assumes a false identity for the sole purpose of deceiving others . . . because he must hide from himself and from everyone else the inadequacies of his actual self." But while he is a liar, a cheat and a manipulator, Kaplan suggests, he is "not a mere criminal." He is (quoting Phyllis Greenacre, whom Kaplan calls "one of the few psychoanalysts who have investigated the character of the impostor") "a very special type of liar who imposes on others fabrications of his achievements, position, or worldly possessions. This he may do by misrepresenting his official (statistical) identity, by presenting himself with a fictitious name, history or other items of personal identity either borrowed from some actual person or fabricated according to some imaginative conception of himself."

With the "rare exception of Pope Joanna," Kaplan writes, "who is said to have reigned as pontiff in the ninth century until she gave birth while riding in a religious procession, so far as we know all *full-fledged* impostors [as opposed to episodic or demi-impostors] are males. . . . He knows that he is not the person he pretends to be, but he feels that he *must* be some person greater or more magnificent than the ordinary mortals he sets out to deceive. His behavior is driven and repetitious. His very existence depends on the success of his trickery. To be a full-fledged impostor is a full-time occupation rather than a ploy for social or material gain."

It doesn't happen overnight, Kaplan writes. "He starts out as the spoiled darling of the nursery, becomes a liar and a cheat in boyhood, and then in early adolescence is an arch manipulator. The average adolescent boy often experiences himself as a pretender. It is not at all unusual for a boy on the verge of manhood to try to prove himself by assuming grandiose postures and roles. Every teenager and adult, male or female, will occasionally manipulate others to advance his or her psychological cause. But for the potential and eventually full-fledged impostor, lying, cheating, manipulating are a way of life. The impostor lies even when there is no immediate practical gain."

Parents, Kaplan says, "consciously or unconsciously" support his fraudulence. Teachers are more confounded by him—the "lone wolf" who operates outside of any group loyalties, but who often provokes delinquencies in others—than by rowdies, vandals, or abusers of drug and alcohol. Smooth as he is, he "is neither saint nor daring hero but an angry, frightened boy who must dissemble in order to cloak the pathetic nobody he imagines himself to be. His deceptions aim at enhancing the illusion that he is a powerful person, so powerful, in fact, that he can fool the grown-ups who are in authority. In a broad sense he is trying to do away with the genital and generational differences that make him feel so inadequate."

His behavior "follows a script that is one of several versions of a family-romance fantasy that must be enacted over and over again. This universal childhood fantasy has as its central theme the idea of being a foundling in a family of provisional parents. Most young children construct such a fantasy as a defensive maneuver to soften the humiliations and allay the anxieties generated by the Oedipal drama. The average child merely imagines that he is a foundling reared by foster parents who are the temporary substitutes for his absent biological parents. He merely fantasizes that he is an unacknowledged aristocrat in a mundane world. When he arrives at puberty he relinquishes the idealizations of infancy and childhood" and gives up his family romance. But when the liar, cheat and manipulator arrives at puberty, he "has become absorbed in his fantasy. He must now live out the scenario of his childhood family romance. He becomes an impostor."

While "typical" scenarios, Kaplan writes, are "reflected in the Frog Prince, Dick Whittington, Snow White, Cinderella myths," a different sort exists as "the model of the impostor's family romance." Kaplan mentions two. "The Master Thief" tells of a young man who pretends to be rich (but whose real family is poor) and "returns to the kingdom of his birth after many years of wandering the earth as a master thief." The king of the kingdom extends three challenges to the young man—all of which he accepts: "to steal his favorite horse from the stable; to steal the bed sheet from under the king and queen while they are asleep and to remove the wedding ring from the finger of the queen; and, third, to kidnap the parson and the sexton from the king's chapel." Failure to do these things would mean the gallows, and no reward for success is even mentioned. But he risks his life anyway, just to prove he can outwit the king. "In accordance with fairy tale tradition," Kaplan writes, "he succeeds in pulling the wool over the king's eyes. . . . But does the master thief get to marry the princess? Is he restored to the kingdom of his birth? No. The king pays tribute to his clever antics but wisely sends the master thief on his way," and he is never heard from again. "Since fairy tales are the morality legends of childhood, warnings to the wicked and the greedy, an obvious master thief may be admired for his cleverness, but he must not be rewarded."

In the story of "Jack and the Beanstalk," the thief's imposture takes the form of "an innocent, dutiful boy whose thievery is not only moral but an act of justice and rightful retribution." Jack lives with "his poor, hardworking mother in a humble cottage. His father is dead and thus neatly out of the way as a competitor for the mother's affections." Jack and his mother are forced to sell Milky White, their cow and "last remaining worldly possession." But instead of receiving money for the cow, Jack proudly returns home from town with some magical beans, expecting his mother to shower him with praise for his clever bargaining skills. Not only does she not do that, but she flings the beans out the window and sends a humiliated and deflated Jack off to bed.

Later that night, though, Jack peers outside his window and sees that the most amazing beanstalk has risen up out of the ground, stretching far into the sky. "The deception has been converted into a victory," Kaplan notes. "Now Jack can really prove himself worthy of his mother's trust and admiration."

Bent on revenge, Jack decides to climb the beanstalk and

slip into the castle of the Giant who lives there—ready to devour anyone caught trespassing, but *especially* little boys like Jack. Instead of finding himself cooked by the Giant's wife for dinner, Jack is able, with the wife's help, to steal the Giant's bag of gold, his goose that lays golden eggs, and his singing Golden Harp. The harp tries to warn the Giant of Jack's presence, but not in time. Jack is already on his way back to earth, back to his mother, clutching the Giant's possessions in his hands. The Giant pursues Jack, but Jack reaches home, grabs a hatchet and chops down the beanstalk, bringing the mighty and wicked Giant toppling down with it. Jack and his mother, Kaplan writes, "need never worry again. The look of admiration returns to his mother's eyes."

"Every imposture is an enactment of a Jack and the Beanstalk legend," Kaplan writes, "the redemption aspect of the family romance. The impostor must impose his false personality and achievements on others again and again in order to maintain the illusion that he is not small and insignificant, that he is worthy of his mother's admiration, that, moreover, he is entitled to trick the father, overthrow him, and rob him of his powers. Though many adolescents engage in reenactments of infantile emotional scenarios so as to rectify the injuries of the past, the impostor's role playing is designed to actualize an illusory victory. The impostor is the master thief who has given himself the moral permission to do wrong because he has been wronged."

In so many ways, Marc seems to fit the role of the full-fledged impostor.

At Allen-Stevenson, he stood apart from his classmates yet tried to gain their attention and acceptance by being the oddball and responding to their dares; as the Incredible Hulk, he enjoyed breaking out of the closet in which his classmates kept him captive; as an essayist, he enjoyed acting out his dark, Poe-like English compositions.

At Kent, one of his teachers couldn't decide if he was "a genius or a con man or both," and his adviser saw him as someone who was always playing a role ("a drunken Charles Laughton"), refusing to be honest about himself, and becoming, by senior year, "the character he created." He collected keys to buildings and offices and had even considered destroying the plumbing system on the night of his senior prom. He broke into the school store not once, but twice, and though he inveigled another student into joining him, he claimed to the police that he was the innocent who had been led astray.

During the summer of 1977 he (and Larry) stole everything they could lay their hands on, but denied at the time that they had done a thing. He tried to poison his grandfather's oatmeal (he told both Richard Behrens and Bryan Baird), but denied it at his mother's trial (the prosecution believed him because they felt he had no reason to lie at that point—but as Louise Kaplan points out, the impostor "lies even when there is no immediate practical gain"). He testified that he couldn't recall the name of the hotel he stayed at the night before the murder, yet he specifically told Bryan Baird it had been the Hotel Utah. He told David Frankel that he hadn't seen his grandfather's face before he shot him or had a conversation with him, but then told Dr. Moench (and later testified himself) that he did. He testified that he hadn't noticed his grandfather's blood on the floor of the warehouse, but described the amount of it to Behrens and Baird. He claimed under oath that he had taken only one cab to the warehouse and one back to the hotel, but told Baird he had deliberately taken a few each way in order to reduce the possibility of detection.

Marc was determined to kill his grandfather for the same reason Jack had killed the Giant—so that he could forever be assured of his mother's trust and love (". . . just wanted to get home and tell Mom and hoping she would approve—he had done something right for once," Dr. Moench's report read). If he could rid the family of the one person who his mother insisted didn't care about them, he could finally be a genuine hero in her eyes—the man she told him it was time he became. He might have had second thoughts the night before the murder and expressed them in a phone call, but he knew there was no other way. The $200,000 haul of the summer before hadn't satisfied her. He was not going to fail; he was not going to let her and Lavinia live on the street in Harlem. When he left New York, Behrens recalled, "he was in high gear." When he got to the warehouse, he didn't just shoot him once, but twice. He had to make sure he wouldn't have to come back and do it again. He told Bryan Baird that one of

751

the reasons he liked murder mysteries was the uncertainty of how they would turn out. And he also told Baird, in describing the scene that Sunday morning, his oft-read copy of *Death on the Nile* back at the hotel, that it was like being in the middle of one. As far as those unlocked doors that Doug Steele had discovered, all he would tell Baird was that "someone" had come by and "purposefully unlocked" them —implying it was Larry, but not saying so, still leaving open the possibility that he had opened them himself, with the keys Behrens and Larry knew he had.

Why did Marc bring the gun back to New York? That remains one of the many mysteries in the minds of the people involved in this story. Perhaps, as Ernie Jones thinks, it was simply because Frances wanted him to. After all, it had been such an ordeal getting one; Marc had paid good money for it (not a minor point, given the value this family attached to the acquisition of material goods); and revenge against Myles Manning had indeed been mentioned at one point. But perhaps there was another reason—that Marc needed to bring back this freshly fired trophy of his adventure in order to *prove* to Frances that he had done it, that he had killed the evil Giant, that he was indeed worthy of her love (and all the hugs and kisses she gave him that he said he had never experienced before), and that *he* was the reason money could now begin pouring forth from Salt Lake like fine wine and without interruption.

But as Marc soon found out, killing Gramps and removing the fear of destitution did not change life with Mom all that much. There might have been money, but there still were suicide threats and another attempt (around Thanksgiving of 1979) to contend with; there were still interminable, angry phone calls between them while Marc finished his last year at Kent, ultimately letting her down by not getting into an Ivy League college; and there was still the situation, particularly when he was out on bail after his arrest in New York, when he was not allowed to stay at Gracie Square because of what the neighbors might think. He had done her bidding, but he was banished from her world.

As a fugitive in New York during 1981, he loved the freedom and excitement of his Jekyll-and-Hyde existence; he loved being Alexander Bentley one minute, dressing up in a tuxedo and going out to fine meals, and then switching to the working-class role of David Jablonski the next, shuffling around Times Square in baggy trousers and eating Big Macs. He enjoyed walking past Susie Coleman's delicatessen window in his hat and trenchcoat, then phoning her immediately to find out if she had noticed him. The private mail drop; the secret meetings with Richard Behrens in Carl Schurz Park; the purchase of rare coins; his dealings in the stock market; the funds from Granny that made it all possible—both the money she willingly gave him and the money and checks he stole and forged: all of these things were like being in an adventure novel, he told Bryan Baird, or like being a spy in a spy novel.

But even his arrest and conviction did nothing to essentially change his imposture. He told Susie Coleman that the only reason he had "admitted" the murder was to protect Larry, who Susie still believes pulled the trigger. The reason he wanted to confuse her and make her think he was "framed into it," he told Bryan Baird, was so "she'll keep that support system going"—one that ensured she would see him as a martyr, that she would always be available to him, even if his mother would not.

While he made it clear that he felt above his fellow inmates at Utah State Prison, in both intellect and material possessions, he was not above stealing things from them at SSD soon after he arrived, or taking his lawyers' pens when they came to visit. He was, he signed his letter to his friend Claudia, "Marc the magician," who could wangle special privileges with "Ken, buddy" (the warden) and couldn't resist telling other inmates of his outings in Salt Lake with Mike George and Mary Lou—remaining mostly indifferent to the intense jealousy those trips would cause. To Michael Moore and Dan Shaffer, the two inmates who had been in the culinary the day Marc arrived back from *Return of the Jedi,* Marc is a "brilliant gamesman" who told them how much he enjoyed playing Mike George and Ernie Jones around—a person who "thinks solely in terms of profits and losses," has "a tendency to let people underestimate him," and is so "well schooled at being devious and manipulating that the toughest con at the prison is just putty in his hands."

All in all, Moore and Shaffer concluded, when Marc gets

out of prison and changes his name (which he apparently plans to do), "his potential for being successful in business is extreme."

A few days after the verdict in his mother's trial, Marc said over the telephone that anyone trying to plumb the depths of this story would find the waters awaiting him to be "dark, icy and murky." And so they had been, long before his cautionary call. The question of why Marc brought the gun back naturally leads to the question of why, once he did, Frances gave it—as well as the note with Dr. Cavenaugh's name and address—to Richard Behrens.

"Two traits," Freud wrote in "Dostoevsky and Parricide," "are essential in a criminal: boundless egoism and a strong destructive urge." Later in that essay he stated: "It is a fact that large groups of criminals want to be punished. Their super-ego demands it and so saves itself the necessity for inflicting the punishment itself."

In committing parricide, Frances and Marc had, according to Freud, committed "the principal and primal crime of humanity as well as of the individual." If Marc hadn't fully realized that at the time or even shown much remorse, perhaps he got a clearer understanding by reading *The Brothers Karamazov*—which he did during his trial—the novel on which Freud based his essay. "It is in any case," Freud continued, "the main source of the sense of guilt, though we do not know if it is the only one. . . ." In an earlier essay, "Criminals from a Sense of Guilt," Freud went even further in discussing misdeeds in general. He argued that "the sense of guilt was present before the misdeeds in general. He argued that "the sense of guilt was present before the misdeed, that it did not arise from it, but conversely—the misdeed arose from the sense of guilt. These people might justly be described as criminals from a sense of guilt." By committing the crime, the person's "sense of guilt was at least attached to something."

In a story filled with intriguing ifs and whys, everyone realized (and the police conceded) that if Marc or Frances had thrown the gun away, the case would never have been solved. But they didn't, and it was. Interestingly enough, Marc had brought a batch of chemicals home from Kent around the same time. Frances promptly threw those into the East River, but not the gun. It is one thing to give a loyal friend documents to hide while enmeshed in a messy divorce and quite another to ask him to find a hit man, buy a gun, keep him fairly well briefed of all the plans, and then give him the murder weapon. But even if Frances had told Richard Behrens to get rid of it, why did she allow him and Marc to take her car down to Chambers Street in lower Manhattan and buy a cover and cleaning material for it? Even if, for argument's sake, she didn't know *where* they had gone, Marc had taken a picture of Behrens going into the store to remind her. She asked Behrens to destroy the picture, but did not ask him for the gun back. Frances was intelligent enough to know that those were not the actions of a man who was planning to get rid of his newest acquisition.

If some of Frances's and Marc's behavior can be attributed to "boundless egoism"—a quality neither of them lacked— and sheer arrogance (Frances told Behrens that she knew suspicion would be immediately cast on her, Marc and Larry, but that the police would *never* be able to prove it and the bullets were most likely smashed), there is evidence beyond what has been mentioned, and beyond Marc's telling Dr. Moench that at first he wanted to be caught, to suggest they both had a strong desire, however unconscious, to be caught and punished for what they had done. Vittorio Gentile testified that he had lunch with Frances at Gino in the spring of 1978 and learned of her intentions. What he did not say—other than how incredulous he was—was that Frances had come by to see him the day after the murder and simply told him that her father had died. (Aside from the dealings with Behrens, this also explains why she arrived in Salt Lake City the day after Marilyn and Elaine.) What Gentile also didn't say—but did to Mike George—was that he had been seeing Marc once a month both before and after the murder. While Gentile still insists that he didn't know what had happened to Marc (or to Larry too, for that matter) until George and Harman "surprised" him at his office in December of 1981, that seems highly unlikely—especially since an article on Marc's arrest in New York ran on October 28 in the *Daily News* (the paper Gentile reads), and Marc saw him while he was out on bail.

But even if Frances and Marc felt that knowledge of their actions was safe with Behrens and Gentile, it wasn't confined to them. In the winter of 1979, Marc was studying one night at Kent with John Kantor, the boy who eventually broke into the school store with him. They often studied together, and on one occasion Marc boasted that he had once written a paragraph of "high English vocabulary," sent it to the *New York Times,* and received $5,000 for his effort. Other than thinking of Marc as "a diabolical genius," Kantor didn't know whether to believe him or not.

But on this particular night, Marc had an even larger claim to make: he said that his grandfather had been done away with the previous summer and "that *he* had done it so cleverly—time had elapsed and there were no clues to him," Kantor recalled. "It just came out in a series of things he said he was able to accomplish: 'I can get into this or I've done this,' like it was no big deal. He had gotten pretty comfortable talking about his mischievous acts—like getting into the business office and picking the safe. It was simply a challenge to him."

At the time, Kantor didn't believe him—until he was on his way back to college and read about Marc in the paper. And even though he was angry at Marc for accusing him of being the instigator behind the school store break-ins (he ironically remembers Frances saying at the time that "Marc always tries to blame his troubles on someone else"), he still felt sorry for Marc. "He was so young, he could have accomplished more with his life. If Mrs. Schreuder had been a little more intelligent, if she had worked for a few years, it would have worked out with her father. Marc was capable of doing this, but there had to be a reason. He probably needed that little push from his mother. If he were a little older, he probably could have done it on his own."

By the time Marc broke into the Kent school store in late May of 1979, his "confession" to Kantor was not the only reference he made to the summer before—but it was the only direct one. This was roughly the same period in which his friend Jack Hartman decided Marc was "demonstrably insane" (an impression certainly not hindered by Marc's telling him he thought he was losing his mind); Hartman observed Marc washing his face with ammonia; Marc suggested Hartman kill himself by drinking a vial of cyanide in the chemistry lab (which Hartman later interpreted as a suicide wish of his own); and Marc thought of blowing up the school's plumbing system.

Aside from his "confession," none of these incidents by themselves necessarily mean Marc was sending out a cry for help or punishment. But when he broke into the school store, he wasn't doing it because he couldn't live without the cash, sneakers and pens that he stole, or because, as he told his adviser, he was angry with the school. The significant thing is that he broke in *twice;* and even after the second time, knowing that the first one was bound to have been reported, he hung around the campus. It was after graduation, and he could have left. But he chose to stay—part of the evidence of *this* particular adventure in his room with him—practically waiting, it seemed, for the police to come and arrest him.

On the surface, a preppie breaking into his school store is relatively insignificant in the realm of national crises. But it wasn't for Marc: that gesture not only enabled Marc to be punished for the break-in, and to be officially acknowledged for his larceny; but it enabled him, as Freud suggested, to attach, or begin to attach, his guilt over the murder to something tangible—and to punish his mother through public embarrassment, through his being virtually erased from the history of the school, and through being unable to attend Trinity College that fall. More than twenty years after Frances was suspended from Bryn Mawr, Marc was eerily mirroring her own delinquent behavior.

Had Marc's and Frances's "lapses" stopped with the school-store incident, they still might not have been caught. But Frances had already begun withdrawing Richard Behrens's money out of their joint account at Chase Manhattan. She not only knew Behrens was beginning to write to everyone—including her and her mother—about the money, but, as it turns out, knew that Behrens had begun calling Marilyn even before he started writing letters, because Behrens told her he was. Still, she did nothing, almost daring him, it seemed, to expose her.

He filed suit and she denied the charges. He later testified that she was amazed that he had turned in the gun and had kept it for as long as he had, but the fact is that Marc *knew* Behrens still had it. Behrens informed him of that—"By the way, I still have something that belongs to you"—during his struggle to get his money back, and Marc told him that he'd been meaning to come by and pick it up. If Marc knew, Frances knew. After he was arrested and out on bail, Marc lamented to Behrens that he hadn't collected it and "melted that down."

The weekend after Joel Campbell and John Johnson had traveled to Hartford in late October of 1980 and advised Marc he was a suspect, Marc took a bus to New York. He frantically rang Behrens's buzzer to no avail, but did manage to reach him on the phone. When Marc told him, "I see that you and Marilyn have been busy," Behrens simply suggested he call Marilyn and hung up. Even if Marc still thought Behrens had the gun at that point (which Behrens didn't), Marc went back to Trinity as if nothing had happened. Two cops from Salt Lake City don't travel two thousand miles to Hartford, Connecticut, more than two years after a homicide and after the case was, for all intents and purposes, closed, unless they have *something*. Arrogance aside, Marc was smart enough to realize that.

Yet even after he got a "second chance" when his case was dismissed in Connecticut and his mother and grandmother implored him to leave the country, offering him money if he would, he didn't. He told Behrens he might go to Brazil and spend the rest of his life merrily dancing the samba, and even told David Frankel he might flee too, but he didn't. Nor did he flee after he was let out on bail in Salt Lake. Marc had read enough murder mysteries to know the case usually gets solved—sooner or later—and that, in the end, the good guys win and the bad ones go to jail.

Frances was every bit as clever and devious as Marc was. After all, nearly everything Marc and Larry knew they had learned from her. ("We learned from the best," Larry said.) The theft of Richard Behrens's $3,688.43 was more than just another act of larceny for Frances. Even if she had taken the money as a form of revenge (because Myles Manning had proved to be a stiff), it was more than that. And it was more than just another potato chip she couldn't resist. Nor did she steal his money because she disliked him; no one could have been a more loyal friend than he had been—or a more patient one. More than a year elapsed from the time he first discovered the withdrawals until the time he filed suit against her. In this story of ifs, if Richard Behrens had been solvent, he said, he never would have turned her or the gun in. And it's true: he held on to that gun for more than two years and never once used it to blackmail her or anything else. Other than the dunning letters he wrote, the most threatening thing he did was remind Marc he still had the .357. Of all the ifs, the most striking one is this: if Frances had done as Doug Steele later suggested—"given Behrens his money back with interest, and kissed him twice"—she would still be on the board of the New York City Ballet, and the gun would probably still be a museum piece on the shelf of his apartment.

But all her life no one had been able to stop her, so in the end she stopped herself, even before Marc did. Frances needed to be punished for what she'd done, just as much as Marc did. Frances needed to be acknowledged for what she'd accomplished, just as much as Marc did. And for them, the murder of Franklin Bradshaw was exactly that: an accomplishment. Marc had done it for her, and Frances had done it for the one person she had, in her own way, tried all her life to please, for the one person she could not do without—Berenice.

Spoken or unspoken, conscious or unconscious, it doesn't matter. The request was there. If Marilyn, Elaine and Frances all understood their mother's deep unhappiness, no one was in a better position—or had more reason—to try to change that than Frances.

This was her mother's hope, and Frances had fulfilled it, had finally done something right. By killing her father and pleasing her mother, the child no one ever wanted had, at long last, secured a permanent place in their lives.

"Antisocial acting out in a child is unconsciously initiated, fostered and sanctioned by the parents, who, through a child's acting out, unconsciously achieve gratification of their own poorly integrated forbidden impulses." A.M. Johnson expressed this in a widely cited essay, "Specific Factors

Determining Anti-Social Acting Out," and the psychoanalyst Brian Bird expounded on it in his paper "A Specific Peculiarity of Acting Out."

"This thesis," Bird wrote, "which I believe holds good for acting out in general, has several implications. The first point is that acting out, although personally motivated, is also a direct action response to stimulation by another person. A second point, similar to the first but not exactly the same, is that the acting-out person, by means of his behavior, aims either to please or to influence another person, or perhaps to do both. A third characteristic is that the influence extended from one person to another in the acting-out situation is largely unconscious, and that many forms of nonverbal communication make this mutual two-way influence possible."

"It is a matter of indifference," Freud wrote in "Dostoevsky and Parricide," "who actually committed the crime; psychology is only concerned to know who desired it emotionally and who welcomed it when it was done." In speaking of Dostoevsky, Freud said, "A criminal is to him almost a Redeemer, who had taken on himself the guilt which must else have been borne by others. There is no longer any need for one to murder, since *he* has already murdered; and one must be grateful to him, for, except for him, one would have been obliged oneself to murder."

Elaine and Marilyn weren't the only ones who wanted to know if their mother had had any involvement in—or had given some kind of approval to—the murder of their father. So did Doug Steele.

"What was the position of Grandma?" he asked one day after Frances's trial, sitting in his office at the warehouse and remarking how pleased he was by the verdict. "Why was she fighting so hard with all the evidence coming at her? In my own mind, I still don't know how much, if anything, she knew ahead of time. There's still a little doubt in my mind." Steele leaned back in his chair and rubbed his eyes, weighing his next statement as if it were a stick of dynamite that he reluctantly had to plant. "But I'll tell you this," he slowly began. "She was too close to Frances. She was too close to the action. For a long time, I just couldn't get myself to think there was anything involved there. Right to this day, I have a hard time considering it."

From his Salt Lake insurance office around the same time, Craig Bradshaw was saying how, in his mind, he had questioned Berenice "when she alibied for Larry that morning." Are you part of it, he thought, or are you so confused that you're willing to lie? "I gave her the benefit of the doubt, and decided she'd been put through so much that she's confused and desperate enough to do what she has to do to keep her family. . . .

"At this point, it doesn't matter. The damage has been done. I know my family has been damaged by it. But it's history. They'll have to live with themselves. He was an old man, but he wasn't ready to die."

Craig Bradshaw was right. Trite as it may sound, the damage had been done and the survivors would have to live with themselves. In the end, what one feels about this story is perhaps even more important than what one knows. Whether an old woman can reunite with two of her daughters in the future is more important now than who unlocked those doors that Saturday night. The kind of life that Lavinia Schreuder—not to mention Marc, Frances and Larry—will lead in the years to come is more important now than the fact that Franklin Bradshaw *did* make a new will, which was *stolen* shortly before he died. He had kept it in his file cabinet and showed it to his half sister, Sylvia Jean Christensen, a few months before the murder. "He explained," she said one day after Frances's trial, "that I would be hearing that he had taken Frances out of his will—and he wanted me to hear why. I saw it. Wayne Hacking and Wally Glover were going to be over the whole company. Frank told me that he told Frances and the kids that he was cutting them out. I told Berenice [after Frances's trial] and she was surprised that I'd seen it."

Marc, as it happens, told Bryan Baird about the new will. "His grandfather had just barely gotten the will out, and his mother wanted to find out if she was in it. His grandmother told his mother about it. I believe Larry had taken it and had given it to his mom. He found it in his grandfather's file cabinet at the warehouse. He broke into the cabinet and took it. He either gave it to his grandmother and she gave it to Marc's

761

mother or he gave it straight to his mother. Marc said that his grandmother and mother had been talking about ways of stopping the changing of the will—ways of being kept in and getting a good sum—and I think the subject of murder had been brought up.''

"It's awfully hard," Sylvia Jean said, "for Berenice to admit she was wrong, which she would be doing if she walked away from Frances. Bradshaws are very strong-willed. I was always the poor relation from Tooele, but I will say this: I sure hope I never leave my children enough money for them to fight over."

One month before Marilyn turned in the gun to Ed Regan at New York's 20th Precinct, before there had been any arrests made, Berenice, tired and bitter from all the legal wranglings over Franklin's estate, had written Marilyn one of her most revealing letters:

. . . The last two years have been a nightmare for me. I feel like I'm on a merry-go-round, in a fantasy world, nothing is real—something is missing. It is the ones left behind who must suffer. Life plays tricks on us. I say this over and over. [Not] in all my wildest dreams could I [have] imagined my life would end like this.

It is fun having all the things I want, going to all the places that have interested me in my studies but there is something very essential, very important missing—a united family, a harmonious family. The nastiness, the "behind-the-scenes" negotiations, one playing against the other—all of it uncalled for, all of it unnecessary.

But the bitterness, violence, & hate has been there for a long, long, time & nothing anyone can say or do will ever change this condition.

My family is split right down the middle. I can not be on two sides. I can not be of two opinions. The bitter ordeal for me was to choose. Right or wrong I went to the side where I felt I was needed & I was needed very much.

I love each one of my three daughters the same—not one more than the other. Each one of us have our good points & our failings. The failings I prepared to overlook while love lingers upper most in my heart and mind.

All this sudden wealth means nothing if it encouraged any one of my daughters to turn from me. I hope & pray when the settlement is

over you can at least resume some measure of respect & feeling for
me, as I have for you. . . .

Marilyn, you have been a wonderful daughter to me—always—I
love you very much. I feel very sad about what has happened to us.
When I think of you my heart leaps in my throat & I can't keep the
tears back—this is another tragedy in my life and I've had plenty of
them. I'm looking for a brighter day.

> All my love for you,
> MOTHER

More than three years later, the brighter day Berenice said
she was looking for still eluded her grasp—partly because her
own stubborn pride and martyrdom and, most of all, her guilt
would not allow her to do more than pay lip service to finding
it.

On a cold, dark, snowy day in January of 1984, she met an
acquaintance for lunch at a Chinese restaurant in Manhattan
and began talking about all that had happened, about the past
few months since Frances had been in prison, and about what
she felt the future would hold.

Dressed in black (the color she favored so much it almost
seemed her uniform) and nearly eighty-one, she had trudged
ten blocks in the snow to get there, amused by the fact that
in all the years she'd been coming to New York, New Yorkers were still falling over each other to jump into taxis
when a good brisk walk would do all of them some good.
Warmed by a cup of tea, she brightened as she spoke of
her plans to return to China in the spring. And as she
did, first talking about her previous trips to the Orient, it
was easy to see why Franklin had once fallen for her nearly
sixty years before. She was still the knockout from Iowa
who could light up a room, still the teenage girl who shyly
waited in the corner of the train station at Redmond, Oregon, the day Arthur Tuck came home with thirty-two firsts
and searched for her in the crowd. Yet it was also easy to
see why Bertha Beck had once said she was two people:
charming and funny one minute, headstrong and indomit-
able the next. Above all, though, she was as tragic and
lonely a figure as she insisted, over and over, her life had
been.

During November she had gone out to the prison, bearing flowers and satin sheets for Frances, only to find that some days her daughter refused to see her or, even when she did, had little to say.

In early December, Marilyn, knowing that her mother would be in New York to watch Lavinia dance in *The Nutcracker,* decided to seize the slight glimmer of hope her mother had expressed in her October 23 letter—that they would see each other in the future—and phoned her at Gracie Square to invite her to Sunday lunch. Berenice said she would come and Marilyn was elated. But the next afternoon the doorman in Marilyn's building gave her a letter that had been hand-delivered.

Dec 3 1983

Dear Marilyn:

You hit me just after I had had 2 glasses of wine & felt like a crying binge. Now I must tell you how I feel in my calmer moment.

You have crucified my daughter (your own sister), ruined our family name & caused untold agony & pain to the whole family. And what was gained by it? . . . The tragedy & suffering goes on. . . .

Dad was a proud man. He would not have wanted this mess. How do you think I feel having my family humiliated & torn like this? My heart bleeds for Frances. She has not done the things she is accused of. The lies, deceit & blackmail that went on in this trial are appalling & unbelievable. Those Salt Lake officers & lawyers were out to "feather their own nest"—financially & publicly—even to destroying the life of an innocent woman. An innocent woman faces life in prison for something her son did. Now he is going scot-free in a couple of years. He did the shooting, he is the one who should spend his life in prison. The guilty ones—Behrens, Manning & Marc—should be in prison.

Frances is a sick person & should be treated for her illness, not thrown into prison. You have no human feeling or you could not have done this to her.

I am sorry but I can not accept your help at this time. What would my lawyers, the relatives & public think if you & I started "budding" at this time? Not now Marilyn.

Sorry,
Mother

764

Three weeks later, on Christmas Day, Berenice was back in Utah. Despite all the things she had said about Marc, she decided to stop by and see him at the prison before spending the rest of the day with Frances. Marc was not expecting her, she said, and cried when he saw the fruitcake she had brought for him. After spending about ten minutes with Marc, she left and did not tell Frances where she had been.

"I don't love him and I don't hate him," she said, sitting in the den at 10 Gracie Square later that January afternoon, the snow becoming heavier outside. "I feel sorry for him. He told me he was not going to testify. I think what he did was horrible."

But what Marc had done was not all that was on her mind that afternoon. "You know, I think the natives turned against those New York lawyers. I didn't want them for the appeal, but Frances did. I've already given them one hundred thousand dollars to get started and now they want another hundred. They didn't earn their million and yet they're still gouging me. Thirty lawyers in all," she said, repeating her statement of four months before, "and not a Good Samaritan among them. Why, just the other day that Frankel phoned here, trying to get me to pay an outstanding bill, and I said, 'Forget it. Oh, no.' For once my back bristled and I had the guts to say no."

Asked if it was possible she knew Frances was guilty but could never admit it to herself or accept it, Berenice stared at her visitor a long time, before politely saying she didn't care to comment on that. As for a new will her husband might have prepared, she said she had *never* heard of one and *never* knew about those memos either (forgetting her testimony that she had "heard whispers" of both). "My husband said," she stated, 'You're never going to know anything about my business'—and I didn't. I've been told since he died that he wanted to divorce me. I wish he would have told me. I would have been most happy to oblige him. He would say to me, about the autobiography I wrote, 'You didn't make it happy.' And I said, 'I wasn't happy.' He wanted to cover everything up. Those were struggling days—days when he was struggling to get ahead. It would have been a bare existence if I'd have left with the kids."

She suddenly began talking about Lavinia and saying how she felt it was good for Lavinia "to be away from Frances for a while. She just loves attention. She's in the height of her glory. She's just so free. Nobody's nagging her. But Frances phones her *every* night at eleven o'clock and keeps her on the phone for two hours. She never asks to speak with me," she said, starting to raise her voice, "only Lavinia. I don't know why the prison doesn't limit her on that phone. Our next phone bill will be big enough to choke an ox.

"I think Frances has Lavinia brainwashed. I read the transcript of that tape. This is what has been drummed into me: 'I'm a bad mother and a bad grandmother.' I don't force myself on Lavinia, but she won't accept me."

As for Jeanie, the young woman who was taking care of Lavinia, Berenice said that she and Lavinia were very close. "But she doesn't lift a broom or anything. When Lavinia leaves in the morning, so does she. When I first came back here and she saw that I was preparing my own meals, she said, 'Mrs. Bradshaw, I was worried that you would expect me to cook for you.' Can you imagine? I'm not senile yet. This place hasn't been cleaned for months. Why, just yesterday I was down on my hands and knees, scrubbing and polishing. I don't think this couch [the one she was sitting on] has been moved an inch in all the years they've lived here. Frances is just totally irresponsible in that way. She had three bathtubs sitting downstairs for three years. And I've got workmen here now installing them."

She said she was thinking of selling the co-op and buying a smaller apartment, but hadn't decided; she knew that if Frances ever found out, "she'd have a heart attack." In any case, Berenice insisted, she just couldn't stand to have the place unfinished. She offered to take her visitor on a tour of the upstairs and slowly led the way, a cat named Tiffany lazily trailing behind. "This is Frances's room," she announced as soon as they walked in, "and that's the window they *said* she tried to escape from."

"It looks like someone is living here," the visitor said.

"Lavinia and Jeanie are sleeping in here while Frances is away."

She led the way down the dimly lit hall to Lavinia's room. It was pretty and tidy—a little girl's room, filled with bright colors and toys. "Why, she has enough toys," Berenice said, "to open up a store."

Around the corner was another bedroom. Except for a bare mattress, there was nothing in it. "This was Marc's room. Larry came up in November and took all of Marc's things with him." Whenever Marc got out of prison, he wouldn't be coming back to 10 Gracie Square. Of that, everyone was certain.

"Where is Larry's room?"

"Larry never lived here," she said abruptly. "He was already in prison before we moved in."

She walked back toward the stairs and into the bedroom located between Frances's and Lavinia's. "And this is my room," she said. "Mine is the smallest. I call myself Cinderella."

She and her visitor made their way back downstairs. The workmen had already left. The snow had let up a bit, but daylight was fading quickly and the den felt much colder than it had when they first arrived back from the restaurant. Berenice put on a sweater and closed her eyes for a few minutes, her head resting on the back of the couch.

"You know," she said, "when Frances is all fixed up, she is a beautiful woman, she looks like Elizabeth Taylor. She'd always get invited to things of high caliber, and when I was in town I'd go with her. We were both members of The Huguenot Society and The Americans of Armorial Ancestry. We once went to a reception for the King and Queen of Denmark at the World Trade Center. I miss those things—the teas and other occasions we would go to. Lavinia is dancing in *Harlequinade* tonight at Lincoln Center, and I'm going to see her. If Frances had been here, we would have gone together."

A few more minutes passed in silence. She then got up and inched toward the window, staring out onto the East River, and southward to the Queensboro Bridge, its lights like bright stars shining in the distance. Lost in thought, she said nothing for a while, then spoke her mind: "Why didn't he throw that gun into the Great Salt Lake or into the river here? It was so arrogant of him to bring the gun back. I *begged* him to leave the country but he wouldn't. He even had a fake passport he paid ten thousand dollars for, but he wouldn't leave. He was determined to stay in New York. But he obviously wasn't very clever, was he? Even when he impersonated other people, they finally found him."

A barge was making its way past the window and caught her eye. "Marc's problem," she began again, "is that he was too much a pansy. If I were he, I would have gotten on a ship and shipped out to sea.

"You couldn't get this family out of New York. They went hungry here for years. They suffered here for years. But you couldn't have got them out of New York with a derrick."

She had exhausted herself, and still had a full evening ahead of her. For the first time all day, she looked her age. She had no idea how her daughter's appeal would turn out, but she was going to fight on. Just the week before she had hired a private investigator to try to find "new information."

"But even if Frances is vindicated," she said, "I have no idea what effect it will have on her and Lavinia's future. I think it's a scar the rest of Frances's life. How are they going to overcome that?"

Since the old woman's visitor did not have an easy answer, he offered none. But he had lived with the story long enough to know this: that whenever Frances was released from prison, Berenice, if she was still alive, would be waiting for her.

Epilogue

In his closing argument, Mike Rosen predicted that Richard Behrens would seek the $10,000 reward Marilyn had offered on behalf of the estate. On January 10, 1984, Behrens officially did, requesting the money in a letter to Steve Swindle. But by the end of the year, having gotten nowhere with either Swindle or a petition he hired a Salt Lake lawyer to file, he returned to New York's Civil Court on December 27 as his own lawyer—four years after he had gone there to sue Frances—and filed suit against Marilyn. On his way home, he went to a thrift shop and bought a blue pinstripe Hickey-Freeman suit—to wear in the event the case ever came to trial. It didn't. The matter is still pending.

Eddie Dean submitted a bill to the County Attorney's Office after Frances's trial, but it has never been paid. Myles Manning realized a lifelong dream to have his own truck, but later complained to Dean that the truck was in constant need of repair. How the two of them ever got together, Steve Klein says, "remains one of the great mysteries of Western civilization."

Jeff Morris was moved back to Minnesota after Frances's trial and continued to maintain that his meeting with her took place as he'd described it. But shortly before Christmas of 1984, he confessed that he had made up the story, that he had read about the case in *Newsweek,* that his "knowledge" of Frances's having a daughter in the ballet was a lucky guess, and that for $5,000 he would be happy to explain how a con man such as himself passed polygraph tests. "As a master of deceit," he wrote, "I have redundantly and studiously read the following publications: (1) Sigmund Freud's *Group Psychology and the Analysis of the Ego;* (2) Machiavelli's *The Prince;* and (3) Nicholas Capaldi's *The Art of Deception.*" Of the three, he wrote, Freud's is "the most highly recommended . . . if a person wants to learn how to control and manipulate masses. I can attest to this, for I have mesmerized a number of groups myself." Asked his future plans when he got released from prison, Morris said that he was seriously considering taking some courses at the Dale Carnegie Institute.

In violation of his parole, Larry drove to nearly every state in the country during 1984—including Utah. He called his grandmother from Wyoming in June to let her know he was on his way. Despite her warning that he should "stay out of Utah, your family is in prison," and that she was going to call the sheriff (which she did), he came anyway, rented a house a few blocks from hers, and tried to see Marc, but not Frances. Because the prison had learned of his parole violation and he was not on Marc's visiting list to begin with, he was turned away. Six months later, off parole and still depressed because a girl named Dawn Moatz had left him, he came back to Salt Lake and planned to start classes at the University of Utah on January 2, 1985. But when that day arrived, having spent another Christmas by himself, he was in California, seeking work. By June of 1985, Larry had returned to Salt Lake and was beginning to display the same paranoid behavior that he had at Lehigh when he attacked Fred Salloum. With the assistance of state psychiatrists, Mike George, whose involvement with the entire case never waned, had Larry involuntarily committed.

The meeting between Marc and Frances that the warden of the Utah State Prison had thought might take place never did. While Marc waits for a parole date from the Board of

Pardons, Frances went before the board on November 7, 1984, and was given a date in October of 1996.*

On November 15, at three in the morning, she and some other women prisoners were transferred to the Idaho Correctional Institution in Orofino. Shortly afterward, Berenice wrote an anonymous letter to Salt Lake's two newspapers; entitling it "Human Rights," she protested the way the women were "swooped down on" and claimed that they were neither dangerous nor a menace to society. "Unfortunate circumstances," she wrote, "have brought them to this horrible existence."

In late March of 1985, Frances was returned to Utah. Her appeal for a new trial was argued before the Utah Supreme Court in June, but a decision will not be handed down until sometime in 1986.

In mid-June of 1985, Marilyn Reagan received an unexpected phone call. Her mother was in New York and wanted to see her. Pleased but cautious, Marilyn learned that Berenice desired a reconciliation—the one thing that Marilyn had hoped for all along. How permanent this reuniting of mother and daughter—which Berenice made painfully clear did not signify a backing away from her support of Frances— will be, remains to be seen. But it already has had one positive result: it has brought Lavinia into contact with an aunt she had never met.

---

*Utah has indeterminate sentencing. A person sentenced to life generally serves a minimum of fifteen years, but two of the three women convicted of first-degree murder before Frances served less than that, and the third, triumphant on appeal, was released after two years. Unless Frances's appeal is successful, she will serve thirteen years.

Notes

The factual material in this book is drawn primarily from the hours of interviews I conducted with more than 250 people, many of whom graciously allowed me to intrude upon their lives numerous times. Nearly all of these people agreed to speak on the record, though some—whose pseudonyms are John Kantor, Jack Hartman, Gary Perman, Bob Brown, Vicky Brown, Ted Berman—asked that their real names not be used, and a handful of others that their identities be no more specific than, for example, "a former classmate."

In addition to the interviews, the majority of which were tape-recorded, and my own observation, I drew on a vast array of other material: court transcripts and exhibits; police reports; appointment calendars; telephone logs and records; letters; books (including the unpublished autobiographies of Berenice Bradshaw, John Bradshaw and Bertha Beck); newspaper and magazine articles; photographs; jail and hospital reports; school records and yearbooks; and other memoranda and documents.

Since this book is not intended to be a scholarly work and I am not a historian, I did not feel that a page-by-page notes section would either serve a useful purpose or be appropriate to the story I have tried to tell. As often as possible, I identified my sources within the text itself; in the instances where I felt to do so would interrupt the flow of the narrative,

I list those additional sources of information here (and briefly identify those people whose names do not appear in the book itself).

PROLOGUE

Author's interviews with Bertha Beck, Craig Bradshaw, Nancy Jones, Doug Steele.

PART ONE

Oscar Wilde epigraph from *A Woman of No Importance*.

CHAPTER 1

Author's interviews with Doug Steele, Bertha Beck, Berenice Bradshaw, Marilyn Reagan, Elaine Drukman, Nancy Jones, Bryan Baird.

Other sources: *Salt Lake Tribune; Utah!* (a travel guide); *Utah: A Guide to the State* by Ward J. Roylance (revised and enlarged, Salt Lake City, Utah Arts Council, 1982); *Utah's History* by Richard D. Poll, Thomas G. Alexander, Eugene E. Campbell and David E. Miller (Provo, Utah, Brigham Young University Press, 1978); *Salt Lake City: The Gathering Place* by John S. McCormick (Woodland Hills, California, Windsor Publications, 1980); *The Mormon Experience: A History of the Latter-day Saints* by Leonard J. Arrington and Davis Bitton (New York, Vintage Books, 1980); the autopsy report on Franklin J. Bradshaw; Officer Larry Stott's testimony at trial of Marc Schreuder; Marc Schreuder's testimony at trial of Frances Schreuder; that state's exhibits at trial of Marc Schreuder.

CHAPTER 2

Author's interview with Bertha Beck.

Other sources: *The Mormon Experience;* "The Prophet Joseph Smith's Testimony" (a pamphlet distributed by the Mormon Church); Azer Briggs's biographical sketch of his father (Azer Richard Briggs); Beck's autobiography; *Utah; Lehi Centennial History: 1850–1950* (Lehi, Utah, Free Press Publishing Company, 1950); John F. Bradshaw's autobiography.

CHAPTER 3

Other sources: "A Branch of the Jewett Family in America" (a booklet researched and compiled by Dorothy Haas

Singleton, edited by Berenice Jewett Bradshaw, 1972); Berenice Bradshaw's autobiography.

CHAPTER 4
Author's interviews with Bertha Beck, Marilyn Reagan.

CHAPTER 5
Author's interviews with Bertha Beck, Marilyn Reagan, Elaine Drukman, Wally Glover, Don Bradshaw.

CHAPTER 6
Author's interviews with Berenice Bradshaw, Elaine Drukman, Marilyn Reagan, Richard Behrens.

Other sources: *Salt Lake Tribune* (article on epilepsy).

CHAPTER 7
Author's interviews with Marilyn Reagan, Elaine Drukman, Don Bradshaw, Bertha Beck, Scott Flandro (son of Claire Flandro), Berenice Bradshaw, Neil Swan, Doug Steele, Nancy Jones, Neal Bernson (Bradshaw employee), Ed Drury (Bradshaw employee), Wayne Hacking, Wally Glover, Mason Drukman, Claire Flandro, Mrs. Floyd Oberle (friend of Franklin and Berenice Bradshaw), Bob Kunkel (Utah oilman who occasionally did consulting work for Franklin).

Other sources: Berenice's autobiography and *Utah*.

CHAPTER 8
Author's interviews with Marilyn Reagan, Berenice Bradshaw, Elden Rasmussen (East High teacher of Frances's), Scott Flandro.

Other sources: Frances's East High records..

CHAPTER 9
Author's interviews with Marilyn Reagan, Elaine and Mason Drukman.

Other sources: Berenice's autobiography.

CHAPTER 10
Author's interviews with Bryn Mawr faculty members and classmates of Frances's (who requested anonymity), Camilla Jones Tatem, Vittorio Gentile, Marilyn Reagan, Elaine Drukman, Berenice Bradshaw, Howard Bradshaw, Nancy Jones.

Other sources: letter to author from Katharine Hepburn.

CHAPTER 11

Author's interviews with Marilyn Reagan, Vittorio Gentile, Robert Reagan.

Other sources: wedding invitation to marriage of Frances Bradshaw and Vittorio Gentile; Vittorio's testimony at Frances's trial; birth certificate of Lorenzo Jewett Gentile; affidavit of Marilyn Reagan (July 12, 1963, Supreme Court, New York County); letter from Franklin to Art and Bertha Beck.

CHAPTER 12

Author's interviews with Vittorio Gentile, Marilyn Reagan, Berenice Bradshaw.

Other sources: Alfred Albelli's articles in the New York *Daily News; Harper's Bazaar* (November 1983); letters from Franklin to Frances; Berenice's autobiography.

CHAPTER 13

Author's interviews with Larry Bradshaw, Berenice Bradshaw, Richard Behrens, Marilyn Reagan, Mike George, Mason Drukman.

Other sources: letter from Chemical Bank to Frances, copy to Franklin.

CHAPTER 14

Author's interviews with Vittorio Gentile, Robert and Marilyn Reagan, Berenice Bradshaw.

Other sources: court papers of *Napolitano* v. *Gentile*.

CHAPTER 15

Author's interviews with Berenice Bradshaw, Marilyn Reagan, Elaine Drukman, Doug Steele, Larry Bradshaw.

Other sources: letters from Frances to Berenice and to Franklin; from Franklin to Frances; from Berenice to Frances; Berenice's autobiography.

CHAPTER 16

Author's interviews with Marilyn and Robert Reagan, Berenice and Larry Bradshaw, Vittorio Gentile, Bryan Baird.

Other sources: court papers of *Schreuder* v. *Schreuder;* Frederick Schreuder's September 1974 letters to Judge Edith

Miller of New York's Family Court; letters from Berenice to Franklin; Berenice's autobiography.

CHAPTER 17

Author's interviews with Marilyn Reagan, Bryan Baird, Henry Boehm, Michael Moore, Berenice, Larry and Craig Bradshaw, Vittorio Gentile, Elaine Drukman, Richard Behrens, Susie Coleman, Andrew and Bobby Fuleki, Doug Steele, Neil Swan, Neal Bernson.

Other sources: *New York Times* (piece on Allen-Stevenson); 1976 Allen-Stevenson yearbook; Marc Schreuder's testimony at trial of Frances Schreuder; Dr. Louis G. Moench's testimony at trial of Marc Schreuder and written report of meetings with Marc in May and June of 1982 (defense exhibit at trial); Berenice's autobiography; letters between Franklin and Frances.

CHAPTER 18

Author's interviews with Elaine and Mason Drukman, Larry Bradshaw, Marilyn Reagan, Richard Behrens.

Other sources: Berenice Bradshaw's autobiography.

CHAPTER 19

Author's interviews with Bryan Baird, Bob Brown, Hart Perry (Kent School faculty member), Judson Scruton, Nancy Jones, Doug Steele, Steve Swindle, Berenice Bradshaw, Claire Flandro.

Other sources: Dr. Louis G. Moench's testimony at trial of Marc Schreuder and his written report; Marc's testimony at trial of Frances Schreuder; David Frankel's testimony at Marc's trial; Berenice's autobiography.

CHAPTER 20

Author's interviews with Doug Steele, Berenice Bradshaw.

Other sources: Berenice's letters to Larry.

CHAPTER 21

Author's interviews with Berenice Bradshaw, Nancy Jones, Doug Steele, Neil Swan, Ed Drury, Neal Bernson, Wally Glover, Larry Bradshaw, John Kantor, Jack Hartman, Marilyn Reagan, Richard Behrens, Craig Bradshaw.

Other sources: Marc Schreuder's testimony at trial of Frances Schreuder; Dr. Louis G. Moench's testimony at Marc's trial and his written report; phone records; checks.

CHAPTER 22

Author's interviews with Berenice Bradshaw, Elaine and Mason Drukman, Doug Steele, Don Bradshaw, Neil Swan, Neal Bernson, Ed Drury, Larry Bradshaw, Nancy Jones.

Other sources: Neil Swan's statement to the Salt Lake City police.

CHAPTER 23

Author's interviews with Dan Schindler, Neil Swan, Doug Steele, Lt. Roger Kinnersley, (then) Sgt. Brent Davis, Joel Campbell, Don Bradshaw, Larry Bradshaw, Elaine and Mason Drukman, Marilyn and Robert Reagan.

Other sources: Salt Lake City police reports (including the statements of Dan Schindler and Kirk Taylor and the transcripts of interviews with Berenice and Larry).

CHAPTER 24

Author's interviews with Neil Swan, Elaine and Mason Drukman, Wally Glover, Doug Steele, Marilyn Reagan, Bertha Beck, Joel Campbell, Larry Bradshaw.

Other sources: Salt Lake City police reports (including transcripts of interviews with Clive Davis, Swan, Elaine, Marilyn, Frances); Franklin Bradshaw's death certificate; copies of Craig Bradshaw's memorial-service speech and the memorial-service announcement.

CHAPTER 25

Author's interviews with Marilyn Reagan, Steve Swindle, Wayne Hacking, Bertha Beck, Roger Kinnersley, Joel Campbell, Major Willie Stoler (Salt Lake City police), Brent Davis, Captain Harry Patrick (SLC police).

Other sources: SLC police reports (including correspondence from Interpol).

CHAPTER 26

Author's interviews with Doug Steele, Marilyn Reagan, Don Burgi (probate clerk of Salt Lake County), Elaine and Mason Drukman, Steve Swindle.

Other sources: the probate file of Franklin Bradshaw's estate; FBI report of interview with Elaine.

CHAPTER 27

Author's interviews with Larry Bradshaw, Dean Robert

Cohen (of Lehigh University), Robert and Marilyn Reagan, Jack Hartman, Peter Bragdon (former head of admissions, Kent School), Vittorio Gentile, Don Bradshaw, Elaine Drukman, FBI agent in New York (who requested anonymity), Ted Berman (Kent School classmate of Marc's), John Kantor, Hart Perry, Trooper James Caputo, Berenice Bradshaw, Steve Swindle, Bryan Baird.

Other sources: *The Freshman Register* (of Lehigh University); court papers (relating to Larry's change of name from Schreuder to Bradshaw); Lehigh University records; the probate file of Franklin Bradshaw; Marc Schreuder's testimony at trial of Frances Schreuder; Connecticut State Police reports; Dr. Louis G. Moench's written report.

CHAPTER 28

Author's interviews with Larry Bradshaw, Joel Campbell, Rob Rouland, Harold Smith, William Kinch, James Ammend, Mark Refowich, John Gombosi, Stanley Vasiliadis.

Other sources: affidavit of Dave Dubosky; Bethlehem Police reports (including statements of Farid Salloum, Kenneth Heinick, Keith Conley, Michael Weaver, Judy Sare, Tom Morog, Lynne Andreach, Kathy Ignar, Joe Griffin); Dr. David Marvi's report of conversation with Frances Schreuder; testimony given at Larry's trial (by Morog, Ignar, Andreach, Conley, Sergeant Neil Schlottman, Officer Pedro Torres, Kinch and Ammend); the *Brown and White* (Lehigh University's newspaper); Northampton County Public Defender files.

CHAPTER 29

Author's interviews with Stanley Vasiliadis, Larry Bradshaw, James Onembo, Deputy Warden Robert Olander (Northampton County Prison), Harold Smith, Chester Reybitz, Mark Refowich.

Other sources: Northampton County Public Defender files; Allentown State Hospital reports; Northampton County Prison reports; transcripts of Larry's trial and other hearings related to his case.

CHAPTER 30

Author's interviews with Gary Perman, Larry Bradshaw,

Steve Swindle, Bertha Beck, Berenice Bradshaw, David Richardson, Marilyn and Robert Reagan, Richard Behrens.

Other sources: court records of Behrens's suit against Frances Schreuder; telephone conversation with Mary Porter.

PART FOUR

Epigraph from *The Scarlet Pimpernel*.

CHAPTER 31

Author's interviews with Marilyn Reagan, Elaine and Mason Drukman, Joel Campbell, Richard Behrens, Ed Regan, Major Willie Stoler, Frank Nicolosi, John Johnson, Susie Coleman, Bryan Baird, Mike Schweighoffer, Bob Beltrandi, Mike George, Trinity classmate (who asked anonymity).

Other sources: court testimony of Behrens, Reagan, Campbell and Marc Schreuder at preliminary hearings and trials of Marc and Frances Schreuder; New York City and Salt Lake City police reports; Trinity College catalogue; *Hartford Courant;* Connecticut Historical Society.

CHAPTER 32

Author's interviews with Ernie and Mary Lyne Jones, Marilyn Reagan, Joel Campbell, Richard Behrens, Major Willie Stoler, Nick Miller, Ron Nelson, John Snow, Jerry Register, Malcolm McPhail, Bruce Stanley, Bryan Baird.

Other sources: Salt Lake City police reports (including transcripts of interviews with Shara Vestal, McPhail, Snow, Stanley, and John Cavenaugh); "Profile/Midland, Texas" (distributed by the Midland Chamber of Commerce); article on Midland in *World* (published quarterly by Peat, Marwick, Mitchell & Co.); Dr. Louis G. Moench's testimony at trial of Marc Schreuder and his written report.

CHAPTER 33

Author's interviews with Ed Regan, Joel Campbell, Don Nelson, Richard Behrens, Mike Schweighoffer, Bob Beltrandi, Stanley Stadnicki (warden of the Morgan Street jail), Susie Coleman.

Other sources: Hartford police reports; Morgan Street jail records.

CHAPTER 34

Author's interviews with Spencer Austin, Ted Carey, Ernie Jones, Joel Campbell, Richard Behrens, Jim Conway, Marilyn Reagan.

Other sources: Salt Lake City police reports; Behrens's testimony at trials and preliminary hearings of Marc and Frances Schreuder; Reagan's testimony at trials.

CHAPTER 35

Author's interviews with Richard Behrens, Marilyn Reagan, Spencer Austin, Ernie Jones.

Other sources: testimony of Behrens at trials and preliminary hearings of Marc and Frances Schreuder; testimony of Marc at trial of Frances; Behrens's notarized statement; transcript of Behrens's deposition by James Wade of Robinson, Robinson & Cole.

CHAPTER 36

Author's interviews with Marilyn Reagan, Richard Behrens, Joel Campbell, Jim Conway, Ted Carey, Ernie Jones, Nancy Jones, Spencer Austin, Doug Steele, Allen Sullivan, Larry Bradshaw, a confidential source, Chester Reybitz, Mark Refowich.

Other sources: invoice from Mutual Investigative Service Inc.; internal Van Cott, Bagley memorandum (regarding meeting between Nancy Jones and Conway).

CHAPTER 37

Author's interviews with Ed Regan, Ernie Jones, Richard Behrens, Fred Seligman, Allen Sullivan.

Other sources: New York City police reports; Hartford court papers.

CHAPTER 38

Author's interviews with Ernie Jones, Mike George, Joel Campbell, Marilyn Reagan, Ron Nelson, Chester Reybitz.

Other sources: New York Telephone.

CHAPTER 39

Author's interviews with Fred Seligman, Richard Behrens, Allen Sullivan, Bryan Baird, Mike George, Ernie Jones, Spencer Austin.

Other sources: Seligman's papers; testimony of Behrens,

Marc Schreuder and George at preliminary hearings and trials of Marc and Frances Schreuder; Salt Lake City police reports.

CHAPTER 40

Author's interviews with Mike George, Ernie Jones, Carolyn Karoliszyn-Morris, Allen Sullivan, Richard Behrens, Larry Goldman, Bryan Baird, Michael Muntenau (manager of the Hotel Seville), Susie Coleman.

Other sources: transcript of John Cavenaugh interview; testimony of Jane Ufier (American Airlines representative) at Marc Schreuder's trial; Marc's testimony at Frances's trial.

CHAPTER 41

Author's interviews with Mike George, Malcolm McPhail, Jerry Register, Ed Regan, Ernie Jones, Richard Behrens, Allen Sullivan, Bob Beltrandi, Stephen Klein, Gerald Bauman, Frank Juliano, Braulio Martinez (manager of East 85th Street Citipostal), David Frankel, Larry Goldman, Bryan Baird.

Other sources: Don Harman's written summary of interviews with Malcolm McPhail and Bruce Stanley; transcript of interviews with Register and Dr. and Mrs. Cavenaugh; Klein's written report.

CHAPTER 42

Author's interviews with David Frankel, Norman Ostrow, Larry Goldman, Mike George, Stephen Klein, Gary Perman, Richard Behrens, Ernie Jones, Carolyn Karoliszyn-Morris, Ed Regan, Ron Hoffman, Trinity College classmate, Vittorio Gentile.

Other sources: Frankel's testimony at trial of Marc Schreuder.

CHAPTER 43

Author's interviews with Mike George, Paul Van Dam, Myles Manning.

Other sources: transcript of Myles Manning interview with Don Harman and George.

CHAPTER 44

Author's interviews with Mike George, Ernie Jones, Ernie Cruz, Stephen Klein, David Frankel, Allen Sullivan.

Other sources: Salt Lake jail records for Marc Schreuder.

CHAPTER 45

Author's interviews with David Richardson, Larry Goldman, Allen Sullivan, Richard Behrens, Mike George.

Other sources: 1983 *Nutcracker* program (Chujoy quote from his book *The New York City Ballet,* second edition, New York, Alfred A. Knopf, 1955); court transcripts.

CHAPTER 46

Author's interviews with Ernie Jones, Mike George, confidential source, Mary Lou Kaiser, Allen Sullivan, Stephen Klein, Berenice Bradshaw, Larry Goldman, Richard Behrens, Ron Nelson.

Other sources: *Salt Lake Tribune;* court transcripts.

CHAPTER 47

Author's interviews with Judge Jay Elmer Banks, Richard Behrens, Marilyn Reagan, Judge Banks's clerk.

Other sources: court transcripts.

CHAPTER 48

Author's interviews with Stephen Klein, David Frankel, police officers from New York's 19th Precinct, confidential source, Gary Perman, Ernie Cruz, Mike Shaw, Daniel Casagrande (associate in Shaw's law firm), Ed Regan, Ernie Jones, Larry Goldman, Berenice Bradshaw, East End Avenue merchants, Mike George, Larry Bradshaw.

Other sources: Klein's written report and testimony at Frances's trial; Frankel's testimony at Marc's trial; New York *Daily News; New York Post; Salt Lake Tribune.*

CHAPTER 49

Author's interviews with Mike George, Edward Dean, Myles Manning, David Richardson, New York City Ballet board member (who requested anonymity), Ernie Jones, Berenice Bradshaw, Kevin Kurumada, Paul Van Dam, Michael Moore, Dan Shaffer, Salt Lake jail employees (who requested anonymity), Mary Lou Kaiser, Bryan Baird, Dave Walsh, Judge Jay Elmer Banks, Judge James Sawaya.

Other sources: Ernie Jones interview with Jack Ford of KSL-TV; written report of Dr. Louis G. Moench.

CHAPTER 50

Author's interviews with Cathy Gallegos (Judge Sawaya's court reporter), Mike Carter (reporter for the *Salt Lake Tribune*), Dave Walsh, Ernie Jones, Nancy Jones, Judge Sawaya, Marilyn Reagan, Mike George, Mary Lyne Jones, Nedra Wright (secretary in the Salt Lake County Attorney's Office), Edward Dean.

Other sources: court transcripts.

CHAPTER 51

Author's interviews with Ted Carey, David Frankel, Shane Smith (colleague, at the time, of Joe Tesch), Ernie Jones, Mike George, Mike Carter, Dr. Louise J. Kaplan, John Nielsen, Dave Walsh.

Other sources: court transcripts; *Salt Lake Tribune.*

CHAPTER 52

Author's interviews with Dr. Lee Coleman, Ernie Jones, Cathy Gallegos, Judge Sawaya.

Other sources: court transcripts.

CHAPTER 53

Author's interviews with Ernie Jones, Mike George.
Other sources: court transcripts; *Salt Lake Tribune.*

CHAPTER 54

Author's interviews with Robert Vansciver (Salt Lake attorney), Mike Carter, John Johnson, Roxanna Bennett (officer at Utah State Prison), Richard Behrens.

Other sources: letter from Behrens to Larry Goldman (regarding meeting with the two Washington attorneys).

CHAPTER 55

Author's interviews with James Onembo, Mike George, Dave Teclaw (Hopkins Police Department), five Minneapolis police officers (who had had experience with Jeff Morris), Jeff Morris.

Other sources: Dr. Louis G. Moench's written report of

meetings with Marc Schreuder; psychiatric reports on Jeff Morris.

CHAPTER 56

Author's interviews with Mary Lou Kaiser, Roxanna Bennett, John Peters (inmate in SSD at Utah State Prison), Susie Coleman.

Other sources: Marc Schreuder's testimony at Frances's trial.

CHAPTER 57

Author's interviews with Jeff Morris, Steve Bartlett (Mike George's colleague who administered polygraph test), Berenice Bradshaw, Cathy Gallegos, Paul Van Dam, Howard Cerny, Irving Erdheim, Kevin Kurumada, Ernie Jones.

Other sources: Salt Lake jail records.

CHAPTER 58

Author's interviews with Michael Moore, Dan Shaffer, Bryan Baird, Pat Naylor, Mark Refowich, Harold Smith, Ernie Jones, Mike George, Jeff Morris, Mike Rosen, David Richardson.

Other sources: Bethlehem police reports; inventory list of contents in Larry Bradshaw's trunk; court transcripts; *Salt Lake Tribune.*

CHAPTER 59

Author's interviews with Mike George, Susie Coleman, Mark Refowich, Larry Bradshaw.

CHAPTER 60

Author's interviews with Jeff Morris, Sam and Elaine Drukman, Ernie Jones, Michael Rosen.

Other sources: probably cause statement (regarding Morris's attack on Allen Arbesfeld); court transcripts.

CHAPTER 61

Author's interviews with Larry Bradshaw, Bryan Baird, Roxanna Bennett, Leon Ames (inmate on Dog Block, Utah State Prison), Michael Moore, Dan Shaffer, Mike George, Mona Ladue, Vittorio Gentile, Ernie Jones, Wally Bugden,

Michael Rosen, John Peters, Bertha Beck, David Frankel, Paul Van Dam, Doug Steele.

Other sources: court transcripts; Dr. Louis G. Moench's testimony at trial of Marc Schreuder and his written report.

CHAPTER 62

Author's interviews with Paula Giese, Michael Rosen, Jeff Morris, Mike George, James Wise (Morris's cellmate at Utah State Prison), Ray Droddy (blockmate of Morris's), John Nielsen, Bryan Baird, Michael Moore, Dan Shaffer.

Other sources: affidavit of Paula Giese.

CHAPTER 63

Author's interviews with David Richardson, Larry Bradshaw, Bryan Baird.

CHAPTER 64

Author's interviews with Michael Rosen, Ernie Jones, Bryan Baird, Mike George, Jeff Morris, Edward Dean, Richard Behrens, Allen Sullivan, Stephen Klein, Harry Klekas, Dave Shewell (Judge Baldwin's clerk), Bob Lewis.

CHAPTER 65

Author's interviews with Sergeant Morris Anderson, Mike George, Jeff Morris.

Other sources: court transcripts.

CHAPTER 66

Author's interviews with Paul Van Dam, Berenice Bradshaw, John Lang, Kevin Kurumada, Jay Schulman.

CHAPTER 67

Author's interviews with John Lang, Kevin Kurumada, two of Frances's Bryn Mawr classmates, Ernie Jones, Dave Walsh, Wally Bugden, Bryan Baird.

Other sources: court transcripts.

CHAPTER 68

Author's interviews with Ernie Jones, Mike George, Wally Bugden.

PART SEVEN

Epigraph from "Musée des Beaux Arts."

CHAPTER 69

Author's interviews with Kevin Kurumada, Michael Rosen, Wally Bugden, Ernie Jones, Mike George, Bob Lewis, Berenice Bradshaw, Vittorio Gentile, Paul Van Dam.

Other sources: court transcripts.

CHAPTER 70

Author's interviews with Mike George, secretary in Salt Lake County Attorney's Office (who requested anonymity), Wally Bugden, Ernie Jones, Rob Denton, Richard Behrens.

Other sources: affidavits of Wally Bugden and Rob Denton; court transcripts.

CHAPTER 71

Author's interviews with Stephen Klein, Ernie Jones, Mike George, Bob Lewis, Edward Dean.

Other sources: court transcripts.

CHAPTER 72

Other sources: court transcripts.

CHAPTER 73

Author's interview with Mr. and Mrs. Fred Weber.

Other sources: court transcripts.

CHAPTER 74

Author's interviews with Bertha Beck, Berenice Bradshaw, Mary Lyne and Ernie Jones, Mike George, Dave Walsh, Fred Weber.

Other sources: court transcripts.

CHAPTER 75

Author's interviews with Mike George, Bryan Baird, Ken Shulsen, Bertha Beck, Berenice Bradshaw.

Other sources: court transcripts.

CHAPTER 76

Author's interviews with Kevin Kurumada, Harry Klekas, Salt Lake jail employees (who requested anonymity).

Other sources: *Salt Lake Tribune;* court transcripts; Salt Lake jail records.

CHAPTER 77

Author's interviews with Salt Lake jail employees (who requested anonymity), Kristen Edwards, Laura Williams.

Other sources: the prosecution's notes on jury selection.

CHAPTER 78

Author's interviews with Claudia Schauerhamer, Mary Holloway (inmate at Utah State Prison), Bryan Baird.

CHAPTER 79

Author's interviews with Claire Flandro, Berenice Bradshaw, Mrs. Floyd Oberle, Salt Lake jail matron (who requested anonymity), Laura Williams, Kristen Edwards, Florence Gouge (Salt Lake jail matron who accompanied Frances to Utah State Prison).

Other sources: court transcripts; Salt Lake jail records.

CONCLUSION

Author's interviews with a Bryn Mawr classmate of Frances's (who requested anonymity), Marilyn Reagan, Mae Hacking, Doug Steele, Bertha Beck, Mike George, Larry Bradshaw, Richard Behrens, Bryan Baird, Mike Carter, Vittorio Gentile, John Kantor, Berenice Bradshaw, Don Bradshaw, Claudia Schauerhamer, Ernie Jones, confidential source.

Other sources: the FBI's *Uniform Crime Reports;* BBC program "Men of Ideas" (Sir Isaiah Berlin comment, 1/19/78); "The Impostor: A Masculine Pursuit of Perfection" —chapter from *Adolescence* by Louise J. Kaplan (New York, Simon and Schuster, 1984); Sigmund Frued's "The Exceptions" and "Criminals from a Sense of Guilt" (two of three essays under the heading "Some Character-Types Met with in Psychoanalytic Work," from the *Complete Psychological Works of Sigmund Freud,* Volume 14, London, Hogarth Press, 1955) and "Dostoevsky and Parricide" (from the Hogarth Press edition, Volume 21); Alice Miller's *Prisoners of Childhood* (New York, Basic Books, 1981), Berenice Bradshaw's autobiography; letters from Robert Bradshaw to Franklin and from Frances to Berenice; telephone call with Marc Schreuder; A. M. Johnson's essay "Specific Factors Determining Anti-Social Acting Out" (from *Journal of the*

American Orthopsychiatric, No. 24. 1954); Brian Bird's essay "A Specific Peculiarity of Acting Out" (from Journal of the American Psychoanalytic Association, Volume 5, No. 4, October 1957)

EPILOGUE

Author's interviews with Richard Behrens, Steve Swindle, Marilyn Reagan, Edward Dean, Jeff Morris, Larry and Berenice Bradshaw, Claudia Schauerhamer.

Other sources: telephone call with Marc Schreuder.

Marc Schreuder and I spoke on the telephone about six times in the course of my work on this book; we met unexpectedly the night before his mother's trial; and we exchanged a couple of letters. None of these things resulted in interviews in any real sense, because his lawyer Joe Tesch, acting on Marc's behalf, wanted an indeterminate sum of money before I would be allowed to sit down with Marc. I declined their request for what I believe to be sound journalistic reasons, and they were able to obtain that money elsewhere.

Mike Rosen told me before Frances's trial that if she was acquitted there was a possibility I would be able to interview her. Even though she was found guilty, I requested an interview with her on three separate occasions. She never responded.

As for Lavinia, who had her twelfth birthday in April of 1985, I decided early on not to try to interview her—a decision that I still feel was a proper one.

Acknowledgments

It began, at least for me, on March 19, 1982. I was on my way home from CBS News when I learned that a woman named Frances Schreuder had been arrested earlier that day on Manhattan's Upper East Side. The allegations seemed too incredible to be true, but I began to pursue the story nonetheless, having no idea at the time that it would compel me to write this book—or of the extent to which it would take over my life.

To all the people whose names appear in the book—and to those whose don't—I want to express my deep, though still inadequate, gratitude. With the exception of the previously mentioned situation with Joe Tesch and Marc, these "collaborators," as Truman Capote called them once, asked for nothing and were promised nothing. My only assurances to them were that I would go wherever the story took me—and that I would ultimately tell it with the utmost care. Though some of these people will doubtless disagree with some of what they read here, and others may regret speaking with me at all, I tried to do that.

There are a number of other people—people who didn't figure in the story itself, but without whose support my task would have been considerably more difficult. Though I can't name all of them (and some would not want me to), I do want to thank the following, and I hope that they know why: Ken Auletta, Ann Beattie and her mother, Charlotte Beattie (whose postcards were a constant reminder that a world did indeed exist beyond the walls of my apartment), Susan Bolotin, David Broder, Janet Brown, Fred Coleman (my father), Michael Coleman (my brother), Roger and Marge Colloff, Jean Courtney, Mary de Bourbon, Joni Evans, Alexis Fernandez, Marcy Frosh, David Goehring, Ashbel Green, Ken Green, Kate Green, Jim Griffin, Sylvia Harris (my mother), Andrew Lack, John Lane, Gloria Loomis, Sterling Lord, Brenda and Lori Marsh, Michele Marsh, James McCourt, Harry Moses, Esther Newberg, Robin Nollet, John and Francis O'Brien, Sheila Parker, Jody Perkins, Sara Rimer, Kathy Robbins, Catherine Roberts, Mary and Paul Rooney, Marly Rusoff, Howard Stringer, Barbara Thompson, Amanda Urban, Tom Victor, Vincent Virga, Irene Webb, Howard Weinberg.

A special note of thanks to Ron and Elaine Carlson and Crystal Craig, who opened up their homes to me in Salt Lake and became my friends; to Mike Carter of the *Salt Lake Tribune* and Jack Ford of KSL-TV, who tolerated my phone calls long before they ever met me; to Dr. Louise Kaplan, Dr. Robert Evans and Judy Coleman, for the many hours they spent both listening and responding to what I had to say; to Nan Talese, the sister I never had; and to Robert Lindsey, for all the things that one phrase simply cannot convey, and who made sure that I got this done.

My agent, Owen Laster, is one of the most decent, professional people I have ever known, and I am pleased he found room for me on his list of clients.

At Atheneum, Pat Knopf and Liv Blumer believed in this book long before they ever read it; Harry Ford, Barbara Campo and Mary Flower handled it with care; Susan Richman and Sharon Dynak made people aware of it; and Tom Stewart not only lived up to his reputation as an extraordinary editor, he exceeded it. Whatever the book's flaws, they are mine, not Tom's.

And, finally, to my wife, Kathryn Court, who always understood why I had to do it, and who put up with more—much more—than I had any right to expect. Thanks.

Picture Credits

About the Author

Jonathan Coleman, who first began investigating the Bradshaw murder in 1982 for CBS News, has interviewed more than 250 people, from family members to hit men to the mysterious figure who broke the case. Coleman has uncovered startling new details in this powerful, harrowing portrait of how one American family—a family that seemed to have everything—collapsed in a final, bloody tragedy.